the politics of **GAY RIGHTS**

Also in the series

IMPROPER ADVANCES
Rape and Heterosexual Conflict in Ontario, 1880–1929
by Karen Dubinsky

A PRESCRIPTION FOR MURDER
The Victorian Serial Killings of Dr. Thomas Neill Cream
by Angus McLaren

THE LANGUAGE OF SEX
Five Voices from Northern France around 1200
by John W. Baldwin

CROSSING OVER THE LINE
Legislating Morality and the Mann Act
by David J. Langum

SEXUAL NATURE/SEXUAL CULTURE
edited by Paul R. Abramson and Steven D. Pinkerton

LOVE BETWEEN WOMEN
Early Christian Responses to Female Homoeroticism
by Bernadette J. Brooten

THE TRIALS OF MASCULINITY
Policing Sexual Boundaries, 1870–1930
by Angus McLaren

THE INVENTION OF SODOMY IN CHRISTIAN THEOLOGY
by Mark D. Jordan

SITES OF DESIRE/ECONOMIES OF PLEASURE
Sexualities in Asia and the Pacific
edited by Lenore Manderson and Margaret Jolly

SEX AND THE GENDER REVOLUTION, VOLUME I
Heterosexuality and the Third Gender in Enlightenment London
by Randolph Trumbach

TAKE THE YOUNG STRANGER BY THE HAND
Same-Sex Relations and the YMCA
by John Donald Gustav-Wrathall

CITY OF SISTERLY AND BROTHERLY LOVES
Lesbian and Gay Philadelphia, 1945–1972
by Marc Stein

THE

CHICAGO

SERIES ON

SEXUALITY,

HISTORY,

AND

SOCIETY

Edited by
John C. Fout

the

POLITICS *of*

GAY RIGHTS

Edited by Craig A. Rimmerman,
Kenneth D. Wald, and Clyde Wilcox

THE UNIVERSITY OF CHICAGO PRESS
CHICAGO AND LONDON

298819

CRAIG A. RIMMERMAN is professor of political science at Hobart and William Smith colleges and author most recently of *The New Citizenship: Unconventional Politics, Activism, and Service* (1997). KENNETH D. WALD is professor of political science at the University of Florida and author of *Religion and Politics in the United States*, 3d ed. (1997). CLYDE WILCOX is professor of government at Georgetown University, author most recently of *Onward Christian Soldiers? The Religious Right in American Politics*, 2d ed. (forthcoming), and coeditor most recently of *Women in Elected Office: Past, Present, and Future* (1998).

The University of Chicago Press, Chicago 60637
The University of Chicago Press, Ltd., London
© 2000 by The University of Chicago
Chapter 2 © 2000 by John D'Emilio
All rights reserved. Published 2000
Printed in the United States of America
09 08 07 06 05 04 03 02 01 00   1 2 3 4 5

ISBN: 0-226-71998-7 (cloth)
ISBN: 0-226-71999-5 (paper)

Library of Congress Cataloging-in-Publication Data

The politics of gay rights / edited by Craig A. Rimmerman, Kenneth D. Wald, and Clyde Wilcox.
     p. cm.—(The Chicago series on sexuality, history, and society)
Includes bibliographical references and index.
ISBN 0-226-71998-7 (cloth : alk. paper)—ISBN 0-226-71999-5 (pbk. : alk. paper)
     1. Gay rights—United States. 2. Homosexuality—Political aspects—United States. 3. Religion and politics—United States. 4. United States—Politics and government—1989– 5. United States—Social conditions—1980– I. Rimmerman, Craig A. II. Wald, Kenneth D. III. Wilcox, Clyde, 1953– IV. Series.

HQ76.8.U5P65   2000
305.9′0664′0973—dc21

                                                        99-055589

To all those who have been
the target of hate crimes

CONTENTS

List of Contributors / ix
Preface / xv

1. The Context of Gay Politics
Kenneth D. Wald / 1

I. THE GAY MOVEMENT

2. Cycles of Change, Questions of Strategy: The Gay and
Lesbian Movement after Fifty Years
John D'Emilio / 31

3. Beyond Political Mainstreaming: Reflections on Lesbian and
Gay Organizations and the Grassroots
Craig A. Rimmerman / 54

4. Where Rhetoric Meets Reality: The Role of Black Lesbians
and Gays in "Queer" Politics
Keith O. Boykin / 79

5. Lesbian and Gay Policy Priorities: Commonality and
Difference
Jean Reith Schroedel and Pamela Fiber / 97

II. THE OPPOSITION

6. Antigay: Varieties of Opposition to Gay Rights
John C. Green / 121

7. The Gay Agenda Is the Devil's Agenda: The Christian
Right's Vision and the Role of the State
Didi Herman / 139

8. Direct Democracy and Gay Rights Initiatives after *Romer*
   Todd Donovan, Jim Wenzel, and Shaun Bowler / 161

III. THE ISSUES

9. DOMA and ENDA: Congress Votes on Gay Rights
   Gregory B. Lewis and Jonathan L. Edelson / 193

10. Gays and AIDS: Democratizing Disease?
    Mark Carl Rom / 217

11. Sex/uality and Military Service
    Francine D'Amico / 249

IV. THE ARENAS

12. The Politics of Gay Rights at the Local and State Level
    James W. Button, Barbara A. Rienzo, and Kenneth D. Wald / 269

13. Lesbian and Gay Politics in the States: Interest Groups, Electoral Politics, and Policy
    Donald P. Haider-Markel / 290

14. Gay and Lesbian Issues in the Congressional Arena
    Colton C. Campbell and Roger H. Davidson / 347

15. Sex and the Supreme Court: Gays, Lesbians, and Justice
    Sarah E. Brewer, David Kaib, and Karen O'Connor / 377

16. Gay Rights in the Public Sphere: Public Opinion on Gay and Lesbian Equality
    Clyde Wilcox and Robin Wolpert / 409

Index / *433*

CONTRIBUTORS

SHAUN BOWLER teaches in the Department of Political Science at University of California, Riverside. He is coauthor of *Demanding Choices: Opinion, Voting, and Direct Democracy* (1998, with Todd Donovan) and coeditor of *Citizens as Legislators: Direct Democracy in the United States* (1998, with Todd Donovan and Caroline J. Tolbert).

KEITH BOYKIN is author of *One More River to Cross: Black & Gay in America* (1996) and *Respecting the Soul: Daily Reflections for Black Lesbians and Gays* (1999). He served two years in the Clinton administration as special assistant to the president and director of specialty media and two and a half years as the executive director of the National Black Lesbian and Gay Leadership Forum. His writings are published in several books, including *Atonement* (1996), *Gay Men at the Millennium* (1997), and *Dangerous Liaisons* (1999). A graduate of Dartmouth College and Harvard Law School, Keith was editor in chief of the daily newspaper at Dartmouth and a general editor of the *Harvard Civil Rights–Civil Liberties Law Review*. He is currently an adjunct professor of government at American University in Washington.

SARAH E. BREWER is a graduate student in the School of Public Affairs at American University and received her B.A. from Eckerd College. Her research focuses on campaigns and elections, especially women campaign consultants.

JAMES W. BUTTON is professor of political science at the University of Florida. He is author of *Blacks and Social Change* (1989), which received the V. O. Key Award, and coauthor of *Private Lives, Public Conflicts: Battles over Gay Rights in American Communities* (1997, with Barbara Rienzo and Kenneth Wald). He is currently researching the politics of innovation in school health programs for minority and poor youth.

COLTON C. CAMPBELL is assistant professor of political science at Florida International University. He is coeditor of *New Majority or Old Minority? The Impact of Republicans on Congress* (1999, with Nicol C. Rae). He served as a 1998–99 American Political Science Association congressional fellow in the office of U.S. Senator Bob Graham of Florida.

FRANCINE D'AMICO teaches political science at SUNY, College at Cortland, and at LeMoyne College in Syracuse. She is coeditor of *Women, Gender, and World Politics* (1994, with Peter Beckman), *Women in World Politics* (1995, with Peter Beckman), and *Gender Camouflage: Women and the U.S. Military* (1999, with Laurie Weinstein).

ROGER H. DAVIDSON, professor emeritus of government and politics at the University of Maryland, serves as visiting professor of political science at the University of California, Santa Barbara. He is coauthor of *Congress and Its Members*, 7th ed. (1999, with Walter J. Oleszek), and coeditor of the *Encyclopedia of the United States Congress* (1995, with Donald C. Bacon and Morton Keller), among many other publications.

JOHN D'EMILIO is professor of Gender and Women's Studies at the University of Illinois, Chicago and served as the founding director of the Policy Institute of the National Gay and Lesbian Task Force. He is author of *Sexual Politics, Sexual Communities: The Making of a Homosexual Minority in the United States, 1940–1970* (1983) and *Making Trouble: Essays on Gay History, Politics, and the University* (1992) and coauthor of *Intimate Matters: A History of Sexuality in America*, 2d ed. (1997, with Estelle Freedman). He is currently preparing a biography of civil rights leader and pacifist Bayard Rustin.

TODD DONOVAN is associate professor of political science at Western Washington University. He is coauthor of *Demanding Choices: Opinion, Voting, and Direct Democracy* (1998, with Shaun Bowler) and *Citizens as*

Legislators: Direct Democracy in the United States (1998, with Shaun Bowler and Caroline J. Tolbert). He has also published a number of book chapters and articles on initiatives, including papers in *Journal of Politics, American Journal of Political Science,* and *American Politics Quarterly,* and has published papers on election systems minority representation.

JONATHAN L. EDELSON is an operations research analyst at the Internal Revenue Service in Washington, D.C.

PAMELA FIBER is a Ph.D. student in the Department of Politics and Policy at Claremont Graduate University and an instructor in the Department of Politics at California State University, Fullerton. Her fields of research include American politics with an emphasis on the law and public policy. She has given conference papers and published works on fetal policymaking and reproductive rights. She is currently working on a dissertation examining campaign finance issues.

JOHN C. GREEN is the director of the Ray C. Bliss Institute and professor of political science at the University of Akron. He has written extensively on religion and politics in the United States; he is coauthor of *Religion and the Culture Wars* (1996) and *The Bully Pulpit: The Politics of Protestant Clergy* (1997, with James L. Guth).

DONALD P. HAIDER-MARKEL is assistant professor of political science at the University of Kansas. He has authored and coauthored several articles and book chapters on gay and lesbian politics, abortion, hate crimes, and citizen militia groups, some of which have appeared in the *Journal of Politics, Political Research Quarterly, Social Science Quarterly,* and *Demography.*

DIDI HERMAN is professor of law and social change at Keele University in the U.K. She is author of *Rights of Passage: Struggles for Lesbian and Gay Equality* (1994) and *The Antigay Agenda: Orthodox Vision and the Christian Right* (1997).

DAVID KAIB is a graduate student in the School of Public Affairs at American University. His research focuses on public law.

GREGORY B. LEWIS is professor of public administration at Georgia State University and director of the joint Ph.D. program in policy studies of

Georgia State University and the Georgia Institute of Technology. His research, which has focused on the effects of race, sex, sexual orientation, and other personal and job characteristics on the careers of public employees, has appeared in several journals. Currently his research focuses on public opinion on gay rights issues. He has recently been appointed to the National Research Advisory Board of the Gay and Lesbian Alliance Against Defamation (GLAAD).

KAREN O'CONNOR is professor and chair of the Department of Government at American University. She is author of *No Neutral Ground: Abortion Politics in an Age of Absolutes* (1996) and coauthor of several books, including *Women, Politics and American Society*, 2d ed. (1998, with Nancy E. McGlen) and *American Government: Continuity and Change*, 5th ed. (forthcoming, with Larry Sabato). She is president-elect of the Southern Political Science Association and editor of *Women & Politics*.

BARBARA A. RIENZO is professor of health science education at the University of Florida. She has published numerous articles and chapters on sexuality education and school health programs. She is coauther of *Private Lives, Public Conflicts: Battles over Gay Rights in American Communities* (1997, with James Button and Kenneth Wald). She is currently working on research on the politics of school-based health care.

CRAIG A. RIMMERMAN is professor of political science at Hobart and William Smith Colleges, where he teaches courses in American politics, environmental and urban policy, democratic theory, and gay and lesbian politics. He spent the 1992–93 academic year as an American Political Science Association congressional fellow in the Washington, D.C., offices of Senator Tom Daschle (D-S.D.) and Representative Barbara Kennelly (D-Conn.). He is the author of *Presidency by Plebiscite: The Reagan-Bush Era in Institutional Perspective* (1993) and *The New Citizenship: Unconventional Politics, Activism, and Service* (1997), and the editor of *Gay Rights, Military Wrongs: Political Perspectives on Lesbians and Gays in the Military* (1996). He is currently working on a book examining the state of the lesbian and gay movement in the United States.

MARK CARL ROM is an associate professor of government and public policy at Georgetown University. He is author of *Public Spirit in the Thrift Tragedy* (1996) and *Fatal Extraction: The Story behind the Florida Dentist Accused of Infecting His Patients with HIV and Poisoning Public Health* (1997), and coauthor of *Welfare Magnets: A New Case for a National Welfare Standard* (1990, with Paul E. Peterson), among other book chapters and articles. While at Georgetown, he has three times been selected by the students as the outstanding faculty member in the Graduate Public Policy Institute. His dissertation, *The Thrift Tragedy: Are Politicians and Bureaucrats to Blame?* was the co-winner of the 1993 Harold Lasswell Award from the American Political Science Association as the best dissertation in the public policy field.

JEAN REITH SCHROEDEL is associate professor and chair of the Department of Politics and Policy at Claremont Graduate University. Her research and teaching interests focus on American politics, public policy, and gender politics. She is author of *Alone in a Crowd* (1985), *Congress, the President and Policymaking* (1994), and *Is the Fetus a Person?* (forthcoming).

KENNETH D. WALD is professor of political science and director of the Center for Jewish Studies at the University of Florida. He is coauthor of *Private Lives, Public Conflicts: Battles over Gay Rights in American Communities* (1997, with Barbara Rienzo and James Button) and articles on gay political mobilization in the *American Journal of Political Science* and *Urban Affairs Review*. His *Religion and Politics in the United States*, now in its third edition, has also been published in Chinese and Indian editions.

JAMES WENZEL is assistant professor of political science at the University of California, Riverside. He has published several book chapters on initiatives and has published papers on judicial politics and behavior.

CLYDE WILCOX is professor of government at Georgetown University. He is the author, coauthor, editor, or coeditor of more than 20 books on religion and cultural politics, campaign finance, gender politics, and other topics, most recently *Prayers in the Precincts: The Christian Right in the 1998 Elections, Women in Elected Office: Past, Present, and Future,* and *Political Science Fiction*.

ROBIN WOLPERT has taught political science at Georgetown University and at the University of South Carolina. She has published a number of articles and chapters in the general area of judicial politics and is now studying law at Cornell University.

While this book was being written, the brutal murders of two gay men—Matthew Shepard and Billy Jack Gaither—received considerable public attention. Their murders were particularly heinous. Shepard was beaten and tied to a fence post outside Laramie, Wyoming and left to die in freezing temperatures. Gaither was beaten to death and then burned. Shepard's murder, in particular, prompted a national debate over the wisdom of a federal hate crimes law called the Hate Crimes Prevention Act, which would afford federal agencies jurisdiction over bias incidents.

But what received little public attention in the aftermath of the two murders is the need for education at all levels that fosters the acceptance and understanding of difference. This book has been written with that goal in mind. We have come together—straights and gays, academics and activists—to contribute to that important educational goal. We also hope that our readers will better understand the Christian Right's challenge to the lesbian, gay, and bisexual movement, and how the movement is responding to that challenge at the national, state, and local governmental levels. We hope, too, that the arguments contained within the pages of this book are discussed and debated in college classrooms as well as in the larger public sphere. As political scientists, we believe that we are making important contributions to our discipline, as well, and opening up further avenues of inquiry for future political science research.

But we also recognize and celebrate the interdisciplinary and multi-perspective approach that is apparent in this book, one that is needed for addressing the complex phenomenon of lesbian and gay rights.

We thank our editor at the University of Chicago Press, Doug Mitchell, for his enthusiastic support of this project from start to finish. We could not have asked for a better and more diligent editor with whom to work. His associate, Matt Howard, did an excellent job in addressing a number of important details as the book headed toward publication. Leslie Keros, production editor at the Press, took great care in the production of the manuscript, and we also appreciate the careful work of Robert Caceres of Macximum Editorial Services. In addition, we appreciate the thoughtful comments offered by two anonymous reviewers in response to the manuscript's first draft. We know that our book is much improved as a result of the considerable amount of quality time and thought that each reviewer devoted to their careful reading of the entire book. Without our contributors, of course, there would be no book. Thanks to all of them for responding to our revision requests and deadlines in a timely manner.

Craig Rimmerman thanks Dawn Feligno and Lois Judson—secretaries extraordinaire—for their efforts in helping to bring this project to fruition. In addition, he acknowledges the valuable discussions with his students in his Sexual Minority Movements and Public Policy course at Hobart and William Smith Colleges, conversations that helped to convince him that this book needed to be written. Ken Wald is particularly grateful to those pioneering scholars who made this book possible by paving the way for empirical scholarship on gay and lesbian politics. Their willingness to instruct him by virtue of both their research and personal communications has been an inspiration. Clyde Wilcox thanks Rachel Goldberg, his student assistant, who did a superb job in readying the book for final publication.

In the end, this book has truly been a sustained collaborative effort. We believe that it serves as a model in the academy and in the larger society for the kind of crucial coalition building that is needed to challenge the climate of fear, misunderstanding, and hate that contextualizes almost all bias crimes. We dedicate this book to those who have been the targets of hate crimes as a result of their sexual orientation. In doing so, we hope that its mere existence is a source of optimism about the future.

Craig A. Rimmerman *Ithaca, New York*
Kenneth D. Wald *Gainesville, Florida*
Clyde Wilcox *Washington, D.C.*

THE CONTEXT OF GAY POLITICS

Kenneth D. Wald

This volume provides an overview of the gay rights struggle in American politics.[1] It covers the strategies and ideology of both the advocates and opponents of gay civil rights,
explores the key political issues in which gays and lesbians
have been involved, and offers an accounting of the various political arenas in which lesbian and gay interests have
been contested. Although there has been no shortage of
scholarship about gay politics in recent years, most of the
published work "consists of memoirs from the front lines
or 'how to' manuals on political activism" (Fleischmann
1998, 54).[2] These valuable and necessary genres often fail
to connect with the scholarly concerns of mainstream research in social science. By offering this volume, we hope
to help overcome the isolation of scholarly research about
gays and lesbians in the political arena.

In seeking contributions to this volume of original essays, we were driven by three goals. First, as the next section will recount, we wanted studies that treated gay politics not as an end in itself but as a specific "case" of more
general political phenomena. We think the political activity associated with gay and lesbian mobilization is not only
important in its own right but is significant because it can
address broad questions about public life in the contemporary United States. Many of the studies reported here fit
comfortably into the realms of public policy analysis, minority group politics, legislative studies, interest group
politics, and other fields of scholarship. The studies in this

volume raise the same issues and employ the same language used in other research on these topics.

Our second goal was to present research that was accessible to students or scholars seeking a disinterested perspective on one of the most contentious and important struggles in contemporary politics. By suggesting that much contemporary research has been inaccessible, we mean in part that it is often found in specialized journals or edited collections that may not be widely available. But more fundamentally, much of the scholarship is steeped in a language and tradition of cultural theory that most general readers may find difficult to decode (Chauncey 1998). Although the authors in this volume draw on a variety of theoretical traditions, methodological approaches, and academic disciplines, their goal was to write essays comprehensible to readers without an intensive background in gay studies.

Third, this volume is distinct because it focuses on politics. Our dependent variable—that which we want to understand—is the political world and how it copes with the demands of gays and the equally powerful claims of gay rights opponents. One might think that a movement based on the premise that "the personal is political" would have produced a large body of scholarship on the role of sexual orientation in public life. Nonetheless, when he remarked on "how little analytical work has been undertaken on contemporary lesbian/gay/bisexual activism and its political impact," David Rayside (1998, xiii) underlined the need for studies of this nature. We thus sought to assemble a set of essays focused on the political dimensions of the gay rights movement.

Although it was not one of our selection criteria, the essays in this volume also exhibit the diversity that characterizes the study of the gay rights movement in the United States. Some of our authors are identified with the lesbian and gay movement and have written extensively on the subject, but others, not affiliated with the gay movement, are new to the field of study; their contributions mark their first venture into this subject matter. Most of our authors are political scientists by training, but we have tried to avoid disciplinary parochialism by including historians and legal scholars and encouraging our contributors to draw on approaches from other disciplines such as sociology and anthropology. Even though most of the authors work in the academic world, the list of contributors also includes activists who have helped shape the struggles that are written about in these pages.

Along with personal diversity, the authors also bring to this volume a variety of analytic approaches. The methods in the articles encompass such diverse practices as historical analysis, case study research, textual criticism, and survey methodology. The articles run the gamut from interpretive essays built on literature reviews to quantitative analyses of original data. In the former case, authors are able to draw from the results of well-developed scholarly traditions. By necessity, other chapters present new data to illuminate issues that have seldom been explored in previous research on gays and lesbians. We regard this eclecticism as a positive quality because it mirrors the complexity of the gay experience and the many theoretical approaches with which scholars have approached the phenomenon. Gay politics has too many facets to be studied satisfactorily from any single perspective or with only one research tool.

In the next section I will explain the reasons scholars have become interested in the study of gay politics and how such research speaks to the enduring concerns of political science. Following that section, the chapter turns to a broad overview of the factors that have increasingly drawn gays into the political process and conditioned their success. This discussion entails the reasons for gay political mobilization, the political resources available to gays, lesbians, and their allies, and the accessibility of the political system to gay and lesbian claimants. There follows a brief account of the organization of the book and a preview of the content of the chapters. I conclude with an interim assessment of the responsiveness of the American political system to gay and lesbian efforts.

WHY STUDY GAY POLITICS?

The interest in gay-related political activity is part of a larger trend to focus public and scholarly attention upon gays and lesbians. Although some gay activists attempted to build a social movement well before the 1960s, it was the 1969 rebellion at New York's Stonewall bar that first caught public attention and inspired the modern gay rights movement (Duberman 1993). What began as a fairly routine police raid on a gay bar generated spontaneous acts of public resistance that eventually became a powerful symbol, the foundation of a new gay pride and self-assertion. Precisely because of their long tradition of invisibility, the newly assertive gays of the Stonewall era seemed "like ghosts who suddenly materialized" to confront public authority in an open challenge (Deitcher 1995, 21). The gay and lesbian consciousness revolution inspired and was accompanied by a growing scholarly interest in the history and experience of gay men, lesbians, and bisexuals. By the 1980s, a recognizable "gay studies" scholarly movement began to explore all facets of homosexuality in the United States

(Abelove, Barale, and Halperin 1993). Gay studies is now a recognized subfield of scholarly inquiry, legitimizing the kind of research reported in this volume.

The publication of a book of this nature also owes much to the politicization of sex at the end of the century. To a remarkable degree, perhaps to a greater extent than ever before, the agenda of American political life has recently been focused on matters of sexuality. In discussions about the problems of young people (a frequent topic of national debate), there is much concern about teenage sexuality, unwed mothers, sexually transmitted diseases, the distribution of birth control devices, and the sexual exploitation of children. Female sexuality has produced strong public debate over such diverse subjects as abortion, sexual harassment, and changes in fertility. Activists who believe in the theory of cultural decline have raised alarms over indecency in the mass media, music, advertising, and the Internet. In the ultimate sexual spectacle, a president whose marital fidelity was widely questioned, was impeached and put on trial for charges stemming from intimate liaisons with a White House intern. Given the salience of sexual matters in contemporary political debate and the concern with defining and regulating sexual behavior, we should not be surprised to find that questions about homosexuality, too, have become part of the public agenda in the United States.

Few issues in American politics, sexual or not, inspire as much passion as the struggle over civil rights for gays and lesbians. Whether it is about gays and lesbians being allowed to serve openly in the military, to marry, to adopt children, to receive partner benefits, or to gain legal protection from discrimination in housing and employment, the debate is often heated and intense. The rhetoric and tactics on both sides are often extreme, stretching and occasionally obliterating altogether the norms of civility in public discourse (Bull and Gallagher 1996). The passion associated with the issue stems from the clash of fundamental social values and the clash of social movements. The case for gay rights evokes values such as equality, autonomy, and individual freedom—deeply held values that provide support for policies to extend civil rights protection to disadvantaged minorities. Yet gay rights also evokes in many Americans the value of moral traditionalism, which is an important source of opposition to gay rights. When he declared that "what is morally wrong can never be politically right," a British statesman of the nineteenth century articulated the mindset that fiercely resists laws protecting the civil rights of gays, lesbians, and bisexuals.

The conflict between these opposing values is further intensified because it is embodied in social movements. Social movements have become such a prominent part of the political landscape that we sometimes have trouble distinguishing this particular form of political activity from related genres such as parties, interest groups, or protests. Social movements are distinct because they (1) rest upon a mass base of individuals, groups, and organizations linked by social interaction; (2) organize around a mix of political and cultural goals; and (3) rely on a shared collective identity that is the basis of mobilization and participation (Diani 1992). Such movements have transformed the American social and political landscape in the twentieth century, giving such disparate groups as African Americans, environmentalists, the physically disabled, and women a new means of pursuing social and political equality. The willingness of social movements to operate outside the conventional framework of party politics and interest group activity—to take their grievances into the streets—further separates their style of action from politics as usual, but also adds a potentially incendiary element to political life.

Both gays and their opponents pursue their conflict through the medium of social movements. Although we may speak of *a* social movement, which implies a single actor with a common purpose, social movements are by nature decentralized and composed of organizations with competing strategies and ideologies that attract individuals with varying commitments to democratic norms. The gay and lesbian rights movement has spawned a set of competing organizations (profiled in Craig Rimmerman's chapter), some of which advocate working within traditional political structures to gradually change policies, while others support more confrontational tactics and more radical goals. Some organizations within that broad movement focus on single issues like AIDS, or represent a subset of the gay community, such as African Americans or Latinos or lesbians, while others address the entire spectrum of gay-lesbian life. These groups also differ on whether gays and lesbians should pursue their interests in coalition with a broader array of groups or exist essentially as "single issue" organizations devoted solely to advancing the needs of homosexuals. Like the black civil rights campaign that had such a profound influence on the struggle for gay liberation, the gay rights movement harbors organizations with distinctive tactical repertoires. Alongside broad-based groups with comprehensive action plans, there are organizations that specialize in litigation, lobbying, media analysis, electioneering, and other specific techniques. On the opposite side of the political spectrum, as John Green demonstrates convincingly in his chapter, the groups that challenge the gay rights movement are no less a social movement with multiple and competing organizations and tactics. While some Christian Right organizations, such as Oregon's Citizen's Alliance, have as their central organizing rationale an opposition to gay rights, others like the Christian Coalition use gay rights issues in fundraising appeals but do not stress the issue in the legislative agenda. Similarly, some activists seek to root out and fire gay and lesbian schoolteachers and to remove from school libraries and curriculums any books that sympathetically or even neutrally portray gay couples. Other Christian Right groups merely oppose any expansion of gay and lesbian rights. When two social movements clash so openly over fundamental social values, political conflict is inevitable.

The undeniable passion that suffuses the issue is apparent to anyone who has witnessed a public debate on the subject, but it makes the topic of gay rights merely interesting, not intrinsically important. Why should scholars and students who have no personal stake in the controversy study this subject? As political scientists, the editors and authors were drawn to this topic because it raises issues that are central to the perennial concerns of our discipline. At the macro level, for example, the attempts by gays to alter their status through political means gives us the opportunity to study how small, weak and despised groups can use political means to challenge larger and stronger political forces who enjoy the support of entrenched social values. The ability of the Christian Right to defeat many gay initiatives addresses precisely the same question because it, too, has emerged from obscurity to the limelight in a process that defies much conventional wisdom about the conditions that breed political influence. The clash of social movements over gay rights thus forces us to ask fundamental questions about the nature and distribution of power in the United States, which *is* a central concern of political science.

At the middle range of scholarly analysis, the studies in this volume also demonstrate that the entry of gays and lesbians into political life provides many opportunities to apply, test, and refine our theories of political behavior. Schroedel and Fiber invoke theories of gender differences in political attitudes to explain disparities between the political priorities of male and female homosexuals. By highlighting the role of social dislocation in clearing the way for rapid advances in gay status, D'Emilio attests to the significance of the political opportunity structure in the progress of social movements. Campbell and Davidson show how the time-honored technique of using experts to provide legitimacy or cover for policies that make politicians nervous helped Congress formulate legislation to combat AIDS. Students of interest groups have shown us important differences between organizations that use what are called "insider" techniques versus those that rely on an "outsider" strategy. Rimmerman applies this distinction to the many interest groups that pursue the collective interests of gays and lesbians. Herman's analysis of the religious ideology of the antigay movement constitutes a powerful argument against the emerging hypothesis of Christian Right learning and moderation. In exploring referendums on gay-related issues, Donovan, Wenzel, and Bowler both point to parallels with earlier episodes of social backlash against other unpopular minorities and rely on a theory of political entrepreneurship developed in the study of other public policy questions. Haider-Markel organizes his examination of openly gay public officials around concepts of descriptive and substantive representation that have been widely deployed in prior studies of political elites. Button, Rienzo, and Wald draw extensively on social movement theory to explain the adoption patterns of gay rights ordinances. In the study of congressional action on two pieces of legislation critical to gays and lesbians, Lewis and Edelson consider the conditions under which public opinion affects public policy, the linkage issue that concerns students of public opinion. Rom shows that the AIDS issue had some unique properties that encouraged activists to pursue unconventional tactics but that public policy toward the disease was most responsive when the interests of AIDS activists coincided with other elite actors. That lesson is a staple of coalition politics. The chapter by Brewer, Kaib, and O'Connor, focusing on the judicial reaction to gay initiatives, addresses both the question of litigation as a political strategy and the manner by which groups are able to put their concerns on the agenda of legal decision-makers. Wilcox and Wolpert show that public opinion toward the gay political movement is centrally influenced by underlying views about homosexuality, confirming the finding that public opinion on political issues is driven primarily by affective attitudes toward the groups who are engaged in conflict.

These chapters demonstrate conclusively that the political travails of gays and lesbians belong on the scholarly agenda of minority group politics in the United States. The questions asked in this volume about gays and lesbians are the same queries we raise about other minority groups, notwithstanding the qualities that undeniably distinguish gays from blacks, Latinos, women, the disabled, and other minority groups that have also entered the political realm. Furthermore, studying gay mobilization through the lens of concepts developed in other areas of political science raises the possibility that case studies of gay mobilization will yield stronger and more accurate theories of the political process. This is a long way of saying that one does not have to be gay to appreciate the significance of gay involvement in public life.

HOW TO UNDERSTAND GAY POLITICS

In mystery novels, solving a crime means finding a suspect with the motive, means, and opportunity to commit an illegal act. Although we are trying to comprehend a political struggle rather than a criminal act, the same three factors are a useful way of organizing the inquiry about political struggles over gays and lesbians. This framework addresses the question of why gays and lesbians have turned to the political realm for remedial action, what resources are available to them in this endeavor, and how the political system is likely to respond to these initiatives. The goal of this endeavor is not to develop a definitive model of gay political action nor to solve the puzzle of gay mobilization, but simply to call attention to the dimensions of gay and lesbian political activity—its origin, nature, and impact. It sets the stage for the more detailed studies in the individual chapters.

Motive: Repression and the Struggle for Collective Identity

In understanding the stigma that still attaches to homosexuality, it is worthwhile recalling Herbert Butterfield's famous warning against a linear interpretation of history, that is, against understanding the past as the progressive unfolding of trends. Rather than mimic a straight line, Butterfield argued, human experience was a matter of cycles, of fits and starts, of progress and regress. Thus it has been for people engaged in homosexual activity. The historical record does not reveal a simple evolution from a primitive past in which homosexuality was condemned and forbidden to an enlightened present where the sexuality of gays and lesbians is treated as a purely personal concern. Nor is it accurate to contrast a golden age in the distant past when homosexuality was accorded social acceptance with a modern reign of terror imposed sometime in the Middle Ages and persisting ever since. The position of gays and lesbians has differed widely across space and time. In some cultures at some times, same-sex erotic relationships were accepted with a degree of equanimity. The rigid distinction between "homosexual" and "heterosexual" was recognized as a massive oversimplification, and there were social spaces where homosexual interactions were relatively sheltered. In response to various social forces, these periods of tolerance often gave way to eras of intense homosexual persecution.

For most of the twentieth century, however, tolerance and openness have not marked the condition of gays and lesbians in the United States. Rather, homosexuality has been regarded as a "problem" in need of a solution. Whether homosexuality was regarded as "a sin, a sickness, or a crime," and unsure whether it represented "a genetic defect, a mental disorder, or a learning disability," the culture nonetheless treated it as something that needed governmental regulation (Harbeck 1992, 1). Perceived by most of the public as a threat to the moral order, gays and lesbians were harshly restrained by law. One symptom of this status was the almost universal practice of American states and local communities to criminalize gay sexual conduct under antisodomy codes. Well into the 1960s and beyond, these codes permitted criminal prosecution of persons found to be engaged in same-gender sex. The laws were often enforced with zeal against people who congregated in gay bars, bath houses, and movie theaters, or cruised for homosexual partners in more public locales such as beaches, parks, and restrooms. These formal prosecutions, which often relied on undercover police officers who induced illegal behavior by posing as potential partners, were also accompanied by informal sanctions that could range from isolated acts of harassment to murderous physical assaults known colloquially as "gay-bashing."

The degree to which gays and lesbians still face legal restrictions may not be fully appreciated today (Harvard Law Review 1990; Rubinstein 1993). At the national level, the U.S. Supreme Court ruled in 1986 that the Constitution confers no legal protection on sexual congress between people of the same gender (*Bowers* 1986). Despite widespread repeal of antisodomy statutes in the 1970s, private sexual contact between adults of the same gender remains a criminal act in twenty states. In some states, the laws have been voided by state courts but remain on the books. The state and local laws, even if left unenforced, remain as a tool that can be wielded selectively against gays and lesbians. Moreover, they constitute a powerful affirmation that society rejects on principle the expression of erotic love between members of the same sex. When the expression of physical intimacy between consenting adults of the same sex carries the threat of incarceration, it suggests the depth of social hostility to gays and lesbians and the willingness to embody it in law.

The criminalization of sexual activity between consenting adults of the same gender sends a powerful message about the marginal legal status of gays and lesbians. So too does the failure to criminalize attacks on gays and lesbians under state laws against hate crimes. All but ten states have passed laws that intensify the penalties for criminal attacks motivated by the individual characteristics of the victim or group. Such laws are one way society affirms support for victims of persecution and, by specifically condemning attacks based on religion, race, and ethnicity, embraces racial, cultural, and ethnic diversity. Although a significant proportion of gays have reported experiencing hate-motivated violence and gay rights advocates often lobbied actively for such legislation, the legislative sponsors of hate crimes laws have sometimes found it politically necessary to exclude sexual orientation from coverage. This means that attacks on sexual orientation are not singled out for special censure in seventeen states with hate crimes laws or in the ten states with no such laws in force. Although hate crimes inspired by the sexual orientation of the victim are still punishable under other laws, the exclusion of such crimes from the list of hate crimes can easily be interpreted as a sign that such attacks are not seen by society as particularly heinous or worthy of condemnation.

Gays continue to experience a number of additional legal disabilities beyond the criminalization of same-gender sex and the refusal to criminalize hate crimes against gays. As Lewis and Edelson show in chapter 9, on the assumption that homosexuality left individuals open to blackmail, government agencies routinely treated gays and lesbians as security risks or as otherwise unsuitable for federal employment until the 1970s. This left gay and lesbian federal employees with a choice between remaining closeted so they could continue to work at jobs requiring clearance or coming out openly and risk losing their jobs precisely because they had revealed a forbidden sexual orientation. Despite President Clinton's ringing endorsement of ending the military ban on gays and lesbians during the 1992 campaign, he had to settle for a much less far-reaching revision known as the "don't ask, don't tell" policy. For all its apparent innovation, the new policy continues to make homosexual conduct—but not heterosexual activity—grounds for expulsion from the armed forces. As D'Amico recounts in chapter 11, the military leadership has exercised this option with apparent enthusiasm. The law also disadvantages gays in many family matters. While this too has been changing in response to determined lobbying and litigation, state law still allows unequal treatment based on sexual orientation in the realm of adoption, foster parenting, child custody, inheritance, visitation, and other matters related to family status. The message of such restrictions (that gays are incapable of being good parents or role models for children) further reveals the extent to which homosexuality carries a legally reinforced stigma.

Gays may be singled out for legal disadvantage in several realms, as the foregoing analysis underlines. Moreover, they may be denied coverage under the civil rights protections otherwise available to minority groups. While ten states and approximately 150 local governments have laws and policies that incorporate sexual orientation in antidiscrimination law (a development explored by Button, Rienzo, and Wald in chapter 12), the vast majority of Americans live in jurisdictions that do not provide such protection. Even when state or local law forbids discrimination based on sexual orientation, the victims of illegal practice may lack the means to obtain redress. Enforcement mechanisms are often spotty. Furthermore, at the federal level, there are no laws prohibiting discrimination against gays and lesbians.[3] In practice, the absence of penalties for discrimination based on sexual orientation means that employers, landlords, and credit agencies are free to take that characteristic into account when hiring, selling, and extending credit. Access to such vital social resources as housing, jobs, and loans may be denied to gays and lesbians who have no legal recourse and no institutional support in seeking restitution.

Upon hearing such accounts, students may protest that surely gays are entitled to civil rights protection under the Constitution. Those who regard gay civil rights initiatives as unnecessary have often deployed precisely that argument. This line of reasoning fails to distinguish between the fundamental protections that are guaranteed to all citizens by the Constitution—the various rights enumerated in the first ten amendments—and the absence of specific provisions based on sexual orientation. Gays, like other Americans, do indeed have constitutional protection for free speech, religious practice, and against self-incrimination. But the Constitution has been interpreted to permit what is sometimes called "rational" discrimination by government. In that spirit, the Supreme Court has permitted governments to criminalize consensual homosexual sex and the military to treat gays and lesbians differently from other members of the armed forces. Absent specific legislation that prohibits discrimination based solely on sexual orientation, gays do not enjoy constitutional protection against most forms of discrimination.[4]

The reality of life for many gays and lesbians is marked by a powerful stigma against homosexuality. Depending upon one's point of view, the stigma may reflect a kind of moral panic known as homophobia or constitute a rational cultural reaction to a dangerous social force. But the reality of stigma underlying the litany of disadvantages encountered by homosexuals should make it clear why gays and lesbians have turned to political action. Simply put, the law has often been both the symbol and the effective instrument of gay oppression. If the political process is one source of the problematic conditions facing homosexuals, then it requires little imagination to understand why gays and lesbians perceived political activity as a potential route to liberation. The same instrument that permitted the passage of laws and policies penalizing gays and lesbians could, in principle, be used as a means of achieving a more equitable legal status. Both the fact of gay oppression and its basis in law help to explain the motive for gay rights mobilization.

Means: The Resources Available to Gays and Lesbians

It is easier to nurture grievances than to develop effective means for resolving them. Notwithstanding the harshness of the situation facing gays and lesbians, it was not until the 1970s that a social movement devoted to resolving their problems began to achieve a modicum of success. Why some groups emerge as a political force when they do and others languish for decades without redress is a complex matter. Part of the explanation lies in the resources, tangible and intangible, available to those that would put the group's grievances on the political agenda and seek governmental solutions. As the "resource mobilization" approach to social movements has taught us, groups that are well-endowed with collective identity, dense networks of preexisting social ties, financial resources, skilled leadership, and powerful organizations generally have an advantage over lesser-endowed groups when it comes to political attention and impact (Zald and McCarthy 1979). An additional resource—a sense among group members that they constitute an oppressed minority deserving of better treatment—is no less important for being intangible.

The degree to which the gay and lesbian movement can draw on potent resources is very much a matter of contention between advocates and opponents of gay rights. At a minimum, there would be agreement that gays and lesbians have certainly increased their resource base relative to prior periods in American life. To be openly gay, to run organizations that are recognized as legitimate, and to engage in overt political action on behalf of gay causes, are all possible today but would not have been so a generation ago. We can also point to advances in the formulation of an open gay identity, greater organizational diversity, an expanding infrastructure of services and businesses that cater primarily to gay consumers, and other signs of collective life. Yet to assert that gays have increased their resources is not to say that they constitute a politically powerful force in American life or even match the power level achieved by other minority groups. Kenneth Sherrill (1993; 1996) has enumerated the disadvantages still facing gays as they attempt to use political means to obtain redress of grievances.

The first problem is numbers. Judging by survey data (Singer and Deschamps 1994, 9–12), only around 3 percent of adults consider themselves primarily lesbian, gay, or bisexual.[5] Even if the true percentage is closer to the 10 or 15 percent figure that emerges in some studies, that figure is a significant barrier to success in a political system where numbers matter. Groups without large numbers may sometimes exert an influence beyond their size due to exceptionally high levels of cohesion. For gays, however, the reality of social stigma undermines political cohesion and reinforces the problem imposed by small numbers. John D'Emilio in chapter 2 considers "the defining feature of gay experience" to be the isolation and invisibility that gays experience by virtue of growing up without a supportive gay community. Unlike political identities rooted in ethnic heritage, race, or other traits, gay identity is not transmitted within the family nor routinely celebrated and reinforced by "an elaborate network of social and religious structures" (Sherrill 1996, 469). Indeed, as we noted above, gay identity is routinely stigmatized as aberrant, perverse, and immoral. This means that many gays are to some degree "closeted," hiding their sexual orientation from family, friends, and coworkers. Moreover, as Sherrill notes, gays are usually isolated from one another until adulthood. Despite the notoriety of certain gay neighborhoods in a few large cities, most gays do not live in ghettoized gay environments. Psychologically, this isolation and stigmatization may produce a crippling level of self-hatred. Politically (the impact we explore in this volume), these experiences undermine the formation of a common political identity and discourage people from mobilizing to achieve common goals.

The next two problems cited by Sherrill, affection and safety, have already been mentioned in the discussion of the motives for gay mobilization. By virtually every tangible indicator available to us, it is clear that gays remain disliked by a large share of the public at a very visceral level. Beyond sheer numbers, a most instructive and ironic datum is that 60 percent of subscribers to *OUT,* a serious magazine for gays and lesbians, request their copies in plain brown wrappers (Pettit 1994). As Wilcox and Wolpert demonstrate in chapter 16, the hostility of the public to gays is paramount because political action often reflects general attitudes to the groups who are engaged in struggle. Gays face an uphill battle in pursuing political success. The awareness of public hatred and the fear of violence that often accompanies it undermine efforts to develop an effective gay political identity. Gays are disinclined to risk retaliation by open identification with the movement, and potential allies from outside the gay community may think twice about allying their fortunes with such a despised population. That may explain why many gay officials hide their sexual orientation until they have built up considerable public trust, or why gay candidates have not been elected to public office in due proportion to the size of the gay community or enjoyed the same level of political success as blacks, Latinos, and other minority groups.[6]

The final problem is rooted in wealth. In estimating the financial status of homosexuals, opponents of gay rights have seized on marketing studies of people who subscribe to gay-oriented magazines. From statistics about the affluence of the readership, these opponents paint an exaggerated portrait about a "politically powerful minority" composed of citizens with "high disposable income" who operate through "a rich and powerful homosexual lobby in Washington."[7] Recognizing that magazine readers are not a representative sample of the larger population, the critics of this approach have turned instead to data from more representative surveys that include a question about gay identity. These data reveal a community that is financially disadvantaged relative to comparable heterosexuals (Badgett 1995). The claim that gays need less income because they do not have children to support also evaporates in the face of evidence to the contrary. Many gays do have children and may also have parents who need financial assistance as they age. Moreover, fear of public identification and concern about pervasive housing discrimination may force gay and lesbian couples to maintain two residences, an expense seldom encountered by heterosexual couples.

To better grasp the resource base of gays and lesbians, consider Sherrill's instructive contrast between gays and American Jews, another minority that constitutes about 3 percent of the population. American Jews are widely regarded as a model of what a determined minority can achieve in the political sphere (Goldberg 1996). Jewish organizations have led the effort to erase from the law almost all forms of overt anti-Semitism and have used the courts to undermine the legal advantages once enjoyed by Christians. Any public figure who publicly attacks Jews risks severe retaliation and a loss of respect. Hate crimes against Jews are likely to be punished swiftly and severely. On the positive side of the ledger, Jews have been elected to public office out of all proportion to their share of the population and have attained high leadership positions in government, industry, and academia. The nation's political parties and their candidates go out of their way to obtain the support of Jewish activists, contributors, and voters, wooing them openly and continuously. The major foreign policy priority of American Jews, the security of Israel, has been an important component of American policy in the Middle East. To achieve these ends, American Jewry has created and funded a plethora of religious, political, and charitable associations.

The political power of the gay community does not come close to matching the impressive resource base assembled by American Jews. Nor does it stack up favorably to the resources enjoyed by the religiously motivated opponents of gay rights. The American religious community is itself deeply divided by the question of homosexuality, and it is difficult to unambiguously classify the position of some of the largest and most powerful religious traditions on this difficult issue (Hartman 1996). Furthermore, given the tradition of local autonomy in American religious organization, individual congregations and religious leaders may take positions at odds with national or international church authorities. If we simply consider the one wing of the American religious mosaic that has been the most outspokenly opposed to gay political rights, evangelical Protestantism, the resource imbalance between gays and their opponents is clear. Approximately one-fourth of adult Americans with a religious affiliation are associated with evangelical congregations, and this movement boasts a large number of organized structures with substantial resources. Evangelicals have become one of the largest single religious voting blocs within the Republican coalition and support a number of political organizations that have earned reputations for effective political action. The resources available to gays and lesbians are simply not in the same league as their evangelical opponents.

Opportunity: The Political Opportunity Structure

Precisely because of the pervasiveness of antihomosexual feeling in the United States and the severe resource imbalance just described, some gay activists have doubted the utility of the political process. Why should gays compete on a playing field that is not level? Instead of struggling to deal with the symptoms of homophobia (repressive laws), these activists contend that the goal should be to root out the causes, the negative attitudes toward gays and lesbians. From this perspective, gays need to wage a "cultural" struggle to alter their status in the hearts and minds of Americans (Vaid 1995). Even with this common assumption, there remain substantial differences on how to implement a cultural strategy. Should gays strive to show how "normal" they are, how much their lives and aspirations resemble that of heterosexuals? Some advocates of this assimilationist model have given priority to seeking official legitimation of same-sex marriage as the best way to normalize gays in the minds of heterosexual Americans. Other advocates of the gay and lesbian cause believe in a more pointed and radical cultural offensive. In their minds, gays need to confront society directly, showing themselves as they are, rather than conforming to middle-class notions of respectability. By "acting out," it is alleged, gays will shatter the prejudice that consigns them to second-class citizenship. In this effort, gays also need to build bridges to other oppressed groups—blacks and other people of color, women, the disabled, et cetera.

The advocates of political action do not necessarily reject the notion that gays should pursue cultural activities, but they believe the movement should still focus its priorities on attaining political power and legal victories. The basis for this strategy is partly the recognition that gay disadvantage is crystallized by unequal legal treatment. Gays should, in a sense, fight the problem where it exists. But there is another reason why some activists stress the utility of a political and legal battle. Experience has taught that the law is itself a powerful instrument of political socialization. While law may reflect public attitudes, they argue, it is equally true that the law molds attitudes. This argument received powerful validation from the civil rights struggle of blacks in the 1950 and 1960s. By forcing white Americans to confront African Americans on the job, in public spaces and other venues where segregation once ruled, the law changed fundamental racial beliefs. Scholars continue to debate the extent of racism in American public opinion, but there is no question that Americans have lost their abstract belief in racial separation as changes in the law altered patterns of behavior. By sending the signal that discrimination is legally wrong, the community changes its view of the victims of discrimination and helps reduce the stigma against them. The advocates of political action by gays, lesbians and bisexuals believe the same outcome will occur once the law is altered to make it possible for gays and lesbians to identify their sexual orientation without suffering legal penalties. By pursuing a political strategy, it is argued, gays will both redress the symptoms of discrimination and reduce the underlying hostility on which that discrimination is based.

The choice between cultural and legal strategies depends heavily on judgments about the prospects for gays to succeed in conventional political activity. Research on other minorities suggests that the attainment of legal change through political activity is possible, but that it depends on a cluster of factors known collectively as the "political opportunity structure" (Tarrow 1994). Can the minority find support for its efforts among other population groups and attain in coalition the numbers it lacks on its own? Are political elites divided such that one segment of leadership may adopt the cause of the minority? Does the governmental structure offer places where minorities may overcome their numerical disadvantages to contest successfully for policy change? The experience of the women's movement, environmentalism, African Americans, and other social movements indicates that favorable conditions may indeed produce significant political and legal changes in status.

To date, the evidence suggests that the success of gays into the political process depends on the venue. In activities where resources such as numbers and wealth are critical, gays often run up against the "tyranny of the majority" identified by Alexis de Tocqueville. The electoral process has not been kind to gays and lesbians. Through mid-1996, for example, the National Gay and Lesbian Task Force (1996) reported that voter referenda on gay rights produced just 17 victories against 46 defeats. This poor record probably reflects a number of factors, but there is little doubt that gays are disadvantaged in competing for electoral support. Gays begin such campaigns with the disadvantage of popular antipathy and can only overcome it by turning out in huge numbers and inducing allies from other groups to do the same. To pass antigay initiatives or to repeal gay rights laws by referendum, the church-based opponents of gay rights can draw upon the natural organizing capacity of religious communities—their physical meeting places, telephone networks, regular gatherings, paid leadership, and moral credibility. By contrast, the gay community has to create political structures from scratch. There is simply no standing organizational equivalent within the gay community.

In the policy-making arenas of government, gays may face a slightly more level playing field (Haider-Markel and Meier 1996). If gays are sufficiently concentrated and organized to represent an important constituency in even a single district that elects a representative to the local governing body, they may find a patron for their cause. With patient negotiation and discussion, the patron may be able to assemble a coalition that is capable of passing some kind of remedial legislation. That has been the process by which civil rights legislation has been extended to sexual orientation in the ten states and more than 150 local communities mentioned above. But even at this level, one step removed from the electoral process, the stigma against homosexuality may operate as a powerful barrier to effective coalition. Kenneth Sherrill (1993, 100) cites former Senator Bill Bradley of New

Jersey as a case in point. In voting for a law that merely authorized the federal government to collect information on crimes of violence against gays and lesbians, Bradley went to extraordinary lengths to disassociate himself from the presumed beneficiaries of this action. It is difficult to conceive of another group who would have received the same treatment from the tolerant and urbane Senator Bradley. In states and communities with the initiative (a device that permits voters to repeal laws at the ballot box via referenda or propositions), the voters may overturn the actions of a legislative body. Thus the relatively greater success enjoyed in the governmental realm may be undone by popular electoral pressure.

Most minorities have found the judicial branch to be the one most open and accessible to claims that run against the grain of public opinion. Federal judges do not face election and are, in theory, freer than legislators or elected executives to rule on behalf of minority groups that seek legal protection. Perhaps because of that reputation for openness, gays have frequently turned to the courts for protection against various forms of discrimination. The results have been mixed. The state-level courts have often overturned antisodomy laws in the name of privacy and equal treatment. In the Cincinnati and Colorado cases, where voters not only repealed gay rights laws but set higher thresholds for including sexual orientation in protective legislation, the Supreme Court resoundingly rejected this action on equal protection grounds (Keen and Goldberg 1999). Yet while courts possess the greatest leeway to act on behalf of oppressed minorities, judges are hardly immune to public attitudes, and more than one judge has sent the message that gays do not enjoy public respect. Courts continue to deny visitation or guardianship to gay parents, hand out light penalties to persons convicted of vicious physical assaults on gays, and gratuitously repeat antigay prejudices and stereotypes. Apart from the *Romer* decision that struck down the Colorado legislation, the Supreme Court has remained tellingly silent on other gay-related political issues and has upheld state statutes against sexual practices associated with homosexuality. If the Courts are generally more receptive to claims by gays and lesbians than the other branches of government, they often fall far short of being friendly to homosexuality.

PLAN OF THE BOOK

This volume is organized into four parts. The chapters in the first part explore the gay community and the social movement that champions the cause of gay rights. In his overview, the distinguished historian John

D'Emilio provides a concise account of the development and progress of the homophile movement in the aftermath of World War II and follows that movement through various incarnations into the contemporary era. D'Emilio emphasizes that the progress of the movement has been neither uniform nor linear. Rather, the pulse of gay politics has alternated between cycles of intense accomplishment produced by major social and political dislocation and periods of relative quiescence in which gay activism advances and retreats in a lower key way. The distinction between "leaping" and "creeping," his name for the two cycles, also incorporates differences of political style. In the breakthrough periods of leaping, the agenda is dominated by bold, even radical visions of change marked by bold assertions of gay identity. In the creeping cycle that follows, political activism by gays deemphasizes militancy in favor of "dialogue, negotiation and moderation," often within a civil rights framework. Rather than choose between these modes of action, D'Emilio regards both as essential and suggests that the apparently quiescent periods of creeping lay the foundation for the episodes of radical political action that follow.

Since 1994, D'Emilio argues, the gay movement has been engaged primarily in the low-key, relatively mainstream political action typical of the creeping cycle. The next chapter explores the nature and consequences of this political style for gay progress. Craig Rimmerman offers a profile of the major organizations that dominate the assimilationist wing of the gay movement. He discusses each organization's purpose and relationship to the broader movement, the funding sources and social background of contributors and members, the central issues pursued by each group, and the major ends of its activity. Because all these organizations embrace a strategy that relies on gay access to elected officials, a classic insider approach, Rimmerman cautions that they need to learn important lessons from highly publicized incidents when even national leaders deemed sympathetic to gay causes have abandoned the movement. Gay initiatives cannot be entrusted solely to such insiders, Rimmerman believes, and must be sustained by a grassroots base of vibrant organizations capable of mobilizing gays and supporters on short notice.

The final chapters in part 1 raise questions about the representativeness of the gay movement by highlighting politically relevant race and gender differences among gays. Keith Boykin, a leader in efforts to broaden the inclusiveness of gay political action, concludes in chapter 4 that "black lesbians and gays do not play a meaningful role in the gay and lesbian political movement." African Americans played a pioneering role in stimulating gay consciousness, both by providing the model of the civil rights movement and by nurturing talented and forceful role models such as Lorraine Hansberry, Bayard Rustin, and James Baldwin. Nonetheless, the contemporary gay movement largely ignores its African-American constituency when it selects political priorities or chooses tactics. Boykin argues that the organized gay movement is squandering a valuable resource and offers several suggestions for promoting a more inclusive and representative movement. Jean Schroedel and Pamela Fiber (chapter 5) reach similar conclusions about the role of lesbians in the gay movement. They alert us to the importance of a lesbian separatist movement from the outset of modern gay political organizing and note that the gender integration of the gay movement is a relatively recent development. Despite the increasing prominence of women in gay organizations, they argue, those organizations continue to give priority to issues that disproportionately influence gay males and assign lower priorities to the particular concerns of lesbians. By means of a content analysis of Internet sites and a mail survey of openly gay elected officials, Schroedel and Fiber demonstrate significant divergence in the policy values that concern the men and women of the gay movement.

Part 2 provides a parallel analysis of the countermovement against gay and lesbian rights. The chapters focus upon the political organizations and strategies of the opposition. Foremost among these opponents, John Green argues in chapter 6, are the social traditionalists of the evangelical Protestant tradition whose major political embodiment is the Christian Right. This social movement is no less diverse than the gay movement with which it is locked in combat. Green divides the religious opposition into three categories based on whether the organization pursues instrumental, reactive, or proactive opposition. The instrumental opponents deploy antigay rhetoric as one weapon in an arsenal, aiming ultimately at the acquisition of political power. Reactive opposition (rejection of specific gay initiatives) is more concentrated and typically pursued by specialized organizations. The concept of proactive opposition refers to efforts to inhibit the gay community by closing off opportunities for political advance and putting the gay rights movement on the defensive. As Green's case studies illustrate, each strategy may yield significant dividends under favorable circumstances.

Didi Herman attempts to penetrate the worldview of Christian traditionalism in chapter 7. She explores the theological foundation of the movement in the premillennial strain of Protestant Christianity and shows how adherents of this perspective interpret homosexuality as part of a broader satanic force that includes feminism, environmentalism, and secularism. In her chapter on the political philosophy of the Christian Right, she parts company with those observers who have detected a maturing and moderation in the Christian Right, which is something akin to the creeping phase that D'Emilio located in gay political activity. Rather, Herman concludes, the antigay movement remains distinctive and radical in its goal of a Christian state with sweeping power to repress what it regards as immoral behavior.

The opponents of gay rights have capitalized on one important component of the political opportunity structure: the citizens' initiative that permits groups to place legislation directly on the ballot by obtaining a requisite number of voter signatures. Chapter 8 by Todd Donovan, Jim Wenzel, and Shaun Bowler examine the efforts by antigay groups to use this device in the battle over sexual orientation. At one level, the proliferation of antigay proposals at the state and local level seems to confirm the fears of those who regard the political arena as unremittingly hostile to gay and lesbian progress. But upon closer inspection, the authors report that the outcome of such initiatives hinges on the specifics of the proposal presented to voters. "Incremental" referendums that roll back recent gay advances in antidiscrimination protection are usually successful. The record is much more mixed for nonincremental policy changes, such as efforts to freeze existing laws or erect barriers against subsequent advances by the gay movement. The final class of referendums, proposals that involve radical departures from existing law that would implement new policies that penalize gays, have repeatedly failed to attract majority support from the electorate. Donovan, Wenzel, and Bowler speculate that advocates of these proposals may be driven less by the hope of success than by the publicity and resources such campaigns bring to the antigay movement.

The chapters in part 3 explore the specific issues around which gays and their opponents have mobilized. Gregory Lewis and Jonathan Edelson examine two recent civil rights initiatives on behalf of gays and lesbians, the campaigns for state-sanctioned gay marriage and the effort to bar employment discrimination in the federal government. Two gay men challenging the monopoly of marital status by heterosexuals in Hawaii largely imposed the first issue upon the organized gay community. The probability of the success of this lawsuit provided antigay organizations with a powerful weapon in the form of a campaign in defense of traditional marriage, a campaign that national gay organizations felt little alternative but to fight. One lesson from this chapter is that the gay community does not have the freedom to choose its own policy agenda.

On the other hand, the campaign against employment discrimination based on sexual orientation was a perennial item on the agenda of gay organizations. Despite their different provenance, these two issues were linked in 1996 when advocates of gay rights sought to weaken the proposed federal law against gay marriage by including the "Employment Non-Discrimination Act" in the bill. Despite their efforts, as Lewis and Edelson report, the "Defense of Marriage" bill passed but the antidiscrimination provision was stripped from the bill and was narrowly defeated in a separate Senate vote.

As several contributors note in earlier chapters, the AIDS epidemic was a critical factor in the emergence of the most recent wave of gay activism. Mark Rom (chapter 10) examines the politics of the crisis and concludes that AIDS, while not the first politicized disease, was the "most democratic" disease as measured by the degree to which the victims refused to cede control over policy making to medical experts and public officials. AIDS was one of the arenas in which gay activists clashed most intensely over the value of insider versus outsider political strategies. AIDS had contradictory impacts upon gay activism. On the one hand, because the disease was initially associated with the gay community, it stimulated a high level of activity by a wide range of gay participants and provided a rallying cry around which different segments of the community could coalesce. As Rom recounts, AIDS inspired an unprecedented wave of community organizing that has left a lasting impact. On the other hand, the disease itself decimated the community and its leadership, consumed attention that might have been devoted to other gay causes, and provided the opponents of gay progress with a particularly vivid symbol around which they could counter-mobilize through the means discussed in part 2.

Part 3 concludes with Francine D'Amico's review of gay exclusion policy in the U.S. Armed Services. This chapter provides an intensive account of how the military formulated and justified its traditional policy of excluding gays from service. She recounts the events that brought that policy under challenge and how the campaign to end gay exclusion metamorphosed into a confused and ambivalent policy known colloquially as "don't ask, don't tell." What was justified as a neutral standard has in operation proven itself to be a highly punitive policy that has made military life harsher and more uncertain for gays and lesbians, with disproportionate impact upon women.

In part 4, the contributors look at the different arenas where issues relevant to gays and lesbians are contested. Despite the focus of attention on national political debates over the issues discussed in part 3, much of the governmental activity affecting the lives of gay men and lesbians takes place outside Washington in cities, counties, and states. For that reason, chapter 12 by James Button, Barbara Rienzo, and Kenneth Wald examines the outcomes of efforts by gay and lesbian activists to pass antidiscrimination legislation based on sexual orientation in local governments. Such legislation has become law in well over one hundred cities and counties across the United States, often in the face of determined opposition by religious conservatives and some business leaders. Based on a survey of officials in communities with such protective legislation, they conclude that the laws cover relatively few areas of life and are enforced without much zeal in many areas, undercutting their impact. On the other hand, local observers reported that these laws did in fact reduce the incidence of discrimination, made gays and lesbians more comfortable in their communities, and often paved the way for more expansive policies such as domestic partner benefits. The report from the states in Donald Haider-Markel's essay (chapter 13) discusses the growing presence of gays in state legislatures—as lobbyists and activists and as elected officials. What difference has this made? Using both case studies and quantitative analysis, the author describes the extensive efforts undertaken by gay activists across different sets of issues: antidiscrimination protection, hate crimes laws, repeal of antisodomy laws, and the same-sex marriage controversy. As a rule, Haider-Markel found that the level of membership in gay organizations at the state level was a powerful influence on the passage of antidiscrimination legislation and hate crimes laws, and it also delayed the passage of bans on same-sex marriage. Taken together, these chapters offer some hope to advocates of conventional political activity at the local and state level.

The next two chapters in part 4 illuminate the status of gay concerns at the national level, focusing on Congress (chapter 14 by Colton Campbell and Roger Davidson) and the federal courts (chapter 15 by Sarah Brewer, David Kaib, and Karen O'Connor). Campbell and Davidson report that Congress had seldom considered gay concerns until AIDS forced the issue on the national agenda. Even then, a lack of familiarity with the issue and distaste for dealing openly with such controversial matters encouraged legislators to resort to an expert National Commission to help them frame an official policy. The outcome was a policy that stressed treatment and research (the goals of gay activists) rather than the punitive antigay measures proposed by social conservatives. By the time the issue of same-sex marriage made it to the congressional agenda, Congress was not reluctant to take up the issue but the outcome was overwhelming passage of the Defense of Marriage Act. The difference outcomes in the two policy areas, Campbell and Davidson argue, was partly due to the Republican takeover of Congress in 1994 and the less sympathetic atmosphere to gays and lesbians thereafter. Nonetheless, gays remain in a position to exert some influence because of their increasing involvement in congressional campaigns.

Despite the reputation of the legal process as relatively friendly to unpopular minorities, at least in comparison with the legislative process, Brewer, Kaib, and O'Connor conclude that the Supreme Court "has been notoriously reluctant to enter the legal fray" by hearing cases that raise issues about gay and lesbian rights. The Court has been petitioned on many occasions by several special purpose organizations created expressly to stimulate judicial support for gay rights and modeled in large part upon the success of the African-American community in its successful legal crusade against racial segregation. Despite these appeals, the courts had generally refused to consider such cases until in 1986 it shocked and angered gay activists by upholding the constitutionality of Georgia's criminal law against sodomy in *Bowers v. Hardwick* (1986). Apart from endorsing basic political rights for gays and lesbians when it struck down an antigay amendment added by referendum to the Colorado constitution, the Court has generally shown itself just as unwilling as Congress to deal with issues of concern to gays and lesbians. The confidence in the judicial arena as a relatively neutral forum where gay and lesbians have a level playing field may be misplaced.

In the final chapter, Clyde Wilcox and Robin Wolpert consider the factor that underlies reactions to gay political priorities at all levels of government: the force of public opinion. While conservative groups have attempted to portray gays and lesbians as immoral people who have freely chosen to practice a deviant lifestyle, the supporters of gay rights have tried to frame the issue in terms of equality and fairness. The underlying assumption of gay advocates has been that homosexuality is a relatively fixed orientation that does not involve free choice. Although gays and lesbians enjoy a relatively poor public image as described above, the data suggest a gradual improvement in public understanding. The emotional reaction to homosexuality and beliefs about its origins prove to be the major direct influences on public evaluations of gays and lesbians and individual preferences about policies designed to reduce discrimination against gays and lesbians. As expected, religious traditionalists hold the most negative views of gays and lesbians and support restrictive public policies. These findings suggest that the way Americans frame the question—whether homosexuality is a moral problem or a condition that unfairly imposes legal disability—largely determines how Americans react to the campaign for gay rights. To the extent that scientific research determines whether gayness is a matter of choice or a biologically-driven orientation, the authors speculate, public attitudes are likely either to harden or to become more sympathetic to gay liberation.

SUMMARY

Taken together, the studies that make up this volume attest to the considerable political progress made by gays and lesbians since the emergence of the social movement dedicated to gay rights in the late 1960s and 1970s. Although the record of achievement falls far short of the wishes of the movement's most ardent advocates, it still marks a substantial improvement over the conditions faced by the pioneers of gay political organizing in the 1950s.

Nonetheless, when we compare the advances of the gay rights movement to the other social movements that emerged from the tumultuous 1960s, the glass symbolizing gay rights appears only half full. Environmentalism, once the preserve of cranks and tree-huggers, is now enshrined as a high value in American public policy and has attained something of the status of a "motherhood" issue. Although it has not stopped environmental degradation altogether, the social movement dedicated to preserving nature has claimed a strong voice in American public life. The women's movement can rightfully take credit for establishing gender equality as a consensus goal in policy if not in fact. The civil rights movements pursued by African Americans, Latinos, and other racial and ethnic minorities have also borne fruit in the form of ameliorative public policies, a changing public climate, and acquisition of government office. Even movements that were relative latecomers to the political arena, such as the crusades on behalf of consumers and the disabled, can point to impressive legislative accomplishments and a supportive climate in public opinion.

By comparison, the movement on behalf of gays and lesbians has lagged. Unlike most of the other social causes that emerged in the recent past, the campaign for gay and lesbian rights has yet to achieve unquestioned public legitimacy. Political opponents feel free to defame gays and lesbians with insensitive language and slanderous charges they would not dare use against any other social movement. The primary goal of the movement, to attack discrimination based on sexual orientation by changing law and policy, has yet to be realized in any arena beyond the state and local level. Even many of the successes reveal weaknesses. AIDS had initially to be "degayed" before Congress would treat it with the urgency it demanded, and gays were often incorporated under hate crime legislation that passed only because groups with more social acceptability were publicly identified as the main beneficiaries. Sometimes depicted as a juggernaut, the gay rights movement is perhaps better portrayed as a caravan of covered wagons slowly making its way across hostile territory, forced to stop every few miles and circle the wagons to ward off enemy attacks.

If the gay rights movement has achieved less than parallel movements that emerged at the same time, a fair assessment, that reflects the social reality that gays had (and have) a greater distance to traverse than most social movements. In their efforts to fight discrimination and obtain a place at the table, gays face a political system that is famous for its complexity and decentralization, offering to advocacy groups both opportunities for advance and obstacles to success. If the period since the Stonewall Rebellion is any indication, it seems that gay and lesbian organizations will continue to press forward with their demands and their opponents, no less determined, will exploit every avenue of resistance in an ongoing political struggle.

NOTES

1. I am grateful for the constructive comments and suggestions of my coeditors, my colleague Jim Button, and the external reviewers of the manuscript. It should be understood that all references to "gays" are a linguistic shorthand meant to incorporate gay men, lesbians, and bisexuals.
2. For some important exceptions, see the recent works by Hertzog (1996), Rayside (1998), and Bailey (1998).
3. By executive order, President Clinton has extended antidiscrimination protection to gay and lesbian federal employees but this protection does not have permanent status.
4. There are many who do believe the Constitution should be understood to prohibit discrimination based solely on sexual orientation, just as it has been read since 1954 to forbid discrimination by race (Gerstmann 1999; Karst 1993). The federal courts have not accepted this interpretation. Moreover, it required the passage of the Civil Rights Act (1964) and the Voting Rights Act (1965) to achieve effective implementation of the rights that African Americans enjoyed under the Constitution.

5. There is a sharp distinction between engaging in homosexual activity and claiming homosexual orientation (Murray 1996, chap. 1). The former category is much larger than the latter. That, plus the undeniable feeling of danger in revealing gay identity, accounts for what experts believe is the considerable underestimate of the gay population in most studies.

6. Until the recent election of Tammy Baldwin from Wisconsin, no openly gay man or woman had been elected to Congress. The few openly gay congressional representatives came out publicly well *after* their election.

7. The first two quotations are taken from Justice Antonin Scalia's dissent in *Romer v. Evans,* the 1996 Supreme Court decision reviewed in chapters 8 and 15. The comment about the powerful Washington lobby is taken from a June 1996 "Legislative Action Alert" issued by Beverly LaHaye, chairman of Concerned Women for America.

REFERENCES

Abelove, Henry, Michele Aina Barale, and David M. Halperin, eds. 1993. *The lesbian and gay studies reader.* New York: Routledge.

Badgett, M. V. Lee. 1995. The wage effects of sexual orientation discrimination. *Industrial and Labor Relations Review* 48:726–39.

Bailey, Robert. 1998. *Gay politics / urban politics.* New York: Columbia University Press.

Bowers v. Hardwick, 478 U.S. 186 (1986).

Bull, Chris, and John Gallagher. 1996. *Perfect enemies: The religious right, the gay movement and the politics of the 1990s.* New York: Crown Publishers.

Chauncey, George. 1998. The ridicule of gay and lesbian studies threatens all academic inquiry. *Chronicle of Higher Education* 44 (3 July): 40A.

Deitcher, David, ed. 1995. *The question of equality: Lesbian and gay politics in America since Stonewall.* New York: Scribner.

Diani, Mario. 1992. The concept of social movement. *Sociological Review* 40:1–25.

Duberman, Martin. 1993. *Stonewall.* New York: Dutton.

Fleischmann, Arnold. 1998. Acting locally: What works. *Harvard Gay and Lesbian Review* 5:54–55.

Gerstmann, Evan. 1999. The constitutional underclass: Gays, lesbians, and the failure of class-based equal protection. Chicago: University of Chicago Press.

Goldberg, J.J. 1996. *Jewish power: Inside the American Jewish establishment.* Reading, Mass.: Addison-Wesley.

Haider-Markel, Donald P., and Kenneth J. Meier. 1996. The politics of gay and lesbian rights: Expanding the scope of the conflict. *Journal of Politics* 58:332–49.

Harbeck, Karen. 1992. Introduction to *Coming out of the classroom closet*, edited by Karen Harbeck. New York: Harrington Park Press, 1–7.

Hartman, Keith. 1996. *Congregations in conflict: The battle over homosexuality*. New Brunswick, N.J.: Rutgers University Press.

Harvard Law Review. 1990. *Sexual orientation and the law*. Cambridge: Harvard University Press.

Hertzog, Mark. 1996. *The lavender vote: Lesbians, gay men, and bisexuals in American electoral politics*. New York: New York University Press.

Karst, Kenneth L. 1993. *Law's promise, law's expression*. New Haven: Yale University Press.

Keen, Lisa, and Suzanne B. Goldberg. 1999. *Strangers to the law: Gay people on trial*. Ann Arbor: University of Michigan Press.

Largent, Steve, et al. 1996. Can government save the family? *Policy Review* 79 (Sept.–Oct.): 43–47.

Murray, Stephen O. 1996. *American gay*. Chicago: University of Chicago Press.

National Gay and Lesbian Task Force. 1996. The record on gay-related referenda questions (leaflet). Washington, D.C.: NGLTF.

Pettit, Sarah. 1994. In or out? *Newsweek*. 22 August, p. 14.

Rayside, David. 1998. *On the fringe: Gays and lesbians in politics*. Ithaca, N.Y.: Cornell University Press.

Rubinstein, William B., ed. 1993. *Lesbians, gay men and the law*. New York: New Press.

Sherrill, Kenneth. 1993. On gay people as a politically powerless group. In *Gays and the military*, edited by Marc Woshinsky and Kenneth Sherrill. Princeton: Princeton University Press, 84–120.

———. 1996. The political power of lesbians, gays and bisexuals. *PS: Political Science and Politics* 29:469–73.

Singer, Bennett L., and David Deschamps, eds. 1994. *Gay and lesbian stats*. New York: New Press.

Tarrow, Sidney. 1994. *Power in movement: Social movements, collective action and politics*. New York: Cambridge University Press.

Vaid, Urvashi. 1995. *Virtual equality: The mainstreaming of gay and lesbian liberation*. New York: Anchor Books.

Zald, Mayer N., and John D. McCarthy, eds. 1979. *The dynamics of social movements: Resource mobilization, social control and tactics*. Cambridge, Mass.: Winthrop.

I. THE GAY MOVEMENT

CYCLES OF CHANGE, QUESTIONS OF STRATEGY:
THE GAY AND LESBIAN MOVEMENT AFTER FIFTY
YEARS

John D'Emilio

Fifty years have elapsed since Harry Hay, an American
Communist living in southern California, entertained the
guests at a gay party by spinning out a plan for an imagi-
nary political organization of homosexuals. In the in-
tervening half century, gay men and lesbians have taken
Hay's idea and run with it. They have built thousands of
organizations—local, statewide, and national—dedicated
to the proposition that they deserve the same rights and
ought to be treated with the same respect as other Americans.

Many of these organizations have been explicitly political. They work to influence the outcome of elections; affect
the content of party platforms; lobby for or against the
passage of new laws and the repeal of existing ones; re-
shape the interpretation of the law through litigation; negotiate with bureaucrats to change the policies of government agencies; and pressure public officials through noisy
demonstrations. Many more of these organizations are not
directly involved in the political process. Lesbians and gay
men have created community centers, social service organizations, institutions for religious worship, sports
leagues, health clinics, newspapers, magazines, bookstores,
and publishing companies. More social and cultural than
political in their expressed missions, these organizations
nonetheless feed into the stream of overt political activity.
By fostering stronger community ties and a collective
awareness of belonging to a minority group, these organizations constitute a foundation on which to build sustained

political engagement. In other words, the relationship of the gay movement and the gay community is close and interdependent.

Over the course of five decades, the work of all of these organizations, along with the actions of individuals and the support of mainstream groups and institutions, has dramatically changed the place of gay men and lesbians in American politics, law, society, and culture. Enough has happened over a long enough time to make it possible to do more than simply describe change. Half a century of public engagement over the status of gays and lesbians offers the opportunity to observe cycles of activity, suggest patterns of change, and draw conclusions that go beyond single campaigns, particular issues, and discrete local studies.

In this chapter I propose to do three things. First, I will offer a brief overview of the history of the gay and lesbian movement in the United States, sketching with broad brush strokes the main contours of political activity and change. Second, I will address the issue of the velocity and intensity of change by teasing out from the historical record some sense of cyclical patterns. Third, I will turn to questions of strategy, not in relation to individual goals or issues but more broadly—to the underlying strategic assumptions that have guided much of the movement's work in different eras. I will end by pointing to some of the implications this analysis may have for contemporary choices facing gay and lesbian political activists.

AN HISTORICAL OVERVIEW

Post–World War II Origins

The gay movement was born from the tension created by a brief interlude of freedom quickly followed by intense repression. By disrupting typical patterns of heterosexual sociability, World War II dramatically accelerated the development of a shared group identity among lesbians and gay men. The increased sex segregation, the geographic mobility, and the temporary freedom from the constraints of family allowed large numbers of young men and women, in a concentrated period of time, to explore their sexual desires and discover communities of men and women like themselves (Berube 1990). The effects can be seen in the immediate postwar years: a growth in the number of gay and lesbian bars; the appearance of a spate of novels with gay and lesbian themes; the release of the Kinsey study of male sexual behavior in 1948 and the attention its findings on homosexuality received; the courageous efforts of some veterans to challenge the discharges they received for homosexual conduct; the publication in 1951 of *The Homosexual in America,* a plea for understanding and tolerance of an unrecognized minority group in America (Kinsey et al. 1948; Cory 1975; D'Emilio 1983, chap. 2).

But the postwar years also brought an intensely conservative reaction. Most often thought of as a political era of virulent anticommunism at home, the broad phenomenon known as McCarthyism witnessed as well an attack on homosexuals at every level of government and in a wide array of institutions. The Senate investigated the employment of "sex perverts" by the government; the military conducted witch hunts against gays and lesbians; the FBI began surveillance of the gay community; postal authorities opened the mail of suspected homosexuals. In cities around the country, police harassed and arrested lesbians and gay men, while the press reported the names of these targets of overzealous law enforcement officials. Throughout the 1950s, hundreds of gays and lesbians daily experienced trouble with the police, other government agencies, or their employers (Senate 1950; D'Emilio 1992, chap. 3).

In this setting, Harry Hay and a few other leftist gay men formed a secret organization, the Mattachine Society, in Los Angeles in 1951, dedicated to "liberating one of our largest minorities from . . . persecution" (D'Emilio 1983, 9). Although they envisioned a radical organization that would mobilize masses of homosexuals to make change, the conservative temper of the 1950s led the organization, and the inchoate movement it was launching, in a more moderate direction. The Mattachine Society, along with the Daughters of Bilitis ("DOB"), a lesbian organization formed in San Francisco in 1955, spoke in softer, gentler tones. Making a plea for tolerance, they focused on education and information. Each organization published a magazine, established chapters in several cities, held public forums, and made contact with sympathetic professionals in law, medicine, and religion. As a counterpoint, a small group of more defiant gays published a magazine, *ONE,* that offered a sassier, bolder, and brasher voice—so much so that, after the postal authorities confiscated copies of it as obscene, the editors of *ONE* challenged the action and won a Supreme Court ruling that protected their right to publish material about homosexuality. It was the only significant legal victory of the 1950s (D'Emilio 1983, chap. 7).

The accommodationist stance of the Mattachine and DOB was very much suited to the times. It allowed the groups to take root, thus beginning a tradition of formal lesbian and gay organization that remains continuous to the present day. But the approach of these first activists also did not promise much in the way of change.

Provoked by the heroism of the southern civil rights movement and the idealistic rhetoric of the Kennedy presidency, the temper of the country began to shift in the early 1960s. The changed mood affected the outlook of the gay movement. In the northeast, a group of newer recruits began to speak with greater self-assurance. For instance, activists such as Frank Kameny, Barbara Gittings, and Jack Nichols boldly rejected the dominant medical view of homosexuality as an illness and confidently asserted the inherent health and goodness of their sexual orientation. Through letter-writing, meetings, public picketing, and litigation, they also directly challenged the discriminatory practices of the federal government, which banned the employment of lesbians and gay men in all federal jobs and denied them security clearances in the private sector. By the late 1960s, they had won two key cases in federal court that began the process of overturning the ban (D'Emilio 1983, chap. 8; *Scott* 1965; *Norton* 1969).

In San Francisco, meanwhile, a combination of police repression and political scandals was provoking greater militancy among activists there. In 1961, Jose Sarria, a drag performer in one of the city's gay bars, ran for the Board of Supervisors in response to the police attacks on the gay subculture. His campaign led to the birth of San Francisco's first gay community newspaper as well as the formation of a trade association among gay bar owners. Before long, activists were in dialogue with some of the city's liberal Protestant ministers, were meeting regularly with public officials, and were holding candidate nights during fall electoral campaigns (D'Emilio 1992, chap. 4).

By the late 1960s, gay and lesbian activists across the country were creating tighter networks among themselves. Fledgling groups appeared in as many as two dozen cities. Their basic goals of fair employment practices and the repeal of sodomy laws had won the endorsement of mainstream organizations like the American Civil Liberties Union which, increasingly, was advocating for this still-small social movement. Court cases in a number of states had provided gay bars with some protection against harassment, while the Supreme Court had further narrowed the applicability of obscenity statutes to homosexual material. Prodded by activists, dissenting voices within the medical profession were beginning to challenge the reigning orthodoxy that viewed homosexuality as disease (D'Emilio 1983, chap. 11).

From Stonewall to AIDS

Even as these developments reoriented the focus of the gay movement away from the cautious educational efforts of the 1950s toward a more active engagement with law, politics, and public policy, the leading edge of social protest in the United States had moved far beyond the liberal, though militant, reform efforts of most gay activists. Black Power, the New Left, the antiwar movement, an emerging women's liberation movement, the youth counterculture: together these were creating a profound generational divide in which many adolescents and young adults broke sharply with mainstream values. Espousing a rhetoric of revolution, radicals in a variety of movements set themselves against not only the American government, but most forms of institutional authority (Gitlin 1987; Anderson 1995).

The Stonewall Riots of June 1969—when the drag queens and other patrons of the Stonewall Inn in Greenwich Village fought the police who were raiding the bar—became the catalytic event that allowed young gay men and lesbians to draw the connection between their own status as homosexuals and the larger political critique that the movements of the 1960s were making about American society. Taking advantage of the extensive networks of communication that radicals of the 1960s had built, they created a new kind of gay and lesbian movement. Adopting organizational names such as the Gay Liberation Front, Radicalesbians, and Third World Gay Revolution, these activists brought anger, militancy, and an anarchic kind of daring to the goal of gay and lesbian freedom. They conducted sit-ins in the offices of newspapers and magazines that purveyed demeaning images of homosexuals; they marched in the street to protest police harassment; they disrupted the conventions of psychiatrists who proclaimed them to be sick; they occupied campus buildings to win concessions from university administrators. Proclaiming the necessity of "coming out of the closet" as the first essential step toward freedom, they acted on their beliefs by being as visible as they could in every sphere of life. They also produced a new kind of writing about homosexuality: one that used the language of oppression, that analyzed sexuality and gender roles as mechanisms of inequality, and that argued for the relationship between gay oppression and other forms of social injustice (Altman 1971; Jay and Young 1992; Duberman 1993; Teal 1971; Kissack 1995).

The message of gay liberation and lesbian feminism proved infectious, and it spread very quickly. On the eve of Stonewall, almost twenty years after the founding of the Mattachine Society, there were perhaps fifty gay and lesbian social change organizations in the United States. By 1973, four years after Stonewall, there were over eight hundred. The impulse to work in an organized way for change spread quickly from large cities like New

York, San Francisco, and Los Angeles, and from liberal university communities like Berkeley, Madison, Ann Arbor, and Cambridge, to cities and towns in every region of the country.

The gay men and lesbians motivated by Stonewall and the protest movements of the 1960s left an important legacy, one in which the notion of coming out as the key to change and pride as a stance towards one sexual identity were central. These characteristics were adopted by virtually all the individuals and groups comprising the post-Stonewall movement. But the radical sea that spawned gay liberation was already drying up by the early 1970s. As the decade wore on, most of the organizations campaigning for gay freedom eschewed revolutionary rhetoric and instead tended to adopt one of two approaches to social change: (1) the reform of laws, public policies, and institutional practices so that lesbians and gay men enjoyed fair and equal treatment, and (2) the building of institutions designed to create a strong, cohesive, and visible community (Marotta 1981). The two purposes, of course, were intimately related since a well-organized, articulate, and mobilized community has a greater ability to change laws and public policies. And, to describe many of these organizations as "reform-oriented" says little about the tactics they wielded, which ranged from drafting legislation, lobbying elected officials, and registering voters to picketing, marching, and civil disobedience.

For instance, Lambda Legal Defense and Education Fund, an "ACLU" for gays and lesbians, was founded in 1973 with the purpose of using litigation to make change. The National Gay Task Force, also founded in 1973, worked with federal bureaucrats to change policies in areas such as immigration and the issuance of security clearances, and also sought to mobilize gays and lesbians to run as delegates to the national conventions of the major political parties. Locally, an organization like the Gay Activist Alliance of Washington, D.C. worked to change police practices and campaigned for gay-friendly candidates for office. Around the country, gays and lesbians created community centers; they published newspapers and opened bookstores; they formed bowling and softball leagues, and attended services at gay churches and synagogues; they staffed their own health clinics. And they also began to form caucuses and mobilize within institutions such as religious denominations, colleges and universities, professional associations of various kinds, and labor unions.

Not surprisingly, the higher visibility, the more extensive level of organization, and the new language of pride and respect sparked a significant degree of change in the decade after Stonewall. By the early 1980s, roughly half the states had repealed their sodomy statutes; more than three dozen municipalities, including some of the nation's larger cities, had prohibited discrimination on the basis of sexual preference or orientation; and some political figures of national stature spoke out in favor of gay rights (Button et al. 1997, chap. 3). Building on work that had started before Stonewall, activists succeeded in persuading the American Psychiatric Association in 1973 to eliminate homosexuality from its list of mental disorders; two years later, the federal Civil Service Commission dropped its blanket ban on the employment of lesbians and gay men (Bayer 1981). During the Carter presidency, a delegation of gay and lesbian leaders were invited to the White House to discuss their goals, and in 1980 the Democratic Party included a gay rights plank in its national platform. A good number of court cases had been won which seemed definitively to establish that gay and lesbian organizations enjoyed the constitutional protections of the First Amendment.

Even as the gay and lesbian community grew more visible and became more densely organized, the almost utopian sense of optimism that followed in the wake of Stonewall was fading. By the early 1980s, the nation's politics and social climate were growing more conservative, as witnessed by the election of Ronald Reagan to the White House in 1980 and the Republican majority in the Senate. The further repeal of sodomy statutes virtually stopped in the 1980s, and the passage of civil rights protections for homosexuals slowed as well. At the same time that legislative advances became less common, a more aggressive opposition to the gay movement coalesced. First coming to national attention in 1977, through the campaign led by Anita Bryant to repeal gay rights legislation in Dade County, Florida, an antigay Christian conservatism mounted similar successful campaigns in a number of localities. In Congress, conservative Republicans proposed a Family Protection Act designed in part to fortify the legislative barriers against gay equality (Deitcher 1995, chap. 2).

Coincident with the rise of these outside threats were the internal divisions that compromised the ability of activists to mobilize their constituents and have the movement speak with a unified voice. Since the early 1970s, male sexism had led many lesbians to organize separate groups for women; by the end of the 1970s, a similar process was underway among gay people of color antagonized by the persistence of white racism in the institutions of the gay community. Differences also regularly emerged between those who pursued mainstream methods of lobbying, education, and negotiation and those who urged more militant, confrontational tactics; between those whose work gave priority to opening up mainstream institutions to gays and lesbians and those who valued the building of almost "nationalist" communities; and between those who saw homophobia and gay oppression as self-contained issues needing political attention and those who saw gay freedom coming only through a broader multi-issue struggle for social justice.

In the short run these conflicts variously bred anger, frustration, and the fracturing of a movement still too weak to achieve its full range of goals. In the longer run, the efforts to respond to them promised a more densely organized community, with the experience of employing a fuller range of tactics to make change, involving participants who reflected the social complexity of American society. For beneath all the particular campaigns and conflicts there remained one overriding fact in the early 1980s: the vast majority of lesbians and gay men, more than a decade after Stonewall and a generation after the founding of the Mattachine Society, remained "in the closet." Many were willing to socialize within gay and lesbian worlds, but kept their identity a secret from outsiders; many others even maintained a distance from any of the institutions of the gay community.

AIDS and Its Impact

The biggest challenge, perhaps because completely unexpected, soon became the source of renewed political momentum for the gay and lesbian movement. In 1981, the Centers for Disease Control first reported the mysterious outbreak of fatal illnesses among clusters of gay men in a few major urban areas. Soon labeled Acquired Immuno-Deficiency Syndrome, it spread during the 1980s with alarming rapidity among gay and bisexual men. In contrast to some other recently identified medical conditions—Legionnaire's Disease and Toxic Shock Syndrome—the media gave AIDS little attention, and government, especially in Washington, was loathe to devote resources to combating the epidemic. When combined with the antigay rhetoric that the epidemic spawned, AIDS initially highlighted the vulnerability and relative political weakness of the gay and lesbian community (Shilts 1987).

But AIDS also unleashed vitally new constructive energy. Within a few years, gays and lesbians had built a nationwide infrastructure of organizations that provided health care and social services, assisted in scientific research, spearheaded prevention campaigns, and engaged in spirited public advocacy to combat the epidemic and the discrimination entwined with it. The fight against AIDS had startling effects: It brought many more gays and lesbians out of the closet, as the life-and-death nature of the epidemic overcame the fear of coming out; it led to renewed cooperation among lesbians and gay men; it provided a more visible platform for lesbians and gays of color and more resources for them to build organizations of their own to fight AIDS. Eventually, policymakers at every level of government and in a host of other mainstream institutions opened their doors to gay men and lesbians wearing the hat of AIDS activist. And, once opened, it became easier for activists to use this new access to address issues of homophobia and gay oppression (Andriote 1999; D'Emilio 1992, chap. 20).

The effects can be seen most clearly through two events in 1987: the national march on Washington to fight AIDS and to promote equality for gays and lesbians; and the birth of ACT UP ("AIDS Coalition to Unleash Power"). In 1979, activists had organized a first national march; generous estimates put the crowd at one hundred thousand. Now, eight years and many deaths from AIDS later, well over half a million men and women assembled from around the country. For many the experience was so powerful that they returned home with a determination not only to halt the spread of AIDS but to live openly as gay or lesbian. Meanwhile, a new militancy was spreading among AIDS activists, which found expression in the direct action group, ACT UP. In local communities and in Washington D.C., members engaged in confrontational tactics in order to prod public officials to take more vigorous action against the epidemic (Kramer 1989; Crimp 1990; Vaid 1995, chap. 3).

Although the AIDS movement and the gay movement were not identical, the boundary between them has always been indistinct and permeable. Thus, the activism that AIDS had engendered also translated by the late 1980s into a more dynamic movement for gay and lesbian liberation. Locally, for instance, the pause in the passage of municipal gay rights laws yielded to an upsurge in the number of cities adopting such measures. State legislatures joined the parade, too, as several of them extended legal protections based on sexual orientation, and many more enacted statutes punishing hate crimes against lesbians and gay men. At the national level, activists participated in two key coalitions which brought them historic legislative victories in 1990: passage of the Hate Crimes Statistics Act, which mandated that the FBI collect statistics on hate-motivated violence, including that based on sexual orientation; and the Americans with Disabilities Act, whose provisions banned discrimination against people infected with the HIV-virus that causes AIDS.

Other indicators of change were also emerging by the early 1990s. Mainstream news media were devoting more substantial coverage to the lesbian and gay community so that issues of sexual identity became woven into the fabric of what was deemed newsworthy (Alwood 1996, chap. 14). Out-of-the-closet candidates were running for political office and winning, while a few members of Congress who had been closeted were able to secure reelection after coming out (DeBold 1994). Campaigns to win legislative protection against discrimination were increasingly complemented by the efforts of employees in the workplace and through unions to secure on-the-job guarantees. Notions of equality expanded to encompass not just the rights of individuals, but also those of the family unit as gays and lesbians fought for domestic partnership recognition, legal marriage, and access to adoption. Finally, in 1992 a major political party for the first time nominated for president a candidate, Bill Clinton, who openly campaigned for the support of the gay community and promised to take action around issues important to this constituency. And, within days of Clinton's inauguration, a gay issue—the military ban against homosexuals—moved to the front and center of national politics (Mixner 1996).

The 1992–93 political season also saw the opponents of gay rights coalesce into a political force more potent than ever. While the Democrats nominated Clinton, the Republican national convention of August 1992 witnessed virulent homophobic rhetoric and the incorporation of explicitly antigay planks into the party platform. That fall, in Colorado and Oregon, militant antagonists of the gay movement campaigned for voter approval of statewide ballot initiatives that would have repealed and prohibited legislative remedies against discrimination based on sexual orientation. Early in 1993, a bipartisan coalition in Congress quickly took the initiative on the military issue away from the president and the gay community suffered a major defeat. By the mid-1990s, the Christian Right had built a powerful network of organizations that made fomenting fear of homosexuals a central element of their strategy (Bull and Gallagher 1996).

The Current Moment

In the wake of the military debacle, leaders of the gay and lesbian movement were forced to pause and take stock. On the one hand, there was no question that the community's quest for equality now occupied a recognized place on the political agenda. Issues such as workplace equity, marriage and parenting rights, and the responsiveness of the public schools to its gay students and personnel remained prominently in the public eye, as they were debated in local communities and state legislatures across the country. Especially in the realm of popular culture, a new kind of plateau had been reached. Particularly on television, but in Hollywood as well, gays and lesbians were becoming a standard fixture. No longer framed as monsters, nor relegated to an occasional walk-on role, they were increasingly a regular part of the social landscape.

On the other hand, there was a fractiousness to the debate about homosexuality that highlighted the lack of social consensus and that often produced political stalemate, contradiction, or both. For instance, by the mid-1990s, state capitols had become the site of ongoing legislative debate on gay issues, but the measures that were introduced and passed were equally likely to be gay-friendly or gay-hostile (NGLTF 1997; 1998). Even at the level of the Supreme Court the absence of consensus was striking. In the historic *Romer v. Evans* decision in 1996, a majority of the court ruled that gay rights laws cannot be banned. "A state cannot so deem a class of people a stranger to its laws," wrote Justice Anthony Kennedy, in a strong enunciation of elemental principles of fairness (Eskridge and Hunter 1997, 93). Yet even as it issued this decision, the nation still lived with the consequences of a decision ten years earlier, in *Bowers v. Hardwick*, in which the Court upheld the constitutionality of sodomy laws that, historically, have provided much of the justification for discrimination against gay people (Rubinstein 1993, 132).

Without question, this overview has tended to flatten the story of the gay and lesbian movement. It offers a view of the forest, and renders indistinct the wealth of detail and variety to be found in all the trees. It ignores, for instance, differences in regional experience; it gives scant attention to vigorous, often contentious, debates within the gay and lesbian community; it emphasizes general patterns at the expense of local particularity. But with these limitations recognized, the account I have offered does also provide a thumbnail sketch of the broad contours of change.

CYCLES OF CHANGE

Students of American reform have long attempted to understand what provokes change in American politics, why some eras witness rapid mobilization of citizens and major alterations in policy, and what happens to social movements during "the doldrums," those periods of quiescence when a society does not seem responsive to agitation for change (Rupp and Taylor 1987). One study of American politics has noted that change occurs "both incrementally and in bursts," leading the authors to conclude that a "punctuated equilibrium" best describes how new policy agendas get set and implemented (Baumgartner and Jones 1993, 235–36). A study of feminism in the last generation has commented on the importance of understanding how social movements "endure," how there are periods when a movement seems to be "in abeyance" and other times when movements "change relatively rapidly" (Whittier 1995, 255–57).

In looking at the history of the gay and lesbian movement over the last fifty years, it is abundantly clear that the velocity of change–within the movement and in the implementation of its goals—has not been steady. In fact, careful scrutiny suggests something very different. For the gay and lesbian movement, change has come in the form of alternating cycles of what we might colloquially describe as "leaping" and "creeping." Identifying these cycles, whose rhythms seem at first glance to be thoroughly unpredictable, can help us make sense of the course of the lesbian and gay movement. It may also contribute to a deeper appreciation of the processes of change in social movements more generally and in American politics as well.

The first leap forward came in the late 1940s and early 1950s and was marked by the appearance of the Kinsey studies of human sexuality, Donald Webster Cory's manifesto for homosexual rights, and the founding of the Mattachine Society. An awareness of oppression had crystallized in the minds of a few, and some of them had resolved to do something about it in a collective and organized way. But it was almost as if the effort required to launch a movement exhausted all of the available political opportunity. For well over a decade, a small core of brave people crept along, one very small step at a time. They were floating the new idea that homosexuals were the targets of unjust treatment. They were standing up for themselves, initiating a social dialogue, and experimenting with different kinds of strategies, but they could not succeed at much more than that.

The second great leap forward came in the handful of years around the Stonewall Riot. Galvanized by the radical upheavals of the 1960s and further inspired by the image of rioting drag queens, a cohort of young adult gays and lesbians adopted a stance of confident, almost defiant pride toward their sexual identities. They adopted the imperative to come out as the key element in the new movement they were building. And, taking the need for militant political action as a given, they targeted the key institutions that seemed complicitous in the oppression of gays and lesbians. Since many forms of institutionalized authority in the United States were wobbling as a result of a decade of protest, these gay radicals were able to accomplish a lot in a short period of time.

But the revolution that gay liberationists and lesbian feminists saw on the horizon never arrived, and for the next long stretch of time, gay and lesbian activists once again crept along. Incorporating both pride and coming out into the core sense of what it meant to be gay, these activists formed organizations, built community institutions, persisted in their efforts to affect law, public policy, and mainstream institutions, and generally maintained a higher level of visibility than their pre-Stonewall predecessors. What they lacked, and what the previous leap forward had not yet provided, were two key ingredients for a successful social movement: a mass constituency and an organizational infrastructure capable of successfully mobilizing it.

Coming in the wake of the AIDS epidemic, the third leap forward was roughly bounded by the 1987 March on Washington and the debate over the military exclusion policy in 1993. Like gay liberation of the Stonewall era, activists in these years frequently used militant direct action tactics. But unlike the two earlier periods of leaping ahead, this one witnessed movement and community organizations sinking secure roots in every region of the country. The movement for gay and lesbian equality also shifted in these years from being a predominantly volunteer effort to one in which many organizations were able to hire paid staff. In other words, the resources of the movement expanded enormously in these years, and the results could be seen not only in an even higher level of visibility, but in the string of successes that were achieved at the local, state, and national level. Gay issues in this period became a permanent part of the world of politics and public policy, and gay people became a regularly visible part of American cultural and social life. But the failure to repeal the military ban in 1993 and the presence of an ever-stronger organized conservative force in American politics put the brakes on change before this leap could reach the longer range goal of forging a new majority consensus around the place of gays and lesbians in American society.

Something to notice about the periods of leaping ahead is that they cannot solely—or even primarily—be explained by the will, the grit, or the savvy of activists themselves. Rather, they are provoked by social or political turmoil that creates new openings for change, or new motivations to act. The first leap forward occurred in the context of the intense social disruptions of World War II and the equally intense repression of the early Cold War. The second grew out of a decade of tumultuous political and cultural protest that threw into question many of the core beliefs of Americans. The third leap was a result of the sudden and rapid spread of a terrifying epidemic that made survival itself seem to be at stake. These upheavals admittedly did not in themselves lead to political gains for gay men and lesbians; the decisions of individuals to act were still necessary. But it is difficult to imagine these intense periods of concentrated progress occurring without some preceding dramatic circumstances. And, while it is probably true that societies can expect periods of disorder and disruption to recur, their timing and form are unpredictable.

A second thing to notice about these alternating cycles is that they seem to be characterized by different sorts of approaches to change. For instance, the moments of leaping seem tailored to radical visionaries willing to use bold, often militant, methods. By contrast, in the eras when a movement creeps along, militancy may work in very particular local circumstances, but as a general approach to making change the arts of dialogue and negotiation seem to dominate these times. Of course, some might claim that radical visions and militant tactics are themselves the causes of the shift from creeping to leaping. At some point the ideas and the model serve as inspiration for large numbers of people, who then initiate a period of dramatic forward movement. Or, alternately, some might argue that, if only the militants toned things down, the big gains made during an era of leaping might keep happening. But, as a description of what has happened, rather than as an explanation of why things happened, it does seem to be true that radical visions and militant action characterize the moments of leaping ahead, while dialogue, negotiation, and moderation describe the dominant approach during the longer periods of creeping along.

A final point to make about these alternating cycles of change is that each accomplishes something essential. It is easy to see this in relation to the periods in which a political movement leaps forward, but it might seem questionable about the far less dramatic eras of creeping along. Perhaps a climbing analogy will help: the eras of leaping are comparable to intense stretches of climbing upward to reach a new height; the eras of creeping represent the work of constructing a solid base camp so the next height can be scaled. In other words, what happens during the long stretches of incremental, almost imperceptible change, during which the landscape around us does not seem to vary, is critical for the future. The choices one makes during these periods will help shape how far ahead, and in what direction, a movement or a community is able to leap during the next period of tumultuous change. In the 1950s and 1960s, activists kept alive a young social movement: surely that is something worth achieving. For much of the 1970s and 1980s, another larger cohort of activists stayed out of the closet, built community institutions in which the message of gay liberation could be nurtured, and accumulated enough local victories to make change seem possible and desirable: certainly that, too, had value. In the movement's last leap forward, activists reached the goal of putting their issues on the table of mainstream politics and achieving sustained cultural visibility, a significant achievement. We are now in the middle of the next era of creeping along: what are its chief characteristics? What, in other words, are the current goals of the moment and what strategies have emerged to achieve them?

GOALS AND STRATEGIES

Antigay ideologues often speak about "the gay agenda." In the way they use the phrase, a tone of menace often attaches to it, as if there is something self-evidently threatening or surreptitious about the notion itself. In fact, gay and lesbian Americans do have an agenda, although we might more profitably think of it as the set of goals toward which the gay movement is heading. Despite the wide diversity of the gay and lesbian community, and the often fractious debates that occur within it, there has been over the last few decades an amazingly broad consensus about a core set of goals. It would be very hard to dispute the claim that the overwhelming majority of activists —and probably a large majority of gay men and lesbians—agree that the following set of goals are highly desirable: the repeal of sodomy statutes criminalizing homosexual behavior; the removal of the medical classification of homosexuality as a disease; the elimination of discriminatory provisions and practices at every level of government and in every institution of civil society; fair and accurate representation of gay life and gay issues in the media; due process of law, especially in relationship to the behavior of law enforcement personnel toward lesbians and gays; recognition of family relationships; and protection against hate-motivated violence.

"Broad consensus" does not, however, mean unanimity; it leaves room for wide disagreement about priorities and about the mechanisms to achieve these goals. Most gay conservatives, for instance, look askance at civil rights laws as a way of eliminating discrimination because they are philosophically opposed to the expansion of governmental powers, while many gays on the left have tended to underemphasize work to end the military ban. Political moderates and liberals see a single focus on gay issues as a sufficient way to go about eliminating homophobia, whereas gays and lesbians who define themselves as politically progressive emphasize the importance of linking the fight against homophobia and heterosexism to social movements fighting against racism, sexism, and economic injustice. There may be consensus that gay family relationships ought to be recognized, but for some this means the right to marry, and for others it means broadening our understanding of what constitutes a family.

If a goal describes a destination, strategy describes how we propose to arrive. Strategy can be simply described as the overall plan we have for moving toward goals beyond our immediate reach. Nations, corporations, sports teams, families, individuals: every unit of people from the smallest to the largest needs strategy. Strategies can be effective or ineffective (which we learn, unfortunately, only after the fact); they can be bold or cautious, simple or complex; they can have a shelf life of a week or a decade, depending on the goal.

Above all, strategy is something that every individual, group, or institution always has, whether articulated or not. When strategy is articulated, it has a better chance of proving effective because its articulation implies that some conscious assessment of conditions has occurred, that human intelligence has been applied to the goals at hand. But even when strategy is not articulated, it can be discerned through the patterns that emerge upon examination of the actions that individuals or groups make.

Thinking about strategy for a social movement is trickier than studying it at the level of the organization or, even, the nation. Corporations have CEOs, nonprofits have executive directors, and both have boards of directors. Policies get set and then carried out. A democratic nation, like the United States, has citizens who elect legislatures and executives who then propose, enact, and execute laws. Organizations and nations experience debate, factionalism, and dissension from within; they experience conflict, pressure, and opportunity from without. But they also have boundaries, lines of authority, policies, and procedures which make them definable units of analysis.

But social movements? A congeries of organizations and individuals, social movements lack boundaries, lines of authority, policies, and procedures. Membership in a movement can be declared at will; participants can be responsible to no one but themselves. The frequency with which individuals are described in the gay press as "self-appointed leaders" in itself suggests how anarchic the gay and lesbian movement is.

Under these circumstances, is it even possible to speak meaningfully of strategy for the gay and lesbian movement beyond analysis of particular goals and campaigns? I think it is, though its discovery will not come by finding the one key manifesto or the joint declaration issued by major organizational leaders. Paradoxically, despite the apparently radically democratic structure of the movement, one can discern in different periods a quite broad agreement about a core outlook that constitutes in effect a strategic approach to change. This core outlook, or underlying strategic assumption, is most clearly evident during the stretches of time in which the movement is creeping along. Almost by definition, the periods of leaping ahead are characterized by such an abundance of restless chaotic activity that strategy seems too structured a concept to have much meaning.

The core outlook, or strategic approach, of the period from the early 1950s through the mid-to-late 1960s is best encapsulated by the phrase "give us a hearing." The phrase has the tone of a pleading in that action depends on the cooperation of individuals and institutions that are neither gay nor gay-friendly, but it also has the structure of a command, which leaves room for more militant approaches to the issue at hand. Either way, as plea or command, the phrase reflects the dominant fact of political, social, and cultural life in the 1950s and 1960s. Gays and lesbians were not setting the terms in which their lives were discussed or understood. Laws, institutional policies, the shape of social life, and the cultural representation of love, romance, and sexual desire: all presumed heterosexuality as normative.

"Give us a hearing" also efficiently describes the chief methods by which activists hoped to achieve what was the key goal of the era: to break the consensus that viewed homosexuality as dangerous, deviant, and wrong. Before Stonewall, almost all the energy of the movement went toward two activities: publishing material that would offer a counter to hegemonic views of homosexuality, and making contact with professionals in law, government, medicine, and the church whose views they hoped to influence.

"Here we are" effectively captures the core outlook for the period of creeping along that stretched from the early 1970s through the mid-to-late 1980s. It suggests both place ("here") and collectivity ("we"). It takes the form of a simple statement of fact. But try to imagine the inflection in the voice: there is an insistence in the tone that suggests a mix of defiance, determination, and a lurking uncertainty as to how secure the place and the collectivity actually are. The urge to transform that uncertainty into a clear statement of fact explains the dominant strategic impulse of this era: a dual commitment to coming out and building community.

Among activists, coming out of the closet became the gay equivalent to a biblical injunction. Those who remained in the closet had a shadow cast over their moral character. Their integrity was suspect, their courage lacking, their identity uncertain. Meanwhile, those who had come out possessed a compelling need to have others join them. While it was emotionally liberating to drop the pretense of heterosexuality and reveal the secret of one's sexual identity, safety—and future success—demanded that the number of open gays and lesbians grow.

Security also seemed to require that gays and lesbians work intentionally toward building the institutions that could weld all these disparate individuals into a visible, cohesive community. The greater part of what men and women who considered themselves part of the movement did in these decades was directed toward creating and sustaining a public community. Whether they were socializing in or moving to urban neighborhoods perceived to be gay; expending a great number of volunteer hours staffing hot lines, health clinics, or rudimentary community centers; establishing small businesses like bookstores, publishing ventures, or vacation getaways; playing together in softball or bowling leagues or worshipping together in a church or synagogue: large numbers of lesbians and gay men in the 1970s and 1980s devoted themselves to the task of collective visibility through organizations and communities that held an aura of separatism, of incipient queer nationalism, to them.

The quest for visibility and community-building even drove the policy goals that were most avidly pursued from the early 1970s until AIDS seemed to overtake all other issues in the mid-1980s. The elimination of the disease classification of homosexuality, the repeal of sodomy statutes, the adoption of civil rights protections against discrimination, curtailing police harassment of gay meeting places and enlisting law enforcement in the effort to prevent violence against gays and lesbians: all of these goals share a common insistence. "Leave us alone," they seem to imply. Get out of our bedrooms and out of our psyches. "Put a stop to our mistreatment." If they were all achieved, the cost of coming out would be reduced dramatically. And they would make gay communities safer, thus accelerating the process of community building.

Coming out and community building have had enormous staying power as core strategic impulses. Both seem to speak directly to what is perhaps the defining feature of gay experience, the fact that almost all gay men and lesbians are neither raised in nor socialized at an early age into a gay community. The imprint of those critical years of isolation, especially when compounded by the historic invisibility of homosexuality in everyday social

life and in popular culture, creates an insistent need for the alternative—
for visibility and the connection that community provides. Hence, the great
enthusiasm that greeted the coming out of Ellen DeGeneres's TV sitcom
character in 1997, and the decision of some sectors of the movement to
plan a great public rally in the nation's capital in the year 2000, despite
the absence of a concrete political agenda that a rally might contribute
toward advancing.

Yet even as coming out and community building remain powerful impulses, the current period of creeping along has seen a dramatic shift in
the specific issues that are animating the gay community. Matters like civil
rights protections and sodomy law repeal certainly remain on the agenda,
but since the eruption of the debate over the military exclusion policy in
1993, the weight of gay and lesbian advocacy efforts have tilted toward a
new cluster of issues: family, school, and work. The recognition of same-
sex relationships either through domestic partnership arrangements or the
legalization of same-sex marriage; the assertion of the right to parent, the
quest for equitable adoption, foster care, and custody policies, and the need
to have the law recognize that some children have two parents of the same
gender; the proliferation of lesbian, gay, and bisexual employee groups
across the country and their efforts to achieve workplace equity; the local
battles over school curricula, the rights of students to organize gay-straight
alliance clubs, the need for gay-supportive counseling and other policies
in order to make schools safe places for students of all sexual identities:
these, more than the old staples of the 1970s, have become the key issues
in the gay community since the early 1990s.

The importance of this shift has been masked by the fact that the issues
can be seen simply as new planks added to a gay political agenda. But in
fact they are qualitatively different. Whereas the issues of the 1970s re-
volved around a demand to be left alone, those of the 1990s call for recognition and inclusion. Instead of a core outlook captured by the phrase "here
we are," the agitation around family, school, and work puts forward a different demand: "we want in." If the former appears as a simple statement
of fact that can be realized through visibility and the creation of public
communities, the latter demands both action and response. It requires, for
its realization, a strategy of winning allies, of building support outside the
community from the people—heterosexuals—whose lives will inevitably
be changed too by the full inclusion of homosexuals in the core institutions
of American society. It also suggests the distance that the movement has

traveled from the days over a generation ago when it would have been thrilled just to receive a hearing.

IMPLICATIONS AND CONCLUSIONS

In this chapter I have attempted to identify temporal cycles of change in the history of the gay and lesbian movement. I have also sought to align the periods of incremental change (what I have described as creeping along) with unifying strategic impulses. Though this analysis by no means accounts for the full range of activity or the various crosscurrents that inevitably exist in any period of time, it does, I believe, provide a reasonably accurate overview of the movement's history and political evolution.

It also suggests that the current moment in which we find ourselves— that is, in a third era of creeping along—displays strategic incoherence. In previous periods, goals, methods, and strategic vision worked in tandem with one another. Today, the gay and lesbian movement still places high value on a strategic vision that emphasizes coming out and community building, but the actual goals toward which activism is directed—goals around family, school, and work encapsulated by the outlook "we want in"—will not best be served by primary emphasis on coming out and building community. Access to and equity within the key structures of American life will instead require that winning allies becomes a priority. Coming out, of course, is a necessary precondition for this, but coming out has been so absorbed into the value structure of contemporary gay life that it hardly needs to be the movement's main rallying cry. As for community building, it can in serious ways work counter to achieving success in these other areas. Community building easily becomes insular and separatist. It can unwittingly foster an isolation and marginalization that runs contrary to the imperative of political engagement, particularly of the sort that involves winning support from outside one's own community.

These comments are meant to be descriptive rather than prescriptive. That is, I am making no judgment on the suitability of the goals that seem to be animating large numbers of gay men and lesbians in recent years. But, to the degree that success in achieving these new issues matter to their advocates, they will be better served by adopting methods of organizing designed to attract supporters and build coalitions. Otherwise, when the next moment of dramatic opportunity arrives, the movement will find itself too poorly positioned for a great leap into the future.

REFERENCES

Abbott, Sidney, and Barbara Love. 1972. *Sappho was a right-on woman.* New York: Stein and Day.

Adam, Barry. 1995. *The rise of a gay and lesbian movement.* Rev. ed. New York: Twayne.

Altman, Dennis. 1971. *Homosexual oppression and liberation.* New York: Outerbridge and Lazard.

Alwood, Ed. 1996. *Straight news: Gays, lesbians, and the news media.* New York: Columbia University Press.

Anderson, Terry H. 1995. *The Movement and the Sixties.* New York: Oxford University Press.

Andriote, John-Manuel. 1999. *Victory deferred: How AIDS changed gay life in America.* Chicago: University of Chicago Press.

Baumgartner, Frank R., and Bryan D. Jones. 1993. *Agendas and instability in American politics.* Chicago: University of Chicago Press.

Bayer, Ronald. 1981. *Homosexuality and American psychiatry.* New York: Basic Books.

Berube, Allan. 1990. *Coming out under fire: The history of gay men and women in World War II.* New York: The Free Press.

Bowers v. Hardwick, 478 U.S. 186 (1986).

Bull, Chris, and John Gallagher. 1996. *Perfect enemies: The religious right, the gay movement, and the politics of the 1990s.* New York: Crown.

Button, James W., Barbara A. Rienzo, and Kenneth D. Wald. 1997. *Private lives, public conflicts: Battles over gay rights in American communities.* Washington, D.C.: Congressional Quarterly Press.

Cory, Donald Webster. 1975. *The homosexual in America: A subjective approach.* New York: Arno Reprint.

Crimp, Douglas, and Adam Ralston. 1990. *AIDS demographics.* Seattle: Bay Press.

DeBold, Kathleen, ed. 1994. *Out for office: Campaigning in the Gay '90s.* Washington, D.C.: Gay and Lesbian Victory Fund.

Deitcher, David, ed. 1995. *The question of equality: Lesbian and gay politics in America since Stonewall.* New York: Scribner.

D'Emilio, John. 1983. *Sexual politics, sexual communities: The making of a homosexual minority in the United States, 1940–1970.* Chicago: University of Chicago Press.

———. 1992. *Making trouble: Essays on gay history, politics, and the university.* New York: Routledge.

Duberman, Martin. 1993. *Stonewall.* New York: Dutton.

Echols, Alice. 1989. *Daring to be bad: Radical feminism in America, 1967–1975.* Minneapolis: University of Minnesota.

Eskridge, William, and Nan D. Hunter. 1997. *Sexuality, gender, and the law.* Westbury, New York: Foundation Press.

Faderman, Lillian. 1992. *Odd girls and twilight lovers: A history of lesbian life in twentieth-century America.* New York: Penguin Books.

Gitlin, Todd. 1987. *The Sixties: Years of hope, days of rage.* New York: Bantam.

Jay, Karla, and Allen Young. 1992. *Out of the closets: Voices of gay liberation.* New York: New York University Press.

Kinsey, Alfred, Warell B. Pomeroy, and Clyde E. Martin. 1948. *Sexual behavior in the human male.* Philadelphia: W. B. Saunders.

Kissack, Terence. 1995. Freaking fag revolutionaries: New York's gay liberation front, 1969–1971. *Radical History Review* 62:104–34.

Kramer, Larry. 1989. *Reports from the Holocaust: The making of an AIDS activist.* New York: St. Martin's.

Marcus, Eric. 1992. *Making history: The struggle for gay and lesbian equal rights, 1945–1990.* New York: HarperCollins.

Marotta, Toby. 1981. The politics of homosexuality. Boston: Houghton Mifflin.

Martin, Del, and Phyllis Lyon. 1972. *Lesbian/Woman.* San Francisco: Glide Publications.

Mixner, David. 1996. *Stranger among friends.* New York: Bantam.

National Gay and Lesbian Task Force Policy Institute. 1997. *Capital gains and losses: A state by state review of gay, lesbian, bisexual, transgender, and HIV/AIDS-related legislation in 1997.* Washington: NGLTF Policy Institute.

———. 1998. *Capital gains and losses: A state by state review of gay, lesbian, bisexual, transgender, and HIV/AIDS-related legislation in 1998.* Washington: NGLTF Policy Institute.

Norton v. Macy, 417 F.2d 1161 (D.C. Cir. 1969).

Romer v. Evans, 517 U.S. 620 (1996).

Rubinstein, William, ed. 1993. *Lesbians, Gay Men, and the Law.* New York: New Press.

Rupp, Leila J., and Verta Taylor. 1987. *Survival in the doldrums: The American women's rights movement, 1945 to the 1960s.* New York: Oxford University Press.

Scott v. Macy, 349 F.2d 182 (D.C. Cir. 1965).

Shilts, Randy. 1982. *The mayor of Castro Street.* New York: St. Martin's.

———. 1987. *And the band played on: Politics, people, and the AIDS epidemic.* New York: St. Martin's.

———. 1993. *Conduct unbecoming: Gays and lesbians in the U.S. military.* New York: St. Martin's.

Signorile, Michelangelo. 1993. *Queer in America: Sex, the media, and the closets of power.* New York: Random House.

Streitmatter, Rodger. 1995. *Unspeakable: The rise of the gay and lesbian press in America.* Boston: Faber and Faber.

Teal, Donn. 1971. *The gay militants.* New York: Stein and Day.

U.S. Senate. 1950. Committee on Expenditures in Executive Departments. *Employment of homosexuals and other sex perverts in government.* 81st Cong. 2d sess. Washington: Government Printing Office.

Vaid, Urvashi. 1995. *Virtual equality: The mainstreaming of gay and lesbian liberation.* New York: Anchor Books.

Whittier, Nancy. 1995. *Feminist generations: The persistence of the radical women's movement.* Philadelphia: Temple University Press.

3

BEYOND POLITICAL MAINSTREAMING: REFLECTIONS ON LESBIAN AND GAY ORGANIZATIONS AND THE GRASSROOTS

Craig A. Rimmerman

In recent years, the lesbian and gay movement has embraced a narrow form of identity politics that is rooted in a top-down, hierarchical approach that embraces the language and framework of liberal democratic institutions, interest group liberalism, and pluralist democracy. In doing so, there have been increasing conflicts among those who consider themselves assimilationists, who typically embrace "insider" political strategies, and liberationists, who are often associated with "outsider" and grassroots political strategies. These conflicts raise several interesting questions: Given that liberal democracy has provided a certain degree of lesbian and gay rights, what are its limits? To the extent that the lesbian and gay movement continues to work within the broader context of "interest group liberalism," will it not always merely pursue a reformist strategy embracing a narrowly focused identity politics? To what extent have the national lesbian and gay political organizations embraced such a narrow strategy and how "successful" has such a strategy been? What are the implications of this analysis for future movement strategy? The concluding section addresses this important question.

This chapter will evaluate the broader issues of movement strategy within the context of describing and evaluating the approaches to political and social change embraced by several national organizations—Human Rights Campaign, the National Gay and Lesbian Task Force, the National Black Lesbian and Gay Leadership Forum, the Log Cabin Republicans, the Lambda Legal Defense and

Education Fund, and the Gay and Lesbian Victory Fund. In doing so, the chapter explores the tensions between a nationally based political strategy and the much-needed grassroots organizing at the state and local levels that is central to any successful political and social movement. The goal is to make the case for both insider and outsider political strategies that recognize the importance of liberal and radical approaches to movement organizing. My analysis is rooted in personal interviews with members of the lesbian and gay community conducted over the past three years and critical evaluations of primary and secondary source material.[1]

ASSIMILATIONIST AND LIBERATIONIST POLITICAL STRATEGIES

Much of the work of the national lesbian and gay organizations has relied on an insider, assimilationist strategy, one that strives for access to those in power and is rooted in an interest group and legislative lobbying approach to political change. As Donald Haider-Markel (1997, iii–iv) correctly suggests, this strategy "has resulted in congressional activity driven more by gay interest groups and the opposition than by changes in public opinion, or grassroots resources."

Gay and lesbian groups that are organized around sexual orientation issues face several disadvantages as they enter into mainstream political processes. They often lack the resources of most interest groups with whom they are competing at all levels of government. Kenneth Sherrill argues persuasively that "gay people are saddled with the burdens of cumulative inequalities," and as a result the mainstream political process "is far more likely to deprive [lesbian/gay/bisexual] people of our rights than to protect those rights" (1996, 469). In addition, they are part of a larger political and social movement that is often bitterly divided over appropriate strategy. Indeed, there is considerable disagreement within the movement itself over whether even to work within existing political institutions. However, as David Rayside astutely suggests, political mainstreaming has interacted with and coincided with other aspects of movement politics in interesting and complicated ways:

> Engagement with the political mainstream has not led the gay and lesbian movement in a uniformly less radical and more bureaucratic direction. It co-exists with other strands of activism more wary of or antagonistic to that mainstream. One strategy can as easily provoke as supplant others; each depends on the others. In that sense, mainstreaming can never wholly coopt a social movement, for a movement is always more than a single organization,

a single set of political networks, or a uniform strategy. It is, as William Gamson put it, a field of action, encompassing an enormous range of cultural, social, and political work. (Rayside 1998, 3)

In the late 1980s and early 1990s, the insider/outsider political strategy that Rayside describes was practiced with considerable success by ACT UP ("AIDS Coalition to Unleash Power"). ACT UP embraced a political strategy rooted in an "enormous range of cultural, social, and political work," characterized by well-publicized demonstrations and protests from the outside, that were designed to force policy-makers into negotiation with AIDS activists over the lack of appropriate governmental response at all levels of government. After the conversations had begun, ACT UP launched an insider strategy, where participants demanded access to mainstream decision-making channels "to advise and monitor future policy" (Oppenheimer 1997, 303 n. 6). The fiery street activism practiced by ACT UP, which was the central element of its outsider style of unconventional politics, was a return to the liberationist approach practiced by the Gay Liberation Front during the Stonewall Era of the 1960s and early 1970s. The AIDS epidemic had short-term financial and community pressures for the gay and lesbian community, as well as the larger movement. As a result, there were enormous pressures to institutionalize. These pressures had consequences for ACT UP, just as they did for the earliest generation of AIDS organizers and activists.[2]

Political mainstreaming has, of course, been a part of the lesbian and gay movement for the past fifty years. Indeed, author and activist Urvashi Vaid contends that to the extent that the movement embraced a civil rights strategy with the founding of the Mattachine Society in 1950, it established the foundation for a civil rights strategy today. "By pursuing the path of civil rights, we consciously chose legal reform, political access, visibility, and legitimacy over the long-term goals of cultural acceptance, social transformation, understanding, and liberation" (Vaid 1995, 106). In doing so, the movement has practiced mainstreaming through three major political strategies: participation in local and national electoral campaigns; working on behalf of legal reform and litigation; and lobbying for the passage of nondiscrimination laws. The goal of each of these strategies is to win civil rights for lesbian and gay people and integrate them into the political, legal, and social mainstream. The central problem with this civil rights strategy is that access to the system becomes far more important than the actual treatment of lesbians and gays within that system.

The importance of access to politicians underlies the mainstream, assimilationist approach to political and social change. Those who advocate this approach believe that it is much preferred to "outsider" political strategies because such strategies are far too utopian and counterproductive. But relying solely on the mainstream, assimilationist approach is far too limited, and helps explain the failure of the movement to overturn the military's ban on lesbians and gays in the military in 1993. A hierarchical, top-down approach to political change may also explain why federal legislation to block same-gender marriage was passed by Congress and signed into law by President Clinton in 1995. What contributed to the movement's failures in both of these areas was a political strategy that largely ignored grassroots organizing at the state and local levels (Haider-Markel 1997, 42). Rayside also makes the obvious point that the lesbian and gay movement cannot even take the possibilities of assimilation for granted "because gays and lesbians are located on the fringe of the political mainstream." As a result, they do not have the necessary leverage, especially when compared to the vast organizational resources of the Christian Right, to force their issues on the national policy agenda (Rayside 1998, 8).

Given all of this, it is no surprise that many lesbian and gay activists have rejected the mainstream political process that is associated with the assimilationist approach. As Kenneth Wald points out in the introduction to this volume, some activists believe that the continued existence of anti-homosexual feeling in the United States, coupled with their severe resource disadvantages when compared with their opponents on the Christian Right, leads them to reject the mainstream political process, especially at the national level. Vaid contends that the mainstream political process has led to a state of "virtual equality." She describes "virtual equality" in this way:

> In the state of virtual equality, gay and lesbian people are at once insiders, involved openly in government and public affairs to a degree never before achieved, and outsiders, shunned by our elected officials unless they need our money or votes in close elections. (Vaid 1995, 4)

Indeed, the critique suggests that there is a considerable gap between access and power, as national organizations with access to President Clinton can attest. Activists who subscribe to this perspective tend to embrace a cultural, liberationist strategy, one that attempts to address the negative attitudes towards lesbians and gays in meaningful ways. In order to do so, what is required is a shift from an emphasis on *political* change to *cultural* change. It is important to recognize, as well, that the political and cultural approaches are not mutually exclusive. Even Vaid recognizes the importance of pursuing a political strategy, but instead of embracing a hierarchical top–down approach to political change, she would eschew concentrating our efforts on the national level for organizing at the state and local levels— at the grassroots. The ultimate goal is to expand the overall purpose of the movement: "gay civil rights must be seen as part of a broader focus on human rights, sexual and gender equality, social and economic justice, and faith in a multiracial society" (180). This expansion must also include integration of "queer cultural and political strategies" into the framework of the lesbian and gay movement (195).

To be sure, there has been considerable debate within the broader movement over whether the assimilationist or liberationist approaches should guide overall movement strategy. Much of this debate has centered on the role of our national organizations. In order to fully understand the nature of this debate and to evaluate the various strategies embraced by our national organizations, we must describe the various organization's goals, structures, and issues of particular interest. In doing so, we will establish the foundation for a critical discussion of a possible future political and social strategy, one that emphasizes grassroots political and social change, in the final section of this chapter. It is to a discussion of the national organizations that we now turn.

THE NATIONAL ORGANIZATIONS

In the 1980s, lesbian and gay activists became much more actively involved in mainstream politics at the national level, due to several factors. Prior to the 1980s, many activists did not believe that the federal government would be responsive to lesbian and gay concerns. There were exceptions to this, of course, but for the most part, lesbian and gay activists concentrated their reform efforts at the local level. But with the spread of the AIDS epidemic and the Republican ascendancy in national politics, which threatened previous movement accomplishments, lesbian and gay activists recognized the importance of having a national presence in the mainstream political and policy process. Indeed, the AIDS epidemic made that national presence essential (Rayside 1998, 284–285).

These developments led to the growth of already existing and newly created nationally based organizations, all of which embraced mainstream politics to a certain extent. Rayside correctly describes the consequences of this growth in this way:

The six largest groups went from a combined budget of $3.2 million in 1987 to $8.8 million in early 1991, reflecting both the development of resources within gay and lesbian communities and the opening up of opportunities for activist entry into national politics. To some extent, organizational growth was accompanied by specialization in each of the primary channels of mainstream activism: the instigation of legal challenges through the courts; the lobbying of legislators and officials; the promotion of lesbian and gay electoral candidates; and the participation in partisan networks. (Rayside 1998, 285)

The national organizations discussed here have been chosen for their diversity, for their overall commitment to lobbying and/or public education, for their focus on litigation, and for their support of the mainstream electoral process.

Human Rights Campaign

Founded in 1980, the Human Rights Campaign Fund (HRCF) has developed into an aggressive lobbying and education-based organization. It largely works in the mainstream, national political and policy process. HRCF grew out of the earlier work of the Gay Rights National Lobby, an organization that was created in 1978 to lobby Congress and organize a national network of lobbyists at the local level.

HRCF's period of greatest growth occurred during the late 1980s and early 1990s. In early 1991 HRCF had a budget of $4.5 million, five times what it had four years earlier when the March on Washington took place in 1987. It ranked among the fifty largest Washington, D.C. PACs as of mid-1992. By the 1996 elections, HRCF had changed its name to Human Rights Campaign (HRC) after conducting marketing surveys that indicated that potential contributors would think more highly of the organization if "Fund" was dropped from its title. At this point in the organization's history, HRC had a full-time staff of sixty, a budget of ten million dollars, and 175,000 members. The organization raises much of its funding through highly publicized and visible dinners in over twenty cities throughout the United States. Some of these dinners attract over a thousand people, each of whom pay at least $150.00 (Rayside 1998, 287).

The organization became even more aggressive in its fundraising, membership, and overall visibility when former Apple Computer executive Elizabeth Birch replaced Tim McFeeley as executive director in 1995. Birch had also been associated with the National Gay and Lesbian Task Force and brought several of her associates with her. Under Birch's leadership, HRC not only changed its name but also developed a new website, moved into a sleek new headquarters reminiscent of corporate America, and published a glossy magazine.

HRC's central activities include lobbying the federal government on lesbian, gay, and AIDS concerns, participating in election campaigns, educating the general public, organizing volunteers, and offering expertise and training at the state and local level. The latter provided direct benefits in 1994, when HRC's "Americans Against Discrimination" project assisted states and communities across the United States who had been targeted by antigay initiatives sponsored by the radical right. The project, which was cochaired by former Oregon Governor Barbara Roberts and retired Arizona Senator Barry Goldwater, was most helpful in defeating antigay initiatives in Idaho and Oregon in 1994. HRC's political action committee offers financial and in-kind contributions to Democratic, Republican, and Independent candidates for federal office. It also makes available political expertise in organizing, fund raising, and outreach in the lesbian, gay, and bisexual community. To this end, HRC contributed more than $1,090,429 to lesbian and gay-friendly candidates, political parties, and other PACs during the 1995–1996 election cycle.

In 1996 the *Washington Blade* concluded that HRC "is the largest—and most influential—national Gay political organization." David Mixner, a longtime gay political consultant and activist, believes that "there's not a question that they have evolved dramatically over the last five years to a more influential player in Washington. There's still room for growth, but Elizabeth Birch is taken very seriously by major political players in the city." To lesbian activist Mandy Carter, who worked for HRC for three-and-a-half years, much of HRC's strength comes from the organization's recognition that the movement needs electoral politics and street politics in order to be successful. She believes that HRC "got it a long time ago that . . . our presence in Washington is necessary" (Freiberg 1996a, 1). One long-time gay activist said, "Elizabeth Birch has moved HRC in the direction of being more than a PAC, and has aggressively used the financial clout of the [lesbian and gay] community to get a seat at the table" (interview, February 19, 1997).

With this kind of success also comes greater scrutiny and criticism. The organization is often criticized for being elitist and catering largely to upper-class lesbian and gay concerns. These critics argue that HRC spends too little time on political activity and is more concerned with hosting fancy dinners for wealthy contributors and potential contributors (Haider-Markel 1997, 129). Of all the national organizations, HRC may well be the most hierarchical, as it has no local organizations. HRC does have field directors in each region of the country, who attempt to coordinate the group's activities. From the vantage point of those movement activists who wish to see a more decentralized structure, the central problem is that "the executive board makes all decisions for the organization and individual members do not have a formal means of communicating issues or concerns to HRC leaders" (129).

However, HRC has begun to respond to these criticisms in tangible ways. It has selected coordinators in more than a dozen states and fifty congressional districts in an effort to galvanize grassroots support. In doing so, it has also increasingly attempted to build ties to local lesbian and gay organizations in an attempt to form lasting and meaningful partnerships (130).

What kinds of organizing initiatives has HRC sponsored? Like many other organizations, HRC recognizes the importance of getting people to come out of the closet. With this in mind, it sponsors the National Coming Out Project, which encourages lesbians and gays to inform others about who they are. HRC also sponsors a five-thousand-member Field Action Network, which trains and organizes grassroots volunteers. These volunteers are often recruited by HRC staff to assist in local congressional or Senate campaigns. HRC staff also assist candidates by providing campaign advice. In addition, HRC has organized "Speak Out Action Grams," a direct-mail organizing campaign designed to pressure congressional members (130).

What issues have been most important to HRC in recent years? The organization has fought for the passage of the Employment Non-Discrimination Act (ENDA), which would ban sexual-orientation discrimination in employment as a part of federal law. It has continued to advance awareness, funding, and education on HIV. In addition, it has tried to promote the passage of lesbian and gay marriage at the federal level. Finally, it has been generally quite supportive of President Clinton. In the words of one HRC strategist, "Clinton has transformed this country for the better on gay and lesbian issues" (interview, February 5, 1997).

HRC's recent efforts reveal both the importance and limitations of an insider, largely hierarchical, nationally-based political strategy. HRC thrives on access to politicians and has consistently taken "a safe, middle-of-the-road approach" to political change (Vaid 1995, 92). To gain an understanding of another approach to political and social change, we turn to a discussion of the National Gay and Lesbian Task Force.

National Gay and Lesbian Task Force

Founded in November 1973 to "fill the void where no national work was being done on behalf of gays" (interview, February 6, 1997), the National Gay Task Force was the nation's leading gay political group. The organization was formed by New Yorkers who had been associated with the Gay Activists' Alliance. Those involved were New York City Health Administrator Harold Brown (who had recently come out publicly), Professor Martin Duberman, publicist Ronald Gold, longtime activist Franklin Kameny, and Dr. Bruce Voeller. The organization's initial goals were to bring "gay liberation into the mainstream of American civil rights" and to "focus on broad national issues" (Thompson 1994, 82). In its early years, the Task Force enjoyed several major accomplishments:
- it convinced the American Psychiatric Association to end the classification of homosexuality as a mental illness;
- it challenged the media's portrayal of gays;
- it persuaded then U.S. Rep. Bella Abzug (D-NY) to introduce the first gay civil rights bill in Congress;
- it initiated the first meeting in the White House between gay leaders and a top presidential adviser in the administration of President Jimmy Carter.

In addition, the Task Force provided advice to local groups and served as a clearinghouse for information. At this point in its history, however, the organization was an elite organization with a narrow membership base, and it was cautious in its choices over strategy. In the late 1970s and early 1980s, the group experienced organizational and debt problems. Its annual budget for 1980 was only $260,000, reflecting the organization's small size. The Task Force moved to Washington, D.C. in 1986 and also changed its name to the National Gay and Lesbian Task Force. The catalyst for the organization's growth was the March on Washington for Lesbian and Gay Rights in October 1987. At this point in the organization's history, the Task Force largely addressed issues of violence, privacy, and AIDS (Rayside 1998, 285). During the late 1980s and through the mid-1990s, the Task Force sponsored the Gay and Lesbian Violence Project, a yearly project that reported the numbers of lesbians and gays who were victims of gay bias crimes.

At the end of the 1980s, the Task Force devoted more attention to the ban on lesbians and gays in the military as well as family issues. The latter included "questions of relationship recognition, adoption, foster care, and reproductive rights." The organization diversified its national leadership considerably, as lesbians such as Urvashi Vaid (who served as Executive Director from 1989 to 1993), Peri Jude Radicec, and Tanya Domi played major roles. Virginia Apuzzo had been Executive Director of the Task Force from 1982 to 1986. The racial composition of the organization's staff also became much more diverse in the late 1980s. There was also a much greater emphasis on the intersection of race with lesbian and gay politics. By late summer 1996, the organization had forty thousand members, a yearly budget of $2.4 million, and twenty-two full-time staff.

Today the organization addresses an array of issues, including antigay ballot initiatives and referenda, violence against lesbians and gays, general homophobia, sodomy laws, antidiscrimination policies for lesbians and gays, legal protections for lesbian and gay families, and AIDS research funding. The overall goals and strategy are decided within the Washington, D.C. national office. The Task Force is not constituted as a federation of local chapters, but the group's literature contends that it is building a grassroots movement. It "holds an annual Creating Change Conference, started its Youth Leadership Training program in 1993, has built partnerships with more than 120 local groups through its cooperating Organization program, and coordinates the activities of local and state groups through its 'activist alert' network" (Haider-Markel 1997, 126). The goal of the Creating Change Conference is to make contacts with activists at the grassroots. Because the Task Force has no local chapters or local committees that plan annual fundraising dinners like HRC, it must develop these kinds of creative and innovative grassroots projects.

In recent years, the Task Force has practiced both insider, mainstream politics as well as more radical, direct action politics, often at the grassroots. As one staffer pointed out, "NGLTF has been on the inside and outside from time to time" (interview, February 6, 1997). Unlike HRC, which has had a more focused and clear political and policy agenda over the years, NGLTF has embraced various political strategies over the course of the past fifteen years. This has led some to question just what role the Task Force is playing in the larger lesbian and gay movement. Indeed, an October 1996 article on the organization, which appeared in *The Washington Blade*, was titled "NGLTF's Identity Crisis" (Freiberg 1996b, 1, 31, 33). Torie Osborn, who served as Vaid's immediate successor as Executive

Director, argues that there is a "gap between the reality and the potential" at the Task Force. Osborn believes that the organization has the potential to be a "mobilizing force" by organizing around cutting-edge lesbian and gay rights issues. But the Task Force has failed to fulfill this potential because "they're an organization without a vision" (Moss 1996, 45).

However, most would agree that the Task Force has occupied a niche on the progressive left of the political and ideological spectrum. The organization's progressive political leanings have led to tensions between itself and other national groups, notably the Human Rights Campaign, which occupies a more centrist position on the political and ideological spectrum.

At this time, the Task Force is devoting more attention to statewide organizing. The assumption here, in the words of one staffer, is that "state-level politics are far more important than politics at the national level over the next four years, and there are opportunities to move forward incrementally at the state level" (interview, February 6, 1997). The Task Force Policy Institute, which was founded by historian and activist (and chapter 2 author) John D'Emilio in 1995, has also embraced this state-level focus to a large extent. The Institute "is a think tank dedicated to research, policy analysis, and strategic projects that advance equality for GLBT people." It is involved in a number of strategic projects, including the "Equality Begins at Home Campaign," a week-long organizing effort of more than 250 rallies, lobby days, caravans, town meetings, and other grassroots actions on behalf of lesbians and gays in every state, which took place in March 1999. The idea for utilizing actions and marches "was proposed to the Federation of Statewide GLBT Political Organizations to increase visibility and capacity of state organizations through coordinated national days of action" ("Task Force Report" 1998, 3). The campaign was ultimately organized by the Federation of LGBT Statewide Political Organizations and coordinated by the Task Force.

Of all the national organizations, perhaps the Task Force is most committed to grassroots political and social change. Yet like HRC, the Task Force also embraces the hierarchical model of decision-making to the extent that its national office is in Washington, D.C., and a board of directors ultimately makes decisions about the day-to-day running of the organization. When the Task Force moved from New York to Washington in 1986, it recognized the importance of having a serious lobbying presence. This was largely prompted by the AIDS crisis. Indeed, Vaid argues that "there is no question that AIDS forced the gay and lesbian movement to institutionalize, nationalize, and aggressively pursue the mainstream" (Vaid 1995, 74).

The National Black Lesbian and Gay Leadership Forum

The National Black Lesbian and Gay Leadership Forum was originally founded in 1988 by veteran civil rights activists Ruth Waters and Phill Wilson as a Los Angeles–based local organization. The Leadership Forum's original goal was to address issues facing the black lesbian and gay community. It was also created to focus on racial concerns that had not been satisfactorily addressed by national groups such as the Human Rights Campaign Fund, the National Gay and Lesbian Task Force, and the Lambda Legal Defense and Education Fund (Haider-Markel 1997, 22). The Leadership Forum's first conference took place in 1988 and was very well attended by people from all over the country. The conference addressed racism in the gay community and homophobia in the straight black community. As one organization official said, "The good turnout reflected a growing desire for black lesbians and gays to come together to organize" (interview, February 28, 1997).

Since 1995, the organization has restructured itself from a local to a national one. Keith Boykin, Executive Director from 1995 to 1998 (and author of chapter 4 in this volume), writes of his dismay in visiting the Washington, D.C. chapter of the National Lesbian and Gay Journalists Association (NLGJA), HRC, and NGLTF in the early 1990s and finding almost no representation of people of color. As Boykin argues in the next chapter, separate national organizations that address the concerns of blacks and lesbians and gays are needed because of the inability of other national organizations to represent their concerns adequately. He quotes Tim Mc-Feeley on HRC's efforts to promote diversity and greater representation of blacks, shortly after McFeeley ended his five-year tenure as Executive Director: "I think we've done a good job, and I think it needs to always be examined and the question needs to be raised." But then McFeeley added, "I think HRC is clearly defined as a white person's organization. HRC will not be as comfortable a place to black gay people as their own" (Boykin 1996, 230).

As Boykin points out, McFeeley's statement provides a clear justification for the existence of organizations such as the National Black Lesbian and Gay Leadership Forum. Boykin believes that McFeeley's attitude is shared by other national organization leaders as well, a prevailing view which heightens the importance of the organization's day-to-day efforts.

Today, the Leadership Forum hosts a yearly national conference that has become an important source of income, publicity, and networking. One of its first major projects was the creation of a Los Angeles–based AIDS Prevention Team, designed to offer services to African-American gay and bisexual men locally. Since the late 1980s, the Leadership Forum has extended its AIDS prevention programs to the national level through U.S. Centers for Disease Control and Prevention grants (Haider-Markel 1997, 22).

The organization's Washington, D.C. headquarters were opened in 1995, and the Leadership Forum's budget doubled from $450,000 in 1996 to $850,000 in 1997, reflecting increased fundraising activity. Today it lobbies on behalf of black lesbians and gays before Congress and the White House, the news media, universities, and churches. Other recent efforts include the development of a Women's Health Program and the creation of a black gay community center at the Leadership Forum's D.C. office, which houses an array of materials and records pertaining to black lesbian and gay history. The Leadership Forum has also targeted young people by creating its first national youth council. When asked to identify its top priorities for 1997–1998 by the *Washington Blade*, the Leadership Forum response was (1) "working with the black church to help transform attitudes within the black community," and (2) "working with the mainstream media to encourage 'fair and accurate' representation of black gay people" (Haider-Markel 1997, 22–23).

The Leadership Forum's major operating and staffing decisions are made by a seventeen-member board of directors composed of members throughout the United States. Former Executive Director Boykin has justifiably received credit for exercising important leadership and fundraising abilities. But he also recognizes that the Leadership Forum must rise above the efforts of a single individual if it is to be successful. At its February 1998 annual meeting, Boykin told members gathered for a plenary session, "It's time to stand up. It's time to dare to be powerful. I don't want the organization to fall by the wayside because of one individual" (Smith 1998a, 1). At the same meeting, the Leadership Forum Board announced that Jubi Headley Jr., formerly an executive assistant and press secretary to openly gay Cambridge, Massachusetts Mayor Kenneth Reeves, would replace Boykin. But Headley's tenure lasted less than four months when he resigned June 5, 1998, apparently due to the Leadership Forum's continued financial problems and its inability to pay his salary in a timely manner. In announcing his resignation, Headley also said that the Leadership Forum needed to restructure if it wished to remain viable in the future. In practice, this restructuring meant the elimination of the Executive Director's position and the establishment of "a five-person 'management team' that could put financial emphasis on 'program delivery'" (Smith 1998b, 1).

The Leadership Forum has played an invaluable role in the mainstream political and policy process by insuring that black lesbians and gays are granted a seat at the table when the movement's national organizations meet to plan coordinated strategy. Like all of the other organizations discussed thus far, the Leadership Forum is vulnerable to the critique that its primary activities are too grounded in national-level politics. But like the Task Force, the Leadership Forum is attempting to make progress at the grassroots as well. However, the organization faces considerable difficulties in doing so, to the extent that financial concerns and structural organizational concerns remain problems. Perhaps the greatest accomplishment that the Leadership Forum might make in the immediate future is to inspire black lesbians and gays to kick the closet doors down, recognize that they are not alone, and realize that they have an organization working on their behalf.

Log Cabin Republicans

Founded in 1993, the Log Cabin Republicans are a national group that represents lesbian and gay Republicans. A considerable amount of their organizing work is done by more than fifty chapters located throughout the United States. Some of these local chapters were formed long before the national organization was even created (Haider-Markel 1997, 22). Indeed, the earliest such club was formed in California in 1978 as a response to the Briggs antigay initiative (interview, February 10, 1997).

All the local clubs joined together as the Log Cabin Federation in 1990. Over the course of the next two years, Rich Tafel, the new head of the Federation, and veteran conservative organizer Marvin Liebman gained considerable media attention. The Federation's third annual meeting at the 1992 Republican National Convention in Houston brought together fifteen clubs from ten different states. However, Log Cabin activists were still outsiders in a party more responsive to the Christian Right.

In early 1993, a small group of individuals formed a Washington, D.C.-based organization that acted as a lobbying group and served as clearinghouse for information about legislators and legislation. Within two years, it merged with the Log Cabin Federation (Rayside 1998, 291). One of the central goals of the organization has been "to convey the idea that gay rights and the party's philosophy [is] not inimical" (Bull and Gallagher 1996, 79). The organization's first major political success was the election of Governor William Weld in Massachusetts. Weld appointed lesbians and gays to visible positions throughout his administration and confronted challenging issues such as gay teen suicide rates (Bull and Gallagher 1996, 80). In many ways, he was one of the most progay governors in the United States.

Among the Weld administration's appointees was Rich Tafel, who later became the Executive Director of the Log Cabin Republicans. Since 1993, Tafel has presided over the growth of the organization and has guided the organization through its greatest political controversy. By early 1997, Log Cabin Republicans had a $700,000 budget, a paid staff of six, and a membership numbering over ten thousand (interview, February 10, 1997).

The Log Cabin Political Action Committee is an arm of Log Cabin Republicans, and it raises money for Republican candidates who support gay and AIDS issues. It contributed $76,000 to national, state, and local candidates in the 1996 elections.

Until June 1998, the Log Cabin Republicans were the only national gay organization that was affiliated with one of the two major political parties in the United States. Obviously influenced by the success of the Log Cabin Republicans, Rep. Barney Frank (D–Mass.) announced the creation of the National Stonewall Democratic Federation, a national organization with direct ties to the Democratic party.

The Log Cabin Republicans received considerable media publicity and scrutiny when openly lesbian reporter Deb Price revealed that in August 1995 then-presidential candidate Bob Dole returned a one-thousand-dollar contribution from the group. Dole and his campaign were widely criticized for returning the contribution. The mainstream press wondered publicly "whether Dole had hurt his overall chances of winning the presidency by appearing to be 'pandering' to the religious right faction of the Republican party" (Chibbaro, Jr., September 1, 1995, 1). Eventually he accepted the donation, blamed the returned check on his staff, and accepted a Log Cabin endorsement.

The Dole incident produced considerable turmoil within the organization, especially since the Log Cabin Republicans ultimately decided to endorse his presidential candidacy. This kind of turmoil likely faces the organization in the future, as it tries to navigate its role within a Republican party bitterly divided over social issues.

But the Log Cabin Republicans have an important role to play in supporting Republican lesbian and gay candidates at the national level. HRC supports a limited number of Republican lawmakers, such as Rep. Nancy Johnson (R-Conn.), Rep. Christopher Shays (R-Conn.), and Senator James Jeffords (R-Vt.). The Log Cabin Republicans can help support additional lesbian and gay candidates for national, state, and local offices (interview, February 10, 1997). They will also continue to lobby on AIDS and ENDA. But perhaps most importantly of all, they can potentially use their political mainstreaming strategy and their decentralized organizational structure in various state and local chapters throughout the United States to educate about lesbian and gay concerns.

Lambda Legal Defense and Education Fund

Founded in 1973, the Lambda Legal Defense and Education Fund is the oldest of the national lesbian and gay groups. It is one of four that pursues gay-related court challenges. The others are the National Center for Lesbian Rights, which has offices in New York and San Francisco; the ACLU's Lesbian and Gay Rights Project; and the Servicemembers Legal Defense Network, which was formed in 1993 with the specific goal of assisting armed forces military personnel who face possible discharge from the military.

Underlying all of these groups' various approaches to mainstream political and social change is a rights-based strategy that seeks greater equity through the legal system. The Lambda Legal Defense and Education Fund specializes in lesbian, gay, and AIDS-related cases, but generally takes only those cases "which, if successful, can provide a breakthrough ruling that can benefit the greatest number of Gays and people with AIDS" (Haider-Markel 1997, 22). Similar to the strategy used by the National Association for the Advancement of Colored People (NAACP), Lambda usually acts as legal counsel or co-counsel for its clients or by filing amicus curiae briefs in cases that might set legal precedent or alter current law. Lambda handles a wide array of cases, including those dealing with child custody, the right to marry, job discrimination, inheritance rights, and sodomy laws. In 1996, for example, Lambda served as the co-counsel for those opposed to the Colorado antigay rights ballot initiative, which the U.S. Supreme Court ultimately struck down. Lambda also served as co-counsel to Margarethe Cammermeyer's successful effort to prevent the Army from discharging her after she publicly revealed that she is a lesbian (Haider-Markel 1997, 127–28).

What kind of strategy does Lambda pursue? The organization seeks, first and foremost, legal change and protection for lesbians and gays. Education can then follow, once basic civil rights are guaranteed. A supervising staff attorney in Lambda's Los Angeles office, Jon Davidson, argues that "the ultimate goal in this work has not been to change what [people] believe about homosexuality. . . . They can believe whatever they want to." To Davidson, the central goal is to make sure that "the government treats everyone equally regardless of sexual orientation" (128).

With this in mind, Lambda has led key challenges to the Pentagon's "don't ask / don't tell" military policy through a series of high profile court cases. One such case, *Able v. United States*, is likely to force the issue before the U.S. Supreme Court. Lambda has also provided counsel in the Hawaii lawsuit "seeking to allow same-sex couples to obtain a state marriage license." The organization has also represented clients in an array of other cases involving AIDS discrimination, challenges to sodomy laws, and domestic partner rights. One of its major legal accomplishments was its landmark victory in a Wisconsin federal court that compels public schools to respond more forcefully in protecting gay students from harassment and assault (Haider-Markel 1997, 22).

Lambda has headquarter offices in New York City and regional offices in Atlanta, Chicago, and Los Angeles. Its staff comprises fourteen attorneys with a network of supporting attorneys throughout the United States. There is a national board of directors composed of board members from throughout the United States. From 1992 to 1997, the organization's budget almost doubled, from $1.6 million to $3.1 million (Freiberg 1997, 1). The budgetary increase is not surprising, given that many movement leaders believe that a legal strategy is integral for expanding lesbian and gay civil rights.

Kevin Cathcart, Lambda's executive director, says that in recent years, "The courts have been a relatively successful place for Lesbians and Gay men to go—a more successful place in many ways than political avenues have been for expanding Lesbian and Gay rights" (18).

One criticism of Lambda and the other legal groups is that they fail to link their legal work with the larger political movement. For example, Urvashi Vaid points out that Lambda's regular Legal Issues Roundtables can only be attended by lawyers. She was allowed to participate as an attorney, but was not invited in her capacity as the director of NGLTF (Vaid 1995, 133). Vaid correctly believes that there must be better coordination between political groups and gay legal groups if the movement's overall goals are to be advanced successfully.

Lambda has done some excellent work in recent years in an effort to link legal organizing and political organizing. For example, the organization assembled a large coalition of community, media, and political groups growing out of its work to challenge Hawaii's marriage law. Lambda has also worked with political activists in extending its Marriage Project to encompass political organizing and public education strategies to challenge the antigay referenda it has confronted in the courts (Vaid 1995, 134). In this way, Lambda has pointed the way to a new model of political and social change rooted in cooperation among national and local organizations that take into account the importance of the grassroots.

Gay and Lesbian Victory Fund

Since its creation in 1991, the primary goal of the Gay and Lesbian Victory Fund (GLVF) has been to elect openly lesbian and gay officials to all levels of government. The organization's book, *Out for Office,* argued in 1994 that "gay men and lesbians are the most underrepresented group in electoral politics," and asked, "If we don't support our own, who will be there for us" (DeBold 1994, p. xiii)?

The founder and first director of the Victory Fund, William Waybourn, had been influenced by the organizing efforts of Emily's List, the Washington, D.C.-based PAC that helped Ann Richards defeat Clayton Williams in the 1990 Texas governor's race. As a native Texan, Waybourn was well aware that Richards credited Emily's List for playing an integral role in the early portion of her successful campaign. To Waybourn, such an organization needed to exist at the national level for lesbians and gays as well. He contacted Vic Basile, who had formerly served as Executive Director of the Human Rights Campaign Fund, to see if he would be interested in joining forces. Basile agreed and together they worked to secure the support of lesbian and gay donors throughout the United States. Their efforts produced the Victory Fund's first board of directors, composed of individuals who had accumulated considerable political and fundraising experience. More importantly, these were individuals who were committed to giving $10,000 each initially to fund the creation of the Victory Fund (Rimmerman 1994, 215; Rimmerman 1999).

Unlike other national lesbian and gay organizations discussed in this chapter, the Victory Fund is the only one that exists solely to recruit and elect openly lesbian and gay candidates to public office at all levels of government. "The Victory Fund is a peculiarly American formation, one that illustrates the prominence of money in United States elections and the need for candidates to raise funds outside party channels" (Rayside 1998, 287). Given that all told there are some half a million elected offices at all levels of government in the United States, the Victory Fund has a chance to play an important role in assisting openly lesbian and gay candidates who seek election to public office.

How does the Victory Fund decide who will receive the organization's electoral support? What criteria is used when deciding which candidates to support? The process, which is a thorough and rigorous one, has largely remained the same over the course of the organization's existence. In the early stages of its decision-making process, an outside consulting firm provides independent evaluations of the races in question. After carefully reviewing the evidence, the Victory Fund staff makes recommendations about which candidates to support to the board of directors. Spirited debate and discussion often follows, after which the board decides which candidates merit Victory Fund support. Candidates desiring Victory Fund support must meet the following published criteria:

- must be openly lesbian or gay;
- must endorse the Federal Gay/Lesbian Civil Rights Bill in a public manner, as well as similar state and local antidiscrimination laws or legislation;
- must advocate aggressive public policies and positions relevant to AIDS education, treatment, and research, as well as lesbian and gay health and wellness;
- must have a strong base of support outside of the lesbian and gay community;
- must be strongly prochoice;
- must demonstrate the ability to organize and to raise money;
- must have a viable candidacy (i.e., a legitimate chance to win) (Rimmerman 1999; interview, February 26, 1997).

During the 1996 election cycle, some 180 candidates contacted the organization for support. The Victory Fund decided to support thirty-two of these candidates, twenty-two of whom won. These numbers represent considerable progress on behalf of the organization. For example, during the 1992 election cycle, some seventy-two candidates contacted the Victory Fund asking for its support and the organization decided to give financial and organizational support to thirteen candidates at all levels of government (Rimmerman 1999). It gave roughly $500,000 to these thirteen candidates. In the 1994 off-year elections, the Victory Fund backed twenty-seven candidates, with some $800,000 in contributions, and fourteen of those won. Perhaps its greatest success was during the 1997 off-year elections, when ten of the fifteen openly lesbian and gay candidates backed by the Victory Fund achieved electoral victories and another three forced run-off elections (Haider-Markel 1997, 21).

The success and resulting publicity that the organization has received has had positive consequences for membership as well. In 1991 the Victory Fund had only 181 members, but by 1994, there were some 3,500 members, who contributed more than $1.3 million by 1996. The organization ranked as the fifteenth largest independent PAC in the United States during the 1996 election cycle and gave more than $400,000 to candidates (Haider-Markel 1997, 132).

The Gay and Lesbian Victory Fund has had three Executive Directors during its short existence—William Waybourn (1992–1995), David Clarenbach (1996–1997), and Brian Bond (1996-present). As a former Democratic National Committee official, Bond brings with him significant political organizing expertise but also a partisan background that concerns some members of other national organizations, given that the Victory Fund supports candidates of any party who meets the organization's published criteria. The executive director of the Victory Fund is responsible for the day-to-day running of the Washington-based organization and coordinates its political and fundraising strategies.

What lies ahead for the Victory Fund? As the organization heads into the next election cycle, it faces a number of important issues. The possibility of campaign finance reform looms in the background, which could mean an end to bundling, the primary way that the Victory Fund receives contributions and distributes money to its chosen candidates. Nonconnected ideological PACs, such as the Victory Fund, are able to avoid the $5,000 spending limitation by requiring their members to earmark their contributions to candidates who have been identified by the Victory Fund for support. How does this work in practice? Victory Fund contributors will write their checks, for example, to "Barney Frank for Congress," and the checks are then gathered and bundled every two days so that the Frank campaign has the cash flow it needs throughout the electoral process (Rimmerman 1994, 219; Rimmerman 1999).[3] Organization leaders also worry that they do not have the financial base needed to support all candidates running for office who deserve their attention. In addition, they wish to aggressively help

those candidates who are already in office and who seek election to higher office (interview, February 26, 1997). The fact that the Victory Fund has these worries so soon after its formation is a testimony to its accomplishments and the fact that incremental progress has been made in encouraging openly lesbian and gay officials to run for public office. But the fact remains that there are only two openly gay representatives and one openly lesbian representative in the entire Congress. Questions remain, as well, about what such elected officials can actually accomplish working within mainstream political structures to bring about necessary political, social, and cultural change.

IMPLICATIONS FOR THE FUTURE

This chapter began with these important questions: To the extent that the lesbian and gay movement continues to work within the broader context of "interest group liberalism," will it not always merely pursue a reformist strategy embracing a narrowly focussed, identity politics? To what extent have the national lesbian and gay political organizations embraced such a narrow strategy and how "successful" has such a strategy been? The analysis here suggests that for the most part, the national lesbian and gay organizations have embraced a political strategy rooted in an insider, assimilationist approach to politics, one that strives for access to those in power. By its very nature, this approach embraces an interest group and legislative lobbying approach to political change.

What are the implications of this analysis for future movement strategy? First and foremost, we must recognize that the national organizations do not always have to pursue a narrowly focused identity politics. In order to broaden their political and cultural strategy, the national organizations must recognize that any meaningful movement has to build in grassroots organizing and education at both the community and state-wide levels. There are signs that the national organizations see the importance of doing so. For example, HRC offers expertise and training to state and local activists, who face the daily challenge of combating the power and organizational resources of the Christian Right. NGLTF launched a "Celebrating Our Families" campaign in spring 1998, which was rooted in addressing community concerns about family issues and building support for families that celebrate sexual difference. Its Youth Leadership Training program is a model for how to build partnerships with local youth groups throughout the United States, and its Equality Begins at Home Campaign signals a serious commitment to organizing at the state and local levels. The National Black Lesbian and Gay Leadership Forum is committed to working with black churches throughout the United States to help transform attitudes regarding homosexuality in the black community. By its very nature, this project will rely on grassroots organizing and support. The Log Cabin Republicans will continue to use their decentralized organizational structure by relying on their local organizations to educate people in local communities about broadening the base of the Republican party to include openly lesbian and gay people, while fostering an atmosphere that celebrates difference and diversity. Lambda Legal Defense and Education Fund has potentially provided a model for grassroots organizing by assembling a large coalition of community members, media officials, and political group representatives in an effort to challenge Hawaii's marriage law.

The Gay and Lesbian Victory Fund has worked to elect openly lesbian and gay officials at all levels of government. In this way they, too, are committed to embracing grassroots political and social change.

The movement must learn from recent mistakes, most notably from the debacle concerning gays in the military (chapter 11 in this volume). At the outset of that important national debate, the mainstream lesbian and gay movement trusted Bill Clinton far too much. Many national organization members were thrilled that a supposed "friend" had been elected to the White House (Rimmerman 1996, 121). Some national organization leaders were even invited to the White House in spring 1993, a meeting where the President promised to eventually overturn the ban. National organization leaders believed him, thus accepting access to the president as evidence of his commitment to their cause. As we now know, this faith was sorely misplaced.

The movement's inability to persuade the President and members of Congress to overturn the ban is also a reminder that it could have done much more to rally support at the grassroots in ways that might have influenced wavering members of Congress. In addition, the movement might have done more for its cause by articulating a shared agenda, linking the concerns of lesbians and gays with other oppressed groups, and ultimately building coalitions at all levels of politics to bring about more meaningful change. This is all especially important, given the enormous resources of the Christian Right, resources that were used with considerable effectiveness in the military debate.

Ultimately, all movements face the problems associated with the trend towards institutionalization, many of which have been discussed in this chapter. But it also needs to be recognized that the lesbian and gay movement has achieved legislative and legal progress as a result of the access to power that institutionalization provides. As we know, the move towards institutionalization has caused enormous fissures within the movement itself. The conflicts over institutionalization have had consequences for the national organizations as they attempt to find common ground where they might work together. Perhaps these conflicts and a collective recognition of the enormous resources of the Christian Right will ultimately produce a common purpose, one that celebrates the importance of building a truly participatory and democratic lesbian and gay movement from the grassroots.

NOTES

1. The author wishes to thank an array of national movement leaders, who gave their quality time in the form of personal interviews and thus provided invaluable material for this chapter. All interviewees were guaranteed anonymity as a part of the interviewing process.
2. Unfortunately, space constraints and the overall focus of this chapter limit my discussion of ACT UP and other grassroots groups here. However, another grassroots organization that deserves attention is Queer Nation. Founded in New York City in 1990, Queer Nation began by organizing large demonstrations against gay bashings. As sociologist Steven Epstein correctly points out, "Many present and former members of ACT UP, who had been mobilized by AIDS but wanted to work on other issues affecting their communities, flocked to Queer Nation Meetings" (Epstein 1999, 60–61). Both ACT UP and Queer Nation were particularly effective in garnering mainstream media attention. For an overview of ACT UP, see Rimmerman (1998, 36–40); for good discussions of both ACT UP and Queer Nation, see Epstein (1999, 30–90).
3. One Victory Fund official defended bundling when he argued "that there is nothing more grassroots and democratic than bundling. Campaign finance reform should not take away democratic forms of contributions" (interview, February 26, 1997).

REFERENCES

Able v. United States, 44 F.3d 128 (2d Cir. 1995).

Boykin, Keith. 1996. *One more river to cross: Black and gay in America.* New York: Anchor Books.

Bull, Chris, and John Gallagher. 1996. *Perfect enemies: The religious right, the gay movement, and the politics of the 1990's.* New York: Crown Publishers.

Chibbaro, Lou, Jr. 1995. Bob Dole tells Log Cabin: "No thanks!" *Washington Blade,* 1 September.

DeBold, Kathleen, ed. 1994. *Out for office: Campaigning in the Gay '90's.* Washington: Gay and Lesbian Victory Fund.

Epstein, Steven. 1999. Gay and lesbian movements in the United States: Dilemmas of identity, diversity, and political strategy. In *The Global Emergence of Gay and Lesbian Politics: National Imprints of a Worldwide Movement,* edited by Barry D. Adam, Jan Willem Duyvendak, and Andre Krouwel. Philadelphia: Temple University Press.

Freiberg, Peter. 1996a. With success comes scrutiny. *Washington Blade,* 23 August.

————. 1996b. NGLTF's identity crisis. *Washington Blade,* 25 October.

————. 1997. Courting gay civil rights. *Washington Blade,* 3 January.

Haider-Markel, Donald P. 1997. *From bullhorns to PACS: Lesbian and gay politics, interest groups, and policy.* Ph.D. diss., University of Wisconsin–Milwaukee, Political Science.

Moss, J. Jennings. 1996. Where have all the radicals gone? *The Advocate,* 10 December.

Oppenheimer, Joshua. 1997. Movements, markets, and the mainstream. In *Acting on AIDS: Sex, drugs, and politics,* edited by Joshua Oppenheimer and Helena Reckitt. London, England: Serpent's Tail Press.

Rayside, David. 1998. *On the fringe: Gays and lesbians in the political process.* Ithaca: Cornell University Press.

Rimmerman, Craig A. 1994. New kids on the block: The WISH list and the Gay and Lesbian Victory Fund in the 1992 elections. In *Risky business? PAC decisionmaking in congressional elections.* Armonk, N.Y.: M. E. Sharpe.

————. 1996. Promise unfulfilled: Clinton's failure to overturn the military ban on lesbians and gays. In *Gay rights, military wrongs: Political perspectives on lesbians and gays in the military,* edited by Craig A. Rimmerman. New York: Garland Publishing, Inc.

————. 1998. ACT UP. In *Encyclopedia of AIDS: A social, political, cultural, and scientific record of the HIV epidemic,* edited by Raymond A. Smith. Chicago: Fitzroy Dearborn Publishers.

————. 1999. "The Gay and Lesbian Victory Fund comes of age: Reflections on the 1996 elections." In *After the revolution: PACS, lobbies, and the Republican Congress,* edited by Robert Biersack, Paul S. Herrnson, and Clyde Wilcox. Needham Heights, Mass.: Allyn and Bacon.

Sherrill, Kenneth S. 1996. The political power of lesbians, gays, and bisexuals. *PS: Political Science and Politics* 29:469–73.

Smith, Rhonda. 1998a. Forum picks new director. *Washington Blade,* 20 February.

————. 1998b. New executive director resigns. *Washington Blade,* 29 May.

Task Force Report. 1998. National Gay and Lesbian Task Force (Spring).

Thompson, Mark, ed. 1994. *The long road to freedom.* New York: St. Martin's Press.

Vaid, Urvashi. 1995. *Virtual equality: The mainstreaming of gay and lesbian liberation.* New York: Anchor Books.

Washington Blade, 1997. A look at the largest gay political organizations. 12 December.

Personal Interviews

February 5, 1997: Human Rights Campaign Official

February 6, 1997: National Gay and Lesbian Task Force Official

February 10, 1997: Log Cabin Republicans Official

February 19, 1997: Human Rights Campaign Official

February 26, 1997: Gay and Lesbian Victory Fund Official

February 28, 1997: National Black Lesbian and Gay Leadership Forum Official

December 7, 1998: Lambda Legal Defense and Education Fund Official

4

WHERE RHETORIC MEETS REALITY: THE ROLE OF BLACK LESBIANS AND GAYS IN "QUEER" POLITICS

Keith O. Boykin

The words "diversity" and "inclusion" have been so over-used in the language of lesbian and gay politics that one might expect the "queer community" to shine as an exemplar in multicultural representation, effortlessly integrating communities of color and their causes and concerns into the larger liberation struggle. Unfortunately, the politically correct rhetoric differs greatly from the politically incorrect reality.

In reality, black lesbians and gays play no meaningful role in the lesbian and gay political movement. Putting aside the movement's inclusive rhetoric and the often strategically placed representation of selected people of color, the predominantly white lesbian and gay community actually engages in many of the same racially backward practices as the heterosexual population it hopes to enlighten. As historian Barbara Tuchman has written, "Every successful revolution eventually puts on the robes of the tyrant it deposed." The lesbian and gay political movement—inasmuch as it can be considered a success in challenging some conventional social values—provides no exception to Tuchman's rule.

I introduce the issue of black lesbian and gay representation here to initiate a candid and long overdue dialogue and not merely to cause contention within the already contentious LGBT (lesbian, gay, bisexual, transgender) community. I plan to explore the LGBT community's approach to race relations as one area in which "queer" politics seems to belie professed philosophies. I argue that the community fails to practice what it preaches regarding diversity and inclusion and I provide a strategy for changing this reality.

Three arguments are put forth in this chapter: (1) that black lesbians and gays do not play a meaningful role in lesbian and gay politics, (2) that it serves the interests of both white and black lesbians and gays that blacks should play a more significant role, and (3) white lesbians and gays and African-American heterosexuals and homosexuals can change the current reality by taking specific steps to ensure greater inclusion.

As the three points suggest, this is a discussion more about what is called "gay racism" than about "black homophobia," the latter of which seems to be the preferred topic that many white lesbians and gays would have black gay men and lesbians address. This censorship of expression is itself a form of racially insensitive bias toward people of color practiced within the LGBT community.

For simplicity, I use a variety of terms including "gay," "lesbian," "homosexual," and "same-gender-loving" when referring to gay men and lesbians. I also use the term "LGBT" to refer to the widening circle of people included in the community. Finally, I use the terms "African American" and "black" interchangeably.

BLACK LESBIANS AND GAYS DO NOT PLAY MEANINGFUL ROLE IN GAY POLITICS

The argument that black lesbians and gays do not play a meaningful role in gay politics should be understood in the context of a history that contradicts the current reality. Black lesbians and gays throughout the twentieth century have been very involved in shaping "gay" consciousness, but much of this involvement seems to have taken place outside the boundaries of the gay rights movement itself. From the Harlem Renaissance to the civil rights movement to the Stonewall Rebellion to the AIDS crisis, same-gender-loving African Americans have played a significant role in shaping society's understanding and definition of homosexuality and gay politics.

If homosexual identification can be considered a twentieth-century phenomenon, then perhaps no period of modern history may be more significant to its early development than the Harlem Renaissance. Certainly, the Renaissance's newfound openness toward bisexuality and homosexuality was virtually absent of overtly gay political messages such as those found in the post-Stonewall gay liberation time period. But despite its seemingly apolitical context, the Harlem Renaissance paved the way for more open and frank public conversation about sexuality than had ever happened before and therefore marked a significant milestone in the development of the later lesbian and gay political movement.

Black lesbians, gay men, and bisexuals played a leading role in the drama that unfolded in Harlem during the 1920s and 1930s. The music, literature, poetry, and creative performances of the day reveal a world of greater openness and sexual expression than had previously existed in black America. Historian Eric Garber has noted that "[h]omosexuality was clearly part of this world." Well-known artists such as Bessie Smith, Mabel Hampton, Wallace Thurman, Bruce Nugent, Claude McKay, Countee Cullen, Alain Locke, and Langston Hughes either wrote, talked, performed, or thought about same-sex sexual behavior. Many of them were known to have engaged in homosexual sexual activity themselves and were most likely homosexual or bisexual, as we now understand those terms. Their sexual liberation—though it may appear circumscribed by today's standards—actually helped open America's closet door about homosexuality.

The civil rights movement, roughly from 1954 to 1968, provides another historical reminder of the role of African Americans in defining the gay rights movement today. The developments of the civil rights era affected the burgeoning homosexual political movement in at least two significant ways: by creating a climate that enabled the gay rights movement, and by producing black lesbian and gay heroes who took center stage in America's racial morality play.

The movement's street protests, civil disobedience tactics, and challenges to authority awakened America's consciousness to the unfulfilled promises of the early dreams of the republic. Dr. Martin Luther King Jr. and other black civil rights activists cleverly used the rhetoric of America's own early patriots to remind the country of its values, and recalled a place where everyone is endowed "with certain inalienable rights" including "life, liberty, and the pursuit of happiness."

In a relatively conservative nation where change was not to be encouraged for "light and transient causes," as Thomas Jefferson had written, King taught Americans that change was not always to be feared. Moreover, the civil rights movement encouraged oppressed people and their oppressors to embrace change as their patriotic duty to the betterment of America. The climate that they created in their struggle for civil rights was itself a gift to American activism, and it enabled the subsequent development of the antiwar movement, the women's rights movement, and the gay liberation movement. As activist Bernice Johnson Reagon wrote in her essay in the 1983 anthology *Home Girls,* "[t]he civil rights movement was the first powerful movement of our era. Black folks started it, Black folks did it, so everything you've done politically rests on the efforts of my people."

The climate created by the civil rights movement also enabled the development and maturation of black lesbian and gay legends such as Lorraine Hansberry, Bayard Rustin, and James Baldwin. Through their writings and speaking, they not only challenged white America to accept black people; they also challenged black America to accept them as homosexuals and a part of the black community. Perhaps unwittingly, they were among the early gay rights activists, and not because they chose this role but rather because of the honesty with which they led their lives.

Hansberry, Rustin, and Baldwin were well known, but of course they are not the only black lesbians and gays in the modern era to have contributed to the gay and lesbian political movement. Audre Lorde produced literature so expressive and unique that she became a cultural icon in both the black community and the gay community. Melvin Boozer helped to push the Democratic Party in its politics on gay issues when he told the 1980 Democratic Convention that he understood the pain of both racism and homophobia. Phill Wilson has articulated the interests of black gay men living with AIDS as he has played a leading role in the fight against the disease nationally and internationally.

Many other black lesbians and gays toiled in obscurity for years in their communities. The black gay and lesbian oral tradition has long celebrated the courageous role that black and Latino drag queens played in defying the New York City police during the now famous 1969 raid at the Stonewall Bar in Greenwich Village. The Stonewall Rebellion, as it later came to be known by some in the gay community, marked the defining moment in the modern gay rights era. Later, black lesbians and gay men involved in multiracial organizations helped to educate white gays and lesbians about the black experience, and black men and women stung by the AIDS crisis mobilized their communities throughout the 1980s and 1990s. In addition, many black lesbians and gays have formed their own local, regional, and national organizations to educate, empower, and affirm the black LGBT community.

Despite the hope and optimism that one might expect from the historically influential role of black lesbians and gays in the gay rights movement, the dream of racial inclusion and sensitivity within the movement has today still not been realized. Instead, the black LGBT community continues to be exploited by the larger community. Black lesbians and gays have been tokenized, ignored, or simply patronized while the predominantly white gay and lesbian community has defined values, issues, agendas, and symbols without meaningful black contribution.

White lesbians and gays, particularly those in positions of responsibility within the movement, tend to interact with their black counterparts using the model of a paternalistic relationship. Paternalism, as used here, refers to the practice of treating people in a manner that provides for their needs without giving them rights or responsibilities. Notice that even the needs of the group provided for are determined by the father figure. The tone of this relationship might best be expressed by the once popular child rearing philosophy that "children are to be seen and not heard." In such relationships, children are viewed almost as trophies to help demonstrate the parent's love and compassion to the outside world. But the child's development is often a secondary concern and best understood in the context of how the development reflects on the parent. A well-mannered child with good grades, for example, is to be valued because he casts a positive light on his parents.

Following the paternalistic child-rearing approach, black lesbians and gays are often treated as though they are to be seen (when appropriate, to demonstrate the gay community's progressiveness) but not heard (in making important decisions).

As African Americans have gained in political power since the 1970s, white leaders have been forced to deal with newly elected and appointed black power figures. In urban America, as white flight has drained white families out into the suburbs, cities have become increasingly populated by blacks and single whites, many of whom are gay or lesbian. As an unexpected consequence of the white flight, a symbiotic relationship eventually developed in which black big city mayors began to court predominantly white lesbian and gay communities and organizations for political and financial support, and white lesbians and gays began to seek the political and moral support of black politicians for the gay rights agenda.

By the 1980s, black big city mayors like Tom Bradley in Los Angeles, David Dinkins in New York, Harold Washington in Chicago, Maynard Jackson in Atlanta, and Marion Barry in Washington came to understand the need to win the support of gays and lesbians in order to win a significant portion of the white vote in multi-candidate elections. Energized by their new influence and the urgency of the growing AIDS crisis, the white lesbian and gay community in the 1980s began to demand more from these black politicians. They asked for and won the support of black politicians on issues ranging from antidiscrimination laws to domestic partnership rights to repealing antisodomy ordinances to increased funding for care and treatment of people living with AIDS.

In some cities, black lesbians and gays played a significant role in initiating this dialogue with black politicians. In many other places, however, the faces of gay and lesbian urban politics were most likely to be white. Black lesbians and gays often lacked the financial resources to make a significant financial contribution to political leaders, they lacked the access to other resources that would open the doors of political power, and they were less likely to be "out of the closet" about their sexual orientation, especially to other blacks. Many white lesbian and gay city dwellers had escaped their small-minded suburban backgrounds by relocating to big cities, but black lesbians and gays often were native to their urban communities, making it more difficult for them to "come out" without fear of discovery or repercussion.

A few openly lesbian and gay African Americans became prominent in some of these cities, and it suited the interests of the white lesbian and gay communities to include them. After all, if the lesbian and gay movement hoped to win the support of black elected officials, it would seem appropriate to demonstrate its own representation of black gays and lesbians. Out of this three-way relationship between black leaders, white lesbians and gays, and black lesbians and gays, the practices of *triangulation* and *tokenization* began to develop.

Politically and financially weaker than their white counterparts, black lesbians and gays found themselves left out of the equation between the gay community and the black leadership. For the most part, blacks did not control the gay newspapers, bars, nightclubs, political organizations, and other media that would have enhanced their political power by giving them a tool for swift and effective mass communication of political messages. The whites who did control these institutions became the gatekeepers for access to political power. Their access gave them the power to determine which black lesbians and gays to include in the process, and not surprisingly they chose to tap those blacks who appeared to reflect their own gay-oriented values. In effect, white gay men and lesbians maintained the power to decide which black lesbians and gays were suitable to be leaders.

Black lesbian and gay leaders selected this way have sometimes played a tenuous role in the gay rights political drama. On the one hand, they have gained public credibility as African-American spokespeople for the

LGBT cause, but on the other hand, if they are perceived as too closely connected to the white community and distant from the black community, their credibility is undermined among other African Americans. They become particularly susceptible to criticism from more "black-identified" or "Afrocentric" homosexuals who have a reputation for being tied to the black community. This "credibility gap" between the black and white homosexual communities should cause concern for the mainstream LGBT movement that expects to capitalize on the involvement of people of color.

The interests of the LGBT community are well served by the public presence of black people in the gay rights struggle by creating the appearance that blacks are actively involved in the movement at all levels. The reality is far different. In contrast to the strategically manipulated perception, only a handful of African Americans have played key leadership roles in the major mainstream LGBT political organizations in the country. These organizations—the five most recognized nationally—include the Human Rights Campaign (HRC), the National Gay and Lesbian Task Force (NGLTF), the Lambda Legal Defense Fund, the Gay and Lesbian Alliance Against Defamation (GLAAD), and the Gay and Lesbian Victory Fund. A few blacks in these organizations have served in very significant roles such as director of development or director of finance and exercised a high level of responsibility over administrative and financial functions. Two organizations (Lambda and NGLTF)—have employed black development directors, and one—(HRC) has employed a black director of finance. Despite these indicators of change, at the time of this writing, very few of the African Americans in these organizations serve in key policy-making roles about the philosophy, strategy, and direction of the community. In addition, none of these large organizations has ever employed an African American as executive director.

I do not suggest that blacks employed in nonpolicy roles cannot influence policy decisions, but instead I focus on policy positions because the people employed in these roles are hired specifically for the purpose of making such decisions.

On the board level, the records have been mixed. All of the major organizations profess to strive for gender and racial diversity on their boards of directors, but some have been more successful than others. Some have met with limited success because of the high-dollar fundraising requirements expected of their board members while others appear to be limited by the lack of contact with or knowledge of suitable candidates. The most likely prospects for board membership are also likely to be approached by other boards too, creating a competition for the "best" candidates of color. For whatever reason, the racial composition of board memberships seldom match the proportional representation in the larger community.

Despite the emphasis on racial representation in political organizations, tokenism is just as widely practiced and perhaps more widely felt in the context of the gay media. Even as the gay media has grown rapidly in the past decade, black lesbians and gays have been consistently tokenized in their representation. Gay newspapers, magazines, cable television programs, and radio shows have often presented African American images only when pressed to do so, or as a once-a-year effort to "cover" Black History Month in February. When lists are published of the "100 most influential" or "50 most important" or "25 most historically significant" lesbians and gays, a select few blacks—the "usual suspects"—have often been represented in token form, but often their inclusion appears to be something of an afterthought. Even when it's not, the whole decisionmaking process of compiling such lists is always inherently suspect on any number of grounds, including the absence of black lesbians and gays from the news rooms and editorial boards of so many gay media establishments. Their absence only ensures that African Americans will react suspiciously to editorial decisions.

Just as pernicious as the practice of tokenism is the tendency among white "queers" to ignore or patronize African Americans. Often when decisions are made that affect the entire LGBT community, white-run organizations and officials don't bother or don't remember to contact African Americans for their input. Instead, they make their decisions in a racial vacuum, mistakenly content that their commitment to progressive values is expansive enough to include the interests of all oppressed people within their community. As with many forms of prejudice, often the decision to ignore black lesbians and gays is not really a decision at all but instead an omission. But the fact that the prejudice is unconsciously practiced does little to lessen the severity of the blow to those impacted.

Consciously or unconsciously ignoring the input of black lesbians and gays is tantamount to exclusion. Sometimes the exclusion occurs because some person or a group of people simply fail to notice the absence of black people in the room or on the advance list of participants. The racial dynamic that allows this to happen is itself troubling, because it indicates that black people are not, and have not been, the "players" in the decisionmaking. If they were, surely their absence would be felt or noticed just as the absence of a representative from one of the big five organizations would quickly be observed. Ironically, some in the white community have interpreted the absence of black participants as a problem for black people and not for whites. In other words, they have argued that black lesbians and gays must play a more visible role in the community without recognizing that white exclusion has created the black absence in the first place.

The recent trend against "identity politics" expressed by some gay progressive intellectuals raises troubling issues as well. The critique of "identity politics" appropriately suggests that our community must move beyond organizing tactics that focus solely on our identities, whether race, gender, sexual orientation, or some other identity. In its best form, the argument suggests the LGBT community might appropriately tackle such class problems as economic injustice, corporate greed, capitalistic manipulation of political power, or even the systematic diminution of organized labor. In its basest form, however, the argument against "identity politics" seems to rail against the perceived problem in the ever devolving "Balkanization" of our society. Thus the development of more identity organizations only separates us as communities from those values we supposedly share in common. This second argument--already disingenuous when expressed by white male heterosexual conservatives—seems reductionist and hypocritical when expressed by gays and lesbians, especially when directed at people of color within the lesbian and gay community.

On a number of separate occasions in my years as an activist, I remember being questioned by white gay men and lesbians who asked why we need a black lesbian and gay organization. As they put it, "Why can't we all be part of the same community?" The question, coming from an openly gay or lesbian person, is so shallow that it almost answers itself. The community they would have black lesbians and gays embrace is, first of all, a community based on identity politics itself. It is not the human identity they embrace, but the lesbian and gay identity. The question they pose could just as easily by asked of them: "Why can't gays and lesbians just be part of the mainstream community?" In answer to both questions, the oppression practiced by people in the larger communities excludes or ostracizes members of the subcommunities from fuller participation in the mainstream.

Unfortunately, some white gays and lesbians fail to notice the parallels and see the problem only through their own frame of reference. Thus when black lesbians and gays organize, they are practicing division, but when white lesbians and gays organize, they are merely organizing. Similarly, in other contexts, when blacks exclude whites it's considered "segregation," but when whites exclude blacks it's merely natural. The absence of black people from the table has become so common that many people don't even recognize it or consider it a problem.

Just as problematic as the practice of tokenizing or ignoring black lesbians and gays is the increasing tendency to patronize them. When this happens, white lesbian and gay leaders actually pretend to help black lesbians and gays when they really aren't, or they feign concern about the plight of African Americans without ever really doing much to make a difference. Some organizations, nationally and locally, have begun genuine outreach efforts to involve more people of color. Many of these efforts are destined to fail if they do not first understand the economic, social, and psychological barriers that prevent blacks from participating. If, for example, these organizations assume that blacks and other people of color have not participated merely because they were unfamiliar with the organizations then they will miss the larger problem that people of color often don't participate because they don't feel comfortable in these white-gay environments. Many of the presumably well-intentioned efforts to embrace blacks—such as inviting prominent black speakers to organizational functions, hosting gospel concerts, or conducting diversity training—may generate some initial interest among blacks but are not likely to make a significant, long-term impact as isolated events unless accompanied by a long-term commitment to and interest in the development of the black lesbian and gay community.

The practice of patronizing black lesbians and gays may provide the classic example of the paternalistic "seen and not heard" model of white relations with blacks. As a result, "queer" issues are selected that do not necessarily represent the interests and concerns of black lesbians and gays, and names and symbols are selected that discount them. This is not to suggest that the issues that are chosen are not important, but only that they are often selected either without the consultation, input, or concern for how they affect the segment of the community that is African American. Two such issues—same-sex marriage and the Millennium March—provide dramatic illustrations of the challenge. The recent popularity of the same-sex marriage issue was generated largely by the judicial and political proceedings stemming from a celebrated court case in Hawaii. Activists and legal organizations in that state and nationally quickly responded to the Hawaii case by mounting a strategic media and political response to accompany the legal response. The Lambda Legal Defense Fund assigned one of its top lawyers in New York to the case and helped to coordinate a coalition of like-minded organizations to champion the cause. When some activists in the coalition raised concerns about whether same-sex marriage should be the defining issue for the LGBT movement, they were told that the "train had left the station" and it was too late to stop it. The gay community didn't choose this issue at this time, they were told, the issue chose them.

It may be true that the gay community did not purposefully choose to make same-sex marriage the defining gay issue in 1996 and 1997, but it quickly became the dominant issue nonetheless. Reasonable arguments can be made both for and against making same-sex marriage a cause celebre for the community, even by those who do not doubt that securing marriage rights would ultimately benefit everyone in the LGBT community. The question about same-sex marriage is one of priorities, not propriety. It was certainly proper for the LGBT community to respond to a crisis that threatens it, but it is less clear that marriage should become the priority issue within the community. Such determinations of priority might appropriately be made after consultation among various organizations who have presumably also consulted with their membership and constituents. While leaders must make organizational priorities all the time, they need not determine community priorities (as distinct from organizational ones) without the input of the community affected. Some organizations organized and participated in town meetings to gauge the sense of the community, but few of these town meetings ever took place in the black community. One that took place in the white-gay community of West Hollywood merely ratified the perception that openly identified white gay men and lesbians supported the cause, as they comprised 99 percent of the meeting's participants. When HRC and Gay Men of African Descent (GMAD) organized a joint event about marriage in New York, the event took place in the predominantly white-area of Chelsea and even there the sentiment among the black participants was decidedly mixed. When the National Black Lesbian and Gay Leadership Forum (NBLGLF) surveyed its membership about the issue, virtually no one expressed enthusiasm for making marriage a priority in the community. Despite the concerns, the gay community marched on with the issue.

In February 1998, HRC and the Universal Fellowship of Metropolitan Community Churches (UFMCC) jointly agreed that it was time to organize another initiative—a march on Washington. At the behest of organizer Robin Tyler, the two organizations agreed to provide funding for the planning of the march and helped make preliminary decisions about its course.

Without consulting any other organizations or the general community in advance, they decided to hold the march in the year 2000, to label it the "Millennium March," and to focus its theme on the issues of "faith and family." That process of deciding to hold a nationwide march without the reasonable input of other organizations has been widely criticized in other writings, and I will not repeat those arguments in this context. More to the point of this chapter is the exclusion of African Americans from the process. (In the interest of full disclosure, I should reveal that I served my last week as executive director of NBLGLF during the same week when HRC and UFMCC announced the march, and I was involved in discussions that week that led to NBLGLF's preliminary decision to sign on for the announcement of the march since the event was presented as a fait accompli.)

I do not claim to know whether African-American lesbians and gays support another march on Washington, and I don't know that any polls or surveys have been conducted on this issue. As with most of these issues, reasonable arguments can be made on either side. Nevertheless, when a grassroots coalition of veteran African-American LGBT activists raised concerns, their issues were patronizingly addressed as a momentary diversion from the planning for the inevitable. The black activists included, among others, such notables as Mandy Carter, a longtime field organizer for HRC and NBLGLF; Barbara Smith, a black lesbian feminist writer and early LGBT organizer; and Nadine Smith, a Tampa area LGBT activist who co-chaired the 1993 March on Washington. Partly in response to their concerns and the concerns of NBLGLF executive director Jubi Headley, HRC and UFMCC held a series of conference calls and meetings to address issues of process and inclusion. In September 1998, seven months after the march was announced, the ad hoc coalition of black LGBT activists and others took out a two-page advertisement in the *Washington Blade* newspaper to voice their view that their concerns had still not been addressed.

The first lesson from the Millennium March and the same-sex marriage controversies is that the white-dominated LGBT community has and will continue to select the LGBT community's priorities and then ask for input afterwards, once the "train has left the station."

The priorities of the white LGBT community often do not reflect the priorities of black lesbians and gays, first, because black lesbians and gays often identify more with traditional black community issues than they do with gay issues, and second, because black lesbian and gay issues are not always "political" issues. Black lesbians and gays are just as likely to be concerned about affirmative action or racial discrimination or unemployment as they are about repealing sodomy laws or outlawing antigay discrimination. In some instances, they are more likely to be concerned about traditional race issues than about "queer" issues that don't seem to matter to them, such as same-sex marriage. Even when black lesbians and gays are focused on gay issues, they are often bread-and-butter issues of daily life and existence. Many do not accept the rhetoric about the importance of "coming out" and instead are focused more on the matters of family, community, church, and economics.

The idea behind an event to focus on "faith and family" might have been perfectly suited to the black LGBT community had black people been involved in the process. The black church plays an enormously influential role in the black lesbian and gay community, but most black lesbians and gays worship at traditional black churches, not at gay-identified churches. Religion and church are still very racially segregated in America, among heterosexuals and homosexuals, so the selection of a nonblack church to cosponsor a march raises the issue about involving the black church as well. If the purpose of selecting only one church is to unify everyone around our commonality instead of our difference, then this approach neglects the long history of difference practiced by the white community. Whenever the white LGBT community wants to minimize racial differences, it resurrects the language of "coalition politics," but its words often fall onto the deaf ears of a black community that knows too well that white lesbians and gays do not support black issues that don't involve gay rights.

The notion that we can all be one community seems hypocritical to many black people who perceive a white community that historically and continually disregards African Americans. This helps to explain the recent popularity of the black-identified "same-gender-loving" (SGL) movement, which consciously avoids the oppressive language of the white "queer" community. Terms such as "gay" or "lesbian" are perceived as vestiges of white Eurocentric dominance. Cleo Manago, a leader of the SGL movement, has defined gay as "the mainstream white (patriarchal) homosexual community." According to Manago, "In the midst of a need for affirmation and acknowledgment from the 'gay' community, same-gender-loving Black people are subject to sexual objectification, discrimination, white supremacist treatment and indifference."

The term "queer" is even more unpopular among African-American gays and lesbians, whether or not they identify with the SGL cause, yet white "queers" persist in defining the LGBT movement with a language that offends most blacks. The SGL movement also objects to the symbols of white gayness, including the pink triangle, the rainbow flag, and the lambda symbol, none of which is African- or black-identified. These concerns will continue to create obstacles for the efforts by the mainstream LGBT movement to include more blacks as blacks feel increasingly isolated from the "queer" community.

As a result of the paternalism, tokenism, and indifference to the black LGBT community, black lesbian and gays no longer play a meaningful role in lesbian and gay politics. As I have mentioned, they have even become triangulated out of the equation involving black (heterosexual) leaders as well-funded white lesbians and gays have used their resources against the interests of their black counterparts. But despite the current state of racial affairs in the LGBT community, many blacks and whites do agree that black lesbians and gays should play a meaningful role in the movement, even though they don't already.

BLACK LESBIANS AND GAYS SHOULD PLAY MEANINGFUL ROLE IN GAY POLITICS

At a winter 1997 meeting in New York City organized by HRC and GMAD, a black man in the audience stood up during the question period and asked why black gays and lesbians should support the same-sex marriage issue while HRC had an abysmal record of hiring blacks to top positions or appointing them to its board of directors. As I understood the man's question, he seemed to support same-sex marriage, but did not support HRC. HRC's field director Donna Red Wing responded to the accusations by indicating that progress was being made and more changes were coming. The man in the audience said that he was not fully satisfied with the response, but the incident revealed two separate explanations of why both sides might want black lesbians and gays to play a role in gay politics.

First, white organizations and leaders desperately need black participants to help advance their cause. While many have managed to navigate around this problem by involving blacks in figurehead capacities, such tokenism is becoming less convincing to prove their sincerity as blacks and others have become more conscious of its practice. Black participation helps the white LGBT community tap into the civil rights tradition, portrays a progressive and integrated community, and helps to persuade black heterosexual leaders to support the gay community's agenda. Second, and just as importantly, blacks themselves should play a meaningful role in gay politics, in part, because the decisions made affect them too.

The audience member at the New York meeting may have missed the point that by opposing same-sex marriage rights solely for the purpose of challenging HRC, he may have been, at some level, opposing his own struggle for justice. As I have said before, reasonable people can and have disagreed about the importance of the same-sex marriage issue, but for those who do support this issue, they must be careful not to conflate their support for the issue with support for an organization that also supports the issue. I do not wish to suggest that people of color should acquiesce to the interests of the white LGBT community by ignoring or failing to raise racial concerns. However, if a particular organization does not represent one's concerns, then another more suitable organization could be supported instead. But why oppose the Employment Non-Discrimination Act (ENDA) or same-sex marriage, as some have, merely because you disagree with one of the messengers on other important issues? The issues of employment rights and same-sex marriage do not belong to HRC or Lambda or any other organization.

Most of the participants, of all races, in the racial dialogue in the LGBT community actually acknowledge the need for greater representation of people of color at the decision-making tables. Even if their acknowledgment merely reflects lip service to the politically correct expectation, white lesbians and gays are also quick to state their support for greater racial inclusion. But despite the mutual benefit to blacks and whites by achieving civil rights for lesbians and gays, I believe the responsibility rests primarily on the white LGBT community, as I will explain in the final section of this chapter.

A STRATEGY FOR GREATER INCLUSION OF BLACK LESBIANS AND GAYS

No single strategy or approach, by itself, is guaranteed to bring about meaningful change in the gay community's racial dynamics. Those interested in advancing the racial dialogue must be willing to try a number of different approaches to the problem. Still, because of the long-term pattern of neglect, ostracism, and exclusion practiced by whites toward blacks, the white LGBT community has farther to go to reach black lesbians and gays than the black community does. Certainly, the work of coalition building requires mutual cooperation and a fair amount of trust, but "mutual" does not mean "equal." In this context, I place the heavier burden on the white community instead of the black community. White lesbians and gays, first of all, still control the LGBT community's resources. Second, white lesbians and gays must overcome a long legacy of distrust that they themselves have created and left behind in their interactions with blacks. Until the white LGBT community recognizes and accepts this heavier burden and stops trying to place the blame of failed race relations on the shoulders of blacks, then progress will not be made. This is a critical first step to bridge the chasm of misunderstanding.

In the course of my discussions with white LGBT leaders and organizations, I have developed eight recommendations for greater and more meaningful inclusion of black lesbians and gays. I will briefly explain each of the recommendations here, but I will limit my in-depth comments to the last recommendation—the issue of triangulation—which is most relevant to this chapter.

1. *Treat racial inclusion as a serious issue.* Executive directors, board members, and others in policymaking and hiring roles in organizations should incorporate diversity into their strategic planning process and view this issue as seriously as they view meeting their budgetary and fundraising goals.

2. *Go beyond tokenism.* Organizers must seek to involve black activists who can and will make a meaningful contribution to their organization and the movement. It's not enough to select a few token black representatives without involving people with serious responsibility.

3. *Provide for increased visibility of blacks.* Internally, more blacks should be visible to those who work for the operation, and externally more blacks should be visible in the media and at public events. Moreover, white lesbians and gays should not be the only spokespeople for gay organizations.

4. *Listen to black viewpoints.* The Millennium March is just one example of how white organizations don't listen to black people's concerns. Organizers must learn to listen to the concerns of blacks (and other people of color) without responding defensively to these concerns.

5. *Support black organizers and organizations.* White organizations should not be in the business of selecting which black leaders are acceptable. Instead, indigenous, autonomous black LGBT leaders (who are not beholden to white gay organizations) should be involved. Nor should white organizations assume they know what black organizers and organizations need without asking first. The white LGBT community must learn to see its issues more broadly than the simple white gay agenda and learn that other issues such as affirmative action, women's rights, civil rights, and class issues need to be addressed as well.

6. *Self-educate.* The responsibility for white education about racial issues

rests with the white community, and it should not become the burden of the black community. As Audre Lorde explained in her famous address, "The Master's Tools Will Not Dismantle the Master's House," educating the oppressor is "an old and primary tool of all oppressors to keep the oppressed occupied with the master's concerns. . . . This is a diversion of energies and a tragic repetition of racist patriarchal thought."

7. *Go beyond "the usual suspects."* We've passed the time for excuses from white gays and lesbians about why they can't find good black people. Those who are genuinely committed will find ways to identify, recruit, hire, sustain, nurture, and promote black activists in meaningful leadership roles in their organizations. This means they have to stop looking in their own self-selective insular circles to find black people and start looking in other places.

8. *End the triangulation paradigm.* The strategy for inclusion I put forward relies heavily on this final point—eliminating the model of triangulation by involving each of the three parties (black homosexuals, white homosexuals, and black heterosexuals) in retriangulating its direction until the problem is resolved. In other words, instead of pushing black lesbians and gays out of the loop, I suggest putting white lesbians and gays out of the loop until they learn to include their black counterparts in the mix. Of course, some will perceive this as "reverse discrimination," but actually that is not what I have in mind. Instead, I have devised an approach that is intended to force cooperation, not discrimination. Moreover, since the black LGBT community still does not control the resources of the community, it's hard to imagine a scenario that allows it to discriminate—with all the implications of power involved in the use of that word—against whites. What black lesbians and gays can do, however, is to leverage their political access, power, connections, and affinity with black heterosexual leaders to guarantee that they are involved in the decision-making process.

Thus black mainstream leaders should insist that white lesbians and gays only deal with them with other black lesbians and gays involved. These black leaders should demand that black lesbians and gays be present in meetings when important decisions are being made, and they should consult with black lesbian and gay leaders before meeting with white lesbians and gays. When white lesbians and gays approach them without the involvement or the obvious consultation of black lesbians and gays, then the black mainstream leaders should politely refuse to talk to them until they correct the problem. This approach should be adopted by black mayors and municipal officials as well as members of the Congressional Black Caucus.

Black lesbians and gays will play a role in the new equation by helping to enforce appropriate behavior by the other two parties. Black lesbians and gays should hold accountable their own black leadership and white lesbians and gays by demanding their inclusion in the decision-making process. Where some black lesbians and gays may not have the experience or background necessary to participate in certain activities, they should insist that others with the experience commit to training them. At the same time, for this strategy to work, black lesbians and gays must continue to build, support, and grow their own institutions independent of the white LGBT community, both as a way of empowering and affirming black lesbians and gays and as a means to demonstrate and flex the community's political power in dealing with the other two parties in the triangle.

Aside from the independent goals achieved by black autonomy and empowerment, another primary goal to be achieved is the greater inclusion of black lesbians and gays in the LGBT political movement. This is where the white lesbian and gay community becomes involved. The white LGBT community and organizations must finally diversify their leadership, decision-making processes, and activities by including more African Americans, in addition to other people of color. Some will complain, as they have in the past, that they have tried everything possible but they cannot locate a single qualified black person anywhere in the country. Let them complain. Only when these white leaders understand that their political access and power depends on their ability to locate, recruit, train, support, and involve black lesbians and gays will this goal actually become the genuine priority it never was before.

REFERENCES

Boykin, Keith. 1996. *One more river to cross: Black and gay in America*. New York: Anchor Books.

Dynes, Wayne R., ed. 1990. *The encyclopedia of homosexuality*. New York: Garland Publishers.

Garrow, David. 1988. *Bearing the cross: Martin Luther King Jr. and the Southern Christian Leadership Conference*. New York: Vintage Books.

Hemphill, Essex, ed. 1991. *Brother to brother: New writings by black gay men*. Boston: Alyson Publishers.

Smith, Barbara, ed. 1983. *Home girls: A black feminist anthology*. New York: Kitchen Table—Women of Color Press.

5

LESBIAN AND GAY POLICY PRIORITIES: COMMONALITY AND DIFFERENCE

Jean Reith Schroedel and Pamela Fiber

Many gay men and some lesbians and feminists assume that it is reasonable to expect lesbian and feminist support for, or participation in, gay political and cultural organizations and projects, and many people think it is reasonable to expect that gay men will understand and support feminist and lesbian causes. But both of these expectations are, in general, conspicuously not satisfied (Frye 1983, 128).

INTRODUCTION

Although the 1992 presidential election brought gay and lesbian policy concerns onto the national agenda for the first time, the lesbian and gay rights movement[1] had been actively engaged in community building and political mobilization throughout the preceding four decades. The prevalence of antigay attitudes within the broader society is a major reason that gays and lesbians have found it difficult to get their policy concerns addressed. Not only are these attitudes widespread and socially permissible, they also are legally sanctioned. (See chapter 1 of this volume for evidence and details.) Lesbians and gay men face barriers and discrimination in employment, housing, and healthcare, as well as scrutiny and abuse by law enforcement and the legal justice system.

One of the strongest bonds helping to forge a common "gay" identity, community, and political movement is the shared oppression based on sexual orientation. "The creation of a movement among individuals, most of who previously accepted collective invisibility, the mobilization of political resources by members of the community, and the opening of opportunities for participation by local political regimes resulted in the increasing participation of lesbians and gay men in municipal politics" (Rosenthal 1996, 45). To a large extent, the current national movement for "gay rights" reflects traditional forms of interest group politics and evolved out of smaller local and regional movements (Haider-Markel and Meier 1996).

Despite the common experience of living within an often hostile society, divisions based upon sex, race, and class make the creation of a unified movement difficult (Vaid 1995). These cleavages are not new. The tension between the need for unity and commonality in the movement versus the pursuit of issues significant to one segment of the community to the exclusion of others has been evident from the beginning. Although the focus in this research is on differences between gay men and lesbians, it is important to recognize that other divisions exist. As Hamilton (1992, 13) pointed out, "the media in its coverage of queer issues has given white gay men the most vocal spots and attention. It's going to take a long time for Black lesbians to feel safe enough to come forward and join this group."[2]

In the first part of this chapter we briefly summarize attempts over the past four decades to build a unified lesbian/gay movement, as well as the sources of strain that have undercut those efforts. Next we examine the policy aims of the current "gay" rights movement and assess the extent to which it articulates the policy priorities of both lesbians and gay men. Finally, we analyze data obtained from the first national survey of openly gay and lesbian elected officials to determine whether gay male officeholders and lesbian officeholders have the same policy priorities.

THE CREATION OF A GAY AND LESBIAN MOVEMENT

Although Cruikshank (1992) traces the history of a political movement for gay and lesbian rights in the United States back to the 1890s, we will only focus on developments since World War II.[3] The origins of the homophile movement (1945–1969) can be traced to a group of gay leftists including Harry Hay, who founded the Mattachine Society in 1951. Although the Mattachine Society's primary goal was to develop a strong group consciousness "free of negative attitudes" (Rivera 1984), lesbians were uncomfortable with the gay male ethos of the group. This discomfort led to the formation of the Daughters of Bilitis in 1955. Although the Daughters of Bilitis worked cooperatively with the Mattachine Society in many cities, it strongly defended the need for a separate women's group within the homophile movement (Stein 1994, 64).

In the 1950s and 1960s, "most lesbian and gay male activists would come to think of themselves as both members of the same community and members of sex-specific communities. But the balance of these two senses changed dramatically over time" (65). Within the homophile movement, lesbian attempts to shape the political agenda were largely unsuccessful, and gay men tended to downplay the differences between the two groups. For gay men, "community" was found in gay-friendly bars and bath houses (Bronski 1987); neither of which were frequented by lesbians. Although lesbians joined with gay men in rallying against police raids and violence directed at gay male bar and bath house patrons, over time they became angry at continually having their needs ignored by the male dominated homophile movement (Hamilton 1992; Stein 1994). The gender hierarchy that existed within the heterosexual world was replicated within the homophile movement. Lesbians were expected to fulfill traditional women's roles within groups—coffee making and secretarial tasks (Frye 1983; Phelan 1989). A lesbian active in the homophile movement described the social rules as follows: "There wasn't a women's movement yet so there wasn't anything to have a conflict about. We knew our place—we were always the coffee makers. . . . There was a clear set of chores for women" (Stein 1994, 68).

The Development of a Lesbian Separatist Movement

The reemergence of a women's movement in the 1960s led to increased conflicts about women's roles within the homophile groups and contributed to the development of a strong lesbian separatist movement (Hamilton 1992; Taylor and Whittier 1992; Cruikshank 1992; Stein 1994; Blasius 1994; Rosenthal 1996).[4] As lesbians came to see their social status as defined by patriarchal social and cultural norms, many came to believe that lesbian separatism was "the logical outcome of feminism, the quintessential expression of the personal as political" (Taylor and Whittier 1992, 108) and that gay men were representatives of the patriarchy (Hamilton 1992). The defection of lesbians into separatist groups severely weakened homophile groups that ostensibly represented both gay men and lesbians.[5]

Lesbian feminism promoted group consciousness and solidarity among women, utilizing "boundary strategies" to create separate institutions and develop a distinct women's culture. Instead of protesting police harassment of bar patrons, the political priorities of the new lesbian separatist groups included issues such as the sexual abuse of children, rape, pornography, and "the harmful effects of growing up in a sexist culture" (Cruikshank

1992, 136). Despite the shared experience of being homosexual in a pre-dominantly heterosexual world, many lesbians came to believe that sexual oppression eclipsed this commonality and precluded the formation of polit-ical alliances with gay men (Taylor and Whittier 1992). By creating women only cultural events, institutions, businesses, and even language, lesbian feminist culture attempted to place women's lives and experiences at the center of the movement (Phelan 1989; Daly 1990; Penelope 1992; Cruik-shank 1992).[6]

The Re-creation of a Unified Movement

Probably the biggest single impetus for reuniting lesbians and gay men into a common movement was the discovery of AIDS in the early 1980s. The initial unwillingness of Congress and the Reagan and Bush administra-tions to fund basic AIDS research and provide treatment to HIV-positive individuals led to the creation of a self-help AIDS activist movement.[7] The most successful AIDS organizations have been composed of gay men, who were subsequently joined by lesbians (Blasius 1994, 157). Although the disease has wreaked havoc within the community, it has helped galvanize support from segments of the community that in the past would never have considered working together (see chapter 10). Even though few lesbi-ans have been infected with HIV, it remains an important political cause for both lesbians and gay men. Not only have many lesbians lost friends to the disease, they recognize that the antihomosexual backlash triggered by the AIDS epidemic affects them as well as gay men (Cruikshank 1992; Adam 1995; Blasius 1994).[8]

In many states and localities, lesbians and gay men have found common interests in battling against the enactment of antigay initiatives such as Colorado's Amendment Two, which would have prohibited government from including sexual orientation in their antidiscrimination and civil rights statutes.[9] Although the movement has been galvanized by attacks from groups like the Moral Majority and the Traditional Values Coali-tion(Haider-Markel and Meier 1996), mobilization also has occurred through the politicization of sexuality. Blasius argues that simply the act of living as a homosexual is "by definition political" (1995). Through the act of "coming out," a lesbian or gay man creates a relationship with the broader gay and lesbian community. Because the broader society has la-beled the lesbian and gay community as "deviant," "pathological," and "perverse," one of the major challenges of the movement is the construc-tion of a positive group identity (Phelan 1989; Taylor and Whittier 1992;

Blasius 1995; Wald, Button, and Rienzo 1996). "Such construction occurs through a shaping of individual subjective and interpersonal identity, by recourse to a structure of power relations within society" (Blasius 1994, 3). This construction is evident in both political and legal discourse.

In *Bowers v. Hardwick* (1986), the Supreme Court held that Georgia's sodomy law was constitutional, reasoning that the right to privacy that covered both contraceptive use (*Griswold* 1965) and the decision to have an abortion (*Roe* 1973) did not apply to homosexuals because there was no "connection between family, marriage, or procreation." Justice White then went on to point out that the proscription against sodomy had existed in the United States since the founding of the republic and that the Court needed to respect the majority's sentiment that such conduct was immoral. Even though sodomy laws are infrequently invoked, Abby Rubenfeld, the director of the Lambda Legal Defense Fund argues "sodomy laws are the bedrock of legal discrimination against gay men and lesbians" (Cain 1993). Because sodomy laws criminalize consensual acts within the private sphere of the home, they stigmatize all homosexuals as a criminal and deviant group.

To combat the social construction of homosexuality as deviant, lesbian and gay groups have followed a two-pronged strategy of building a positive self-identity within the community and campaigning to extend civil rights protection to lesbians and gay men (Taylor and Whittier 1992; Adam 1995). "Seen in terms of subordination and stigmatization, the gay and lesbian civil rights claim is strong. Gay men and lesbians live in a regime of formal inequality, where it is lawful to deny people employment, housing and access to public accommodations solely because of their sexual orientation under the law of all but eight states" (Schacter 1994, 298). The addition of sexual orientation to civil rights laws would also affect child custody decisions, visitation rights for noncustodial parents, adoption laws, marriage, and statutes that restrict sexual relations between individuals of the same sex (Cole and Eskridge 1994; Blasius 1994; Cruikshank 1992; Newton 1994; Schacter 1994; Adam 1995; Garfield 1995; Riccucci and Gossett 1996; Vaid 1995).[10]

TENSION WITHIN THE MOVEMENT

Although many recognize the need for a united movement, tensions still remain. "In the relational dimension of everyday life, there is still a delicate balance between separatism and friendship involving lesbians and gay men (this is even more the case in urban areas where the lesbian and gay community has become more elaborated)" (Blasius 1994, 200). By articulating needs of both lesbians and gay men, the contemporary Queer movement is one attempt at bridging some of the distance between lesbians and gay men (Hamilton 1992). However, divisions based on gender, as well as those from race, education, income, and social status, continue to pose obstacles to "community" building (Vaid 1995; Rosenthal 1996).

Many lesbians who have chosen to once again work in "gay" rights organizations believe they are relegated to second-class status. Urvashi Vaid, the former Executive Director of the National Gay and Lesbian Task Force (NGLTF), recalls a male colleague suggesting that the way to raise money was to "hire a nice white man with a cute ass as your development director" (Vaid 1995, 276). Despite the NGLTF's efforts directed at repealing sodomy laws, raising funds for AIDS research, and combating discrimination against people with AIDS and HIV—all of which primarily affect gay men—a male staffer told Vaid that he as a gay man was opposed to funding lesbian-specific projects (277).

As a result, some lesbians have begun to question whether they should be heavily involved in efforts to repeal sodomy laws and halt the spread of AIDS, neither of which significantly impact lesbians. Most of the existing sodomy laws in the United States are defined in terms of male sex, both heterosexual and homosexual.[11] In a telling section about gay men's attitudes toward safe sex practices needed to avoid HIV infection, Hamilton writes, "Their safe sex practices are forced down our throats (recall how many times you've seen the proper way to put a condom on a penis) and they've never even heard of a dental dam. This from the same men who we've joined in the fight against AIDS???" (Hamilton 1992, 15).

Despite the growing integration of men and women into a single movement, scholarly research on the "gay" community as a whole only pays minimal attention to lesbian concerns (Rust 1992). Part of the reason is that women are less likely than men to give up their heterosexual identity on the basis of one or two homosexual experiences and are therefore often missed by survey researchers. An additional reason why isolating specific "lesbian" policy issues is problematic is that some lesbians identify more with their biological sex than their sexual orientation (Stein 1994). Moreover there is a great deal of overlap between a lesbian policy agenda and feminist one, because many lesbian issues also affect heterosexual women.

Lesbians are unique in that some of their policy aims are congruent with those of gay men while others are more congruent with those of feminists.

However, some of the issues in each of these categories disproportionately affect lesbians. For example, while all women need to guard against breast cancer, studies showing higher rates of the disease among women who do not give birth make it of greater concern to lesbians. In a similar vein, although both gay men and lesbians have a shared interest in laws that protect the rights of homosexual parents, a higher proportion of lesbians are parents than are gay men.

Differentiating Lesbian Policy Issues from Gay Male Issues

Although gay men and lesbians have a common interest in the enactment of civil rights protections for homosexuals, their interests diverge when it comes to issues that primarily affect women. Lesbians, like heterosexual women, are discriminated against in the workplace. They too encounter the "glass ceiling" in business; the devaluation of jobs traditionally performed by women, such as daycare workers, teachers, home health aides, and nurses; sexual harassment;[12] lower pay than comparably situated male workers; and a shortage of affordable, quality child care (Schneider 1989; Fried and Reinelt 1993; Badgett 1995a). Lesbian families face the same economic pressures as heterosexual families, especially with regard to the costs and quality of child care, health care, and education.[13] Along with heterosexual women, lesbians care about issues related to the sexual exploitation of women in pornography, rape, sexual violence, and abuse. Many lesbian separatists consider pornography an exhibition of "uncompromising women-hating" (Frye 1983, 136). In contrast, many gay men consider some forms of pornography, sexual contact between the young and old, and consensual sadomasochism to be "central to the predominantly male gay liberation movement" (Taylor and Whittier 1992, 116).

Lesbians and gay men have radically different views about reproductive issues and health care priorities. Although many lesbians strongly support abortion rights, gay men have refused to take it on as a demand because it is "not a gay issue" (Moss 1996). Even though the gay and lesbian movement has been a strong proponent of safe sex practices for men, either heterosexual and homosexual (Perkins 1990), lesbian safe sex practices have been neglected (Hamilton 1992; Rebecca Cole and Sally Cooper Lesbian Exclusion from HIV / AIDS Education, <www.hrc.org>). Lesbian groups believe that the medical and scientific establishment dismisses the validity of their health concerns (Advancing a Lesbian Health Agenda 1998). In particular, lesbians appear to be more prone to developing certain types of cancer (e.g., breast cancer). With the notable exception of the Human Rights Campaign, few "gay" rights groups have lesbian health issues on their policy agenda.[14]

Lesbian Issues and the Policy Agenda of "Gay" Rights Groups

Because the Internet has become an important resource for community building, the dissemination of information, and mobilization among gays and lesbians, we used it as a way to identify the policy priorities of "gay" rights groups. We did key word searches for "gay" and "homosexual" on five of the major Internet search engines (Alta Vista, Excite, Infoseek, Lycos, and Yahoo) to find the web sites of national gay, lesbian, and homosexual organizations. Most of the sites provided up-to-date information about legislation (pending and passed at both the state and federal) and court cases affecting the gays and lesbians, as well as information about social events and mobilization efforts (gay pride parades, etc.).[15]

The nonlesbian-specific web sites included information about a wide range of policy issues including: the legalization of same-sex marriages and domestic partnerships; sodomy laws; adoption; immigration; hate crimes and law enforcement; discrimination in the workplace, the military, education, and access to housing; and AIDS prevention, funding, and treatment. Although many of these policy issues deal with problems that affect both gay men and lesbians, quite a few addressed concerns that predominantly concern gay men. The most obvious example is the national campaign to repeal state laws that criminalize sodomy. Because same-sex acts involving women are often not prohibited by sodomy statutes and even in states that criminalize same-sex relations involving women, police rarely arrest women, so the issue is of little direct interest to lesbians. In a similar vein, most of the AIDS-related information was directed at gay men (i.e., promoting safe sex through the use of condoms) and increasing funds for research, treatment, and prevention.

The nonlesbian-specific web sites made almost no mention of issues that solely affected lesbians. For example, the key word searches brought up medical issues, but nearly all focused on AIDS and the genetics of sexual orientation. The medical needs of the lesbian community were largely ignored. Of the twenty-three "homosexual" sites chosen for analysis, only two (Human Rights Campaign and Gay and Lesbian Activists Alliance) included lesbian-centered issues under health concerns. The HRC site included a general statement about the importance of lesbian health[16] and the GLAA site discussed lesbian safe sex issues related to AIDS.[17]

Although the Internet is a powerful tool, only those with access to computers and Internet connections can make use of it (Chapman and Rhodes 1997). Although many studies have shown a strong positive relationship between income and Internet access,[18] none have specifically focused on differences in access among gay men and lesbians. However, there is little reason to expect that these income-related differences in access do affect patterns of use within the gay and lesbian community. According to Badgett (1995b), lesbian earnings are lower than heterosexual women, who in turn usually earn less than gay and straight men, so it is likely that lesbians have less access to the Internet than gay men. If so, it is possible that as greater sectors of the community become hooked up to the Internet, lesbian issues will get more attention in the web sites.

COMMONALITY AND DIFFERENCE IN THE PRIORITIES OF LESBIAN AND GAY ELECTED OFFICIALS

Although we uncovered evidence that lesbians and gay men share some common concerns, we also found some important areas of difference, most notably in terms of policy priorities. In this section, we analyze data from the first national survey of openly gay and lesbian elected officials to determine whether their policy preferences also diverge along gender lines. We were particularly interested in discovering the areas of common concern to both lesbian and gay officeholders and what issues are significantly more important to one group. Because elected officials do not solely represent the gay and lesbian community, we divided our policy questions into two groups: general policy areas and gay and lesbian policy issues.

The original data used in this study was obtained through a mail survey sent to openly gay and lesbian elected officials serving in state legislatures, county and municipal offices, and local school boards. William Waybourn, the executive director of the Gay and Lesbian Victory Fund provided an initial list of elected officials, and additional names were provided by gay and lesbian officeholders and their staff.[19] The first batch of surveys were sent in 1994 with follow-up mailings continuing into early 1995. Sixty of the seventy-four elected officials filled out and returned the surveys for a response rate of 81 percent. Although twenty states and the District of Columbia are represented, 41 percent are from the West. There were more than twice as many male respondents as female (41 to 19) and 90 percent are white. Although the ages of the officials ranged from thirty-one to fifty-eight years of age, the mean age was forty-four. Their level of educational attainment is extremely high—nearly 62 percent have post-graduate or professional degrees. With the exception of two gay men, who listed their party affiliation as Republican, all the others identified themselves as Democrats. Although nearly three quarters represented urban electoral constituencies, none classified their district as primarily composed of gay or lesbian voters. Estimates of the percentages of gays and lesbians in the populace ranged from 1 percent to 45 percent.

General Policy Priorities

Focussing solely on gay and lesbian issues would be easy, but a mistake. Gay and lesbian elected officials are not solely the representatives of that community, but must represent a broad constituency whose interests are far more diverse than what is typically considered "gay" issues. As Barney Frank noted, "The single most important piece of advice that I can give to openly gay or lesbian candidates is to resist the effort that will almost certainly be made to portray you as someone who will focus almost all of your energies on gay and lesbian issues to the exclusion of all other issues" (1994, 147). Glen Maxey, who was first elected to the Texas House of Representatives in 1991 from a majority Hispanic and African-American district, consciously avoided the single issue label by trying to be identified as the candidate of many disparate groups—(e.g., the environmental candidate, the teachers' candidate, the women's candidate, etc.) (Maxey 1994, 159).

Because gay and lesbian officials must deal with a variety of issues (many of which have little or nothing to do with sexual orientation), one survey question asked them to identify how important they considered a broad range of policy areas and interests to be. Although most of the items on the list were unconnected with sexual orientation, we did include a few "gay" related items so that we could compare the importance of those issues and interests with other non-gay-related items. The list of policy areas/ interests included the following: elderly, children, labor, law enforcement/ crime, jobs, education, health care, transportation, environmental issues, housing, business, political party, women, racial minorities, gays, lesbians, people with AIDS, and people with disabilities. For each area or interest, they marked whether it was of "major importance," "medium importance," "minor importance," or "not of importance to my office." The results are summarized in table 5.1.

As the table shows, there are significant differences between the policy priorities of the gay male elected officials and the lesbian elected officials. Although there are a variety of techniques for assessing the degree of differ-

Table 5.1 Policy Priorities of Gay and Lesbian Elected Officials

Policy	Importance to Gay Men (n = 41)				Importance to Lesbians (n = 19)			
	Major (%)	Medium (%)	Minor (%)	Not Important (%)	Major (%)	Medium (%)	Minor (%)	Not Important (%)
Elderly	35.9	35.9	15.4	27.8	27.8	44.4	22.2	5.6
Children	64.1	15.4	10.3	10.3	66.7	22.2	5.6	5.6
Labor	20.5	41.0	23.1	15.4	22.2	50.0	22.2	5.6
Crime	46.2	35.9	10.3	7.7	52.9	35.3	11.8	0.0
Employment	30.8	23.1	33.3	12.8	50.0	33.3	5.6	11.1
Education	52.5	17.5	12.5	17.5	44.4	33.3	5.6	16.7
Health	33.3	30.8	12.8	23.1	50.0	27.8	11.1	11.1
Transportation	23.1	33.3	23.1	20.5	33.3	33.3	22.2	11.1
Environment	43.6	28.2	17.9	10.3	66.7	22.2	5.6	5.6
Housing	41.0	25.6	15.4	17.9	50.0	22.2	22.2	5.6
Business	33.3	35.9	20.5	10.3	22.2	44.4	27.8	5.6
Political party	10.3	10.3	25.6	53.8	0.0	27.8	33.3	38.9
Women	41.0	35.9	17.9	5.1	77.8	11.1	5.6	5.6
Minority	46.2	33.3	15.4	5.1	44.4	44.4	5.6	5.6
Gays	64.1	30.8	5.1	0.0	50.0	44.4	0.0	5.6
Lesbians	61.5	30.8	7.7	0.0	52.9	41.2	0.0	5.9
AIDS	61.5	20.5	15.4	2.6	61.1	27.8	0.0	11.1
Disabled	48.7	38.5	12.8	0.0	33.3	44.4	16.7	5.6

ence between the two groups of officeholders, we will focus on the following: the rank ordering of items classified as having major importance, and analysis of variance (ANOVA).[20] Even though we obtained responses from nearly all of the gay and lesbian elected officials serving in state legislatures, local offices and school boards, the relatively small N size means that one must be careful to avoid overgeneralizing. Despite this qualifying statement, some important differences emerged between the policy priorities of the two groups of elected officials.

Although there was some overlap in the rank ordering of general policy areas / interests, it was more the exception than the rule. Perhaps the most striking difference is that lesbians ranked women's issues as their top priority while gay men gave it a ranking of number 10 to 11, tied with housing issues. The top priorities for the gay male elected officials were children's issues and gay issues, which tied for the top ranking. Lesbians gave children's issues a ranking of 2 to 3, which is fairly close to the ranking it was given by their male counterparts. However, they ranked gay issues far lower as part of a four-way tie for positions 7 through 10. One notable commonality in the rankings is that both gay men and lesbians ranked political parties in *last* place, although one possible explanation is the fact that two-thirds of the officials were elected in nonpartisan races.

While useful because they provide us with a general sense of the policy priorities of gay and lesbian elected officials, neither the rank orderings nor the percentages of respondents in each category help in determining whether any of the differences between the two groups are statistically significant. An ANOVA model reveals that only two of the policy priority differences between the gay male elected officials and the lesbian elected officials are significant, and then only barely so (.1 level). Employment policy issues, which lesbians considered more important than gay men, had a significance of .093. The statistically most significant difference was on women's issues, which again lesbians considered far more important than did the gay male elected officials, was nearly significant at the .05 level (.059).

Although many scholars (Frankovic 1977; Saint Germaine 1989; Thomas and Welch 1991; Thaemert 1994; Thomas 1994) have found differences in the policy priorities of male and female elected officials, this is the first research to show that statistically significant differences also occur among lesbian and gay male elected officials. While this research shows that one cannot assume a commonality of interests based on the shared experience of being homosexual in a predominantly heterosexual society, it is also worth emphasizing that there were no statistically significant differences on the other issues.

Gay and Lesbian Policy Issues

Although lesbian and elected officials must be concerned about a wide array of policy issues, one would expect gay and lesbian issues to be far more important to them than to heterosexual politicians. However, there is little reason to expect lesbian and gay elected officials to agree on the relative importance of different items. As we have shown in earlier sections, some policies affect the entire community while others differentially impact either gay men or lesbians. In this section we analyze the relative importance of the following gay and lesbian policy issues:

* gays and lesbians in the military,
* fighting antigay state and local initiatives,
* increased funding for AIDS education, treatment, and research,
* combating discrimination against people with AIDS/HIV,
* winning federal civil rights protection,
* passing and enforcing hate crimes legislation,
* repealing sodomy laws,
* protecting parental rights of lesbians and gay men,
* supporting school programs aimed at lesbian and gay youth,
* lesbian health care issues.[21]

The elected officials were asked to mark whether each item was of "major importance," "medium importance," "minor importance," or "not of importance to my office." The results are summarized in table 5.2.

As the table shows there are some areas of commonality and some significant differences between the priorities of lesbian and gay elected officials. Again, we assessed the differences using the rank ordering of items classified as having major importance and an analysis of variance (ANOVA).

Both gay men and lesbians consider fighting antigay state and local initiatives to be a high priority, with the former ranking it the top priority and lesbians giving it the second highest ranking. However, the top priority of lesbians, protecting parental rights, was ranked seventh by gay male elected officials. In general, lesbian and gay male elected officials shared a high concern for policies that dealt with civil rights issues for homosexuals. Both groups also made increased AIDS funding a priority. Their rank orderings diverged on some other issues that differentially impacted the two groups. However, only three items had rankings that were at least

Table 5.2 Gay and Lesbian Policy Priorities of Elected Officials

Policy	Importance to Gay Men (n = 41)				Importance to Lesbians (n = 19)			
	Major (%)	Medium (%)	Minor (%)	Not Important (%)	Major (%)	Medium (%)	Minor (%)	Not Important (%)
Military	32.5	57.5	10.0	0.0	15.8	63.2	10.5	0.0
Antigay state law	90.0	10.0	0.0	0.0	78.9	63.2	10.5	0.0
AIDS funding	75.6	24.4	0.0	0.0	70.6	29.4	0.0	0.0
Discrimination against PWAIDS	68.3	31.7	0.0	0.0	66.7	27.8	5.6	0.0
Federal civil rights	62.5	35.0	2.5	0.0	68.4	23.3	5.3	0.0
State/local civil rights	75.0	25.0	0.0	0.0	77.8	11.1	11.1	0.0
Hate crime law	50.0	44.7	2.6	2.6	33.3	61.1	5.6	0.0
Repeal sodomy	56.8	21.6	21.6	0.0	21.1	36.8	31.6	10.5
Parental rights	57.5	40.0	2.5	0.0	84.2	15.8	0.0	0.0
Same-sex marriage	29.3	43.9	22.0	14.9	42.1	36.8	21.1	0.0
School programs	58.5	31.7	9.8	0.0	57.9	36.8	5.3	0.0
Lesbian health	32.5	55.0	12.5	0.0	57.9	36.8	5.3	0.0

NOTE: The cells give the percentages of gay male officeholders and lesbian officeholders who rank the policies as having major importance, medium importance, minor importance and not of importance to them.

three gradations apart when broken down by sex. In addition to parental rights, lesbians ranked the legalization of same-sex marriage significantly higher than gay men did (a rank ordering of 9 as opposed to 12). However, gay men were far more concerned about repealing sodomy laws than were lesbians (a rank ordering of 8 versus a rank ordering of 11).

The ANOVA models indicated that there are more pronounced policy differences among the gay and lesbian elected officials on gay-related policy issues than on the more general policy issues. Not only were there differences between the lesbian and gay elected officials on more policy issues, the significance of the differences was greater. The greatest difference was on the importance of repealing sodomy laws, an area that 56.8 percent of the gay elected officials classified as of major importance but only 21.1 percent of their lesbian counterparts did the same. According to the ANOVA model, the likelihood of the differences on sodomy laws occurring within the same population is .009. The other policy issues with statistically significant differences and the likelihood of those differences occurring randomly are as follows: protecting parental rights (.042), policies dealing with gays and lesbians in the military (.053), and lesbian health care issues (.071).

Concluding Thoughts

Although the data and anecdotal evidence compiled in this study are quite clear in demonstrating the existence of sex based divisions within the gay and lesbian community, interpreting the results is a murkier proposition. One must confront the perennial problem of whether the glass is half empty or half full. While the cleavages are a source of concern, there are other indications that gays and lesbians have forged very real and important common bonds. In particular, the importance that lesbians give to fighting AIDS is a clear indication of their willingness to go beyond more narrow definitions of self interest and unite with gay men in a common struggle. In a similar vein, the creation of coalitions to fight against antigay initiatives and enact civil rights measures is another indication of a commonality of purpose.

However, the results of the survey of gay and lesbian elected officials indicate a clear pattern of divergence on many of the policy issues that primarily affect one sex. On general policy issues, statistically significant differences only occurred on employment issues and women's issues. However, more differences were evident on policies specifically relating to gays and lesbians. The most pronounced differences were on repealing sodomy laws, protecting parental rights, gays and lesbians in the military, and lesbian health concerns. Ultimately, a determination of whether the glass is half empty or half full will depend upon whether the community as a whole (and their elected representative) recognize that the common requires them to fight for the interests of the opposite gender as much as their own. In short, only time will tell whether commonality or difference will triumph.

NOTES

The authors would like to express appreciation to the Fletcher Jones Foundation and the G. E. Bradshaw Foundation for the financial support that made this research possible. We would also like to thank Bruce Snyder, Daniel Jordan, and Erik Root for research assistance and William Waybourn, Charles Cox, and Kathleen DeBold of the Gay and Lesbian Victory Fund for their help in identifying openly gay and lesbian officeholders.

1. While it is clear many scholars in the field use the term "gay" politics to refer to both female and male homosexual politics (see, e.g., Wald, Button, and Rienzo 1996), the term does not capture lesbian women in the mainstream perspective. Further, there is a specific word that solely refers to female homosexuals "lesbian," but no equivalent word that solely refers to homosexual men. Cruikshank (1992, 4) notes that "popular usage of 'gay' sometimes conflates the term with gay men." In this article, we will use both terms—"lesbian" and "gay" to refer to the broader movement or solely use "gay" but place it in parentheses to gain the reader's attention. Issues or groups that are specific to lesbians will be characterized as "lesbian."

2. Many scholars have noted that the needs of ethnic and racial minorities have often been ignored by mainstream "gay" rights groups (Frye 1983; Perkins 1990; Cruikshank 1992; Rust 1992; Adam 1995; Vaid 1995; Rosenthal 1996). Urvashi Vaid, an Indian-American, experienced discrimination within the movement on the basis of her sex, skin color, and ethnicity. According to Vaid, the following comment sums up the reaction of many to her selection as executive director of the National Gay and Lesbian Task Force, "How could they have selected that radical woman, who's practically a nigger" (Vaid 1995, 275).

3. Cruikshank (1992) divides the movement into three periods: (1) 1890s to World War II period of homosexual emancipation, (2) post-war to the Stonewall Riot of 1969 period of the homophile movement, and (3) the post-Stonewall period of the gay and lesbian liberation movement.

4. "Lesbians in the gay rights and gay liberation movements found themselves in the position of women in the civil rights, anti-war and new left movements: conceptual appendages and organization housekeepers/secretaries/sexual partners. In the gay movements, this conceptual annexation took the form of

denial by male leaders that lesbians faced problems unique to them and due to their status as women" (Phelan 1989, 36).

5. For example, Rosenthal (1996) attributes the decline of the Buffalo chapter of the Mattachine Society in the late 1970s to the decision of lesbians to leave the group and establish a lesbian feminist organization.

6. Lesbian feminist culture is a conscious attempt to create an alternative women's space (or "wimmin's" space) that is separate from the dominant misogynist culture. The creation of a new language is central to the women's culture (Daly 1990; Froman 1992).

7. For an analysis of how antigay attitudes affected Congress's response to the AIDS epidemic, see Schroedel, Jean Reith and Daniel R. Jordan (1998, 107–32).

8. As Weeks (1993, 23) noted, "It was an historic accident that HIV disease first manifested itself in the gay population of the east and west coasts of the United States, and subsequently in similar populations throughout the west. But that chance shaped, and has continued to form, the social and cultural response to AIDS." In fact, the original name applied to the virus was GRID (Gay Related Immune Deficiency). The popular media turned this designation into the "gay plague" or the "gay cancer."

9. Colorado voters' passage of Amendment Two had reverberations across the country. Antigay groups considered it a major victory and organized similar campaigns in other states, which in turn helped mobilize lesbian and gay activists into a national campaign to defeat such initiatives and pass laws adding sexing orientation to state and local civil rights statutes (Wald, Button, and Rienzo 1995; Garfield 1995).

10. The implications of simply ending one of these unequal social practices, the prohibition on same-sex marriage, are staggering. Because they cannot legally get married, homosexual couples usually are unable to obtain health care benefits for both partners. Badgett (1995b) estimates that employer paid medical benefits mean that a working lesbian or gay man in a relationship receives a compensation package of several thousand dollars less per year than a comparably situated married person. Moreover, only one member of a homosexual couple can have legal parenting rights for children, and some states restrict adoption to only married heterosexual couples. The 1993 decision by the Hawaiian state supreme court in *Baehr v. Levin* that bans on same-sex marriage violated the equal protection clause of the state constitution has sparked widespread legal debates over whether same-sex relationships can be proscribed and treated differently than heterosexual ones. Although the case has been appealed to the Supreme Court, twenty-five states have enacted laws prohibiting same-sex marriages.

11. According to Justice Blackmun's notes in *Bowers v. Hardwick*, sodomy is: "The carnal knowledge and connection against the order of nature, but man with man, or in the same unnatural manner with woman" (cited in Perkins 1990, 18).

12. In a study of the prevalence of sexual harassment against lesbians in the workplace, 33 percent reported being sexually propositioned, 34 percent reported being pinched or grabbed, and 67 percent indicated that coworkers had made comments about their bodies or physical appearance (Schneider 1989, 222).

13. Although polls show that lesbians are less likely to be parents than are heterosexual women, the differences are relatively small. In the 1996 voter exit poll, 31 percent of lesbians and 37 percent of heterosexual women had children under 18 years of age in their households. In another poll, 67 percent of lesbians and 72 percent of heterosexual women identified themselves as parents and 32 percent of lesbians and 36 percent of heterosexual women said they had children under 18 years of age in the household.

14. The Human Rights Campaign includes lesbian health concerns on its list of the top four policy issues: "renewing America's commitment to fighting HIV/AIDS, ending workplace discrimination, launching a rapid response to anti-gay hate legislation and focusing attention on lesbian health issues."

15. For a sample of the national sites, see: And Justice for All, The Advocate, Gaynet, GaySource, Gay and Lesbian Activists Alliance (GLAA), Gay and Lesbian Alliance Against Defamation (GLAAD), Gay and Lesbian Association of Retired Persons (GLARP), GLBT-Workplace, Gays and Lesbians for Individual Liberty (GLIL), GLSEN, GLWeb, High Tech Gays, Human Rights Campaign, International Gay and Lesbian Association (IGLA), Lambda Legal Defense and Education Fund, National Gay and Lesbian Task Force (NGLTF), ONE, OutBox, PlanetOUT, Parents, Families and Friends of Lesbians and Gays (P-FLAG), Queer Press International, QueerPolitics, TurnOUT. We also found many regional sites, that covered specific to cities, states and counties. For example, see Oregon Right to Pride, San Diego Democratic club, Massachusetts Gay and Lesbian Political Caucus, Dallas Gay and Lesbian Alliance, Empire State Pride Agenda, FACES of South Dakota, Freedom Coalition of Kansas, and the Gay and Lesbian Alliance of Alabama.

16. The Human Rights Campaign's web site included the following statement: "As women, lesbians face many of the same barriers and discrimination experienced by heterosexual women dealing with the medical and scientific communities. In addition, lesbian and bisexual women face a medical and scientific establishment that often dismisses the validity of our health concerns and ignores our existence in treatment and education interventions."

17. The Gay and Lesbian Activists Alliance web site included the following statement: "The needs of women with HIV/AIDS are also often ignored. City agencies which dispense birth control or barriers for disease prevention also need to provide dental dams and/or other barriers for safe lesbian sexuality."

18. According to a 1996 survey by the National Telecommunications and Information Administration, nearly half of all urban households with incomes above

$35,000 had computers, but only 8 percent of those with incomes below $10,000 did (Chapman and Rhodes 1997).

19. While it is possible that we missed a few openly gay men and lesbians, who were serving as state legislators, local elected officials, or school board members at the time, it is unlikely that more than a handful were excluded.

20. Analysis of variance is a statistical test used to determine whether there are significant differences between sample means, which is used to estimate the likelihood of significant differences within the corresponding populations. See Bohrnstedt and Knoke (1994, 121–37) for a good introduction to the procedure.

21. We consulted with Kathleen DeBold of the Gay and Lesbian Victory Fund in compiling the list of gay and lesbian policy issues.

REFERENCES

Adam, Barry D. 1995. *The rise of a gay and lesbian movement.* Rev. ed. New York: Twane Publishers.

Badgett, Lee. 1995a. Economic issues for lesbians and bisexual women. <www.iglss. org>.

Badgett, M. V. Lee. 1995b. The wage effects of sexual orientation discrimination. *Industrial and Labor Relations Review* 48:726–39.

Baehr v. Levin, 852 P.2d 44 (Haw. 1993).

Blasius, Mark. 1994. *Gay and lesbian politics: Sexuality and the emergence of a new ethic.* Philadelphia: Temple University Press.

Bohrnstedt, George W., and David Knoke. 1994. *Statistics for social data analysis.* 3d ed. Itasca, Ill.: F. E. Peacock Publishers, Inc.

Bowers v. Hardwick, 478 U.S. 186 (1986).

Bronski, Michael. 1987. Eros and politicization: Sexuality, politics and the idea of community. *Radical America* 21:45–56.

Bunch, Charlotte. 1989. Not for lesbians only. In *Feminist Frontiers II,* edited by Laurel Richardson and Verta Taylor. New York: McGraw-Hill, Inc.

Cain, Patricia A. 1993. Litigating for lesbian and gay rights: A legal history. *Virginia Law Review* 79:1551–641.

Cerullo, Margaret. 1987. Night visions: A lesbian/gay politics for the present. *Radical America* 21 (2–3): 67.

Chapman, Gary, and Lodis Rhodes. 1997. Nurturing neighborhood nets; computer networks. *Massachusetts Institute of Technology Alumni Association Technology Review* 7 (100): 48.

Cole, David, and William N. Eskridge Jr. 1994. From hand-holding to sodomy: First Amendment protection of homosexual expressive conduct. *Harvard Civil Rights-Civil Liberties Law Review* 29:319.

Commentary. 1992. Why I think gay men are sexist. *Off our backs* 22 (9): 15.

Cruikshank, Margaret. 1992. *The Gay and Lesbian Liberation Movement*. London: Routledge, Chapman and Hall Inc.

Daly 1990. Gyn | Ecology: The meta-ethics of radical feminism. Boston: Beacon Press.

Frank, Barney. 1994. Reaching a Broader Audience. In *Out for office: Campaigning in the Gay '90s,* edited by Kathleen DeBold. Washington D.C.: Gay and Lesbian Victory Fund.

————. 1996. Why party politics matters. *Harvard Gay and Lesbian Review* 3 (2).

Frankovic, Kathleen. 1977. Sex and voting in the U.S. House of Representatives: 1961–1975. *American Politics Quarterly* 5 (3): 315–31.

Fried, Mindy, and Claire Reinelt. 1993. A family policy for "all kinds of families." *Social Policy* 23 (4): 65.

Froman, Creel. 1992. *Language and Power*. Highlands, N.J.: Humanities Press.

Frye, Marilyn. 1983. *The politics of reality: Essays in feminist theory*. Freedom, Cal.: The Crossing Press.

Garfield, Daniel J. 1995. Don't box me in: The unconstitutionality of Amendment 2 and English-only amendments. *Northwestern University Law Review* 89 (2): 690.

Griswold v. Connecticut, 381 U.S. 479 (1965).

Haider-Markel, Donald P., and Kenneth J. Meier. 1996. The politics of gay and lesbian rights: Expanding the scope of the conflict. *Journal of Politics* 58 (2): 332.

Hamilton, Amy. 1992. Queer notions. *Off Our Backs* 22 (9): 15.

Hartman, Keith. 1993. Conference of openly gay politicians meets in Chapel Hill. *Christopher Street* 195, 4 January.

Henry, William A. III. 1991. To "out" or not to "out." *Time,* 19 August.

Hunt, Ronald J. 1992. "Gay and lesbian politics." *PS: Political Science and Politics* 25 (2): 220.

Knopp, Lawrence. 1987. Social theory, social movements, and public policy: Recent accomplishments of the gay and lesbian movements in Minneapolis, Minnesota. *International Journal of Urban and Regional Research* 11 (2):243.

Maxey, Glen. 1994. Running against the Right. In *Out for Office: Campaigning in the Gay '90s,* edited by Kathleen DeBold. Washington D.C.: Gay and Lesbian Victory Fund.

Moss, J. Jennings. 1996. Coming out of the Republican closet—One lesbian at a time. *The Advocate,* 29 October.

Newton, David E. 1994. *Gay and lesbian rights: A reference handbook*. Santa Barbara, Cal: ABC-CLIO, Inc.

Penelope, Julia. 1992. *Call me lesbian: Lesbian lives, lesbian theory*. Freedom, Cal.: The Crossing Press.

Perkins, Penny. 1990. Lesbians and sodomy laws. *Visibilities* 4 (2): 18.

Phelan, Shane. 1989. *Identity politics: Lesbian-feminism and the limits of community.* Philadelphia: Temple University Press.

———. 1992. Social Constructionism, Sexuality, and Politics. *Women and Politics* 12 (1): 73.

———. 1993. (Be)Coming out: Lesbian identity and politics. *Signs: Journal of Women in Culture and Society* 18 (47): 65.

Rand. 1993. *Sexual orientation and U.S. military personnel policy: Options and assessment.* Santa Monica, Cal.: Rand Corporation.

Roe v. Wade, 410 U.S. 113 (1973).

Riccucci, Norma M., and Charles W. Gossett. 1996. Employment discrimination in state and local government: The lesbian and gay male experience. *American Review of Public Administration* 26 (2): 175.

Rivera, Rhonda R. 1984. Review of *Sexual politics, sexual communities: The making of a homosexual minority in the United States, 1940–1970,* by John D'Emilio. *University of Pennsylvania Law Review* 132 (2/3): 91.

Robson, Ruthann. 1987. Discourses of discrimination and lesbians as (Out)Laws. *Radical America* 24 (4): 39.

Rosenthal, Donald B. 1996. Gay and lesbian political mobilization and regime responsiveness in four New York cities. *Urban Affairs Review* 32 (1): 45.

Rust, Paula C. 1992. The politics of sexual identity: Sexual attraction and behavior among lesbian and bisexual women. *Social Problems* 39 (4): 366.

Saint-Germaine, Michelle A. 1989. Does their difference make a difference? The impact of women on public policy in the Arizona legislature. *Social Science Quarterly* 70 (4): 956–68.

Schacter, Jane S. 1994. The gay civil rights debate in the states: Decoding the discourse of equivalents. *Harvard Civil Rights-Civil Liberties Law* 29:283.

Schneider, Beth. 1989. Peril and promise: lesbians' workplace participation. In *Feminist Frontiers II,* edited by Laurel Richardson and Verta Taylor. New York: McGraw-Hill, Inc.

Schroedel, Jean Reith, and Daniel R. Jordan. 1998. Senate voting and social construction of target populations: A study of AIDS policy making, 1987–1992. *Journal of health politics, policy and law* 23 (1): 107–32.

Stein, Marc. 1994. Sex politics in the city of sisterly and brotherly loves. *Radical History Review* 59:60.

Taylor, Verta, and Nancy E. Whittier. 1992. Collective identity in social movement communities: Lesbian feminist mobilization. In *Frontiers in Social Movement Theory,* edited by Aldon D. Morris and Carol McClurg Mueller. New Haven, Conn.: Yale University Press.

Thaemert, Rita. 1994. Twenty percent and climbing. *State Legislatures* 20:28–32.

Thomas, Sue. 1994. *How women legislate.* New York: Oxford University Press.

Thomas, Sue, and Susan Welch. 1991. The impact of gender on activities and priorities of state legislators. *Western Political Quarterly* 44:445–56.

Vaid, Urvashi. 1995. *Virtual equality: The mainstreaming of gay and lesbian liberation.* New York: Doubleday.

Wald, Kenneth D., James W. Button, and Barbara A. Rienzo. 1995. Where local laws prohibit discrimination based on sexual orientation. *PM: Public Management* 77:14.

————. 1996. The politics of gay rights in American communities: Explaining antidiscrimination ordinances and policies. *American Journal of Political Science* 40 (4): 1152.

Weeks, Jeffrey. 1993. AIDS and the Regulation of Sexuality. In *AIDS and Contemporary History,* edited by Virginia Berridge and Philip Strong. Cambridge: Cambridge University Press.

West, J. 1988. Homosexuality and social policy: The case for a more informed approach. *Law and Contemporary Problems* 51 (1): 181.

II. THE OPPOSITION

6

ANTIGAY: VARIETIES OF OPPOSITION
TO GAY RIGHTS

John C. Green

Efforts to expand legal protection to gays, lesbians, and bisexuals, or "gay rights" in shorthand, have become a staple of American politics at the end of the twentieth century. Indeed, some observers argue that gay rights had become the civil rights issue of the 1990s (Gallagher and Bull 1996, xi). These efforts and their proponents have met with strong opposition. In some respects, this opposition resembles resistance to civil rights for African Americans and women. It also has its own peculiar features because it is deeply embedded in religious traditionalism and the Christian Right (Wilcox 1996; Button, Rienzo, and Wald 1997).

This chapter is a description of the major forms opposition to gay rights has taken in recent times, using interview and documentary evidence.[1] First, the importance of the Christian Right as the major source of opposition is established, and then three major forms of opposition are identified (instrumental, reactive, and proactive) based on differences in the motives, means, and methods of Christian Right activism. All three kinds of opposition can contribute to the strength of the Christian Right, although each also has its liabilities. The most common kind of opposition, reactive, is likely to be even more important in the near future.

SOCIAL TRADITIONALISM AND OPPOSITION
TO GAY RIGHTS

Opposition to gay rights is rooted in various kinds of social traditionalism (Button, Rienzo, and Wald 1997, chap. 6).

Of course, "tradition" is a problematic notion in the United States, given the country's modern cast, intense individualism, great diversity, and dynamic nature. But precisely because of the unsettled character of American society, social stability and conventional arrangements are often prized and strenuously defended (Wiebe 1975). If accepted for long enough and bolstered by the substantive values of enough people, such arrangements can take on the patina of "tradition," even though they may not be especially old. Social traditionalism has by and large opposed homosexuality, often harshly (Bawer 1994), although the attitudes of the American public are increasingly ambivalent toward gay rights.

Attempts to change the conventional treatment of homosexuals regularly challenge three important sources of tradition: organized religion, groups and institutions concerned with maintaining social order, and the business community. Organized religion is the most potent source of opposition, and here social convention is reinforced by religious values. Simply put, most religious groups in the United States have long believed that homosexual behavior is morally wrong. These views are frequently rooted in sacred texts and codes of sexual conduct derived from those texts. There are, however, enormous differences on how these beliefs are defined and applied, with some religious groups attaching intense stigma to homosexuality and others adopting a more latitudinarian approach.

Evangelical Protestantism, one of the largest religious traditions in the United States (Kellstedt et al. 1996), is especially prone to stigmatize homosexuality. Evangelical theology puts a special stress on individual morality and assigns to social institutions, including the government, responsibility for fostering individual moral behavior. Historically, these beliefs played an important role in establishing social convention regarding homosexuals, and Evangelicals have been especially attached to those conventions. In recent times, Evangelicals have been the mainspring of opposition to gay rights, often joined by other theologically conservative churches, such as the Mormons. Much of this opposition has been carried forward by the Christian Right, a social movement concentrated among religious traditionalists.

It is important, however, to distinguish between the Christian Right and its religious base. Evangelicals are diverse in religious terms and not all are stridently antigay (Wald 1997, 186–88). Other important religious traditions are even more divided on this issue. For example, mainline and black Protestants, Roman Catholics, and Jews all contain elements that are critical of homosexuality, although not usually with the fervor of Evangelicals. But within these groups there are also elements tolerant of gay rights, and still others that are strong proponents. In fact, some of the strongest advocates for the gay community are found among the theological liberals in all these groups (Melton 1991). For this reason, gay rights often generates intense conflict within religious institutions.[2]

Groups and institutions with a special interest in social order often oppose gay rights as well, but usually more on the basis of social convention than substantive beliefs (Diamond 1995). For instance, some secular conservatives stress the maintenance of social control and thus find gay rights problematic. Thus organizations as diverse as the John Birch Society and the Free Congress Foundation frequently speak out on the issue. Similarly, the military and police are frequently suspicious of gay rights because of the fear that changes in social convention will undermine their missions. However, there is some diversity here as well. Some conservatives are libertarian in focus and sympathetic to all manner of individual rights. And within the military and police there are also individuals who believe that gay rights will improve the performance of their institutions.

The business community also has a pragmatic approach to gay rights, reflecting social conventions (Button, Rienzo, and Wald 1997, 187–89). On the one hand, many businesses oppose gay rights because of the fear that such changes will increase their costs. Small businesses are especially sensitive to such changes due to their low profit margins. Researchers have discovered that small business owners are very common among antigay activists, although this may reflect religious sentiments as well as economic interests (Lunch 1997). On the other hand, some businesses value gay employees and customers, and major corporations are most likely to accept gay rights for these reasons (Griffith 1998). Because of these divisions in the business community, business associations such as the National Federation of Independent Businesses and the Chamber of Commerce rarely take public positions on gay rights, and when they do, it is usually to urge the avoidance of controversy that can hurt the business climate.

All of these groups can be aroused to oppose gay rights, depending on how much the proposed changes challenge their traditions. Indeed, the magnitude of the challenge appears to be a key variable in the breadth of the opposition. For example, modest extensions of employment law to cover sexual orientation typically produce less opposition than major policy changes such as the legalization of same-sex marriage. Given the divisions over gay rights found within most religious communities, advocates of social order and the business community, such groups are unlikely to lead the opposition to gay rights under normal circumstances. Not surprisingly, then, opposition to gay rights is spearheaded by the groups most united and hostile to homosexuality. The Christian Right is the chief vehicle for such opposition, and as we shall see, differences within the Christian Right account for the major varieties of opposition to gay rights.

THE CHRISTIAN RIGHT AND OPPOSITION TO GAY RIGHTS

The Christian Right is a social movement concentrated among Evangelical Protestants and dedicated to restoring "traditional values" in public policy (Green 1996; Wilcox 1996).[3] The current movement arose in the late 1970s in response to perceptions of "moral decay" in American society. Chief among the "decaying traditions" was the patriarchal family, defined as two, legally married heterosexual adults and their children. Changes in women's roles, the legalization of abortion, and the spread of sexual permissiveness were central to this perception of moral decay, as were changes in social arrangements that once supported the traditional family, including schools, law enforcement, and popular culture.

Gay rights represents both kinds of changes: homosexuality occurs outside the ideal of the traditional family, and legal protection for homosexuals challenges conventional arrangements supportive of such families. For these reasons, opposition to gay rights was one of the original pillars of the Christian Right. Organized opposition existed prior to the rise of the contemporary movement (Diamond 1995) and may well have been a precursor to it (Crawford 1980). However, the advent of the Christian Right increased the level, intensity, and sophistication of the opposition.

Like other social movements the Christian Right can be understood in terms of the motives, means, and methods of its activists (Green, Guth, and Hill 1993; Green, Guth, and Wilcox 1998). Variations in these factors help account for the different kinds of opposition by the Christian Right. "Motives" are the grievances that provide the rationale for movement activism. As we have noted, opposition to gay rights is a potent motive for Christian Rightists, but such grievances come in different forms (Lienesch 1993). Perhaps the most common view is that homosexuals engage in sinful behavior, and thus the defense of gay rights is tantamount to condoning immorality. Sexual orientation is assumed to be a matter of individual choice, and gays should be encouraged to make "better" choices. Holders of this position are not necessarily hostile to homosexuals (though usually critical of their advocates) and often feel sympathy for them, including an urge to help gays change their "lifestyles."

A less common but more intensely held view adds to immorality the notion that homosexuals are dangerous, and that if protected by law, they will threaten the entire community. Homosexuals are seen as purveyors of disease such as AIDS, and crime such as pedophilia. Holders of this view are frightened by gays and hostile to their advocates. A small minority of Christian Right activists add to immorality and danger yet another idea: homosexuals are subversives bent on undermining society. The gay community is seen as actively recruiting individuals, especially the young, to their "cause," which range from fostering the "new world order" to serving the forces of evil. Holders of this view are deeply hostile to all aspects of the gay community.

"Means" refers to the resources that allow the movement to pursue its grievances, and the most important of these resources are movement organizations. Like other movements, Christian Right organizations are products of entrepreneurial leaders who identify sympathetic clienteles and mobilize resources. Because of the importance on individual leaders, these organizations are diverse, competitive, and often short-lived (Wald 1997, 249–51). There are at least three different kinds of organizations in the contemporary Christian Right, and each is linked to one of the three common grievances regarding gay rights.

The largest and best known movement organizations are "general purpose" groups, such as the Christian Coalition and Focus on the Family. The primary goal of these groups is to gain political power; the strategy is to organize activists at the grassroots to pressure the political system. Both pragmatic and opportunistic, general purpose groups seek to harness opposition to gay rights to their broader purpose, and judging from surveys of their membership, they draw broadly on activists who believe homosexuality is immoral (Guth et al. 1994).

Another kind of organization is the "limited purpose" group. Usually based in localities or regions, such organizations are vehicles for specific confrontations. Limited purpose groups are frequently created to oppose gay rights initiatives; good examples include the Colorado for Family Values and Take Back Cincinnati, organizations that conducted antigay rights campaigns in Colorado and Ohio, respectively. Judging by public statements and interviews with participants, such groups draw heavily on activists who see gays as a danger to the community.

Yet another kind of organization are "specialized" groups. These organizations resemble general purpose groups in national scope, but they resemble the limited purpose groups in stressing a particular constituency or issue. Some such organizations specialize in opposition to gay rights; good examples are the Traditional Values Coalition and The Report, an antigay "research" and propaganda group. Specialized antigay groups apparently draw most heavily from activists who view gays as subversive. Specialized antigay groups have an ambiguous relationship with a large network of groups dedicated to "converting" and "healing" homosexuals, such as Exodus International. While both kinds of groups often cooperate with one another, the latter are far less hostile to individual gays.

"Methods" refers to the opportunities for the movement to redress its grievances by the deployment of resources. The Christian Right employs a number of methods to achieve its purposes, and they are frequently linked to types of movement groups and grievances regarding gay rights. A great portion of movement activity is dedicated to building organizations, such as raising funds and recruiting activists. Such organizations can then be used for the "three L's" of modern politics: lobbying, litigating, and electioneering. In recent times, the Christian Right has focused on electoral activities because the numbers of religious traditionalists in the mass public are a potent source of power. In addition, the movement often tries to influence public opinion on issues it cares about, including homosexuality and gay rights. General purpose groups have the broadest repertoire of methods, while limited purpose tend to focus on one activity. Specialized antigay groups also do a number of things, but concentrate on propaganda.

THREE KINDS OF OPPOSITION

In sum, the Christian Right contains within it a variety of motives, means, and methods that influence its opposition to gay rights. If the movement is often the spearhead of opposition to gay rights, then it is fair to say there are different kinds of spears, with different kinds of effects. We can usefully summarize this diversity by imaging three ideal types of opposition to gay rights: instrumental, reactive, and proactive. Each reflects a different mix of motives, means, and methods.

Instrumental opposition is the use of antigay rhetoric to obtain political power. The chief motive for such efforts is to implement a broad agenda of traditional morality, of which opposition to gay rights is one part. The chief means of implementing this ideology is mobilizing resources to support general purpose organizations. Such organizations allow for a wide range of methods in politics. From this vantage point, activists can negotiate with other interests over "traditional values," including the treatment of homosexuals.

Reactive opposition is the rejection or repeal of specific proposals regarding gay rights. The chief motive for such efforts is to prevent changes in the law that are seen as dangerous to the community. The chief means for such opposition is the "mobilization of outrage" in a narrow context, and then reaching out to other kinds of traditionalists. Thus, gay rights is the only focus of the activity, the methods employed arise directly from the occasion, and the effort dissipates once the controversy has passed. Such efforts allow activists to maintain or restore the status quo ante regarding gay rights.

Proactive opposition is the preemption of attempts to promote gay rights. The chief motive of such efforts is to limit the ability of gay rights advocates to pursue their objectives. The chief means of such opposition is the mobilization of bias against the "special interests" of the gay community; organization and resources arise from the prospect of stalling a subversive enemy. The methods employed also vary with the context, but the focus is constricting the politics surrounding the issue, thus eliminating the opportunities for the advancement of gay rights.

The impact of these forms of opposition can be usefully summarized by a sports metaphor.[4] The primary impact of instrumental opposition is to "field a team" of Christian Right activists who may oppose gay rights as part of their broader agenda. These efforts are successful to the extent they interject movement activism into political process. The primary impact of reactive opposition is "playing defense" by directly resisting gay rights; its success depends on mobilizing a large enough coalition of traditionalists in favor of the status quo. Finally, proactive opposition is "offense as defense," seeking to preempt gay rights proposals by law. Here success requires broad public acceptance of gay rights advocates as an illegitimate "special interest."

Instrumental Opposition: Fielding a Team

In terms of sheer volume, instrumental opposition to gay rights by the Christian Right probably outpaces all other forms of antigay activity. Homosexuality and gay rights is a common element for nearly all movement organizations and general purpose groups such as the Christian Coalition and Focus on the Family. Instrumental opposition is most clearly evident in the organization-building efforts of these groups and is least obvious in their public activities. Of course, for limited purpose and specialized antigay groups, instrumental and substantive opposition are largely one in the same. However, these groups are much smaller and often locally focused, while the general purpose groups are larger and nationally focused (Anti-Defamation League 1994).

The most common form of instrumental opposition is direct mail fundraising, which takes place largely within the confines of these organizations and their prime constituencies. As a fundraising technique, direct mail of all sorts relies on strident appeals and hot button issues (Godwin 1988). Indeed, it is quite common for political groups on all sides of a controversy to use strongly worded appeals to raise funds, including fearful denunciations of each other. Gays and gay rights are favorite targets of direct mail of Christian Right groups—much as the Christian Right is a target of fundraising by a variety of liberal groups.

A review of Christian Right fundraising letters from the 1990s illustrates the extent of this practice.[5] General purpose groups, like the Christian Coalition, mention gay rights in about three-quarters of their appeals. About one-half of these mentions, or a little less than two-fifths of the total, discuss the issue in some detail, and in about one-half of these, or about one-fifth of the total, gay rights is the focus of the letter. The great bulk of the more detailed mentions concern advocates of gay rights rather than homosexuals in general, and when this occurs, the remarks are usually quoting information from a specialized antigay group.

These figures can be contrasted in two ways. First, mention of abortion is nearly universal and far more strident in the fundraising efforts of general purpose organizations. Second, the direct mail of limited purpose and specialized antigay groups nearly universally mentions gay rights, and is far more vitriolic in tone and substance. Although nearly all Christian Right leaders have at one time or another made strong statements about gays and gay rights, usually for internal purposes, such comments are standard fare for specialized antigay groups (Anti-Defamation League 1994, 131–38).

This pattern extends to other activities of Christian Right groups as well. For instance, the publications and press releases of general purpose organizations regularly mention gay rights, but with less frequency and intensity than the other kinds of groups. Gay rights also plays an important role in the construction of voter guides and legislative score cards of general purpose groups. For instance, in 1994 about one-third of Christian Right voter guides mentioned gay rights in some way. General purpose groups sometimes endorse and support the activities of limited purpose and specialized antigay groups, but until recently, have rarely initiated such efforts themselves.

Gay rights is much less visible in the public agendas of general purpose groups (Reed 1996). For example, the legislative proposals of the Christian Coalition and Focus on the Family in the 1990s had only brief mentions of gay rights. Much to the surprise of observers, general purpose organizations publicly down play hostility to homosexuals, and some Christian Right leaders have criticized their colleagues for their strident antigay rhetoric. This disjunction between the sentiments expressed inside and outside of these organizations raises some questions about the integrity of these groups and their leaders.

The most likely answer to these questions lies with the pragmatism of the general purpose groups. On the one hand, attacks on gay rights are used internally because they are effective in raising money and mobilizing activist support. On the other hand, a softer tone is used for external purposes, including cooperating with secular conservatives and Republican politicians, because it is more effective in coalition building. This balance of internal and external communication strategies is hardly unique to the Christian Right. However, it does carry serious liabilities: harsh internal language can undermine external relations, while a civil tone in public debate can alienate core activists.

Instrumental opposition does not appear to directly foster connections with other kinds of traditionalists outside of the Evangelical camp (Guth et al. 1994). If movement donors and activists are any guide, relatively few mainline Protestants, Catholics, or Jews participate in these organizations. Similarly, secular conservatives are rare, with little overlap with groups like the John Birch Society or the Free Congress Foundation. Many Christian Right activists are involved in small business and some have military and police backgrounds, but these individuals are also deeply religious. So, these groups do not build a broad conservative alliance within their ranks; instead, they are one distinct element that can participate in such an alliance (Green 1996).

What are the political effects of instrumental opposition to gay rights? To the extent that the issue helps build strong movement organizations, it can produce a cadre of grassroots activists who can oppose gay rights should the opportunity arise, even if the parent groups do not seek or initiate such actions. The volume and persistence of instrumental opposition suggests it is quite effective in this regard. Along these lines, general purpose groups can become repositories of information and expertise for opposing gay rights, much of it generated by specialized antigay groups. Likewise, to the extent that the issue helps elect or appoint movement supporters to office, it contributes to a government that is at least unsympathetic and often hostile to gay rights. Thus, from the grassroots to Capitol Hill, instrumental opposition can create beacons around which other traditionalists rally in specific confrontations. As one movement activist put it: "We are fielding a pro-family team; when we need to play against the gay rights, we'll be ready."

Reactive Opposition: Playing Defense

Christian Right activists are frequently involved in outright opposition to gay rights proposals, whether or not they are on the "teams" of general purpose organizations. Most such battles are fought in direct reaction to proposals made or changes achieved by gay rights advocates and their allies. Not surprisingly, these efforts are waged mostly by limited purpose groups founded during specific confrontations, sometimes aided by specialized antigay and general purpose organizations.

There is a logic to reactive opposition. Throughout most of the United States, conventional treatment of homosexuals is the norm and barely attracts public attention. Even if local citizens hear about gays rights from the news media or from the instrumental opposition by movement groups, it may not arouse any immediate concern. In fact, in many places the mobilization of bias is so strong against gay rights that the issue never arises. But once it does, mobilization in defense of the status quo can be sudden and intense.

The typical pattern is for gay rights advocates to propose or produce a change through legislative channels (Haider-Markel and Meier 1996). Opposition arises at once and pressure is brought to bear on public officials to oppose the change. The longer the controversy persists, the more likely it is to generate organized opposition. If a proposal actually becomes law, then the opposition hardens and expands the scope of conflict, often taking the form of a referendum or recall election if these tools are available, or devolving into electoral politics if not. Key factors in the intensity of the reaction is the magnitude of the change propose and the traditionalism of the community (Button, Rienzo, and Wald 1997, 173–77).

Reactive opposition tends to begin with activists who have had some previous experience in antigay activities.[6] These core activists then mobilize sympathetic religious communities, many of whom may never had been politically active. At this point, core activists often seek technical information and assistance from the broader Christian Right, usually from specialized antigay groups. Here is where the organizing efforts of general purpose groups and the propagandizing of specialized antigay groups can make a big difference. Finally, the core activists seek support from other traditionalists in the community. Here other religious groups, secular conservatives, and especially the business community are quite important. Each can provide critical resources to a local effort, but more importantly, the absence of opposition from these quarters can allow such an effort to proceed unhindered.

A good example of reactive opposition occurred in Austin, Texas in 1994 (*New York Times* 1994). Austin is the capital of Texas, the home of the University of Texas, and reputed to be the most liberal city in Texas. In 1993, the city council enacted a domestic-partnership policy for city employees that included gays. The reaction was swift. Led by a local Baptist minister who had been previously active on the issue, a limited purpose group called Concerned Texans Inc. collected enough signatures to put a repeal measure on the ballot, and then waged an effective campaign on its behalf. Aided by local churches and expertise from Christian Right groups (but apparently little money), the drive mobilized a large section of the electorate, winning by a margin of 62 to 38 percent. Although few nonreligious groups endorsed the drive, a focus on public expenditures apparently secured substantial behind-the-scenes support from secular conservatives and the local business community. The effort then disbanded after the election.

School boards are often a special focus of reactive opposition, and some cases have drawn considerable national attention, engaging the support of both specialized antigay and general purpose groups (Gallagher and Bull 1996, 219–20, 254–56). For example, in 1995 a gay member of the Des Moines, Iowa school board was defeated by local effort aided by Bill Horn, an activist for the antigay project, The Report, and an infusion of cash from the state Christian Coalition. Another example occurred in New York City in 1991, when a coalition of conservative Catholics, Jews, and Protestants, including the Christian Coalition, campaigned against a sex education curriculum, Children of the Rainbow, that included mention of homosexuality.

Although reactive opposition is most common at the local level, it also occurs at the federal and state level. Probably the best known example of the former is the outcry against President Clinton's attempt to end the ban on gays in the military in 1993 (Rimmerman 1996). Here the Christian Right was very active, but it was joined by a broad coalition of traditionalists, especially the military itself. Other examples include the perennial efforts of social issue conservatives in Congress to restrict the activities of the National Endowment of the Arts and to require that AIDS-prevention efforts not encourage or condone homosexuality.

A recent example of reactive opposition may be a harbinger. In February 1998, a referendum in Maine repealed a gay rights statute passed in 1997 by the legislature and signed by the governor (Goldberg 1998). The Christian Civic League of Maine, a one-hundred-year-old state organization, and the Christian Coalition of Maine, backed by its national office, collaborated to put the referendum on the ballot and campaign on its behalf. The referendum passed by a slim 51 to 49 percent margin with a 33 percent turnout, which was rather high for an off-year election but well short of typical turnout in contested elections in Maine. The coalition assembled thus appeared to be smaller and narrower than most successful reactive opposition. This campaign may reflect opportunism on the part of the Christian Coalition, which received a boost from the effort. But it may also signal a new involvement of general purpose organizations in reactive opposition.

Overall, reactive opposition has been quite successful. For example, Gamble (1997) found that antigay activists prevailed in the vast majority of referenda since the 1970s; such success has been especially common at the local level (Donovan and Bowler 1998). Of course, reactive opposition does not always succeed and gay rights advocates regularly seek new venues for change (Wald, Button, and Rienzo 1996). Since the 1970s, there has been something of a seesaw battle between proponents of gay rights and reactive opposition, with the former making gains and the other reacting. As one antigay activist put it: "We police the boundaries. It is an endless task just to hold the line." Or in the words of another: "We are always playing defense and in most of the country that is not a bad place to be."

Proactive Opposition: Offense as Defense

Not all opponents of gay rights are content to "play defense." Extreme views on homosexuality and frustration with reactive opposition have led some Christian Rightists to advocate proactive opposition. "We want to take the battle to the enemy," one activist proclaimed, and another remarked, "the best defense in a good offense." The goal here is to preempt the expansion of gay rights by constricting political opportunities through propaganda and legal restrictions.

The lack of success for most proactive opposition is largely due to its stridency. For example, the intense propaganda of specialized antigay groups, complete with "research" and "scientific facts," frequently fails to persuade the broader public to support additional restrictions on the gay community (Diamond 1996). Although such propaganda can arouse the core constituencies of the Christian Right, it often alienates other traditionalists. Similarly, proactive ballot initiatives, as opposed to reactive efforts, have generally fared poorly (Gallagher and Bull 1996, 21–25); legislative attempts to preempt gay rights efforts have not been particularly successful either, with some notable exceptions (Dupuis 1998).[7]

In the 1990s, a wave of proactive opposition appeared with a new twist: specialized antigay organizations developed more politic arguments for preempting gay rights. Operating under the slogan "no special rights," the argument claimed that extending legal protection to homosexuals was, in effect, granting new rights to a "special interest." The goal of these arguments was to maintain the status quo in political rather than policy terms. Despite the failure of most of these efforts, this new rhetoric has been embraced by general and limited purpose Christian Right organizations, and may become a staple of instrumental and reactive opposition in the future.

A good example of this new phase of proactive opposition occurred in the summer of 1998, when a coalition of fourteen movement organizations spent some $400,000 on full-page advertisements in the *Washington Post*, *New York Times*, and *USA Today*. Called the "The Truth in Love Campaign," these ads promoted efforts to "convert" homosexuals to heterosexuality, featuring testimonials by former gays and highlighting the therapies that "healed" and "rescued" them. This campaign was led by Janet Folger, the director of The Center for Reclaiming America, a group associated with televangelist Dr. D. James Kennedy and strongly opposed to gay rights. The list of cosponsors included general purpose groups, such as the Christian Coalition.

These ads ignited a storm of controversy over the origins of sexual orientation, much of it raising serious doubt about the efficacy of therapies designed to change homosexuals. However, the political message of the ads was clear: homosexuality is an individual choice, not a personal condition, and thus not deserving of legal protection. The more positive tone of the message was part and parcel of the "no special rights" strategy and designed to preempt gay rights activism by attacking a common rationale for it (Miller 1998).

The fullest expression of this new strategy appeared in a series of ballot proposition in four states: Oregon (1992 and 1994); Colorado (1992); Idaho

(1994); and Maine (1995) (Donovan and Bowler 1997). These proposals were developed by specialized antigay groups and had explicitly political goals: prohibiting the enactment of state or local gay rights legislation of any sort. While general purpose groups backed most of these measures, they were not directly involved in their origins or implementation (see subsequent chapters in this book for more details).

Only the 1992 Colorado proposition succeeded, obtaining 53 percent of the vote. Efforts to capitalize on the Colorado victory were largely unsuccessful, however, and were undermined further in 1996 when the U.S. Supreme Court ruled the Colorado initiative was unconstitutional in *Romer v. Evans*. The Court's ruling invalidated the particular strategy behind these referenda by prohibiting the enactment of measures that legally preempted efforts to protect gay rights (Asseo 1996). However, the Court took no position on the content of gay rights measures themselves, a fact that will surely redirect proactive opposition into other channels.

This wave of proactive opposition also found expression in the legislative process, especially after the Republicans gained control of the Congress and a number of state legislatures in the 1994 election. While most proposals to prohibit "special rights" for gays were not successful (Dupuis 1998), one important exception illustrates the phenomenon and its potential: the Defense of Marriage Act (DOMA), which was passed by large margins in the Congress and signed by President Clinton in 1996 (CQ Almanac 1996).

DOMA sought to preempt the possibility that same-sex marriages would be legalized by indirect means. A state court case in Hawaii had ruled that the state's ban on same-sex marriages was unconstitutional, opening up the prospect that same-sex marriages would have to be recognized by other states under the full faith and credit provision of the U.S. Constitution. To prevent such a possibility, DOMA declared that states were not forced to recognize same-sex marriages if sanctioned by other states. It also defined marriage as "a legal union between one man and one woman as husband and wife," thereby precluding gay couples from participating in federal tax or social programs. Following the logic of *Romer v. Evans*, some legal scholars believe DOMA may also be unconstitutional (Tribe 1996).

Nevertheless, DOMA was unusually popular, drawing widespread support from many groups beyond the Christian Right. Both the magnitude of the challenge to traditional treatment of homosexuals (same-sex marriages) and the indirect nature of this challenge (via state courts) were critical in assembling such broad-based support for such a sweeping measure.

Under most circumstances, this kind of proactive opposition would have been very difficult for the Christian Right to achieve.

THE FUTURE OF OPPOSITION TO GAY RIGHTS

The gay community and its allies may not see much difference between these three kinds of opposition. After all, each is hostile to homosexuality and can hinder the advancement of gay rights. But as we have seen, opposition to gay rights is not of one piece, with differences arising from the different motives, means, and methods of the antigay activists. Instrumental opposition helps "field a team" of activists unsympathetic to gay rights by mobilizing traditionalists. Reactive opposition is "playing defense" against gay rights proposals fueled by fear of homosexuality, arising in particular contexts. Proactive opposition is "offense as defense" by hardcore specialists in antigay politics, seeking to constrict the politics of gay rights and thus preempt further battles. All such opposition tends to be led by the Christian Right and supported by its base among religious traditionalists, especially Evangelical Protestants. Other sources of opposition are modest by comparison, although they can be aroused by severe challenges to their traditions.

What about the future? Instrumental opposition is likely to continue as long as the Christian Right is in operation, because it helps "field a team" of activists. In fact, any decline in the movement may actually intensify this kind of opposition as the entrepreneurial leaders seek to maintain their organizations. However, instrumental opposition imposes limits on the capacity general purpose groups to participate in broader conservative coalitions.

Proactive opposition has been slowed and redirected by negative public reaction to specialized antigay groups and the Supreme Court. Indeed, except in cases where gay rights advocates overreach and arouse a broad-based opposition, there are likely to be few attempts to preempt progay rights political activity in the immediate future. Proactive opposition has not been eliminated, however, because of the strategic gains "playing offense" offers to antigay activists—as can be seen in the popularity of the "no special rights" rhetoric. Thus, like instrumental opposition, proactive opposition has both costs and benefits for the movement, especially for specialized antigay groups.

Given these trends, there may be an expansion of reactive opposition in the near term. Continued activism by the gay community and its allies will surely provide further opportunities for reactive opposition, and general purpose and specialized antigay groups may bring greater coordination and sophistication to local limited purpose organizations. Thus, the 1998 Maine initiative may be a model for the future. "Playing defense" patrols the boundaries of social convention and provides tangible victories, both of which help sustain and expand the broader movement. All this suggests the seesaw battle for gay rights will continue well into the next century.

NOTES

1. This chapter is based in large part on three dozen interviews conducted in 1996 and 1997 with Christian Rights activists from across the country. Although few would be classified as movement leaders, all had been very active since the late 1980s, including opposing gay rights at the local, state, and national levels. The interviewees were promised anonymity. The essay also draws on two decades of movement documents collected by the author.
2. In the 1990s, many mainline Protestant churches experienced bitter internal battles over the role of gays, especially ordination of practicing homosexuals. While formally separate from opposition to gay rights, these battles have fed into these conflicts.
3. In common discourse, this movement is referred to as the "religious right," and from its inception, the Christian Right aspired to be a true "religious right," mobilizing religious traditionalists from all backgrounds. So far, the movement has largely failed to meet this goal.
4. This sports metaphor arose repeatedly in interviews with Christian Right activists.
5. These statistics and those that follow are based on a collection of several hundred fundraising letters, voter guides, and other Christian Right documents. The numbers must be viewed with some caution since these collections are neither random samples nor comprehensive.
6. This sequence of events was recounted in numerous interviews with Christian Right activists; it fits the "community protest model" of policy change well (Button, Rienzo, and Wald 1997, 17).
7. A good example is the case of arts funding in Cobb County, Georgia (Gallagher and Bull 1996, 179–87). Such incidents are not always about gay rights per se, although they are clearly hostile to gays. The "defense of marriage" acts at the state and federal levels are another good example.

REFERENCES

Anti-Defamation League. 1994. *The religious right.* New York: Anti-Defamation League.

Asseo, Laurie. 1996. Gay-rights forces win major test at high court. Associated Press. 11 January.

Bawer, Bruce. 1994. *A place at the table: The gay individual in American society.* New York: Simon and Schuster.

Button, James W., Barbara A. Rienzo, and Kenneth D. Wald. 1997. *Private lives, public conflicts: Battles over gay rights in American communities.* Washington, D.C.: CQ Press.

Congressional Quarterly Almanac. 1996. New law discourages gay marriages. Washington D.C.: CQ Press.

Crawford, Alan. 1980. *Thunder on the right.* New York: Pantheon.

Diamond, Sara. 1995. *Roads to dominion.* New York: Guilford Press.

———. 1996. *Facing the wrath.* Monroe, Maine: Common Courage Press.

Donovan, Todd, and Shaun Bowler. 1997. Direct democracy and minority rights: Opinions on antigay and lesbian ballot initiatives. In *Antigay rights: Assessing voter initiatives,* edited by Stephanie L. Witt and Suzanne McCorkle. Westport, Conn.: Praeger.

———. 1998. Direct democracy and minority rights: An extension. *American Journal of Political Science* 42:1020–24.

Dupuis, Martin. 1998. *State legislative response to Hawaii's same-sex marriage case.* Paper delivered at the annual meeting of the Midwest Political Science Association, Chicago.

Gallagher, John, and Chris Bull. 1996. *Perfect enemies: The religious right, the gay movement, and the politics of the 1990s.* New York: Crown Publishers.

Gamble, Barbara S. 1997. Putting civil rights to a popular vote. *American Journal of Political Science* 41:245–69.

Godwin, Kenneth. 1988. The direct marketing of politics. Chatham, N.J.: Chatham House.

Goldberg, Carey. 1998. Maine voters repeal gay rights law. *New York Times,* 12 February.

Green, John C., James L. Guth, and Kevin Hill. 1993. Faith and election: The Christian Right in congressional campaigns, 1978–1988. *Journal of Politics* 55: 80–91.

———. 1996. *Understanding the Christian Right.* New York: The American Jewish Committee.

Green, John C., James L. Guth, and Clyde Wilcox. 1998. Less than conquerors: The Christian Right in state Republican parties. In *Social movements and American political institutions,* edited by Anne Costain and Andrew McFarland. Lanham, Maryland: Rowman and Littlefield.

Griffith, Victoria. 1998. Gay Rights: Welcome to Your Friendlier Company. *Financial Times,* 8 March, p. 1.

Guth, James L., John C. Green, Lyman A. Kellstedt, and Corwin E. Smidt. 1994. Onward Christian soldiers: Religious activist groups in American politics. In

Interest Group Politics, 4th ed., edited by Allan Cigler and Burdett Loomis. Washington, D.C.: CQ Press.

Haider-Markel, Donald P., and Kenneth J. Meier. 1996. The politics of gay and lesbian rights: Expanding the scope of conflict. *Journal of Politics* 58:332–49.

Kellstedt, Lyman A., John C. Green, Corwin E. Smidt, and James L. Guth. 1996. The puzzle of evangelical Protestantism, in *Religion and the culture wars,* edited by John C. Green, James L. Guth, Corwin E. Smidt, and Lyman A. Kellstedt. Lanham, Maryland: Rowman and Littlefield.

Lienesch, Michael. 1993. *Redeeming America: Piety and politics in the new Christian Right.* Chapel Hill: University of North Carolina Press.

Lunch, William J. 1997. Oregon: The Flood Recedes. In *God at the grassroots,* edited by Mark J. Rozell and Clyde Wilcox. Lanham, Maryland: Rowman and Littlefield.

Melton, J. Gordon. 1991. *The churches speak on homosexuality.* Detroit, Mich.: Gale Research.

Miller, Mark. 1998. Going to war over gays. *Newsweek.* 27 July, p. 27.

Reed, Ralph. 1996. *Active Faith.* New York: Free Press.

Rimmerman, Craig A. ed. 1996. *Gay rights, military wrongs.* New York: Garland Publishers.

Romer v. Evans, 517 U.S. 620 (1996).

Tribe, Laurence. 1996. Toward a less perfect union. *New York Times.* 25 May, p. 32.

Verhover, Sam Howe. 1994. Texas capital ends benefits for partners. *New York Times,* 9 May, A6:6.

Wald, Kenneth D. 1997. *Religion and Politics in the United States.* 3d ed. Washington D.C.: CQ Press.

Wald, Kenneth D., James W. Button, and Barbara A. Rienzo. 1996. The politics of gay rights in American communities: Explaining antidiscrimination ordinance and policies. *American Journal of Political Science* 40:1152–78.

Wiebe, Robert H. 1975. *The segmented society.* New York: Oxford University Press.

Wilcox, Clyde. 1996. *Onward Christian soldiers?* Boulder, Colo.: Westview Press.

7

THE GAY AGENDA IS THE DEVIL'S AGENDA:
THE CHRISTIAN RIGHT'S VISION AND THE
ROLE OF THE STATE

Didi Herman

Gay rights activism, from its first stirrings, has met with vigorous resistance. While some adversaries attack the extension of rights to lesbians and gay men on economic or libertarian grounds, it is the religious opposition that has taken the lead and provided the foundation of antigay activity. For conservative religious believers, homosexuality was a sin condemned, in no uncertain terms, in holy scriptures. Lesbian and gay rights were akin to "adulterer's rights" or "murderer's rights." Many people experienced the cultural normalization of homosexuality, of which the acquisition of formal equality was only a symptom, as an attack on everything in which they believed.

The close correlation between religious orthodoxy and opposition to gay rights has been confirmed in a multitude of statistical studies and experiential research (Wald, Button, and Rienzo 1996; Kirkpatrick 1993; Seltzer 1992; Shapiro 1993, 42–48). A religious, antigay perspective is shared by many conservative believers of the major American faiths—Christianity, Judaism, and Islam (Nugent and Gramick 1989; Prager 1993). The mainstreaming of gay and lesbian sexuality shook the foundations of orthodox religious belief. For strict observers, there could be no tolerance of what was scripturally condemned, and the increasing acceptance of homosexuality became a sign of godlessness and impending calamity. The opposition of the orthodox, then, became the primary obstacle to the progress of gay rights. The more the lesbian and gay rights movement gathered momentum and achieved successes, the more the disquiet of the orthodox increased.[1]

At the same time as the lesbian and gay rights movement was gaining strength and a groundswell of religious opposition fermenting, a different political movement was also coming to the fore. From initial public stirrings in the 1970s, the Christian Right[2] was, by the 1990s, one of the most vibrant and effective social forces in the United States. The history, politics, and significance of the Christian Right's activism has been chronicled ably by many scholars.[3] While commentators are divided as to the potential power of the Christian Right,[4] all are agreed that this is a movement worth watching.

For those interested in the progress and politics of lesbian and gay rights, the Christian Right is not only deserving of notice, its activities are of the utmost importance. For by the 1980s, the Christian Right had made antigay activity central to its political practice and social vision. From the 1970s onwards (there were six antigay referenda in 1977 and 1978 alone), the Christian Right mobilized grassroots opposition to homosexuality, and gay rights had been dealt setbacks locally and nationally. Local gay rights ordinances were repealed and in some cases banned permanently; statewide initiatives prohibiting future, similar legislation were launched; state gay rights legislation and proposed legislation was challenged or killed (Bull and Gallagher 1996; Herman 1997a). In some cases, specific antigay statutes were proposed or enacted. While orthodox believers of other faiths may oppose gay rights with a similar fervor, it is the Christian Right that has instigated and led the public antigay agenda in the United States. In this area, there is little evidence of the "religious right realignment" suggested by Hunter (1991, 47–48).

The purpose of this chapter is to analyze how the Christian Right's antigay agenda relates to its wider ideological politics. I define the Christian Right as a broad coalition of profamily organizations (e.g., Focus on the Family, Concerned Women for America, Traditional Values Coalition) that have come together to struggle for their socio-political vision in the public sphere. These organizations, and their activist leaders, are predominantly committed to a conservative, largely premillennial, Protestant Christianity (Herman 1997a, 9–14). I argue that the intensity of antigay activity in the United States cannot be fully understood without giving adequate consideration to a somewhat neglected field of study: the Christian Right's underlying theological vision, particularly its premillennial foundation.

I begin by briefly outlining the basic elements of conservative premillennialism. The next section of the chapter considers the ways in which the Christian Right articulates the struggle for gay rights to a wider "Satanic" conspiracy involving, among others, feminists, environmentalists, and secular humanists. For Christian Right writers and activists, anti-Christian forces, of which lesbians and gay men make up only one part, are intent on using the state to achieve the complete removal of Christianity from the public sphere.

The final section of the essay considers the Christian Right's understanding of the state and its own role vis-à-vis the state. The Christian Right is often described as either antistatist or theocratic. I suggest that both these analyses have merit, and they are not as contradictory as they might appear.

PREMILLENNIALISM

Over 60 percent of Americans have no doubt that Christ will return (Gallup and Castelli 1989, 66). Of these, many millions are premillennialists—they believe that the bible prophesies the end of the world, followed by the second coming of Christ and the arrival of the "millennium." A smaller number are postmillennialists: Christ will not return until God's Kingdom rules on earth for one thousand years. Postmillennialism is not an eschatological perspective espoused by many Christians in the United States today. Premillennial understandings largely (although not entirely) animate the Christian Right and its potential constituents and are the subject of my analysis here. Note that Christian Identity and similar extreme movements embrace a different form of millennialism (Barkun 1990).

Premillennialists find the predominant authority for their eschatology in the final book of the New Testament, The Revelation of John. Most historians view The Revelation as an inspiration to believers during intense persecution by Roman tyrants at the time of writing, 81–96 C.E. (Gager 1983). However, orthodox Christians have for centuries considered it a prophetic blueprint for the earth's end, Christ's return, and the ultimate rule of the saints over the world as heaven (Boyer 1992). That these things will happen is beyond question; several million American believe it deeply. The disputed matter is *when*, not *if*.

Various versions of the end-times scenario have flourished throughout the history of Christianity (Boyer 1992; Bull 1995).[5] Apocalyptic eschatology has been both populist and radical; early white settlers in the "new world" brought a mix of pre- and post-millennialist perspectives of many centuries' duration (Lippy 1982). By the early 1900s, "new world" optimism (Glanz 1982) had given way to doomsday forecasting and premillennialism had become the dominant theology, which continues to be the case today.

Historically, there have been various versions of the end-times scenario. Broadly, in order for Christ to reappear, a series of events will occur. The Gospel must be preached around the world and, as a result of this "Great Commission," as it is known, many new adherents will be brought into the fold. At a certain point, this task will be complete, and "true believers" will be "raptured"—they will literally ascend to heaven to sit with Christ and watch the horrors unfold. This period will also see the rise of the Antichrist—the charismatic leader who will unite huge regions of the world behind him in an anti-Christian mission for global power.

The earth will then be plagued by terrible disasters—floods, fires, earthquakes, wars, and so on. Many millions of people will die horrible, excruciating deaths. At this point, thousands of Jews will see the light and convert (however this is far too late for Rapture and most of them will perish in the disasters and final battles). As regional power blocs engage in war, Christ and the saints return. They kill all nonbelievers, including the Antichrist, and usher in the peace and harmony of the millennium. During this period, according to Billy Graham, "Jesus Christ will be the King over all the earth in His theocratic world government" (1983, 227). At the end of one thousand years, Satan rises again, only to be defeated by Christ once and for all. The earth is then no more; only heaven exists.

Popularly, speculation about the end-times has generated a wealth of bestselling literature aimed at predicting and representing the end of earth. Historically, the Antichrist was argued to be embodied in the Ottoman Empire ("the Turk") and in the Pope himself (Boyer 1992, 61–62, 153). In the first half of this century, signs were seen in the ascendancy of fascist dictators, the expansion of Soviet communism, the creation of the Israeli state (the Second Temple must be rebuilt), and the nuclear arms race. The premillennial worldview embodies both what Hofstadter (1966) has called a political "paranoid style" (meaning very imaginative, rather than mentally unbalanced) and a fear of conspiracy that runs deep in American culture (Davis 1971; Johnson 1983). It also helps to shape, in important ways, the stances and understandings believers take on social and political issues generally (Lienesch 1993).

Conservative premillennial eschatology informs many of the political positions adopted by the Christian Right in the United States. For example, the Christian Right's enthusiastic support for Israel (Mouly 1985), particularly in light of its continued anti-Semitism, makes little sense without an understanding of the role Jewish people must play at the world's end (Henry 1971; Pieterse 1992; Ariel 1991). Pat Robertson's writing reflects this sort of pro-Israel anti-Semitism (1990, chaps. 11, 12). Similarly, the Christian Right's pro-defense and patriotic stance is, for many, linked to the preordained role the United States is destined to play in the final days (Boyer 1992, chap. 7; Cassara 1982), and even antienvironmentalist ideologies are significantly determined by conservative eschatology (Guth et al. 1995).

Finally, premillennialism is not simply, or solely, an eschatology; it is also visionary. Come the millennium, justice and equality will reign everywhere. Poverty, race hatred, and sinful corruptions will be no more. At its heart, conservative Christianity is utopian; hence its appeal, power, and significance as a social force to be reckoned with (Herman 1997b).

THE GAY MOVEMENT AND THE SECULAR HUMANIST CONSPIRACY

From the first Christian Right treatises on gay issues (Rueda 1982), writers sought to portray the lesbian and gay movement as an elite cadre of well-to-do professionals insinuating themselves into the fabric of American institutional life. The movement is portrayed as organized and powerful, and its agenda, dangerous in the extreme. This representation was part of a deliberate strategy to create hostility to the gay movement on the part of "regular folk" (by definition, not gay) (Herman 1997a, chap. 3).

According to James Dobson and Gary Bauer, authors of the influential text *Children at Risk,* "today there are few political and social movements as aggressive, powerful, or successful as 'gay rights' advocates" (Dobson and Bauer 1990, 107). Others echo these sentiments: "the homosexual movement in America is perhaps the most well organized and most disciplined pressure group in the country today" (Dannemeyer 1989, 22); "they're talented and ruthlessly aggressive in the pursuit of their goals" (McIlhenny, McIlhenny, and York 1993, 17); "we are talking about a very powerful and wealthy group of individuals who have a clear strategy and agenda" (Farrar 1994, 117). Material published by a range of Christian Right organizations also characterizes the movement as a whole in this way.

The media particularly is represented as being in the pocket of the lesbian and gay rights movement.[6] According to Focus on the Family's *Citizen* magazine, for example, gay activists, during the Colorado campaign for an antigay amendment, managed to manipulate the media into printing a series of inaccuracies and misleading distortions all leading to a negative characterization of the individuals and organizations supporting the amendment while at the same time showing only positive images of the gay movement.

But it is not only the media that Christian Right activists argue has become "gay." Other key institutions of American life have been seized (it is not clear from whom, other than an amorphous "them"), including: the arts and education establishments, the military, and the government itself. Christian Right literature very clearly argues that this takeover has been both secretive and a fait accompli: "we don't even know we've been conquered" (Dannemeyer 1989, 121). Here, the Christian Right implicitly recognizes the ability of gays to "pass" as straight, in an echo of a classic anti-Semitic charge (Herman 1997a, chap. 2). Yet at the same time, Christian Right literature is replete with images of lesbians and gays who "flaunt" their sexuality in the most public of ways. There is, therefore, a tension present in Christian Right depictions of all the modern social movements between the enemy as both "secret infiltrator" and an "in your face," outrageously immoral actor. For many, HIV/AIDS education in particular was used by the gay movement as a cover for homosexual designs on youth (Knight 1995a; Woodall 1995).

The investing of the gay movement with such dual potency serves to highlight imminent danger, increase fear, galvanize reaction, and construct the counter-identity of the conservative Christian activist (Herman 1994, chap. 5). It also helps to erect an important division for the Christian Right: "gay militants" vs "gay others." Others may include duped troops, conservative gays, quiet, closeted lesbians and gay men who disapprove of the movement's agenda, and the so-called "ex-gays" (Pennington 1989).

To conservative Protestants, and particularly for those active in the Christian Right, the gay movement, while powerful and dangerous, is not acting alone, and its agenda is not solely devoted to gay issues. For the Christian Right, the success of lesbians and gay men is intimately linked to that of several other groups, particularly feminists, environmentalists, and New Age spiritualists, all of whom are seen to be linked in an anti-Christian drive for power. For some, class politics continues to play an important role as well.

> You have the extreme environmentalists, the extreme labor movement . . .
> the homosexual debate is the actual frontlines. It's the no man's land, during
> world war one, between the trenches, it's where the actual hand to hand

combat is goin' on right now. They're almost the vanguard of the effort on behalf of what we call the "radical left." They also have a religious left too. The abortionists, and the radical feminists, the homosexual activists, the environmentalists, the extreme labor movement, and so forth, and that's the coalition out there that is advancing that agenda. (Mabon, Oregon Citizen's Alliance, 1994)

These links are found everywhere in Christian Right literature, one of the most detailed studies being Texe Marrs' *Big Sister Is Watching You* (1993). Primarily an antifeminist tirade directed at Hillary Clinton and her band of "feminazis," *Big Sister* offers portraits of Clinton women appointees, each of whom is described as a member of a secret cabal. Significantly, however, these women are not simply, or only, "radical feminists." Marrs insists, or insinuates, that most are lesbians, New Age spiritualists (Marrs has also penned *Dark Secrets of the New Age* in 1987), and economic conspiracists (e.g., members of the Federal Reserve and Trilateral Commission). The Christian Right believes these links have also been forged at the international level. As Doris Buss has argued (1998), the Christian Right's activities at the 1992 United Nations Women's Conference in Beijing were largely directed towards showing third world countries that gay rights and women's rights were part of a western liberal, atheistic, colonization project.

Kevin Tebedo, a former activist with Colorado for Family Values, goes further by arguing that "the politics of homosexuality is Marxism-Leninism," which he defines as "a political view that makes the state God" (Tebedo 1994). Tebedo's view that Marxism is alive and well and the logical culmination of new social movement politics belies the notion that the Christian Right has moved away from an anticommunist politics in the post–Cold War era. Indeed, Tebedo and others have no faith that communism has died; they insist that its values (and cadres) are actively seeking (and winning) political power (Kintz 1994).

Yet, at the same time as Christian Right activists and literature construct their enemy as a monolithic and united opposition, in other discourses, principally the Christian Right's pragmatic rights rhetoric, the Christian Right is keen to identify divisions between social movement aspirations. For example, in campaigning against gay rights, the Christian Right has sought to convince recipients of race-based rights that the currency of rights is being devalued by gay opportunists (Herman 1997a, chap. 5). Still, it is important to recognize that even these forces —whether united or divided—do not act alone; on the contrary, they are in the service of Satan who, behind the scenes, is orchestrating their performance. While this might seem an exaggeration, as I discussed earlier, premillennial conservative evangelicals believe fervently in the apocalyptic scenario. They see all around them signs of impending finality. It is therefore understandable and consistent that they view opposing social movements as a Satanic conspiracy (Davis 1971; Johnson 1983). In tract after tract the lesbian and gay movement is described as a "malevolent force" (Dannemeyer 1989, 18) and the gay agenda as "symbolic of the all-encompassing plan of the kingdom of darkness as a whole" (McIlhenny, McIlhenny, and York 1993, 232). Pat Robertson has explicitly linked homosexuality to the "antichrist" (1982, 88–89).

Conservative evangelicals in America liken themselves to the biblical people of Israel, standing up to the Philistines and other opponents with God on their side (Grant and Horne 1993; Meigs 1995). Steve Farrar also employs biblical analogies, arguing that modern Satanic forces bear a striking resemblance to the old testament people of Baal:

1. Baal worshippers were pro-choice after the child was born.
2. Baal worshippers held the environment in high esteem and considered Baal as the one who determined and controlled the environment. . . .
3. Baal worship encouraged and promoted rampant sexual immorality, particularly homosexuality, as a normal and natural lifestyle.
4. Baal worship sought to coexist as a legitimate religious viewpoint alongside Judaism. (Farrar 1994, 115)

During interviews I conducted when working on *The Antigay Agenda* (1997), I asked several Christian Right acitivists if they believed gay rights was part of a wider Satanic conspiracy. They agreed that it was. "From a religious perspective, and from what I read of my Bible, I would conclude the same. Yes" (Loretta Neet, Oregon Citizen's Alliance, 1994). "If those behaviors are contrary to [a] biblical or God's perspective in that sense, well you'd have to say yes, he is an influence there" (Will Perkins, Colorado for Family Values, 1994). "I believe that there is evil. Real honest to goodness evil. [There] is an opposite side of God" (Kevin Tebedo, Colorado for Family Values, 1994). "If you're not working for God, you're working for Satan" (Jim Woodall, Concerned Women for America, 1995). "I believe in the personification of evil. . . . I know the ultimate struggle is between good and evil, between God and the devil, and I do believe that we do side with one or the other in this cosmic, ageless struggle that's been going on. . . . you're either advancing the principles of either a set of moral absolutes or a divine being, or you're advancing the principles of immoral absolutes or immoral principles, or an unholy being" (Mabon, Oregon Citizen's Alliance, 1994).

For the Christian Right, anti-Christian conspiracies are not confined within the nation's borders. The evil forces, of which the gay movement is part, are a world-wide phenomenon, and Christian Right literature is replete with analyses of how global power (re)alignments and international organizations such as the United Nations and the European Union fit into the end-times scenario (Herman, forthcoming).

The uniting theme here is Godlessness: a failure to comply with conservative Christian tenets is synonymous with atheism, and atheism is most definitely a Satanic strategy. The gay agenda is the secular agenda is the liberal agenda is the devil's agenda. In the eyes of the Christian Right, American anti-Christian forces coalesce around their efforts to seize the state and control state practice. Let me turn, then, to considering the relationship between the Christian Right and the state.

THE CHRISTIAN RIGHT AND THE STATE

How does the Christian Right understand the state (Marty and Appleby 1993)? Like most oppositional movements, the Christian Right views the state as a monolithic, institutional bloc of power. Unlike most other movements, however, the Christian Right believes the state exercises rights and privileges that are God's alone. The state, in Christian Right literature, comprises government and a range of other institutions, including: public schools and hospitals; the legal system; public funding bodies; and quasi-public media (e.g., National Public Radio and the Public Broadcasting System). According to the Christian Right worldview, these state structures operate with one voice and one agenda: anti-Christian secular humanism. At the same time, however, Christian Right practice belies the omnipotence of this representation as Christian Right activists seek, with some success, to win control of state bodies at the local level (e.g., school and hospital boards).

The Christian Right's understanding of the state involves, I would argue, three primary, and contradictory, beliefs. First, the state is "too big"; state bureaucracies over-interfere in the lives of individuals and the work of the church. Second, the Founding Fathers did not intend the state to be atheistic; indeed, religious faith, and more particularly, the Christian faith, lies at the heart of the Constitution and the American polity itself.

Third, and following from the second, the state has a duty to act as a moral leader; not to usurp the church, but to imbue its activities with the values and principles of Christianity (or, its euphemism, "the Judeo-Christian tradition"). For many conservative Christians (but not all), this includes, indeed necessitates, that the state legislate morality. The attack on the "Big Brother" state is what aligns the Christian Right with both the economic right and the populist revolt against a perceived gigantic, corrupt, and biased government (Crawford 1980). However, the two final postulates, that the U.S. state is fundamentally a Christian state and has a duty to act in accord with Christian principles, stand in some contradiction to the first, for they entail an activist, interfering state, furthering a very specific moral agenda. Arguably, neither the economic right, nor the majority of American people, support such a program.

Regulation: Big Government

This aspect of the Christian Right's state politics is perhaps the most well known. In keeping with conservative economic and social thought generally, the Christian Right argues that the state is overextended and its reach too penetrative of commercial and civil life. But more than this, for many on the Christian Right, the American state has become identified with a range of totalitarian characteristics formerly reserved to describe foreign, socialist governments.

Welfarist policies are discussed by the Christian Right as if they were Soviet desensitization programs, lulling the populace into laziness and soporific ignorance (e.g., Christian Coalition 1995, chap. 7; Robertson 1993, 179–83). Public funding of the arts is represented as furthering official state liberalism; hence the Christian Right call to defund the Public Broadcasting System, the National Endowment for the Arts, and other similar organizations (e.g., Christian Coalition 1995, chap. 9; Dobson and Bauer 1990, chap. 11; Knight 1995b).

The Department of Education is also a prime target of the Christian Right. Officials there and within the National Education Association, the Christian Right argues, contrive and impose an anti-God agenda, aimed at instilling socialist values and indoctrinating the youth of America (e.g., Dugan 1991; Robertson 1993, chap. 9; Family Research Council 1995). Similarly, the Bureau of Alcohol, Tobacco, and Firearms is seen to weave an increasingly tangled web of red tape in its efforts to prevent individuals from exercising their constitutional rights. Arguably, the extreme right crystallized this view with the bombing of Oklahoma federal offices in 1995.

The Christian Right also takes a public stand against state interference in religious freedom. Occasionally, this interest is overtly self-serving and hypocritical, as when the Christian Right vociferously spoke out against the FBI's handling of the Branch Davidian community at Waco in 1993 (Marrs 1993). The Christian Right is no friend to religious cults and "their" state would likely have taken exactly the same actions. Nevertheless, the U.S. government is represented by the Christian Right as either an aspiring (or already installed) monolithic, left-wing bloc of power, stamping out all dissension, controlling and manipulating peoples' very thoughts. Pat Robertson expresses it thus:

> What you have to realize is that the goal of the Radical Left is never to build up society but to tear down existing structures and replace them with a massive social bureaucracy. . . . The dialectic of socialism is that existing orthodoxies are constantly being replaced by new ones. That is what the liberal wing of the Democratic party in this country is dedicated to doing. . . . The cultural elites who orchestrate and bring about change are a privileged cadre here, just as they were in the Soviet Union—a small, well-educated core of liberal leaders who are entitled to have the fantastic dreams, while the rest of us do as we are told. That elite cadre, or politburo, was one of the principal instruments of Marxism, expressed in the principle of "the dictatorship of the proletariat." It is hardly different from the inner circle of the president's cabinet in Washington today. . . . the Radical Left controls all of the citadels of power—the presidency, the Congress, many courts, public education, the universities, the press, the motion picture and television industry, the major foundations, and the National Council of Churches. (Robertson 1993, 197–98, 301)

Thus, as the Cold War cooled down, the Christian Right and others came to identify a new "enemy within"—the American state itself. Forces once seen largely as external threats are now viewed as wielding complete power over a disenfranchised and downtrodden people. In previous decades, the U.S government was, for many Americans, including most conservative Christians, a glorified focus of patriotism; while there may have been bad apples within, the basket itself was beyond reproach. Now, this reverence has evaporated as the Christian Right agenda and state priorities have increasingly diverged. The state itself is now a symbol of un-Americanism: it has been hijacked by feminists, homosexualized by gay activists, and rendered impotent by peaceniks and environmentalists. Furthermore, the former patriots are now the subversives—a shift starkly highlighted in the 1995 Oklahoma bombing, the 1996 stand-offs with the "freemen" communities, and continuing threats by right-wing militia groups.

The gay rights case *Romer v. Evans* illustrates the manner in which the Christian Right believes conservative faith has been marginalized by elite, liberal state institutions. In 1992, the Colorado electorate passed Amendment 2, a citizen's initiative denying state-sponsored civil rights protections to lesbians and gay men in the state (Herman 1997a, chap. 6). Gay rights activists immediately brought a constitutional challenge to the law, an injunction was imposed by the court, and the measure never implemented. In the subsequent litigation, conservative Christian forces, now represented by a state government that had little sympathy with them, lost the argument at all levels, including, finally, the U.S. Supreme Court in 1996. For Christian Right activists, judicial rejection of populist attempts to reign government in only confirmed what they already knew to be true: the courts, and the state, are in the hands of the enemy.

The idea that there is "too much" state controlling too many aspects of life is not new to conservative Christianity. However, what is different now about both the Christian Right's representation of the state and popular antistatist feeling in general, is this disidentification from the state and its objectives. Furthermore, the state is now identified as being controlled by a liberal (or Marxist) elite, intent on pursuing its own agenda through governmental prerogatives: "As secularism triumphs, the god of the state eats away at the religious symbols of yesteryear" (Staver 1995, 178). But for many on the Christian Right, the state does not simply need to be rolled back; rather, ownership must be transferred. Indeed, as I will argue below, many on the Christian Right would welcome an activist, interventionist state, provided that the state's agenda was their own.

Restoration: Church and State

An integral part of the Christian Right's state agenda involves the production of a revisionist historiography. Christianity, the Christian Right contends, was the foundation upon which America was built. This history begins with a reinterpretation of Columbus. He was not an explorer, but a missionary: "He wasn't primarily looking for a trade route to the Indies at all, he was looking to bring the gospel of Jesus Christ into the western hemisphere" (Marshall 1993). Similarly, the Pilgrims were not fleeing religious persecution, they were evangelists, coming to spread God's word amongst the natives (Barton 1993a).

Following from this, Christian Right historians maintain that the

Founding Fathers were devout believers, the populace at the time was resolutely God-fearing, and the Constitution itself a statement of religious values and principles (Staver 1995; Whitehead 1994).[7] The First Amendment, prohibiting the "establishment" of religion, was never intended to secularize the state; rather, its drafters simply sought to ensure that no one Christian denomination could use the state for its own ends, and, in the process, persecute others. Many prominent Christian Right scholars and several Christian Right organizations propagate this message.[8]

The predominant theme of the Christian Right revisionist historiography is to reject the expression "wall of separation," used first in a letter by Thomas Jefferson in 1802, and relied on subsequently by the state and its courts. The Christian Right contends that the separation of church and state is a "myth" that has no foundation in the original construction of American constitutionalism.

> Every one of us was taught the pilgrims came to America for freedom of worship—that is flatly not true. . . . they were led to America by the lord Jesus himself to propagate the gospel among the Indians, which they did. And to become themselves stepping stones for the furtherance of the gospel to the outermost parts of the earth. They were missionaries. . . . They had a vision of a new society based on the word of God. . . . The only time in human history that free Christian men and women had the opportunity to build a whole new society based on the biblical principles of self-government was at Plymouth, in 1620. And that's exactly what they did. (Marshall 1993; see also Barton 1993b; LaHaye and LaHaye 1994, chap. 3)

Thus, this perspective is more than just a critique. It is also visionary. In other words, the Christian Right seeks to *restore* Christianity to the American polity. The word "restoration" is used consistently by the revisionists. Its connotations aptly signal the project in which the Christian Right is engaged: to rebuild America as a Christian nation. Indeed, many Christian Right activists view this project as divinely inspired (e.g., LaHaye and LaHaye 1994; Robertson 1993); it is God's desire that the United States fulfill this role in the world (Marshall 1993). It is interesting to note that proslavery Protestants of the nineteenth century similarly had "God on their side" (Smith 1994; Crowther 1992).

What relationship, then, does antigay politics have to this revisionist historiography? First, the Christian Right historians "prove" that the true character of the state is a Christian one, and that it is the duty of the state to promote Christian values. Second, the restorationists demonstrate that

Christian values are at the heart of the American polity itself, indeed they are the reason for the very existence of the nation. For the State to condone, indeed to endorse, sin is in itself an abomination. Finally, the Christian Right historians provide a justification for a state-activist conservative agenda: the state must be reoriented towards combating secularism, in all its guises, as the Founders would have wished.

To complete this project, the Christian Right needs not a minimalist state but an expansive and activist one. I would argue that it is far more accurate to view the Christian Right (but not all conservative Christians by any means) as hoping for, and indeed building (restoring), a *Christian state*—a Christian state that will actively promote Christian tenets through its law-making powers. The Christian Right pays lip service to neoconservative economic theory requiring a "lean, mean, state," but their aspiration and agenda is to take control of the existing state in order to "restore" its Christian character. While some state action would certainly be rolled back (eg, welfare policies, progay initiatives), other areas of state practice would be extended dramatically. The Christian Right is not so much against the state as it is for the Christianization of worldly states generally. As Keith Fournier, director of the American Center for Law and Justice, has said, urging Christian action today: "Constantine opened the door in ancient Rome and the Christians of that age transformed the whole empire" (1995).

The Christianization project is evident throughout the Christian Right agenda. For example, Focus on the Family and the Family Research Council advocate governmental activism in a wide range of areas, including: abortion; divorce; pornography; family tax incentives; penal sanctions; and antigay measures. Similarly, Tim and Beverly LaHaye support laws banning abortion, homosexuality, pornography, and instituting the establishment of "decency standards" throughout the arts and entertainment industries (1994, 269). Christian Right voter's guides rate candidates according to whether they support such things as tax relief for married couples, antiabortion measures, legislation requiring young women to obtain parental consent prior to having an abortion, a statutory ban on any form of euthanasia, and, of course, antigay rights legislation.[9]

The Christian Coalition's 1995 *Contract with the American Family* provides yet another example of this mendacity. Although the *Contract* is replete with images of "big government out of control," the Coalition's actual agenda requires massive governmental intervention. For example, the *Contract* promotes legislation to: expand religious and parental rights (including "right to know" legislation); provide "family-friendly tax relief" (including child and married couple tax credits); ban abortion; control and restrict pornography on the Internet and cable television; and impose mandatory drug and HIV testing on prison populations. The huge and complex bureaucracy needed to implement these and other Christian Right measures would surely make up for that lost from cuts to welfare and arts subsidies.

The tensions this state activist agenda throws up for the Christian Right alliance with the secular "new right" minimalists are perhaps obvious. So serious are these potential conflicts that intensely pragmatic organizations, such as the Christian Coalition, prefer to keep this activist agenda much in the background, emphasizing instead liberty issues such as freedom of worship that superficially may involve a reduction in state regulation (Wilcox 1996, 145). This shift has the added benefit of making Christian Right politics more palatable to the evangelical pietists—an important, potential Christian Right constituency put off by calls for the "legislation of morality."

But, in my view, it is incontrovertible that the Christian Right aspires to govern a Christian state. Although it has been suggested that the Christian Right's newer pragmatic discourse indicates a shift in Christian Right aspirations (Moen 1994; Rozell and Wilcox 1996), I would argue that this shift is tactical rather than ideological (Herman 1997a, chap. 5). "It would be nice [if the government] professed Christ" (Woodall 1995). "I would like to see America governed by biblical principles" (Knight 1995a). Interestingly, this agenda in itself poses questions for conservative Protestant theology. The Christian Right (and conservative Protestants generally) are and have been premillennialists for most of this century. The eschatological centrality of premillennialism is that the world will descend into greater and greater chaos, degeneration, and war before Christ returns. Activist conservatives have never taken this to mean that they must withdraw and simply await rapture; however, the task of building God's Kingdom *now* was always associated with *postmillennialism*—a theology insisting that Christ will only return when Christianity rules the earth.

Arguably, these eschatologies, once starkly separate and antagonistic, have, in the form of the Christian Right, come together in a kind of cloudy synthesis. Pre- and post-millennialists work side by side in Christian Right organizations, and it would appear as though many Christian Right activists have come to accept that they must strive to establish the United States as a Christian nation now (Fournier 1993; LaHaye and LaHaye 1994; Robertson 1993).

CONCLUSION

Many critics of the Christian Right argue that its "real" agenda is to create a theocracy. This is no doubt the requirement of certain conservative Christian perspectives, most notably the Reconstructionists (Herman 1997a, chap. 7). However, to the extent that the Christian Right continues to be dominated by premillennialism, the most one can say, I would argue, is that the question is unsettled. If one believes that the world will descend into a final abyss and then it will end as Jesus returns, then the possibility of establishing His reign on earth now is simply not there. Furthermore, some members of the Christian Right sincerely believe in the "good" of separation of church and state. However, the more the Christian Right actively seeks to impose its orthodoxy on government, to take control of the state, and to use state power to achieve religious ends, the more theocracy becomes the necessary culmination of these efforts, despite its public disavowals.

Ironically, however, the more the Christian Right moves in this direction, the less support it may have from the American people. For although Americans are amongst the most Christian in the world, they are also, it would seem, amongst the most libertarian—and this is a source of antipathy to both the Christian Right and the gay rights agendas. In one opinion study, for example, while 78 percent of respondents believed the President should be a moral and spiritual leader, and 84 percent agreed that governmental policies should reflect moral values, 91 percent expressed the view that "individual freedom was critical to democracy."[10] And, although 93 percent of those surveyed believed in God or a universal spirit, only 34 percent thought that the Bible was God's literal word (Sheler 1994). While the Christian Right has had some success tapping into a populist revolt against the aspirations of new social movements, only a small minority of Americans may stay with the Christian Right as its activist, interventionist, and fundamentally orthodox agenda becomes more apparent.

NOTES

Some parts of this chapter have been previously published in Herman (1997a).

1. That is not to say that there are not orthodox lesbians and gay men—of course there are. However, my focus here is on antigay politics, not gay activism within orthodoxy (Thumma 1991). See also White's (1994) personal account.

2. I have elsewhere discussed various ways of defining this term (Herman 1997a,

9–14). When I use the term *Christian Right* I refer to a broad coalition of "pro-family" organizations that have come together to struggle for a conservative Christian vision in the political realm. Note that this chapter does not focus on the tensions and divisions within the Christian Right (but see Herman 1997a).

3. See, e.g., Bromley and Shupe, eds. (1984), Bruce (1990), Diamond (1989, 1995), Hunter (1991), Jorstad (1987), Liebman and Wuthnow, eds. (1983), Lienesch (1993), Moen (1992, 1994), Rozell and Wilcox (1996), Wald (1991), and Wilcox (1992, 1996), to name just a very few.

4. For example, contrast Diamond (1989) and Hertzke (1988) with Moen (1989) and Bruce (1990, 1994).

5. Klaus Koch has provided a useful definition of the genre. Characteristics he identifies include: urgency of expectation; cosmic catastrophe; presence of angels and demons; new salvation possible; and the ultimate enthronement of God and his Kingdom (1983, 21–24). For further discussion of the rhetorical dimensions of the genre, see Brummet (1984). In addition to Boyer's (1992) exhaustive study of the apocalyptic genre, the details of this scenario have been analyzed, critically and otherwise, by a range of theologians, historians, sociologists, journalists, and others, including Chandler (1984), E. Dobson and Hindson (1986), Pieterse (1992), and Wilson (1977).

6. The American Family Association, for example, constantly monitors the perceived "progay bias" of the media in articles in its *AFA Journal*. See also its leaflet, "Top sponsors of pro-homosexual programs" (1994a).

7. This story stands in some contrast to Bellah's famous account of "civil religion" (1967).

8. One of the most important Christian Right historians is David Barton (1992), president of Wallbuilders, a leading organization constructing this revisionist historiography. Wallbuilders describes itself as "an organization dedicated to the restoration of the moral and religious values on which America was built" ("A word about Wallbuilders," in *The Wallbuilder Report*, Summer 1995). Barton appears regularly on the Christian Right circuit. He is a frequent guest, for example, on James Dobson's *Focus on the Family* radio program. He also appears on the roster of experts relied on by the extreme right-wing movements, such as Christian Identity (Anti-Defamation League 1994, 54–56). Other important figures in this genre include Peter Marshall, Gary DeMar (1995), and John Whitehead (1994), President of the Rutherford Institute (and an advisor to Paula Jones in her legal action against Bill Clinton). Other organizations include The American Center for Law and Justice (Virginia) and The Foundation for American Christian Education (San Francisco).

9. See, for example, "Oregon Christian Voter's Guide," Traditional Values Coalition (Oregon), 1994.

10. For a discussion of religious belief and church/state understandings, see Jelen and Wilcox (1995).

REFERENCES

American Family Association, 1994a. Homosexuality in America (leaflet).

American Family Association, 1994b. Top sponsors of prohomosexual programs (pamphlet).

Anti-Defamation League. 1994. *The religious right: The assault on tolerance and pluralism in America.* New York: Anti-Defamation League.

Ariel, Yaakov. 1991. Jewish suffering and Christian salvation: The evangelical-fundamentalist holocaust memoirs. *Holocaust and Genocide Studies* 6:63–78.

Barkun, Michael. 1990. Racist apocalypse: Millennialism on the far right. *American Studies* 31:121–40.

Barton, David. 1989. *The myth of separation: What is the correct relationship between church and state?* Aledo, Tex.: Wallbuilders.

———. 1993a. A grateful nation. In *America's Christian Heritage* (audiotape). Colorado Springs, Colo.: Focus on the Family.

———. 1993b. Our spiritual heritage. In *America's Christian Heritage* (audiotape). Colorado Springs, Colo.: Focus on the Family.

Bellah, Robert. 1967. Civil religion in America. *Daedalus* 96:1–21.

Boyer, Paul. 1992. *When time shall be no more: Prophecy belief in modern American culture.* Cambridge: Harvard University Press.

Bromley, David G., and Anson Shupe, eds. 1984. *New Christian politics.* Macon, Ga.: Mercer University Press.

Bruce, Steve. 1990. *The rise and fall of the new Christian Right: Conservative Protestant politics in America 1978–1988.* Oxford: Clarendon.

Brummet, Barry. 1984. Premillennial apocalyptic as a rhetorical genre. *Central States Speech Journal* 35:84–93.

Bull, Chris, and Gallagher, John. 1996. *Perfect enemies: The religious right, and the gay movement, and the politics of the 1990s.* New York: Crown.

Bull, Malcolm, ed. 1995. *Apocalypse theory and the ends of the world.* Oxford: Blackwell.

Buss, Doris. 1998. Robes, relics, and rights: the Vatican and Beijing Conference on Women. *Social and Legal Studies* 7:339–63.

Cassara, Ernest. 1982. The development of America's sense of mission. In *The apocalyptic vision: Interdisciplinary essays on myth and culture,* edited by L. P. Zamora. Bowling Green, Ohio: Bowling Green University Popular Press.

Chandler, Ralph Clark. 1984. The wicked shall not bear rule: The fundamentalist heritage of the new Christian Right. In *New Christian Politics,* edited by D. Bromley and A. Shupe. Macon: Mercer University Press.

Christian Coalition. 1995. *Contract with the American family.* Nashville, Tenn.: Moorings.

Crawford, Alan. 1980. *Thunder on the right: The "new right" and the politics of resentment.* New York: Pantheon.

Crowther, Edward R. 1992. Holy honour: Sacred and secular in the Old South. *Journal of Southern History*, 58:619–36.

Dannemeyer, William. 1989. *Shadow in the land: Homosexuality in America*. San Francisco: Ignatius.

Davis, David Brion. 1971. *The fear of conspiracy: Images of un-American subversion from the revolution to the present*. Ithaca, N.Y.: Cornell University Press.

DeMar, Gary. 1993, 1995. *America's Christian history: The untold story*. Atlanta: American Vision.

Diamond, Sara. 1989. *Spiritual warfare: The politics of the Christian Right*. Boston: South End.

———. 1995. *Roads to dominion: Right-wing movements and political power in the United States*. New York: Guilford.

Dobson, Ed, and Ed Hindson. 1986. Apocalypse now?: What fundamentalists believe about the end of the world. *Policy Review* 38:16–22.

Dobson, James, and Gary Bauer. 1990. *Children at risk*. Dallas: Word.

Dugan, Robert P. 1991. *Winning the new civil war*. Portland, Ore.: Multnomah.

Family Research Council. 1995. Freeing America's schools: The case against the U.S. education department. *Family Policy*, April.

Farrar, Steve. 1994. *Standing tall: How a man can protect his family*. Sisters, Ore.: Multnomah.

Fournier, Keith A. 1993. *Religious cleansing in the American republic*, American Center for Law and Justice (pamphlet).

———. 1995. Christ and Caesar. *Law and Justice* 4 (1): 4.

Gager, John G. 1983. *The origins of anti-Semitism: Attitudes toward Judaism in pagan and Christian antiquity*. New York: Oxford University Press.

Gallup, George, Jr., and Jim Castelli. 1989. *The people's religion: American faith in the 90's*. New York: Macmillan.

Glanz, Dawn. 1982. The American West as millennial kingdom. In *The apocalyptic vision in America: Interdisciplinary essays on myth and culture*, edited by L. P. Zamora. Bowling Green, Ohio: Bowling Green University Popular Press.

Graham, Billy. 1992, 1995. *Storm warning*. Dallas: Word.

———. 1983. *Approaching hoofbeats: The four horsemen of the apocalypse*. London: Hodder and Stoughton.

Grant, George, and Mark A. Horne. 1993. *Legislating immorality: The homosexual movement comes out of the closet*. Chicago: Moody.

Guth, James L., John C. Green, Lyman A. Kellstedt, and Corwin E. Smidt. 1995. Faith and the environment: Religious beliefs and attitudes on environmental policy. *American Journal of Political Science* 39:364–82.

Henry, Carl F., ed. 1971. *Prophecy in the making*. Carol Stream, Ill.: Creation House.

Herman, Didi. 1994. *Rights of passage: Struggles for lesbian and gay legal equalit*. Toronto: University of Toronto Press.

————. 1997a. *The antigay agenda: Orthodox vision and the Christian Right*. Chicago: University of Chicago Press.

————. 1997b. "And then I saw a new heaven and a new earth": Thoughts on the Christian Right and the concept of "backlash." In *Dangerous territories: The backlash in education*, edited by L. Eyre and L. Roman. New York: Routledge.

————. Forthcoming. The New Roman Empire: European envisionings and American Premillenialists. In *British Journal of American Studies*.

Hertzke, Allen D. 1988. *Representing God in Washington: The role of religious lobbies in the American polity*. Knoxville: University of Tennessee Press.

Hofstadter, Richard. 1966. *The paranoid style in American politics and other essays*. London: Jonathan Cape.

Hunter, James Davison. 1991. *Culture wars: The struggle to define America*. New York: Basic Books.

Jelen, Ted G., and Wilcox, Clyde. 1995. *Public attitudes toward church and state*. Armonk, N.Y.: M. E. Sharpe.

Johnson, George. 1983. *Architects of fear: Conspiracy theories and paranoia in American politics*. Los Angeles: Jeremy P. Tarcher.

Jorstad, Erling. 1987. *The new Christian Right, 1981–1988*. Lewiston: Edwin Mellen.

Kintz, Linda. 1994. Motherly advice from the Christian Right: The construction of sacred gender. *Discourse* 17:49–76.

Kirkpatrick, Lee A. 1993. Fundamentalism, Christian orthodoxy, and intrinsic religious orientation as predictors of discriminatory attitudes. *Journal for the Scientific Study of Religion* 32:256–68.

Knight, Robert. 1995a. Interview by author, 11 September 1995. Mr. Knight is a spokesperson for the Family Research Council.

————. 1995b. The national endowment: It's time to free the arts. *Insight*, Family Research Council.

Koch, Klaus. 1983. What is apocalyptic? An attempt at a preliminary definition. In *Visionaries and their apocalypses*, edited by P. D. Hanson. Philadelphia: Fortress.

LaHaye, Tim, and Beverly LaHaye. 1994. *A nation without a conscience*. Wheaton, Ill.: Tyndale House.

Lawrence, Bruce B. 1989. *Defenders of God: The fundamentalist revolt against the modern age*. San Francisco: Harper and Row.

Lechner, Frank L. 1990. Fundamentalism revisited. In *In gods we trust: New patterns of religious pluralism in America*, edited by Thomas Robbins and Dick Anthony. New Brunswick, N.J.: Transaction.

Liebman, Robert C., and Robert Wuthnow. 1983. *The new Christian Right: Mobilization and legitimation*. Hawthorne: Aldine.

Lienesch, Michael. 1993. *Redeeming America: Piety and politics in the new Christian Right*. Chapel Hill: University of North Carolina Press.

Lippy, Charles H. 1982. Waiting for the end: The social context of American apocalyptic religion. In *The apocalyptic vision in America,* edited by L. P. Zamora. Bowling Green, Ohio: Bowling Green University Popular Press.

Mabon, Lon. 1994. Interview by author. Mr. Mabon is spokesperson for the Oregon Citizen's Alliance.

Marrs, Texe. 1993. *Big sister is watching you: Hillary Clinton and the White House feminists who now control America—and tell the President what to do.* Austin, Tex.: Living Truth.

Marshall, Peter. 1993. Recovering America's Christian heritage, in *America's Christian Heritage* (audiotape). Colorado Springs, Colo.: Focus on the Family, 1993).

Marty, Martin E., and R. Scott Appleby. 1993. *Fundamentalisms and the state.* Chicago: University of Chicago Press.

McIlhenny, Chuck, Donna McIlhenny, and Frank York. 1993. *When the wicked seize a city.* LaFayette, La.: Huntington House.

Meigs, Anna. 1995. Ritual language in everyday life: The Christian Right. *Journal of the American Academy of Religion* 63:85–103.

Minnery, Tom. 1993. Feeding frenzy! *Citizen* 7 (8): 1–3.

Moen, Matthew C. 1992. *The transformation of the Christian Right.* Tuscaloosa: University of Alabama Press.

———. 1994. From revolution to evolution: The changing nature of the Christian Right. *Sociology of Religion* 55:345–57.

———. 1995. Political and theological adjustment in the U.S. Christian Right. *Contentions* 4:75–90.

Mouly, Ruth W. 1985. *The religious right and Israel: The politics of armageddon.* Chicago: Midwest Research.

Nugent, Robert, and Jeannine Gramick. 1989–1990. Homosexuality: Protestant, Catholic and Jewish issues. *Journal of Homosexuality* 18:7–46.

Pennington, Sylvia. 1989. *Ex-Gays? There are none!* Hawthorne, Cal.: Lambda Christian Fellowship.

Pieterse, Jan P. Nederveen. 1992. The history of a metaphor: Christian Zionism and the politics of apocalypse. In *Christianity and hegemony,* edited by J. P. N. Pieterse. New York: St. Martin's.

Prager, Dennis. 1993. Homosexuality, the Bible and us—a Jewish perspective. *The Public Interest* 18 (3–4): 60–83.

Robertson, Pat. 1990. *The new millennium.* Dallas: Word.

———. 1993. *The turning tide: The fall of liberalism and the rise of common sense.* Dallas: Word.

Robertson, Pat, and Bob Slosser. 1982. *The secret kingdom.* Nashville: Thomas Nelson.

Romer v. Evans, 517 U.S. 620 (1996).

Rozell, Mark J., and Clyde Wilcox. 1996. *Second coming: The new Christian right in Virginia politics.* Baltimore: Johns Hopkins University Press.

Rueda, Enrique. 1987. *Gays, AIDS and you.* Old Greenwich, Conn.: Devin Adair.

Seltzer, Richard. 1992. The social location of those holding antihomosexual attitudes. *Sex Roles* 26:391–98.

Shapiro, Susan. 1993. Straight talk about gays. *U.S. News and World Report,* 5 July.

Sheler, Jeffrey. 1994. Spiritual America. *U.S. News and World Report,* 4 April, 48–59.

Smith, R. Drew. 1994. Slavery, succession, and southern Protestant shifts on the authority of the state. In *Journal of Church and State* 36:261–76.

Staver, Mathew D. 1995. *Faith and freedom.* Wheaton, Ill.: Crossway.

Sutton, Neil. 1994. The homosexual agenda from Stonewall to the White House. Family First.

Tebedo, Kevin. 1994. Interview by author, 3 November 1994. Mr. Tebedo is a former activist with Colorado for Family Values.

Thumma, Scott. 1991. Negotiating a religious identity: The case of the gay evangelical. *Sociological Analysis* 52:333–47.

Wald, Kenneth D. 1991. Social change and political response: The silent religious cleavage in North America. In *Politics and religion in the modern world,* edited by G. Moyser. London: Routledge.

Wald, Kenneth D., James W. Button, and Barbara A. Rienzo. 1996. The politics of gay rights in American communities: Explaining antidiscrimination ordinances and policies. *American Journal of Political Science* 40:1152–78.

White, Mel. 1994. *Stranger at the gate: To be gay and Christian in America.* New York: Simon and Schuster.

Whitehead, John W. 1994. *Religious apartheid: The separation of religion from American public life.* Chicago: Moody.

Wilcox, Clyde. 1992. *God's warriors: The Christian Right in twentieth-century America.* Baltimore: John Hopkins University Press.

———. 1994. Premillennialists at the millennium: Some reflections on the Christian Right in the twenty-first century. *Sociology of Religion* 55:243–61.

———. 1996. *Onward Christian soldiers: The religious right in American politics.* Boulder, Colo.: Westview.

Wilson, Dwight. 1977. *Armageddon now! The premillennarian response to Russia and Israel since 1917.* Grand Rapids, Mich.: Baker House.

Woodall, Jim. 1995. Interview by author. Mr. Woodall is vice president of Concerned Women for America.

8

DIRECT DEMOCRACY AND GAY RIGHTS INITIATIVES AFTER *ROMER*

Todd Donovan, Jim Wenzel, and Shaun Bowler

Previous chapters in this section have detailed the agenda and efforts of antigay political activists and Christian Right political organizations. One pattern that emerges from these accounts was the use of the institutions of direct democracy by the opponents of gay rights. Although few states' policies have been changed as a direct result of these antigay ballot initiatives, some of the campaigns received tremendous media attention and have led many to question the merits of a political tool that allows for the vilification of a minority group (Linde 1992). As we note below, from 1978 to 1998 there was a series of contentious antigay initiatives on state ballots. A U.S. Supreme Court ruling that reversed a voter-approved Colorado initiative (*Romer v. Evans*, 1996), however, may seriously constrain the scope of antigay activists efforts via the ballot box.

This chapter assesses the status of gay rights initiatives after the 1996 *Romer* decision and examines their possible effects. We propose that *Romer* will do less than might be hoped to change how frequently direct democracy is used as a tool of opposition to gay rights. Instead these initiatives are likely to remain an enduring—albeit altered— political tool for opponents of gay rights. In the discussion that follows we suggest that more is at stake for state-level antigay activists than winning elections or producing immediate changes in public policy via direct democracy. Rather, we suggest that these initiative contests can also be seen as an arena where antigay political entrepreneurs compete in a game that involves building political capital, establishing and mobilizing a base of supporters, moving mass opinions about gays and lesbians, and, eventually, constraining the discretion of elected legislators.

ANTIGAY INITIATIVES: 1978–1998

Since the 1920s, most western U.S. states (and a few other nonwestern states) have established procedures by which a group obtaining a required number of signatures may place legislation directly before the state's voters[1] (Magleby 1984). Direct and representative democracy have both long been used to constrain the rights and liberties of minorities in America (Cronin 1989). Initiatives are distinctive since the scope of discourse about direct democracy's policy questions often extends beyond an elected legislature to engage the mass public in a very immediate expression of majority rule.

To some extent, citizen's initiatives that attack gay rights reflect the repetition of earlier cycles of political activity directed at other minorities. Movements against various minorities via the statewide initiative process have waxed and waned throughout the twentieth century, often corresponding to a more generalized social backlash associated with political gains of a specific minority group (Gamble 1997). Racial desegregation of schools and integration of housing and accommodations in the 1960s, for example, spawned a number of state and local ballot measures during that period. Those initiatives were designed to roll back legislative gains made by African Africans (Bell 1978; Wolfinger and Greenstein 1968). Similarly, increased accommodation for language minorities led to a series of "Official English" initiatives in the 1980s (Citrin 1990; Citrin et al 1990). In each case, legislative gains made by minorities were subjected to direct public evaluation after political activists succeeded in gathering enough signatures to force a public vote.

Eleven antigay initiatives and two additional statewide referendums have appeared on various state ballots since 1978. The first major initiative appeared in California, not long after a majority of national survey respondents began reporting for the first time that they were tolerant of basic political and economic rights for homosexuals (Donovan and Bowler 1997). The 1978 California initiative was authored by John Briggs, conservative Republican state senator who had unsuccessfully proposed a similar bill in the state legislature. The Briggs Initiative was designed to rid public schools of homosexual teachers by virtually requiring local districts to fire known homosexuals. Laws existing at the time placed no such overt requirement on districts. Early opinion polls showed the measure was heavily favored, but after liberal and conservative elites (including Ronald Reagan) united to criticize the measure during the campaign, it was eventually defeated (Donovan and Bowler 1997).[2]

Subsequent antigay ballot measures from 1978 to 1988 typically proposed undoing housing and employment protections that had been passed by relatively progressive city and county councils in cities such as Seattle, Eugene, St. Paul, and San Jose. Of seventeen initiatives identified on local ballots during this period, twelve proposed repealing protections that had recently been extended to gays. The remaining five proposed extending rights to gays. Foreshadowing future statewide battles, these antigay initiatives were often backed by local evangelical Christian conservatives who had not previously been active politically. Eight of these twelve antigay initiatives passed, returning local policy to the previous existing status quo (Haider-Markel 1997, Appendix E). The initiative battles nevertheless polarized the political environment of communities such as Dade County and San Jose, where the leaders of newly established mass-attendance churches subsequently became influential players in local candidate elections due to their ability to mobilize voters.

It is important to note that direct citizen's initiatives have primarily been a tool of opponents, not proponents, of gay rights. It has been difficult, furthermore, for progay groups to win via the ballot box. Four of the five local proposals qualified by progay groups between 1978 and 1986 that would have created new protections for gays and lesbians were defeated— passing only in Boulder with a 51 percent majority (Haider-Markel 1997, appendix E). This suggests that it has been easier for opponents of gay rights to use local initiatives to repeal recent changes in the policy status quo than it has been for progay activists to change the local status quo via direct democracy (i.e., introduce new protections that legislatures have not).

As table 8.1 illustrates, state-level antigay initiative experiences echo this local-level pattern. In addition, antigay activists cannot easily use direct democracy to produce nonincremental changes in policy. We divide state antigay initiatives into three categories. The first includes measures that propose to reverse a legislative, judicial, or executive branch change in recent status quo policy about gay rights, and thus return policy to the status quo. We classify these as *incrementalist* proposals. The second class of initiatives proposes to repeal established gay rights policies and constrain future legislative action, so we classify these as *nonincremental* policy

Table 8.1   Classification of Statewide Antigay Initiatives, 1978–1998

Effect of Proposed Laws:
1) Reverse recent laws, court decisions, or executive actions
   (incrementalism, return to recent status quo)

State/Year	Sponsors	Election Result
Alaska, 1998[+]	State legislature	(68% in favor)
Hawaii, 1998[+]	State legislature	(69% in favor)
Maine, 1998*	Christian Civic League	(51% in favor)
Oregon, 1988	Oregon Citizens Alliance	(57% in favor)
		Avg. = 61%

2) Repeal existing local protections; prevent future protections
   (non-incremental change; roll-back protections and freeze future acts)

State/Year	Sponsor	Election Result
Colorado, 1992	Colorado for Family Values	(53% in favor)
Idaho, 1994	Idaho Citizens Alliance	(49% in favor)
Maine, 1995	Concerned Maine Families	(47% in favor)
Oregon, 1994	Oregon Citizens Alliance	(44% in favor)
		Avg. = 48%

3) Adopt new restrictions on gay rights
   (radical change from status quo, new conservative policies)

State/Year	Sponsor	Election Result
California, 1978	Sen. John Briggs	(41% in favor)
California, 1986	Lyndon Larouche	(29% in favor)
California, 1988	Rep. William Dannemeyer	(32% in favor)
California, 1988	Rep. William Dannemeyer	(34% in favor)
Oregon, 1992	Oregon Citizens Alliance	(43% in favor)
		Avg. = 35%

[+] A legislative referenda to amend a state constitution.
* A citizen's referenda to repeal a legislative act. The policy was not directly drafted by a citizen's group.

changes. The final category includes measures that propose the adoption of new policies that constitute a *radical* departure from the state's existing policies. Proposals in this class include laws requiring that gay teachers be fired, requiring mandatory AIDS testing, and requiring quarantine of AIDS victims.

The table illustrates a gradual trend over time away from the more radical proposals. Nearly all of the "first wave" of antigay state initiatives, starting with Briggs in California and continuing through Oregon's Measure 9 in 1992, fall into the "radical policy change" category. Between 1986 and 1988, for example, three controversial initiatives targeting AIDS victims qualified for the California ballot: two by the religious conservative U.S. Representative William Dannemeyer (R) and one by fringe political figure

Lyndon Larouche. These three measures included a call for mandatory AIDS testing and forced quarantine of people testing positive for the disease. All of these proposals were rejected by very large vote margins. A fourth, moderate, AIDS-testing initiative was proposed by law enforcement elites in 1988 requiring testing only of criminals convicted of violent crimes. The measure was not seen as antigay and was approved by California voters in 1988 (Donovan and Bowler 1997).

That same year in Oregon, however, antigay activists successfully used direct democracy to repeal a new executive-branch ruling that protected state employees from job actions based on their sexual orientation. The 1988 Oregon measure involved a relatively incremental change in administrative policy, returning state discrimination protections to the status that existed prior to the extension of protections to state employees (the initiative was later reversed by the Oregon Court of Appeals).

With one exception (Oregon in 1992), contemporary antigay state initiatives have had a slightly less radical edge than those on ballots prior to 1990, although most ballot measures from 1992 to 1996 continued to propose nonincremental changes in gay rights polices. Most proposed state laws eliminating long-standing local ordinances protecting gays and lesbians. Two of the initiatives from this period appeared in Oregon, where the drafting, circulation, and qualification of antigay initiatives became something of a cottage industry. Most of this activity is associated with the efforts of Lon Mabon and his Oregon Citizen's Alliance ("OCA"). The OCA found its base of support in Christian churches and was particularly active outside of the state's major metropolitan area. In 1992, the OCA qualified for the state ballot Measure 9, a proposed law that declared homosexuality "abnormal, wrong, unnatural and perverse" while equating it with pedophilia. Measure 9 also banned categorical civil rights protections based on sexual orientation and sexual preference (Donovan and Bowler 1997). Such a proposal represented a sharp departure from existing state law.

Two years later, the OCA was back on the ballot with Measure 13, a bill similar to Measure 9 but with slightly less caustic denunciations of homosexuality. The 1994 Oregon proposal would have repealed Portland's local gay rights ordinance, which dated back to 1974 (Haider-Markel 1997, appendix C). Both initiatives were soundly defeated. In June of 1996, shortly after the *Romer* decision, the OCA withdrew from circulation another initiative that combined the ban on categorical protections with a prohibition of gay marriage and a prohibition of teaching that sexual behavior constituted "differences" similar to race, gender or religion. The *Romer* decision would have likely made the proposed initiative unconstitutional (Beggs 1996). By 1997, Mabon had two more initiatives circulating in Oregon, including "The Family Act," a bill that defined a "government approved" family as constituting only a man and woman in marriage, with children.[3]

Although numerous citizen petitions for antigay initiatives and referendums circulated in states other than Oregon in the 1990s (including at least four unsuccessful ones in Washington), only four qualified for state ballots beyond Oregon prior to 1999. These include a 1994 OCA-influenced initiative that was narrowly defeated in Idaho and the successful 1992 Colorado initiative backed by James Dobson's organization, Colorado for Family Values ("CFV"). CFV was the state branch of Dobson's national organization[4] involved in Christian radio broadcasting, education issues, and political lobbying. The national organization was reported to have a $70 million dollar budget in 1992, having moved to Colorado Springs in 1989 (White 1992). The CFV's Colorado initiative measure subsequently became the subject of the *Romer* decision (Witt and McCorkle 1997). Like the 1994 Oregon initiative, the central provisions of the Idaho and Colorado proposals involved the repeal and prohibition of laws prohibiting discrimination based on sexual orientation. The Colorado law repealed local ordinances, including laws from Boulder and Aspen, which had been in effect since 1975 and 1977, respectively (Haider-Markel 1997, appendix C). Two other antigay rights measures were on the state ballot in Maine, one in 1995 (similar to the Colorado, Idaho, and 1994 Oregon initiatives) and another in 1998. Maine's 1995 initiative would have repealed a three-year-old Portland gay-rights ordinance (Haider-Markel 1997, appendix C).

An overview of table 8.1 shows that initiative proponents are rarely successful in winning these elections. Of eleven statewide initiatives from the last two decades that are readily classifiable as antigay, only three (27 percent) passed.[5] Of these three, two failed to survive legal challenges (Maine's 1998 referendum had not been tested). When referenda written by a legislature are considered with initiatives, the pass rate increases to 5 of 13 (38 percent), matching the overall average. All of the ballot measures that might be seen as radical departures from the status quo were solidly rejected by voters. Proposals in this category were supported by only 35 percent of voters on average. Antigay activists have fared slightly better when they propose less radical, nonincremental changes, such as banning the extension of future civil rights protections to gays. These measures received on average of 48 percent support. Again, voters rejected all but one of the measures in this class—the one approved being rejected by the Supreme Court in *Romer.*

Incrementalist proposals were far more popular, averaging over 60 percent voter support. Indeed, the only place where antigay activists have succeeded in directly reversing policy is through the repeal of protections that had been recently extended to gays in Maine. (Like the 1992 Colorado initiative, the 1988 Oregon measure was rejected by an Oregon court (Donovan and Bowler 1998a, 268).) The propositions in Alaska and Hawaii that received widespread support prevented a change in future marriage policy, and, as such, did not reverse established policy.

THE STRATEGIC ENVIRONMENT FOR BALLOT PROPOSITIONS

The Maine case reveals something of the strategic environment that antigay initiative activists operate within, and illustrates how the same state might reject one antigay measure while passing another.

In 1995 antigay activists in Maine placed a measure on the state ballot that proposed freezing extensions of state and local civil rights protections, and in future only including extensions that embraced the categories of race and sex, thereby effectively denying gays future discrimination protections via state law. The measure would have also overturned local protections adopted by Portland and one other town. Voters rejected this proposal. After the 1995 vote, the state legislature acted to prohibit discrimination based on sexual orientation in housing, employment, public accommodation, and credit. A petition to repeal the new law was quickly qualified by conservative religious groups, including the Christian Civic League and the Christian Coalition of Maine (George 1998). This led to a special 1998 referenda election where voters narrowly approved (by less than five thousand votes) the measure overturning the legislature's new antidiscrimination law.

After this election, Maine became the only state in the country to overturn an existing state gay rights law via direct democracy. The Maine case raises the question of how a state's voters could apparently defend gay rights in one election while rejecting them in a second. One answer to this question illustrates why ballot proposals made by antigay activists might be moving away from attempts at radical policy change and moving toward a more incrementalist approach.

Maine voters were faced with no fewer than three possible choices regarding gay rights between 1995 and 1998. Figure 8.1 illustrates the nature of these choices. Before 1995, status quo policy was that Maine law

Vote Needed to Produce Left, Right, or Status Quo Outcome

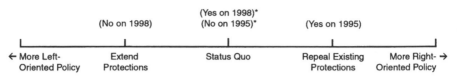

Figure 8.1 Nature of Choices Presented to Main Voters, 1995–1998

provided no protections against discrimination based on sexual orientation—but local governments could pass laws, and nothing prohibited state protections in the future. A "yes" vote on the 1995 ballot measure would have effectively shifted public policy to the right by enacting these prohibitions. In contrast, the Maine Legislature's post-1995 move to protect gays from some forms of discrimination shifted policy away from the status quo, to the left. A "yes" vote on the 1998 Maine referendum would produce a shift back to the right that was effectively a return to the status quo.

The 1998 Maine measure passed, while the 1995 measure failed, for at least two reasons. First, direct democracy voters are often likely to select the status quo policy (the options presented by approving the 1998 referenda and rejecting the 1995 initiative) over proposed departures from it (Bowler and Donovan 1998). It would not be inconsistent, then, for the same Maine voter to vote "yes" in 1998 (an antigay vote) and "no" in 1995 (a progay vote). Second, turnout was quite low in Maine's 1998 special election. With the antigay measure being the only item on the ballot, less than a third of voters came to the polls (George 1998), increasing the chance that politically mobilized Christians composed a disproportionately large share of the electorate.

Evidence from Oregon suggests that the seemingly contradictory electoral outcomes in Maine (one election "progay," another "antigay") might not simply be a function of differences in turnout across elections or shifting mass preferences about gay rights. We suggest that contests in each state illustrate that a large proportion of voters have fairly stable preferences for some status quo course of events.

Figure 8.2 presents a stylized representation of the nature of choices presented by various statewide gay rights ballot measures in Oregon. The Oregon experience demonstrates that antigay initiative proponents per-

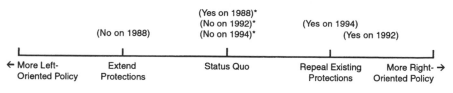

Figure 8.2 Nature of Choices Presented to Oregon Voters, 1988–1994

sisted in proposing measures that might be seen as radical departures from status quo policy, but even Lon Mabon's initiatives displayed some evidence of strategic moderation after 1992. Having repealed the governor's administrative act in 1988, the OCA sought more radical change and proposed Measure 9 in 1992—an attempt to shift a state's status quo policy sharply rightward. After Measure 9's defeat, Mabon and the OCA returned to the ballot in 1994 with an initiative similar to Measure 9, but stripped of some of Measure 9's more inflammatory language in an attempt to make the proposal appear less extremist. Voters approved the 1988 measure, and rejected the 1992 and 1994 measures. Once again, all three elections resulted in the maintenance of status quo gay rights policies.

All of this suggests that if voters are presented with a menu of different gay rights proposals, those policy proposals closest to the status quo will be more likely to pass. Progay and antigay activists thus face a strategic decision about which sort of choices to put before these voters. Experience suggests that antigay forces have more success asking voters to return to some recent status quo than they have asking voters to depart from it.

After the series of state-level defeats in the 1980s and 1990s, antigay activists may be turning to more incremental policy proposals that have a better chance of being marketed as maintaining a status quo. In 1997, for example, activists in several states were circulated petitions banning the recognition of "same-sex" marriages, anticipating that a Hawaii State Supreme Court decision allowing such marriages could require all states to recognize them.[6] Such initiatives would likely be an easier "sell" since they could be framed as defending an existing policy, rather than being seen by many voters as a call for radical change. These marriage-related petition efforts were largely preempted by Congress and by state legislatures eager to defend "traditional" families from any expansion of the definition of marriage. State legislatures in Alaska and Hawaii referred antigay marriage proposals to voters in the Fall of 1998. Legislators responded to anticipated (Hawaii) or actual state court rulings that found same-sex marriage to be protected by state constitutions (Abrahms 1999). The 1998 ballot propositions provided means for amending each state's constitution to prohibit same-sex marriage, and each received support from over two thirds of the states' voters. The Utah-based Mormon Church contributed half a million dollars to the campaign in favor of the Alaska ballot measure (Ruskin 1998).

POLITICAL ENTREPRENEURS AND THE INITIATIVE INDUSTRY

Most antigay initiatives fail, and most of those that pass are rejected by courts (Donovan and Bowler 1998a, 268–69). Moreover, although antigay activists might have some electoral success at the local level, there are reasons to expect that they will have a more difficult time convincing a larger electorate to treat gays unfavorably. For example, it has been demonstrated that progay rights measures are more likely to be adopted in larger political jurisdictions (Wald, Button, and Rienzo 1996), in part because minorities such as gays and lesbians are less likely to be victims of majority tyranny in larger, more socially heterogeneous, jurisdictions. Empirically, antigay measures are far more likely to pass in small localities than at the state level (Donovan and Bowler 1998b). Yet antigay activists continue to file proposals.

On one level this presents a puzzle: why would antigay activists persist in such attempts? We do not intend to understate the moral incentives, ideological motivations, and antigay animosity that might also drive these antigay initiative proponents. But at least part of the explanation for such persistence may lie in the opportunities the initiative process provides for political entrepreneurs to begin to mobilize support and build political capital.

The initiative process provides opportunities for entrepreneurial, non-mainstream politicians (from the left, right, or center) to gain access to political resources they might otherwise be denied. These resources, including media attention, an expanded base of contributors, and major opportunities to frame public debate about policy issues, allow these politicians to build a stock of political capital that can be used in future political battles. We suggest that this creates incentives for circulating petitions that go beyond the short-term prospect of electoral success, creating a situation where there are established groups in some states ready to file antigay rights ballot measures. Antigay activists are neither the first, nor the most prominent, to use the process as a vehicle for wider political ambitions. Perhaps the most famous entrepreneur of recent years was not someone associated with antigay initiatives but with taxation—Howard Jarvis.

Jarvis gained fame for authoring Proposition 13, the landmark 1978 California property tax-cut initiative that precipitated a national tax revolt (Sears and Citrin 1982). Before 1978, Jarvis may have had genuine "populist" roots, promoting other less-known, low-budget antitax causes before Proposition 13. Experienced campaign professionals even say that his 1978 campaign may have been the last vestige of "grassroots" direct democracy in California (McCuan et al. 1998), but even his 1978 effort relied upon the professional campaign industry and well-financed interests, to the point that Smith (1998) categorizes entrepreneurs such as Jarvis as *"faux* populists." After 1978, Jarvis and his associates made a professional, profitable business out of ballot initiatives. Through a series of initiative petition efforts, he developed a base of supporters who could be continually targeted with directed mail fund-raising appeals in future campaigns. Jarvis's organization also supplied "content" for a booming initiative industry that would guarantee ballot qualification of any "citizen's" initiative if the proponent was able and willing to pay the cost of gathering signatures. By the 1990s, the minimum costs for this was over $500,000 per initiative in California. (Lee 1997; Bowler, Donovan, and Fernandez 1996).

Jarvis clearly affected public policy through his initiative efforts. But, regardless of policy effects, direct democracy provided him the arena in which to be a successful political entrepreneur and establish himself as an political figure nationally. This provided, among other things, the opportunity to maintain an enduring political organization. Jarvis was not alone as a direct democracy political entrepreneur—environmentalists, consumer advocates, term-limit activists, and others have sustained themselves in politics by maintaining organizations skilled at playing the game of initiative politics.

Antigay activists have not been able to use initiatives to attain the same level of national stature that Jarvis had in the early 1980s, but it does appear that some rely upon the direct democracy arena to sustain their own personal visibility and generate momentum for their political organizations. Lon Mabon is the primary example. While attracting national attention (and financial resources) with his antigay initiatives in Oregon, Mabon's OCA attempted to secure control of the state's Republican party. It also established political organizations in neighboring states (the Idaho Citizens' Alliance and Citizens' Alliance of Washington) during this period for the purpose of qualifying antigay measures in those states. The Idaho measure, sponsored by former OCA official Kelly Walton (Witt and McCorkle 1997), was narrowly defeated, and the Washington petitions failed to attract sufficient signatures.

Although they have not passed a single state initiative in the 1990s, in one respect the OCA's efforts have paid off rather handsomely. In addition to their base of small contributors, the OCA reportedly became one of the top beneficiaries of LifeLine, a Christian long-distance telephone company. The company claims that AT&T, MCI, and Sprint support the "homosexual movement," the "homosexual lifestyle," and sponsor "gay friendly" events.[7] LifeLine directs their marketing appeals to Christians who would prefer to have their long-distance dollars going to "those organizations serving Christ and building His Kingdom."[8] The company says it returns 10 percent of its customers' bills to conservative, pro-Christian organizations (including Christian Coalitions and over forty "right-to-life" groups) and that $250,000 per month goes to its top twelve recipients (an average of over $20,000 per month, per group). In addition to the OCA, LifeLine's top twelve list includes The Rutherford Institute (an organization that attracted attention for funding Paula Jones's legal team in her civil suit against President Bill Clinton and for promoting the conspiratorial idea that a cocaine-addicted Clinton had Vincent Foster killed in order to hide an affair Foster allegedly had with Hillary Clinton).[9]

Lacking the level of access to mainstream media that incumbent elected officials and representatives of major religious organization might enjoy, politicians such as Mabon and Lyndon Larouche can remain in the public eye by occasionally proposing new ballot initiatives. The announcement of newly drafted initiatives, the attention of associated initiative petition drives, as well as a possible campaign (if the measure qualifies), are all opportunities for building the political capital of enhanced public visibility and an expanded base of potential contributors.

The process can also provide advantages for marginalized politicians like Dannemeyer or Briggs. Antigay initiatives can increase their public visibility among "core supporters"—particularly those who will be contacted for campaign contributions in any bid the politician might make for higher office. In fact, a majority of the thirteen antigay state ballot measures were sponsored or advocated by politicians who sought higher elected office soon after their respective antigay campaigns. John Briggs and William Dannemeyer sought the Republican nomination for the U.S. Senate in

California in different years, and Lon Mabon ran in the 1996 Republican U.S. Senate primary in Oregon. Larouche continued to run for President. Gary Bauer, a conservative Christian activist and eventual presidential candidate, used his Washington, D.C.-based American Renewal group[10] to raise $50,000 for the campaign to pass Alaska's same-sex marriage ban (Ruskin 1998). None of these candidates won a nomination.

At this point we should consider the use of direct democracy from the point of view of progay groups. After all, if there are rewards that flow to those who promote initiatives, then in principle at least we should be just as likely to see rival entrepreneurs sponsoring as many progay initiatives as antigay ones. But we do not. Before moving to consider the impact of *Romer*, then, we should address the question of this imbalance between the use of the initiative by progay and antigay groups.

With the notable exceptions of Prohibitionists and the women's movement early in the twentieth century (Banaszak 1996), and perhaps environmentalists in the last part of the century, most modern initiatives are not the product of social movements promoting their goals. Outside of these striking examples, however, more contemporary attempts have probably been made to use direct democracy as a roadblock than as a vehicle for the advancement of minority interests. In part, of course, this is definitional. As a majoritarian institution, direct democracy requires majorities of voters to support a particular policy and, by definition, minority groups are disadvantaged. Because of this we are less likely to see attempts to build entrepreneurial movements around minorities, unless active antiminority efforts can attract majority support. As we have seen, this has been harder for antigay groups to accomplish than might be thought at first.

But, in part, the relative infrequency of attempts to mobilize around progay initiatives may reflect a strategic choice by a minority group that finds pursuing their cause through the legal process a more successful one. The judicial arena, after all, is one where minority rights are entrenched, while the arena of direct democracy is one where majority rule prevails. As many feared, the initiative process has been the scene of repeated attempts to roll back a variety of social gains, and not just those made by gays. To a considerable extent the courts have played their role as they should as protectors of minority rights and repeatedly defused or overturned attempts to reverse social advances made by a variety of groups. And, again, this pattern is not restricted to the battles over gay rights, as court decisions over California's anti-immigration Proposition 187 show.

Romer shows one example of how courts operate as a bulwark in favor of gay minority rights and could, in principle, greatly shape the incentives facing antigay groups.

ROMER V. EVANS

From 1992 to 1995, antigay activists filed initiative petitions in Arizona, Colorado, Florida, Idaho, Maine, Mississippi, Missouri, Nevada, Oregon, and Washington to ban or repeal laws that protected gays and lesbians from discrimination.[11] One of the major slogans used to attract signatures (placed directly on official petitions) was "equal rights, not special rights," the implication being that the extension of antidiscrimination protections to certain classes of citizens constituted an extraordinary legal status to which most people were not entitled.[12] The overt argument was that although race, religion, and gender might constitute necessary categories of citizens requiring protections against discrimination, sexual orientation did not. Sponsors of antigay initiatives argued if that ugly people and short people suffered from discrimination yet were protected only by existing laws, why should homosexuals require "special" protections?

Sponsors of Colorado's Amendment 2 also argued that the law merely prevented "special rights" from being extended to gays and lesbians. As noted above, Colorado voters approved the initiative, which overturned local protections against discrimination based on sexual orientation in housing, employment, education, public accommodations, health and welfare, and other services. Prior to 1992, a small number of Colorado communities (including Aspen, Boulder, and Denver) had adopted such ordinances. The initiative amended the state constitution in banning action by any Colorado governmental agency (legislative, executive and judicial) that would protect persons from discrimination based on their "homosexual, lesbian or bisexual orientation, conduct, practices or relationships."[13] Amendment 2 eliminated the handful of existing local ordinances that offered protections based on sexual orientation, but, more importantly, it placed an absolute bar to the ability of gays, lesbians, and bisexuals to seek such protection in the future. Indeed, with the passage of Amendment 2, the only recourse open to this newly created class of persons was to appeal to the same Colorado voters for another constitutional amendment to overturn Amendment 2.

Local communities and gay and lesbian citizens affected by the initiative (including Richard Evans, an employee of the City of Denver, and tennis player Martina Navratilova) appealed to the Colorado courts, arguing that the initiative was an unconstitutional denial of equal protection. The Colorado Supreme Court ruled in favor of the gays and lesbians holding that "the Equal Protection Clause of the Fourteenth Amendment to the United States Constitution protects a fundamental right to participate equally in the political process" and "that any legislation or state constitutional amendment which infringes on this right by 'fencing out' an independently identifiable class of persons must be subject to strict judicial scrutiny."[14]

The Fourteenth Amendment's equal protection clause requires that governments (local, state, and federal) treat citizens in similar ways and requires that states defend any law that treats citizens differently by classifying them into groups (based on age, gender, race, etc.). Governments nonetheless frequently classify people into groups for the purposes of conferring benefits and exacting penalties. For example, under most circumstances Social Security benefits are available only to those over the age of sixty-five. Similarly, the Federal Aviation Administration imposes a mandatory retirement age for airline pilots and welfare recipients must meet income and work requirements. In general laws of this sort, whether adopted via initiative or by a legislature, are constitutional provided they have some "rational relationship" to a government objective (e.g., maintaining the solvency of the Social Security system or promoting airline safety). This "rational basis" standard requires only that the government be able to identify a reasonable objective of a policy and demonstrate that the policy is rationally related to the achievement of the stated goal. As a matter of policy, the Supreme Court has been unwilling to second guess these sorts of governmental actions, even those that are demonstrably unwise or unfair.

Problems arise, however, when government seeks to classify individuals on the basis of "suspect" criteria, the most obvious of which is race. Statutes or policies based on these "suspect classifications" must withstand a much stricter degree of judicial scrutiny. Rather than simply needing to demonstrate a rational relationship to a governmental objective, "if they [suspect classifications] are ever to be upheld, they must be shown to be *necessary* to the accomplishment of some permissible state objective, independent of the racial discrimination of which it was the object of the Fourteenth Amendment to eliminate" [emphasis added] (*Loving* 1967, 11). Notice that no longer must the policy simply be rationally related to the achievement of a legitimate state end: it must be *necessary* to the achievement of the goal. The Court has gone further still, ruling that not only must the state's interest be legitimate, it must be *compelling*. Thus, for a race-based statute to withstand "strict scrutiny" the state must show that the law was the least restrictive means of accomplishing a compelling state interest.

In deciding *Evans* the Colorado Supreme Court, rather than declaring sexual orientation a "suspect class," identified a fundamental right: the "right to participate equally in the political process," and then held Amendment 2 to a strict standard of judicial scrutiny. The state was unable to demonstrate that Amendment 2 was the least restrictive means of accomplishing a compelling state interest and a Colorado trial court held the amendment unconstitutional. The Colorado Supreme Court affirmed the trial court's decision.

Colorado appealed the state supreme court decision to the U. S. Supreme Court, arguing among other things that the statute did not offend the Fourteenth Amendment because it did not deprive the gay community of anything. Rather, the state contended, by denying special rights to gays, lesbians, and bisexuals Amendment 2 simply put them on the same legal footing as all other citizens of Colorado. Moreover, if these individuals found themselves in need of some sort of protection they could avail themselves of the general protections available to any citizen of Colorado. Indeed, the state argued, to preclude discrimination of gays on the part of employers and landlords was to in effect interfere with employers' and landlords' freedom of association and their free exercise of religion.

The U.S. Supreme Court was not persuaded and in 1996 ruled 6–3 that the Colorado law violated the equal protection clause of the Fourteenth Amendment. Rejecting the state's arguments. The majority wrote:

> In any event, even if, as we doubt, homosexuals can find some safe harbor in laws of general application, we cannot accept the view that Amendment 2's prohibition on specific protections does no more than deprive homosexuals of special rights. To the contrary, the amendment imposes a special disability upon those persons alone. Homosexuals are forbidden the safeguards that others enjoy or may seek without constraint. (*Romer* 1996, 1626)

Perhaps more interesting for our purposes is the rationale Justice Kennedy employed in rejecting Amendment 2. Recall that the Colorado Supreme Court had held Amendment 2 up to strict scrutiny, demanding that the policy address a compelling state interest in the least restrictive manner possible. Justice Kennedy, however, scrupulously avoided the use of a strict scrutiny standard. Rather, he stated:

We have attempted to reconcile the principle with reality by stating that, if a law neither burdens a fundamental right nor targets a suspect class, we will uphold the legislative classification so long as it bears a rational relation to some legitimate end.

Amendment 2 fails, indeed defies, even this conventional inquiry. First the amendment has the peculiar property of imposing a broad and undifferentiated disability on a named group, an exceptional, and as we shall explain, invalid form of legislation. Second, its sheer breadth is so discontinuous with the reasons offered for it that the amendment seems inexplicable by anything but animus toward the class that it affects; it lacks a rational relationship to legitimate state interests. (1627)

What is Justice Kennedy trying to tell us in *Romer?* Is he telling us that provisions such as Amendment 2 place an unconstitutional burden on the fundamental right to participate in the political process, while simultaneously targeting a suspect class of citizens? We think not. Rather, the flaws the Court finds with Amendment 2 seem to be that the state has imposed a broad sanction on a particular segment of society and cannot offer a rational explanation tying Amendment 2's political excommunication of homosexuals to some legitimate state interest. Perhaps what is most interesting in the *Romer* majority's opinion are its rather conspicuous silences. The status of a "right to participate equally in the political process" that figured so prominently in the Colorado court's opinion is simply not at issue, nor is the Court willing to extend "suspect class" status to gays, lesbians, and bisexuals.

Justice Kennedy takes a dim view of what he considers the animosity toward homosexuals that underlies Amendment 2. The majority's somewhat tepid support for the political rights of homosexuals stands in contrast to the position taken by the dissenters. In his dissent, Justice Scalia attached a very limited scope to Amendment 2, concluding that it "prohibits *special treatment* of homosexuals and nothing more." Contending that homosexuals possess a degree of political influence that is far out of proportion to their numbers, Justice Scalia states that "Coloradans are . . . *entitled* to be hostile toward homosexual conduct" (1630) and on the basis of that hostility to use the initiative process to "counter both the geographic concentration and the disproportionate political power of homosexuals" (1633).

The broad sanctions against homosexuals found in Amendment 2 and the lack of any rational explanation for the sanctions put the initiative (and others like it) directly in violation of the equal protection clause. By extension, similar initiatives from Idaho, Maine (1995), and Oregon (1994) would have been declared unconstitutional had they passed. Although this decision cannot compel any legislature to extend categorical protections to gays, it makes it rather more difficult for antigay activists to use a state's initiative process to reverse protections against discrimination granted by local governments. The decision is also important because of its forceful rejection of the main argument that antigay initiative proponents had been using from 1992 to 1995. According to the Court, allowing a class of citizens to seek protection from government does not constitute "special rights."

In sum, the Court found that Amendment 2 suffered from two flaws: First, it singled gays out for special attention. This in and of itself may well not have proved problematic had the burden posed by the amendment been structured more narrowly. The combination of singling out homosexuals and then imposing what amounted to an absolute bar to the group's access to the political arena simply pushed the majority too far. As a result, the decision in *Romer* was extremely narrow: in essence, it forbids states from foreclosing gays from using the political process.

This line of reasoning has two major implications. First, it is easy to imagine a somewhat less restrictive yet still quite broad policy, or one that deals with a less sensitive topic, that would pick up the support of at least two or three of the justices in the *Romer* majority. Consider *Bowers v. Hardwick*, for example. Justice White's majority opinion focused almost exclusively on what he perceived as a request to grant Constitutional protection to the practice of homosexual sodomy. This, of course, he refused to do. Never mind that heterosexuals might engage in sodomy—the idea of homosexuals doing so was sufficiently troublesome that White was unable to accept the privacy issue that formed the basis of Hardwick's claim. This example is notable because it signaled the Court's willingness to allow homosexuals to be singled out for the imposition of burdens not applied to heterosexuals thus implying that there is still scope for legal challenges to claims of gay rights.

Second, the Court's decision in *Bowers* still appears to have strong support among the justices. In the briefs filed by Evans in *Romer* a discussion of the possibility of overturning *Bowers* was conspicuous by its absence. In oral arguments, the Court questioned how its ruling on *Bowers* would be affected by a decision in favor of Evans, but Evans's attorneys took great pains to distance themselves from any discussion of *Bowers*, a fact Justice Scalia was careful to point out in his dissent.[15]

Romer seems to have little to say about the use of the initiative process to incrementally roll back advances homosexuals may make through the legislature. The problem with Amendment 2 was not that progay attempts to influence policy failed, but that they were foreclosed from the attempt in the first place. Assuming for the moment that the legislatures (or city councils) are responsive to progay attempts to alter policy, there seems to be nothing in *Romer* that would prevent antigay forces from continuing to use the initiative process to incrementally roll those gains back to the status quo ante.

Although this ruling will limit the use a specific category of state and local antigay initiatives (those patterned after Amendment 2), it will not end the initiative efforts of antigay political entrepreneurs completely, since the legal door has not been fully closed to antigay laws, provided they are crafted with more care than Amendment 2. It is to the politics of antigay movements post-*Romer* we turn next.

ANTIGAY INITIATIVE POLITICS AFTER ROMER

We have suggested that antiminority initiatives tend to come in cycles of backlash against the political success of various minority groups. As a cycle, these efforts tend to have a distinct beginning and end. They begin when political activists who resist recent minority gains in legislatures take to the initiative process. Efforts via the initiative are often relatively short-lived, however. For example, Court rejection of a 1978 Washington state school desegregation initiative ended a wave of initiatives on ballots in this arena. Five statewide initiatives attacking desegregation of housing and public accommodations appeared between 1964 and 1968, but Supreme Court rulings (*Reitman* 1967) and federal legislation in the late 1960s superseded these and future initiatives of this type. Five statewide "English only" measures appeared on state ballots from 1986 to 1988, but none have appeared since a Supreme Court ruling directed the issue back to the Arizona courts (*Arizonans* 1997). Given this historical experience, we might expect that the *Romer* decision could spell the end of initiatives attacking gay rights.

Given the greater frequency of local ballot proposals, it is worth examining state and local cases in order to detect trends in the use of antigay ballot measures. As shown in figure 8.3 (which does *not* include measures that would have expanded gay rights), a fairly consistent number of ballot measures designed to restrict the rights of gays and lesbians were initiated between 1978 and 1992, with a peak after the 1992 Colorado and Oregon

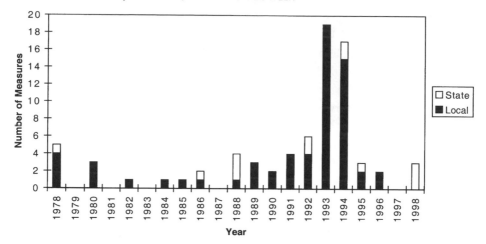

Figure 8.3 Frequency of State and Local Antigay Ballot Measures
SOURCE: Haider-Markel 1997.

initiatives appeared. This post-1992 surge in activity reflects the nationalization of efforts by antigay groups noted above, and by a large number
of local measures appearing in Oregon in 1993 and 1994 that were copied
from the statewide initiative (Measure 9) that voters rejected in 1992. The
OCA placed local versions of Measure 9 in towns and counties where
the state initiative had received substantial support. After 1994, we see a
marked decline in antigay ballot activity. This trend, combined with the
Romer decision, might suggest that America's experience with antigay ballot measures might have run its course.

Yet figure 8.3 also illustrates that antigay measures have not disappeared
after *Romer*. Although *Romer* might make it difficult to ban gays from *seeking* civil rights protections from legislatures, there are numerous areas of
policy that antigay activists appear poised to target with initiatives. Initiative petitions challenging gay adoptions were filed in Washington and other
states but failed to qualify. In mid-1999, state affiliates of Focus on the
Family mobilized contributors to fund "action to stop the homosexual
assault on schoolchildren, marriage and society." At issue were policies
that affected gay and lesbian adoption, discussion of same-sex marriage
in school curriculum, and gay and lesbian clubs in public schools. State
legislatures in Alaska and Hawaii referred antimarriage propositions to voters in November 1998. Had other legislatures and the U.S. Congress not
passed various "Defense of Marriage Act" (DOMA) laws in 1997 and 1998

several additional initiatives could have appeared on state ballots addressing gay marriages in 1998.

Despite the results of marriage referendums in Alaska and Hawaii, there is evidence suggesting that other state's electorates might not be as quick to prohibit legal status for gay and lesbian families. Opinion polls from California found that 60 percent of voters were opposed to gays having "regular" marriages. Yet almost 66 percent of these respondents favored "granting legal recognition to domestic partners in the areas of family rights such as hospital visitation rights, medical power of attorney and conservatorship" and six in ten supported granting financial benefits to domestic partners (Trounstine 1997). It is not certain, or even likely, that an initiative banning the recognition of Hawaii's gay marriages would have passed in California. While the legislature addressed the issue in March 1997, only 49 percent of survey respondents supported a proposed law banning the Hawaii marriages (Trounstine 1997), and the "Yes" side in an initiative contest nearly always loses support over the course of an actual campaign (Bowler and Donovan 1994, 1998). Likewise, polls found strong opposition to Oregon's proposed DOMA in April 1997 (*The Oregonian* 1997). After three divisive antigay initiative campaigns in that state, only 37 percent of that state's voters reported being in favor of the proposed Oregon DOMA.

After most antimarriage ballot petitions are rendered moot—not by court action or higher-level policies preventing such initiatives, but by elites embracing the antigay policies—opponents of gay rights can move on to other proposals. At the state and local level, antigay activists can continue their incrementalist attempts at repealing recent gains made by gays and lesbians, particularly as more communities move to adopt domestic partner ordinances and antidiscrimination policies. A 1997 referenda petition in Santa Clara County, California succeeded in suspending such an ordinance (Trounstine 1997). Antigay activists used petitions in 1998 to force public votes on antidiscrimination ordinances passed in Fayetteville, Arkansas and Ft. Collins, Colorado (voters rejected both, overturning each city's ordinances). *Romer* appears only to bar initiatives that deny gays and lesbians from seeking the regular "protections" that all citizens enjoy from government. The Supreme Court's refusal to grant certiorari in an appeal of the 6th Circuit's decision about a 1993 Cincinatti initiative (*Equality Foundation* 1998) allows, de facto, that initiatives limited to banning "special" status for gays and lesbians are constitutional. Unless the courts subsequently rule that *Romer* somehow also prevents these measures and those repealing progay policies on a piecemeal basis, *Romer* cannot bring an end to the politics of antigay ballot measures.

SOCIAL AND POLITICAL EFFECTS OF ANTIGAY INITIATIVES

Up to this point we have noted that although few of these initiatives pass, antigay activists continue to promote them as part and parcel of entrepreneurial attempts to become "players." Despite incentives—both entrepreneurial and moral—to propose such propositions that go beyond short-term ballot success, such groups do need success if they expect to remain politically active over the long haul. The relative moderation of recent ballot proposals can be understood as attempts to produce some (albeit incremental) success in affecting policy.

But the effects of ballot campaigns are not restricted to the groups that propose them, nor to public policies: there are also important consequences for the mass public, for gays and lesbians, and for states that experience these campaigns. One of the more frequently cited consequences, according to those who contest these initiatives, is that violence against gays and lesbians might increase in states during antigay campaigns (Associated Press 1998; Agler 1993; National Gay and Lesbian Task Force 1997). Systematic research on this is lacking, however.

Another consequence relates to the effect initiative campaigns have on mass opinions about minority groups targeted by an initiative. Many scholars of public opinion assume that mass attitudes are malleable during election campaigns and are therefore shaped by elites in politics and the media (Converse 1964; Key 1966). This being the case, elite rhetoric about initiatives targeting gays can be expected to affect people's opinions about gays. Depending upon the intensity of a particular campaign, citizens can be exposed to information that alters their opinions about people who are made the subjects of the campaign (Converse 1962; Zaller 1992).

Other studies show that vote decisions about initiatives are influenced by positions taken by elites (Lupia 1994; Karp 1998). We have found that antigay ballot initiatives typically fail at the state level when major Democrat and Republican elites (party leaders, governors, U.S. senators) are united and unequivocal in their condemnation of the measure (Donovan and Bowler 1997). In the case of the Colorado measure that passed and the Idaho initiative that nearly passed, major state-level officials from the Republican Party either endorsed the antigay initiative or remained silent about it.[16]

Partisan exploitation of this issue can change how people think about gays and how they think about policies affecting gays. For example, Zaller (1991, 1992) notes that if elite messages display clear partisan differences, then the public can be expected to respond in a manner consistent with messages supplied by elites they identify with. Shifts in national opinions about gays from 1992 to 1994 suggest that Republican voters did respond to antigay cues from their party. It has been shown that Republican Party voters nationally shifted to opinions less tolerant of "gay and lesbian lifestyles" and that the effect was most pronounced among GOP voters in states where antigay initiatives were filed (Wenzel, Donovan, and Bowler 1998). Hence one of the more important consequences might be the least visible.

Initiatives and referenda have long been advocated by populists who see it as the "gun behind the door" of the legislature. Initiatives exist, the reasoning goes, to prod a legislature into passing laws elected officials might not like but the public nevertheless want, such as term limits and tax rebates (Lascher, Hagen, and Rochlin 1996). It has been shown that the mere existence of the initiative device can affect the mix of policies that elected officials adopt (or do not adopt) across the 50 states (Gerber 1996; Matsusaka 1995). By this reasoning, it is the threat of a possible initiative and the legislature's anticipation of initiatives, rather than actual initiatives that appear on ballots, that ultimately affects state policy. Knowing the "gun is behind the door," elected officials in initiative states take greater care to insure they are passing policies that will not be challenged by citizen legislation. Initiative processes, even if seldom used, might thus drive a state's public policies closer to actual mass preferences. The rush of many state's legislatures to pass DOMA-like policies could have thus been accelerated in some places by antigay activists threatening to circulate marriage policy initiatives.

As far as public policies are concerned, there is little to be feared from this indirect effect of initiatives if the state's electorate is reasonably tolerant of homosexuals. Legislators would move toward mass preferences in anticipation of the public's vote on possible initiatives, and antigay initiatives that actually make the ballot would fail. If, however, a state's electorate is less than tolerant, then it is not only actual initiatives that reach ballots, but legislative anticipation of the threat of initiative that can possibly lead to state gay rights policies that are less tolerant of gays and offer fewer protections. This potential for indirect influence on policy, coupled with evidence that campaigns can move mass opinions about groups targeted by initiatives, are perhaps the most serious consequences of state-level antigay initiatives. We can conceive of some states where antigay political entrepreneurs use the threat of initiatives, not simply to pass laws, but rather to mobilize mass opinion against further extension of rights to gays and lesbians while constraining the range of policy remedies available via the legislature.

CONCLUSION

We have argued that *Romer* should alter but not eliminate the presence of antigay measures from state ballots. As we have noted here, and as other chapters also illustrate, there is an enduring, organized opposition to homosexuality and gay rights in America. The citizen's initiative is only one of its political tools, but it is one that provides them with substantial public visibility. Like other groups that have operated in America outside of the political mainstream, direct democracy is an effective vehicle for attempting to shape public policy. The initiative has populist roots, after all, and was designed to allow groups with limited access to the legislature (e.g. prohibitionists, environmentalists, social reformers) to nevertheless affect the policy agenda.

Conservative, politicized Christians appear to be well positioned for using the initiative as a method for advancing their policy goals. Although they have some supporters in many legislatures, in most states they are unable to control the legislative agenda. As a result, present and future antigay activists are likely to seek "outsider" tactics such as the popular referenda and the citizen's initiative. This does not mean that they can pass many state initiatives. We have shown that only the more incrementalist proposals seem to be approved by a majority of voters. And in the future, only those strategically tailored to avoid conflict with the *Romer* ruling will have any chance of serious consideration.

But passing initiatives, and using the initiative to shape public debate and opinions about homosexuality, are different matters. Up to the late 1990s, Christian political entrepreneurs have dominated the use of initiatives and set much of the tone for statewide discourse about gay rights in many states. There is evidence, however, that this might be changing. In 1997 advocates of gay rights qualified a statewide antidiscrimination initiative in Washington State, and in 1998 local groups qualified similar antidiscrimination ordinances for local ballots in two Maine communities.[17] These measures would protect gays from discrimination in employment and housing (with exceptions granted for religious institutions in Washington). Although voters rejected the Washington measure, some proponents were hopeful that by placing a progay issue on the ballot, they could recapture control of public discussion about civil rights. Other gay and lesbian activists in the state, however, feared that placing the issue on the ballot would only serve to create a lightning rod for further conflict. Voters in South Portland, Maine approved that city's 1998 antidiscrimination ordinance, while Ogunquit, Maine narrowly defeated another.

Initiatives have had more success shaping public policy in another area of concern to some gay men: medical use of marijuana. The coauthor of California's successful 1996 medical marijuana initiative, Dennis Peron, claimed the initiative was motivated by a need to provide legal access to marijuana for chronically ill patients. He wrote Proposition 215 after his lover died of AIDS, and most of the twelve thousand members of his Cannabis Buyers Club are people with AIDS or HIV (Booth 1997). Peron enlisted many members of the club in the initiative campaign and estimates that most of the people working on behalf of the California initiative and another Arizona initiative (that also passed) were gay men (Ferguson 1997).

Although Peron saw medical marijuana as a political issue of major concern for the gay community, the fact that gays were active on the initiative was kept low-key during the campaign in order that the medical question not be seen as a gay issue. By keeping the issue defined this way, Peron was able to use the statewide initiative to shape public policy—something that antigay activists have had little success at. These campaigns in Washington and California illustrate that gay and lesbian political activists need not always regard statewide initiatives as something that they must only defended against, but rather something that can be used to shape policy proactively.

NOTES

1. Petitions may place original legislation on a ballot or refer bills passed by a legislature to voters.
2. Early polls can be a poor measure of outcomes on ballot initiatives. See Magleby (1989) and Bowler and Donovan (1994).
3. The draft ballot title read: "Amends Constitution: Government-Approved Family May Include Only Man/Woman Marriage, Children." <www.sos. state.or.us/elections>. Accessed March 28, 1998.
4. In 1992, CFV's Colorado Springs-based advisory board included Focus on the Family's Randy Hicks, in addition to University of Colorado football coach Bill McCartney and U.S. Senator Bill Armstrong. McCartney gained national

    attention as the leader of the Promise Keeper's, a Christian men's movement that held revival meetings in sports arenas. See White (1992).

5. This compares to a 38-percent pass rate for all state initiatives from 1898 through 1992 (Magleby 1994).

6. The Constitution's full faith and credit clause (article 4, sec. 1) requires mutual recognition of other states laws. Anticipating the Hawaii Court's ruling, the state's Senate and House voted in March of 1997 to ban same-sex marriages, but the Senate bill extended the benefits of marriage to people that could not apply for marriage.

7. This includes sponsoring the TV programs "Married with Children" and "Rosanne," sponsoring the Gay Games in New York and observing Gay and Lesbian Awareness Week. In March 1998, the company's description was posted at its own website: <upstel.net/~cld/why.html>.

8. This according to the company's posting in March of 1998 at <upstel.net/~cld/about.html>

9. The Rutherford Institute maintains a website at <www.rutherford.org>. Background on the institute's activity with antigay causes and with Paula Jones is archived online at *Salon Magazine,* accessible at <www.salon.com/search/>. Accessed March 28 1998.

10. Bauer's organization was also reported as being the Washington, D.C.–based Campaign for Working Families.

11. The Arizona, Mississippi, Missouri, Nevada, and Washington initiative petitions failed to attract enough signatures for ballot listing. The Florida initiative was struck down by that state's court prior to any election.

12. The sponsor of Washington's Initiative 608 incorporated as "Equal Rights, Not Special Rights." For examples of initiatives formally using this language, see Washington's I-166 and I-669, archived at: <leginfo.leg.wa.gov/pub/billinfo/initiatives/>. Some media coverage also adopted the proponent's "special rights" terminology (Larrabbee 1995).

13. Amendment 2, titled "No Protected Status Based on Homosexual, Lesbian, or Bisexual Orientation," reads:

> Neither the State of Colorado, through any of its branches or departments, nor any of its agencies, political subdivisions, municipalities or school districts, shall enact, adopt or enforce and statute, regulation, ordinance or policy whereby homosexual, lesbian, or bisexual orientation, conduct, practices or relationships shall constitute of otherwise be the basis of or entitle any person or class of persons to have or to claim any minority status, quota preferences, protected status or claim of discrimination. This Section of the Constitution shall be in all respects self-executing. (Colorado Const. art. 2, sec. 30b)

14. *Evans v. Romer,* 882 P.2d 1335, 1339 (Colo. 1994) (*Evans II*), *citing Evans v. Romer,* 854 P.2d 1270, 1282 (Colo. App. 1993) (*Evans I*).)

15. Another major thread in the dissent noted that a number of states have made a point of specifically outlawing the practice of polygamy. Again, Justice Scalia made a point of noting that when it comes to restricting practices of this sort, states are well within their rights to do so. In light of this consider what might occur should the Court be called on to hear a challenge to a state or federal Defense of Marriage Act. From a strategic standpoint, Justice Scalia has three votes (his and those of Justices Rehnquist and Thomas) to start and must pick up only two more to complete a majority. His dissent in *Romer* goes a long way toward laying the foundation for doing so. Thus it is not difficult to imagine a challenge to a DOMA-like statute failing by a 5-4 or 6-3 vote.

16. In Idaho, some Republican officials and party leaders refused to speak against that state's initiative. Some lobbied the state GOP to prevent it from taking a position against the initiative (Donovan and Bowler 1997). Prior to the Colorado campaign, Colorado Senator Bill Armstrong (a CFV supporter) was reported to have written a letter (made public) calling gays and lesbians "a grave threat" (White 1992).

17. In Ogunquit, Maine, the ordinance reached the ballot as a result of an initiative by gay rights activists. In South Portland, Maine, council members referred the ordinance to voters. Two other gay rights measures appearing in November 1998 were qualified by petitions organized by antigay groups challenging ordinances passed by councils in Fayetteville, Arkansas and Ft. Collins, Colorado.

REFERENCES

Abrahms, Yvonne. 1999. Harvard conference focuses on obstacles to gay marriage. *Boston Globe,* 14 February, B5.

Agler, Elizabeth. 1993. Antigay initiative campaign threat cited: Increase in hate crimes sets stage for campaign. *Idaho Statesman,* 4 June.

Arizonans for Official English v. Arizona, 117 S. Ct. 1055 (1997).

Associated Press. 1998. Intolerance in Maine. *Boston Globe* (web edition). 5 March, 21:35. <www.globe.com>.

Banaszak, Lee Ann. 1996. *Why movements succeed or fail: Opportunity, culture and the struggle for women's suffrage.* Princeton: Princeton University Press.

Beggs, Charles. 1996. Antigay ballot initiative dropped in Oregon. *Boston Globe* (web edition). 6 June. <www.globe.com>.

Bell, Derrick. 1978. The referendum: Direct democracy's barrier to racial equality. *University of Washington Law Review* 54:1–29.

Booth, William. 1997. At this club, the third floor is high. *Washington Post.* 21 January, A03.

Bowers v. Hardwick, 478 U.S. 186 (1986).

Bowler, Shaun B., and Todd D. Donovan. 1994. Opinion change on ballot propositions. *Political Behavior* 16:411–35.

———. 1998. *Demanding choice: Opinion and voting in direct democracy.* Ann Arbor: University of Michigan Press.

Bowler, Shaun B., Todd Donovan, and Ken Fernandez. 1996. Political marketing and the California initiative industry. *European Journal of Marketing* 30 (10/11): 173–85.

Citrin, Jack. 1990. Language politics and American identity. *Public Interest* 99: 96–109.

Citrin, Jack, Beth Reingold, Evelyn Walters, and Donald P. Green. 1990. The "Official English" movement and the symbolic politics of language in the United States. *Western Political Quarterly* 43:535–60.

Converse, Philip. 1962. Information flow and the stability of partisan attitudes. *Public Opinion Quarterly* 26:578–99.

———. 1964. The nature of belief systems in mass publics. In *Ideology and discontent,* edited by David Apter. New York: Free Press.

Cronin, Thomas. 1989. *Direct democracy: The politics of initiative, referendum and recall.* Cambridge: Harvard University Press.

Donovan, Todd, and Shaun Bowler. 1997. Direct democracy and minority rights: opinions on antigay and lesbian ballot initiatives. In *Antigay initiatives,* edited by Stephanie L. Witt and Suzanne McCorkle. Greenwood, Conn.: Praeger.

———. 1998a. Responsive or responsible government? In *Citizens as legislators: Direct democracy in the United States,* edited by Shaun Bowler, Todd Donovan, and Caroline Tolbert. Columbus: Ohio State University Press.

———. 1998b. Direct democracy and minority rights: An extension. *American Journal of Political Science* 42 (3), July.

Equality Foundation of Greater Cincinnati, Inc. v. City of Cincinnati, 128 F.3d 289 (6th Cir. 1997), *cert. denied,* No. 97-1795 (October 13, 1998).

Evans v. Romer, 882 P.2d 1335 (Colo. 1994).

Ferguson, Sarah. 1996. The battle for medical marijuana: A home-grown reform movement is beginning to challenge the status quo. *Nation.* 6 January.

Gamble, Barbara. 1997. Putting civil rights to a popular vote. *American Journal of Political Science* 41:245–69.

George, Robert. 1998. Gay rights supporters regrouping in Maine. *Boston Globe,* 7 March, B01.

Gerber. Elizabeth. 1996. Legislative response to the threat of popular initiatives. *American Journal of Political Science* 40 (1), February.

Haider-Markel, Donald P. 1997. *From bullhorns to PACs: Lesbian and gay politics, policy and interest groups.* Ph.D. diss., University of Wisconsin–Milwaukee, Political Science.

Hibbits, Tim. 1997. Majority oppose same-sex marriage ban. *Oregonian*, 19 April.

Karp, Jeffrey. 1998. The Influence of Elite Endorsements in Initiative Campaigns. In *Citizens as legislators: Direct democracy in the United States*, edited by Shaun Bowler, Todd Donovan and Caroline Tolbert. Columbus: Ohio State University Press.

Key Jr., V. O. 1966. *The responsible electorate*. Cambridge: Harvard University Press.

Larrabbee, J. 1995. Gay rights measure put to test in Maine. *USA Today*. Archived at <www.usatoday.com/news/washdc/elect/states/maine/n95me011. htm>.

Lascher, Edward L., Michael G. Hagen, and Steven A. Rochlin. 1996. Gun behind the door? Ballot initiatives, state policies, and public opinion. *Journal of Politics* 58:760–75.

Lee, Eugene. 1997. Hiram's Dream—"The people's rule" and the 21st Century. In *Governing the Golden State*, edited by Gerald Lubenow. Berkeley, Cal.: IGS Press.

Linde, Hans. 1992. When the initiative is not "Republican government": The campaign against homosexuality. *Oregon Law Review* 72:19–45.

Loving v. Virginia, 388 U.S. 1, 11 (1967).

Lupia, Arthur. 1994. Shortcuts versus encyclopedias: Information and voting behavior in California insurance reform elections. *American Political Science Review* 88:63–76.

Magleby, David. 1984. *Direct legislation: Voting on ballot propositions in the United States*. Baltimore: Johns Hopkins University Press.

———. 1989. Opinion formation and opinion change in ballot proposition campaigns. In *Manipulating Public Opinion*, edited by M. Margolis and G. A. Mauser. San Diego: Harcourt, Brace and Co..

———. 1994. The United States. In *Referendums around the world*, edited by David Butler and Austin Ranney. Washington D.C.: American Enterprise Institute.

Matsusaka, John G. 1995. Fiscal effects of the voter initiative: Evidence from the last 30 years. *Journal of Political Economy* 103 (3): 587–623.

McCuan, David, Todd Donovan, Shaun Bowler, and Ken Fernandez. 1998. California's political warriors: Grassroots professionals and the initiative process. In *Citizens as legislators: Direct democracy in the United States*, edited by Shaun Bowler, Todd Donovan, and Caroline Tolbert. Columbus: Ohio State University Press.

National Gay and Lesbian Task Force. 1997. NGLTF statement responding to double killing. Archived at <www.teleport.com/~gerrit/murders_dir/ngltf. html>. December 5.

Reitman v. Mulkey, 387 U.S. 369 (1967).

Romer v. Evans, 517 U.S. 620, 116 S. Ct. 1620 (1996).

Ruskin, Liz. 1998. Ballot funding outlined. *Anchorage Daily News,* 7 October. <www.adn.com/stories/T98100766.html>.

Sears, David, and Jack Citrin. 1982. *Tax revolt: Something for nothing in California.* Cambridge: Harvard University Press.

Smith, Daniel. 1998. *Tax crusaders and the politics of direct democracy.* New York: Routledge.

Trounstine, Philip. 1997. Poll shows gay-rights support exception: Same-sex marriages. *San Jose Mercury News.* 3 March.

Wald, Kenneth, James Button, and Barbara Rienzo. 1996. The politics of gay rights in American communities: Explaining antidiscrimination ordinances and policies. *American Journal of Political Science* 40:1152–78.

Wenzel, Jim, Todd Donovan, and Shaun Bowler, eds. 1998. Direct democracy and minorities: Changing attitudes about minorities targeted by initiatives. In Shaun Bowler, Todd Donovan, and Caroline Tolbert, ed., *Citizens as Legislators: Direct Democracy in the United States.* Columbus: Ohio State University Press.

White, Jerry. 1992. Christian hate groups take root in Colorado: Fundamentalist Christians mount attack against gays and lesbians. National Lambda News Service. 11 March. Archived at <www.qrd.org/qrd/usa/colorado/1992/CO-cfv>.

Witt, Stephanie, and Suzanne McCorkle, ed. 1997. *Antigay Initiatives.* Greenwood, Conn.: Praeger.

Wolfinger, Raymond, and Fred Greenstein. 1968. The repeal of fair housing in California. *American Political Science Review* 62:753–69.

Zaller, John. 1991. Information, values and opinion. *American Political Science Review* 85:1215–38.

———. 1992. *The nature and origins of mass opinion.* Cambridge: Cambridge University Press.

III. THE ISSUES

9

DOMA AND ENDA: CONGRESS VOTES ON GAY RIGHTS

Gregory B. Lewis and Jonathan L. Edelson

As a small, unpopular minority, lesbians and gay men have tried to pick political battles that avoid the power of the public's antipathy. The movement has had noticeable successes with lawsuits, executive orders, and local ordinances, where gay rights advocates have been able to advance arguments based on principles of personal freedom and equality to a limited number of potentially sympathetic decision-makers. Opponents have often succeeded by expanding the scope of the conflict (Haider-Markel and Meier 1996; Schattschneider 1960)—moving conflicts from courtrooms to legislatures, from legislatures to ballot boxes, and from gay-friendly enclaves to larger, less sympathetic publics, and by shifting the argument from freedom and equality to morality.

The Defense of Marriage Act (DOMA) represents an expansion of the scope of conflict on a grand scale. In September 1993, the state supreme court of Hawaii ruled that the state's refusal to grant marriage licenses to same-sex couples was presumptively an unconstitutional form of sex discrimination (because it denied women, but not men, the right to marry a woman) that would need to be justified by a "compelling state interest." DOMA shifted the argument from an issue of sex discrimination in a courtroom in a gay-friendly state to a debate over an assault on a fundamental pillar of Western civilization in the Republican-controlled Congress. The conclusion was foregone, but the battle unexpectedly gave the gay movement a near-victory on the more popular civil rights issue of employment discrimination.

In this chapter, we briefly discuss trends in public opinion toward the civil liberties, sexuality, and relationships of lesbians and gay men. We then look at how these trends help explain why the movement was able to shift from judicial to legislative strategies on employment rights, but was reluctant to pursue even a judicial strategy on gay marriage. We examine the congressional debates in the context of expansion of conflict. Finally, we explore the connections between state opinion on gay rights issues and congressional votes.

PUBLIC OPINION ON GAY RIGHTS ISSUES

Gay men and lesbians are an unpopular minority. In 1965, 70 percent of a national survey labeled homosexuals as "more harmful [than helpful] to American life"; only 1 percent took the opposite position (Yang 1997). In several surveys since 1984, three-quarters or more consistently rated gay men and lesbians between 0 and 50 on their feeling thermometer, where "0–50 means you don't feel favorable and don't care too much for" a particular group—typically making them the least popular group asked about (Sherrill 1993, 98).

Despite their antipathy, Americans increasingly support civil liberties for gay people. Between 1973 and 1996, the percentages saying that "a man who admits he is a homosexual" should "be allowed to teach in a college" and "to make a speech in your community" and who would *not* favor taking "a book he wrote in favor of homosexuality . . . out of your public library" rose steadily by 28, 20, and 15 percent, respectively. By 1996, substantial majorities (75 percent, 81 percent, and 69 percent, respectively) supported each of these rights. Between 1977 and 1996, the percentage saying "homosexuals should . . . have equal rights in terms of job opportunities" rose 27 percent (to 83 percent). Public support for the employment rights of homosexuals varies substantially by occupation, but is rising in all occupations, as is the percentage disagreeing that school boards should have the right to fire gay teachers.

Such beliefs do not necessarily translate into support for gay rights laws, however. In 1996, 60 percent favored "laws to protect homosexuals against job discrimination," far lower than the 83 percent saying "homosexuals should . . . have equal rights in terms of job opportunities." When questions ask about *extending* "fair housing and fair employment laws" or "laws which protect the civil rights of racial or religious minorities . . . to protect the rights of homosexuals," support drops to slightly less than half. Trends in support for laws are not especially clear; 60 percent also said in 1977 that "homosexuals should be guaranteed equal treatment under the law in jobs and housing."

When the questions shift to gay people's sexual or romantic relationships, acceptance drops markedly, and progress toward greater acceptance is erratic. In thirteen surveys from 1973 through 1991, between 67 percent and 75 percent of respondents said that "sexual relations between two adults of the same sex" were "always wrong." Disapproval seemed to dip in the late 1970s, rise in the early 1980s, then dip again, but always quite slowly. Surprisingly, given almost twenty years of stability, the percentage saying "always wrong" dropped 15 percent between 1991 and 1996 (to 56 percent), suggesting the first major decline in disapproval. *Moral* disapproval, however, has held steady: in 1978, 1992, 1993, 1994, and 1996, a consistent 52 percent to 55 percent said that "homosexual relationships between consenting adults are morally wrong."[1] In fifteen surveys between 1977 and 1994 asking whether "homosexual relations between consenting adults should . . . be legal," about half said they should not.

With half the population viewing gay sex as immoral and favoring its criminalization, it would be surprising to find a majority willing to sanctify gay relationships under the mantle of marriage. Rogers (1998) reviews the wide variety of wordings with which pollsters have asked about gay marriage. Only one survey found more than one-third support (39 percent said "homosexuals should . . . have equal rights to marry one another"), probably because the question focused some respondents on equality rather than on marriage. Otherwise, most surveys found fewer than 30 percent in favor and more than 60 percent opposed. Americans accept the validity of gay couples more than these figures might suggest, however. In two *Newsweek* polls in 1996 and 1997, only 34 percent favored "legally sanctioned gay marriage" and only 38 percent agreed to adoption rights, but majorities supported Social Security benefits and inheritance rights for gay spouses (55 percent and 61 percent, respectively).

PUBLIC OPINION AND MOVEMENT STRATEGIES

Gay rights advocates can expect a more sympathetic hearing on civil liberties than on sexuality and relationships, especially if their audience is political elites rather than the general public. (Political tolerance is strongly related to both education and political activism (Bobo and Licari 1989; Gibson and Tedin 1988).) Judicial fora are particularly appealing, as they offer the hope of excluding arguments of morality and focusing debate on constitutional principles of freedom and equality. If gay rights advocates can establish that a government restriction involves a "fundamental right" (e.g., to free speech, privacy, or marriage) or unequal treatment on the basis of a "suspect" or "quasi-suspect" classification (e.g., race and sex, respectively), the courts will submit the policy to "strict" or "heightened" scrutiny. Under such standards, the government must show that its policy is "precisely tailored" to achieve a "compelling state interest" or "substantially related to a legitimate state interest" (Gerstmann 1999). Even under the low standard of "rational" review, the government must show that its policy is rationally related to a legitimate government interest and not motivated by "animus" or popular prejudice.

Gay rights advocates have also quietly persuaded political elites to change government policy, more frequently on employment discrimination issues than on gay relationships or sexuality. As public support for gay rights has increased, or in geographical or issue areas where support for gay rights is especially strong, advocates have more hope of success in directly political conflicts. Still, Haider-Markel and Meier (1996) argue that when gay rights opponents are able to expand the scope of conflict to popular political fora, morality politics trumps interest group politics and gay rights advocates typically lose.

Employment Discrimination

By the mid 1950s, federal, state, and local laws and executive orders barred known homosexuals from at least one-fifth of the nation's jobs (Brown 1958). Early opposition emerged through lawsuits challenging federal dismissals of individual veterans, who, under federal law, could be fired only if that promoted "the efficiency of the service." In the key judicial victory (*Norton v. Macy* 1969, 1164–65), the D.C. Court of Appeals ruled that "the notion that it could be an appropriate function of the federal bureaucracy to enforce the majority's conventional code of conduct in the private lives of its employees is at war with elementary concepts of liberty, privacy, and diversity"; to justify firing a gay employee, the government "must demonstrate some 'rational basis' for its conclusion that a discharge 'will promote the efficiency of the service.'" This "rational nexus" test was extended to all federal dismissals of homosexuals by a class-action judgment four years later (*Society for Individual Rights, Inc. v. Hampton* 1973) and has been widely adopted for state and local employees as well.

To achieve stronger nondiscrimination protections for public employees and even basic protections for private employees (who generally could be fired "at will"), gay rights advocates needed to expand beyond judicial decrees to legislation and executive orders. Haider-Markel and Meier (1996) argue that gay rights advocates have generally attempted to institute protections quietly, to minimize the political salience of the issue. Gay rights opponents have forced popular votes in at least sixty-nine initiatives or referenda on repealing or preventing gay rights protections, however, with three-fourths of the ballots leading to defeats for gay rights advocates (Haider-Markel 1997; Gamble 1997). Thus, because gay rights issues are highly likely to become politically salient, cities that provide protections tend to have strong gay communities who want them and socially liberal populations who are unlikely to oppose them (Wald, Button, and Rienzo 1996; Haeberle 1996).

Forty local governments passed gay rights ordinances in the 1970s, another forty did so in the 1980s, and at least fifty have done so in the 1990s. Gay rights ordinances passed first in large cities and university towns, which are locations most likely to have both gay power and a receptive political environment. As public acceptance of civil liberties for homosexuals grew, the types of cities passing ordinances diversified (Wald, Button, and Rienzo 1997). State-level protections came more slowly, as they required a broader political base. The first protections came primarily through executive orders, and only two state legislatures (in Wisconsin and Massachusetts) had passed gay rights laws by 1990 (Haider-Markel 1997). Only eleven states have passed gay rights laws (and Maine recently repealed its law by referendum), eight of which are in New England or on the Pacific Coast, the two regions where public condemnation of homosexuality is weakest (Tiemeyer 1993, 493). Federal gay rights bills have been introduced in every congressional session since 1974, but did not even receive a committee hearing for two decades.

Indeed, the expansion of protections for gay workers has been particularly quiet at the federal level. President Carter reportedly considered issuing an executive order banning antigay discrimination in federal employment (Shilts 1993), but instead U.S. Office of Personnel Management Director Alan Campbell issued a memorandum declaring that discrimination on the basis of sexual orientation was a prohibited personnel practice (Lewis 1997). Unions and gay employee groups have lobbied individual federal agencies to specifically include sexual orientation in their antidiscrimination policies (with clear support from President Clinton); although most agencies had added such language by 1997, the changes seldom garnered much press. On May 28, 1998, when President Clinton issued an executive order banning sexual orientation discrimination in federal civilian employment, it was not a major policy change, as it merely expanded and regularized protections most federal employees already enjoyed. Nonetheless, he signed the order without fanfare on an afternoon when the media was focused on Pakistan's detonation of a nuclear bomb.[2]

When Congress enters the debate and the forum grows more public, gay rights advocates generally lose. For example, Congress prohibited the expenditure of federal funds on AIDS prevention efforts that targeted gay men with "safe sex" information, for fear that it would "promote homosexuality" (see chapter 10) and it gutted Clinton's plan to lift the ban on gays in the military (see chapter 11). Clinton's executive order offers an interesting example and counter-example of this pattern: efforts to keep the executive order quiet failed to prevent a congressional effort to overturn the order, but the House rejected by a wide margin (252–176) the Helfley amendment, which would have prohibited the expenditure of federal funds to implement Clinton's executive order.

Gay Relationships

As the Supreme Court rejected what it chose to define as a "facetious" claim that homosexuals have "a fundamental right . . . to engage in sodomy" (*Bowers v. Hardwick* 1986) and as the public overwhelming rejects homosexual relations as "always wrong," neither courts nor legislatures seemed likely to grant gay sexual and romantic relationships the status of marriage. Nonetheless, gay couples have intermittently pressed lawsuits and gay organizations have lobbied governments and employers to recognize gay relationships. Gay marriage cases stretch back to the early 1970s, when litigants unsuccessfully sought marriage licenses in Minnesota (*Baker v. Nelson* 1971), Kentucky (*Jones v. Hallahan* 1973), and Washington (*Singer v. Hara* 1974). The most important claims were constitutional ones. First, the litigants argued that their "fundamental right to marry" (established in a line of cases guaranteeing marriage rights to interracial couples, "deadbeat dads," and prisoners) demanded "strict scrutiny" of the ban on same-sex marriage. The courts denied that a fundamental right to marry someone of the same sex existed, however, since marriage by definition required a man and a woman. Second, the litigants argued that they were being denied equal protection of the laws based on their sex or sexual orientation, which would again require heightened scrutiny. *Loving v. Virginia* (1967) had found race discrimination in Virginia's antimiscegenation law, even though it applied equally to blacks and whites, because whites (but not blacks) were prohibited to marry blacks and blacks (but not whites) were prohibited to marry whites. The courts did not see an analogous case of sex discrimination when the law prohibited a man but not a woman from marrying a man. Likewise, they refused to grant "quasi-suspect" status to sexual orientation, thus requiring only rational review, easily met by the state's interest in procreation (Leonard 1994).

Though gay marriage cases largely disappeared from the courts until the 1990s, lobbying for recognition of gay relationships has grown stronger. Beginning with the *Village Voice* in 1982, public and private employers have increasingly extended benefits to their workers' domestic partners, similar to those they grant spouses and children. By 1995, 421 cities and states, 96 private-sector companies, and 68 institutions of higher education offered some form of domestic partner benefits, and the number was rising steadily (Winfield and Spielman 1995, 97–98). Such policies could be extremely unpopular. Even in San Francisco, probably the city where gays have the greatest political strength, city voters overturned council-passed domestic partner benefits in 1989 (they were later reinstated). A Texas county decided to risk its economic development by denying tax incentives to a new Apple Computer facility because the company offered domestic partners benefits.

Thus, when three lesbian and gay couples decided to challenge Hawaii's marriage laws, most gay political and litigation groups were not enthusiastic. The plaintiffs had few new arguments that had not been rejected by state courts twenty years earlier. Gay rights organizations were reluctant to enter a battle where they saw little chance of success, a greater chance of setting bad precedents, and the danger of political backlash. Though the Lambda Legal Defense and Education Fund (LLDEF) joined the case as co-counsel when the possibility of judicial success became clear (then started warning other organizations to prepare for a national backlash if the lawsuit succeeded), no other group had a full-time marriage project director by mid-1996 (Rotello 1996; Bull and Gallagher 1996; Rubenstein 1997).

Baehr v. Lewin was primarily an equal protection case, arguing discrimination on the basis of sex and sexual orientation. In its historic 1993 decision, the Hawaii Supreme Court rejected the sexual orientation claim (citing *Hardwick*) but accepted the sex discrimination claim (and the analogy to race discrimination) that other courts had rejected in the 1970s. Because Hawaii's constitution included an equal rights amendment, sex was a "suspect" category (rather than merely "quasi-suspect," as under the federal constitution), so discrimination on the basis of sex was subject to "strict scrutiny"; the state supreme court sent the case back to the lower court to allow the state "to show that the statute's sex-based classification is justified by compelling state interests and the statute is narrowly drawn to avoid unnecessary abridgments of constitutional rights" (*Baehr v. Lewin* 1993, 67). The trial was not held until September 1996, but most observers thought the handwriting was on the wall: governments can rarely justify unequal treatment under the strict scrutiny standard.

Such an unpopular decision could not be constrained to the courtroom for long. The scope of the conflict began widening almost immediately. The Hawaii legislature amended state law to specify that only male-female couples could receive marriage licenses, and opponents of gay marriage proposed a constitutional amendment clarifying the state legislature's right to do so. (Hawaii voters overwhelmingly passed the amendment in November 1998.) Other state legislatures, fearing that their own residents would seek recognition of same-sex marriages they obtained in Hawaii, began amending their marriage laws to deny that possibility. By February 1998, twenty-six states and Puerto Rico had statutes banning same-sex marriage and eleven more were considering similar legislation.

THE EMERGENCE OF GAY MARRIAGE AS A MAINSTREAM POLITICAL ISSUE

The issue leapt onto the national agenda in early 1996. As in previous campaigns against gay rights advances, leadership came from the Christian Right. A coalition of eight conservative religious groups (including the Christian Coalition) promoted its Marriage Protection Resolution at a large political rally in Iowa three days before the presidential caucuses. All the Republican candidates signed the resolution, and three addressed the rally (Berke 1996).

Same-sex marriage offered social conservatives proof of the dangers of the "gay agenda," but it also offered Republicans the potential either to define Clinton as an extremist or to estrange him from an important voting bloc. Lesbians and gay men were credited with donating three million dollars to Clinton's 1992 campaign, and 72 percent had voted for him, making them one of the most consistent Democratic voting blocs (D'Emilio 1996). Clinton could not afford to offend them too much, but gay marriage was clearly too radical a proposition for the American public. (Clinton defused the issue by expressing his opposition to gay marriage and willingness to sign DOMA, even while he attacked the bill as unnecessary and divisive.)

Republicans needed to play the gay issue carefully, taking a strong enough position to hold and energize the Christian Right without alienating the average voter. They appeared to bungle the issue in 1992, when Patrick Buchanan's "culture war" convention speech attacking gay activists convinced many Americans that the party had crossed the line into bigotry and mean-spiritedness. The debate over gays in the military reaffirmed the potential of the issue, however. Strong military and congressional opposition to the policy change, a powerful grassroots campaign led by the Christian Right, and weakness in the Clinton and gay rights camps gave Republicans a stunning victory over Clinton in his first months in office and led him to change his position in ways that demoralized many lesbian and gay supporters but did not win back conservative voters (Rayside 1996; Wilcox and Wolpert 1996; Rimmerman 1996). Colin Powell's distinction between discrimination based on race and on sexual orientation (because "skin color is a benign, nonbehavioral characteristic") also protected conservatives from charges of bigotry. Gay marriage gave Republicans a far easier target. The public overwhelmingly opposed gay marriage, and the "obviousness" of heterosexual marriage would make it harder to charge bigotry.

CONGRESS CONSIDERS GAY MARRIAGE AND EMPLOYMENT RIGHTS

Three months after the Iowa rally, the thrice-married Bob Barr (R-Ga.) introduced the Defense of Marriage Act (DOMA). DOMA denied recognition to same-sex marriages for federal purposes[3] and declared that states were free to refuse recognition to same-sex marriages (and their effects) validly performed in another state.[4] Proponents forwarded several arguments for expanding the conflict. First, judicial decision-making on this issue was "profoundly undemocratic"—gay rights lawyers had convinced two activist judges on the Hawaiian supreme court "to foist the newly coined institution of homosexual 'marriage' upon an unwilling Hawaiian public," 70 percent of whom opposed gay marriage.

Second, the federal government needed to prevent a single state from imposing its will on the other forty-nine and the federal government. Some proponents argued that the full faith and credit clause of the Constitution would automatically force all states to recognize any Hawaii-sanctioned gay marriage, but most presented this as a danger rather than a certainty. Although the general rule is that a marriage is valid everywhere if it is valid in the state where it was performed, states can refuse to recognize validly performed marriages that violate "the strong public policy" of the state where the couple lives.[5] Many states were amending their laws to establish that strong public policy, and proponents argued that DOMA would strengthen their positions.

In addition, the House Judiciary Committee reported that the words "marriage" and "spouse" appeared in hundreds of sections of federal statutes and regulations, but without clear federal definitions. Thus, gay marriages validated by Hawaii would presumably qualify under federal law, contrary to Congress's expectations and desires when they passed those laws. Failing to clarify federal definitions could "throw open the doors of the U.S. Treasury" and provide benefits to gay couples that were intended "to promote, protect, and prefer the institution of [heterosexual] marriage" (House 1996).

Third, DOMA proponents argued for switching the grounds for decision-making from discrimination to morality. In the words of House floor leader Charles Canady (R–Fla.), "What is at stake in this controversy [is n]othing less than our collective moral understanding . . . of the essential nature of the family." DOMA proponents repeatedly extolled marriage as a "cornerstone," "foundation," "bedrock," and "fundamental pillar," not only of America, but of any civilized society, and excoriated any attempt to declare gay relationships to be their "moral equivalent." The less moderate attacked homosexuals as immoral, lustful, and promiscuous.

DOMA opponents attacked the bill as a purely political issue trumped-up during an election year, arguing that the Hawaii supreme court's preliminary decision was too far in the past (September 1993) and its final decision too far in the future (probably late 1998) to justify precipitate federal action. Barney Frank, the openly gay floor leader of the opposition in the House, proposed amending DOMA to grant federal recognition of same-sex marriages only if they had been validated by legislative or popular vote, thereby, he claimed, eliminating any problems with the undemocratic nature of the judicial process. His amendment failed overwhelmingly. Opponents also argued that DOMA undercut rather than strengthened state sovereignty. Frank argued that "every single sponsor of this bill" believed that the "strong public policy" exception already gave the states all the protection DOMA would provide. Opponents labeled DOMA as federal intrusion into family law (historically the preserve of the states) by second-guessing the states' definitions of marriage. DOMA opponents further argued that a marriage license does not grant government's moral approval any more than a divorce decree does, and that the real basis for opposition to gay marriage was discrimination—but on the basis of sexual orientation, rather than sex, as had been decided by the Hawaii supreme court.

Gay rights supporters attempted to widen the conflict from clearly unpopular gay marriages to more palatable protections against employment discrimination. In both houses, supporters attempted to amend DOMA to include the Employment NonDiscrimination Act (ENDA), which prohibited discrimination on the basis of sexual orientation for most employees. The House disqualified the amendment as not germane, but Senate proponents and opponents reached a compromise to allow a free-standing vote on ENDA (as a bill rather than as an amendment). This probably increased support for both bills: Senators could demonstrate support for gay rights by voting for ENDA, freeing them up to vote for DOMA. A pro-ENDA vote seemed less liberal when combined with a pro-DOMA vote, and ENDA supporters would not have to deal with backlash from its passage, since House leaders were unlikely to allow a floor vote on ENDA even if it passed the Senate.

DOMA passed quickly and easily. The House Judiciary Committee held a hearing one week after its introduction and passed it 20–10 one month after that. A month later, the House passed it by a 5-to-1 margin (342–67). The Senate took another two months to approve it by a 6-to-1 margin (85–14). Seven months after the Iowa rally, DOMA was law. In contrast, federal gay rights bills languished in committees for twenty years before receiving a hearing. Gay rights opponents are more effective than advocates in placing their issues on the congressional agenda, though often in reaction to supporters' gains in smaller arenas. ENDA's narrow defeat (49–50) provided a symbolic victory for advocates in the midst of a major rout, but the bill saw no real action in the next congressional session; ENDA clearly reached the Senate floor as an adjunct to DOMA, not on its own.

Congressional Voting Patterns

The voting on these gay rights bills was clearly partisan. About one-third of Democrats voted against DOMA in each house, but only one Republican did so (Steven Gunderson (R-Iowa), who is openly gay). In the Senate, 87 percent of the Democrats but only 13 percent of the Republicans voted for ENDA.

Individual characteristics also played a role. Research on attitudes toward homosexuality in the general population indicates that women are more gay-supportive than men, and that Jews and the nonreligious are more supportive than Catholics, who tend to be more supportive than Protestants, especially fundamentalists. Although minorities and whites do not differ much in their attitudes toward homosexuals, minorities are more likely to support laws to protect gay rights (e.g., Herek 1988; Kite and Whitley 1996; Schwanberg 1993). In line with those findings, congressional females were more likely than males to oppose DOMA (35 percent versus 13 percent in the House, 38 percent versus 12 percent in the Senate) and to support ENDA (75 percent versus 48 percent). Racial and ethnic minorities voted against DOMA more than did whites (48 percent versus 11 percent in the House, 75 percent versus 12 percent in the Senate). Jews were the most likely to take the progay position on DOMA in both House and Senate and on ENDA (11 percent, 50 percent, and 100 percent, respectively); followed by Catholics (17 percent, 19 percent, and 62 percent, respectively); and by Protestants (12 percent, 10 percent, and 38 percent, respectively).

How large a role did public opinion play? A simple reading of the polls might have led one to expect overwhelming victories for both DOMA and ENDA—support for the general principle that "homosexuals should . . . have equal rights in terms of job opportunities" (83 percent) was even higher than opposition to gay marriage (less than 70 percent). As noted above, however, public support for legislation to prohibit job discrimination is much lower, however, perhaps especially if the proposed legislation is federal—even a 1996 poll sponsored by a key gay rights organization found only 55 percent support for ENDA[6] (Lewis and Rogers 1999). People also have real questions about hiring homosexuals into particular occupations: ENDA would have guaranteed the employment rights of lesbian and gay elementary school teachers, for instance (a fact that was mentioned repeatedly by Senate ENDA opponents) but a 1996 Gallup poll was the first ever to find a (small) majority willing to accept gays in the elementary classroom. If one uses the "toughest" employment discrimination questions as the gauge of public support, the split vote on ENDA is not surprising.

An alternative approach to assessing the impact of public opinion on congressional gay rights votes is to examine whether interstate variation in public opinion affected the votes of individual Senate and House members. In the most sophisticated modeling of congressional voting on gay rights issues, Haider-Markel (1997) finds that member partisanship and ideology are the strongest predictors of their votes, but that constituency opposition to gay rights also has a clear effect. He bases his measure of constituency opinion on the demographic characteristics of the district, however, rather than a more direct measure.

In this section, we take advantage of two large series of surveys on gay employment issues to develop state measures of attitudes toward gay rights. While we were unable to match the huge samples Wright, Erikson, and McIver (1985) used to compute state liberalism scores, two separate series gave us sufficiently large samples to develop reasonably reliable measures of public opinion by state (Jones and Norrander 1996). Eight Times-

Mirror polls from 1987 through 1993 yielded 15,368 usable responses on whether "school boards should have the right to fire teachers who are known homosexuals." Six Gallup polls from 1977 through 1992 gave us 7,297 usable responses on hiring homosexuals into a variety of occupations. We computed state scores for each set of polls, then combined them.

First, for the Times-Mirror polls, we gave scores of 0 to those who "completely agreed" that "school boards should have the right to fire teachers who are known homosexuals," and scores of 25, 50, 75, and 100 to those who said "mostly agree," "don't know," "mostly disagree," and "completely disagree," respectively. We regressed these scores on dummy variables for each state (using Pennsylvania as the reference group) plus dummy variables representing the year of the survey (because the percentage disagreeing with the statement rose steadily and substantially over this period). Our sample includes a minimum of eleven cases per state, with all but Alaska and Wyoming having over twenty cases.

The state coefficients are differences in public opinion between each state and Pennsylvania (table 9.1). Thus, Hawaii had the most progay public opinion—scores thirty points higher (on a one-hundred-point scale) than scores for Pennsylvania in the same year. Massachusetts, Connecticut, New Jersey, and Maryland were the next-most gay-supportive, with scores nineteen or twenty points higher than Pennsylvania's. Mississippi was the least gay-supportive, with scores twenty-six points below the Keystone State and fifty-six points below Hawaii.

Second, for the Gallup polls, we gave respondents twenty points for each of the five occupations (doctors, salespersons, elementary school teachers, clergy, and the armed forces) into which they said homosexuals should be hired. The scale runs from zero to one hundred and can be interpreted as percentage acceptance.[7] We regressed this score on dummy variables for each state (again using Pennsylvania as the reference group) and survey year. The state coefficients are shown in the second column of table 9.1. Massachusetts and Connecticut again score very high, accepting gays into nineteen points and seventeen points more of the occupations than respondents in Pennsylvania; Mississippi again brought up the rear, nineteen points behind Pennsylvania and thirty-eight points below Massachusetts.

As the two state opinion measures are strongly correlated ($r = .59$), we took the simple average of the two scores our final measure, presented in column 3.[8] This measure ranges from a high of 19.5 for Massachusetts to a low of −22.5 for Mississippi, with Pennsylvania as before held to a score of 0. A few states with few respondents (e.g., Wyoming, North Dakota, and Hawaii) differed substantially across the surveys, but only two states

Table 9.1 Progay Public Opinion and Congressional Votes by State

State	Fire Teacher?	Job Index	Mean	Senate (% progay)	House (no. on DOMA)
Massachusetts	20***	19***	19.5	100	5/9
Connecticut	20***	17***	18.5	50	1/6
Hawaii	30***	6	18.0	100	2/2
Nevada	14	17*	15.5	50	0/1
New Jersey	19***	11***	15.0	50	2/13
Maine	14**	16*	15.0	50	0/1
Maryland	19***	10**	14.5	50	0/8
New Hampshire	8	17*	12.5	0	0/2
Vermont	10	15	12.5	50	1/1
California	13***	10***	11.5	100	22/52
Oregon	14***	9*	11.5	75	1/5
Wisconsin	15***	4	9.5	75	1/9
New York	11***	7**	9.0	75	10/29
Minnesota	8*	7*	7.5	25	1/8
Montana	9	6	7.5	25	1/1
Washington	11***	3	7.0	25	1/8
Illinois	3	8**	5.5	100	2/19
Rhode Island	10	1	5.5	75	1/2
Virginia	1	10**	5.5	50	2/11
Delaware	6	3	4.5	25	0
Michigan	5	3	4.0	25	3/16
Ohio	7**	−1	3.0	75	2/18
Colorado	1	5	3.0	0	2/6
Arizona	4	2	3.0	0	0/6
Iowa	−3	8	2.5	25	0/5
Nebraska	10*	−6	2.0	50	0/3
Missouri	2	1	1.5	0	0/7
Wyoming	−21	24	1.5	25	0/1
North Dakota	9	−8	.5	50	0/1
Florida	−4	4	0.0	25	2/20
Pennsylvania	0	0	0.0	25	3/19
New Mexico	−11	5	−3.0	25	0/3
Kansas	−1	−6	−3.5	0	0/3
Georgia	−5	−3	−4.0	0	2/10
Utah	−3	−5	−4.0	0	0/3
Indiana	−4	−6	−5.0	0	0/10
Texas	−7**	−3	−5.0	0	0/29
North Carolina	−1	−12	−6.5	0	0/11
West Virginia	−11**	−5	−8.0	25	0/3
Louisiana	−11***	−5	−8.0	0	0/6
Idaho	−6	−11*	−8.5	0	0/2
South Carolina	−7	−15***	−11.0	25	0/6
Alabama	−10**	−13**	−11.5	0	0/7
Oklahoma	−14***	−11*	−12.5	0	0/5
Tennessee	−15***	−11**	−13.0	0	0/8
Arkansas	−17***	−10*	−13.5	50	0/1
Kentucky	−13***	−15***	−14.0	0	0/6

Table 9.1   (continued)

State	Fire Teacher?	Job Index	Mean	Senate (% progay)	House (no. on DOMA)
Mississippi	−26***	−19***	−22.5	0	0/4
South Dakota	−10	—	—	25	0/1
Alaska	−1	—	—	0	0/1

Difference from Pennsylvania significant:
*.05 level.
**.01 level.
***.0001 level.

(Ohio and Nebraska) had significantly higher scores than Pennsylvania in one poll but (insignificantly) lower scores in the other.

In line with previous regional analyses of opinions on gay issues (e.g., Tiemeyer 1993), the most progay third of the states are concentrated in New England and along the Pacific Coast, with a number in the Middle Atlantic and along the country's northern border. Massachusetts, Connecticut, and Hawaii emerge as the states with the most progay public opinion. The Deep South is staunchly antigay, though the more urban Southern states of Florida, Georgia, and Texas do not differ substantially from Pennsylvania.

State opinion shows up clearly in the Senate and House votes. In table 9.1, we gave each state twenty-five points for each Senate vote against DOMA and for ENDA. Four states (Massachusetts, Hawaii, California, and Illinois) had perfect scores; two were in the top three states in terms of public opinion, the third was in the top ten, and Illinois was well within the top half. Of the five states with scores of seventy-five (two votes for ENDA, one against DOMA), three (Oregon, Wisconsin, and New York) were in the top third and the other two (Rhode Island and Ohio) were in the top half. Gays got only eleven of the ninety-eight votes from the twenty-five states in the bottom half of the table (including two from Clinton's home state of Arkansas).

Table 9.2 demonstrates the pattern more simply. We divided the states into three groups: the most negative (Mississippi to New Mexico), the most positive (Washington to Massachusetts), and the most average (Pennsylvania to Illinois). In the Senate, 82 percent of those from the most negative states voted consistently antigay (against ENDA and for DOMA); in contrast, 50 percent of those in the middle states and only 16 percent in the most positive states did so. On the other hand, 28 percent of those in the most positive

Table 9.2 Congressional Votes by State Opinion on Gay Rights and by Party

	All			Republicans			Democrats		
	Negative	Average	Positive	Negative	Average	Positive	Negative	Average	Positive
Senate									
Antigay	82	50	16	96	81	50	44	14	0
Pro-ENDA	18	33	56	4	19	50	56	50	59
Anti-DOMA	0	17	28	0	0	0	0	36	41
Gamma		.72			.77			.61	
House									
Pro-DOMA	81	61	41	99	84	77	53	30	6
Some anti-DOMA	17	27	29	1	16	22	42	42	35
Anti-DOMA	2	12	31	0	0	1	4	28	58
Gamma		.53			.59			.68	

states, 17 percent of those in the average states, and none of those in the most negative states took the progay line (for ENDA and against DOMA).

Controlling for party did not weaken the relationship between public opinion and votes (measured by the gammas). For instance, none of the Democrats in the most negative states voted against DOMA and none of the Democrats in the most positive states voted against ENDA. Public opinion mattered, even among senators of the same party.

For the House, table 9.1 presents the number of votes against DOMA in each state and the size of its delegation. Only eight of the sixty-seven votes against DOMA came from the bottom twenty-five states—votes from the large cities of Pennsylvania, Florida, and Georgia. In contrast, thirty-three came from the top ten states. Hawaii and Massachusetts were the only two states where a majority of members voted against DOMA. The other three stand-out states were California and New York (both in the top third), which delivered twenty (of fifty-two) and ten (of twenty-nine) votes, respectively; and Texas (in the bottom third), where none of the twenty-nine members voted against DOMA.

House members had four roll-call votes on which to express some qualms about the bill. Although only 67 members voted against DOMA, 133 voted against the rule for the debate, 103 voted for the Frank amendment described above, and 164 voted to recommit the bill. In table 9.2, a progay vote on any of those issues is counted as "some anti-DOMA." The House pattern mirrors that in the Senate. The percentage taking the consistently pro-DOMA stance dropped from 81 percent in the most negative states, to 61 percent in the average states, to 41 percent in the most positive states. This basic pattern held up within members of each party. Indeed, the gammas suggest that the effect of public opinion was a bit stronger within each party than overall.

To determine whether the impact of public opinion holds up after controlling for member characteristics, we ran simple regressions. For House members, our dependent variable was a one-hundred-point "progay" scale, with members scoring twenty-five points for each progay vote on the four roll-calls described above. Our key independent variable was the state public opinion measure. Because this was less appropriate for the House, where individual districts may differ substantially from statewide patterns, we added district population density (thousands of persons per square mile), because public support for gay rights is stronger in large cities. We included dummy variables coded 1 for Democrats (and Independents), men, Jews, Catholics, liberal Protestants,[9] and whites. Finally, we added the member's 1994 Americans for Democratic Action (ADA) score as a measure of liberalism. As several members were missing 1994 ADA scores, we ran separate models with and without member ideology.

Even without ADA score, the model explained 63 percent of the variation in the House votes (table 9.3). Partisanship had the strongest impact: Democrats scored thirty-nine points higher than comparable Republicans. With the second strongest beta-weight, state public opinion made a real difference: a one-point rise in state attitudes was associated with a one-point expected rise in member score. As expected, progay voting rose significantly with population density. Whites scored twenty-two points lower than comparable minorities; men, thirteen points lower than comparable women; and Jews and liberal Protestants, fifteen and nine points higher, respectively, than other comparable Protestants. All these differences (except the religious ones) were significant at the .001 level.

Table 9.3   Regression Analysis for House and Senate Votes

	House		Senate	
	Model 1	Model 2	Model 1	Model 2
Democrat	39***	−8	38***	9
	(.000)	(.126)	(.000)	(.305)
State opinion	1.0***	0.7***	1.0***	0.7*
	(.000)	(.000)	(.001)	(.031)
Population density	3.7***	1.7*	—	—
(Natural logarithm of	(.000)	(.021)		
population per square mile)				
Male	−13***	−4	−8	−7
	(.001)	(.311)	(.365)	(.433)
White	−22***	−13**	−23*	−20*
	(.000)	(.003)	(.061)	(.089)
Jewish	15**	9	17*	13
	(.006)	(.102)	(.069)	(.146)
Liberal Protestant	9*	8*	7	4
	(.037)	(.071)	(.267)	(.519)
Catholic	−3	−4	3	4
	(.277)	(.210)	(.675)	(.591)
ADA score		0.8***		0.5***
		(.000)		(.000)
Intercept	16	10	38	24
Adjusted R²	.63	.71	.59	.64
Sample Size	402	315	94	90

***Significant at .001 level.
**Significant at .01 level.
*Significant at .05 level (one-tailed test).
Numbers in parentheses are exact significance levels.

DOMA appears to have been even more clearly an ideological than a party vote. Adding ADA score to model 2 caused most of the other variables to lose strength. (Much of the effect of party, race, sex, and religion is associated with ideology—Democratic, urban, female, minority, and Jewish representatives are all more likely to be liberals, and liberalism is the clearest determinant of DOMA votes.) The state public opinion measure retains two-thirds of its strength, however, and remains significant at the .001 level. Population density also continues to have a statistically significant effect (at the .05 level). The more gay-supportive the state and the more urban the district, the more likely a member was to oppose DOMA, even controlling for member ideology. (In addition, whites were more likely than comparable minorities, and liberal Protestants were less likely than other comparable Protestants, to vote for DOMA.)

Senators had two major opportunities to vote on gay rights: DOMA and ENDA. We gave them fifty points for each "correct" vote. In model 1, party was again the key determinant: Democrats scored thirty-eight points higher than comparable Republicans. State public opinion was again the second-strongest determinant, with a one-point rise in public support associated with a one-point rise in member score. Whites scored twenty-three points lower than comparable minorities and Jews scored seventeen points higher than nonliberal Protestants (both significant at .05 in one-tailed tests). In model 2, ADA score was the primary predictor of these votes on gay rights. Adding ideology to the mix decimated the effect of party, which lost statistical significance. The impact of state public opinion also fell by a third, but remained statistically significant. Whites remained less likely than minorities of the same ideology to vote for gay rights. In both houses, then, votes against DOMA tended to come from liberals in gay-friendly states (and urban districts, if representatives), many of whom had experienced discrimination as women or as racial, ethnic, or religious minorities.

CONCLUSION

Although attitudes toward lesbians and gay men remain quite negative, variation in public opinion creates issue and geographic niches with sympathetic audiences for gay rights. These niches have been growing steadily for three decades. Attempts to expand civil liberties for gay people raise fewer objections than do efforts to decriminalize their sexual behaviors or legitimize their romantic relationships. Expansion of the decision-making arena from the judiciary to the executive branch to the legislature to popular referenda has typically meant closer attachment to public opinion and a lower probability of finding a sympathetic niche. Raising the decision-making level from local to state to federal government has required a broader base of public support, decreasing the odds of success for a small, unpopular minority. Employment protections emerged first from the courts, then from some local governments in the most supportive environments, then expanded to more cities and to state governments in the most supportive regions. At the federal level, employment protections have come from the courts and the executive branch, frequently agency-by-agency with little public fanfare; expanding the conflict to include Congress has decreased the chances of success.[10]

Gay marriage advocates have needed to deal with overwhelmingly unfavorable public opinion. The courts have generally been so unsympathetic to the issue that the leading gay litigation groups largely abandoned the issue, leaving leadership to isolated litigants, who experienced no success in the courts until Hawaii. The conflict then jumped almost overnight from a courtroom in a gay-supportive state to the floor of Congress, making a defeat for gay marriage advocates inevitable. The gay-supportiveness of localities and states affected their representatives' positions on DOMA, but until the nation becomes much more gay-friendly, gay marriage has little hope of political success.

NOTES

The authors are grateful to American University for funding the purchase of several of the data sets used in this chapter, to the Pew Charitable Trust for giving us data from the Times-Mirror polls, and to the Roper Center for Public Opinion Research at the University of Connecticut for providing the Gallup polls.

1. The 1993 and 1996 surveys ask about "homosexual relations between adults."
2. Though the executive order appears to have been finalized weeks before, the timing of its signing was so abrupt that even openly gay congressman Barney Frank, a key proponent of the executive order, was not notified in time to attend.
3. "In determining the meaning of any Act of Congress, or of any ruling, regulation, or interpretation of the various administrative bureaus and agencies of the United States, the word 'marriage' means only a legal union between one man and one woman as husband and wife, and the word 'spouse' refers only to a person of the opposite sex who is a husband or a wife."
4. "No State . . . shall be required to give effect to any public act, record, or judicial proceeding of any other State . . . respecting a relationship between

persons of the same sex that is treated as a marriage under the laws of such other State . . . or a right or claim arising from such relationship."

5. Thus, if Hawaii legalized same-sex marriage and a lesbian couple from Utah got married during a Hawaiian vacation, Utah could refuse to recognize their marriage on their return if it had a strong public policy against such marriages. However, if a Hawaiian gay couple married in their home state and a California lesbian couple married during a Hawaiian vacation (and such a marriage did not violate California's strong public policy), and if both couples moved to Utah years later, standard marriage law would force Utah to accept the marriages, as the state did not have a significant relationship with either couple at the time of the wedding (Strasser 1997). On the other hand, since several state courts determined that same-sex marriages do not exist by definition, the Utah court might still decide that there was no marriage to recognize (Leonard 1994).

6. In the 1996 poll commissioned by the Human Rights Campaign, 70 percent thought "gays and lesbians should be protected from discrimination in the workplace," but only 55 percent responded favorably to the follow-up question: "There is a measure before Congress called the Employment Non-Discrimination Act, which would extend current civil rights protections in the workplace to cover gays and lesbians. Do you favor or oppose this bill?"

7. All five occupations loaded heavily on a single factor, which explained 62 percent of the variance in responses. The index had a reasonably high reliability (Cronbach's alpha − .84). Alaska and South Dakota had no respondents, and five more states had under 20 (Hawaii had 4, Delaware 7, Wyoming 9, North Dakota 16, and Vermont 17).

8. Each measure has its own strength. The Gallup poll includes questions on five occupations, making it a more reliable measure for individual respondents than the single Times-Mirror question. Luckily, the one question is about gay schoolteachers, a flashpoint in virtually every fight over nondiscrimination policy. Times-Mirror had more than twice as many respondents as Gallup, increasing its reliability as a measure of state opinion.

Though public opinion on gay employment may seem a weak proxy for attitudes toward gay marriage, marriage looks enough like simply a "hard" gay rights issue that any good measure of support for gay rights will probably serve adequately. In the Senate, everyone who opposed DOMA voted for ENDA, suggesting that voting against DOMA was simply three times harder than voting for ENDA. It has been argued that the public debate on gay rights ordinances does not depend on the particular provisions of the ordinance but on the general issues of homosexuality and gay rights (Button, Rienzo, and Wald 1997). *Newsweek* polls in 1996 and 1997 asked seven questions on gay relationships and discrimination, covering issues from "legally sanctioned gay marriages" to "special legislation to guarantee equal rights for gays." All seven items loaded heavily on the main factor, which explained 48 percent of the variation. A scale of all seven items was reliable (alpha = .82) and gained from all seven items.

9. Episcopalians, Congregationalists, and Unitarians were classified as liberal Protestants. In an alternative specification of religion, we ranked denominations on an eight-point conservatism-liberalism scale (Green and Guth 1991), yielding a significant coefficient in Model 1 for the House but insignificant effects in the Senate. Model fit was slightly better with the three dummy variables.

10. The gay movement appears to have made inroads in Congress on employment issues. Congress recently rejected an amendment overturning Clinton's executive order regularizing protections of federal employees from discrimination on the basis of sexual orientation. Still, congressional unwillingness to legislate in favor of discrimination in federal employment, where protections already exist, does not guarantee willingness to pass new legislation creating new protections in the economy generally.

REFERENCES

Baehr v. Lewin, 852 P.2d 44 (Haw.), *reconsideration granted in part*, 875 P.2d 225 (Haw. 1993).

Baker v. Nelson, 191 N.W.2d 185 (Minn. 1971).

Berke, Richard L. 1996. Fight for religious right's votes turns bitter. *New York Times*, 10 February, p.1.

Bérubé, Allan. 1990. *Coming out under fire: The history of gay men and women in World War II*. New York: Free Press.

Bobo, Laurence, and Frederick C. Licari. 1989. Education and political tolerance: Testing the effects of cognitive sophistication and target group affect. *Public Opinion Quarterly* 53 (3): 285–308.

Bowers v. Hardwick, 478 U.S. 186 (1986).

Brown Jr., Ralph S. 1958. *Loyalty and security: Employment tests in the United States*. New Haven: Yale University Press.

Bull, Chris, and John Gallagher. 1996. *Perfect enemies: The religious right, the gay movements, and the politics of the 1990s*. New York: Crown Publishers, Inc.

Button, James W., Barbara A. Rienzo, and Kenneth D. Wald. 1997. *Private lives, public conflicts: Battles over gay rights in American communities*. Washington, D.C.: CQ Press.

D'Emilio, John. 1996. *Power at the polls: The gay / lesbian / bisexual vote*. Washington, D.C.: National Gay and Lesbian Task Force.

Eskridge, William N., Jr. 1996. *The case for same-sex marriage: From sexual liberty to civilized commitment*. New York: The Free Press.

Gamble, Barbara S. 1997. Putting civil rights to a popular vote. *American Journal of Political Science* 41:245–69.

Gerstmann, Evan. 1999. The constitutional underclass: Gays, lesbians, and the failure of class-based equal protection. Chicago: University of Chicago Press.

Gibson, James L., and Kent L. Tedin. 1988. The etiology of intolerance of homosexual politics. *Social Science Quarterly* 69 (September): 587–604.

Green, John C., and James L. Guth. 1991. Religion, representatives, and roll calls. *Legislative Studies Quarterly* 16 (4): 571–84.

Haeberle, Steven H. 1996. Gay men and lesbians at city hall. *Social Science Quarterly* 77 (1): 190–97.

Haider-Markel, Donald P. 1997. *From bullhorns to PACs: Lesbian and gay politics, policy and interest groups.* Ph.D. diss., University of Wisconsin–Milwaukee, Political Science.

Haider-Markel, Donald P., and Kenneth J. Meier. 1996. The politics of gay and lesbian rights: Expanding the scope of the conflict. *Journal of Politics* 58 (2): 332–49.

Herek, Gregory M. 1988. Heterosexuals' attitudes toward lesbians and gay men: Correlates and gender differences. *Journal of Sex Research* 25 (4): 457–77.

Jones v. Hallahan, 501 S.W.2d 588 (Ky. 1973).

Jones, Bradford S., and Barbara Norrander.1996. The reliability of aggregated public opinion measures. *American Journal of Political Science* 40 (1): 295–309.

Kite, Mary E., and Bernard E. Whitley Jr. 1996. Sex differences in attitudes toward homosexual persons, behaviors, and civil rights: A meta-analysis. *Personality and Social Psychology Bulletin* 22 (4): 336–53.

Leonard, Arthur S. 1994. Lesbian and gay families and the law: A progress report. *Fordham Urban Law Journal* 21:927–72.

Lewis, Gregory B. 1997. Lifting the ban on gays in the civil service: Federal policy toward gay and lesbian employees since the Cold War. *Public Administration Review* 57 (September/October): 387–95.

Lewis, Gregory B., and Marc A. Rogers. 1999. Does the public support equal employment rights for gays and lesbians? In *Gays and lesbians in the democratic process: Public policy, public opinion and political representation,* edited by Ellen D.B. Riggle and Barry L. Tadlock. New York: Columbia University Press.

Loving v. Virginia, 147 S.E.2d 78 (Va. 1966), rev'd, 388 U.S. 1 (1967).

Norton v. Macy, 417 F.2d 1161 (D.C. Cir. 1969).

Pacelle, Richard. 1996. Seeking another forum: The courts and gay and lesbian rights. In *Gay rights, military wrongs: Political perspectives on lesbians and gays in the military,* edited by Craig A. Rimmerman. New York: Garland Publishing, Inc.

Rayside, David M. 1996. The perils of congressional politics. In *Gay rights, military wrongs: Political perspectives on lesbians and gays in the military,* edited by Craig A. Rimmerman. New York: Garland Publishing, Inc.

Rimmerman, Craig A. 1996. Promise unfulfilled: Clinton's failure to overturn the military ban on lesbians and gays. In *Gay rights, military wrongs: Political perspectives on lesbians and gays in the military,* edited by Craig A. Rimmerman. New York: Garland Publishing, Inc.

Rogers, Marc A. 1998. A theoretical and empirical analysis of americans' attitudes toward gays and lesbians. Ph.D. diss., American University.

Rotello, Gabriel. 1996. To have and to hold: The case for gay marriage. *Nation.* 24 June, pp. 11–18.

Rubenstein, William B. 1997. Divided we litigate: Addressing disputes among group members and lawyers in civil rights campaigns. *Yale Law Journal* 106 (April): 1623–81.

Schattschneider, E. E. 1960. *The semi-sovereign people.* New York. Holt, Rinehart, and Winston.

Schwanberg, Sandra L. 1993. Attitudes toward gay men and lesbian women: Instrumentation issues. *Journal of Homosexuality* 26 (1):99–136.

Sherrill, Kenneth. 1993. On gay people as a politically powerless group. In *Gays and the military: Joseph Steffan versus the United States,* edited by Marc Wolinsky and Kenneth Sherrill. Princeton: Princeton University Press.

Shilts, Randy. 1993. *Conduct unbecoming: Gays and lesbians in the U.S. Military.* New York: St. Martin's Press.

Singer v. Hara, 522 P.2d 1187 (Wash. App. 1974).

Smith, Rhonda. 1998. R.I. nears repeal: GOP governor expected to sign bill. *Washington Blade,* 5 June, 1, 22.

Society for Individual Rights, Inc. v. Hampton, 63 F.R.D. 399 (N.D. Cal. 1973).

Strasser, Mark. 1997. *Legally wed: Same-sex marriage and the Constitution.* Ithaca: Cornell University Press.

Tiemeyer, Peter E. 1993. Relevant public opinion. In *Sexual orientation and U.S. military personnel policy: Options and assessments,* National Defense Research Institute, 191–208.

U.S. House of Representatives, Judiciary Committee, Defense of Marriage Act, Report 104-664, 104th Cong., 2d sess. July 9, 1996.

Wald, Kenneth D., James W. Button, and Barbara A. Rienzo. 1996. The politics of gay rights in American communities: Explaining antidiscrimination ordinances and policies. *American Journal of Political Science* 40 (4): 1152–78.

Wilcox, Clyde, and Robin M. Wolpert. 1996. "President Clinton, public opinion, and gays in the military." In *Gay rights, military wrongs: Political perspectives on lesbians and gays in the military,* edited by Craig A. Rimmerman. New York: Garland Publishing, Inc.

Winfield, Liz, and Susan Spielman. 1995. *Straight talk about gays in the workplace: Creating an inclusive, productive environment for everyone in your organization.* New York: American Management Association.

Wright Jr., Gerald C., Robert S. Erikson, and John P. McGiver. 1985. Measuring state partisanship and ideology with survey data. *Journal of Politics* 47:469–89.

Yang, Alan S. 1997. Attitudes toward homosexuality. *Public Opinion Quarterly* 61: 477–507.

10

GAYS AND AIDS: DEMOCRATIZING DISEASE?

Mark Carl Rom

AIDS has changed the politics of the gay community.
Gays united to educate themselves about the disease and
to care for those who were afflicted. They mobilized to
seek more money for medical research to understand this
disease, cure it, and ultimately prevent it. They were galvanized to seek changes in the ways drugs are developed,
tested, and marketed. They were provoked to seek changes
in medical standards of care and the ways these standards
are devised. They demanded changes in the ways that persons with disabilities—and this disease could be disabling
in so many ways—are treated by their employers.
Through this activism, gays have achieved numerous
changes in public health policy. The main question this
chapter considers is whether gay activism has had a
broader impact on the public health policy *process.* Did
gays activism on AIDS make the process more democratic?

This chapter examines several ways that gays responded politically to the AIDS epidemic and considers
some of the major policy changes that have resulted.[1] First,
I consider issues in democratization. Second, I outline
some of the sources and limits to gay political power regarding AIDS. Next, I describe the politics of some of the
AIDS issues of greatest concern to the gay community.
Finally, I explore some of the broader implications of gay
activism on AIDS and consider whether this activism has
democratized public health policy more broadly or is limited to an interest group response to a particular disease.

DEMOCRACY

Imagine that health policy is made in a big room with many tables, with each table making specific policy decisions. What would it mean to make the process more democratic?[2] For our purposes, democratization means increasing participation (the numbers of people vying for chairs at the tables), increasing access (the number of chairs at the tables), or increasing equality (so that the voices expressed from each chair have similar weight). These three situations are typically related. Chairs are unlikely to be added unless individuals mobilize to demand them; voices are unlikely to be equalized unless those at the table demand that they be.

Gay activism towards AIDS can have several impacts on democracy. A first, more limited one, would occur if gays themselves participated more, gained access to the tables where decisions regarding AIDS were made, and obtained a more equal voice in those decisions.[3] A second, broader impact, would occur if gay activism induced others to participate, gain access, and equalize voice in AIDS policy. A third, even larger consequence would be if gay activism on AIDS helped encourage greater democratization of public health policy more broadly defined.

DISEASE AND POLITICS

Disease can mobilize several types of groups to political activity. It can impel the afflicted themselves—those persons who have contracted the illness (for infectious diseases) or manifest the ailment (for cancers and chronic conditions, among others). Disease can also activate those who do not themselves bear the illness but who nonetheless have seen its toll on lovers, friends, or family members. Finally, disease can engage those who have perhaps little direct stake in the disease itself, but who are active in the controversies for other political reasons.

The politics of AIDS involves all three groups. Part of the power of gay activists stems from the fact that AIDS linked the infected and the affected. Gay activists were also able, eventually, to bring in others who sympathized with the fight against AIDS. Precisely because gays are a sexually-identified group, however, their activism brought religious and social conservatives into AIDS politics in ways that gays could hardly have hoped (Bull and Gallagher 1996). Whereas other ailments (heart disease, cancers, etc.) could be seen by most merely as illnesses that should be eradicated, AIDS was seen by certain elements as divine retribution for sinful behavior. In this view, it was not the disease that should be eliminated but the behaviors—or perhaps even groups—most closely linked to the disease.

Gays and their allies, as well as those who opposed homosexuality, all attempted to frame the political definition of AIDS that best suited their interests and ideologies.[4]

In considering the politics of AIDS the reader must remember that, despite the wishes of some, AIDS was never just a disease nor merely a medical problem. AIDS has always been intimately connected with broader and more controversial political issues involving sexuality, self-determination, civil rights, and moral values. When some gays opposed the shutting down of bath houses, they did so because they feared the loss of the freedoms that allowed them to be left alone, not because they favored illness (Shilts 1987; Bayer 1991b). When advocates of traditional public health measures called for mandatory HIV testing, most gays opposed this as a needless and reckless intrusion into their civil rights (Bayer 1991b). When gays sought educational programs to promote safer sex, opponents portrayed this as advocacy for "the homosexual lifestyle." If there has been an uncontroversial issue in AIDS, I am not aware of it.

All diseases are not politically equal, however, nor equally political. AIDS was perhaps unique in its ability to unify and mobilize a group of activists to seek policy remedies. AIDS activists were unrivalled in their ability to generate momentum for their cause through direct action, inside lobbying and, especially, the ability to create a high media profile. The reasons for the high political salience of AIDS involve both the ailment and the audience. The disease is especially mediagenic, especially when it struck someone perceived as straight (Kinsella 1989; Colby and Cook 1991). It typically involved sex or drugs. It was uniformly horrible and fatal (at least during its first decade), and it usually struck down those in the prime of their lives. AIDS was spread sexually, at least among gays, and this sexual aspect helped unite gays who, after all, were already united because of their sexual orientation. The places AIDS first struck with full force (San Francisco and New York City) were the homes of the most visible and vocal gay populations. These populations, and the communities they had built, faced immediate, direct, and dire consequences from this disease.

GAY ACTIVISTS AND ACTIVISM

Gay activism on AIDS did not spring from a vacuum. An active gay liberation movement had existed since at least 1969 with the Stonewall Inn riots in New York. By the late 1970s, the gay community in San Francisco had elected an openly gay politician (Harvey Milk) to the board of supervisors, had one of the city's more powerful grassroots organizations (the Harvey Milk Gay Democratic Club), and, with one-in-four registered voters, had the potential to form the largest single voting bloc in the city (Shilts 1987, 13). At least in the largest cities, prior to AIDS there was already gay political activism on issues of special concern to the gay community (D'Emilio 1983; Altman 1982; Adam 1987). This activism left a strong imprint on subsequent gay reactions towards AIDS.

Gay leaders certainly also knew, and took cues from, the civil rights movement regarding goals and strategies (Vaid 1995). Like African Americans, gays were understandably skeptical about the idea that the government would act in their best interests, and they knew that their interests would only be considered if they demanded they be. Gay activists have argued that governmental neglect of AIDS was actually intentional because, by letting the disease run its course, the public would free itself both of sexual deviancy and a medical threat (Poirer 1988). It is no accident that many members of ACT UP ("AIDS Coalition to Unleash Power") embraced Malcolm X's slogan of "By any means necessary" (Wachter 1992). Like civil rights leaders, since the onset of AIDS gay activists have wanted both to be free from discrimination and also to receive their fair share of social resources.

Political activists in this socially marginalized group did well resemble the typical American political participant, but for their sexual orientation. The gays who were politically active on AIDS, especially during the early years of the epidemic, were overwhelmingly white, middle-class, well-educated men, though perhaps a bit younger than the average Rotarian. As in other American political issues, race, gender, and class mattered. Those who participated most had more at stake and more political resources to bring.

Women and minorities, gay and straight, have played notable roles in AIDS politics, of course. These roles came later, slower, and were often smaller. To be sure, women both lesbian and straight provided valuable aid as caregivers, in groups such as the Gay Men's Health Crisis and in organizations as diverse as ACT UP and the AIDS Action Council. But AIDS did not pose the same threat to lesbians as it did to gays, nor rally the same support from straight women.

Minority activism was even more modest. As late as 1987 the claim could still be made that "[t]here has been little organized Black or Hispanic response [to AIDS]. The major Black and Hispanic institutions have done little or nothing, and there has been no grassroots flowering of AIDS-related organizations" (Friedman *et al.* 1987). White gays, for their part, did little to recruit minorities to their organizations, except for efforts in groups such as "Men of All Colors Together" and the Gay Men's Health Crisis (Kayal 1993, 99; Vaid 1995, 24). And while AIDS did little to unite women or minorities, persons with AIDS (PWAs) from these groups generally had even fewer political resources than their uninfected counterparts.[5]

If gays had some of the political resources necessary for political efficacy, they lacked other prerequisites of political power, as Wald discusses earlier in this volume (Wald 1999). Gays are relatively few in number and these numbers were cut by AIDS itself.[6] Gays are a socially stigmatized group, and doubly so through their connection with the epidemic.[7] Still, gays could muster a core of highly motivated, politically savvy, resourceful individuals to seek political power over this epidemic.

ORGANIZATIONS AND AIDS

Much gay activism has been channeled through political organizations, and hundreds of mainly gay organizations have been active in the struggle against AIDS (see HRC 1999a, 1999b). For example, the AIDS Action Council, and its subsidiary, National Organizations Responding to AIDS, represent five hundred AIDS organizations nationwide in their political activities. The New York AIDS Coalition represents two hundred organizations in that state alone (Kayal 1993, 186). By 1994, the National AIDS Clearinghouse had compiled a list of over eighteen thousand AIDS service organizations across the country (Burkett 1995, 145). Like the nonprofit world more generally, however, many of these organizations are constantly in flux, sprouting and dying, merging and splitting, being reorganized and renamed. Four especially long-lasting and well-known gay groups are the Gay Men's Health Crisis (GMHC), the AIDS Coalition to Unleash Power (ACT UP), the Human Rights Campaign (HRC), and the Lambda Legal Defense Fund. These groups are worth discussing because they illustrate the different political strategies and targets gays have used to confront AIDS, with the GMHC emphasizing self help, ACT UP public demonstrations, HRC mainstream political action, and Lambda litigation.

Gay Men's Health Crisis

The GMHC is the oldest and best established gay organization focused on AIDS; it is also the largest and most recognized.[8] Founded in 1981 in New York City, the GMHC mainly provides AIDS education, counseling, and social services to assist the sick "in much the same way that a family, community, or group of friends would" (Kayal 1993, 2; GMHC 1999). It represents an effort to address AIDS apart from the government; although the GMHC does take political stands, it is first and foremost a community devoted to caring for its members. As a former executive director noted, GMHC was "founded *by* the gay community *for* the gay community—and I was confident GMHC would *always* be there for the gay community" (Braff 1990, 2). The GMHC "would ultimately serve as a model of communal self-help efforts in both the United States and Europe" (Bayer 1995, 135). Communal self-help groups have been around for centuries, of course, but the GMHC and similar AIDS organizations represent an unusually well-organized and established response.

The GMHC is a mainstream organization: it seeks to build the boat, not rock it. In the early 1990s, it was the largest nongovernmental distributor of AIDS information in the world (Kayal 1993). It is also thoroughly institutionalized, as it has grown into a large and complex organization. By the late 1990s, the GMHC served more than 7,500 clients annually with a staff of over two hundred and nearly seven thousand volunteers; it had a $22 million yearly budget, with two-thirds of the funds coming from private donors (GMHC 1999). One indication of its presence in the AIDS establishment is that it "appears *de riguer* for all levels of government to include a representative of GMHC in any major AIDS-related group they establish" (Kobasa 1990, 286).

ACT UP

The AIDS Coalition to Unleash Power was established, in part, as a reaction to what was seen as the political inactivity of the GMHC (Arno and Feiden 1992; Fabj and Sobnosky 1993; Wolfe 1994). Although a speech by Larry Kramer, one of the founders of the GMHC, is reputed to have triggered the formation of ACT UP, the hundreds who attended the first meeting demonstrate that he touched powder ready to explode.[9] Explicitly antihierarchical, ACT UP's protocols keep it from having a board of directors, elected leaders, or paid staff. Each meeting is run by a facilitator chosen by the audience. In practice, anyone attending the meetings can vote. ACT UP meetings have consequently been described as "a bold experiment in participatory democracy and an exercise in creative chaos" (Arno and Feiden 1992, 76). ACT UP's main political goal has been to increase access to new drugs for people with AIDS.[10]

If the GMHC wanted to nurture the afflicted, ACT UP wanted to overthrow the establishment (see ACT UP 1999). If the GMHC wanted to quietly persuade, ACT UP wanted to embarrass, harass, or intimidate officials into taking action. If GMHC aspired to be—and became—and "insider" organization, ACT UP wanted to remain an "outside" agitator; suspicious, indeed, as to whether one could become an insider without selling out (see chapter 3 in this volume). With the pink triangle (used in Nazi Germany to identify gays) as its symbol and the words "Silence = Death" as its motto, ACT UP preferred direct and shocking action to subtle responses.

ACT UP has been less successful at establishing a permanent institutional presence, however. In part, ACT UP avoided organization building efforts; in part, its confrontational tactics alienated substantial elements of the gay community; Jennings and Anderson 1997); in part, many of its most active members were lost to the disease. As a result, ACT UP has declined in importance in recent years.

Human Rights Campaign

Founded in 1980, the HRC is the largest gay and lesbian political organization in the nation, with over two hundred thousand members. As noted in chapter 2, the HRC engages in a wide variety of mainstream political activities; for instance, it lobbies the federal government on gay, lesbian, and AIDS issues; participates in election campaigns (it gave over $1 million to federal candidates in 1996, and claims that 84 percent of the candidates it favored won). HRC also organizes volunteers and provides expertise and training at the state and local level. It has a political website that could easily have been established for the AARP or the NRA (HRC 1999a). It rates each member of Congress on issues important to the HRC and provides an easy way for individuals to send personalized messages to their representatives via email. AIDS is only one of the HRC's concerns, however; "Sound AIDS policy" is currently listed third among the HRC's political goals, behind protection from job discrimination and hate crime.

Lambda Legal Defense Fund

Lambda is a national organization committed to achieving full recognition of the civil rights of lesbians, gay men, and people with HIV/AIDS through "impact litigation" (that is, lawsuits whose goal is setting precedent, not just winning the case at hand), education, and public policy work. Lambda carries out its legal work principally through test cases selected for the likelihood of their success in establishing positive legal precedents that will affect lesbians, gay men, and people with HIV/AIDS. Lambda claims to have brought the first AIDS discrimination case to court, and Lambda's legal staff of attorneys, supplemented by volunteers, continues to work on a wide range of cases, with a docket averaging over fifty cases at any given time (Lambda 1998).

INSTITUTIONS AND STRATEGIES

Like all other political actors in the United States, gays could attempt to influence public policy through various political institutions at various levels of government. Gays could target elected politicians, bureaucrats, or judges within local, state, or national governments. Gay activism could also encompass the entire range of political behaviors. To change AIDS policies, gays could vote, raise funds, write letters, file lawsuits, seek publicity, conduct research, lobby officials, advertise, seek appointments, provide care, and raise hell, among others. Finally, the activities could be focused on various types of AIDS policy: research, treatment, prevention, and discrimination, among others. The type of action used, and the institution to which it was directed, reflected strategic choices as well as spontaneous outbursts.[11] Some forms of political action dominated, however, and for good reason. Let us now consider the strategic choices faced by gays.

Elected Officials

Gays have had limited influence over elected officials. In only a few places (such as San Francisco) could gays expect to have much direct influence over many elected officials by virtue of their voting power.[12] In no state, however, and certainly not in Congress, could gays by themselves expect to have much electoral clout, although they may constitute important parts of the electoral coalitions for some individual legislators. They tended to be active in Democratic party politics. (By the 1980 election, the gay caucus at the Democratic National Convention, with seventy members, was larger than the delegations of twenty states (Shilts 1987, 13).) Yet gays had little to show for their involvement in presidential elections through the 1980s. Presidents Reagan and Bush had little to do with either gays or AIDS. Gays were an important element in Clinton's election, with an estimated 72 percent of gays and lesbians voting for him (D'Emilio 1996), and he has been much more active on AIDS issues than his predecessors.[13] Clinton appointed an AIDS "czar" to lead a newly formed National AIDS Programs Office (NAPO).[14] NAPO, meanwhile, has been given little power or money; it attempts to coordinate policy rather than developing and administering it.

From nearly the beginning of the epidemic, gay political activity has had more electoral influence on at least a few members of Congress. Phil Burton, a Democrat from San Francisco who almost became Speaker of the House in 1976, was an early ally of gays as they sought federal funding for research (Shilts 1987, 162, 186–87). Barbara Boxer, San Francisco's other representative in the 1980s, also aligned herself with San Francisco's most important grassroots—and gay—organization, the Harvey Milk Club (13, 254). Neither representative made AIDS a top priority, however (526).

Two other congressional allies had more interest and more influence. Los Angeles Representative Henry Waxman was one of the most liberal members of Congress, and the Gay and Lesbian Services Center was in the heart of Waxman's district (143). Waxman, as chair of the Health Subcommittee, was also in a position to make his support on AIDS issues count. A final vigorous advocate for gays regarding AIDS was Manhattan Representative Ted Weiss. Weiss had a substantial gay constituency and aggressively monitored the administration's AIDS activities, especially those of the Centers for Disease Control (CDC). Only Waxman has been able to provide a lasting voice to gays on AIDS, however; Burton and Weiss both died in office, while Boxer moved to the Senate. Meanwhile, the few publicly gay members of Congress—Barney Frank, Steve Gunderson, Gerry Studds—have kept a rather low profile on AIDS policy.[15]

Gays nonetheless had their supporters in Congress, and these supporters have mainly been liberal Democrats (Haider-Markel 1997). In 1998, the House of Representatives held votes on five issues of special importance to gays (HRC 1999a). Democrats, on average, received a score of 3.95 (with each vote in support of the HRC preference counted as 1). Republicans, in contrast, had average scores of 0.79. Both parties, moreover, were highly polarized: over 70 percent within both parties mainly supported (Democrats scoring 4 or 5) or mainly opposed (Republicans scoring 0 or 1) the HRC preferences in 1998.[16]

Because of their limited electoral clout, gay activists wanting to influence national legislation typically faced two possible strategies. Gays could rely on sympathetic individual legislators to promote gay interests by, for example, holding hearings or tucking in AIDS spending provisions into larger bills. Alternately, gays could try to influence the legislature as a whole by building coalitions with other groups having similar interests vis-à-vis AIDS. In any case, the willingness of antigay legislators to block legislation that appeared in any way to reward gays has induced gay leaders usually to make moderate and broad-based appeals when dealing with elected officials.

Judges

Gays have also achieved limited success from the courts in obtaining their policy goals regarding AIDS (Burris et al. 1995). Courts are, of course, limited institutions; unlike legislators, they cannot initiate policy but must respond to cases that are brought to them. Moreover, while courts are inherently political, they are less subject to direct political action than are legislators and bureaucrats. Nonetheless, the courts can be used to seek protection from discrimination, and those infected with HIV have sought such protection many times.

The response from the courts has been mixed. In a 1992 study conducted for the U.S. Public Health report that noted the "unprecedented flood of litigation" concerning AIDS, the author concluded, "There is still a basic fear, often an irrational fear, in society [regarding AIDS] that is being litigated in the courts. The problem is [that] many of the judges are reinforcing and perpetuating the stereotypes." Unfortunately, those stereotypes have not vanished entirely in subsequent years. HIV-positive health care workers continued to face discrimination throughout the 1980s, for instance, as courts tended to allow them to be fired because they posed risks to their patients, though it is not clear that even a single patient has been accidentally infected by a health care worker (Rom 1997).

Bureaucrats

The policymakers most sympathetic to gay concerns regarding AIDS, but with limited ability to act on these concerns, have been public health officials. By and large, public health officials favored the same health measures that gays sought. The general reason for this agreement is that public health officials typically believe that their effectiveness depends on the co-operation of the citizens—health officials see themselves more as doctors than as police. A more specific reason is that health officials, especially those at the CDC, had developed good working relationships with the gay community. Even before AIDS, the CDC sent representatives to national meetings of gay organizations, for example, and had worked closely with gays in the hepatitis B vaccine trials that began in 1980 (Etheridge 1992, 326–27). Division between gays and health officials have existed, however; one highly visible conflict concerned issues surrounding HIV in the medical workplace (Rom 1997).

There is thus no single politics of AIDS. Gay activism, and prospects for success, has depended in part on how gay interests were structured, how these interests were expressed in the political process, and how the various governmental institutions responded to these interests. Let us now examine the differing politics of prevention, care, spending, drugs, and discrimination.

THE POLITICS OF PREVENTION

One might hope that this would be the simplest political topic in AIDS policy. Surely everyone, not just gays, must have a stake in preventing the spread of AIDS. Certainly we know how to prevent its spread. As HIV is transmitted through infected blood, semen, or vaginal fluids, preventing its spread means keeping individuals from coming into contact with those fluids. Prevention has nevertheless been among the most controversial topics in AIDS politics.

The main sexual problems are these: persons can avoid the risk of contracting HIV by remaining celibate or by maintaining a mutually exclusive relationship, while they can greatly reduce risks by using "safer sex" practices (such as condoms). The former ways are completely effective and, moreover, they accord with the moral or religious principles of many people. However, a large proportion of the American public is neither celibate nor sexually exclusive. The safer sex approach reduces risk but does not eliminate it. Moreover, those who favor chastity or monogamy can portray safer sex education as government-supported education in immorality. Much of the political discussion about AIDS prevention has bogged down in claims about morality and effectiveness.[17]

The gay movement fostered large gay enclaves, especially in New York and San Francisco, by the end of the 1970s. These communities formed as gays sought protection from harassment but also to celebrate homosexuality. As a result, these cities developed subcultures favoring high levels of sex with multiple partners. When AIDS first started spreading, but before it was known to be an infectious disease, its sexual implications were subjects of heated debate. Many gays worried that AIDS was connected with unfettered sexual play and urged restraint; others saw any effort to limit sexual expression as being fundamentally antigay and a threat to the gay movement. Writing in the *Native*, New York's gay newspaper, one doctor noted: "Within the gay community, a . . . crisis of ideology is threatening to explode. With much confusion on all sides, advocates of sexual 'fulfillment' are being opposed by critics of 'promiscuity'" (Mass

1982, 11). On the one side were those who refused to give up casual sex with the argument, "I refuse to blight my life—supposedly—to preserve it" (*New York Native* 1983a, 5). The sober response, as from Larry Kramer: "I am sick of guys who moan that giving up careless sex until this blows over is worse than death. How can they value life so little and cocks and asses so much? Come with me, guys, while I visit a few of our friends in intensive care. . . . Notice the looks in their eyes, guys. They'd give up sex forever if you could promise them life" (*New York Native* 1983b, 1).

Much of this early intramural debate concerned how homosexuals should live their own lives. The major policy debate concerned whether public establishments fostering sexual encounters (especially bath houses) should be closed. Some gays saw bath houses as a central part of gay culture and, moreover, an ideal place to provide information about AIDS. Others saw them as health hazards that profited mainly their commercial owners. But in an early introduction to AIDS politics, health officials moved very slowly to shut them down (Shilts 1987; Bayer 1991b).

The federal government did little, especially during the early years, to prevent the spread of HIV. Legislation was introduced but not enacted (Haider-Markel 1997). To be sure, conservatives within Congress, as well as the Reagan and Bush Administrations, opposed sexually explicit prevention programs. The gay community, for its part, did little to promote them. Part of the reason for this, perhaps, was strategic: so long as social conservatives had political power (and they have held it, at least in the Senate, throughout virtually the entire course of the epidemic), it made little political sense for gays to press for federally funded safer sex programs.[18] In 1987, for instance, Senator Jesse Helms (R-N.C.) was able to insert an amendment to the AIDS funding bill prohibiting the CDC from funding any activities that "promote or encourage, directly or indirectly, homosexual sexual activities"; he also obtained language forbidding prevention programs that targeted homosexual behavior (*CQ Almanac* 1987, 457). In doing so, Helms waved sexually explicit educational comic books produced by the Gay Men's Health Crisis that, in fact, had not been produced using federal funds. Helms and his allies skillfully used AIDS prevention activities to paint homosexuals in the light that made the straight public most uneasy, making it difficult for health-minded members of Congress to support prevention (Bailey 1992).[19] Indeed, "moralizing" issues in gay politics has been a consistently successful strategy for conservatives (Haider-Markel and Meier 1996).

It is noteworthy that the GMHC sued the government, and won, to strike down the Helms amendment. Although the GMHC won that particular battle, a legal strategy would be quite limited: the federal government cannot be forced through litigation to conduct AIDS prevention programs (Burris 1993).

Gays themselves have given little attention to prevention issues (Wachter 1992; Bailey 1995; HRC 1999a, 1999b), which upon analysis reveals more than one Catch-22. The gays who have most reason to make prevention the highest policy priority are those who are already infected, but they would benefit little from this; their main political concerns, naturally, concerned such things as research and treatment. For the rest, it is quite natural that if you didn't know anything about prevention, you had no idea to campaign for it, but if you *did* know about prevention you had no reason seek more of it. The main political advocates of prevention programs have thus not been gays, but public health officials who have professional reasons for advocating prevention. Prevention thus lacks a core constituency among gays, and as a result, prevention programs have accounted for less than 20 percent of federal spending on AIDS (Burris 1993, 88).

THE POLITICS OF CARE

When AIDS first emerged in New York and San Francisco, the number of gays with the disease grew exponentially. As these men grew increasingly ill, they needed more and more help—medical care, social services, spiritual attention, and comfort. These needs could be met in three main ways. In a purely individual approach, the PWAs ("persons with AIDS") could seek these things through their own personal resources, friends, and family. Alternately, PWAs and their allies could try to obtain these necessities by changing public policies so that the government provided them. Finally, gays could join together in broader community to deliver these services themselves rather than relying on the government. All three approaches are political in that they express ideological or strategic views about the appropriate way (i.e., personal, governmental, or communal) to address problems. Gays in San Francisco, already politically active and powerful (at least locally), emphasized the governmental track. New York gays favored the community-based method.

At the beginning of the 1980s, gays also had strategic reasons for preferring voluntary, communal approaches to the problems of AIDS. While gays had special reasons for distrusting the government, the public as a whole also entered into an antigovernmental mood. Reagan was elected in 1980, in part, on a platform calling for less government and more volunteerism. During his eight years in office, the Reagan administration was not a sympathetic audience for gays seeking help.

So especially during the early years of AIDS, gays sought to fashion their own response to the growing epidemic. The most prominent response, the Gay Men's Health Crisis (GMHC) of New York, was the first organized response to AIDS on the east coast. By the early 1990s it "offered direct personal support to about 35 percent of all New Yorkers with AIDS [and had] outreach services in every borough" (Kayal 1993, 2).

Although the GMHC does some political lobbying, its main emphasis has always been on AIDS prevention and care. The GMHC, moreover, offered gays a way to "bear witness" by helping unite those who offered care with those who received it, and at the GMHC large numbers did both. The name itself is illuminating, focusing as it does not on an illness but on the community: not AIDS, but Gay Men's Health. The GMHC has helped served as a model for similar organizations that sprung up in other cities, such as the AIDS project in Los Angeles, NO AIDS in New Orleans, AIDS Atlanta, the AIDS Arms Network in Dallas, and the Kaposi Sarcoma Education and Research Foundation in San Francisco (237).

The importance of these gay efforts to provide care to PWAs should not be underestimated. During the early years of the epidemic, "the vast bulk of the cost of the AIDS epidemic has been borne by vast amounts of unpaid labor donated by community organizations founded by gay activists, as well as by private charities and a few local governments—and *not* by the federal government" (Krieger and Appleman 1986, 31–32). At least for the GMHC, this is still true, as two-thirds of its budget still comes from private sources, not counting the several million dollars worth of donated labor it receives each year (GMHC 1999).

Those who volunteer at GMHC are, typically, openly gay males. A 1986 survey showed that roughly three-fourths of GHMC volunteers were unconcerned that this work identified them as gay, a supporter of gay rights, and an AIDS activist. Most were active in the gay rights struggle; they volunteered because they felt a sense of communal responsibility to do so (Kayal 1993). A later survey showed similar results, while also showing that gay volunteers did so for diverse reasons: "Many gay people apparently volunteer as a way of acting on humanitarian values, helping the gay community in particular, establishing important social contacts and identities, or as an outgrowth of personal experiences with HIV" (Omoto and Crain 1995, 205).

THE POLITICS OF SPENDING

While a few members of Congress had electoral reasons to assist gays, they also had gay staffers who worked to ensure that their bosses did assist them. Michael Housh, a Milk Club activist, worked for Barbara Boxer, while Phil Burton hired Bill Kraus, a prominent San Francisco gay activist, for his staff. Tim Westmoreland was Henry Waxman's chief of staff. (In the early 1980s, these were just about the only openly gay staff members working for the Congress (Shilts 1987).) As anyone with experience on Capitol Hill knows, staffers can make a difference. Shilts concluded that "virtually all the money that funded the early scientific advances on AIDS can be credited almost solely to these two gay men [Kraus and Westmoreland]" (187).

The early funding provided for AIDS does show the power that a few insiders can assemble in the Congress. In 1982 the federal government was spending a trivial amount on AIDS research; the Reagan administration had vetoed a half-million-dollar supplemental appropriation as "too costly." Kraus got an appointment with Burton to discuss funding, but Burton simply asked Kraus how much he wanted. Kraus's back of the envelope answer: $5 million for the Centers for Disease Control, $5 million of the National Institutes of Health. Burton's response: "Let's ask for $5 million and $10 million." Waxman aide Westmoreland put this into legal language and the bill was introduced; it was then incorporated into a larger supplemental appropriations bill (187).

Waxman was the first to conduct oversight on the government's response to the AIDS epidemic, holding hearings in Los Angeles in April 1982 and in Washington in May 1983. He made it clear that he was "very disappointed with the Administration's response" (290). Immediately after this hearing, Westmoreland, Housh, and Susan Steinmetz (a Weiss staffer) met to discuss strategy. They concurred that if Congress was to increase AIDS funding, they needed to find direct evidence that health officials needed more money, and so began to conduct a comprehensive investigation of federal AIDS policy for Weiss's subcommittee (Panem 1988, 31–35). The evidence was damning (House 1983). Weiss concluded:

> Tragically, funding levels for AIDS investigations have been dictated by political considerations rather than by the professional judgments of scientists and public health officials who are waging the battle against the epidemic. The inadequacy of funding, coupled with inexcusable delays in research activity, leads me to question . . . this Administration's commitment to an urgent resolution to the AIDS crisis. (Weiss 1983)

Waxman subsequently introduced a bill to create the Public Health Emergency Fund (note that AIDS was *not* in the title) to increase federal funding for AIDS. Once again, this bill was incorporated as an amendment to a much larger supplemental spending bill, where it was enacted.

Whatever congressional antipathy towards gays existed, in fact federal funding for AIDS grew dramatically in the early years of the epidemic, and by 1995 the U.S. Public Health Service spent more on AIDS ($2.7 billion) than on any of the other ten most lethal diseases (Johnson 1997).[20] The Department of Health and Human Services (HHS) accounts for the vast bulk of federal AIDS research, prevention, and treatment programs, and spends about three-fourths of the federal dollars on AIDS (Johnson 1997).

HHS funding for AIDS has grown considerably over time. The largest percentage growth came in the early years, when the total spending was so modest. AIDS funding increased by over 2600 percent (from $200,000 to $5.5 million) between 1981 and 1982, by another 400 percent in 1983, and it continued to double in 1984, in 1985, in 1986, and again in 1987. During the next decade the increases were more modest in percentage terms (with growth between 4 and 24 percent). The two largest increases in dollar terms came in 1988 and 1994, with AIDS spending growing by over $450 million in each of those years.

Whether the federal government spent enough to combat AIDS will inevitably be a matter of debate. If the question is posed as "Did the government spend enough to find a cure or to stop the spread of AIDS or as much as it would have to stop a similar disease that mainly affected straight men?" then the answer is pretty clearly: No, it did not. Still, others believe that the government spends too much on AIDS relative to other serious diseases (Knight 1998). No clear metric exists, unfortunately, for determining what the appropriate amount of spending should be.[21]

In Congress, it is relatively easy to insert a minor provision into a major bill—after all, what's a couple of million in a trillion dollar budget?—and this can be done through the work of a few. It is a different game to enact broader, stand-alone, legislation (Elving 1995). If gays can count on a few members of Congress and their staffers to advocate for additional funding for AIDS, then gays would need to broaden their coalition substantially if they were to have much luck persuading Congress to enact legislation and the president to sign it.

Gays did have many potential, and potentially powerful, allies. Public health officials generally supported gays on issues involving AIDS. Surgeon General C. Everett Koop, a popular and respected conservative, argued that moral judgments had no place in a public health debate—a position gays certainly found sympathetic to their cause. Admiral James Watkins, the first director of a Reagan-appointed presidential commission on AIDS, also advocated (among the commission's 579 recommendations) confidentiality in testing, antidiscrimination protections for those testing positive, and much greater spending for voluntary testing, HIV education, and medical research. A joint panel of the National Institutes of Health and the National Academy of Sciences had similar recommendations (*CQ Almanac* 1988, 300).

Gays faced a major dilemma on Capitol Hill, however. In one of the great ironies of AIDS politics, gays have had much less to fear from the congressional majority than from a small but highly vocal antigay minority, especially Jesse Helms in the Senate and William Dannemeyer in the House.[22] Just as it is relatively easy for a few individuals to insert special interest provisions into legislation, it is also possible for individuals to block legislation from being considered. As a result, gays had better luck when they worked quietly within Congress and avoided, when possible, much emphasis on the word "gay" than when they used more militant tactics that might be more successful elsewhere.[23]

So if AIDS funding grew rapidly during the mid-1980s, it did so without much explicit discussion in Congress of the disease or how it was spread. In 1987, for example, the year that Congress approved the greatest increase in AIDS funding for research, the Senate leadership decided not to bring a separate AIDS bill to the floor (even though a Senate committee had unanimously approved the bill) because Helms threatened to offer numerous amendments requiring, among other things, mandatory HIV testing, a proposal that is anathema to gays (*CQ Almanac* 1987, 20).

Not until 1988 did Congress enact its first significant policy outlines for addressing AIDS, and even then the measures were attached to a much broader spending bill.[24] At that time, gay advocates, public health officials, and their supporters in Congress, sought intensive public education programs coupled with confidential blood testing and counseling of high-risk individuals. Helms, Dannemeyer, and their allies wanted mandatory testing with the names of those infected reported to public health authorities and to the infected persons' sexual partners. Helms and Dannemeyer also opposed any educational programs that promoted homosexual activity "directly or indirectly" (and, they would argue, any literature that discussed homosexual activity was interpreted as promoting it). Once again, Helms threatened to block the entire bill unless "controversial" measures, such as a voluntary testing program with guaranteed confidentiality of test results, and antidiscrimination protections for infected individuals, were removed (*CQ Almanac* 1988, 296). "Judging by the debate, Helms and his allies were vastly outnumbered by those who favored widespread dissemination of AIDS information to the people at greatest risk. However, they were able to craft their proposals so that members found it politically impossible to vote against them" (302).

Even after both House and Senate approved AIDS legislation, it almost stalled because Helms refused to allow the Senate to appoint members to a conference committee to resolve the differences between the bills of the two houses. The legislation's sponsors then dropped the provisions Helms most objected to (involving confidentiality and counseling), wrapped the bills into an omnibus health bill, and approved the legislation by voice vote. Thus a radical antigay minority had major responsibility for the law. As Republican Senator Lowell Weicker summarized it, "I'm not happy with the package, because I don't like Jesse Helms setting AIDS policy for this country" (306).

Helms tried to do so again in 1990, when the Congress enacted its first major AIDS law, the Ryan White Comprehensive AIDS Resources Emergency Act. True to form, Helms and Dannemeyer attempted to obstruct and amend, with some success, but the Congress ultimately enacted the bill by wide majorities (95–4 in the Senate, 408–14 in the House) (*CQ Almanac* 1990, 582). The purpose of the bill was to increase the availability of care outside of hospitals for persons with AIDS. The bill consequently created several grant programs, with most of the grants going directly to public or private nonprofit health care and social service providers in the areas with the greatest number of AIDS cases, while other grants were given to the states to allocate. Congress authorized $785 million to be awarded to states and various AIDS-service organizations, but appropriated only about $220 million in funds for the first year of the program.

Why did the Congress, which had never before approved an AIDS bill, do so virtually unanimously now? First, the "political stream" was changing (Kingdon 1984). The coalition supporting this bill was much broader, and politically more attractive, than gays alone. To promote this legislation, AIDS lobbyists had assembled an alliance of around 150 organizations representing nurses, doctors, hospital workers, AIDS organizations, mayors, and governors, among others. Second, the "policy window" opened (Kingdon 1984). At a critical point, it became easier for members of Congress to view the bill as less "gay." Ryan White, a straight white teenager from

Indiana who had contracted HIV through a blood transfusion and consequently become a media star as an "innocent victim" after he was banned from school, died in April 1990. Just before he died, and before the Senate began to work on the legislation, Senator Hatch renamed the bill after White. Shortly after White died, his mother came to Congress to lobby for her son's namesake. When she arrived, twenty-three Senators were cosponsoring the bill; when she left, forty-one others had agreed to do so (Burkett 1995, 146).

Finally, this bill allowed Congress to do what it does best: distribute money widely across the country.[25] Every state (and congressional district) had access to HIV funds; the sixteen hardest-hit cities got the lion's share of the funds. Although the money was urgently needed, the Ryan White Act resembled the kind of pork-barrel legislation often so attractive to Congress.[26] This combination of broadening the AIDS coalition, focusing attention on "straight" PWAs (or those perceived as straight, including Liberace and Rock Hudson) and widely distributing program benefits, proved successful in the Ryan White Act.[27]

The Ryan White Act was not simply the first AIDS law; it was the first time Congress had created a federal program targeting a single disease. The act was a remarkable achievement for AIDS activists. It is also now a durable part of the AIDS policy system, growing every year, costing the federal government over one billion dollars—or nearly thirty percent of federal AIDS funding—in 1998 (Johnson 1997).

THE POLITICS OF DRUGS

The Food and Drug Administration is the federal agency responsible for ensuring that safe and effective drugs are available to the American public. It typically did so with caution, putting more emphasis on safety than availability. FDA officials surely understand that they would receive more blame if Americans died because the agency approved a drug that proved to be lethal than if they denied approval to a drug with the potential to save lives. The critical historical precedent for this involved Dr. Frances Kelsey, the FDA examiner who in 1962 refused to approve the drug thalidomide and so avoided the tragedy caused by this drug in other countries. For her service, President Kennedy awarded Kelsey the highest award for distinguished federal civilian service; for its work, the FDA won public respect. As late as the mid-1980s, opinion polls ranked the FDA just behind the National Park Service as the most appreciated federal agency (Holston 1997).

The FDA was hardly approved by all, however. While AIDS was first reported in 1981, through 1986 the FDA had still not approved *any* drug treatments for it. Before the FDA approved the use of AZT in March 1987, over twenty-five thousand Americans had died from AIDS. AIDS activists were especially angered with FDA procedures for testing and approving drugs. The two most controversial aspects of the approval process concerned the FDA's insistence on double-blind trials and, related to this, the length of time it took for drugs to gain approval for marketing.

In double-blind trials, one group of participants receives the trial medication and the other receives a placebo. In observing the treatment effects, neither participants nor investigators know which group received the medication or the placebo. While such trials are considered the "gold standard" in medical research because they allow accurate measurement of the true impact of the medication, they by definition imply that one group of patients will receive a treatment (the placebo) known *not* to work. Those with terminal illnesses are understandably reluctant to be in the placebo group— and understandably furious that scientists insisted on requiring them.

The FDA had long permitted the emergency use of unapproved, investigational new drugs (INDs) for desperately ill patients (Flieger 1995). Under this informal "compassionate use" policy, patients could obtain these drugs (or other medical products) outside the formal clinical studies necessary to test the drug's safety and efficacy. During the 1970s, for instance, thousands of patients were treated with experimental "beta-blockers" for life-threatening heart and lung conditions that were not otherwise treatable.

In 1987 the FDA changed its regulations for INDs (FDA 1988). These changes had two main components. First, the FDA now explicitly allowed INDs to be used for treatment (and not just research) purposes. Second, the FDA accelerated its processes for bringing new drugs and other medical products to market.

The most famous "treatment IND" was AZT. Within one week of receiving initial, promising results of AZT treatment for AIDS, the FDA authorized use of AZT for treatment. As a result, more than four thousand AIDS patients received AZT treatments before the drug was formally approved for sale (Flieger 1995). In fact, the AZT experience was essential for developing the regulations used for INDs. And while the IND regulations were developed primarily in response to AIDS, between 1987 and 1994 twenty-nine drugs had been awarded treatment IND status, for conditions ranging from AIDS and its related infections, control of infection in kidney transplant recipients, severe obsessive-compulsive disorder, Alzheimer's disease, severe Parkinson's disease, various advanced cancers, and respiratory distress syndrome in premature infants (Flieger 1995). As sponsors are allowed to charge for these therapies and most insurers will not reimburse for experimental drugs, patient access to them is still limited.

More broadly, the FDA has streamlined its drug review and approval process. In 1992 the agency created an "accelerated approval" process for drugs that promise large benefits over existing drugs for serious or life-threatening illnesses. This process is used if the drug has an effect on a surrogate endpoint.[28] Under the accclerated approval process, the FDA stipulates the conditions under which the drug can be administered. By 1994, five drugs available through accelerated approval had ultimately been approved: three antivirals for HIV, one drug for an AIDS-related condition, and one drug for multiple-sclerosis (Kessler 1994).

The FDA also created a "parallel track" policy in response to AIDS. This policy allows PWAs whose condition prevents them from participating in clinical trials to obtain investigational drugs shown in preliminary studies to be potentially useful. According to FDA Commissioner Kessler, "tens of thousands of HIV-infected patients have received unapproved therapies through parallel track" (Kessler 1994). Yet Kessler also acknowledged that these patients did not resemble the broader population of PWAs, as 85 percent of those receiving the first drug available through parallel track (D4T) were white, even though by then a majority of PWAs were minorities.

The FDA is apparently trying to push HIV treatments to approval faster than other drugs. Simple comparisons cannot capture the complexity of the approval process; still, at least in 1996 the average approval time for HIV-related treatments was 2.5 months while for all other treatments, the average was 16.5 months. None of the forty-five other treatments was approved as quickly as the three medications for HIV (FDA 1997). The previous year FDA Commissioner Kessler noted that five of the first six AIDS therapies had been approved in six months or less (FDA 1995).

THE POLITICS OF DISCRIMINATION

Discrimination against gays did not begin with AIDS. Much of the political action of gays prior to the onset of AIDS was, in fact, directed towards fighting discrimination. Yet AIDS brought a new wave of discrimination against those infected or suspected of being infected. For the visibly gay, that suspicion was common: in the early 1980s, "a gay man in New York or San Francisco with a limp wrist and a persistent cough could find

himself fired and estranged from family and friends in a very short time"
(Senak 1996, 85). Between 1983 and 1988, for example, thirteen thousand
complaints of HIV-related discrimination were filed at state and local civil
rights agencies. These complaints involved discrimination in health care,
insurance, housing, workplace treatment, and public benefits, among others (ACLU 1990). Accordingly, a major concern of gays and other PWAs
concerned protecting themselves from discrimination (Senak 1996). They
did this both by establishing their own networks for care (such as through
the GMHC) and through legal action.

The principal bulwarks against AIDs-based discrimination are the
Americans with Disabilities Act of 1990 (ADA) and the Rehabilitation Act
of 1973 (Leonard 1993). These laws prohibit discrimination against handicapped persons, subject to certain limitations. The Supreme Court has
made it clear that persons with contagious diseases can be considered handicapped, and subsequently Congress, administrative agencies, and lower
courts have indicated that AIDS and HIV-positive persons can also receive
protection as handicapped individuals.

While the ADA holds that homosexuality or bisexuality are not disabilities, gay men can still be protected by the law if they experience HIV-
related discrimination (even if they are not themselves HIV-positive). For
example, three gay men in New York tried to rent an apartment; the land-
lord first agreed, then withdrew his offer because he feared these men
might develop AIDS. The state superior court consequently ruled that
the men were discriminated against as they were covered by disability law
(Leonard 1993, 302).

Congress has on a few occasions explicitly considered legislation pertaining to AIDS discrimination, but it has never passed any. Interestingly,
a 1994 survey by the Human Rights Campaign found broad bipartisan
support within Congress for the principle that gay and lesbian people
should not be singled out for discrimination in the workplace. Eighty-two
Republicans and 231 Democrats (including majorities of both parties in
the Senate) confirmed that they do not discriminate in their offices on the
basis of sexual orientation (HRC 1999b). While Congress is infamous for
exempting itself from laws it has passed for others, in this case it appears
that lawmakers are practicing themselves what they have been unwilling
to incorporate into legislation.

DEMOCRATIZING PUBLIC HEALTH

Has gay activism regarding AIDS helped democratize health policy?
The answers must be yes. Gay political activism regarding AIDS has cer-

tainly democratized disease in that gays themselves participated more, gained greater access to the places where AIDS policy is made, and demanded that their voices be heard there.

Certainly more gays participate in health politics, and they participate on a more equal basis, than before AIDS. Gays have compelled policymakers to take gay concerns seriously by becoming policymakers themselves, by lobbying policymakers, or by generating publicity to influence them, among other ways. Not all gays did these things to make the system more democratic, of course. Gays wanted their voices to be included in the policy process, to be sure, but some wanted even more for their voices to prevail—even if this meant silencing other voices. ACT UP ("AIDS Coalition to Unleash Power"), in particular, has drawn criticism for its antidemocratic stridency (Leo 1990). When Louis Sullivan, Secretary of the Department of Health and Human Services, tried to address the Sixth International Conference on AIDS in 1990, for example, he was nearly shouted down by ACT UP (Wachter 1991).

Gay activism on AIDS also had the substantive consequence of wresting power away from the government. There was a major element of "do it yourself" philosophy in gay efforts to prevent the spread of AIDS, to care for the infected, and even to do drug research. As an outsider group, with perhaps little reason to believe that the government would take their concerns seriously, gays sought to build their own educational and health care networks, with the Gay Men's Health Crisis organization being a leading example. Much gay activism, especially during the early stages of the epidemic, was directed towards reducing the power of the government to intervene in private lives. Gays resisted all attempts to require compulsory testing for HIV and reporting of those who were infected or to otherwise restrict their hard-earned sexual freedoms (Bayer 1991a, 1991b).

Public health policy was not completely undemocratic prior to the time of AIDS, of course. Already after World War II the FDA began seeking out consumer opinions on standards for food staples, for instance. By the 1970s "consumer representatives" served on the scientific panels advising the FDA; later, the FDA created a consortium of consumer organizations to help nominate lay members for advisory panels (Holston 1997).

Gay activists did help expand access to unproven drugs and also speed FDA approval of new drugs, but gays were by no means the only ones who favored these measures. Political conservatives did not necessarily want some bureaucracy to tell the public what medical treatments it could take. The Competitive Enterprise Institute, for instance, argued that the FDA should cede all authority to keep drugs off the market, and instead should identify drugs as "safe and effective" or "unapproved"—and let consumers make choices about the risks they wanted to accept (Kasman 1989). Similarly, pharmaceutical companies favored expedited approval of new drugs, more for the economic reasons such as reducing uncertainty and expense than for any sympathy with gay activists (indeed, pharmaceutical companies and gay activists often sharply opposed each other regarding drug pricing) (Arno and Feiden 1992). Would gays have achieved expanded access and expedited approval on their own? Perhaps. But having allies with intellectual or material interests in the same goals undoubtedly helped gay efforts.

Still, one should not speak confidently about "gay" anything. As with any other collection of individuals with various backgrounds, beliefs, preferences, and resources, among other characteristics, gays vary in their political interests, activities, and goals. There is no more a single gay politics than a single Catholic, or African-American, or business, or Democratic politics. Consider the debate over whether the FDA should under certain circumstances (e.g., for immediately life-threatening illnesses) allow certain new drugs (for instance, those not judged clearly ineffective or unreasonably dangerous) to be sold.[29] Although a majority of gays apparently favored this policy, the support was hardly unanimous. Jeff Levi, the executive director of the National Gay and Lesbian Task Force, publicly opposed the idea, warning that these drugs could indeed be worse than the disease they intended to treat (Arno and Feiden 1992, 99).

Despite the impact that gay activism had on AIDS policy, the policy process is hardly open to all participants. Journalistic accounts of the gay response to AIDS depict most of the main players as white, well-educated, affluent, and politically savvy (Shilts 1987; Arno and Feiden 1992; Burkett 1996). Less mention is made of the political actions of less white, less educated, or less affluent gays. Public health activists, like the rest of those in the American political choir, still "sing with an upper class accent" (Schattschneider 1960).

Gay activism on AIDS has had broader democratic consequences for health policy. Breast cancer activists in particular have modeled at least some of their political strategies after those of the AIDS activists (Stabiner 1996). Moreover, those "suffering from chronic fatigue, multiple chemical sensitivity, prostate cancer, mental illness, Lyme disease, Lou Gherig's disease, Alzheimer's, and a host of other conditions have [also] displayed a new militancy and demanded a voice in how their conditions are conceptualized, treated, and researched" (Epstein 1996, 348).

In examining gay activism in their struggle against AIDS, we can observe several classic elements of the American political system. Through the politics of care, we see the unwillingness of Americans to rely on their government for all their needs and the readiness to create organizations to provide the services that the community needs. Through the politics of spending, we see the ability of interests to work within the legislative process to obtain greater resources, on a small scale through the work of key staffers and on a larger scale by building coalitions. In the politics of drugs, we see how committed activists—if heard by sympathetic bureaucrats—can change the ways that our government carries out its functions. In the politics of prevention, we see how a devoted minority can thwart policy change, particularly when the change has few dedicated advocates. Throughout, gays have helped demonstrate that the American policy process is capable of being opened, however slowly and incompletely, to those who seek to influence it.

NOTES

1. A large body of literature describes the politics of AIDS, all of which contain discussion of gay activism (Shilts 1987; Bayer 1991, 1995; Wachter 1991; Blasius 1994; Burkett 1995; Epstein 1996; Haider-Markel 1997).
2. For a discussion of various conceptions of democracy, see Dahl (1999).
3. In writing that the impact would be "modest," I do not intend to underestimate the struggle it took gays to gain a place at the table. I do mean that this struggle would have had only a moderate impact on democracy.
4. The "social construction" of policy issues and the populations affected by these issues are considered at length by Schneider and Ingram (1993). Donovan (1993) applies social construction theory to AIDS.
5. For one view of the political divisions between white males, lesbians, and persons of color regarding AIDS, see Vaid (1995, 274–306).
6. Perpetual controversy exists over the proportion of the population that is gay, with estimates typically running between 1 and 10 percent Pollsters for President Clinton estimated that 5 to 6 percent of the public was gay (Vaid 1995, 127).
7. For example, polling data show that gays and lesbians are typically the least popular group appearing in surveys (Sherrill 1993, 98). The public is becoming somewhat more sympathetic towards gays, however (Wilcox and Wolpert 1999).
8. For a discussion of self-help efforts to combat AIDS, see Petrow, Franks, and Wolfred (1990).

9. The view that Kramer did not found ACT UP is strongly stated by Wolf (1997).

10. A more cynical view is presented by Burkett (1995).

11. Gay political activism regarding AIDS was substantially different from activism towards gay rights, for instance (Haider-Markel 1997).

12. Because the *perception* of power can be power, like any other political actor gays have reason to overstate their impact on events. The HRC, for instance, claims that it mobilized 250 volunteers to assist Senator Chuck Robb in his campaign for reelection against Oliver North, and that these volunteers contacted 15,000 voters, or 29 percent of Robb's majority (HRC 1999a).

13. Clinton is hardly popular with all gay AIDS activists, of course; in one ACT-UP event in 1998, protestors gathered at the White House to call Clinton a "murdering liar" (ACT UP 1998).

14. Given that AIDS disproportionately affected gay men, it is perhaps ironic that all three AIDS czars (Kristine Gebbie, Patricia Fleming, and Sandy Thurman) thus far have in fact been czarinas.

15. Not until 1998 was the first candidate openly homosexual before running for office elected to the House of Representatives.

16. Bernie Sanders, the one independent in the House, was counted with the Democrats.

17. Of course there need not be political stalemate on these issues. There is no reason why AIDS education cannot emphasize both fidelity and safer sex practices, and many researchers and public health advocates favor this blended approach.

18. Helms, Dannemeyer, and their ilk opposed gay sex period, whether safe or not.

19. In the view of some, "it is better to let the guilty die of AIDS than to risk encouraging extramarital sex or drug abuse among the innocent" (Perrow and Guillen 1990, 8).

20. Exact figures are difficult to come by, as it depends on how one defines "funding for AIDS" and how one collects data.

21. One must be naïve to think that such a metric can be created because evaluations of spending decisions must ultimately be based on moral criteria. While in principle governments might allocate funds for diseases based on the costs each disease imposes on society and the benefits the spending would yield. Both costs and benefits and impossible to measure objectively. Does the slow death of an affluent, white male impose greater total social costs than the swift death of a young, poor, black girl? Does spending on care produce greater benefits than spending on research?

22. In journalistic accounts of congressional action on AIDS in the 1980s and 1990s, Helms and Dannemeyer are virtually the only ones consistently mentioned as slowing, stalling, opposing, and amending (among other tactics)

AIDS legislation supported by gays, public health officials, and most members of Congress. In addition, while the antigay minority was almost entirely Republican, the Republican party was not entirely antigay. Republican Senator Orrin Hatch, a Mormon from Utah, was an outspoken opponent of Helms on AIDS legislation (CQ Almanac 1988, 302).

23. At the state and local level, gays have been more effective legislatively when they kept the scope of conflict narrow and less effective when the conflicts broadened to become morality politics (Haider-Markel and Meier 1996).

24. These policies were still contained in omnibus health legislation. A summary of the main provisions are in *CQ Almanac* (1988, 297–99).

25. The notion of "distributive politics" is developed by Lowi (1964).

26. While AIDS service organizations were united in the need to obtain additional funds from Congress, they were hardly united in the distribution of these funds. Burkett describes the internecine squabbling among these organizations as they each tried to get their fair share of the limited White Ryan funds (1995, 147–68).

27. This combination has also been called the "degaying of AIDS" (Bailey 1995).

28. A clinical endpoint would be improved health or increased longevity. A "surrogate endpoint" is a condition that leads to the clinical endpoint. A standard surrogate endpoint is blood pressure; CD4 counts are a surrogate endpoint for increased longevity for a PWA.

29. This category of drugs was called Treatment Investigational New Drugs.

REFERENCES

ACT UP (AIDS Coalition to Unleash Power). 1999. <www.actupny.org>.
———. 1998. Political Funeral. <www.actupny.org/reports/SteveMichael.html>.
Adam, Barry D. 1987. *The rise of a gay and lesbian movement*. Boston: Twayne Publishers.
Altman, Dennis. 1982. *The homosexualization of America*. Boston: Beacon Press.
Arno, Peter S., and Karyn L. Feiden. 1992. *Against the odds: The story of AIDS drug development, politics and profits*. New York: HarperCollins Publishers.
Bailey, William A. 1992. "Politics, drug use, and sex: The HIV primary prevention picture in the United States." Paper presented at the 8th International AIDS Conference. Amsterdam, The Netherlands.
———. 1995. The importance of HIV prevention programming to the lesbian and gay community. In *AIDS, identity, and community: The HIV epidemic and lesbians and gay men*, edited by Gregory M. Herek and Beverly Greene. Thousand Oaks, Cal.: Sage Publications.
Bayer, Ronald. 1991a. The politics of prevention. *Health Affairs* 12:87–97.

————. 1991b. *Private acts, social consequences: AIDS and the politics of public health.* New Brunswick, N.J.: Rutgers University Press.

————. 1995. The dependent center: The first decade of the AIDS epidemic in New York City. In *Hives of sickness: Public health and epidemics in New York City,* edited by David Rosner. New Brunswick, N.J.: Rutgers University Press.

Blasius, Mark. 1994. *Gay and lesbian politics.* Philadelphia: Temple University Press.

Braff, Jeffrey. 1990. Diversity and gay identity. *Volunteer* 7:2.

Brandt, A. M. 1988. AIDS in historical perspective: Four cases from the history of sexually transmitted diseases. *American Journal of Public Health* 78:367–71.

Bull, Chris, and John Gallagher. 1996. *Perfect enemies: The religious right, the gay movement, and the politics of the 1990s.* New York: Crown Publishers, Inc.

Burkett, Eleanor. 1995. *The gravest show on earth: America in the age of AIDS.* Boston: Houghton Mifflin.

Burris, Scott. 1993. Education to reduce the spread of AIDS. In *AIDS law today: A new guide for the public,* edited by Scott Burris, Harlon L. Dalton, Judith Leonie Miller, and the Yale AIDS Law Project. New Haven: Yale University Press.

Burris, Scott, Harlon L. Dalton, Judith Leonie Miller, and the Yale AIDS Law Project. 1993. *AIDS law today: A new guide for the public.* New Haven: Yale University Press.

Colby, David, and Timoth Cook. 1991. Epidemics and agendas: The politics of nightly news coverage of AIDS. *Journal of Health Policy, Politics and the Law* 16:215–49.

CQ Almanac. 1987. Washington, D.C.: Congressional Quarterly.

————. 1988. Washington, D.C.: Congressional Quarterly.

————. 1990. Washington, D.C.: Congressional Quarterly.

Dahl, Robert A. 1999. *On democracy.* New Haven: Yale University Press.

D'Emilio, John. 1983. *Sexual politics, sexual communities: The making of a homosexual minority in the United States, 1940–1970.* Chicago: University of Chicago Press.

————. 1996. *Power at the polls: The gay / lesbian / bisexual vote.* Washington, D.C.: National Gay and Lesbian Task Force.

Donovan, Mark C. 1993. Social constructions of people with AIDS: Target populations and United States policy, 1981–1990. *Policy Studies Review* 12:3–29.

Elving, Ronald D. 1995. *Conflict and compromise: How Congress makes a law.* New York: Simon and Schuster.

Epstein, Steven. 1991. Democratic science? AIDS activism and the contested construction of knowledge. *Socialist Review,* 35–61.

————. 1996. *Impure science: AIDS, activism, and the politics of knowledge.* Berkeley: University of California Press.

Etheridge, Elizabeth W. 1992. *Sentinel for health: A history of the Centers for Disease Control.* Berkeley: University of California Press.

Fabj, Valeria, and Matthew J. Sobnosky. 1993. Responses from the street: ACT UP and community organizing against AIDS. In *AIDS: Effective Health Communication for the 90s,* edited by Scott C. Ratzan. Washington, D.C.: Taylor and Francis.

Feinberg, David B. 1994. *Queer and loathing: Rants and raves of a raging AIDS clone.* New York: Viking.

Flieger, Ken. 1995. FDA Finds New Ways to Speed Treatments to Patients. <www.fda.gov/fdac/special/newdrug>.

Food and Drug Administration. 1988. Making drugs available for life-threatening diseases. <www.fda.gov/bbs/topics>.

———. 1995. FDA approves first protease inhibitor drug treatment of HIV. <www.fda.gov/bbs/topics>.

———. 1997. *Center for drug evaluation and research: Fact book 1997.* <www.fda.gov/oashi/aids>.

———. 1998a. Expanded access and expedited approval of new therapies related to HIV/AIDS. <www.fda.gov/oashi/aids>.

———. 1998b. When a patient speaks . . . Patient representatives to FDA Advisory Committees. <www.fda.gov/oashi/patrep>.

Friedman, S. R. et al. 1987. The AIDS epidemic among blacks and hispanics. *Milbank Quarterly* 65, supp. 2: 455–99.

GMHC ("Gay Men's Health Crisis"). 1999. <www.gmhc.org>.

Haider-Markel, Donald P. 1997. *From bullhorns to PACS: Lesbian and gay politics, policy and interest groups.* Ph.D. diss., University of Wisconsin–Milwaukee, Political Science.

Haider-Markel, Donald P., and Kenneth J. Meier. 1996. The politics of gay and lesbian rights: Expanding the scope of conflict. *Journal of Politics* 58 (2): 332–49.

Hammonds, Evelynn. 1987. Race, sex, AIDS: The construction of other. *Radical America* 20:28–36.

Holston, Sharon Smith. 1997. The value of patient's perspective in FDA decision processes. Speech to the 10th IMS International Symposium. Brussels. <www.fda.gov/oashi/aids>.

HRC (Human Rights Campaign). 1999a. <www.hrc.org>.

———. 1999b. <www.hrc.org/links/index.html>.

———. 1995. Extremists may pressure GOP to push a divisive agenda: Helms introduces hate legislation targeting gay workers. Press release. <www.hrc.org/hrc/hrcnews>.

Jennings, M. Kent, and Ellen Ann Anderson. 1996. Support for confrontational tactics among AIDS activists: A study of intra-movement divisions. *American Journal of Political Science* 40 (2): 311–34.

Johnson, Judith A. 1997. AIDS: Funding for federal government programs: FY1981–FY1998. Washington, D.C.: Congressional Research Service.

Kasman, Sam. 1989. *Washington Post.* 10 July.

Kayal, Philip M. 1993. *Bearing witness: Gay Men's Health Crisis and the politics of AIDS.* Boulder, Colo.: Westview Press.

Kessler, David A. 1994. Remarks, Institutes of Medicine 25th Anniversary Lecture. <www.fda.gov/oashi/aids>.

Kingdon, John W. 1984. *Agendas, alternatives, and public policies.* New York: HarpersCollins.

Kinsella, James. 1989. *Covering the plague: AIDS and the American media.* New Brunswick, N.J.: Rutgers University Press.

Kirp, David, and Ronald Bayer. 1992. *AIDS in the industrialized countries.* New Brunswick, N.J.: Rutgers University Press.

Knight, Robert H. 1998. How to Overhaul AIDS Spending. Washington, D.C.: Family Research Council. <www.frc.org:80/insight/is95a2ai.html>.

Kobasa, Suzanne C. Ouelette. 1990. AIDS and volunteer associations: Perspectives on social and individual change. *Milbank Quarterly* 68:280–94.

Kramer, Larry. 1990a. A call to riot. *Outweek Magazine,* 14 March, 36–38.

———. 1990b. *Reports from the Holocaust: The making of an AIDS activist.* London: Penguin.

Krieger, Nancy, and Rose Appleman. 1986. *The politics of AIDS.* Oakland, Cal.: Frontline Press.

Lambda Legal Defense Fund. 1998. <www.lambdalegal.org>.

Leo, John. 1990. When activism becomes gangsterism. *U.S. News and World Report,* 5 February, p. 18.

Leonard, Arthur S. 1993. Discrimination. In *AIDS law today: A new guide for the public,* edited by Scott Burris, Harlon L. Dalton, Judith Leonie Miller, and the Yale AIDS Law Project. New Haven: Yale University Press.

Lowi, Theodore J. 1964. American business, public policy case studies, and political theory. *World Politics* 16:667–715.

Mass, Lawrence. 1982. *New York Native.* 21 June–4 July. (Quoted in Bayer 1995, 134.)

New York Native. 1983a. 12–30 January, p. 5. (Quoted in Bayer 1995, 134.)

———. 1983b. 14–27 March, p. 1. (Quoted in Bayer 1995, 135.)

Omoto, Allen M., and A. Lauren Crain. 1995. AIDS volunteerism: Lesbian and gay community-based responses to HIV. *AIDS, identity, and community: The HIV epidemic and lesbians and gay men,* edited by Gregory M. Herek and Beverly Greene. Thousand Oaks, Cal.: Sage Publications.

Panem, Sandra. 1988. *The AIDS bureaucracy.* Cambridge: Harvard University Press.

Perrow, Charles, and Mauro F. Gullen. 1990. *The AIDS disaster: The failure of organizations in New York and the nation.* New York: New York University Press.

Petrow, Steven, Pat Franks, and Timothy R Wolfred, eds. 1990. *Ending the HIV epidemic: Community strategies in disease prevention and health promotion.* Santa Cruz, Cal.: Network Publications.

Poirier, Richard. 1988. AIDS and the tradition of homophobia. *Social Research* 55:461–76.

Rom, Mark Carl. 1995. *Public spirit in the thrift tragedy.* Pittsburgh: Pittsburgh University Press.

Rom, Mark Carl. 1997. *Fatal extraction: The story behind the Florida dentist accused of infecting his patients with HIV and poisoning public health.* San Francisco: Jossey-Bass.

Schattschneider, E. E. 1960. *The semi-sovereign people: A realist's view of democracy.* Hillsdale, Ill.: Dryden.

Schneider, Anne, and Helen Ingram. 1993. Social construction of target populations: Implications for politics and policy. *American Political Science Review* 87 (2): 334–47.

Senak, Mark S. 1996. *HIV, AIDS, and the law: A guide to our rights and challenges.* New York: Insight Books.

Sherrill, Kenneth. 1993. On gay people as a politically powerless group. In *Gays and the military: Joseph Steffan versus the United States*, edited by Marc Wolinsky and Kenneth Sherrill. Princeton: Princeton University Press.

Shilts, Randy. 1987. *And the band played on: Politics, people and the AIDS epidemic.* New York: St. Martin's Press.

Stabiner, Karen. 1996. *To dance with the devil: The new war on breast cancer.* New York: Delacorte Press.

Tocqueville, Alexis de. 1969. *Democracy in America*, edited by J. P. Mayer. New York: Doubleday-Anchor Books.

Truman, David B. 1971. *The governmental process.* 2d ed. New York: Knopf.

U.S. House of Representatives. 1983. *The federal response to AIDS.* Report by the Intergovernmental Relations and Human Resource Subcommittee of the Committee on Government Operations.

U.S. House of Representatives. 1992. *The politics of AIDS prevention at the Centers for Disease Control.* Report by the Intergovernmental Relations and Human Resource Subcommittee of the Committee on Government Operations.

Vaid, Urvashi. 1995. *Virtual equality: The mainstreaming of gay and lesbian liberation.* New York: Anchor Books.

Verba, Sidney, Kay Lehman Scholzman, and Henry E. Brady. 1996. *Voice and equality: Civic voluntarism in American politics.* Cambridge: Harvard University Press.

Wachter, R. M. 1991. *The fragile coalition: Scientists, activists, and AIDS.* New York: St. Martin's Press.

———. 1992. AIDS, activism and the politics of health. *New England Journal of Medicine* 128–32.

Weiss, Ted. 1983. House report documents inadequate response to AIDS. Press Release.

Wolfe, Maxine. 1994. The AIDS Coalition to Unleash Power (ACT UP): A direct model of community research for AIDS prevention. In *AIDS Prevention and Services: Community Based Research,* edited by Johannes P. Van Vugt. Westport, Conn.: Bergin and Garvey.

———. 1997. Make it work for you: Academia and political organizing in lesbian and gay communities. Invited Roundtable Presentation at the Seventh Annual Queer Graduate Studies Conference. New York, New York, 3–5 April. <www.actupny.org/documents/academia.html>.

11

SEX/UALITY AND MILITARY SERVICE

Francine D'Amico

Since its inception, the U.S. military has attempted to control the sexual activities and to constrain the sexuality of those who serve. The policing of what I term "sex/uality" is manifested by the effort to exclude people whom military officials suspect are or who identify themselves as *sexual minorities.*[1] The "Don't Ask, Don't Tell" policy adopted in 1994 promised to end this exclusion by establishing a "zone of privacy" for military personnel that would allow sexual minorities to serve—so long as they do so quietly.

The experience of current and former service members since then indicates that the policy is either misunderstood or being deliberately misapplied by those who must enforce it. Sexuality-based investigations, harassment, discharges, complaints, and legal challenges have escalated over the five years the policy has been in force. Further, the "Don't Ask, Don't Tell" policy disproportionately affects servicewomen, working as a tool of sexual extortion against them. The policy's cumulative effect has been to foster a hostile climate of suspicion and isolation and hence to degrade morale. I recommend that the policy be rescinded and that military law be revised to reduce sexual harassment against servicewomen and to promote greater tolerance for diversity. These steps are necessary to enhance the cohesion of the U.S. armed forces.

EXCLUSION POLICY HISTORY

The U.S. military has policed the sex/uality of its troops since 1778, when the first soldier was drummed out of the service for engaging in same-sex relations (Shilts 1993, 11). During World War I, soldiers found guilty of forcible sodomy were court-martialed, imprisoned, and dishonorably discharged upon completion of their sentence. After the war, the Articles of War were amended to categorize even consensual sodomy as a criminal and dischargeable offense (Burrelli 1994, 17). Subsequently, the armed forces routinely engaged in "dragnets" to purge gay men from the ranks (Murphy 1988).

During World War II, suspected gay recruits or draftees were deemed unsuitable for service based on the medical community's interpretation at the time of homosexuality as a mental illness. Soldiers suspected of being gay were either discharged or, as the war went on, "rehabilitated" and retained for service, in part because the government worried that soldiers and draftees would claim to be gay to avoid their military obligation. Gay veterans argue that military expedience appeared to trump the exclusion policy when demand for personnel was high (Bérubé 1985; Shilts 1993).

Military women's sex/uality has also been scrutinized by policymakers. The women's auxiliary services during both world wars sought to enlist only unmarried women "of good moral character." In contrast to the men, servicewomen suspected of heterosexual promiscuity or lesbianism were discharged, not "rehabilitated" and retained, though commanders could exercise some discretion (Bérubé and D'Emilio 1984). Military service required near-celibacy for women: regulations requiring automatic discharge for marriage and/or pregnancy remained in force until the mid-1970s (D'Amico 1997; Katzenstein, Fainsod, and Reppy 1999; Katzenstein 1998).

Current military law provides several mechanisms for policing service members' sex/uality in the Uniform Code of Military Justice (UCMJ). Article 125 prohibits sodomy, defined as anal or oral penetration, whether consensual or coerced and whether same- or opposite-sex. The maximum penalty for sodomy with a consenting adult is five years at hard labor, forfeiture of pay and allowances, and dishonorable discharge. Article 134, also known as the "General Article," proscribes assault with the intent to commit sodomy, indecent assault, and indecent acts, and prohibits all conduct " 'to the prejudice of good order and discipline in the armed forces' " (Dyer 1990, 56–61, 68). Each offense carries a maximum penalty of five years, except assault with intent, which has a maximum of ten.

During the Cold War, the rationale for the exclusion policy shifted from alleged mental instability to a concern that sexual minorities presented a security risk—the theory was that anyone learning their personal secret could extort them into betraying military secrets. Three studies commissioned by the Pentagon in 1957, 1988, and 1989 found no connection between sexuality and espionage, but these were not made public until released by court order in late 1989 (Dyer 1990). The exclusion policy continued despite these findings and despite the medical community's reassessment beginning in the late 1940s that homosexuality was *not* a mental illness but rather one aspect of the normal range of human sexuality (Shilts 1993, 34, 238).

Some service members contested their discharges openly, which brought media and public attention. On August 30, 1975, Air Force Technical Sergeant Leonard Matlovich, a decorated Vietnam veteran, appeared on the cover of *Time* with the caption, "I Am a Homosexual." As Randy Shilts notes, "It marked the first time the young gay movement had ever made the cover of a major newsweekly. To a cause still struggling for legitimacy, the event marked a major turning point" because Matlovich defied the common stereotypes of gay men (227). His story was made into a television movie in 1978 (302, 321).

Subsequently, other outed and ousted service members began to tell their stories in public and to challenge their discharges in court, and academic studies of sexuality and military service also began to appear (e.g., Gibson 1978; Williams and Weinberg 1971). Reserve Officer Training (ROTC) programs, already unpopular with many liberal academics, came under fire for discrimination based on sexuality. Students, faculty members, and administrators at many colleges and universities sought to ban ROTC programs and military recruiters from campus to protest the exclusion policy (Holobaugh and Hale 1993; Card 1994).

In 1982, the policy was revised to end the practice of giving dishonorable discharges when no violations of the UCMJ were alleged. Department of Defense (DOD) Directive 1332.14 sec. H.1 held that "homosexuality" was "incompatible with military service" and a threat to morale, good order, and discipline (Shilts 1993, 37–38). Here, the rationale shifted from the alleged (and unfounded) *security risk* that suspected lesbian / gay personnel presented to the *comfort level* of nonlesbian / gay personnel; that is, from *competence* to *cohesion* (Herek 1996a, 4). Straight personnel would be uncomfortable because many believed sexual minorities to be sexual predators—hence the focus on "habitability issues" (showers and sleeping quarters). Under this version, the armed forces continued to ask recruits about their sexuality and to investigate and discharge personnel suspected of being sexual minorities. While most received honorable discharges, prison and dishonorable discharge remained a possibility because the UCMJ itself was not revised (US GAO 1992).

Challenges to the exclusion policy continued through the late 1980s and into the 1990s. Organized interest groups, such as the American Civil Liberties Union and the Gay, Lesbian, and Bisexual Veterans of America, supported litigation efforts (Pacelle 1996, 195–226). Part of the strategy to challenge sexuality-based discrimination included reaching out to mainstream America through publicity on cases of "exemplary" service members (Cammermeyer and Fisher 1994; Zuniga 1994). Television talk shows and news analysis programs tackled issues surrounding sexuality, from job discrimination to child custody and marriage, and academic studies proliferated as well (Shilts 1993, 418–26, 640–58; Humphrey 1990, 284–85; Bérubé 1991).

In this context of increasing media and public attention to sexuality-based discharges, presidential candidate Bill Clinton pledged to end the exclusion policy. Early in his first term, Clinton asked the secretary of defense to draft an executive order to end the military's sexuality-based exclusion policy, which he equated with President Truman's executive order to end racial segregation of the armed forces in 1948. The initiative met stiff resistance from within the military and from Congress, and the Clinton administration negotiated a compromise policy that was announced on July 19, 1993. The policy was subsequently codified into law (10 U.S.C. sec. 654) and instituted in its current form by the Department of Defense on February 28, 1994 (Rimmerman 1996, 11–25).

This compromise—"Don't Ask, Don't Tell, Don't Pursue, Don't Harass"—attempts to reconcile two contradictory perspectives on sexuality and military service. On the one hand, the policy seeks to create "a zone of privacy" for service members in which sexuality is "a personal and private matter" that should not be "a bar to military service." On the other hand, the policy declares that same-sex intimate relations by military personnel create "an unacceptable risk to morale, good order and discipline, and unit cohesion," defining *conduct* broadly as committing "a homosexual act," including "entering a homosexual marriage or stating publicly that one is homosexual" (US DOD 1998, 1). Ostensibly, the policy allows people who identify as lesbian, gay, or bisexual to serve so long as they remain in the "military closet."[2]

Under the new policy, recruits and military members can no longer be asked about their sexuality (Don't Ask), people in service must keep their sexual identity to themselves (Don't Tell), military bosses may not investigate their workers' private lives without credible grounds (Don't Pursue), and harassment of service members based on sexuality—that is, verbal as well as physical "gay bashing" and "lesbian baiting"—is prohibited and punishable conduct (Don't Harass).

As the final form of the "Don't Ask, Don't Tell" policy was being hammered out, Randy Shilts published *Conduct Unbecoming* (1993). Like no previous work, this shifted the discussion on military exclusion from a question for individuals who had been discharged to a question for the entire lesbian/gay community. Shilts was not a discharged service member, but his previous publications on the AIDS epidemic (1987) and politician Harvey Milk (1982) brought his analysis legitimacy within the community that had been at best ambivalent and at worst politically divided about challenging sexuality-based discrimination in the military. As the policy debate continued, more service members came forward and more scholars took up the analysis of the issue, providing important data and broadening the discussion (Webber 1993; Scott and Stanley 1994; Herek, Jobe, and Carney 1996; Shawver 1994; Rimmerman 1996).

EXCLUSION POLICY APPLICATION AND IMPACT

How well has the "Don't Ask, Don't Tell" policy worked to create a "zone of privacy" for military members since its enactment? Consider the case of Navy Master Chief Petty Officer Timothy McVeigh, one of the casualties of the new policy. The Navy sought to discharge McVeigh based on information illegally obtained from an anonymous America Online user profile in which he listed his marital status as gay. Even military sociologist Charles Moskos, architect of the "Don't Ask, Don't Tell" policy, stated in a sworn affidavit for the case that the Navy's pursuit of McVeigh violated the intent of the policy. On January 29, 1998, a federal judge ruled in *McVeigh v. Cohen* that the Navy had violated both the "Don't Ask, Don't Tell" policy and the Electronic Communications Privacy Act of 1989. After his reinstatement, McVeigh was promoted but was not returned to his post on a nuclear submarine; he decided to retire after eighteen years of service rather than be "dry-docked" (Osburn et al. 1998, 24–26; Klein and Adams 1998; "After Losing" 1998).

McVeigh is not the only casualty of this policy. According to data released by the Department of Defense, the number of discharges between 1980 and 1993 totaled 19,267. In the five years since the new "Don't Ask, Don't Tell" policy came into force, another 4,429 servicemen and women

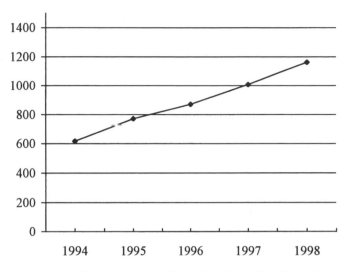

Figure 11.1 Annual Gay Discharges under "Don't Ask, Don't Tell, Don't Pursue" Policy
SOURCE: Servicemembers Legal Defense Network, based on Department of Defense figures.

had been discharged as of February 1999 (fig. 11.1). This brings the total number of people discharged since 1980 to 23,599.

After declining steadily since 1982 and reaching a low point in 1994, the number of discharges began to increase again in 1995 and are now at their highest point in ten years. How do we explain this pattern? A most obvious explanation is that the old policy was suspended by the Clinton administration while the compromise policy was negotiated during 1993–94; recruiters were told not to ask and discharge proceedings were stalled, but investigations continued. Once the new rules were in place, discharge proceedings resumed. However, the Pentagon attributes this flux in the number of discharges not to the policy's temporary suspension but rather to changes in counting methods, the lack of screening of recruits, and an increase in *voluntary disclosure* (US DOD 1998, 4). These explanations are problematic.

While some counting methods have changed, others have not. For example, the Air Force, which once discharged sexual minorities for "fraudulent enlistment," must now record such discharges as based on "homosexual conduct" (4). Yet *recorded* discharges do not accurately reflect the *total* number of service personnel who are forced out or who leave because their sexuality is suspect. Enlisted personnel are often separated during basic training for "inability to adapt to service life," which may serve as code for "suspected of homosexuality." Officers can be forced out without being discharged for "conduct unbecoming." As former Navy officer Jim Woodward reported, in his case, "The code on the paperwork was: separation to inactive duty, active duty obligation complete. They weren't discharging me, they were *deactivating* me, like some frigging battleship" (Humphrey 1990, 164). And career officers are sometimes allowed—or encouraged—to resign their commissions "quietly" to avoid attention (Shilts 1993, 4). Finally, some personnel leave to escape verbal and physical harassment that makes their sexuality suspect, and others simply tire of having to hide who they are in order to serve their country (Osburn et al. 1999, 2).

The Pentagon contends that new recruits unhappy with military life are "telling" voluntarily to get out of their service commitments (Weiner 1998; Winston 1998). While 58 percent of the discharges in 1997 were for personnel with less than one year of service and only 18 percent were for those with more than four years of service (US DOD 1998, 4, 12), this is *not* a new pattern. The vast majority of discharges each year prior to 1994 were also for junior enlisted personnel. Since "telling" risks investigation and court martial under military law, the argument that self-disclosure is voluntary appears suspect.

The Pentagon suggests that the "telling" is voluntary because the discharges are *uncontested*. However, the financial cost of a legal challenge would be prohibitive to most service members, particularly single-term enlisted personnel, who would have to hire their own lawyer while the government's counsel is funded at taxpayer expense. And the personal costs can also be overwhelming: the individual would not only become the focus of media attention and lose all privacy but also risk harassment and bashing. Even winning the case can be a form of punishment, as reinstated military members report that the public outing limits career advancement, increases isolation, and sometimes provokes retaliation from coworkers and supervisors. So it is not surprising that many people do not contest their discharges because they cannot afford to or fear personal or professional repercussions.

Finally, the Pentagon contends that the "telling" is voluntary because the discharges are *uncoerced*. A report issued by the Pentagon in April 1998 identified only three cases of violation of proper investigative procedure and argued that these were "isolated instances," not "widespread 'witch hunts'" (US DOD 1998, 2–3). In a fourth "unique case" of a pretrial agreement (plea bargain), a service member was offered a reduced sentence for identifying other servicemen with whom he'd had consensual sex; one of those he named was an officer who "resigned in lieu of facing a court-martial" for fraternization (7). In four other cases where service members reported antigay harassment or threats, the Pentagon report found that "the commanders promptly took appropriate actions . . . and did not target the victim" of the harassment by launching an investigation into his/her sexuality (6).

The Pentagon's self-confessed numbers don't add up when compared to complaints made by current and discharged service members themselves. The Servicemembers Legal Defense Network (SLDN), a watchdog organization that provides legal aid for those investigated and harassed because of their sexuality, has carefully documented violations of the "Don't Ask, Don't Tell" policy over the past five years. SLDN's latest report finds that violations of the policy increased in 1998, documenting 934 instances in which service members were asked about their sexuality, were subjected to harassment by peers and/or supervisors, and were pursued by military officials. This represents an increase over the 563 command violations for 1997, 443 for 1996, and 182 for 1994. These data are drawn from evidence submitted in legal proceedings as well as internal service memoranda, reports, letters, questionnaires, and training materials, and corroborated complaints from service members.

One reason the Pentagon's numbers do not match SLDN's numbers is because service members, fearing investigation and retaliation, may not report harassment to their commanders. Recognizing this, Ed Dorn, undersecretary of defense for personnel and readiness, issued a memo on March 1, 1997 to clarify that military personnel "must be able to report harassment or threats free from fear of harm, reprisal, or inappropriate or inadequate government response" (US DOD 1998, 6). That is, commanders must investigate the threat, not the sexuality of the person threatened. Yet the Pentagon admits that Dorn's directive may not have had "effective dissemination" to the field. That this clarification may *not* have been widely distributed to commanders with responsibility for enforcing the policy and that it came *three years* into the policy's operation suggest that protecting service members from harassment and gay-bashing is not a priority.

The "Don't Ask, Don't Tell" policy has not reduced the number of sexuality-based discharges. Rather than creating a "zone of privacy" and a climate of tolerance among military personnel, the policy has institutionalized a "military closet" that requires absolute secrecy and celibacy for sexual minorities and encourages harassment and violence against them.

WHOSE CLOSET IS IT?

Not all personnel are equally vulnerable to the exclusion policy. Differences in discharge rates for servicemen and women reflect the gender and race politics of the military institution. For each year since 1980, the proportion of women discharged under the exclusion policy has exceeded the proportion of women in the armed forces overall, such that women have been from two to three times as likely to be discharged as servicemen. For 1998, 826 men and 317 women were discharged under "Don't Ask, Don't Tell." Women thus accounted for 28 percent of exclusion discharges in 1998, yet women were only 14 percent of armed forces personnel in that year.

Why doesn't the military closet created by "Don't Ask, Don't Tell" protect women very well? Women in nontraditional jobs are "presumed lesbian" because they are "gender outlaws" who violate traditional gender boundaries (Chapkis 1988). Military women's sexuality is suspect because of its intimate connection to the social construction of gender (D'Amico and Weinstein 1999; Benecke 1992; Benecke and Dodge 1990; Herbert 1998).

Not all women are equally vulnerable, either. White women were discharged at the highest rate and disproportionately to their presence in the ranks, and women of color other than African-American women were also discharged at a rate disproportionate to their presence, though at a somewhat lower rate than white women. African-American women and white men were discharged in numbers proportionate to their presence in the ranks, and African-American men and other men of color were discharged at rates far below their presence in the armed forces. This pattern suggests that because perceptions of sex/uality are both race-based and gender-based, some personnel have a more difficult time than others in trying to conceal their sexual identity in the institutionalized military closet (D'Amico 1996, 31).

Although military women are disproportionately affected by the exclusion policy, many refused to ally with those who sought to end sexuality-based exclusion during the debate over "Don't Ask, Don't Tell." Instead, military women and their supporters sought to end women's exclusion from combat roles. As a result of this strategy, each group got a compromise policy that no one wanted: women may serve on combat aircraft and in combat ships, but not submarines, special forces, or ground combat units—and sexual minorities may serve in silence, secrecy, and celibacy. Both policies of exclusion were whittled down but not eliminated (Zimmerman 1995, 195–215; Thomas and Thomas 1996, 71–74).

SOCIAL EXPERIMENT? BEEN THERE, DONE THAT

U.S. military policymakers worry that allowing sexual minorities to serve openly would hurt recruitment, retention, unit cohesion, and morale. One of the chief supporters of continued exclusion, Charles Moskos, has argued that the U.S. military is no place for such a dangerous "social experiment" (1994, 53). This argument ignores the integration experiences of other previously excluded groups into U.S. military service, such as African Americans and women (Bianco 1996; Kauth and Landis 1996; Rolison and Nakayama 1994; Thomas and Thomas 1996, 65–84). The lessons to be drawn from both race and sex integration are that military policy can change, but such change takes time and encounters resistance that can be overcome with training, commitment by civilian policymakers and military leaders, and continued political pressure from interest groups and public opinion (D'Amico 1996, 23–35).

Moskos's argument also neglects the experiences of other countries' militaries in ending sexuality-based exclusion. In the 1970s, the Netherlands, Germany, Sweden, Ireland, Denmark, and Norway ended policies excluding sexual minorities from military service, followed by Spain and Portugal in the 1980s and Australia and Canada in 1992. Other countries, such as Belgium, France, and the Republic of Korea, permit service with restrictions; Israel "clarified" its policy in 1993 to remove several restrictions and special requirements. None of these countries report any adverse effect on recruitment, retention, morale, or unit cohesion (D'Amico 1996, 7–23; Gade, Segal, and Johnson 1996, 106–30; RAND, 65–104; US GAO 1993). In addition, countries with policies of inclusion report that self-disclosure remains rare. Indeed, once an exclusion policy is ended, self-disclosure has no further political purpose and little personal benefit (Herek 1996b, 212–17; Shawver 1994).

The experiences of domestic police and fire services in major U.S. cities, including New York, Chicago, Houston, Seattle, San Francisco, Los Angeles, San Diego, and Washington, D.C., suggest that American culture has *already* begun to change and that the military is lagging behind civilian society, *not* leading the way as a "social laboratory" on this issue. These domestic paramilitary organizations approximate the conditions of military service in that each involves command hierarchy, seeks to maintain public security, and requires teamwork in what are often life-threatening circumstances. While there are also significant differences among military, police, and fire services, the similarities suggest that the experiences of metropolitan police and fire departments provide a good (albeit not perfect) vehicle for assessing the impact of an end to sexuality-based exclusion in the U.S. armed forces (RAND 1993, 106–57; Koegel 1996; US GAO 1992).

Moskos's argument also falls short in that the feared effects of "integrating" personnel who identify as sexual minorities would *already* have appeared, because the "Don't Ask, Don't Tell" policy he designed already allows straights and lesbians, gays, and bisexuals to serve side-by-side. But there has been no mass exodus from the armed forces since the policy was implemented in 1994, except the continued enforced outing and ousting of lesbian, gay, and bisexual personnel. If heterosexist/homophobic personnel should leave, that would improve morale and cohesion within the ranks *and* enhance the performance of the armed forces in contemporary missions where dealing with multicultural diversity is requisite.

Instead, the public debate over the "Don't Ask, Don't Tell" policy has brought even more intense scrutiny for "suspect sexuality" within the military by those who seek to exclude people different from themselves. Those who fought the new policy know that recruits are no longer being screened for sexual identity; consequently, their efforts to detect and eject the dreaded enemy from "their" military are more vigilant. This charged atmosphere of suspicion and hostility makes closeting—the very thing the policy requires—more difficult to achieve. Further, closeting is not only less possible because of this heightened scrutiny but also less bearable because of the initial false hope of the freedom Clinton promised (Sullivan 1998).

Uncertainty over the actual constraints of the policy compounds the problem. Is talking about one's sexuality with a military doctor, mental health counselor, or chaplain "telling"? Are such conversations confidential, as they would be in civilian society? This uncertainty increases the isolation of service members, who withdraw socially to avoid suspicion. Most service members do not realize that there is "no physician-patient privilege for communications of any kind between service members and their military doctors" and that military health care professionals may report information to the command without the patient's consent "in order to protect the patient or to ensure the safety or security of military personnel or the accomplishment of the military mission" (US DOD 1998, 8; Barnett and Jeffrey 1996).

Since the policy makes creating the appearance of heterosexuality paramount, women face even greater pressure to prove they are straight by complying with the sexual demands of their peers and/or supervisors, and servicemen must be hetero-promiscuous to avoid suspicion. These pressures present substantial psychological and physical risks, including a potential increase in sexually transmitted diseases. The "Don't Ask, Don't Tell" policy thus appears counterproductive, as it undermines the cohesion it is intended to preserve and puts military personnel at risk.

DOLLARS AND SENSE

The exclusion policy is exorbitantly expensive in terms of the costs of investigation, prosecution, and loss of trained personnel. The SLDN estimates that the policy has cost at least $130 million dollars over the past five years just for training replacement personnel; this does not include the legal costs of investigations and discharge proceedings.

Given these expenses, the Department of Defense tries to "recoup" some of the military benefits discharged personnel have received during service. The "Don't Ask, Don't Tell" policy authorizes recoupment of benefits *only* if conduct punishable under the UCMJ is alleged—so of course finding evidence of such conduct becomes financially important, though the Pentagon denies that investigations occur for this reason (US DOD 1998, 8). Service members who reveal their sexual identity may also be made to repay benefits if the military believes they made the statement to avoid fulfilling a commitment. For example, students in college Reserve Officer Training (ROTC) programs and in the military academies at West Point, Annapolis, and Colorado Springs pledge to serve in exchange for their education. The military may seek tuition reimbursement from students who are outed and ousted, as occurred recently at Cornell University (Osburn et al. 1999, 69–70 and exhibits 19, 20). However, if we end "Don't Ask, Don't Tell," there will be *no* problem of recoupment of benefits. In addition, money previously spent investigating and prosecuting service members and litigating challenges to the exclusion policy can be redirected to more productive areas such as recruiting, and retention will be enhanced seeing that a thousand people will not be drummed out of service each year.

The exclusion policy is also costly in terms of the personal security, dignity, and basic human rights of the women and men who volunteer to serve in our country's armed forces and who also happen to be lesbian, gay, or bisexual. Real people—not just a handful, a dozen, or a hundred, but thousands—have been hurt by this policy, which appears *prima facie* to deny both the First Amendment's protections of freedom of speech and association and the Fourteenth Amendment's guarantee of equal protection of the laws.[3] The policy is based on fear and prejudice rather than military necessity, and in its current form, "Don't Ask, Don't Tell" has proved unworkable: there is no "zone of privacy" for military personnel. The services should move to adopt the sexuality-neutral policy recommended by RAND in its 1993 report, that is, that sexuality is "not germane" to military service (RAND 1993, 1–3, 332–67). This will require that Congress rescind 10 U.S.C. sec. 654 and that the Pentagon revise the UCMJ such that sexual relations between consenting adults is no longer punishable. These changes will be difficult in the current political climate, but the longer the policy continues, the greater the pressure will grow to demand the necessary changes.

NOTES

My thanks to C. Dixon Osburn and Michelle M. Benecke of the Servicemembers Legal Defense Network for permission to use figure 11.1, and to Stacey Sobel at SLDN and reference librarian Janie Wilkins for their research assistance. I am also grateful to all who provided feedback on the chapter manuscript; responsibility for the analysis remains wholly my own.

1. The term "sexual minorities" is used to refer collectively to people who identify as gay, lesbian, bisexual, transsexual, or other varieties of sexuality not conforming to the hegemonic sexual identity of heterosexuality.
2. The term "military closet" refers to the strategies used by sexual minorities who are military personnel to hide their identities in order to protect their friends and partners as well as their own physical safety and careers. Such strategies include "passing" as straight by engaging in heterosexual promiscuity or sham marriages or by participating in gay-bashing to deflect suspicion.
3. Nonetheless, in January 1999, the U.S. Supreme Court for the fifth time declined to review a case challenging the constitutionality of the "Don't Ask, Don't Tell" policy. In refusing to hear the appeals of California National Guard Lt. Andy Holmes and former Navy Lt. Rich Watson, the Court exercised its customary deference to the military on personnel policy issues (Adams 1999).

REFERENCES

Adams, Julia. 1999. U.S. Supreme Court declines to hear case challenging military's gay policy, at <www.sldn.org/scripts/sldn.ixe?page=pr_01_11_99>.

After losing suit, Navy to promote McVeigh. 1998. *New York Times,* 10 May, p. 20.

Barnett, Jeffrey E., and Timothy J. Jeffrey. 1996. Issues of confidentiality: Therapists, chaplains, and health care providers. In *Out in force,* edited by Gregory M. Herek, Jared B. Jobe, and Ralph M. Carney. Chicago: University of Chicago Press, 247–65.

Benecke, Michelle M. 1992. Lesbian-baiting as sexual harassment: Women in the Military. In *Homophobia: How we all pay the price,* edited by Warren Blumenfeld. Boston: Beacon, 167–76.

Benecke, Michelle M., and Kirstin S. Dodge. 1990. Military women in nontraditional job fields: Casualties of the armed forces' war on homosexuals. *Harvard Women's Law Journal* 13:215–50.

Bérubé, Allan. 1991. *Coming out under fire: The history of gay men and women in World War Two.* New York: Plume.

Bérubé, Allan, and John D'Emilio (1984). The military and lesbians during the McCarthy years. *Signs: Journal of Women in Culture and Society* 9:4 (Summer): 759–75.

Bianco, David Ari. 1996. "Echoes of prejudice: The debates over race and sexuality in the armed forces." In *Gay Rights, Military Wrongs,* edited by Craig Rimmerman. New York: Garland, 47–69.

Blasius, Mark. 1994. *Gay and lesbian politics.* Philadelphia: Temple University Press.

Burrelli, David F. (1994). The debate on homosexuals in the military. In *Gays and lesbians in the military,* edited by Wilbur J. Scott and Carson Stanley. New York: Aldine de Gruyter, 17–31.

Cammermeyer, Margarethe, with Chris Fisher (1994). *Serving in silence.* New York: Viking.

Card, Claudia. 1994. Military ban and the ROTC: A study in closeting. *Journal of Homosexuality* 27 (3/4): 117–46.

Chapkis, Wendy. 1988. Sexuality and militarism. In *Women and the Military System,* edited by Eva Isaksson. New York: St. Martin's, 106–13.

D'Amico, Francine. 1997. Policing the U.S. military's race and gender lines. In *Wives and warriors: Women and the military in the U.S. and Canada,* edited by Laurie Weinstein and Christie White. Westport, Conn.: Bergin and Garvey, 199–234.

———. 1996. Race-ing and gendering the military closet. In *Gay Rights, Military Wrongs,* edited by Craig A. Rimmerman. New York: Garland, 3–46.

D'Amico, Francine, and Laurie Weinstein, eds. 1999. *Gender camouflage: Women and the U.S. military.* New York and London: New York University Press.

Dyer, Kate, ed. 1990. *Gays in uniform: The Pentagon's secret reports.* Boston: Alyson.

Gade, Paul A., David R. Segal, and Edgar M. Johnson. 1996. The experience of foreign militaries. In *Out in force,* edited by Gregory M. Herek, Jared B. Jobe, and Ralph M. Carney. Chicago: University of Chicago Press, 106–29.

Gibson, Lawrence E. 1978. *Get off my ship: Ensign Berg vs. the U.S. Navy.* New York: Avon, 1978.

Herbert, Melissa S. 1998. *Camouflage isn't only for combat.* New York: New York University Press.

Herek, Gregory M. 1996a. Social science, sexual orientation, and military personnel policy. In *Out in force,* edited by Gregory M. Herek, Jared B. Jobe, and Ralph M. Carney. Chicago: University of Chicago Press, 3–14.

————. 1996b. Why tell if you're not asked? Self-disclosure, intergroup contact, and heterosexuals' attitudes toward lesbians and gay men. In *Out in force,* edited by Gregory M. Herek, Jared B. Jobe, and Ralph M. Carney. Chicago: University of Chicago Press, 197–224.

Herek, Gregory M., Jared B. Jobe, and Ralph M. Carney, eds. 1996. *Out in force: Sexual orientation and the military.* Chicago: University of Chicago Press.

Holobaugh, Jim, with Keith Hale. 1993. *Torn allegiances: The story of a gay (Army ROTC) cadet.* Boston: Alyson.

Humphrey, Mary Ann. 1990. *My country, my right to serve: Experiences of gay men and women in the military, World War II to the present.* New York: Harper-Collins.

Katzenstein, Mary Fainsod. 1998. *Faithful and fearless: Moving feminist protests inside the church and military.* Princeton: Princeton University Press.

Katzenstein, Mary Fainsod, and Judith V. Reppy, eds. 1999. *Beyond zero tolerance: Discrimination in military culture.* Lanham, Md.: Rowman and Littlefield.

Kauth, Michael R., and Dan Landis. 1996. Applying lessons from minority integration in the military. In *Out in force,* edited by Gregory M. Herek, Jared B. Jobe, and Ralph M. Carney. Chicago: University of Chicago Press, 86–105.

Klein, Rich, and Julia Adams. 1998. Navy drops appeal of decision upholding electronic privacy rights for Master Chief Petty Officer Timothy McVeigh. Servicemembers Legal Defense Network News Release, 12 June. <www.sldn.org>.

Koegel, Paul. 1996. Lessons learned from domestic police and fire departments. In *Out in force,* edited by Gregory M. Herek, Jared B. Jobe, and Ralph M. Carney. Chicago: University of Chicago Press, 131–55.

McVeigh v. Cohen, 983 F. Supp. 215 (D.D.C. 1998).

Moskos, Charles 1994. From citizens' army to social laboratory. In *Gays and lesbians in the military,* edited by Wilbur J. Scott and Carson Stanley. New York: Aldine de Gruyter, 53–65.

Murphy, Lawrence R. 1988. *Perverts by official order: The campaign against homosexuals by the United States Navy.* New York: Haworth/Harrington Park.

Osburn, C. Dixon, Michelle M. Benecke, Kirk Childress, Kelly Corbett, Travis Elliott, and Jeff Cleghorn. 1998. *Conduct unbecoming: The fourth annual report on "Don't Ask, Don't Tell, Don't Pursue."* Washington, D.C.: Servicemembers Legal Defense Network. <www.sldn.org>.

Osburn, C. Dixon, Michelle M. Benecke, Stacey Sobel, and Jeff Cleghorn. 1999. *Conduct unbecoming: The fifth annual report on "Don't Ask, Don't Tell, Don't Pursue."* Washington, D.C.: Servicemembers Legal Defense Network. <www.sldn.org>.

Pacelle, Richard. 1996. Seeking another forum: The courts and lesbian and gay rights. In *Gay Rights, Military Wrongs*, edited by Craig A. Rimmerman. New York: Garland, 195–226.

RAND. 1993. *Sexual orientation and U.S. Military personnel policy: Options and assessment.* Santa Monica: RAND National Defense Research Institute, MR-323-OSD.

Rimmerman, Craig A., ed. 1996. *Gay rights, military wrongs: Political perspectives on lesbians and gays in the military.* New York: Garland.

Rolison, Garry L., and Thomas K. Nakayama. 1994. Defensive discourse: Blacks and gays in the U.S. military. In *Gays and lesbians in the military*, edited by Wilbur J. Scott and Carson Stanley. New York: Aldine de Gruyter, 121–33.

Scott, Wilbur J., and Sandra Carson Stanley, eds. 1994. *Gays and lesbians in the military: Issues, concerns, and contrasts.* New York: Aldine de Gruyter.

Shawver, Lois. 1994. *And the flag was still there: Straight people, gay people, and sexuality in the military.* New York: Haworth/Harrington Park.

Shilts, Randy. 1982. *The mayor of Castro Street: The life and times of Harvey Milk.* New York: St. Martin's.

———. 1987. *And the band played on: Politics, people, and the AIDS epidemic.* New York: St. Martin's.

———. 1993. *Conduct unbecoming: Gays and lesbians in the U.S. Military, Vietnam to the Persian Gulf.* New York: St. Martin's.

Sullivan, Andrew. 1998. Undone by "Don't Ask, Don't Tell." *New York Times,* 9 April, A19 (op ed).

Thomas, Patricia J., and Marie D. Thomas. 1996. Integration of women in the military: Parallels to the progress of homosexuals? In *Out in force*, edited by Gregory M. Herek, Jared B. Jobe, and Ralph M. Carney. Chicago: University of Chicago Press, 71–4.

"The trouble with 'Don't Ask, Don't Tell.'" 1998. *New York Times,* 8 April, A18 (editorial).

U.S. Department of Defense. 1998. Office of the Under Secretary of Defense (Personnel and Readiness). *Report to the Secretary of Defense: Review of the effectiveness of the application and enforcement of the department's policy on homosexual conduct in the military,* 7 April. <www.defenselink.mil/pubs/rpt040798.html>.

U.S. General Accounting Office. 1992. *Defense force management: DOD's policy on homosexuality.* Washington, D.C.: U.S. GAO/NSIAD-92-98, June.

———. 1993. *Homosexuals in the military: Policies and practices of foreign countries.* Washington, D.C.: US GAO/NSIAD-93-215, June.

Webber, Winni S. 1993. *Lesbians in the military speak out.* Northboro, Massachusetts: Madwoman Press.

Weiner, Tim. 1998. Military discharges of homosexuals soar. *New York Times,* 7 April, A23.

Williams, Colin I., and Martin S. Weinberg. 1971. *Homosexuals and the military.* New York: Harper and Row.

Winston, Kevin. 1998. Pentagon's review of "Don't Ask, Don't Tell, Don't Pursue" wins high marks for recommendations, fails for analysis. Servicemembers Legal Defense Network News Release, 10 April. <www.sldn.org>.

Zimmerman, Jean. 1995. *Tailspin: Women at war in the wake of Tailhook.* New York: Doubleday.

Zuniga, José. 1994. *Soldier of the year.* New York: Pocket.

IV. THE ARENAS

12

THE POLITICS OF GAY RIGHTS
AT THE LOCAL AND STATE LEVEL

*James W. Button, Barbara A. Rienzo, and
Kenneth D. Wald*

Although marches on Washington and efforts to eliminate
the ban on gays in the military have captured much of the
publicity, the attention of most lesbian and gay activists
has been monopolized by the political attempts to gain
basic rights for gays in cities and states. The repeal of sodomy laws, the legalization of same-sex marriages, domestic
partner benefits, hate crimes laws, school programs and
policies, and antidiscrimination legislation are all major
goals of the gay movement, and they are also the source
of intense political battles that have been and continue to
be fought almost exclusively at the state and local levels.

The focus of this chapter is primarily on the struggle
to win protection against antigay discrimination in employment, housing, public accommodations, schools, and
other institutions. Such legislative protection has long
been a primary goal of the gay movement. Since there is
no federal antidiscrimination law,[1] the politics of gay rights
has been concentrated in American cities, counties, and
states. In this quest, lesbians and gay men confront significant opposition and hostility, such that the resulting
political conflicts have been likened to a "culture war."
We shall explore the nature and importance of gay rights
laws and other gay supportive policies, their history and
politics of adoption, and the implementation and impact
of protective legislation. We shall also look, somewhat
briefly, at the nature and degree of the opposition movement and why battles over gay rights often represent fundamental conflicts over core American values.

LEGAL PROTECTION FOR LESBIANS AND GAY MEN

As early as the founding of the Mattachine Society in 1951, the gay movement began to consider civil rights. While the more radical forces in the movement pushed for cultural transformation and acceptance, the political moderates pursued a civil rights approach that focused on legal reform, political access, and legitimation. The ultimate goal of this moderate approach was to achieve the integration of gays into mainstream politics and society (Vaid 1995).

The struggle for gay civil rights has been waged mostly through efforts to reform the law. Until relatively recently, government human rights codes purposely excluded lesbians and gays, and as a result, jobs, housing, and public accommodations could be and often were denied to persons because of their sexual orientation. The success of the black civil rights movement suggested, however, that minority groups could protect themselves by legal means against unwarranted discrimination. Comparing their status to that of African Americans prior to the 1960s, lesbians and gay men claimed legitimacy as a deprived minority entitled to basic human rights.

While not all would agree with the comparison to the injustices suffered by African Americans, there is ample evidence that many gays endure a good deal of discrimination. Surveys of gays and lesbians report that most have experienced at least once in their lives some type of victimization because of their sexual orientation, including verbal abuse, physical assault, abuse by police, and vandalized property. Harassment of gay youth, experienced as pervasive and distressing by many, continues to occur unrestricted in most U.S. schools. Even more commonly, lesbians and gay men claim to have faced discrimination in job hiring or promotion, in the process of renting or buying housing, and in public accommodations such as restaurants, motels, and bars. Many other gays report that they feared discrimination, although they did not actually experience it, or purposely hid their orientation to avoid victimization (Comstock 1991; Harbeck 1992; Herek and Berrill 1992).

Mainstream attempts to reduce antigay discrimination have centered on gay rights legislation. Advocates of this approach believed that legal recognition of gays would lead to greater social acceptance and legitimacy. Protected from discrimination, more lesbians and gay men would be willing to come out of the closet with increased feelings of security, confidence, and self-respect. As larger numbers of gays disclosed their sexual orientation, more Americans would come to know and accept them, much as the civil rights laws had broken down the barriers of racial discrimination and created greater integration and understanding.

Opponents of this legalistic approach, however, disagree with these claims. They, and many undecided citizens, believe that gays suffer relatively little discrimination, partly because gays can hide their sexual identity. This situation sets gays apart from blacks and other racial groups that exhibit clearly identifiable characteristics and thus appear to face a great deal more discrimination. Moreover, large numbers of Americans find same-gender sex to be both morally repugnant and a threat to traditional society. In the words of lesbian activist Urvashi Vaid, "We are hated because of how, with whom, and how much (mythic or real) we do it" (1995, 192). Such sexual behavior is considered by many to degrade the moral and social fiber of society. Thus opponents claim that not only is there no dire need for antidiscrimination legislation inclusive of gays, but also that such legislation, if passed, reinforces a lifestyle that is destructive of traditional American norms. (See chapter 7.)

THE QUEST FOR GAY RIGHTS LEGISLATION

The Stonewall rebellion of 1969 sparked the beginning of an active gay political movement for civil rights protections. Prior to this time there were no laws or policies that prohibited discrimination on the basis of sexual orientation in any public or private organization in the country. The post-Stonewall gay movement, however, was relatively small with few significant supporters. Politically organized lesbians and gay men resided primarily in large cities and liberal university communities (D'Emilio 1983).

It is not surprising, therefore, that many of the initial adoptions of gay rights ordinances took place in university settings. In the early 1970s antidiscrimination laws were passed in Berkeley, Palo Alto, Boulder, Ann Arbor, East Lansing, Austin, and Madison, Wis. By 1977 two-thirds of the twenty-eight communities with gay rights legislation were university-dominated cities or counties. As in the case of the black civil rights and women's movements, liberal students and faculty were often in the vanguard of the quest for gay rights.

Large cities with sizable and organized gay populations were also among the first communities to adopt legislation to protect against discrimination based on sexual orientation. These cities included Detroit, Minneapolis, San Francisco, Seattle, and Washington. Other large cities with similar characteristics, such as Atlanta, Chicago, Los Angeles, New York, and

Philadelphia had at least initiated political discussions of such laws by 1975. Thus the pioneers of gay rights laws or policies were localities with significant supportive constituencies consisting typically of liberal university populations and mobilized gay citizens (Button, Rienzo, and Wald 1997).[2]

Progressive states also began to consider civil rights protections for gays. In the mid-1970s New York, Minnesota, Wisconsin, Massachusetts, California, Oregon, Connecticut, Colorado, and Hawaii introduced gay rights bills in their state legislatures, although none of these bills passed. In Pennsylvania, however, Governor Milton Shapp issued an executive order in 1975 to bar discrimination on the basis of sexual orientation in state agencies. The liberal governor had been lobbied for two years by gay activists, and while the executive order was limited to state employees and lacked the force of a law, it was the first such legal action taken by a state.

The legal successes of gays in the early 1970s were also achieved because of the lack of organized resistance. While the Catholic Church offered modest opposition in a few cities, other potential opponents seemed caught off-guard by the sudden emergence of this political issue. Traditional religious groups and other opponents began to mobilize, however, and in 1977 they won a major victory by repealing via referendum the Dade County, Florida ordinance protecting gays. It was the first defeat of gay rights in a major U.S. community. Anita Bryant, a popular singer and devout Baptist, led the coalition of right-wing (primarily religious) forces in Dade County. She contended that such ordinances were a religious abomination and a license for gays to molest children. Bryant's success attracted national attention and propelled her onto an antigay rights crusade that was effective in rescinding similar local laws in Eugene, St. Paul, and Wichita. Moreover, this antigay initiative, with its focus on children, kept proponents from seeking similar protections on behalf of youth in school settings for years to come (Adam 1995).

The conservative opposition to gay rights sparked a further politicization of lesbians and gay men. Gay activists successfully parlayed the attacks on them into greater publicity and increased support for their grievances. In California, for example, a controversial 1978 proposition that would have permitted school boards to expel gay teachers was soundly defeated in a voter referendum. In addition, the steady trend of local adoptions of legal protection for gays continued, and by 1980 forty U.S. communities could claim such legislation.

The decade of the 1980s marked a shift to a more conservative tone in American politics. The new Christian Right emerged as an organized constituency with a strong antigay agenda. The AIDS epidemic broke out, and the stigma of an often fatal disease was conferred on gay men, encouraging many Americans to become less tolerant of homosexuals. However, the disease also pushed a number of gays out of the closet and into the political arena in order to gain government help and protection and in time most Americans, in spite of their attitudes that the gay subculture was immoral, came to support basic civil rights protections for lesbians and gay men. As a result, the 1980s saw some forty additional cities and counties pass gay rights legislation.

Unlike the first communities to adopt human rights codes for gays, the local governments passing such legislation in the 1980s consisted of a mix of large cities, suburban communities adjacent to major cities, and ten counties. Atlanta, Chicago, Philadelphia, and New York, each of which had experienced well-organized opposition and less cohesive gay constituents in the 1970s, finally adopted gay rights legislation. Following a political process known as "diffusion of innovation," suburban governments and counties began to accept the new legislation from larger and more dominant cities. According to this process, once a new law or policy has been widely disseminated and gains legitimacy among decision-makers, it has an increased momentum (Walker 1969). Thus suburban locales and some counties adjacent to or near Los Angeles, San Francisco, Chicago, New York, Seattle, and Washington passed legislation in the 1980s and 1990s following earlier adoptions by central cities.

Policy changes amenable to gays occurred much more slowly at the state level. In 1982, after seven years of debate, Wisconsin became the first state to enact legislation protective of gays. The bill's primary sponsor was a liberal legislator representing the community of Madison, home of the University of Wisconsin. Supporters emphasized the state's progressive tradition in civil rights and the fact that the state's two largest cities already had implemented such legislation. They also were able to defuse religious opposition by gaining endorsements from numerous main-line religious organizations, including the Catholic Archbishop (Haider-Markel and Meier 1996). In 1989, after a legislative battle of nearly two decades, Massachusetts became the second state to adopt a law prohibiting discrimination against homosexuals.

The decade of the 1990s revealed a tremendous upsurge in local laws protective of sexual orientation. By mid-1993 approximately 126 cities and counties had adopted legislation, and by 1996 the figure had increased to an estimated 160 communities. Thus the first seven years of the 1990s produced the adoptions of as many local gay antibias laws as the entire two previous decades. Clearly the diffusion-of-innovation process accounted for some of this dramatic rise in legislation. Perhaps most important, however, was the significant increase in lesbians and gay men coming out of the closet and more urgently demanding government protection from discrimination. As gays began to feel more comfortable in being open about their sexual orientation, more Americans reported that they knew someone who was gay and were thus more accepting of homosexuals and more supportive of gay rights legislation.

As the gay movement expanded, it also became increasingly politicized. Some gays were mobilized by the slow response of government to the AIDS crisis, while others were motivated by a political atmosphere that was more supportive of gays. In the 1992 presidential election, for example, all five leading Democratic contenders actively courted the gay vote, and the election of Bill Clinton signaled unprecedented support for gay rights and other political issues of importance to lesbians and gay men. In addition, the new climate of acceptance and politicization of gays and their allies was felt on the local level: an estimated 120 openly gay officials were elected to local public office by 1993, double the number from 1991.

The communities that implemented gay rights legislation in the 1990s showed great variation in size and region, and were quite different from those cities and counties that passed ordinances in earlier decades. Many adopting communities in the 1990s have been relatively small and suburban in nature, like Brighton, N.Y., Oak Park, Ill., and Rockville, Md. The more conservative regions of the Midwest and South have claimed increased numbers of communities as well, including LaGrange, Ill., Troy, Idaho, Lafayette, Ind., Henderson, Ky., Asheville, N.C., and Virginia Beach, Va. Clearly the gay movement has spread beyond its original coastal confines. A few large cities where gays were just beginning to organize politically also passed antidiscrimination legislation. These cities included Cincinnati, Denver, Kansas City, New Orleans, Phoenix, and Pittsburgh. By the 1990s the community environment supportive of gay rights had changed to one that was less university oriented, smaller in size, had relatively fewer gay residents, and was increasingly found in the Midwest or South. Clearly the local gay rights movement has shifted to a diverse range of cities and counties across America.[3]

The dramatic increase in gay civil rights laws in the 1990s has also been evident at the state level. By 1997 eleven states (and the District of Columbia) had passed some form of statewide legislation banning antigay discrimination. Of these eleven states, nine enacted legislation in the 1990s (California, Hawaii, Minnesota, New Jersey, Rhode Island, Vermont, Connecticut, New Hampshire, and Maine).[4] Protective measures were found, as expected, in the more liberal states like California and Hawaii and most New England states. In addition, by the mid-1990s the governors of eight other states had issued executive orders to prohibit discrimination on the basis of sexual orientation in state employment.

In communities where civil rights protection for gays has been achieved, another important equity issue involving domestic partner benefits has often emerged. The partners of lesbian and gay employees normally do not receive the same medical, pension, and other benefits that are provided to spouses of married workers. Because they cannot legally marry, this practice deprives many gays of sometimes sizable economic dividends. Since the early 1990s lesbian and gay workers have increasingly lobbied for such domestic partner benefits. By 1998 more than sixty cities and counties, including Chicago, Los Angeles, Minneapolis, New York, Philadelphia, San Francisco, and Seattle had adopted policies that provided some benefits for partners of homosexual (and sometimes heterosexual) employees. In addition, in 1997 Hawaii became the first state to offer benefits to partners in same-gender relationships.

While local and state legislation supportive of gays spread throughout the United States, the antigay political backlash that first appeared in the late 1970s gained force in response to the gay successes of the 1990s. The proliferation of gay rights made these ordinances a chief target of the political right. The battles that ensued often took the form of voter referendums on proposals to repeal legislation that protected homosexuals from discrimination. In Colorado, Idaho, Oregon, and Maine, and in cities like Cincinnati, Tampa, and Portland, Me., voters were asked to rescind gay rights. In the most widely publicized referendum of the 1990s, Colorado voters passed decisively a ban on all local gay antidiscrimination laws. Had the results of this referendum not been overturned by the U.S. Supreme Court in 1996, the measure would have repealed gay rights laws in Aspen, Boulder, Denver, and other Colorado cities.

SCHOOLS AND GAY YOUTH

Schools have traditionally been entrusted to promote cultural norms and responsibilities as well as provide education, which means they also perpetuate our society's antigay attitudes and behaviors. Thus it is not surprising that they tend to be heterosexist in nature. This bias is typically institutionalized through schools' omission of homosexuality from a topic of study in the curriculum, from an absence of role models (teachers, counselors), and from lack of visibility in school-sponsored activities (dances). Furthermore, teachers and counselors often lack sufficient knowledge about sexual orientation and share with their students a significant prejudice against homosexuality. Antigay verbal and physical abuse are not only a common experience for students, but occur without negative consequences within most schools. The suffering due to this bias is tremendous both for those merely perceived to be homosexual as well as for gay and lesbian youth, who often first become aware of their sexual orientation in adolescence. As a result, gay youth have been found to be at increased risk of substance abuse, dropping out of school, depression, and suicide (Harbeck 1992; Unks 1994).

In 1989, the federal government issued the *Report of the Secretary's Task Force on Youth Suicide,* which documented the health risks gay youth faced. Its recommendations included a call for schools to institute changes to ameliorate these serious problems in the form of five programmatic interventions (Gibson 1989):

1. Establish and enforce a policy that prohibits harassment based on sexual orientation serves to thwart antigay violence, thereby creating an environment where all students can attend school safely and free of fear.

2. Institute support groups for gay, lesbian, and bisexual students. These groups can decrease the sense of isolation often experienced by these students. They can also be extended to include other students who want to support diversity and decrease prejudice and discrimination.

3. Give gay and lesbian students access to supportive adults, through special counseling services and by identifying openly gay and lesbian teachers and counselors who can be observed as successful and empathetic role models.

4. Include sexual orientation in the curriculum, preferably in a comprehensive way infused through appropriate subjects (history, English, health) as well as through all grade levels. Concomitant with this instruction is the need for schools to provide training for teachers, counselors, and other staff about sexual orientation, since this is a topic about which most school personnel are ignorant and feel incompetent to handle with students.

5. Institute changes in the school environment that promote sensitivity to and acceptance of homosexually-oriented youth, such as being

more inclusive in terminology and opening extracurricular events to gay and lesbian students.

Although public schools are usually the most highly funded and important institutions within local government, they are generally not under the direct jurisdiction of the city or county legislative body and thus are not covered by most gay rights laws or policies. However, contentious local battles over gay issues often focus on youth and schools. Both supporters and opponents of gay rights recognize the distinct potential of schools to affect the future social fabric of American culture through influencing how youth think about gay issues. Consequently, according to lawyer-educator Karen Harbeck, the combination of homosexuality and education evokes "one of the most publicly volatile and personally threatening debates in our national history" (1992, 2).

This potential to elicit controversy is the most formidable barrier to developing programs to address change in U.S. schools today. School administrators and other leaders are fearful that initiating programs that appear to support homosexuality will cause such strife in their communities as to threaten the schools' lifeblood—support for funding—as well as their personal survival in terms of job security. As one school board member in Cincinnati put it, opponents of school programs that deal with homosexuality would "withdraw their children from the schools and beat us at the ballot box" (Button, Rienzo, and Wald 1997, 150). As evidence, many school officials cited New York City's notorious battle over this issue in 1992. The School Chancellor, Joseph Fernandez, supported a multicultural curriculum which included two pages in a 443-page teaching guide that encouraged them to refer to gay and lesbian role models and contained a bibliography that listed three books with content about homosexuality. However, the bulk of the discussion at public meetings and public protests focused on homosexuality. The nationally respected chancellor was subsequently fired by the school board, allegedly due to his support for addressing sexual orientation issues. Fernandez's firing had reverberations across the country in school that were grappling with this issue.

Opponents of dealing with sexual orientation in the schools claim that change supportive of gay youth will lead to increased acceptance of homosexuality. Most of these opponents represent traditional religious organizations that condemn this orientation as immoral. Furthermore, many Americans believe that education about homosexuality will influence individuals to become homosexual. Even though this belief has been repudiated by professionals (medical, psychological, and educational) and by the legal system, strong antigay attitudes persist and are promoted by well-organized conservative political and religious groups. These groups generate formidable opposition to change, especially at the local level. Moreover, gay and lesbian activists have not been willing to press issues on behalf of youth, mainly due to their fears regarding accusations of "recruitment." While advocates for gay rights have successfully influenced some cities and counties to pass antidiscrimination legislation since the 1970s, they have only recently begun to initiate action for change on behalf of youth through the schools.

Intense controversies like that in New York have had significant repercussions and, as a result, most U.S. schools do *little or nothing* to address the issue of sexual orientation. In Raleigh, N.C., for example, although the topic of homosexuality has come up in the schools, the issue has been decidedly suppressed by administrators and school board members. Administrators have repeatedly prohibited community agencies from advertising support services for gay and lesbian youth in high school newspapers. There are no openly gay or lesbian teachers in the schools, nor has there been any in-service education for school personnel on sexual orientation issues. Although members of the school district's health advisory council recognized that homosexuality was a topic that should be addressed, it was quickly dropped from consideration due to the perception that intense objections would be raised in the community.

Nonetheless, school districts within cities or counties that enacted gay rights legislation are more likely to have instituted some policy recommendations on behalf of gay and lesbian youths. In our national survey, about half of school districts in communities with gay rights legislation reported having instruction about sexual orientation, compared with only one-third of school districts without legal protection. Likewise, support groups for gay and lesbian youth were organized within a quarter of school districts in cities or counties with protective legislation, while none of those within communities without legislation reported sponsoring such groups. Other recommended programs showed similar patterns (table 12.1).

In Iowa City, a university-dominated community that adopted gay antidiscrimination legislation in the late 1970s, policy changes in the schools began to take place but only more than a decade later. These changes were initiated in 1992 by a teacher who decided to publicly disclose his sexual identity and approach his district's equity committee with a list of problems identified by other gay and lesbian staff and students. With the strong support of the equity officer and school superintendent, the school dis-

Table 12.1   School Programs Regarding Sexual Orientation in Ordinance/Policy Communities and Comparison Communities

School Programs	Communities with Ordinance/Policy (N = 123) (%)	Communities without Ordinance/Policy (N = 118) (%)
Education/instruction:		
School district (SD) offers sexual orientation education to students? (YES)	50	34
At what level is sexual orientation education offered? (percent below high school)	31	20
SD offers sexual orientation education to staff? (YES)	43	22
SD offers sexual orientation education to parents/school board/community? (YES)	29	13
Support and Services:		
SD offers support groups for gay/lesbian/bi-sexual (g/l/b) students? (YES)	27	2
SD offers special counseling for g/l/b students (YES)	24	1
SD has specific policy prohibiting anti-gay language and behavior? (YES)	23	14

trict instituted several recommended programs to address the issues. Iowa City's schools have implemented policies that protect staff from employment discrimination and students from harassment on the basis of sexual orientation. In-service training about sexual orientation has been conducted for administrators, teachers, and counselors. In 1994 the district passed a policy granting domestic partner benefits for gay and lesbian staff, one of the most coveted requests of gay school personnel.

The vast majority of initiatives that address sexual orientation issues in the states are the result of similar actions that have taken place at the local (school district) level. Although the issue has been raised in several states, few have passed laws or policies on behalf of lesbian and gay youth. One notable exception is Massachusetts. Governor William Weld, a Republican supportive of gay rights as well as other liberal social policies, convened the first state-level Commission on Gay and Lesbian Youth in 1992 in response to the 1989 federal report documenting high suicide rates among gay and lesbian youth. This commission sponsored public hearings throughout Massachusetts that documented problems faced by gay youth, including harassment, isolation, drop-out rates, and suicide. Partly in response to a strong lobbying effort by supportive youth, the legislature subsequently passed the first state law prohibiting discrimination against gay and lesbian students in public schools. The Commission also recommended other programmatic actions to address the problems of gay youth. Four of these were officially adopted by the state board of education. The governor sponsored the first statewide training effort for teachers on lesbian and gay issues. Moreover, the state legislature allocated almost half a million dollars to its Department of Education for HIV / AIDS-related training for school professionals, part of which was used to address the identified needs of gay youth.

The only other states to pass legislation to support gay youth are Iowa and Pennsylvania. Both these states, however, carried out limited efforts without the significant reinforcement of follow-up support found in Massachusetts. On the other hand, most legislation recently proposed at the state-level (the majority of which has not passed) has sought to *prohibit* schools from addressing sexual orientation issues. For example, some state legislation, such as that passed by North Carolina in 1996, specifically prohibits schools from teaching about homosexuality in a positive manner.

UNDERSTANDING THE POLITICS OF GAY ISSUES

The achievement of gay rights legislation in a number of communities and some states, as well as changes in the schools that are supportive of lesbian and gay youth, have provoked a great deal of political conflict and turmoil. Despite this conflict, a significant amount of policy change has occurred in response to demands for legislation protective of gays. What political forces best explain these public policy innovations? Research on social movements, especially the black civil rights and women's movements, has called attention to political and social factors that influence policy change.

Urbanism, and the *social diversity* that accompanies it, have been linked to innovative policies affecting gays. Urban settings are particularly conducive to the development of strong subcultures. Due to the social dislocation of World War II, many gays and other minority groups migrated to major American cities such as New York, San Francisco, Washington, Chicago, Los Angeles, and Boston. Feeling isolated and threatened in smaller communities, lesbians and gay men capitalized on the permissive atmosphere and anonymity found in major urban areas to develop their own neighborhoods (D'Emilio 1983). These gay enclaves were somewhat insulated and protected from the larger culture and, in time, developed the critical mass necessary for political organization. Thus demography, especially city size and diversity, was extremely important in providing the proper setting for the gay political movement and its ultimate achievement of public policies supportive of gays both in city government and the schools.

Mass movements of disadvantaged groups were once viewed as irrational crusades by malcontents that created much disorder but little policy change. Urban race riots and social movements of the poor were sometimes explained in this manner. More recently, however, social scientists have developed a more credible theory of mass movements that has been marked by rational styles and well-organized constituents. Known as *resource mobilization theory,* this approach emphasizes the important role of political and organizational resources of disadvantaged groups in the process of public policy (Mayer 1991). According to this theory, the size and degree of mobilization of the out group are significant requirements. A shared sense of identity and feelings of intense grievances are vital to success, as are such group resources as wealth, organizational capacity, and leadership. Other than sheer numbers of gays, most other characteristics of a politically mobilized constituency also affected policies supportive of homosexuals. Thus it mattered greatly if gays were organized politically, if there were openly gay candidates for office and elected officials, and if lesbians and gays participated actively in politics. In a word, gay politics makes a difference at the local and state levels.

Groups excluded from power, however, must depend on more than just their own efforts to achieve political success. Resources outside the group, such as helpful allies and a supportive political climate, are also crucial. This emphasis on outside factors is known as the *political opportunity structure* (Tarrow 1991). The women's movement, for example, could not have achieved the success it did without a government that was open to new interests and ideas. It also needed active supporters from outside the movement itself. Because gays face considerable public hostility, they must depend on influential allies and a community atmosphere that is open to new demands. Both the local and state adoption of gay rights legislation and school policies addressing issues of sexual orientation were influenced moderately by the political opportunity structure. A gay-friendly political climate, as evidenced in liberal college towns or in states and congressional districts that proved supportive of gay rights, was clearly helpful. Antibias legislation was also dependent on gays having allies and developing political coalitions with additional groups. These supportive interests often included human rights organizations (especially the American Civil Liberties Union), local human relations boards or commissions, liberal church groups, African–American civil rights advocates, liberal women's groups, university or student organizations, the Democratic Party, and environmental groups.

The final factor to influence the establishment of local and state policies protective of gays has to do with the opposition, that is, forces that resist policy innovation and social change. *Communal protest theory* describes reactive groups that emphasize tradition and maintaining the status quo to oppose threatening social practices (Lo 1992). The most significant challenge to the gay rights campaign has been from religious fundamentalists who condemn homosexuality as sinful and a threat to the traditional family. Some local business interests, especially small business owners, also oppose gay demands for fear of loss of economic control and of costly new regulations in the workplace. The most notable opposition to gay rights, however, was from conservative Protestants who proved to be well-organized and who perceived this issue to represent a major conflict with their cultural values. However, even traditional religious groups were not able to stem the tide of gay rights legislation in larger, diverse communities where gays and their allies were organized in sizable numbers.

PHILADELPHIA: GAY POLITICS IN ACTION

An urban setting that is illustrative of the political forces that influenced lesbian and gay initiatives is Philadelphia (Button, Rienzo, and Wald 1997, chap. 2). Known as "the City of Brotherly Love," Philadelphia historically was a haven for many seeking religious and political freedom. In recent decades the city's neighborhoods have become increasingly diverse, with significant numbers of African Americans, Hispanics, Asians, and white ethnics. This sizable city with a socially diverse population was fertile ground for attracting gays and lesbians. Amidst the period of social unrest of the 1960s, a chapter of the Mattachine Society (and later, a Daughters of Bilitis chapter) was organized and gay activists began to challenge discrimination against homosexuals.

In the early 1970s gays in Philadelphia first proposed human rights legislation protective of sexual orientation to the city council. While the city's Commission on Human Relations was supportive, gay activists were relatively few in number, politically inexperienced, and not well organized. Moreover, the city council was moderately conservative, as was the mayor, and opposed to gay rights legislation. Nor was the political climate in the state conducive to such a law. No other city in Pennsylvania had even considered, much less adopted, protective legislation for homosexuals.

Furthermore, when the governor issued an executive order barring discrimination in state employment on the basis of sexual orientation, the state legislature overwhelmingly voted to restrict the employment of gays (this bill was later vetoed by the governor).

Advocates of gay civil rights in Philadelphia, however, were not to be denied. With an emphasis on electoral politics, gays and their allies were able to create a more progressive city council and elect a politically moderate mayor by the late 1970s. They also created the Lesbian and Gay Task Force, an organization that played a key role in the political mobilizing, lobbying, and fund raising necessary to gain passage of local legislation.

By the early 1980s the local political atmosphere for gay civil rights had improved. More than forty communities across the country had adopted gay rights laws or policies. In Philadelphia, the University of Pennsylvania, the city's largest private employer, passed a gay nondiscrimination policy, and Philadelphia's chief administrator issued a similar policy banning such discrimination for city employees. With these changes, gays began to mobilize support for a comprehensive gay rights law. Endorsements for such legislation came from a wide range of local groups including African Americans, women, liberal churches, labor unions, students, progressive businesses, and several prominent public officials.

Opposition to the proposal, much of which came from the Catholic Church, was late in developing and relatively unorganized. With an estimated half a million Catholics in Philadelphia, the church was potentially a powerful political antagonist. Gays and their allies, however, moved the legislation quietly to a city council vote before the opposition could successfully mobilize. In August 1982, the addition to the city's human rights code protective of sexual orientation was approved by a decisive 13–2 council vote and soon became local law. A decade later gay activists and their allies pushed for health and pension benefits for same-sex partners of city workers. Despite more organized opposition from the Catholic archdiocese over this policy, domestic partner benefits were ultimately adopted by a divided city council in 1998.

In 1989 Philadelphia's Lesbian and Gay Task Force began to lobby for inclusion of sexual orientation issues in public schools. They did so by approaching the State Board of Education. By 1992, the Board passed a policy prohibiting discrimination against homosexuality in educational programs, and soon after the state's equity statement was changed to include sexual orientation. These actions encouraged the Task Force to promote similar initiatives at the local level. In 1994, strong leadership of the Task

Force, with assistance from allies both in the schools and in the community, persuaded the city's board of education to pass a policy for "Multicultural-Multiracial-Gender Education" with its stated intention to promote "knowledge about and respect for those of all races, ethnic groups, social classes, genders, religions, disabilities, and *sexual orientations*" (italics added). This was deemed to be a critical step toward incorporating gay issues into all aspects of the city's educational institutions and toward promoting equity and justice for gay students and staff.

However, significant protest, specifically with respect to homosexuality, emerged during the public hearings over the implementation of this policy. Opposing forces, perceived by school board members as "adamantly, even violently opposed" to programs inclusive of sexual orientation, prevailed. As a result, none of Philadelphia's schools have officially implemented curriculum or other supportive strategies that assist students with sexual orientation issues. In addition, the two most supportive school board members have left office, and the committee that fought for passage of the policy and charged with its implementation has been disbanded by a newly hired, unsupportive school superintendent.

IMPACT OF PROTECTIVE LAWS AND POLICIES

One of the most hotly debated issues surrounding gay rights legislation has been the probable effects of protective codes. Gays and their supporters contend that protective codes are necessary to prevent unjustified discrimination in employment, housing, schools, and other areas of life. In the same manner that the civil rights laws of the 1960s successfully stemmed unfair treatment based on race and gender, legislation banning discrimination based on sexual orientation is seen as a crucial step toward the full inclusion of gays in national life. Moreover, such government actions are viewed as essential in granting lesbians and gays greater legitimacy and acceptance in a largely homophobic society.

Critics of gay rights, on the other hand, claim there is no need for protective laws and policies because most gays, due to their middle-class status and ability to hide their identity, rarely face discrimination. Such unnecessary regulations, it is argued, would overly burden local and state governments, schools, and businesses. Unsubstantiated claims of antigay discrimination, often leading to expensive litigation, might strain governmental resources and drive away businesses. Additionally, opponents assert that legislation that provides greater legitimacy to gays is unwarranted for a group that chooses a clearly deviant "lifestyle."

In examining the actual impact of local and state legislation protective of sexual orientation, it is useful to look first at the scope of basic institutions covered by these legal codes. More than 90 percent of cities and counties, and all ten states, with gay rights legislation forbid discrimination in public employment. This is by far the most frequently covered institution. There is much more sporadic coverage of employment in other sectors, with about half the communities (but most states) including private employment in their ordinances. Public accommodations such as restaurants, motels, and retail stores are covered by most local and all state legislation.

Most communities, however, have limited their legal protection of gays in other important sectors of everyday life. This is particularly the case in the area of private resources. Only about one-third of local legislation cover credit agencies, including banks, and small businesses were frequently exempted. Other significant institutions that were commonly omitted from coverage or specifically exempted were religious organizations and schools. There is a prevailing free enterprise ideology that strongly resists government regulation in the private sector. Legal coverage is also limited in this case because many Americans are uncomfortable with the prospect of encountering gays in intimate settings.

Beyond the nature and scope of gay antidiscrimination legislation, the impact of these ordinances depends on their implementation or administration. Effective implementation is influenced first of all by the kind of agency charged with enforcing such laws or policies. At the local level the most common enforcement organization (found in almost one-half of all cities and counties with gay rights legislation) was the human rights board or commission. Established typically during the 1950s and 1960s to enforce the first civil rights laws, these organizations were found in larger communities that maintained specialized, complex bureaucracies for administration of these laws. The second most frequently utilized enforcement agency was the personnel or equal employment opportunity office, reflecting the widespread coverage given to public employment. Small communities were less likely to have specialized enforcement agencies, with administrative responsibility given to the city or county manager, attorney, or clerk. A few communities provided no formal enforcement mechanism in local government but instead relied upon state agencies (if there was a statewide gay rights law) or private litigation in courts.

A common indicator of how well this legislation is enforced is the number of formal complaints of discrimination based on sexual orientation. Our survey of cities and counties with gay rights laws provided such information for 1992. Approximately 40 percent of the communities reported that not a single complaint had been filed in that year. Some 20 percent listed five or fewer formal charges. Only fifteen cities or counties (all of them larger communities) reported ten or more complaints of discrimination based on sexual orientation. Compared to other charges of discrimination, those based on sexual orientation were far fewer in number than claims of race and gender discrimination. Indeed sexual orientation complaints were typically about as frequent as charges of discrimination based on national origin or handicap/disability. A dearth of formal complaints of antigay discrimination has also been reported by most states with gay rights legislation.

The mechanism of enforcement, however, did affect the rate of sexual orientation charges. Independent, specialized enforcement agencies encouraged a higher rate of complaints, but these administrative bodies were limited to large cities (more than 500,000 in population). The small number of complaints reported by most communities and states is due to several factors. The modest enforcement efforts found in many locales have discouraged lesbians and gay men from seeking legal redress of grievances. In addition, in lawsuits claiming discrimination of any sort, the threshold of proof is high and difficult to meet. More fundamentally, gays are often reluctant to take advantage of protective ordinances by filing a formal complaint. Doing so typically forces gays to "come out" publicly in an often hostile environment. When almost half the states criminalize sodomy and few gays feel secure enough to be open about their sexual identity, it is not surprising that antidiscrimination legislation is rarely used.

Despite the low level of formal complaints, other evidence, based on our surveys of public officials, indicates that gay rights laws have had both behavioral and institutional consequences. For lesbians and gay men, the legislation has helped to reduce discrimination in employment and other institutions covered by the legal codes. The law sent a message that antigay discrimination was illegal and therefore not permissible, thus serving to deter in advance unfair treatment. By curbing discrimination, protective legislation made gays feels more comfortable and safe in general. As a result of feeling more secure, lesbians and gay men were more likely to come out or express their sexual identity, and thus not have the stress of hiding a significant part of their lives.

Legislation has been helpful to gays in other ways as well. The political push for civil rights protection proved to be an effective mobilizing strategy for gays and their allies. In addition, the achievement of gay rights often paved the way politically for consideration and adoption of other gay-friendly policies, such as domestic partner benefits. Indeed, the number of local governments providing health, pension, or other benefits to partners of gay employees increased dramatically in the 1990s. Moreover, school districts in localities where gay legislation passed were more likely to have programs and policies that addressed sexual orientation issues than districts where there was no legal protection. Even local police, often abusive of homosexuals in the past, have become more sensitive to gays where protective codes have been adopted.

While business owners and others often claimed that civil rights laws inclusive of sexual orientation would drive away businesses for fear of having to employ or serve gays, such dire economic consequences have not occurred. Gay rights legislation has had little or no effect on business growth and development. Indeed, the drive for gay rights legislation in the public sector has encouraged the adoption of similar protective policies, as well as domestic partner benefits, in growing numbers of businesses. Clearly the workplace has emerged as one of the frontiers of lesbian and gay activism in the 1990s (Woods 1993).

Ultimately local and state legislation has had an impact that goes beyond the more tangible effects of protecting gays and influencing institutions that provide services. The law is a powerful instrument for conferring legitimacy on various groups and ways of living, which is precisely why gay rights legislation has been so bitterly opposed. In the same way that the civil rights legislation of the 1960s granted African Americans greater inclusion in national life, laws banning discrimination based on sexual orientation have acknowledged the right of homosexuals to unfettered membership in the community. Thus legislation has served not only to regulate antigay behavior but also to create a more egalitarian society where lesbians and gay men enjoy greater acceptance and legitimacy.

NOTES

1. In May 1998, President Clinton issued an executive order to protect gay and lesbian federal workers from job discrimination. While a gay rights law covering employment in general has been proposed a number of times in Congress, it has never achieved a favorable vote.
2. Much of the information presented in this chapter is adapted from the authors'

book *Private Lives, Public Conflicts: Battles over Gay Rights in American Communities.* The book presents more complete descriptions, information, and references than are included here.

3. For information on civil rights laws in individual counties and cities, see "Gay, Lesbian, Bisexual, and Transgender Civil Rights Laws in the U.S.," National Gay and Lesbian Task Force, August 1998, accessible at <www.ngltf.org/pub.html>.

4. In February 1998, Maine became the first state to repeal its gay rights law. In a popular referendum, the law was rejected by a 52–48 percent margin.

REFERENCES

Adam, Barry D. 1995. *The rise of a gay and lesbian movement.* New York: Twayne.

Button, James W., Barbara A. Rienzo, and Kenneth D. Wald. 1997. *Private lives, public conflicts: Battles over gay rights in American communities.* Washington, D.C.: Congressional Quarterly Press.

Comstock, Gary David. 1991. *Violence against lesbians and gay men.* New York: Columbia University Press.

D'Emilio, John. 1983. *Sexual politics, sexual communities: The making of a homosexual minority in the United States 1940–1970.* Chicago, Ill.: University of Chicago Press.

Gibson, Paul. 1989. Gay and lesbian youth suicide. In *Report of the Secretary's Task Force on Youth Suicide,* vol. 3. Washington, D.C.: U.S. Department of Health and Human Services.

Haider-Markel, Donald P., and Kenneth J. Meier. 1996. The politics of gay and lesbian rights: Expanding the scope of the conflict. *Journal of Politics* 58:332–49.

Harbeck, Karen M., ed. 1992. *Coming out of the classroom closet: Gay and lesbian students, teachers, and curricula.* Binghamton, N.Y.: Haworth Press.

Herek, Gregory M., and Kevin T. Berrill, eds. 1992. *Hate crimes: Confronting violence against lesbians and gay men.* Newbury Park, Cal.: Sage.

Lo, Clarence Y. H. 1992. "Communities of challengers in social movement theory." In *Frontiers of social movement theory,* edited by Aldon D. Morris and Carol McClurge Mueller. New Haven, Conn.: Yale University Press, 224–47.

Mayer, Margit. 1991. Social movement research and social movement practice: The U.S. pattern. In *Research on social movements,* edited by Dieter Rucht. Frankfort am Main, Germany: Campus Verlag, 47–120.

Tarrow, Sidney. 1991. Comparing social movement participation in Western Europe and the United States: Problems, uses, and a proposal for synthesis. In

Research on Social Movements, edited by Dieter Rucht. Frankfort am Main, Germany: Campus Verlag, 392–420.

Unks, Gerald. 1994. Thinking about the homosexual adolescent. *High School Journal* 77 (1-2): 1–6.

Vaid, Urvashi. 1995. *Virtual equality: The mainstreaming of gay and lesbian liberation.* New York: Doubleday, Anchor.

Walker, Jack L. 1969. The diffusion of innovations among the American states. *American Political Science Review* 63 (Sept.): 880–99.

Woods, James D. 1993. *The corporate closet: The professional lives of gay men in America.* New York: Free Press.

13

LESBIAN AND GAY POLITICS IN THE STATES: INTEREST GROUPS, ELECTORAL POLITICS, AND POLICY

Donald P. Haider-Markel

Outside of statewide ballot initiatives, most research on lesbian and gay politics has focused on local or national politics. In part this is due to a perception that those places are where the action is. At the national level, gay issues tend to attract the media's attention, dragging academics in their wake. And while it is true that local governments have been on the forefront of policies protecting lesbians and gays from discrimination (Wald, Button, and Rienzo 1996), state governments have increasingly addressed a variety of gay-related issues, including the repeal of sodomy laws, antidiscrimination protections, same-sex marriage, hate crimes, domestic partner policy, and AIDS policy (Haider-Markel 1997a). State governments must also sometimes provide the authority for local governments to act on gay issues, or conversely, state governments sometimes pass laws to block local government actions on gay issues.[1] Furthermore, gay issues are increasingly appearing in state elections, including the 1998 California, Minnesota, and Nebraska races for governor (Carlson 1998; Coile 1998; Whereatt 1998). This chapter provides an overview of state activity on these issues, as well as providing for an introductory understanding of gay politics in the states.

The chapter is divided into three sections. Each section summarizes recent research and provides mini-case studies on the patterns of lesbian and gay politics in the states. In the first section I discuss gay movement politics in the states by providing an overview of gay interest group activity. I discuss gay involvement in state electoral politics in the next section, with a particular focus on the election of openly lesbian and gay public officials. The third section examines state policymaking on four gay-related issues: civil rights protections, hate crimes, same-sex marriage, and sodomy laws. State activity in each of these policy areas is summarized, but I also use mini-case studies of the policymaking process to clarify the politics of these issues.

LESBIAN AND GAY INTEREST GROUPS IN THE STATES

Although lesbian and gay groups have been active at the national level for twenty-five years and at the local level since at least the 1950s, few states saw statewide activity by gay groups before the 1980s. In fact, much of the organizing at the state level has only begun to occur since about 1988. Part of the reason gay activity in state government has been inconsistent is because the membership in gay groups varies by the education and income level of the general population, the relative size of the gay population, and public and elite support (Haider-Markel 1997b).

Another reason the strength of gay groups varies across the states is because the movement itself is divided over whether political efforts should focus on the states or on other levels of government. For example, the director of New York state's main gay lobbying group said, "Our movement has been . . . back and forth about a really coordinated focus on the state houses [despite the fact that] many issues affecting our lives are . . . decided by state legislatures." Similarly, in a discussion over the wisdom of a march on Washington, D.C. in the year 2000, the executive director of Montana's statewide gay group said, "The queer community in Montana needs to put pressure on Helena, not Washington, D.C. Montana laws affects Montanans, not a good deal of the federal legislation." Furthermore, increasing activity by Christian Right groups in state legislatures has provided a greater incentive for gays to counter-mobilize in the states (Freiberg 1998a).

Perhaps the increasing involvement of gay groups in state-level politics is best exemplified the "50 State Action" in the spring of 1999, which commemorated the 30th anniversary of Stonewall. The activities came to be known as Equality Begins at Home (EBAH) and included marches, rallies, and lobbying in state capitals. EBAH was planned by The National Gay and Lesbian Task Force (NGLTF) and the newly formed Federation of Statewide Lesbian, Gay, Bisexual, and Transgender Political Organizations (Freiberg 1998a). In all, EBAH produced a week of more than 350 events in all 50 states that included "lobby days" in 24 states, rallies in 31 states, and town meetings in 12 states. Most events focused on hate crimes and nondiscrimination legislation. EBAH is argued to have led to a record amount of gay legislation introduced in state legislatures, the formation of North Dakota's first statewide group, and New Hampshire's repeal of a law banning gays from adopting (Freiberg 1999; NGLTF 1999). EBAH events may have also helped to encourage a record number of 45 state groups to attend the annual meeting of the Federation in July 1999 (NGLTF 1999).

Threats to the gay community in a state often provide the greatest incentive to form and maintain local and statewide organizations. For example, a 1978 California antigay initiative, Proposition 6, motivated gays to form a statewide group called "No on 6" that organized fund raising campaigns, grassroots mobilization, and voter registration. The group raised $1.3 million and defeated the initiative. In the wake of the campaign, lesbian and gay groups formed throughout the state and a number of gay politicians were elected (Haider-Markel 1997a). Three antigay ballot initiatives in Oregon (in 1988, 1992, and 1994) led to the creation of statewide groups to fight the measures (Bull and Gallagher 1996). These groups left an institutional legacy in two Oregon groups—Right to Pride and the Rural Organizing Project (Haider-Markel 1997a).

In Colorado, gay politics has been dominated by the Denver-based organization Equal Protection. This group had successfully lobbied the governor to sign an executive order banning discrimination against homosexual state employees in 1990 (Bull and Gallagher 1996, 100). During the 1992 campaign against the antigay Amendment 2, many smaller groups wanted to form a new coalition to fight the initiative, but Equal Protection took control of the statewide campaign—a pattern that has been replicated in other states (105–6).

The 1994 antigay initiative in Idaho provides another example of gay mobilization to threats. Prior to 1994, Idaho's gay community was fairly invisible outside of Boise, and no groups lobbied the state legislature or governor (Haider-Markel 1997a). To fight the ballot initiative, gays formed the No on One Coalition (NOC). NOC used the opportunity posed by the initiative to create the infrastructure of a movement in Idaho, in part providing the impetus to create Idaho for Human Dignity, the first statewide organization for gays (Bull and Gallagher 1996, 245).

Although gay groups in the states are relatively new, they have already made a significant impact on state politics. Research suggests that these groups have had a significant influence on state adoption of antidiscrimination policies including sexual orientation (Haider-Markel and Meier 1996), progressive AIDS legislation (Colby and Baker 1988; Haider-Markel 1998d), hate crimes laws including sexual orientation (Haider-Markel 1998c), and delaying or preventing consideration and adoption of bans on same-sex marriage (Haider-Markel 1998a). Even so, the ability of gay groups to influence policy in most states is often weakened by Christian Right groups with greater resources. For example, in Florida the Christian Coalition is thought to have more lobbying influence than any other single-issue or social-issue group (Nitkin 1998), and in Michigan, Christian Right groups play a major role in the state Republican party and the policymaking process (Penning 1998).

Examples of gay statewide groups include: the Illinois Federation for Human Rights, the Louisiana Lesbian and Gay Political Action Caucus, Missouri's Privacy Rights Education Project, Montana's PRIDE!, Tennessee's Lesbian and Gay Coalition for Justice, and the Lesbian and Gay Rights Lobby of Texas. By the spring of 1998, thirty-six states had active gay groups involved in statewide politics. One third of these groups have only one paid staff member, another third have more than one paid staff member, and the reminder use all-volunteer staff. Most groups use their own staff or volunteers to lobby state government, but some do hire professional lobbyists (Freiberg 1998a), a pattern similar to that used by other single-issue and social issue groups in the states (Thomas and Hrebenar 1996).

Gay groups in the states tend to focus most of their efforts on lobbying the state legislature, but they also litigate, lobby the executive, and lobby bureaucratic officials, especially education and health officials. Gay groups have also increasingly become involved in electoral campaigns. For example, the Arizona Human Rights Fund, Oregon's Right to Pride, and Virginians for Justice endorse candidates for political office and contribute money to campaigns. In Texas, the Log Cabin Republicans have fought state party officials to gain acceptance within the Republican party and win recognition for gay assistance in the election of moderate Republicans (McNeely 1998). As gay groups increasingly institutionalize themselves within state party and electoral politics, the demand for the election of lesbian and gay officials becomes greater.

OPENLY LESBIAN AND GAY OFFICIALS IN THE STATES

In American politics, a central concern is group representation either through the election of political candidates who belong to a particular racial, ethnic, religious, or gender group, or through the election of candidates that don't belong to these groups but support their interests. Lesbians' and gay mens' concerns over political representation in the policy process may be even more acute since gays are perhaps the most stigmatized numerical minority (Sherrill 1996). Like other groups, gays and lesbians can try to achieve political representation by electing openly gay candidates to public office or by influencing the behavior of elected sympathetic heterosexuals and closeted homosexuals (Haider-Markel 1998b).

Compared to previous decades, the 1990s have seen a virtual explosion in the election of open lesbians and gays to public office. In 1991 there were only fifty-two openly gay elected officials, but by April 1998 there were at least 146 openly gay or lesbian elected officials holding office in twenty-seven states and the District of Columbia (Niedowski 1998; Polman 1998). Prior to 1990 a total of fifty gay officials had served in public offices across America (Haider-Markel 1997a). The same is true of state political offices: in 1998 there were twenty-six openly lesbian or gay elected officials in sixteen states. There were also two openly gay officials holding statewide office, Dale McCormick, the Maine state treasurer, and Ed Flanagan, the Auditor of Accounts for Vermont (see appendix A).[2] During the November 1998 elections, sixty-one gays and lesbians ran for office around the county. Of these candidates, sixteen were incumbents seeking reelection to state offices and twenty were gays challenging incumbents for state offices (Freiberg 1998a). By early 1999 there were twenty-five gay state officials in nineteen states, including the first gay or lesbian elected official elected in Utah. Overall there have only been forty-five openly gay or lesbian state legislators. Although exact figures are not known, by early 1999 an additional fifty-two openly gay or lesbian candidates had run for state offices and lost. By all accounts 1998 was the banner year for gay candidates running for state offices. At least forty-five gay candidates ran for state offices and twenty-five won their races (appendix A).

Like minorities and women before them, successful gay candidates for state offices are increasingly discovering that they must speak to a broader constituency. Without the support of heterosexuals, gay candidates cannot expect to be victorious in diverse state legislative districts or in contests for statewide offices (Fox 1997; Frank 1994; Haider-Markel 1998b). For example, after a Rhode Island race where openly gay incumbent Rep. Michael Pisaturo (D-Cranston) was accused of making gay and lesbian issues his only concern by his losing opponent, Pisaturo said that his win was evidence that "gay baiting doesn't work anymore and a candidate's sexual orientation is much less important to voters than policy positions and advocacy on the issues of the district." Nonetheless, Pisaturo went on to say, "I could not have run solely on lesbian and gay issues and expected to win" (Boyce 1998).

Opponents of gay candidates continue in their attempts to marginalize gay candidates and portray them as representing a special interest group. For example, during the 1994 race for New York attorney general, Republican Dennis Vacco repeatedly insisted that his openly lesbian opponent, Karen Burstein, represented special and narrow interests. Vacco argued: "I have no problems with that sort of agenda, but I think the people of the state should know that that's her agenda." Vacco won the race (Polman 1998). In Connecticut, openly bisexual State Rep. Evelyn Mantilla won a landslide victory in 1998 even though her challenger, Rev. Gabriel José Carrera, tried to appeal to Latino voters by arguing that Mantilla's bisexuality and support of lesbian and gay issues ran contrary to their values (Boyce 1998).

Conservative religious groups, meanwhile, are also targeting gay candidates, attempting to portray them as antifamily and as only concerned about lesbian and gay issues. For example, the president of Gary Bauer's PAC, Campaign for Working Families, argues that gay candidates are running for office to increase their efforts at "promoting homosexuality as an acceptable alternative lifestyle" (Polman 1998). In his 1998 reelection attempt to the Oregon State House, Rep. Chuck Carpenter faced a concerted effort by conservative religious groups to defeat him. Conservatives within the state Republican party recruited ultra-conservative candidate Bill Witt to challenge Rep. Carpenter in the Republican primary. Witt was a founding member of the Oregon Christian Coalition and a major donor to the Oregon Citizen's Alliance, a group that has repeatedly tired to pass antigay ballot initiatives in the state (Gay and Lesbian Victory Fund 1998).

GAY POLITICAL REPRESENTATION

Government officials are elected, in large part, based on their party affiliations, group affiliations, and issue positions. As such, constituents can expect representation based on the extent to which their affiliations and positions coincide with those of their elected officials (Kingdon 1995). When an elected official belongs to a particular ethnic, racial, or religious group, the group can be said to have achieved symbolic or descriptive representation. If the official spends at least part of his or her time representing the policy interests of his or her community, she or he will have achieved substantive representation (Fox 1997; Swain 1993). For example, the election of women to state legislatures has led to the introduction of more state policy concerning women (Thomas 1994), Similarly, elected gay officials at the local-level have played a major role in the adoption of domestic partner policies for gay couples (Haider-Markel 1998b).

Substantive representation, however, is by no means certain, and it can also occur without the election of gay officials. For example, heterosexual Rep. Bella Abzug (D–N.Y.) acted as a policy entrepreneur on the issue of gay civil rights by introducing the first gay civil rights bill in Congress in 1974 and being the main sponsor of similar legislation each year until she left the House in 1977 (Chibbaro 1998). Further, Haider-Markel (1998b) found that sympathetic heterosexual officials can have more influence on the adoption of domestic partner benefit policies than elected gay officials. However, both gay and nongay officials may be constrained in their attempts to act as policy entrepreneurs on gay issues simply because the official may be perceived as responding to the demands of a small disliked group, a tactic that may cost the official his or her seat (Frank 1994; Sharp 1997, 267). Officials may react to these perceptions by making it clear they represent all their constituents. For example, during her first term, Utah's first openly gay elected official, State Rep. Jackie Biskupski, argued: "To say that I am the first openly gay elected official [in Utah] is true, but it's not why I ran. I'm here to represent everyone" (Groutage 1999). However, many lesbians and gays find ways to effectively represent gay concerns without alienating their broader constituency. Below I briefly outline examples of openly gay officials representing the interests of the gay community in the states:

- During the 1997 Washington legislative session, the only openly gay state official, Rep. Ed Murray (D–43–Seattle), introduced several pro-gay measures, including a bill to allow same-sex marriages, a bill banning employment discrimination based on sexual orientation, and a bill for domestic partnership benefits for state employees (Haider-Markel 1998b).
- In 1991 Rep. Gail Shibley (D–66) was appointed to the Oregon House of Representatives. She won a full term in 1992 to become the first open lesbian official in the state. During her tenure she sponsored several gay-related bills, including a bill to ban sexual orientation discrimination in employment, a resolution asking Congress to repeal the ban on gays in the military, and a bill to ban sexual orientation discrimination in public accommodations and housing (Shibley 1994, 97).
- The first openly gay state official in Illinois, Rep. Larry McKeon (D–

Chicago), sponsored bills to ban discrimination in employment and housing based on sexual orientation. Rep. McKeon actively fought for both bills, testifying before legislative committees and building a non-partisan coalition of legislators (Haider-Markel 1998b).[3]

• In Minnesota, openly gay State Sen. Allan Spear was the primary sponsor of S 2183, a 1988 bill that would add sexual orientation to the state's 1983 hate crimes law. Even though it faced opposition from several conservative legislators, S 2183 passed easily in the Senate, 47–7 (Berrill 1992). Senator Spear, who is the longest serving openly gay legislator in the country, was also active in passing the state's antidiscrimination law in 1991 and in delaying the state's adoption of a ban on same-sex marriage. (Vaid 1995, 108)

As these brief examples illustrate, openly lesbian and gay officials in the states can effectively represent the interests of their community. If the trends continue in the election of openly gay candidates in the states, lesbian and gay substantive political representation is only likely to increase. At the same time, these officials are likely to encounter great resistance as Christian Right groups also work to elect their candidates to local and state offices (Persinos 1994).

GAY-RELATED LEGISLATION AND POLICY IN THE STATES

Although the activities of gay activists in the states may serve many purposes, a central concern is often the passage of gay-friendly laws and blocking or repealing antigay legislation and laws. This section examines these efforts in the states. The first part summarizes important forces in gay politics and recent legislative activity on gay issues. The rest of the section examines efforts to pass antidiscrimination laws, pass hate crimes laws, to block laws banning the recognition of same-sex marriage, and to pass legislation repealing state laws prohibiting homosexual sodomy. For each policy type I discuss the forces influencing the policymaking process, present mini-case studies on the policymaking process from select states, and summarize the findings of the case studies in terms of past research on these policy issues.

Important Forces in Lesbian and Gay State Politics

Research on gay politics in the states has consistently found that gay interest group resources influence policymaking on gay-related issues. To varying degrees other factors in the political environment of a state also influence the policymaking process, including the values of political elites, the organizational strength of conservative religious groups, party competition, the preferences of bureaucratic agents, the policy history of a state, partisanship, and issue salience (Haider-Markel 1997a; Haider-Markel 1998a). In other words, depending on the specific issue under review and the scope of political conflict, the pattern of politics for gay issues in the states can resemble that of other "culture war" issues, such as abortion (Mooney and Lee 1995), that of drug and alcohol policies (Meier 1994), but less closely resemble economic or regulatory policies in the states (Berry and Berry 1990; Berry and Berry 1992; Gray 1973; Savage 1978).

The data in table 13.1 allow for a comparison of gay-related policies and the potential resources of gay interest groups in the states. Listed in the table are:

1. state ranking scores based on the number of NGLTF members per 100,000 state population
2. the percent of the state population covered by gay civil rights laws in public employment
3. the year, if any, that a state passed a hate crimes law including sexual orientation
4. the year, if any, that a state passed a law banning the recognition of same-sex marriage
5. the year, if any, that a state repealed (through court or legislative action) its law banning homosexual sodomy.

Table 13.1 Selected Gay-Related Policies and Interest Group Resources in the American States

State	State Rank for Gay Interest Group Resources	Percent of Population Covered by Gay Civil Rights Laws	Hate Crime Law	Ban on Same-Sex Marriage	Sodomy Law (repeal)
AL	47	0	0	96*	0
AK	20	0	0	96	78
AZ	18	37.9	95	96	75
AR	41	.002	0	97	0
CA	2	100	84	0	75
CO	11	100*	0	0	71
CT	4	100	87	0	69
DE	26	0	95	96	73
FL	21	25.1	91	97	0
GA	24	6.2	0	96	0
HI	10	100	0	94	72
ID	36	.0008	0	96	0
IL	17	100*	90	96	61
IN	35	2.24	0	97	76

Table 13.1 *(continued)*

State	State Rank for Gay Interest Group Resources	Percent of Population Covered by Gay Civil Rights Laws	Hate Crime Law	Ban on Same-Sex Marriage	Sodomy Law (repeal)
IA	29	3.9	90	98	76
KS	31	2.4	0	96	0
KY	42	1.13	0	98	92
LA	33	100*	97	96#	0
ME	13	5.2	87	97	75
MD	5	100*	91	0	0
MA	3	100	96	0	0
MI	23	100*	0	96	0
MN	9	100	88	97	0
MS	50	0	0	96*	0
MO	31	16.3	0	96	0
MT	45	0	0	97	96
NE	38	0	97	0	77
NV	27	0	89	0	93
NH	15	100	90	0	73
NJ	7	100	90	0	75
NM	16	100*	0	0	75
NY	1	100*	0	0	75
NC	25	6.8	0	96	0
ND	49	0	0	97	77
OH	30	100*	0	0	72
OK	37	0	0	96	0
OR	19	19.8	89	0	71
PA	22	100*	0	96	80
RI	14	100	91	0	98
SC	46	0	0	96	0
SD	43	17.8	0	96	76
TN	40	0	0	96	96
TX	32	23.3	91	0	82
UT	44	9.3	0	95	0
VT	6	100	90	0	77
VA	8	11.1	0	97	0
WA	12	100*	93	98	75
WV	48	1.33	0	0	76
WI	28	100	88	0	83
WY	39	0	0	0	77

NOTES: Data compiled by the author; ranking of states by potential gay interest group resources was obtained by calculating the number of National Gay and Lesbian Task Force members per 100,000 state population; existing laws are indicated by the year passed; states without a law are indicated by a 0; civil rights laws are only those covering discrimination in public employment; hate crime laws are listed only for those states that include sexual orientation in their law; sodomy laws may have been repealed by the state legislature or overturned in court—in some cases both actions occurred; policies are current as of April 1998.

*Law passed by executive order (not all executive orders are in force).

#Nonbinding legislative resolution.

Overall, states that have the higher levels of gay interest group members tend also to have more progay laws and fewer antigay laws. The time when bans on same-sex marriage were passed, however, offers a better reflection of gay interest group strength than the mere showing that the state has such a policy at all. Sodomy laws, furthermore, still exist in a number of states where gay interest groups are strong, but have been repealed in states where gay groups are weaker. In part this discrepancy is due to the randomness of criminal code convictions and the litigation targets of gay groups—some of the repealed sodomy laws were overturned in court rather than by legislative action.

Summary of Gay-Related Legislation in the States

State legislation concerning lesbian and gay issues has been steadily increasing in the 1990s (see appendix B). Each year gay-related measures in state legislatures surpassed what many believe was a record high in 1995. In 1995 the National Gay and Lesbian Task Force (NGLTF) tracked 105 gay-related bills in the states. Only 16 states considered a total of 41 progay measures and 29 states considered 64 antigay measures.[4] During the 1996 session there were 160 pieces of gay-related legislation of interest to the NGLTF. Only 25 states considered a total of 61 progay bills and 40 states considered the 99 antigay bills. In 1997 the amount of gay-related legislation in 49 states jumped to 248. Some 128 progay measures were considered in 38 states, while 120 antigay measures were considered in 44 states (NGLTF 1997).

A similar 1997 survey by the *Washington Blade*, a gay newspaper, found 233 bills, 122 of which were progay and 111 that were antigay. New York had the most bills with 18 (Jones 1997b). Hate Crime bills represented the largest percentage of progay bills with 35 percent and bans on the recognition of same-sex marriage represented the largest percentage of antigay bills with 66 percent. Of the 1997 bills, 76 percent of progay measures were introduced by Democrats, 16 percent by Republicans, 4 percent by bipartisan teams, and another 4 percent by nonpartisan lawmakers. Republicans outpaced Democrats with their sponsorship of antigay bills, 71 percent to 24 percent—the reminder were bipartisan or nonpartisan (Jones 1997a).

In April 1998 *The Blade* found at least 114 gay-related bills introduced in 29 states—68 were antigay and 46 were progay (Taylor 1998). However, by the end of 1998 the NGLTF found that the number of gay-related had reached 258 bills in 42 states, surpassing the record set in 1997. The Task

Force classified 132 pieces of 1998 legislation as progay and 126 as antigay (NGLTF 1998, 1). The largest single category of bills dealt with HIV / AIDS at 96 bills, 25 addressed civil rights, 17 for marriage, 21 for domestic partners, 20 for hate crimes, 11 for education, and one for sodomy (NGLTF 1998).

During the first month of 1999 a *Washington Blade* survey of state legislation found 113 gay-related bills, about 51 percent more than in January 1998. Progay bills greatly outnumbered antigay bills, 81 were progay and 32 were antigay. Leaders of state groups attributed the increase in progay bills to the increasing political clout of gay interest groups and increasing interaction between groups in different states (Taylor 1999).

My own survey of legislation related to civil rights, hate crime, same-sex marriage, and sodomy through August 1999 revealed at least 176 bills in these four areas alone (appendix B). Interestingly, there were at least 61 bills in 31 states to protect gay civil rights, more than for all of 1998. The highlight was Nevada's passage of a gay civil rights bill on the first try. Also, only 25 bills related to same-sex marriage and 13 bills related to sodomy were introduced. Throughout the country hate crime legislation was introduced following the 1998 murder of a gay University of Wyoming student, Matthew Shepard. In Wyoming alone 7 bills were introduced, though few had much support (Taylor 1999). By August 1999, apparent reaction to the Shepard murder led to the introduction of at least 77 progay hate crime bills (appendix B). However, the only state to pass a new comprehensive hate crimes law covering sexual orientation was Missouri.

Although gay-related legislation appears to be on the increase, the pattern may be similar to that of other "cultural war" issues, such as abortion, where new legislation is leveling off. For example, in 1992 approximately 100 abortion-related bills were introduced in state legislatures—that figure jumped to 220 in 1996, but only increased to 245 in 1998. Also like abortion legislation, gay-related legislation tends to be fairly evenly divided between the favorable and unfavorable.[5] But if the 1999 legislative pattern indicates a trend, gay groups may increasingly be spending more of their time pushing progay legislation and less time blocking antigay legislation.

Civil Rights Policy

Similar to antidiscrimination laws for other minority groups, civil rights protections for lesbians and gays tend to protect against discrimination in one or more of seven areas: public employment, private employment, education, public accommodations, credit, housing, and union practices.

By April 1998 ten states had adopted some form of civil rights protections for lesbians and gays by statute. An additional nine states had provided government employment protections through Executive Orders. Table 13.1 displays the percent of each state's population covered by antidiscrimination laws in public employment and includes local laws. The patchwork of laws covers about half of the U.S. population.

Research on antidiscrimination policies for lesbians and gays suggests that state adoption of these policies is most likely when gay interest groups have significant resources, the salience of the issue is low, partisanship is avoided, conservative religious forces can be neutralized, the policy change can be framed as incremental in nature, and the gay community has the support of political elites (Haider-Markel and Meier 1996; Wald, Button, and Rienzo 1996). Below I examine attempts to pass antidiscrimination laws in Oregon and Wisconsin.

Oregon   Gay activists in Oregon have attempted to pass a gay civil rights law nearly every legislative session since 1973.[6] In an effort to reduce the salience of the issue, gays changed strategies and successfully lobbied the governor to sign an executive order in 1987 that banned sexual orientation discrimination in state employment. Upon hearing of the governor's action, a new conservative group, called the Oregon Citizens' Alliance (OCA), mobilized to repeal the order at the ballot box (Thompson 1994, 329, 397). A group called Oregonians for Fairness formed to fight the 1988 initiative (Measure 8), but their campaign started late and was never able to shape the debate. In the wake of the ballot campaign, activists formed the first permanent statewide group, Right to Privacy (RTP) (Bull and Gallagher 1996, 43, 47; Thompson 1994, 397).[7]

In each legislative session following the 1988 defeat, RTP lobbied to pass gay civil rights legislation. They achieved limited success in 1991 when a progay rights bill passed the state senate with the support of the governor, but the bill stalled in the house (Bull and Gallagher 1996, 44). Meanwhile, OCA continued to fight RTP in the legislature and at the ballot box. In 1992 and 1994 OCA placed measures before the voters to block the passage of local and state gay civil rights laws. Both initiatives were defeated, but by narrow margins.

Following the defeat of the 1994 initiative, RTP successfully lobbied to have another antidiscrimination bill introduced in the legislature. In a May 6, 1995 press release, David Casti of RTP described the situation: "After months of behind-the-scenes work, Right To Privacy has introduced a comprehensive civil rights bill in the Oregon Legislature, prohibiting discrimination on the basis of sexual orientation in employment, housing, public accommodations and real estate transactions." The bill (HB 3459), like many others before it, failed to receive a hearing.

In 1997 a limited gay civil rights bill came closer to becoming law than any gay civil rights bill in Oregon during the twenty-five years they had been introduced. The bill was supported by many high-profile companies in the business community. Openly gay and Republican Rep. Chuck Carpenter was the chief sponsor of the bill (HB 2734), which only covered employment discrimination. When the Republican leadership failed to give the bill a hearing in committee, Carpenter used a rare procedural maneuver—a motion to have the bill go directly to the House floor. The Republican leadership, backed by the OCA, called a recess to avoid voting on the bill (Esteve 1997). Carpenter reached a compromise with the leadership, whereby HB 2734 was allowed to die in committee and new bill was drafted and sent to a different committee. The new bill (HB 3719) was given "priority" status. Even with opposition lobbying by OCA, Carpenter and RTP were able to ensure that HB 3719 passed quickly from the House Commerce Committee by 8–1 and the full House, 40–20 (Chibbaro 1997).

In the senate Rep. Carpenter testified before committees and built bipartisan support, but the bill was again stalled in committee by the Republican leadership. Carpenter teamed up with Democrats in the Senate, who threatened to block Senate activity on any legislation until the gay civil rights bill was put to a floor vote. Carpenter was unable to replicate his Senate victory in the House, and the bill fell one vote short of a majority (Gay and Lesbian Victory Fund 1998).

Wisconsin Wisconsin became the first state to protect lesbians and gays from discrimination in 1982.[8] David Clarenbach (D-Madison) was the main sponsor of the legislation; his cosponsors were four Democrats from safe legislative seats in Milwaukee. The bill simply added the category "sexual preference" to the existing state civil rights laws. Clarenbach introduced the legislation in every session from 1975 to 1981 but did not bring the issue to a vote, thinking that the process required some long-term "softening-up" of political elites on the issue. His strategy had four parts: (1) to present the bill as a civil rights measure consistent with Wisconsin's progressive tradition, (2) to defuse the morality issue by seeking support from main-line religious organizations, (3) to gather bipartisan support for the bill, and (4) to use gay and lesbian activists to do the ground work in building political support. Clarenbach decided to push for passage of the bill in 1981 when his legislation to repeal Wisconsin's sodomy law lost by one vote. Owing to the potential controversy the bill would generate, Clarenbach perceived that he had only one session to pass the bill; if he failed, opponents would have time to counter-mobilize.

Building the supporting political coalition followed the four point strategy. Wisconsin takes a great pride in being the first state to pass progressive legislation. The bill was framed as an incremental extension of protections that the state's two largest cities had already implemented. Using gay and lesbian activists to contact individuals for support resulted in endorsements by the Catholic Archbishop of Milwaukee and by mainstream Protestant denominations. The effort was to isolate the Moral Majority as the sole religious group opposing the legislation. To avoid having the legislation designated as a "Democratic bill" that could be used as a campaign issue, several Republican legislators were persuaded to support the bill. Although the number of Republicans supporting passage was small, the Republicans were highly visible (one later was the Republican candidate for the U.S. Senate, another became Lt. Governor) and provided the margin of victory on several votes. The National Gay and Lesbian Task Force was instrumental in providing resources to gay activists in the state.

The strategy was successful though the margins were close. The legislation passed the lower house by a 49–45 vote. In a compromise for opponents, the Senate Committee on State and Local Affairs and Taxation offered an amendment that specified affirmative action was not necessary in regard to sexual orientation. This compromise passed the Senate in February 1982 by voice vote (the key vote was one of "nonconcurrence" with the Assembly bill, which failed 13–19). The Assembly then accepted the Senate's language, and Republican Governor Lee Dreyfus signed the bill into law on February 25, 1982. Dreyfus reportedly signed the bill immediately to prevent any groundswell of pressure for a veto to materialize. As further illustration that the elite process remained relatively low key, the final passage of the bill occurred in an election year, and it did not become a key issue in either the legislative or gubernatorial races that year.

Summary of Civil Rights Case Studies Each case study supports the findings of prior research, but they also suggest the importance of political elites is incomplete. The quantitative analysis presented in Haider-Markel and Meier (1996) does not pick up the activities and skills of political entrepreneurs such as Clarenbach in Wisconsin. The case studies, capturing changes over time, are also able to illustrate the importance of elections and the changing political fortunes of organized interests.

Other key elements from previous research are also supported by the case studies. When key players were able to prevent the issue from becoming salient to the broader public, gay and lesbian interest groups were able to bring their resources to bear on the process, policy change was framed as incremental, and partisanship was avoided.[9] When partisanship was not avoided and the issue became salient, gay groups were unsuccessful.

Hate Crimes Policy

Of all progay policies, more states have adopted hate crime policies including sexual orientation than any other progay policy. In general, hate crimes laws provide for the enhancement of penalties for crimes motivated by bias, mandate the collection of hate crime statistics, and provide for law enforcement training on hate crimes (Haider-Markel 1998c). By February 1999 at least twenty-two states had adopted hate crimes laws including sexual orientation (see table 13.1). Furthermore, many states have continued to expand and strengthen these laws after their initial adoption. State adoption of these laws is driven by many of the same forces driving state adoption of antidiscrimination laws, with the strength of gay interest groups playing a central role. However, factors such as party competition and the support of bureaucratic agents (in this case, law enforcement officials) appear to play a greater role. Furthermore, gay groups also appear to be more successful in pushing for hate crime policy when they advance their cause by forming coalitions with other groups, such as African-American and women's groups (Haider-Markel 1997a; Haider-Markel 1998c). The mini-case studies below outline the importance of these factors in state adoption of hate crimes laws.

Illinois   Gay activists in Illinois were able to add sexual orientation and physical or mental disability to the state's 1986 hate crimes law in 1990.[10] The key factors in the passage of the bill were a coalition of groups supporting the bill, bipartisan support, and the support of law enforcement organizations. Gay groups organized a coalition that included the National Organization for Women, Planned Parenthood, the Anti-Defamation League, and the Illinois Catholic Conference. The diversity of groups helped to defuse the issue of sexual orientation.

Bipartisan support was achieved by providing legislators with hate crime statistics that had been collected over four years by a Chicago organization. The statistics allowed to supporters to frame the bill as a "law and order" issue and establish that a problem existed. When some Republicans voiced their opposition, the Republican Minority Leader issued a "vote no" directive. Intense lobbying and the concerns raised by Republicans in need of the "gay vote" during the election year lead to the Minority Leader's rescinding of the vote directive. Without the Republicans, the bill would not have passed. Finally, the coalition obtained the support of law enforcement. Particularly key was the effort by Republican Senator Dudyck, a Chicago police officer, to ensure that the sexual orientation clause was not removed from the bill. SB 2267 passed the Illinois House 64 to 51 and sailed through the Senate in a vote of 31 to 13.

Oklahoma Oklahoma has a fairly comprehensive hate crime policy.[11] The principal author of the hate crimes bill was Senator Maxine Horner (D-Tulsa), one of a handful of African-American members in the legislature. Senator Horner was able to create a coalition of African Americans, influential business persons from the relatively small Jewish community, lesbians and gays, and groups such as the National Conference of Christians and Jews. Well-publicized vandalism against Jewish congregations provided much of the motivation for the legislation. Although newspapers only ran a few stories on the incidents, activists were able to capitalize on the citizen interest that the incidents raised. Because the coalition included gay and lesbian activists, the original hate crimes legislation included sexual orientation. A few conservative Republicans in the legislature, however, stated their opposition to the inclusion of sexual orientation. While gays opposed removing sexual orientation, they allowed its removal and still worked within the coalition.

The strategy was to get the bill passed with the hopes of reforming the coalition at some future date to introduce new legislation that would add sexual orientation. While this strategy kept the coalition together and secured the passage of the bill, Oklahoma has still not added sexual orientation to its hate crimes law. The pattern of politics suggests that coalitions and political entrepreneurs play an important role in the passage of hate crimes laws. Senator Horner was able to bring together groups that, if acting alone, may not have been able to gather support for the hate crimes law. The case also shows that coalition building adds in the passage of hate crimes laws, but that the policy may have to be "de-gayed" to lessen opposition. Gay groups continued to work within the coalition, however, demonstrating a strategic understanding that politics is often a series of iterated games.

Summary of Hate Crime Case Studies The case studies suggest that interest groups play an important role in the passage of hate crimes laws, and their efforts are assisted when they are able to form and maintain broad-based coalitions. Coalitions were even more successful when they were able to gain the endorsement or active support of law enforcement. The support of law enforcement greatly assisted the ability of activists to define the issue as a crime issue and defuse opposition.[12]

Competition between political parties also played a role in passage—elections often played a significant role in legislative voting behavior. As the cases demonstrate, broad-based coalitions had an easier time exploiting electoral divisions than single interest groups. Finally, controversy centered on the inclusion of sexual orientation. Coalition partners took different strategies to defuse the opposition, but in each case, the coalition remained intact, regardless of the legislative outcome. This fact illustrates the necessity of gay groups to engage in coalition politics, even when the goals of gays are not achieved in the first attempt.

Same-Sex Marriage Policy

Perhaps more so than any other gay-related policy, same-sex marriage has been a state issue. The first known state legislative action on same-sex marriage came after an April 1975 Arizona Supreme Court decision stating that bans on gay marriage were unconstitutional. The Arizona legislature quickly passed a bill defining marriage as only legal between a man and woman (Thompson 1994). Most importantly, a 1993 ruling by the Hawaii Supreme Court in *Baehr v. Lewin* (now *Baehr v. Miike*) paved the way for legal recognition of same-sex marriages in Hawaii, and perhaps in other states. In response national Christian Right groups organized a national campaign in early 1996 to lobby states for same-sex marriage bans (Dunlap 1996; Haider-Markel 1998a). The organized effort manifested itself mainly through a coalition of groups called the National Campaign to Protect Marriage (NCPM) (Johnson 1996, 3–5; Walker 1996). Groups making up the NCPM helped to distribute a video called *The Ultimate Target of the Gay Agenda: Same Sex Marriage* in state legislatures. Many groups in this coalition also engaged in other independent actions to seek legislative bans on same-sex marriage. For example, Focus on the Family distributed literature on same-sex marriage to state legislatures (Johnson 1996, 7). By May 1998 all but two states (Massachusetts and Nevada) had considered legislation banning the recognition of same-sex marriages and thirty-one had adopted policies banning the recognition of same-sex marriages (see table 13.1). One study suggests that a stunning 209 state bills on same-sex marriage were considered between 1993 and 1998 (Haider-Markel and Lake 1998). The only other gay-related issue that has received so much legislative attention in such a short period of time is HIV/AIDS

(Colby and Baker 1988; Haider-Markel 1997a; Haider-Markel 1998d). Furthermore, in a number of states, including Hawaii, Rhode Island, and Washington, legislation allowing for same-sex marriages was introduced (appendix B).

Research suggests that the consideration and adoption of state laws banning the recognition of same-sex marriages is driven by the resources of gay interest groups, party competition, conservative religious groups, the preferences of political elites, and Christian Right control of state Republican parties (Haider-Markel 1998a; Haider-Markel and Lake 1998). Most importantly, the national campaign by Christian Right groups can be closely linked to diffusion of same-sex marriage bans—both indirectly through the partisanship of legislative sponsors and directly through sponsor ties, group assistance in bill drafting, and lobbying efforts (Haider-Markel 1998a). My reading of past research on other types of policy suggests that no other policy has diffused so rapidly or has been considered and adopted by so many states in one year (Berry and Berry 1990; Berry and Berry 1992; Gray 1973; Mintrom 1997; Mooney and Lee 1995; Savage 1978; Walker 1969). Below I examine the passage of same-sex marriage bans in South Dakota and Washington.

South Dakota   In 1995, South Dakota was one of the first states to introduce a ban on the recognition of same-sex marriages following the 1993 Hawaii Supreme Court ruling. The bill was HB 1184. With no statewide gay group to oppose it, HB 1184 quickly passed the House State Affairs Committee 9–3 and the House 54–13 on February 2. The next day the governor pledged to sign the bill (Wick 1995).

Barry Wick, a local activist following these events, began to mobilize opposition in the gay community. Wick and others testified against the bill before the Senate Health and Human Services Committee. This was the first time gays had publicly lobbied against an antigay law in the state (Wick 1997). HB 1184 passed the Senate Health and Human Services Committee 4–2, but when the bill reached the Senate floor, lobbying by gays and an organized telephone campaign paid off. The Senate voted 18–17 to send the bill back to the Judiciary Committee, where it was tabled in a 4–3 vote—effectively killing it. An attempt on the floor of the Senate to revive the bill failed to receive the required eighteen votes, in part because five Senators abstained from voting. Christian Right groups, led by the South Dakota Family Policy Council, vowed to bring the bill back in 1996 (Wick 1995; Wick 1997).

In October 1995 Barry Wick used funds from donors and the National

Gay and Lesbian Task Force to form Free Americans Creating Equal Status of South Dakota, Inc. (FACES).[13] Wick and volunteers quickly began to build a statewide network of activists. As their effort continued into 1996, religious conservatives teamed up with Rep. Roger Hunt (R–Brandon) again to introduce a same-sex marriage ban in the state House. With almost one hundred activists opposed to the ban present, the House State Affairs Committee tabled the bill in a 7–6 vote, but Hunt was able to use a procedural maneuver called a "smoke-out," whereby a floor vote is taken on whether the bill should come to the floor. The House voted for the procedural maneuver 41–21 on January 26 and passed the bill 49–18–3 four days later.

Lobbying by FACES led to HB 1143's defeat again in the Senate Judiciary Committee (4–2). Despite a FACES letter-writing and telephone campaign, however, Republican legislators backed by religious groups used the same "smoke-out" procedure that was used in the House and passed the bill 26–8. Governor William Janklow signed HB 1143 on February 21, making South Dakota the second state officially to ban the recognition of same-sex marriages (Wick 1997).

Washington Washington passed its ban on the recognition of same-sex marriages in 1998 after over two years of legislative and community debate on the issue.[14] The first bill, HB 2262, was introduced in 1996 by Rep. Bill Thompson (R-Everett). Rep. Thompson had strong ties to conservative religious organizations. Despite heavy lobbying by gay groups, HB 2262 passed the Republican controlled House, 60–36. With the help of Senate Democrats, however, gay groups were able to bottle the bill up in committee.

In 1997 three bills banning the recognition of same-sex marriage were introduced by Republicans, who now controlled both the House and Senate. Gay activists countered by convincing Democrats to introduce two bills that would legalize same-sex marriage in the state. The Legal Marriage Alliance of Washington, a gay activist group, worked closely with the governor and the only openly gay member of the state legislature, Rep. Ed Murray (D-Seattle), to draft the promarriage bills. The main anti-same-sex marriage bill, SB 5398, passed the Washington state Senate by 33–15–1. The House quickly followed and approved SB 5398 with a 63–35 vote after more than an hour of debate. Governor Locke vetoed the bill, noting that Washington courts decided twenty-three years ago that same-sex marriages are invalid. The Senate and House failed to override the governor's veto.

Faced with the defeat of SB 5398, Republicans revived another same-sex marriage bill (HB 1130) and made revisions. One change would place the bill on the ballot. The House passed HB 1130 by 50–48 on March 19. In the Senate gay groups focused their attention on moderate Republicans to have the ballot language removed from HB 1130. Their efforts led to the bill being amended by voice vote; the Senate then passed the amended bill by 30–18–1 on April 16. The House refused to concur with the Senate amendment and the bill died with the end of the session.

By 1998 conservative Republicans were determined to pass a same-sex marriage ban at all costs (Associated Press 1998). The charge was again led by conservative Rep. Bill Thompson (R-Everett) with HB 1130 (the Senate bill was SB 5400). Both bills contained referendum clauses, meaning they would bypass a veto by the Governor and be placed before the people on the November ballot. The House passed HB 1130 by 56–41–1, largely along party lines; faced with a potentially violent battle over the required ballot initiative, legislators began planning to attempt an override of the governor's pending veto. Once it was clear that the governor was likely to veto the bill, Democratic leaders made it known that they would provide the votes to override a veto and prevent the measure form going to the ballot, even though they opposed the bill. With a veto-proof majority, eight Senate Democrats joined the twenty-six Senate Republicans in passing an amended version 34–13 on February 6. Within minutes the House passed the amended version by 60–33. Only one Republican opposed the bill and six Democrats supported it (Ammons 1998).

Shortly thereafter the bill was delivered to the governor, who promptly vetoed it. The governor then actively participated in the process of overriding his own veto by having his lobbyist quickly hand-deliver the veto message back to the legislature. The House immediately voted 65–28 to override the veto and the Senate did the same in a 34–11 vote. Legislative historians said that the events made history—never before had a bill been approved, vetoed and overridden in five hours (Ammons 1998).

Gay officials and Democrat leaders at all levels of government had urged lawmakers to pass the bill to prevent it from going to the ballot. As such, many high-ranking Democrats in the state legislature voted against the ban but for overriding the governor's veto. Even so, many gay activists were angry over the outcome. Much of the gay community's anger was directed at U.S. Senator Patty Murray, who had called on the governor and legislature to pass the ban rather than place the issue on the ballot for the November 1998 elections. Senator Murray and others, including openly gay politicians in the state, believed the ballot question would hurt Democratic candidates (Savage 1998). While it is not entirely clear why the ban and veto override passed in 1998 but not in 1997, some have suggested it was the result of the November 1997 proactive ballot measure on gay civil rights. In 1997 gay activists argued that if the marriage ban went to the ballot it would lead to violence against gays—the governor made similar arguments in his veto message. Once gay activists had placed their own measure on the ballot, however, they had weakened their argument (Savage 1998).

Summary of Same-Sex Marriage Case Studies   As these case studies illustrate, high levels of public opposition to same-sex marriage have made it difficult for gay groups in the states to block the coordinated national effort of Christian Right groups to pass bans on same-sex marriage. The case studies, however, also coincide with the findings of empirical analysis on the diffusion of same-sex marriage laws (Haider-Markel 1998a). The timing of state adoption of same-sex marriage bans is strongly influenced by religious groups, partisanship, and the preferences of political elites. Gay groups, meanwhile, influence the process largely by delaying policy adoption.

Sodomy Laws

While gay activists in the states have focused much of their attention on passing laws to ensure their civil rights and liberties, their efforts to repeal existing laws that limit their personal freedoms have been less frequent and have achieved limited success (Vaid 1995, 14). In particular, gay groups have attempted to repeal existing laws banning homosexual sodomy—laws that are often refer to homosexual acts as "crimes against nature." Homosexual sodomy laws were held to be constitutional by the 1986 Supreme Court decision in *Bowers v. Hardwick*. Although these laws are used infrequently, largely because they are difficult to enforce (Nice 1988), states have used them as the basis for a considerable amount of antigay legislation and in arguments against civil rights protections for gays. For example, in 1995 the Montana Christian Coalition teamed up with conservative state legislators to pass legislation requiring persons convicted of violating the state's "deviate sexual conduct law" to register with the state for life. The provision was removed after a national outcry (National Gay and Lesbian Task Force 1996, 22). Oklahoma legislation in 1978 and 1998 used the state's sodomy law as the basis to ban gays from teaching in the public schools; the 1978 legislation passed, but was overturned in court in 1985 (Brown 1998). Sodomy laws were also used as the legal foundation to deny visitation rights to a lesbian mother in Missouri and to argue against the hiring of gays by the Dallas Police Force (Vaid 1995, 14).

In 1961 Illinois became the first state to repeal its sodomy law. During the 1960s and 70s many other states repealed their sodomy laws during revisions of their archaic criminal statutes (Nice 1988; Vaid 1995, 13). In the 1990s only Nevada has repealed its sodomy law by legislation, and Kentucky, Montana, Rhode Island, and Tennessee saw their sodomy laws overturned in court (see table 13.1). Below I briefly outline attempts to repeal the sodomy law in Rhode Island.

Rhode Island   Led by the Rhode Island Alliance for Lesbian and Gay Civil Rights, gay activists have been trying to repeal the state's homosexual sodomy law since 1984.[15] The Alliance's efforts have been assisted in the 1990s by Rep. Edith Ajello (D-Providence), the presence of two openly gay lawmakers, and a legislature that has been fairly receptive on gay issues (the state has a gay civil rights law, a hate crimes law, and has killed legislation banning same-sex marriage). The 1997 bill, HB 6160, would have repealed the state's "abominable and detestable acts" statute, which is classified as a felony carrying a penalty of seven to twenty years. HB 6160 was tabled in committee.

In September 1997 the negative aspects of the sodomy law increased in salience. Police in North Smithfield, Rhode Island had charged two men with sodomy, even though the encounter had been consensual. The attorney general refused to prosecute the case. Opponents of the law used this case to point out the problems with the law, especially its use in targeting homosexual men (Gregg 1998).

Following these events, 1998 legislation (HB 7585) was introduced in the House to repeal the sodomy law. The sponsor was Rep. Ajello, who has sponsored similar House bills each year since 1992. Rep. Ajello had never forced a vote on the issue because she believed other legislators needed to be educated on the issue before a majority would support passage (Gregg 1998). During the 1998 session Ajello first requested a vote on the bill in the House Judiciary Committee because she believed there was finally majority support for the measure.

The House committee hearings evoked heated testimony, especially between religious representatives. The Rev. Richard Donnelly, a Catholic priest, "said that repeal would be tantamount to changing the name of Providence to Sodom." Meanwhile, the Rev. Janet Cooper Nelson, a United Church of Christ minister, argued that "consenting adult sex is the private business of adults. This law is used purely to invade the privacy of consenting adults." Other supporters of the repeal included the Disability Law Center, the Rhode Island Rape Crisis Center, and the Public Defender's Office (MacKay 1998).

Members of the Alliance argued that the law is too often abused by police and prosecutors. Police use it to attack homosexual behavior in parks while they ignore the same heterosexual behavior in "lovers' lanes" situations. The group also argued that prosecutors "too often use the sodomy law as a trumped-up charge against a defendant for whom they do not have sufficient evidence to win a sexual assault case." In response, the president of the Eagle Forum of Rhode Island said "the drive for repeal is exclusively fueled by the homosexual activists and their allies"; other opponents raised the specter of AIDS, arguing that gays would not get AIDS if they obeyed the law (MacKay 1998).

Following the committee hearings, on March 23, 1998 the *Providence Journal-Bulletin* editorialized for the repeal, mirroring many of the arguments made by the Alliance. Before the committee vote the Alliance made wide use of an e-mail network to mobilize phone calls from members to their legislators. On April 1 Republican members of the House Judiciary Committee tried to kill the bill in a vote of "no passage." The attempt failed in a 6–8 vote. The committee debated the bill further and Rep. Harold Metts (D-19) argued that the bill should be amended to ensure that public sex was still illegal. In a last-minute agreement over the amendment motion, the bill was brought up for a vote on April 9. Rep. Metts's amendment to the bill lost in an 8–8 tie. The full bill passed by 10–6. After a delay by the bill's sponsor to build support in the House, HB 7585 passed the House on May 7 by 49–40–11 with no amendments.

The passage of the sodomy repeal bill in the Rhode Island House follows a pattern similar to that of other gay issues. Interest groups on both sides of the issue played a significant role and political elites were vitally important. One significant difference was the salience of the issue. In this case the issue increased in salience, but the increased attention did not seem to hurt the bill's chances for passage. In fact, reported abuses by the police and editorializing by the main newspaper may have helped the repeal effort.

CONCLUSIONS

Despite a variety of hurdles, lesbians and gays in the states have increasingly begun to create formal organizations and gain access to state government institutions. This access has led to significant electoral, legal, and legislative victories. Gay groups have successfully lobbied for civil rights protections, laws against hate crime, and the repeal of sodomy laws; gay groups have also sometimes succeed in delaying or blocking the passage of bans on same-sex marriage. Like minorities and women, however, at least some of this success has been dependent on the support of heterosexual political elites and interest groups.

Previous research and the case studies presented here suggest that lesbians and gays will continue to be a significant factor in state electoral politics and policymaking. The gay movement will likely continue to make strides at the local level and may even increase its success at the national level. However, broader trends in American politics, especially the devolution of power to the states since the 1980s, means that state governments are likely to become the focal point of the movement in the next decade. Gay groups now exist in a majority of the states, lesbians and gays are increasingly being elected to state offices, and at minimum, gay issues continue to reach the agendas of many state legislatures. Lesbians and gays, however, face considerable opposition in their grassroots efforts in the states. Religious conservative groups, unsupportive politicians, and negative public opinion continue to hinder both the political mobilization of gays and their success in the policymaking process. Also, like other issues that divide a significant portion of the population, such as affirmative action, abortion, and gun control, policy proposals concerning gays will continue to be both positive and negative, especially while religious conservatives maintain power within state Republican parties.

Furthermore, although the successful pursuit of legal change and protections in the states is not *determined* by whether change is pursued within legislatures or at the ballot box, if change is pursued within state legislative and executive institutions, some forces, such as strong interest groups, will be relatively more important to the policy success of gays than other forces (Haider-Markel and Meier 1996). Lessons from antidiscrimination policy, hate crime policy, sodomy laws, and same-sex marriage bans suggest that gays will be most successful in the states if they can frame the issues in terms of rights, effectively mobilize group resources and sympathetic heterosexuals, and demobilize conservative religious groups.

Finally, the study of gay politics in the states has also increased our knowledge of state politics and policy more generally by contributing to research on political representation, state legislatures, and policy theory, including comparative public policy, morality politics, and policy innovation. Future research should further investigate the election of gay officials and their influence on state policy, the dynamic struggle between gay groups and the backlash from conservative religious groups within state legislatures, the history and activities of gay groups in the states, and the intergovernmental nature of advocacy coalitions and policy on both sides of gay politics.

NOTES

1. Examples of this phenomena abound. In 1996 the state of Georgia finally passed a new city charter for Atlanta that allows the city to ban discrimination on the basis of sexual orientation. Conversely, Georgia has also tried to pass legislation blocking Atlanta from offering domestic partner benefits to city employees.

2. The state Democratic Party Chair in Vermont, Steve Howard, is also openly gay and is thought to be the first openly gay person to head one of the major parties in a state.

3. Texas Representative Glen Maxey has faced a similar situation. Maxey again introduced a gay civil rights bill (HB 475) in the 1999 Texas House.

4. By comparison, a 1984 survey of state legislation by the *Washington Blade* found only five antigay measures; a similar survey in 1994 found 24 antigay bills (Vaid 1995, 8).

5. Information is from the National Abortion Rights Action League.

6. Unless otherwise noted, information on Oregon is from Right to Pride and Haider-Markel (1997a).

7. Right to Privacy later changed it named to Right to Pride (RTP).

8. Information on Wisconsin is from 1996 communications with David Clarenbach and the *Wisconsin Legislative Blue Book.*

9. Clarenbach feels that the passage of the 1982 law made gay rights a nonissue in Wisconsin. As evidence he cites that in 1983 the state repealed its sodomy law. In 1988 it passed a hate crimes bill, extended antidiscrimination laws to higher education, and passed a bill of rights for AIDS victims. Furthermore, the 1988 bills were signed into law by a conservative Republican, and the Republican-controlled legislature has failed to pass a ban on same-sex marriage.

10. Information on Illinois is from Berrill (1992) and Haider-Markel (1997a).

11. Information on Oklahoma's hate crime law was collected in an interview with Tom Neal, the editor of Tulsa News, a local gay newspaper.

12. The support of law enforcement was also considered key for the passage of hate crime laws in other states, such as Florida, Maryland, Oregon, and Wisconsin (see Berrill 1992).

13. Since 1995 FACES has expanded its paid membership to over 100. The primary purpose of FACES is educational; the group does not endorse political

candidates. The group operates with an all-volunteer office and lobbying staff (Wick 1997).

14. Unless otherwise noted information on Washington is from the Legal Marriage Alliance of Washington and the Washington state legislature.

15. Unless otherwise noted information on Rhode Island is from The Alliance and the Rhode Island state legislature.

REFERENCES

Ammons, David. 1998. Washington lawmakers ban gay marriage. *Los Angeles Times,* 7 February.

Associated Press. 1998. Conservatives take on social issues. *Lewiston Tribune,* 16 January.

Beggs, Charles E. 1996. Court upholds ban on local antigay ordinances. *Associated Press,* 13 April.

Berrill, Kevin T. 1992. *Countering antigay violence through legislation.* Washington, D.C.: National Gay and Lesbian Task Force Policy Institute.

Berry, Frances, and William D. Berry. 1990. State lottery adoptions as policy innovations: An event history analysis. *American Political Science Review* 84: 395–415.

———. 1992. Tax innovation in the states: Capitalizing on political opportunity. *American Journal of Political Science* 36:715–42.

Boyce, Ed. 1998. R.I. Gov. Almond win re-election; Democrat York's defeat blamed on ignoring "core constituencies." *Newsweek,* 11 November, vol. 8 no. 11.

Brown, Paula. 1998. Oklahoma blasted over vote attacking gays. *Gayly Oklahoman,* 15 April.

Bull, Chris, and John Gallagher. 1996. *Perfect enemies: The religious right, the gay movement, and the politics of the 1990s.* New York: Crown Publishers.

Carlson, Brian. Republican gubernatorial forum focuses on spending. *Daily Nebraskan,* 17 April.

Chibbaro, Lou, Jr. 1998. Bella Abzug dies at 77; Introduced first federal gay civil rights bill. *Washington Blade,* 3 April.

———. 1997. Gay Republican lawmaker forces vote on bill; Oregon representative bucks party line on employment bill. *Washington Blade,* 9 May.

Coile, Zachary. Gay marriage: Davis and Lungren opposed, Harman, Checchi in favor, but say state just isn't ready. *San Francisco Examiner,* 19 April.

Colby, David C., and David G. Baker. 1988. State policy responses to the AIDS epidemic. *Publius* 18:113–30.

Dunlap, David W. 1996. Gay rights advocates question effort to defend same-sex marriage. *New York Times,* 7 June.

Esteve, Harry. 1997. House Republicans bolted Monday from the state capital. *The Register-Guard,* 15 April.

Fox, Richard Logan. 1997. *Gender dynamics in congressional elections.* Thousand Oaks, Cal.: Sage Publications.

Frank, Barney. 1994. Reaching a broader audience. In *Out for office: Campaigning in the Gay '90s,* edited by Kathleen DeBold. Washington, D.C.: Gay and Lesbian Victory Fund.

Freiberg, Peter. 1998a. Fifty-state capital event set for spring of 1999; "It's so important to focus on state issues." *Washington Blade,* 24 April.

———. 1998b. Utah legislature to get its first openly gay member; Massachusetts man loses statewide bid. *Washington Blade,* 6 November.

———. 1999. Capitalizing on local pull: Events at statehouses focus on familiar faces. *Washington Blade,* 2 April.

Gay and Lesbian Victory Fund. 1998. *Press Release: April 9, 1998: Political extremists target openly gay legislator.* Washington, D.C.: Gay and Lesbian Victory Fund.

Gray, Virginia. 1973. Innovation in the states: A diffusion study. *American Political Science Review* 67:1174–85.

Gregg, Katherine. 1998. Legislature drafts bill to repeal oral-sex law. *Providence Journal- Bulletin,* 24 February.

Groutage, Hilary. 1999. Capitol rookie Biskupski keeps her zest for politics: Session rewarding for Utah's first openly gay lawmaker. *Salt Lake Tribune,* March 1.

Haider-Markel, Donald P. 1997a. From bullhorns to PACs: Lesbian and gay politics, interest groups, and policy. Ph.D. diss., University of Wisconsin–Milwaukee, Political Science.

———. 1997b. Interest group survival: Shared interests versus competition for resources. *Journal of Politics* 59 (3): 903–12.

———. 1998a. Bonfire of the righteous: Geographically expanding the scope of the conflict over same-sex marriage. Presented at the annual meetings of the Midwest Political Science Association, April.

———. 1998b. Policy entrepreneurs and the political representation of minority group interests: The case of domestic partner policies. Presented at the annual meetings of the Midwest Political Science Association, April.

———. 1998c. The politics of social regulatory policy: State and federal hate crime policy and implementation effort. *Political Research Quarterly* 51 (1): 69–88.

———. 1998d. State and local government. In *Encyclopedia of AIDS: A social, political, cultural, and scientific record of the epidemic,* edited by Raymond A. Smith. New York: Garland Publishing.

Haider-Markel, Donald P., and Ronald La Due Lake. 1998. The importance of institutional structures on legislative outcomes: Lessons from the American states. Presented at the annual meetings of the American Political Science Association, August.

Haider-Markel, Donald P., and Kenneth J. Meier. 1996. The politics of gay and lesbian rights: Expanding the scope of the conflict. *Journal of Politics* 58:352–69.

Johnson, Hans. 1996. *Wedded to intolerance.* Washington, D.C.: Human Rights Campaign.

Jones, Christopher. 1997a. "Laying the groundwork" pays off in the states. *Washington Blade*, 1 August.

———. 1997b. States approve 10 percent of gay-related bills. *The Washington Blade*, 3 October.

Kingdon, John. 1995. *Agendas, alternative, and public policies.* 2d ed. New York: Harper Collins.

MacKay, Scott. 1998. Move to repeal sex law sparks contentious debate. *Providence Journal- Bulletin*, March 12.

McNeely, Dave. 1998. The parties and gays. *Austin American-Statesman*, 30 June.

Meier, Kenneth J. 1994. *The politics of sin: Drugs, alcohol and public policy.* Armonk, N.Y.: M. E. Sharpe.

Mintrom, Michael. 1997. Policy entrepreneurs and the diffusion of innovation. *American Journal of Political Science* 41 (3): 738–70.

Mooney, Christopher Z., and Mei-Hsien Lee. 1995. Legislating morality in the American states: The case of pre-*Roe* abortion regulation reform. American Journal of Political Science 39:599–627.

National Gay and Lesbian Task Force. 1996. *Beyond the beltway: State of the states 1995.* Washington, D.C.: National Gay and Lesbian Task Force.

———. 1997. *Capital gains and losses: A state by state review of lesbian, gay, bisexual, transgender, and HIV/AIDS related legislation in 1997.* Washington, D.C.: National Gay and Lesbian Task Force.

———. 1998. *Capital gains and losses: A state by state review of lesbian, gay, bisexual, transgender, and HIV/AIDS related legislation in 1998.* Washington, D.C.: National Gay and Lesbian Task Force.

———. 1999. *45 states gather for federation meeting, July 27, 1999.* Washington, D.C.: National Gay and Lesbian Task Force.

Nice, David C. 1988. State deregulation of intimate behavior. *Social Science Quarterly* 69:203–11.

Niedowski, Erika. 1998. Four walk out of the closet and toward the House. *Congressional Quarterly*, 28 April.

Nitkin, David. 1998. Through lobbying, Christian conservatives seek to influence Florida judiciary. *Orlando Sentinel*, 20 April.

Penning, James M. 1998. The Christian Right in Michigan: From social movement to organized interest? Presented at the annual meetings of the Midwest Political Science Association, April.

Persinos, John F. 1994. Has the Christian Right taken over the Republican Party? *Campaigns and Elections,* September: 21–24.

Polman, Dick. 1998. Openly gay candidates the hot topic in U.S. politics; Seeing a more tolerant America, they want straight voters to know they share concerns. *Philadelphia Inquirer,* 3 May.

Savage, Dan. 1998. Don't blame Murray for marriage ban. *Seattle Times,* 7 April.

Savage, Robert L. 1978. Policy innovativeness as a trait of American states. *Journal of Politics* 40:212–24.

Sharp, Elaine B. 1997. A comparative anatomy of urban social conflict. *Political Research Quarterly* 50 (2): 261–80.

Sherrill, Kenneth R. 1996. The political power of lesbians, gays, and bisexuals. *PS: Political Science and Politics* 29:469–73.

Shibley, Gail. 1994. Coming out on every doorstep. In *Out for office: Campaigning in the gay '90s,* edited by Kathleen DeBold. Washington, D.C.: Gay and Lesbian Victory Fund.

Swain, Carol. 1993. *Black faces, black interests.* Cambridge: Harvard University Press.

Taylor, M. Jane. 1998. More states ban gay marriage; Kentucky and Iowa pass laws, Alaska moving quickly. *Washington Blade,* 10 April.

———. 1999. Doubling up in the states; Across the nation, gays go on the offensive. *Washington Blade,* 19 February.

Thomas, Clive S., and Ronald J. Hrebenar. 1996. Interest groups in the states. In *Politics in the American States,* edited by Virginia Gray and Herbert Jacob. 6th ed. Washington, D.C.: CQ Press.

Thomas, Sue. 1994. *How women legislate.* New York: Oxford University Press.

Thompson, Mark. ed. 1994. *The long road to freedom.* New York: St. Martin's Press.

Vaid, Urvashi. 1995. *Virtual equality: The mainstreaming of gay and lesbian liberation.* New York: Anchor Books.

Wald, Kenneth D., James W. Button, and Barbara A. Rienzo. 1996. The politics of gay rights in American communities: Explaining antidiscrimination ordinances and policies. *American Journal of Political Science* 40 (4): 1152–78.

Walker, Jack. 1969. The diffusion of innovations among the American states. *American Political Science Review* 68:880–99.

Walker, Martin. 1996. Gays inch up the aisle. *The Guardian,* 16 April, p. 13.

Whereatt, Robert. 1998. Same-sex marriage issue enters the governor's race. *Minneapolis Star Tribune,* 15 July.

Wick, Barry. 1995. *Press Release: March 1, 1995: South Dakota Gay, Lesbian, and Bisexual Federation declares a draw.* Rapid City, S.D.: South Dakota Gay, Lesbian, and Bisexual Federation.

———. 1997. *The history of FACES of South Dakota.* Rapid City, S.D.: Free Americans Creating Equal Status of South Dakota, Inc.

Openly Lesbian and Gay Elected Officials, by State

State/Locality	Office	Name	Elected	Terms/Years Served and Notes
Arizona	State House	Rep. Ken Cheuvront (D-Phoenix-25)	1994	Reelected 11/96 and 11/98
	State House	Steve May (R-26)	1998	Elected 11/98
California	State Assembly	Sheila Kuehl (D-41 Santa Monica)	1992	3d term; in 11/96, Kuehl chosen as the Speaker Pro Tem; reelected 11/98
	State Assembly	Carol Migden (D-San Francisco)	5/96	Elected to fill rest of Mayor Brown's term; elected for full term 11/96; reelected 11/98
Connecticut	State House	Art Feltman (D-Hartford)	1996	Reelected 11/98
	State House	Patrick J. Flaherty (D-Coventry)	Came out 3/99	
	State House	Joseph Grabarz (D)	1989	Reelected in 1991; served to 1993
	State House	Evelyn Mantilla (D-Hartford)	1997	Came out 6/97 as bisexual; reelected 11/98
Illinois	State House	Lawrence McKeon (D)	11/1996	Reelected 11/98
Maine	State Senate	Dale McCormick (D-18)	1990	3 terms; didn't run in 1996 because of term limit law
	State House	Susan Farnsworth (D-91-Hallowell)	1992	1 term
	State House	Susan Longley (D-11 Waldo County)	1995	Reelected 11/96
	State House	Scott Cowger (D)	1996	First term
	State House	Judy Powers (D)	1996	First term
	State House	Michael Quint (D-Portland)	1996	Reelected 11/98; only gay in 1998
	State Treasurer	Dale McCormick (D)	12/4/96	Two-year term; elected by legislature
Massachusetts	State House	Jarrett Barrios (D)	11/98	First term
	State House	Liz Malia (D)	11/98	First term
	State House	Rep. Elaine Noble (D-Boston)	1974	She was the first openly lesbian Rep. in the U.S.; reelected 11/76
Minnesota	State Senate	Allan Spear (DFL-60)	Came out in 1974	Reelected through 1996; Spear is now the longest-serving openly gay state legislator; he was elected president of the Senate in 1993
Missouri	State Assembly	Karen Clark (DFL-61a)	1980	Reelected every election 11/98
	State House	Tim Van Zandt (D-38-Kansas City)	1994	Reelected 11/96 and 11/98

State	Office	Name	Date	Notes
Montana	State House	Mary Ann Guggenheim (D)	11/98	First Term
	State House	Diane Sands (D)	1996	1st term; elected 11/96
Nevada	State Assembly	Ass. David Parks (D-Las Vegas)	1996	Reelected 11/98
New Hampshire	State House	Jim Splaine (D)	Came out 1997	Reelected 11/98; is his 4th term
New Mexico	State Senate	Liz Stefanics (D-39)	1992	Held office to 1996
New York	State Senate	Tom Duane (D)	11/98	First term
	State Assembly	Deborah Glick (D-66)	1990	5th term; reelected 11/98
Oregon	State Senate	Kate Brown (D)	11/98	from House; also elected Senate minority leader
	State House	Gail Shibley (D-12)	1991	Appointed 1991 and re-elected 1992, 93 and 95
	State House	Kate Brown (D-13)	1994	Reelected 11/96; left for Senate
	State House	Chuck Carpenter (R-7)	1994	Reelected 11/96; lost 98 primary
	State House	George Eighmey (D-14)	1994	Reelected 11/96; forced out by term limit law
	State House	Cynthia Wooten (D-41)	1994	Reelected 11/96
Rhode Island	State Senate	Will Fitzpatrick (D-11)	1992	2 terms; reelected 1994
	State House	David Cicilline (D-Providence)	came out 1999	Reelected 11/98
	State House	Michael Pisaturo (D-Cranston)	1996	Reelected 11/98
Texas	State House	Glen Maxey (D-51)	3/91	
Utah	State House	Jackie Biskpski (D-30)	11/98	1st in state
Vermont	Auditor of Accounts	Ed Flanagan (D)	Came out 1995	First elected in 1992; but not out until 1995; won first term out in 11/96; first openly gay person to hold a statewide office in U.S.; reelected 11/98
	State House	Tom Fleury (D-7-6)	1992	1 term; to 1994
	State House	(William J.) Bill Lippert (D-6)	1994	Reelected 11/96 and 11/98
	State House	Ronald Squires (D-5-Guilford)	1990/92	Came out in 1992; served till his death in 1993
	State House	Rep. Steve Howard (D)	1997	Came out 5/3/97; lost seat 11/98 when he ran for the Senate
	State Democratic Party Chair	Steve Howard (D)	1997	Came out 5/3/97
Washington	State House	Calvin Anderson (D-43)	1987	To 1994
	State Senate	Cal Anderson (D-43)	1994	Died in office 1995
	State House	Ed Murray (D-43)	1995	Reelected 11/96 and 98
Wisconsin	State Assembly	Tammy Baldwin (D-78)	1992	Reelected 1994 and 11/96; left for Congress 1/99
	State Assembly	Mark Pocan (D-78)	11/98	1st term

Known Failed Election Attempts for State Offices

Year	State/Locality	Office	Name	Elected	Terms/Years Served and Notes	Notes
1977	New York	State Assembly	Virginia Apuzzo			57th District
1978	New York	State Assembly	Virginia Apuzzo			57th District
1984	New York	State Assembly	Charles Hitchcock			(Long Island)
1986	Washington	State Senate	Herbert Krohn			(Republican)
1988	Georgia	State House	Dick Rhodes			(Atlanta)
88	Georgia	State House	Gil Robinson			(Atlanta)
1990	Maine	State Senate	Robin Lambert			Republican Primary
90	Massachusetts	State House	Mike Duffy			(Republican)
90	North Carolina	State House	Charles E. Merrill			
1991	Virginia	House of Delegates	Richard Sincere (Libertarian)			Special spring election (49th District)
1993	Virginia	House of Delegates	Bradley Evans			27th District
93	Virginia	House of Delegates	Richard Sincere			49th District
1994	Arizona	State House	Denise Heap			(Dist. 29)
94	California	Secretary of State	Tony Miller			General election; Miller was acting Secretary at the time
94	Massachusetts	State House	Derek Belt (D)			General election
94	New York	Attorney General	Karen Burstein (D)			General election
94	Oregon	State House	Jerry Keene (D)			General election
94	Rhode Island	State House	Mike Pisaturo (D)			General election
94	Wisconsin	State House	Scott Evertz (D)			General election
1996	Arizona	State Senate	Steve May (R-Dist. 25)			Won primary; lost general
96	California	State Leg.	Adam Ross (D)			
96	California	State Assembly	Gerrie Schipske (D-Long Beach)			Won primary; lost general
96	Maine	State House	Corey Corbin			Republican Primary
96	New Hampshire	State House	Randy Kottwitz (D)			Lost general
96	New York	State Leg.	William Barnes (R)			
96	North Carolina	State Leg.	Christopher Cole			
96	North Dakota	State Leg.	Greg Lemke (D)			
96	Oregon	State Leg.	Elly Work (D)			Libertarian

Year	State	Office	Candidate	Notes
96	Vermont	State Senate	David Curtis (D)	Lost general
96	Vermont	State Leg.	Brendan Hadash (D)	
1997	Virginia	Lt. Governor	Bradley Evans	Reform Party
97	Virginia	House of Delegates	Bradley Evans	27th District (write in)
1998	California	Governor	Dennis Peron	Republican primary
98	California	Lt. Governor	Tony Miller	Democratic primary
98	California	State Assembly	Randy Bernard (R)	
98	California	State Assembly	Zeke Zeidler	(53d District)
98	Maine	State House	B. Nolan McCoy (D-S. Portland)	Lost general
98	Maine	State House	John Wade (D-Kennebunk)	Lost general
98	Maryland	State House	James Harrison (R-20)	Lost general
98	Maryland	State House	David "Kip" Koontz (D-3)	Lost general
98	Massachusetts	State Auditor	Mike Duffy (R)	Lost general
98	Massachusetts	State House	Dana Hilliard (D)	Lost general
98	Minnesota	State Treasurer	Wallace "Wally" Swan	Democrat
98	New York	State Senate	Judy Green (D)	Lost general
98	New York	State Senate	Ed Sederbaum (D)	(Queens)
98	Oregon	State House	Chuck Carpenter (R-7)	Incumbent; lost primary
98	Oregon	State House	Elli Work (D)	Lost general
98	Texas	State House	Fred Ebner (R)	Lost general to Glenn Maxey
98	Vermont	State Senate	Steve Howard (D)	Ran from House
98	Vermont	State Senate	Tim Palmer (D)	Lost general
98	Washington	State House	Craig Peterson (D)	Lost general
98	Wisconsin	State Assembly	Curtis Lamon (R)	Lost general
1999				
Pending 2000				
2000	California	State Senate	Sheila Kuehl (D)	incumbent
00	California	State House	Jackie Goldberg (D)	
00	California	State House	Christine Kehoe (D)	

NOTES: Compiled by the author; most information is available in Haider-Markel (1997a), the Gay and Lesbian Victory Fund, the National Gay and Lesbian Task Force, and newspaper accounts. Party and district information was not available for all candidates or officials.

State Government Actions Concerning Gay Civil Rights, Hate Crime, Same-Sex Marriage, and Sodomy, 1993–1999

Year	State	Policy	Pro- or Antigay	Status and Information
1993	Illinois	Civil Rights	Pro	Failed; one vote short of passing in Senate
93	Illinois	SSM	Anti	Died; SB 1042
93	Louisiana	Hate Crimes	Pro	Failed in Legislature
93	Maine	Civil Rights	Pro	Failed; vetoed by Governor
93	Maryland	Civil Rights	Pro	Failed in Committee
93	Maryland	Civil Rights	Pro	Passed; Executive Order
93	Massachusetts	Civil Rights	Pro	Passed; signed by Governor 12/10
93	Minnesota	Civil Rights	Pro	Passed
93	Nebraska	Civil Rights	Pro	Held; LB 395; carried over to 1994
93	New Mexico	Civil Rights	Pro	Died; passed Senate, died in House
93	New York	Civil Rights	Pro	Failed in Senate; passed Assembly
93	Oregon	Civil Rights	Pro	Died
93	Oregon	Civil Rights	Pro	Passed; HB 3500
93	Rhode Island	Civil Rights	Pro	Failed in House; passed Senate 30–17
93	Rhode Island	Sodomy	Pro	Died in Legislature
93	Virginia	Sodomy	Pro	Died in Legislature
93	Washington	Civil Rights	Pro	Died in Legislature HB 1443
93	Washington	Hate Crimes	Pro	Passed
1994	Arizona	Hate Crimes	Pro	Failed in Legislature
94	Arizona	Civil Rights	Anti	Failed; constitutional amendment
94	California	Hate Crimes	Pro	Died in Senate; passed Assembly 67–1 on 8/11
94	California	Hate Crimes	Pro	Passed; SB 1595; signed by Governor 8/31
94	Hawaii	SSM	Anti	Passed; HB 2312; signed by Governor 6/22
94	Hawaii	SSM	Anti	Failed; HB 2366; Senate killed 15–10
94	Hawaii	SSM	Anti	Failed; HB 3709
94	Hawaii	SSM	Anti	Died; SB 3199
94	Idaho	Civil Rights	Anti	Failed at Ballot; Prop. 1
94	Illinois	Civil Rights	Pro	Failed in Legislature
94	Kentucky	Sodomy	Anti	Died; HB 10
94	Louisiana	Hate Crimes	Pro	Failed; HB 129
94	Louisiana	Hate Crimes	Pro	Failed; HB 130
94	Louisiana	Hate Crimes	Pro	Failed; SB 81
94	Louisiana	Hate Crimes	Pro	Failed; SB 156
94	Maryland	Civil Rights	Pro	Failed in House Judiciary Committee
94	Nebraska	Civil Rights	Pro	Died; LB 395
94	New Hampshire	Civil Rights	Pro	Died in Senate; passed House by 226–131; HB 1432
94	New Hampshire	SSM	Anti	Died; no action
94	New Mexico	Civil Rights	Pro	Passed; Executive Order expanded 1985 action
94	New York	Civil Rights	Pro	Failed in Senate; passed House

(continued)

Year	State	Policy	Pro- or Antigay	Status and Information
94	Oregon	Civil Rights	Pro	Failed in Legislature
94	Oregon	Civil Rights	Anti	Failed at ballot; Measure 13
94	Rhode Island	Civil Rights	Pro	Failed in Legislature
94	Rhode Island	Sodomy	Pro	Died in Legislature
94	Virginia	Hate Crimes	Pro	Died in Legislature
94	Virginia	Sodomy	Pro	Died in Legislature
94	Washington	Civil Rights	Pro	Died in Senate; HB 1443 passed House 2/94
94	Washington	Civil Rights	Pro	Passed; nonbinding Senate resolution
94	Wyoming	Hate Crimes	Pro	Tabled by House 3/94
1995	Alaska	SSM	Anti	Died; HB 227
95	Arizona	Hate Crimes	Pro	Failed in Legislature
95	Arizona	Hate Crimes	Pro	Passed
95	Arizona	Hate Crimes	Pro	Passed; SB 1143; signed by Governor 4/19
95	Arkansas	Hate Crimes	Pro	Died; HB 1257
95	California	Civil Rights	Pro	Passed; AB 910
95	California	Civil Rights	Pro	Failed; held for 1996; AB 1001
95	California	Civil Rights	Pro	Failed; held for 1996; AB 1106
95	California	Civil Rights	Pro	Failed; pocket veto; SB 381
95	California	Civil Rights	Pro	Died; SB 806
95	California	Civil Rights	Pro	Died in Senate; SB 970
95	California	Civil Rights	Pro	Passed; SB 1020; signed by Governor 10/10
95	California	Hate Crimes	Pro	Passed; SB 911
95	Colorado	Hate Crimes	Pro	Died; HB 1257
95	Colorado	Hate Crimes	Pro	Died; SB 137
95	Florida	Civil Rights	Pro	Died; SB 2314
95	Florida	SSM	Anti	Failed; amendment to bill that failed
95	Hawaii	SSM	Anti	Died; HB 609
95	Hawaii	SSM	Anti	Died; HB 2172
95	Hawaii	SSM	Anti	Died; HB 2173
95	Hawaii	SSM	Anti	Died; SB 565
95	Hawaii	SSM	Pro	Passed; SB 888
95	Illinois	Civil Rights	Pro	Passed; HB 549
95	Illinois	Civil Rights	Pro	Unknown; HB 2139
95	Illinois	Civil Rights	Pro	Passed; SB 225
95	Illinois	Civil Rights	Pro	Passed; SB 260; signed by Governor 6/23
95	Illinois	Civil Rights	Pro	Died; SB 994
95	Iowa	SSM	Anti	Died; HSB 561
95	Kansas	Sodomy	Anti	Died; HB 2301; passed House
95	Louisiana	Hate Crimes	Pro	Failed; HB 1743
95	Louisiana	Hate Crimes	Pro	Failed; SB 980; Senate passed 21–15
95	Louisiana	Civil Rights	Pro	Failed; HB 2038
95	Louisiana	Civil Rights	Pro	Failed; SB 981

APPENDIX B

(continued)

Year	State	Policy	Pro- or Antigay	Status and Information
95	Louisiana	Civil Rights	Pro	Failed; SB 1045
95	Louisiana	Sodomy	Anti	Died in Senate; SB 1231
95	Maine	Civil Rights	Anti	Failed; LB 310
95	Maine	Civil Rights	Pro	Died
95	Maine	Civil Rights	Anti	Failed at ballot; Question 1
95	Maine	Hate Crimes	Pro	Passed; HB 592
95	Maryland	Civil Rights	Pro	Failed in House committee; HB 213
95	Massachusetts	Civil Rights	Pro	Died; HB 2739
95	Massachusetts	Civil Rights	Pro	Died; HB 2938
95	Massachusetts	Civil Rights	Pro	Died; SB 529
95	Massachusetts	Civil Rights	Pro	Died; HB 3110
95	Massachusetts	Civil Rights	Pro	Died; SB 559
95	Massachusetts	Civil Rights	Pro	Died; HB 5649
95	Massachusetts	Civil Rights	Pro	Died; HB 5255
95	Massachusetts	Sodomy	Pro	Died; SB 1032
95	Montana	Sodomy	Anti	Failed; HB 157; passed and provision removed
95	Montana	Sodomy	Anti	Failed; HB 214; passed and provision removed
95	Montana	Sodomy	Anti	Failed; HB 444; provision removed
95	Nebraska	Civil Rights	Pro	Died; LB 400
95	Nevada	Hate Crimes	Pro	Passed; AB 606; signed by Governor 5/23
95	Nevada	Hate Crimes	Pro	Passed; SB 139; signed by Governor
95	New Hampshire	Civil Rights	Pro	Failed in House
95	New Mexico	Civil Rights	Pro	Passed; HB 482
95	New Mexico	Hate Crimes	Pro	Failed; vetoed by Governor
95	New York	Civil Rights	Pro	Died in Senate; passed Assembly; AB 3801
95	New York	Civil Rights	Pro	Died in Senate; SB 921a
95	New York	Civil Rights	Pro	Died; AB 3584
95	New York	Civil Rights	Pro	Died; AB 3828
95	New York	Civil Rights	Pro	Died; AB 5461; passed Assembly
95	New York	Civil Rights	Pro	Died; AB 6801
95	New York	Civil Rights	Pro	Died; SB 792
95	New York	Hate Crimes	Pro	Died in Senate; passed Assembly; AB 1228
95	New York	Hate Crimes	Pro	Died; AB 4549
95	New York	Hate Crimes	Pro	Died; SB 2774
95	New York	Hate Crimes	Pro	Died; passed Assembly; AB 5405
95	New York	Hate Crimes	Pro	Died; SB 86
95	New York	Hate Crimes	Pro	Died; AB 6560
95	Oregon	Civil Rights	Pro	Failed; HB 3459
95	Oregon	Civil Rights	Pro	Passed; HB 2035; signed by Governor 6/9

APPENDIX B

(continued)

Year	State	Policy	Pro- or Antigay	Status and Information
95	Rhode Island	Civil Rights	Pro	Passed; 95- H 6678; signed by Governor 5/20
95	Rhode Island	Hate Crimes	Pro	Passed; SB 758
95	Rhode Island	Sodomy	Pro	Died in Legislature
95	South Dakota	SSM	Anti	Failed in Senate 13–17; HB 1184
95	Texas	Hate Crimes	Pro	Failed in House by 68–70; passed Senate; SB 141
95	Texas	Civil Rights	Pro	Failed; language removed; HB 999
95	Texas	Civil Rights	Pro	Failed; language removed; HB 1048
95	Utah	Civil Rights	Anti	Passed; HB 103
95	Utah	SSM	Anti	Passed; HB 366; signed by Governor 3/17
95	Virginia	Hate Crimes	Pro	Died
95	Virginia	Sodomy	Pro	Died
95	Wyoming	Hate Crimes	Pro	Died in House; HB 50
1996	Alabama	SSM	Anti	Died; HB 142
96	Alabama	SSM	Anti	Died; SB 45
96	Alabama	SSM	Anti	Died; SB 396
96	Alabama	SSM	Anti	Passed; Executive Order
96	Alaska	Civil Rights	Pro	Died in Senate; SB 228 or SB 282
96	Alaska	SSM	Anti	Passed; SB 308
96	Arizona	Civil Rights	Pro	Died in Senate; SB 1138
96	Arizona	Hate Crimes	Pro	Failed; HB 2050; vetoed by Governor
96	Arizona	Hate Crimes	Pro	Failed; SB 1078
96	Arizona	Hate Crimes	Pro	Died; HB 2109
96	Arizona	SSM	Anti	Died; withdrawn; strike-all to SB 1063
96	Arizona	SSM	Anti	Died; amendment to SB 1362
96	Arizona	SSM	Anti	Passed; SB 1038; signed by Governor 5/1
96	Arkansas	SSM	Anti	Died; HB 1004
96	Arkansas	SSM	Anti	Died; SB 5 (pre-filed for 97)
96	California	Civil Rights	Pro	Failed; AB 1001
96	California	Civil Rights	Pro	Died; AB 2473
96	California	Civil Rights	Pro	Died in House; passed Senate; SB 1822
96	California	Civil Rights	Anti	Failed in Senate 17–17; SB 2110
96	California	SSM	Anti	Failed in Senate 21–20 on 8/19; AB 1982
96	California	SSM	Anti	Failed in Assembly; AB 3227
96	California	SSM	Anti	Died; SB 2075
96	Colorado	Hate Crimes	Pro	Died; SB 191
96	Colorado	SSM	Anti	Failed; vetoed on 3/25; HB 1291
96	Delaware	SSM	Anti	Passed; HB 503; signed by Governor 6/21

APPENDIX B

(continued)

Year	State	Policy	Pro- or Antigay	Status and Information
96	Florida	SSM	Anti	Died; HB 2369 withdrawn
96	Georgia	Civil Rights	Pro	Passed; HB 1502; signed by Governor 2/15
96	Georgia	SSM	Anti	Passed; HB 1278; signed by Governor 4/15
96	Georgia	SSM	Anti	Passed; HB 1580; signed by Governor 4/2
96	Georgia	SSM	Anti	Died; SB 680
96	Georgia	SSM	Anti	Passed; SB 681
96	Georgia	Sodomy	Anti	Died in Senate committee; passed House; HB 694
96	Georgia	Sodomy	Anti	Died in House committee; HB 711
96	Georgia	Sodomy	Anti	Died; amendment to HB 1682
96	Hawaii	Hate Crimes	Pro	Died; SB 2006
96	Hawaii	SSM	Pro	Died; HB 2363
96	Hawaii	SSM	Pro	Died; HB 2365
96	Hawaii	SSM	Anti	Died; HB 2367
96	Hawaii	SSM	Anti	Died; killed in Senate; HB 2524
96	Hawaii	SSM	Anti	Died; HB 2667
96	Hawaii	SSM	Anti	Died; HB 2723
96	Hawaii	SSM	Anti	Died; HB 3256
96	Hawaii	SSM	Anti	Died in conference; HB 3347
96	Hawaii	SSM	Anti	Died; HB 3732
96	Hawaii	SSM	Anti	Died; HB 3801
96	Hawaii	SSM	Anti	Died; SB 2501
96	Hawaii	SSM	Pro	Died; SB 3112
96	Hawaii	SSM	Anti	Died; SB 3114
96	Hawaii	SSM	Anti	Died; SCR 254
96	Hawaii	SSM	Anti	Died; SR 202
96	Idaho	SSM	Anti	Passed; HB 658; signed by Governor 3/18
96	Illinois	Civil Rights	Pro	Passed; Executive Order reaffirmed 1992 Order
96	Illinois	Hate Crimes	Pro	Died; HB 2671
96	Illinois	SSM	Anti	Passed; SB 1140; signed by Governor 5/25
96	Illinois	SSM	Anti	Failed; SB 1773; vetoed in favor of SB 1140
96	Indiana	Hate Crimes	Pro	Died; HB 1225
96	Indiana	SSM	Anti	Failed
96	Iowa	SSM	Anti	Died; HSB 2183; passed House 85–13 on 2/20
96	Kansas	Hate Crimes	Pro	Died in House Committee; HB 2002
96	Kansas	Hate Crimes	Pro	Died in Senate; HB 2659; passed House
96	Kansas	SSM	Anti	Passed; SB 515; signed by Governor 4/10

APPENDIX B

(continued)

Year	State	Policy	Pro- or Antigay	Status and Information
96	Kansas	Sodomy	Anti	Died in Senate committee; HB 2301
96	Kentucky	Sodomy	Anti	Died in House; HB 219
96	Kentucky	Sodomy	Anti	Died in committee; HB 864;
96	Kentucky	Sodomy	Anti	Failed amendment to nonrelated bill in House
96	Kentucky	Sodomy	Anti	Died in Senate committee; HB 493
96	Kentucky	Sodomy	Anti	Failed amendment to nonrelated bill in Senate
96	Kentucky	SSM	Anti	Failed in House; amendment 1 to HB 219
96	Kentucky	SSM	Anti	Died; HB 500
96	Kentucky	SSM	Anti	Died; HB 882; withdrawn
96	Kentucky	SSM	Anti	Failed in committee; amendment to SB 68
96	Kentucky	SSM	Anti	Died; amendment 1 to SB 118
96	Kentucky	SSM	Anti	Died; SB 339; no action
96	Louisiana	SSM	Anti	Passed; HCR 124; nonbinding resolution
96	Louisiana	SSM	Anti	Failed; SR 27; nonbinding resolution
96	Maine	SSM	Anti	Died; SB 531 or LD 1448
96	Maine	SSM	Anti	Died; nonbinding resolution
96	Maine	Hate Crimes	Pro	
96	Maine	Civil Rights		
96	Maine	SSM	Anti	Died; nonbinding resolution
96	Maine	SSM	Anti	Died; LD 1448
96	Maryland	Civil Rights	Pro	Died in committee; HB 67
96	Maryland	Civil Rights	Pro	Failed in House Committee; HB 325
96	Maryland	Civil Rights	Pro	Failed in House Committee; HB 413
96	Maryland	SSM	Anti	Died; introduced HB 1268; 2/15
96	Massachusetts	Civil Rights	Pro	Died; HB 4819
96	Massachusetts	Civil Rights	Pro	Passed; HB 5649; signed by Governor 5/20
96	Massachusetts	Hate Crimes	Pro	Passed; HB 5191; signed by Governor 7/12
96	Massachusetts	Hate Crimes	Pro	Passed; SB 165
96	Massachusetts	Sodomy	Pro	Died in Senate; SB 1032
96	Michigan	SSM	Anti	Held; HB 5661
96	Michigan	SSM	Anti	Passed; HB 5662; signed by Governor 6/25
96	Michigan	SSM	Anti	Passed; SB 937; signed by Governor 6/25
96	Michigan	SSM	Anti	Held; SB 938
96	Minnesota	Civil Rights	Pro	Passed; HF 1856; signed by Governor 5/24
96	Minnesota	Civil Rights	Pro	Died in House; HF 2018
96	Minnesota	Civil Rights	Anti	Died; HF 2159

(continued)

Year	State	Policy	Pro- or Antigay	Status and Information
96	Minnesota	Civil Rights	Anti	Died; SF 1850
96	Minnesota	Civil Rights	Pro	Died in Senate Committee; SF 2843
96	Minnesota	Hate Crimes	Pro	Passed; HF 1648
96	Minnesota	Hate Crimes	Pro	Passed; SB 2186
96	Minnesota	SSM	Anti	Failed; amendment to SF 1996
96	Minnesota	SSM	Anti	Failed; amendment to SF 2067
96	Mississippi	Civil Rights	Anti	Died; HB 135
96	Mississippi	SSM	Anti	Died; HB 1210
96	Mississippi	SSM	Anti	Died; SB 2863
96	Mississippi	SSM	Anti	Passed; Executive Order signed 8/22
96	Missouri	Civil Rights	Pro	Died; HB 854
96	Missouri	SSM	Anti	Died; withdrawn; HB 1255
96	Missouri	SSM	Anti	Died; HB 1454
96	Missouri	SSM	Anti	Died; HB 1458
96	Missouri	SSM	Anti	Passed; amendment to SB 768; signed 7/3
96	Missouri	SSM	Anti	Died; SB 895
96	Missouri	Sodomy	Anti	Died; HB 970
96	Missouri	Sodomy	Pro	Died; HB 1245
96	Nebraska	Civil Rights	Pro	Failed in committee; LB 903
96	Nebraska	Hate Crimes	Pro	Died; LB 919
96	Nebraska	SSM	Pro	Failed; LB 1260
96	New Hampshire	Civil Rights	Pro	Died in House; HB 1294
96	New Jersey	Civil Rights	Pro	Passed; AB 1411; signed by Governor 11/19
96	New Jersey	Civil Rights	Pro	Passed; AB 1499; signed by Governor 11/19
96	New Jersey	Civil Rights	Pro	Died in Assembly; AB 2509
96	New Jersey	Civil Rights	Pro	Passed; SB 695; signed by Governor 11/19
96	New Jersey	Civil Rights	Pro	Died in Senate Committee; SB 1481
96	New Jersey	Hate Crimes	Pro	Died; AB 154
96	New Jersey	Hate Crimes	Pro	Died; AB 691
96	New Jersey	Hate Crimes	Pro	Died; AB 700
96	New Jersey	Hate Crimes	Pro	Died; AB 948
96	New Jersey	Hate Crimes	Pro	Passed
96	New Jersey	SSM	Anti	Held; AB 2193; held over
96	New Jersey	SSM	Anti	Held; SB 1376; held over
96	New Mexico	Hate Crimes	Pro	Failed veto override of SB 615
96	New Mexico	SSM	Anti	Died; SJR 10
96	New York	Civil Rights	Pro	Died; AB 3801 passed Assembly by 85–57
96	New York	Civil Rights	Anti	Died; SB 5071
96	New York	Civil Rights	Pro	Died in Rules Committee; AB 5454
96	New York	Civil Rights	Pro	Died in Health Committee; AB 8504
96	New York	Civil Rights	Pro	Died; SB 910

APPENDIX B

(continued)

Year	State	Policy	Pro- or Antigay	Status and Information
96	New York	Civil Rights	Pro	Died; S 3 921a
96	New York	Hate Crimes	Pro	Died; AB 5404 passed Assembly
96	New York	Hate Crimes	Pro	Died; AB 8972
96	New York	Hate Crimes	Pro	Died; SB 1974
96	New York	SSM	Anti	Held; AB 158 ?
96	New York	SSM	Anti	Died; AB 9861
96	New York	SSM	Anti	Died; SB 1649 ?
96	New York	SSM	Anti	Died; SB 7345
96	New York	Sodomy	Anti	Died; AB 8437
96	North Carolina	SSM	Anti	Passed without Governor; SB 1487
96	Ohio	Hate Crimes	Pro	Died in Senate; passed House; HB 159
96	Oklahoma	Civil Rights	Anti	Died; H.J.R. 1018; constitutional amendment
96	Oklahoma	SSM	Anti	Passed; amendment to HB 2554
96	Oklahoma	SSM	Anti	Passed; HR 1045
96	Oklahoma	SSM	Anti	Passed; SB 73; signed by Governor 4/29
96	Pennsylvania	Hate Crime	Pro	Died in the Senate; SB 701
96	Pennsylvania	Civil Rights	Pro	Died; Schools; SB 2854; no action known
96	Pennsylvania	SSM	Anti	Passed; HB 2604
96	Pennsylvania	SSM	Anti	Passed; amendment to SB 434; signed 10/16
96	Pennsylvania	SSM	Anti	Held; SB 1558
96	Rhode Island	Civil Rights	Pro	Died; HB 8144
96	Rhode Island	Civil Rights	Pro	Passed; HB 8710; establish study committee
96	Rhode Island	Hate Crimes	Pro	Died in House Committee; HB 7335
96	Rhode Island	Hate Crimes	Pro	Died in House Committee; HB 7592
96	Rhode Island	Hate Crimes	Pro	Died in House Committee; HB 7602
96	Rhode Island	Hate Crimes	Pro	Died in House Committee; HB 8041
96	Rhode Island	SSM	Anti	Failed in House Judiciary; HB 7587
96	Rhode Island	Sodomy	Pro	Died in Legislature
96	South Carolina	SSM	Anti	Passed; HB 4502
96	South Carolina	SSM	Anti	Passed; SB 1151
96	South Dakota	SSM	Anti	Passed; HB 1143; signed by Governor 2/21
96	Tennessee	SSM	Anti	Passed; HB 2907; signed by Governor 5/15
96	Tennessee	SSM	Anti	Passed; SB 2305; signed by Governor 5/15
96	Virginia	Hate Crimes	Pro	Died in House; HB 234
96	Virginia	SSM	Anti	Died; withdrawn; HB 1189
96	Virginia	SSM	Anti	Held; HB 1589
96	Virginia	Sodomy	Pro	Died in House; HB1468

APPENDIX B

(continued)

Year	State	Policy	Pro- or Antigay	Status and Information
96	Washington	Civil Rights	Pro	Died; HB 2542
96	Washington	Civil Rights	Pro	Died; HB 2618
96	Washington	Civil Rights	Pro	Died; SB 6534
96	Washington	SSM	Anti	Died in Senate; HB 2262; passed House
96	Washington	Sodomy	Anti	Died in House; passed Senate; SB 6130
96	West Virginia	Civil Rights	Pro	Died; HB 4707
96	West Virginia	Hate Crimes	Pro	Died; HB 4708
96	West Virginia	Hate Crimes	Pro	Died; SB 457
96	West Virginia	SSM	Anti	Died; HB 4730; no action
96	Wisconsin	SSM	Anti	Died; AB 1042
96	Wyoming	SSM	Anti	Failed; HB 412
1997	Alabama	SSM	Anti	Died; HB 482
97	Alabama	SSM	Anti	Died; SB 1
97	Alabama	SSM	Anti	Died; SB 282
97	Arizona	Sodomy	Pro	Died; HB 2538
97	Arizona	Sodomy	Anti	Withdrawn; Sponsor Rep. Debra Brimhall
97	Arizona	Civil Rights	Pro	Died; HB 2431
97	Arizona	Civil Rights	Pro	Died; SB 1464
97	Arizona	Hate Crimes	Pro	Died; HB 2182
97	Arizona	Hate Crimes	Pro	Passed; "strike all" amendment on SB 1047
97	Arkansas	Civil Rights	Pro	Failed; amendment to SB 5 on same-sex marriage
97	Arkansas	Civil Rights	Pro	Died in committee; SB 63
97	Arkansas	SSM	Anti	Passed; HB 1004; Gov. signed 2/13; Act 144
97	Arkansas	SSM	Anti	Passed; SB 5; Gov. signed 2/13; Act 146
97	Arkansas	Sodomy	Pro	Died
97	California	Civil Rights	Pro	Failed in Assembly on 6/3 by 36–40–4AB 101
97	California	Civil Rights	Pro	Failed; Governor vetoed; AB 257
97	California	Civil Rights	Pro	Failed in Assembly by 36–40 on 6/4; AB 492
97	California	Civil Rights	Pro	Failed in Assembly by 37–36 on 6/4; AB 499
97	California	Hate Crimes	Pro	
97	California	Hate Crimes	Pro	Died in Assembly; passed Senate
97	California	Hate Crimes	Pro	Failed in Assembly; AB50
97	California	Hate Crimes	Pro	Died; passed Assembly; AB 51
97	California	SSM	Anti	Failed Assembly committee on 5/7; AB 800
97	California	SSM	Anti	Failed in Senate committee 2–2; SB 911

APPENDIX B

(continued)

Year	State	Policy	Pro- or Antigay	Status and Information
97	California	Sodomy	Pro	Passed; AB 290; revise Megan's Law
97	Colorado	Civil Rights	Pro	Died in committee; HB 1266
97	Colorado	Hate Crimes	Pro	Died in House; Senate passed 18–16; SB 100
97	Colorado	SSM	Anti	Failed; vetoed on 6/5; HB 1198
97	Connecticut	Civil Rights	Pro	Died; HB 7051
97	Connecticut	Civil Rights	Pro	Died; SB 414
97	Connecticut	Civil Rights	Pro	Passed; SB 1121; signed by Governor 6/27
97	Connecticut	SSM	Anti	Died; SB 535
97	Delaware	Hate Crimes	Pro	Passed; SB 53; signed by Governor 7/12
97	Florida	SSM	Anti	Passed; HB 147; effective 6/4
97	Florida	SSM	Anti	Held; SB 272
97	Georgia	Civil Rights	Pro	Unknown
97	Georgia	Sodomy	Pro	Died; Sponsor: Sen. Steve Langford
97	Georgia	Hate Crimes	Pro	Held over to 1998; HB 842
97	Georgia	Hate Crimes	Pro	Died; passed Senate; SR 313
97	Hawaii	Hate Crimes	Pro	Died
97	Hawaii	SSM	Anti	Passed; HB 117; for ballot referendum
97	Hawaii	SSM	Anti	Carried over; HB 182
97	Hawaii	SSM	Anti	Carried over; HB 213
97	Hawaii	SSM	Anti	Carried over; HB 771
97	Hawaii	SSM	Anti	Carried over; HB 1424
97	Hawaii	SSM	Anti	Carried over; HB 1461
97	Hawaii	SSM	Anti	Carried over; SB 36
97	Hawaii	SSM	Anti	Carried over; SB 97
97	Hawaii	SSM	Anti	Carried over; SB 912
97	Hawaii	SSM	Anti	Passed; SB 1800; for ballot referendum
97	Illinois	Civil Rights	Pro	Failed in 60–50 House vote on 4/24; HB 1241
97	Illinois	Civil Rights	Pro	Died in Senate; SB 847
97	Illinois	Hate Crimes	Pro	Passed; HB 1269
97	Illinois	SSM	Pro	Died; no action
97	Indiana	Hate Crime	Pro	Died in Committee; HB 1448
97	Indiana	SSM	Anti	Died; HB 1019
97	Indiana	SSM	Anti	Passed; Strike-out to HB 1265
97	Indiana	SSM	Anti	Died; HB 1889
97	Indiana	SSM	Anti	Died; SB 183; passed Senate
97	Indiana	SSM	Anti	Died; SB 211; passed Senate on 2/10 by 40–9
97	Indiana	SSM	Anti	Died; amendment to SB 490
97	Indiana	SSM	Anti	Failed in conference; amendment to SB 509
97	Iowa	SSM	Anti	Died; HSB 37
97	Iowa	SSM	Anti	Died; HF 382

APPENDIX B

(continued)

Year	State	Policy	Pro- or Antigay	Status and Information
97	Iowa	SSM	Anti	Died; SSB 114
97	Kansas	Sodomy	Anti	Died; HB 215 or SB 215
97	Kansas	Sodomy	Anti	Died; HB 2159
97	Kansas	Sodomy	Anti	Failed; language removed; HB 2169
97	Kansas	Sodomy	Anti	Failed; language removed; HB 2211
97	Kansas	Sodomy	Anti	Died; HB 2232
97	Kansas	Sodomy	Anti	Failed; language removed; HB 2274
97	Kansas	Sodomy	Anti	Failed; language removed; HB 2313
97	Kansas	Sodomy	Anti	Failed; language removed; HB 2367
97	Kansas	Sodomy	Anti	Died; HB 2485
97	Kansas	Sodomy	Anti	Failed; language removed; SB 258
97	Kansas	Sodomy	Anti	Died; SB 261
97	Kansas	Sodomy	Anti	Failed; language removed; SB 291
97	Louisiana	Sodomy	Pro	Died
97	Louisiana	Civil Rights	Pro	Failed in House committee; HB 1819
97	Louisiana	Civil Rights	Pro	Failed in Senate committee; SB 1099
97	Louisiana	Civil Rights	Pro	Passed; resolution for a study
97	Louisiana	Hate Crimes	Pro	Failed in committee; HB 2279
97	Louisiana	Hate Crimes	Pro	Passed; SB 914; signed by Governor 7/97
97	Louisiana	SSM	Anti	Failed in Senate; SB 37
97	Maine	Civil Rights	Pro	Passed; repealed at ballot in 1998
97	Maine	SSM	Anti	Passed; LD 1017; voter petition
97	Maryland	Civil Rights	Pro	Failed in House committee; HB 431
97	Maryland	SSM	Anti	Failed; HB 398; killed in committee
97	Maryland	SSM	Pro	Failed; HB 609; killed in committee
97	Massachusetts	Hate Crimes	Pro	Died in Senate committee; HB 4240
97	Massachusetts	Sodomy	Pro	Died; SB 1032
97	Massachusetts	Sodomy	Pro	Died
97	Michigan	Hate Crimes	Pro	Failed; HB 4674
97	Michigan	Sodomy	Pro	Unknown
97	Minnesota	Civil Rights	Pro	Passed?; exclude gays from 4-H
97	Minnesota	Hate Crimes	Pro	Died in committee; HF 1468
97	Minnesota	Hate Crimes	Pro	Died; SF 1402
97	Minnesota	SSM	Anti	Carried over; HF 16
97	Minnesota	SSM	Anti	Carried over; HF 41
97	Minnesota	SSM	Anti	Carried over; HF 69
97	Minnesota	SSM	Anti	Carried over; HF 395
97	Minnesota	SSM	Anti	Carried over; HF 585
97	Minnesota	SSM	Anti	Carried over; HF 1065
97	Minnesota	SSM	Anti	Carried over; HF 1268
97	Minnesota	SSM	Anti	Carried over; HF 1725
97	Minnesota	SSM	Anti	Carried over; SF 11
97	Minnesota	SSM	Anti	Died; amendment to SF 830

APPENDIX B

(continued)

Year	State	Policy	Pro- or Antigay	Status and Information
97	Minnesota	SSM	Anti	Passed; amendment to SF 1908; signed 6/2
97	Mississippi	SSM	Anti	Died in Senate; HCR 15; passed House on 2/5
97	Mississippi	SSM	Anti	Held; HB 295
97	Mississippi	SSM	Anti	Held; HB 346
97	Mississippi	SSM	Anti	Held; HB 423
97	Mississippi	SSM	Anti	Held; HB 651
97	Mississippi	SSM	Anti	Held; HB 651
97	Mississippi	SSM	Anti	Held; HB 672
97	Mississippi	SSM	Anti	Held; SB 2133
97	Mississippi	SSM	Anti	Passed; SB 2053; signed by Governor 2/12
97	Mississippi	SSM	Anti	Held; SB 2133
97	Mississippi	SSM	Anti	Died; SB 2234
97	Mississippi	SSM	Anti	Died; SCR 524
97	Missouri	Civil Rights	Pro	Unknown
97	Missouri	Sodomy	Pro	Unknown
97	Montana	Sodomy	Pro	Unknown
97	Montana	Civil Rights	Pro	Died in committee; HB 270
97	Montana	Hate Crimes	Pro	Failed in Senate Judiciary Committee; SB 291
97	Montana	SSM	Anti	Passed; HB 323; signed by Governor 4/30
97	Nebraska	Civil Rights	Pro	Held to 1998; LB 869
97	Nebraska	Hate Crimes	Pro	Passed; LB 90; signed by Governor 6/12
97	Nebraska	SSM	Anti	Carried over; filibuster; LB 280
97	Nebraska	SSM	Pro	Failed; LB 407
97	Nevada	Hate Crimes	Pro	Unknown
97	New Hampshire	Civil Rights	Pro	Passed; HB 421
97	New Hampshire	SSM	Anti	Failed in House 261–85 on 3/5; HB 260
97	New Jersey	Hate Crimes	Pro	Passed; AB 691; signed by Governor 9/23
97	New Jersey	Hate Crimes	Pro	Passed; SB 948; signed by Governor 9/23
97	New Jersey	SSM	Anti	Died; AB 2193
97	New Jersey	SSM	Anti	Died; AB 2406
97	New Jersey	SSM	Anti	Died; SB 1376
97	New Mexico	Civil Rights	Pro	Died in House committee; HB 506
97	New Mexico	Civil Rights	Anti	Died; SB 995
97	New Mexico	Civil Rights	Pro	Passed; CSH 399/a; signed by Governor 4/10
97	New Mexico	Hate Crimes	Pro	Died in Senate; passed House; HB 470

APPENDIX B

(continued)

Year	State	Policy	Pro- or Antigay	Status and Information
97	New Mexico	SSM	Anti	Died; HB 640; Rep. Jerry Lee Alwin
97	New Mexico	SSM	Anti	Died; SJR 8
97	New York	Civil Rights	Pro	Died in Senate; passed Assembly on 3/10; AB 2826
97	New York	Civil Rights	Pro	Died in Senate; SB 425
97	New York	Hate Crimes	Pro	Died in Senate; passed Assembly on 2/24; AB 1242
97	New York	Hate Crimes	Pro	Died; SB 572
97	New York	SSM	Anti	Died; AB 158
97	New York	SSM	Anti	Died; AB 4039
97	New York	SSM	Anti	Died; SB 1649
97	New York	Sodomy	Pro	Died; AB 4039
97	New York	Sodomy	Pro	Died; SB 2517
97	North Carolina	Civil Rights	Pro	Failed; HB 758
97	North Carolina	Civil Rights	Pro	Died; SB 632
97	North Carolina	Hate Crimes	Pro	Died; HB 1065
97	North Carolina	Sodomy	Pro	Died; SB 1050
97	North Dakota	Civil Rights	Pro	Passed; SCR 4036; study of discrimination issues
97	North Dakota	SSM	Anti	Passed; SB 2230; signed by Governor 3/25
97	Ohio	Hate Crimes	Pro	Died
97	Ohio	SSM	Anti	Died; HB 160
97	Oklahoma	Civil Rights	Pro	Unknown
97	Oregon	Civil Rights	Pro	Died in House committee; HB 2734
97	Oregon	Civil Rights	Pro	Died in Senate; passed House; HB 3719
97	Oregon	Civil Rights	Pro	Passed; SB 44; relating to transsexualism
97	Oregon	Civil Rights	Pro	Died in Senate; SB 1217
97	Oregon	SSM	Anti	Died; SJR 17
97	Oregon	SSM	Anti	Died; SB 577; passed Senate 20–7–3 on 5/22
97	Pennsylvania	Civil Rights	Pro	Died
97	Pennsylvania	Hate Crimes	Pro	Died; HB 730
97	Pennsylvania	Hate Crimes	Pro	Died; HB 731
97	Rhode Island	Civil Rights	Pro	Unknown
97	Rhode Island	Sodomy	Pro	Failed; HB 6160
97	Rhode Island	Hate Crimes	Pro	Died; HB 5261
97	Rhode Island	Hate Crimes	Pro	Died; HB 6265
97	Rhode Island	Hate Crimes	Pro	Died in Senate; passed House 69–2; HB 6610
97	Rhode Island	Hate Crimes	Pro	Died; SB 0747
97	Rhode Island	SSM	Anti	Failed in committee on 4/10 by 11–5; HB 5808
97	Rhode Island	SSM	Pro	Died; HB 5899

APPENDIX B

(continued)

Year	State	Policy	Pro- or Antigay	Status and Information
97	South Carolina	Hate Crimes	Pro	Died; SB 37
97	South Carolina	Hate Crimes	Pro	Died; SB 55
97	Texas	Civil Rights	Pro	Died; HB 487
97	Texas	Civil Rights	Pro	Died; HB 1519
97	Texas	Hate Crimes	Pro	Died; HB 1116
97	Texas	Hate Crimes	Pro	Failed; HB 2836
97	Texas	Hate Crimes	Pro	Died; SB 80
97	Texas	SSM	Anti	Died; HB 11
97	Texas	SSM	Anti	Failed; HB 3464 was stripped
97	Texas	SSM	Anti	Unconfirmed, SB 334
97	Texas	SSM	Anti	Died; SB 575
97	Utah	Sodomy	Pro	Died; HB 134; Rep. David Ure
97	Vermont	SSM	Anti	Carried over; HB 182
97	Vermont	SSM	Anti	Died; HB 351
97	Virginia	Civil Rights	Pro	Failed in Senate committee 9–2; SB 1079
97	Virginia	Hate Crimes	Pro	Died; HB 2639
	Virginia	Hate Crimes	Pro	Died; SB 1157
97	Virginia	Hate Crimes	Pro	Passed; HJR 561; establishes study panel
97	Virginia	SSM	Anti	Held; HB 1589; signed by Governor 3/15
97	Virginia	SSM	Anti	Passed; SB 884; signed by Governor 3/15
97	Virginia	Sodomy	Pro	Died; HB 2718
97	Washington	Civil Rights	Pro	Died; HB 1044
97	Washington	Civil Rights	Pro	Died; SB 5176
97	Washington	Civil Rights	Pro	Failed at ballot; Initiative 677
97	Washington	SSM	Anti	Failed, but carried over to 98; HB 1130
97	Washington	SSM	Anti	Failed; Governor vetoed; SB 5398
97	Washington	SSM	Anti	Died; SB 5400
97	Washington	SSM	Pro	Died; HB 1203
97	Washington	SSM	Pro	Died; SB 5346
97	West Virginia	Civil Rights	Pro	Died; HB 2505
97	West Virginia	Civil Rights	Pro	Failed; amendment in Senate Judiciary on 3/20
97	West Virginia	Hate Crimes	Pro	Died; HB 2481
97	West Virginia	SSM	Anti	Failed; part of HB 2865
97	West Virginia	SSM	Anti	Died; HB 2179
97	West Virginia	SSM	Anti	Died; SB 302
97	Wisconsin	SSM	Anti	Died in Senate; AB 104; passed House 78–20
97	Wisconsin	SSM	Pro	Died
97	Wyoming	Hate Crimes	Pro	Died; HB 92 or HB 193
97	Wyoming	SSM	Anti	Died; HB 94

APPENDIX B

(continued)

Year	State	Policy	Pro- or Antigay	Status and Information
1998	Alabama	SSM	Anti	Passed; HB 152; signed 5/1
98	Alabama	SSM	Anti	Died; SB 171; deferred to HB 152
98	Alaska	SSM	Anti	Passed; SJR 42; constitutional amendment
98	Arizona	Civil Rights	Pro	Died; HB 2392; passed one house
98	Arizona	Civil Rights	Pro	Died; HB 2394
98	Arizona	Civil Rights	Pro	Died; SB 1346
98	Arizona	Sodomy	Pro	Died; HB 2634; Rep. Winifred Hershberger
98	California	Civil Rights	Pro	Failed; AB 257; vetoed 10/10
98	California	Civil Rights	Pro	Died; AB 1842
98	California	Civil Rights	Pro	Failed; AB 2156; vetoed 9/13
98	California	Civil Rights	Anti	Died; SB 1910
98	California	Hate Crime	Pro	Passed; AB 1999; signed 9/29
98	California	Hate Crime	Pro	Died; AB 2324; passed Assembly
98	Colorado	Civil Rights	Pro	Died; HB 1270
98	Colorado	Hate Crimes	Pro	Died; HB 1268
98	Colorado	SSM	Anti	Withdrawn; HB 1248
98	Connecticut	Civil Rights	Pro	Passed; HB 5673
98	Delaware	Civil Rights	Pro	Died; HB 466
98	Georgia	Hate Crimes	Pro	Died; HB 842
98	Georgia	Sodomy	Pro	Died; SB 442
98	Hawaii	SSM	Anti	Passed; HB 117; placed on ballot
98	Hawaii	SSM	Anti	Passed; SB 1800; placed on ballot
98	Illinois	Civil Rights	Pro	Died; HR 495; passed House
98	Illinois	Civil Rights	Pro	Died; HB 1241
98	Illinois	Civil Rights	Pro	Died; HB 3636
98	Indiana	Hate Crimes	Pro	Died; SB 312
98	Iowa	Civil Rights	Pro	Died; HF 2103
98	Iowa	Civil Rights	Pro	Died; SF 2056; Sponsor Sen. Dvorsky
98	Iowa	Hate Crimes	Pro	Failed; language removed in House committee
98	Iowa	Hate Crimes	Pro	Died or withdrawn; Senate version
98	Iowa	SSM	Anti	Passed; HF 382; signed by Governor 4/15
98	Iowa	SSM	Anti	Passed; SF 2187
98	Kansas	SSM	Anti	Died; HB 2275
98	Kansas	SSM	Anti	Died; HB 2839
98	Kentucky	Hate Crimes	Anti	Died; HB 298
98	Kentucky	Hate Crimes	Pro	Passed; HB 455; signed by Governor 4/14
98	Kentucky	SSM	Anti	Died; HB 11; deferred to HB 13
98	Kentucky	SSM	Anti	Passed; HB 13; signed by Governor 4/2
98	Maine	Civil Rights	Anti	Passed; ballot initiative; repeal

APPENDIX B

(continued)

Year	State	Policy	Pro- or Antigay	Status and Information
98	Maryland	Civil Rights	Pro	Died; HB 68
98	Maryland	Civil Rights	Pro	Died; HB 835; passed House 98–21
98	Maryland	SSM	Pro	Failed; HB 1259; in committee
98	Maryland	SSM	Anti	Failed in House; SB 565; passed Senate
98	Maryland	Sodomy	Pro	Died; Sponsor: Del. John S. Arnick, D–7
98	Michigan	Civil Rights	Pro	Died; HB 5959
98	Michigan	Hate Crimes	Pro	Died; HB 4674
98	Minnesota	SSM	Pro	Died; HF 3773
98	Missouri	Civil Rights	Pro	Died; HB 1719; died in committee
98	Missouri	Sodomy	Pro	Died; HB 1760; died in committee
98	Nebraska	Civil Rights	Pro	Died; LB 869
98	Nebraska	SSM	Anti	Died; LB 280; held from 1997
98	New Hampshire	Civil Rights	Pro	Held; HB 1580
98	New Jersey	SSM	Anti	Died; AB 706
98	New Jersey	SSM	Anti	Died; SB 1281
98	New Mexico	SSM	Anti	Died; SJR 4
98	New York	Civil Rights	Pro	Died; AB 2061
98	New York	Civil Rights	Pro	Died; AB 2826; passed Assembly 87–53
98	New York	Civil Rights	Pro	Died; SB 294
98	New York	Civil Rights	Pro	Died; SB 425-B
98	New York	Hate Crimes	Pro	Died; AB 1242
98	New York	Hate Crimes	Pro	Died; SB 572
98	New York	Hate Crimes	Pro	Died; SB 3427
98	New York	SSM	Anti	Died; AB 158
98	New York	SSM	Anti	Died; SB 1649
98	New York	Sodomy	Pro	Died; AB 4039
98	New York	Sodomy	Pro	Died; SB 2517
98	Ohio	Hate Crimes	Pro	Died; HB 260
98	Ohio	SSM	Anti	Died; HB 160; held from 1997
98	Pennsylvania	Civil Rights	Pro	Died; House version
98	Pennsylvania	Civil Rights	Pro	Died; Senate version
98	Pennsylvania	Hate Crimes	Pro	Died; HB 730; Rep. Cohen
98	Pennsylvania	Hate Crimes	Pro	Died; HB 731; Rep. Cohen
98	Pennsylvania	Hate Crimes	Pro	Died; SB 417; Senator Heckler
98	Rhode Island	Hate Crimes	Pro	Died; HB 7358; passed House
98	Rhode Island	Hate Crimes	Pro	Passed; SB 2025
98	Rhode Island	SSM	Pro	Died; HB 7994
98	Rhode Island	Sodomy	Pro	Passed; HB 7585; signed 6/5
98	Vermont	SSM	Anti	Died; HB 182; from 97 session
98	Virginia	Civil Rights	Pro	Died
98	Virginia	Hate Crimes	Pro	Died; HB 310
98	Virginia	Hate Crimes	Pro	Died; HB 311; Del. James F. Almand
98	Virginia	Hate Crimes	Pro	Died; SB 159

APPENDIX B

(continued)

Year	State	Policy	Pro- or Antigay	Status and Information
98	Virginia	Sodomy	Pro	Died; HB 882; Del. Karen L. Darner
98	Virginia	Sodomy	Pro	Died; SB 583
98	Washington	Civil Rights	Anti	Failed; HB 1043; vetoed
98	Washington	SSM	Anti	Passed; HB 1130; veto override
98	Washington	SSM	Anti	Held; SB 5400
98	West Virginia	Civil Rights	Pro	Died; HB 2505
98	West Virginia	Hate Crimes	Pro	Died; HB 2481
98	West Virginia	SSM	Anti	Died; HB or SB 247
98	West Virginia	SSM	Anti	Died in conference; HB 4469; amendment
98	West Virginia	SSM	Anti	Died; SB 50
98	Wisconsin	SSM	Anti	Died; AB 104; held from 1997
98	Wyoming	Hate Crimes	Pro	Failed; SF 34; failed 2/3 vote
Pending as of 8/99:				
99	Alabama	Hate Crimes	Pro	Failed; HB 14; 3/2/99; Rep. Alvin Holmes
99	Arizona	SSM	Anti	Died; HB 2524
99	Arizona	Sodomy/Family	Pro	Failed; 3 House amendments to SB 1396
99	Arizona	DP	Anti	Died; HB 2524; ban local DP benefits
99	Arizona	DP	Anti	Died
99	Arizona	Schools	Anti	Died
99	Arkansas	Hate Crimes	Pro	Died
99	California	Civil Rights	Pro	Failed; AB 222; Kuehl; education; 40–38
99	California	Civil Rights	Pro	?; AB 1001; Speaker Villaraigosa; Assembly 42–36
99	California	Civil Rights	Pro	?; AB 1541; Fred Keeley, D-Boulder Creek
99	California	Civil Rights	Pro	?; AB 1652; Committee on Labor and Employment
99	California	Civil Rights	Pro	?; SB 513; Richard Alarcon, D-N. Hollywood
99	California	Civil Rights	Pro	?; SB 1237; Martha Escutia, D-Whittier
99	California	Hate Crimes	Pro	?; AB 208; Knox; Assembly 56–19 on 6/2
99	California	Hate Crimes	Pro	?; SB 850; Tom Hayden, D-Santa Monica
99	California	DP Benefits	Pro	Passed; Rule change 13–6; only applies to Legislature
99	California	DP Registry	Pro	?; AB 26; Migden; Assembly 41–32
99	California	DP Benefits	Pro	?; AB 107; Wally Knox; passed Assembly
99	California	DP; taxes	Pro	?; AB 901; Wally Knox, D-Los Angeles

APPENDIX B

(continued)

Year	State	Policy	Pro- or Antigay	Status and Information
99	California	DP Registry	Pro	?; SB 75; Kevin Murray; Senate 23–14 5/25
99	California	DP; leave	Pro	?; SB 118; Tom Hayden, D-Santa Monica
99	California	DP	Pro	?; SB 563; domestic violence
99	Colorado	Civil Rights	Pro	Failed on floor; HB 1245; Gloria Leyba, D-Denver
99	Colorado	Hate Crimes	Pro	Failed; HB 1074; House 32–32; Rep. Tate
99	Colorado	Hate Crimes	Pro	Failed; SB 49 or 99
99	Colorado	SSM	Anti	Failed in committee 6–7; SB 159; Musgrave
99	Connecticut	Civil Rights	Pro	?; HB 1219
99	Connecticut	Civil Rights	Pro	?; HB 1299; telecommunications
99	Connecticut	Civil Rights	Pro	?; HB 5483; education
99	Connecticut	Civil Rights	Pro	?; HB 5811; polygraph
99	Connecticut	Civil Rights	Pro	?; HB 6970; insurance
99	Connecticut	Hate Crimes	Pro	Died
99	Connecticut	SSM ban	Anti	Died; Amend to HB 5966; House
99	Delaware	Civil Rights	Pro	Failed; HB 10; House killed 18–15.
99	Florida	Hate Crimes	Pro	?
99	Florida	DP, Reg. & Ben.	Pro	?; Rep. Tracy Stafford, D-Wilton Manors
99	Florida	DP, Reg. & Ben.	Pro	?; SB 2484; Sen. Daryl Jones, D-Miami
99	Georgia	Hate Crimes	Pro	Died; SB 153; Judiciary Committee
99	Hawaii	Civil Rights	Pro	Held; HB 1163; public accommodations
99	Hawaii	Civil Rights	Pro	Held; HB 1643
99	Hawaii	Civil Rights	Pro	Held; SB 1151; Senate 15–9; public accommodations
99	Hawaii	Civil Rights	Pro	Held; SB 1187; education
99	Hawaii	Civil Rights	Pro	Held; SB 1587
99	Hawaii	Hate Crimes	Pro	Died; HB 289; provide civil action
99	Hawaii	Hate Crimes	Pro	Died; HB 385
99	Hawaii	Hate Crimes	Pro	Died; HB 744; establishes a task force
99	Hawaii	Hate Crimes	Pro	Died; HB 777; defines hate crimes
99	Hawaii	Hate Crimes	Pro	Died; HB 1657; establishes a temporary commission
99	Hawaii	Hate Crimes	Pro	Died; SB 387
99	Hawaii	Hate Crimes	Pro	Failed; SB 605; Senate 25–0 on 3/10; civil action
99	Hawaii	Hate Crimes	Pro	Died; SB 1552; establishes a temporary commission
99	Hawaii	SSM	Pro	Died; HB 717
99	Hawaii	SSM	Anti	Died; HB 775

APPENDIX B

(continued)

Year	State	Policy	Pro- or Antigay	Status and Information
99	Hawaii	SSM	Anti	Died; SB 321
99	Idaho	Hate Crimes	Pro	Failed; HB 36; House State Affairs Committee
99	Illinois	Civil Rights	Pro	Failed; HB 474; House killed 57–59
99	Indiana	Hate Crimes	Pro	Failed in House 44 to 49; HB 1183; Rep. Crawford
99	Indiana	Hate Crimes	Pro	Died in Senate
99	Indiana	Hate Crimes	Pro	Died in Senate
99	Indiana	Hate Crimes	Pro	Died in Senate
99	Indiana	Hate Crimes	Pro	Died in Senate
99	Indiana	Hate Crimes	Pro	Died in Senate
99	Iowa	Civil Rights	Pro	Held; HB
99	Iowa	Civil Rights	Pro	Held; SB
99	Kansas	Hate Crimes	Pro	Died
99	Louisiana	Civil Rights	Pro	Died; SB 999; Irons; employment
99	Louisiana	Civil Rights	Pro	Failed; HB 1917; Schwegmann; employment
99	Louisiana	SSM ban	Anti	Died
99	Maine	Civil Rights	Pro	?
99	Maine	Civil Rights	Pro	?
99	Maine	Civil Rights	Pro	?
99	Maine	Civil Rights	Pro	?
99	Maine	Civil Rights	Pro	?
99	Maine	Civil Rights	Pro	?
99	Maine	Civil Rights	Pro	Held; LD 2239; intro 5/99; would go to ballot
99	Maryland	Civil Rights	Pro	Died; HB 315; passed House 80 to 56
99	Maryland	Civil Rights	Pro	Died; SB 138
99	Maryland	Hate Crimes	Pro	Died; HB 92
99	Maryland	Hate Crimes	Pro	Died; HB 969; passed House 111–23–7 on 3/28
99	Maryland	Hate Crimes	Pro	Died; SB 139
99	Maryland	SSM	Anti	Died
99	Massachusetts	Civil Rights	Pro	?
99	Massachusetts	SSM	Anti	?; HB 472; Rep. John Waters, D-Norwood
99	Massachusetts	SSM	Pro	?; HB 3886; Freedom of Marriage Act
99	Massachusetts	Sodomy	Pro	?; HB 3885
99	Michigan	Civil Rights	Anti	?
99	Michigan	Hate Crimes	Pro	?; Lynne Martinez (D-Lansing)
99	Minnesota	Civil Rights	Anti	Died; amendment to repeal; not added yet
99	Minnesota	Hate Crimes	Pro	Died
99	Minnesota	Sodomy	Pro	?
99	Mississippi	Civil Rights	Anti	Died

APPENDIX B

(continued)

Year	State	Policy	Pro- or Antigay	Status and Information
99	Mississippi	Hate Crimes	Pro	Died
99	Mississippi	SSM	Anti	Died; constitutional amendment
99	Missouri	Civil Rights	Pro	Died
99	Missouri	Hate Crimes	Pro	Died; amend to omnibus crime bill; House passed
99	Missouri	Hate Crimes	Pro	Passed; SB 328; Senate 20–14 on 4/20; House 85–68
99	Missouri	Hate Crimes	Pro	Died; House amend to SB 335; House 88–57
99	Missouri	SSM	Anti	Died; SB 266; Klarich; Passed Senate 3/1/99
99	Missouri	Sodomy	Pro	Died; amendment by Rep. Wilson (D-Columbia)
99	Missouri	Sodomy	Anti	Died; HB 850/851; passed House 139–6
99	Montana	Civil Rights	Pro	Died; SB 328; Sen. Jon Ellingson, D-Missoula
99	Montana	Hate Crimes	Pro	Failed; SB 66; killed in Senate
99	Montana	Hate Crimes	Anti	Died; SB 213; Sen. Lorents Grosfield, R-Big Timber
99	Montana	Sodomy	Pro	Failed; HB 499
99	Nebraska	Civil Rights	Anti	Died
99	Nebraska	Civil Rights	Pro	Died; LB 69; Sen. Chambers
99	Nebraska	SSM	Anti	Died; LB 513; Sen. Jim Jones of Eddyville
99	Nevada	Civil Rights	Pro	Passed; AB 311; Parks; Assembly 30–11; Senate 13–8
99	Nevada	Hate Crimes	Pro	?; AB 53; 3/2 passed Assembly 40–0–2
99	New Hampshire	Civil Rights	Pro	Held over
99	New Hampshire	Hate Crimes	Pro	Passed; strengthens existing law
99	New Jersey	SSM	Anti	AB 706; carried over from 1998
99 998	New Jersey	SSM	Anti	SB 1281; carried over from 1
99	New Mexico	Civil Rights	Pro	Died
99	New Mexico	Hate Crimes	Pro	Failed; vetoed; SB 63; Senate 26–12; House 39–28
99	New Mexico	Hate Crimes	Pro	Died; Senate amendment to Gangs bill; passed 24–14
99	New Mexico	SSM	Anti	Died; constitutional amendment
99	New Mexico	SSM	Anti	Died
99	New Mexico	SSM	Anti	Died; SB 186
99	New York	Civil Rights	Pro	?; AB ; Assembly passed 105–43 on 3/26
99	New York	Civil Rights	Pro	?; SB 425-A
99	New York	Hate Crimes	Pro	?; AB 5405; passed Assembly 113–31

(continued)

Year	State	Policy	Pro- or Antigay	Status and Information
99	New York	Hate Crimes	Pro	?; AB 3427; penalty enhancement
99	New York	Hate Crimes	Pro	Died; Tom Duane?
99	New York	Hate Crimes	Pro	?; SB 1038
99	New York	Hate Crimes	Pro	?; SB 4691
99	New York	SSM	Anti	AB 594; Seminerio; to Judiciary
99	New York	Sodomy	Pro	?; passed Senate
99	North Carolina	Civil Rights	Pro	?; SB 844; local for Orange County; Senate passed
99	North Carolina	Hate Crimes	Pro	Failed; HB ; Insko; House 36–67; local; Orange
99	North Carolina	Hate Crimes	Pro	Failed; HB 884; Matthew Shepard Memorial Act
99	North Carolina	Hate Crimes	Pro	Died; SB 814; Matthew Shepard Memorial Act
99	North Carolina	Sodomy	Pro	Died; SB 759; Sen. Ellie Kinnard, D-Orange
99	Ohio	Civil Rights	Anti	Executive Order; rewrote discrimination EO
99	Ohio	Hate Crimes	Pro	?
99	Oklahoma	Hate Crimes	Pro	Died; provision withdrawn; HB 1211 or 1711
99	Oregon	Civil Rights	Anti	Died; HJR 5; constitutional amendment
99	Oregon	Civil Rights	Anti	Died; HJR 6; constitutional amendment
99	Oregon	Civil Rights	Anti	Died; HJR 36; ban local laws; goes to ballot
99	Oregon	SSM	Anti	Failed; HJR 4; House 32–26–2; S 13–16
99	Oregon	SSM &DP	Anti	Died; HJR 29; constitutional amendment; goes to ballot
99	Pennsylvania	Civil Rights	Pro	?; HB 17; access to library services
99	Pennsylvania	Hate Crimes	Pro	?; HB 44; Rep. Lita I. Cohen
99	Pennsylvania	Hate Crimes	Pro	?; HB 45; Rep. Lita I. Cohen
99	Pennsylvania	Hate Crimes	Pro	?; SB 343; Sen. Wagner
99	Pennsylvania	DP ban	Anti	Failed; amend to SB 652; Egoff; House 194–5
99	Rhode Island	Civil Rights	Pro	?
99	Rhode Island	SSM	Pro	?
99	Rhode Island	DP related	Pro	?; HB 5618l; Pisaturo; funeral plans
99	South Carolina	Civil Rights	Anti	Died
99	South Carolina	Hate Crimes	Pro	Died; HB 3161; Rep. Doug Jennings, D-Marlboro
99	South Carolina	Hate Crimes	Pro	Failed; SB 45; passed Senate; Penalty Enhancement

APPENDIX B

(continued)

Year	State	Policy	Pro- or Antigay	Status and Information
99	Tennessee	Hate Crimes	Pro	Died; HB 1067; Rep. Brown (D-Chattanooga)
99	Tennessee	Hate Crimes	Pro	Died; HB 989; Rep. Jere Hargrove (D-Cookeville)
99	Tennessee	Hate Crimes	Pro	Died; SB 897; Senator Bob Rochelle (D-Lebanon)
99	Tennessee	Hate Crimes	Pro	Died; SB 803; Senator Steve Cohen (D-Memphis)
99	Texas	Civil Rights	Pro	Died; HB 363; education; Rep. Harryette Ehrhardt
99	Texas	Civil Rights	Pro	Died; HB 364; education; Rep. Harryette Ehrhardt
99	Texas	Civil Rights	Pro	Died; HB 475; Representative Glen Maxey
99	Texas	Hate Crimes	Pro	Died; HB 148; Senfronia Thompson
99	Texas	Hate Crimes	Pro	Died; HB 281; Representative Scott Hochberg
99	Texas	Hate Crimes	Pro	Died; HB 938; James Byrd Jr. Act; House 83–61
99	Texas	Hate Crimes	Pro	Died; SB
99	Texas	SSM	Anti	Died; HB 383; Chisum; to State Affairs
99	Texas	Sodomy	Pro	Died; HB 337; Rep. Debra Danburg
99	Texas	Sodomy	Pro	Died
99	Utah	Hate Crimes	Pro	Failed; Sen. Pete Suazo; Senate committee
99	Vermont	Civil Rights	Pro	Held
99	Vermont	Hate Crimes	Pro	Died; HB 214; allow civil action
99	Vermont	Hate Crimes	Pro	Passed; SB 45; all voice vote; allow civil action
99	Vermont	SSM	Anti	Died; HB 479
99	Virginia	Civil Rights	Pro	Died; HB 2718 General Laws Committee
99	Virginia	Civil Rights	Pro	Died; SB 1121
99	Virginia	Hate Crimes	Pro	?; HB 1625; adds sexual orientation
99	Virginia	Hate Crimes	Pro	?; HB 2376; terroristic acts
99	Virginia	Hate Crimes	Pro	?; SB 890; adds sexual orientation and gender
99	Virginia	Sodomy	Pro	?; HB 1504
99	Virginia	Sodomy	Pro	?; HB 2715
99	Virginia	Sodomy	Pro	?; SB 1120
99	Washington	Civil Rights	Pro	Held
99	Washington	Schools	Pro	Died; HB 1765, Rep. Ed Murray (D-Seattle)
99	Washington	Schools	Pro	Died; amend to Education bill; Murray withdrew

APPENDIX B

(continued)

Year	State	Policy	Pro- or Antigay	Status and Information
99	West Virginia	Civil Rights	Pro	Died
99	West Virginia	Hate Crimes	Pro	Died
99	West Virginia	SSM	Anti	Died; HB 2036; Darmon; to Judiciary
99	Wyoming	Hate Crimes	Pro	Died; HB 117; Nicholas
99	Wyoming	Hate Crimes	Pro	Failed; HB 132; Failed on House floor
99	Wyoming	Hate Crimes	Pro	Died; HB 206; Nicholas
99	Wyoming	Hate Crimes	Pro	Died; HB 215; murder only
99	Wyoming	Hate Crimes	Pro	Died
99	Wyoming	Hate Crimes	Pro	Failed; SF 84; enhanced penalties
99	Wyoming	Hate Crimes	Pro	Failed; SF 91; enhanced penalties

NOTES: Compiled by the author from news sources, state legislatures, the National Gay and Lesbian Task Force, and state lesbian and gay groups; SSM = same-sex marriage.

14

GAY AND LESBIAN ISSUES IN THE CONGRESSIONAL ARENA

Colton C. Campbell and Roger H. Davidson

Since the 1969 Stonewall riots in Greenwich Village, gay and lesbian rights have moved from the margins of the political agenda to a more central place in the congressional arena.[1] Gays and lesbians have the potential resources to wield influence, if not necessarily to prevail, on Capitol Hill. These resources include a substantial popular base spread throughout the country but with concentrations in major coastal cities and other urban areas (Hertzog 1996). In recent years "lavender" voters have begun to acquire electoral clout both through votes and through financial contributions, which are key ingredients in gaining access to lawmakers and key congressional staffers (Langbein and Lotwis 1990).

Lesbian and gay political organizations, like the Human Rights Campaign and the Log Cabin Republicans, have become increasingly professional in both organization and political strategy (Thomas 1996; Haider-Markel 1997; see chapter 3). They are engaging in more "inside" lobbying, channeling their efforts through formal decision-making processes within Congress. This includes testifying before committees or subcommittees to place their groups' positions on the record and communicating directly with legislators or their personal staff to promote points of view. Additionally, these groups have adopted newer forms of persuasion such as mounting computer-based campaigns to mobilize grassroots support or bundling campaign contributions for gay candidates. In many instances, lesbian and gay political organizations have begun to employ major public relations efforts in the press to shape public and congressional opinion on gay rights. Yet for every victory these groups attain, subsequent defeats follow, and lesbian and gay groups spend much of their time attempting to block antigay legislation (Haider-Markel 1997).

EARLY POLITICS: THE CONGRESSIONAL CLOSET

For many years sexual politics were limited to those very few lawmakers (and staff members) who were themselves "out of the closet" or who signed on to the issue because of concentrated populations within their electoral districts (Pressman 1983). Before 1998, no openly gay candidate had ever been elected to Congress. The first openly gay members to serve in the House—Representatives Barney Frank (D-Mass.) and Jim Kolbe (R-Ariz.), and former Representatives Robert Baumann (R-Md.), Steve Gunderson (R-Wis.), and Gerry E. Studds (D-Mass.)—either revealed their sexual orientation or were outed after they were in office. In 1998, Tammy Baldwin (D-Wis.), a lesbian, became the first person whose sexuality was well known before her initial election. Her campaign slogan: "A Different Kind of Candidate."

During the 1950s gays and lesbians were victimized by concerns over national security and moral purity (Lewis 1997). In committee hearings legislators routinely questioned federal officials about the employment of homosexuals, characterizing them as moral perverts who endangered national security. The Senate Subcommittee on Investigations recommended that all homosexual civil servants be dismissed as security risks. Many senators denounced "the false premise that what a Government employee did outside of the office on his own time, particularly if his actions did not involve his fellow employees or his work, was his own business" (Senate 1950, 10).

The Senate offered two closely linked arguments to support its conclusion that homosexuals should be excluded from government service. The first pertained to the "character" of homosexuals, who allegedly lacked "emotional stability" and whose "moral fiber" had been weakened by sexual indulgence. The second rationale for exclusion concerned the danger of blackmail which, legislators contended, made homosexuals likely candidates for treasonable activity.

As for gay rights, which entered the agenda in the 1970s Congress traditionally turned aside these issues, under whatever rubric. Measures addressing such issues tended to be introduced toward the end of a legislative session to enable Congress to adjourn without passing or even debating them, or in nonelection years to minimize expected voter backlash (Pressman 1983). At most, Congress engaged in symbolic acts—that is, expressing an attitude of toleration but endorsing no proactive policies, or prescribing policy goals but neglecting to follow through on them. Throughout the 1980s, for example, lawmakers funded AIDS research, education, and prevention activities before they addressed the policy questions involved in trying to slow the spread of the epidemic (Rovner 1987). This afforded members an opportunity to "do something" about AIDS while avoiding the politically profound policy issues surrounding the disease. Such congressional ambivalence toward gay activism reflected the general public's attitudes on the subject; as gay rights became more widely and openly discussed, the issue moved toward a more conspicuous place in the legislative agenda.

Contemporary lawmakers appear more sympathetic to gay rights than were their predecessors. At least anecdotally, this more benign environment provides more access points and potential influence for gay and lesbian organizations. Whereas in the past such groups would achieve influence on Capitol Hill by discreetly lobbying lawmakers with whom they enjoyed proven working relationships and the strongest constituency support, today they can "find an audience or get a meeting almost when or wherever," according to the political director of the Human Rights Campaign, the nation's largest gay rights group.[2] And yet the measurable level of progay support in Congress has declined over the past ten years, partly the result of a backlash created by opposition groups such as the Christian Coalition (Haider-Markel 1997).

As gay rights issues and family-oriented lobbies began to be subsumed within the agenda of the civil rights movement, Congress started to address and frame various types of law reform initiatives, entailing a variety of strategies (Herman 1994; Newton 1994). Stated differently, as the gay movement matured, a branch of the movement increasingly created formal organizations, centered its attention on national institutions, and sought legal policy reform rather than cultural transformation (Haider-Markel 1997). Among these issues have been AIDS research; amending existing antidiscriminatory legislation to include "sexual orientation" grounds to protect jobs and housing or to demand various social benefits currently restricted to heterosexual couples or families; and reforming legislative definitions of "spouse" to embrace gay and lesbian identity within state welfare and tax statutes.

Of the ten thousand or so bills introduced in each Congress, a preliminary search of the workload for the years 1975 through 1999 (94th through

105th Congresses) suggests that in each Congress only a very small proportion of bills—ten to twenty—dealt overtly with gay rights. Hardly any were reported out of committee, much less debated on the floor. These measures were generally worded for or against gay rights: prohibiting employment or housing discrimination on the basis of affectional or sexual orientation; providing civil claims for homosexuals; guaranteeing confidential AIDS testing; setting policy toward gays in the military; prohibiting the use of funds to promote or encourage homosexuality; and allowing organizations in to exclude homosexuals from certain programs and activities involving juveniles.

The preponderance of these bills appear to have been antigay in intent. Haider-Markel's 1997 examination of congressional votes on gay-related issues from the 95th to 104th Congresses reveals similar findings. Other bills would have had an impact, even though they did not overtly deal with gay concerns. These included: proposals for amending the Legal Services Corporation Act to prohibit expenditure of funds to defend or protect homosexuality and gay rights; repealing sections of the Immigration and Nationality Act that restrict homosexuals; and substituting the terms "homosexuality or heterosexuality" for "sexual orientation" as a category for which data are collected on crimes based on prejudice. In some cases, concurrent resolutions have been introduced expressing the sense of Congress that homosexual acts and the individuals who advocate such "conduct" should be denied special consideration or protected status under law.

The first federal legislation to protect homosexuals from discrimination was not introduced until 1974. Comparable measures have been introduced in every subsequent legislative session, but only one has been reported out of committee (Thompson 1994). A limited version of the bill, applying only to employment discrimination, finally reached the Senate floor for a vote in 1996.

After the Republican takeover of the House and Senate, a conservative-led movement fueled by antipathy toward gay rights twice in 1996 set back the legislative gains of gay rights supporters (Wald, Button, and Rienzo 1996). By a lopsided margin, Congress overwhelmingly approved the Defense of Marriage Act, which defines the institution of marriage, authorizes states to disregard same-sex marriages licensed in other states, and denies spousal benefits to same-sex couples. Within a whisper of victory the Senate also narrowly defeated a bill to prohibit antidiscrimination in the workplace, the Employment NonDiscrimination Act (ENDA), which would have prevented employers from firing people based on their sexual orientation.

Yet the bill was crafted to appeal to moderates: it intended to exempt the military, small businesses, and nonprofit religious organizations.

CONGRESS FACES UP TO AIDS

President Reagan initially addressed some of the concerns of gay rights organizations by convening two special commissions on AIDS: the Presidential Commission on the Human Immunodeficiency Virus Epidemic (chaired by retired Admiral James D. Watkins) and the National Commission on AIDS (chaired by June Osborn). The commissions were charged with providing the executive branch with recommendations regarding certain aspects of AIDS policy. Leaders of the AIDS community had expressed outrage at how unqualified and biased most of the Reagan commissions' appointees were, almost all of whom favored mandatory testing for the AIDS virus—a measure overwhelmingly opposed by public officials and by the National Academy of Sciences Panel on AIDS as raising serious ethical and practical problems. Charged Jeffrey Levi, then-executive director of the National Gay and Lesbian Task Force, "They don't have the expertise. . . . [T]he commission should be addressing the policies the government can implement to deal with the epidemic" (Marwick 1988, 169). The presidential commissions were regarded by many in the gay community as dilatory and lethargic, reflecting the Reagan administration's less than assertive attitude toward the disease.

In any event, the president refused to endorse his commissions' final reports, declining to comment. Instead, he directed his drug-abuse advisor, Dr. Donald Ian Macdonald, to review, report, and make recommendations for policy implementation. Macdonald stressed that more than 40 percent of the commissions' 340 recommendations pertaining to the federal government were already being implemented, with another 30 percent to be included in the administration's fiscal 1990 budget request (*CQ Almanac* 1988, 301).

The Reagan plan directed the Food and Drug Administration to take steps to protect the nation's blood supply and instructed the secretary of health and human services to conduct a study of the current system of health care financing and to seek ways to promote out-of-hospital care for AIDS patients. The plan also ordered all federal agencies to adopt AIDS policies based on guidelines to be issued by the Office of Personnel Management. Those guidelines directed federal managers to treat employees with AIDS the same as workers with any other serious illness, and allowed managers to discipline workers who refused to work with those with AIDS.

But Reagan did not issue an executive order to implement the OPM guidelines. Instead, the administration announced that individual directives to each agency would have the same force of law.

This announcement met with ridicule and cynicism from many people throughout the country. Upset by the lack of leadership from the White House, gay rights organizations—following Schattschneider's dictum (1975)—expanded the scope of conflict by turning to the congressional arena.

Congress Creates a Commission

Congress approached the enormity of the AIDS problem in a way not much different than the general public's struggle to understand the illness. Members were initially wary of public opinion about AIDS, leaving it to sympathetic advocates to take the lead in promoting AIDS legislation. In this early period of denial, lawmakers did not see AIDS as a pressing issue. In the second stage members began to recognize the deadly nature of the virus and the broad array of problems and responses that it produced; they sensed that something coherent would have to be done about it. Eventually, a majority in Congress conceded the seriousness of the problems but also recognized that there would be no quick fixes, given the immense technical complexity of the disease (Rovner 1987). According to Representative Barney Frank (D-Mass.), once the dimensions of the AIDS epidemic became known, many representatives "started voting progay because they saw that life-and-death issues were at stake. They had to do the right thing, even though they thought it might hurt them politically" (Schmalz 1992).

Because the majority of initial cases of AIDS in this country were concentrated in the gay community and among intravenous drug abusers, and the early public image of the virus was linked to homosexual men, the disease was known popularly as "GRID" or "gay-related immune deficiency" (Altman 1987). Gays as a group were often perceived as politically irrelevant, largely because they were not seen as a voting constituency capable of swinging a district one way or the other. Indeed, many lawmakers sensed certain political liabilities in the issue and viewed avoidance or denial as the safest course. This accounted in part for the early lack of frank discussion about the epidemic (Dejowski 1989), as well as the timid support in Congress. Lawmakers spent more time debating whether AIDS was an appropriate topic for the political arena than they did about how to deal with the epidemic (Rovner 1987, 2986). Representative Sander M. Levin (D-Mich.) speculated that some of his colleagues were uncomfortable about debating issues such as sex, illegal drug use, and death—all of which are part and parcel of the AIDS epidemic: "I think there's an understandable human tendency to push this aside, to hope it doesn't affect us" (Rovner 1987, 2986).

The characterization of AIDS as being a gay disease was weakened, however, as it became clearer that there was no inherent or necessary connection between AIDS and homosexuality, and that other groups were (and are) equally at risk to the virus (Altman 1986; Watney 1987).[3] (Scientists discovered this when people with hemophilia began getting AIDS, indicating that HIV was caused by a blood-borne infection agent.) This proved an impetus for "de-gaying" the issue, gradually converting Congress's dithering to a more proactive concern. Senator Edward M. Kennedy (D-Mass.), who chaired the Senate Committee on Labor and Human Resources, described this broadened interest: "Recognizing that AIDS and the HIV epidemic has now reached every one of the fifty states and into the territories and possessions of the U.S., the Committee believes that a new and concerted national effort is required to mobilize the resources of this nation to overcome the menace that AIDS poses to the American people and to all future generations" (Senate 1987, 3).

Although the AIDS epidemic had been an urgent public health concern of the nation's medical community for several years, Congress found itself ill-equipped to address the problem. First, few if any members of Congress or their staff aides were in fact knowledgeable about the AIDS virus and the problems associated with it. The vast number of people working on Capitol Hill are generalists, not specialists. Noting that only one member in the House had any medical background (Representative Roy Rowland (R-Ga.)), Representative James Scheuer (D-N.Y.) asserted that a void in expertise and technical certainty with AIDS was impeding legislative action. Conservative Representative Dan Burton (R-Ind.) admitted as much during a House floor debate: "You know, we have 435 Members of this body and 100 Members of the other body. I will tell you from personal conversations with many of them, they are not very conversant with the problems we are facing with AIDS" (*Cong. Rec.* 1987, H22247).

This uncertainty confined early discussion about legislation to generalities instead of specific issues. In 1987, lacking the information and the technical competence to deal with the scientific matters of AIDS legislatively and hampered by its jurisdiction and procedures, the House approved its own fifteen-member commission to study and make policy recommendations regarding all aspects of the AIDS epidemic. The measure,

H.R. 2881, which had eighty-four cosponsors (many of whom were avowed conservatives such as Dan Burton, Robert Dornan of California, and Newt Gingrich of Georgia), and which passed 355–68, was viewed as an alternative technique to satisfy the demand for public policy toward this rapidly spreading disease. Mindful that most policies entail both costs and benefits, and apprehensive that those bearing the costs will hold them responsible, members of Congress often find that the most attractive option is to let someone else make the tough choices. This allows legislators—especially those aiming for reelection—to vote for the general benefit of something without ever having to support a plan that directly imposes large and traceable costs on their constituents or to shift blame for any negative side effects to sensitive issues (Campbell 1996). Thus, the Commission became a device to legitimize congressional action on a distasteful subject.

The idea of the National Commission on AIDS also originated in response to the need felt by gay rights organizations, scientists, and members of Congress for a better governmental device to handle the unprecedented problem (House 1989). Assigning responsibility to a commission of experts seemed more promising than delegating the problem to the executive departments (who by their own admission were incapable of mounting a rapid response to the epidemic) or to Congress's deliberative and political nature, which could not keep pace either.

From the viewpoint of gay rights organizations, a congressional commission would provide a more impartial and bipartisan result than the discredited presidential commission. For Congress, the commission would acquire an understanding of the uniquely complex problems associated with AIDS and its relationship to the human immunodeficiency virus (HIV) without expending an inordinate amount of legislative resources. Representative G.V. (Sonny) Montgomery (D-Miss.), chair of the House Committee on Veterans' Affairs, summarized the merits of a broad-based, knowledgeable, and impartial panel:

> While it is inevitable that the ultimate decision whether or not to implement some of the Commission's recommendations may be based on political factors not considered by the Commission, the Committee believes that the Commission should not conduct itself as a political body. Its analysis and conclusions should be guided by the highest ideals and concern for the persons who are affected by AIDS; its recommendations should not be tempered by a fear of a backlash of public opinion regarding its recommendations. (House 1989, 9)

Consensus among lawmakers on the best approach to treatment, research, education, and prevention was an essential element of effective national policy that was politically too difficult to achieve through normal legislative channels. The commission process was a step toward accommodating this assignment. "It is the hope of the Committee that the Commission serve as a forum for the development of coordinating and consolidating a national consensus for a comprehensive national policy, mapping citizens' preferences and potential choices for the various policy proposals put forth in Congress," the Senate Labor and Human Resources Committee declared subsequently (Senate 1989, 4).

The Commission on AIDS was not without its critics, although they were vastly outnumbered. Cynics scornfully noted that Congress already had available access to extensive expertise on the issue. "We already have a commission in existence to deal with communicable diseases in America," charged Representative William E. Dannemeyer (*Cong. Rec.* 1987, H22243). "It is called the Public Health Services." "Nobody has a monopoly on this. Nobody is omnipotent," answered Representative Burton (H22246). "You know, when we talk about fighting AIDS and looking for a scientific solution to this, we do not ask just one scientific body to do research. We try to get as many well-qualified scientists as we can possible find to research this virus. Policy debate between various commissions may be very healthy and good for coming up with a solution to the policy problem."

Another snag during debate came when a few members objected that the bill had no legislative history and was being rushed through the House, bypassing subcommittees and full committees, without witnesses to testify to the legislative need, the reasons for the commission, or the committee reports. "Would the members believe that the subcommittee of jurisdiction did not even consider this legislation at any time?" charged Representative Dannemeyer (H22242). "If I did not know any better, I would suspect that we were attempting to just railroad this piece of legislation through the House." Other opponents heaped scorn on the fast-tracking. Representative Howard C. Nielson (R-Utah) claimed that the Subcommittee on Health and the Environment had been bypassed by the full Committee on Energy and Commerce and no hearings had been held (H22244). "There have been hearings on this legislation . . . during which our Members discussed extensively the need for this legislation," countered Representative Montgomery (H22245). "The Committee on Energy and Commerce, to which the bill was jointly referred, has also reported the bill, so it has had appropriate committee scrutiny," added Representative Gerald B. H. Solomon (R–N.Y.) (H22248).

H.R. 2881 was sent to the Senate, and then to its Committee on Labor and Human Resources. Eventually, it was attached as an amendment to the Senate's own AIDS bill.

FRAMING THE ISSUE

A second obstacle to early congressional action on AIDS research and treatment was the deep schism among members over the best way to slow the march of the disease, which was transmitted primarily through sexual contact and intravenous drug use. Beneath the political concerns about AIDS was an issue of political framing: between those who saw the disease as a public health disaster that required a nonjudgmental response and those who viewed it as the product of moral turpitude, to be addressed through behavioral change (*CQ Almanac* 1988, 302); that is, a step in redefining AIDS as a health issue against arguments that it was a personal behavior issue.

One side was led by public health experts and their congressional allies, Representative Henry A. Waxman (D-Calif.), chairman of the House Energy and Commerce Subcommittee on Health and the Environment, and Senators Kennedy and Lowell P. Weicker Jr. (R–Conn.). Buttressed by the American Medical Association and federal public health agencies, they urged stepped-up public education efforts and increased access to blood testing and counseling for the AIDS virus. They further pushed for confidential test results and an assurance that those infected with the virus would not be victims of discrimination. "If—on the other hand—we create a program of testing that is punitive, that exposes people to loss of employment or housing," Senator Kennedy argued, "those most likely to be infected will do all in their power to evade the test." "We must not treat the victims of illness as villains. AIDS is spreading like wildfire and ideology can't stop it" (Senate 1987, 5).

The opposing faction was a small but vocal group of conservatives led by Representative William E. Dannemeyer (R–Calif.) and Senator Jesse Helms (R–N.C.). They urged mandatory, routine testing of large groups within the AIDS population, with the names of those infected being reported to public health officials (Rovner 1987, 2986). They also wanted to require that sexual contacts of all those testing positive be contacted and warned of their risk (*CQ Almanac* 1987, 516). Helms and his allies feared that educational efforts aimed at homosexual men and at users of illicit intravenous drugs would have the effect of promoting those activities. Dannemeyer, fixated on the sexual aspect of the problem, distributed to his colleagues publications produced by the New York City-based Gay Men's Health Crisis, which he argued had used federal funds to promote homosexual activity. He also placed explicit materials about homosexual practices in the *Congressional Record.*

The Senate took the lead on AIDS research and treatment issues, leaving the more controversial testing and confidentiality issues to the House (*CQ Almanac* 1988). Members of the Senate Labor and Human Resources Committee in 1987 approved an AIDS bill (S. 1220, initially sponsored by Senator Kennedy) that authorized close to $600 million for fiscal 1988 for AIDS education and treatment and unspecified amounts for research.

Throughout the debate tempers often frayed to the breaking point, and it was apparent just how far apart some members were from one another. At one point when Majority Leader Robert C. Byrd (D-W.Va.) attempted to interrupt consideration of S. 1220 to get a time agreement on two veterans bills, Senator Lowell P. Weicker Jr. (R-Conn.) exploded, "I find it strange that we can pass veterans' legislation so speedily and so cleanly, but somehow we cannot address the greatest threat that has been posed to this nation since World War II" (*Cong. Rec.* 1988, S9303).

Arresting the spread of the HIV epidemic could not, according to the Senate Labor Committee report on S. 1220, "occur as a result of legislative fiat or the adoption of punitive approaches imposed upon individuals" (Senate 1987, 3). As the debate over AIDS heated up, the committee advocated an inclusive policy that would include coordinated action by persons other than Congress (Senate 1987, 5). "I think that it's important that we remember, as we carry on debate and carry out policy related to AIDS, that AIDS represents the ordinary workings of biology—that it's not an irrational or diabolical plague," commented Senator Tom Harkin (D-Iowa). "This is a very, very serious problem. But let's make sure that we approach it rationally and that we base our judgments on facts—not on pernicious mythologies, misperceptions, ignorance or irrational fears" (9).

On other occasions the AIDS fight transcended traditional Democratic-Republican or liberal-conservative lines. In defending an amendment directing that education programs stress the public health benefits of single, monogamous relationships (without stipulating that such a relationship should be heterosexual), Senator Orrin Hatch (R-Utah) pled, "This bill is to help people who need help, and this includes homosexuals." Senator Jesse Helms (R-N.C.) shot back: "The point is, we should not allow the homosexual crowd to use the AIDS issue to promote and legitimize their lifestyle in American society" (*Cong. Rec.* 1988, S9312). Judging by the debate, a large majority of lawmakers responded to the former interpretation, with its elements of equality, impartiality, and moderation. Conservatives, however, were able to craft amendments to S. 1220 that members found politically impossible to vote against.

On October 13, 1988, lawmakers in both chambers passed by voice vote and sent to President Reagan a watered-down version of S. 1220, the Health Omnibus Act (P.L. 100-607). The measure, which the Senate passed 87–4, contained the first significant federal policy outlines for dealing with the AIDS epidemic: it authorized increased research, education, and prevention activities, and the establishment of a temporary advisory commission. The AIDS portion of the measure authorized a minimum of $270 million over three years for AIDS education and a total of $400 million over two years for anonymous blood testing and counseling and for home community-based health services for AIDS patients (*CQ Almanac* 1988, 296). It also authorized $2 million for operating costs for a new congressional AIDS commission. The bill expedited federal AIDS research activities, ordering the hiring of 780 new workers for the Public Health Service, and formally authorized several elements of the federal government's effort against AIDS that had already been launched.

Several more controversial elements contained in another AIDS bill (HR 5142, the AIDS Federal Policy Act) passed the House handily in September, 367–13 (with 51 not voting), but fell short of enactment when conservative senators threatened to filibuster and block the entire package. Congressional conservatives objected to provisions authorizing $1.2 billion for voluntary blood testing and counseling (an amount seen as being too generous as compared with funding for other serious illnesses), with confidentiality of test results. The House then called up the Senate's more limited AIDS bill, substituted its own text, and passed that version. Representatives had struggled with months of private negotiations among committee and subcommittee members and then days of debate over a myriad of amendments before approving the ground rules for debate (*CQ Almanac* 1988, 305). The House accepted H.R. 520 with a vote of 215 to 170, the rule governing debate on the measure, and by voting "the previous question," a procedural step to cut off debate, it derailed threats to the rule 198–182.[4]

In 1990, the 101st Congress cleared fast-track legislation aimed at bolstering aid to areas hit by the AIDS epidemic. Final action came when the Senate approved the conference agreement on the bill by voice vote, less than five months after it was introduced. The legislation was a compromise version of bills passed by both chambers (S. 2240, H.R. 4785) aimed at helping state and local governments coordinate and pay for care for people with AIDS by authorizing $875 million in fiscal 1991 (*CQ Almanac* 1990). AIDS organizations and public health officials belittled this figure as inadequate, charging that Congress was providing far less than that in the spending bill for the Departments of Labor, Health and Human Services, and Education.

President Bush, along with conservative members of both chambers, opposed the measure because of its "narrow, disease-specific approach." (*CQ Almanac* 1990, 582). Senator Helms insisted during the Senate debate that the AIDS crisis was again being exaggerated by a powerful AIDS lobby that was requesting funds necessary to combat diseases that afflicted far larger numbers of people. "What we have is another legislative flagship for the homosexual segment of the AIDS lobby and its apologists in and out of Congress," Helms declared (*Cong. Rec.* 1990, S10248). "I think one of the saddest things is that the taxpayers' money is being proposed to be used to proselytize a dangerous lifestyle. In the meantime, millions of other Americans, gravely ill with Alzheimer's or cancer or diabetes are being cast aside, along with common sense, in the headlong rush to feed the appetite of a movement which will not be satisfied until the social fabric of the nation is irreparably changed."

When the Senate Labor and Human Resources Committee unanimously reported the Senate version, S. 2440, it dedicated the bill to Ryan White, a youth who as a hemophiliac became an advocate for AIDS research before he succumbed to the disease, and to people with AIDS everywhere. "In sum, our nation's health care system was totally unprepared for the advent of AIDS and HIV," the Committee declared (Senate 1990). "Even when the full scope and severity of the epidemic began to be reported in the medical and scientific literature, the planning and funding that would be required to mount an appropriate response lagged."

Sixty-six senators joined Senator Kennedy to co-sponsor the measure: 44 Democrats and 22 Republicans. In states with concentrated gay populations (or progay rights laws)—California, Florida, Hawaii, Maryland, Massachusetts, New Jersey, New York, Oregon, and Rhode Island—both Democratic and Republican senators signed on to the measure. The bill was also endorsed by Majority Leader George Mitchell (D-Maine) and Minority Leader Robert Dole (R-Kan.). S. 2440 cleared the Senate, 95–4. The four dissenting votes came from senators: Jesse Helms, Gordon

Humphrey (R–N.H.), William Roth (R–Del.), and Malcolm Wallop (R–Wyo.).

The House passed its version by a vote of 408 to 14. Members immediately substituted the text of their measure for that of S. 2240 and asked for a conference. The differences in funding levels to cities and approaches to certain programs set the stage for a conference. While the Senate version authorized $300 million annually in fiscal 1991 and 1992 for block grants to states, the House measure authorized $275 million annually and set forth several discrete programs. Conferees went with the House bill's total of $275 million in authorizing funds. They also opted for the House provision requiring half the emergency funds to be distributed within 90 days of when appropriations became available, with the other half to be allocated on the basis of applications from the cities. The compromise also included the Senate block grant program for states and the House initiative to provide funding for early intervention services (*CQ Almanac* 1990).

QUESTIONING THE "TRADITIONAL" DEFINITION OF MARRIAGE

In the waning days of the 104th Congress, the House of Representatives was filled with heated exchanges over an unusual foray into an area of domestic law typically left to the states. The issue of same-sex marriages came to Capitol Hill following a legal challenge in Hawaii brought by three gay couples suing for the right to marry. Fearing that the actions of one state ruling could effectively force all states to recognize same-sex marriages—if, for example, gay couples from Hawaii later moved to another jurisdiction—Republicans crafted the DOMA legislation to thwart that possibility.

Sponsors said Congress needed to act because gay activists were mounting a legal campaign to force recognition of same-sex marriages against the popular will (*CQ Almanac* 1996). Representative James F. Sensenbrenner Jr. (R–Wis.) charged that the issue was less about gay rights than about gay rights groups' "scheming to manipulate the full faith and credit clause to achieve through the judicial system what they cannot obtain through the democratic process" (*Cong. Rec.* 1996, H7484). "I do not think that Congress should be forced by Hawaii's state court to recognize a marriage between two males or between two females. Congress did not pick that fight."

After a contentious two-day markup, the Subcommittee on the Constitution voted 8–4 along party lines to send the measure to the full Judiciary Committee. Mirroring partisan divisions, the full committee by a 20–10 vote approved the bill for floor consideration. All Republicans voted for the measure, joined by two Democrats (Representatives Rick Boucher of Virginia and Jack Reed of Rhode Island); all other committee Democrats opposed the act.

Democrats charged that the bill was premature and calculated to drive a wedge between moderate and liberal Democrats as well as to try to inflame the public within weeks of the presidential election. "Why are we targeting gays and lesbians, blacks and immigrants this year, now, today?" questioned Representative Cynthia McKinney (D-Ga.) "The answer, pure and simple, is politics—election year politics. The Republicans will stop at nothing to win the White House and the Congress. They will fan the flames of intolerance and bigotry right up to November. And if the result is an election won—at the expense of national unity—their attitude is, so be it" (*Cong. Rec.* 1996, H7490).

Debate centered around two main provisions. The first declared that states were not obligated to recognize any same-sex marriages legally sanctioned in other states. Democrats quarreled over the necessity and constitutionality of this proviso. Congressional action, they argued, was unnecessary and an unconstitutional intrusion on state autonomy; Congress would be exceeding its power to regulate aspects of legal reciprocity among states (*CQ Almanac* 1996). "The Defense of Marriage Act compels this Congress to exceed its boundaries of its constitutional authority," explained Representative Jesse Jackson Jr. (D-Ill.). "This bill offends the Constitution, by violating both the full faith and credit and equal protection clauses of this sacred document" (*Cong. Rec.*, H7496). Opponents argued further that the measure was premature, given that no state (not even Hawaii) had yet legalized gay marriage.

Underneath the constitutional concerns about states rights lay a fundamental disagreement about the proper definition of marriage that involved an emotional clash over religious conviction and public morality. Representative John Lewis (D-Ga.), a veteran of the civil rights movement, countered that the bill was a mean-spirited repudiation of the Declaration of Independence's guarantee of the pursuit of happiness. "You cannot tell people they cannot fall in love," he said (*CQ Almanac* 1996, 5–29). "As I walk past the Republican side of the aisle," Representative Anna Eshoo (D-Calif.) declared, "I expect to hear something similar to an old joke from the civil rights era: 'Some of my good friends are gay, I just wouldn't want my son or daughter to marry one'" (*Cong. Rec.*, H7497). "The fact is, it is morally wrong," Representative Tom Coburn (R-Okla.) said of gay unions.

This second provision to DOMA that sparked much debate defined marriage in federal law as a "legal union between one man and one woman as husband and wife" and a spouse as "a person of the opposite sex who is a husband or a wife," thereby precluding homosexual couples from filing joint tax returns or making use of any spousal benefits under Social Security or other federal programs. Sponsors said they wanted to preserve heterosexual values and traditional families and not "succumb to the homosexual extremist agenda" (H7275). Representative Charles Canady (R-Fla.) spoke for many traditionalists when he declared:

> We as legislators and leaders for the country are in the midst of a chaos, an attack upon God's principles. God laid down that one man and one woman is a legal union. That is marriage, known for thousands of years. That God-given principle is under attack. It is under attack. There are those in our society that try to shift us away from a society based on religious principles to humanistic principles; that the human being can do whatever they want, as long as it feels good and does not hurt others. (H7486)

Proponents also argued that legalizing gay marriage would send children a message that homosexuality was appropriate, pushing them away from heterosexual relationships. They invoked concern for Judeo-Christian tenets and other traditional values. Representative Canady asked whether loosening the definition of marriage might send mixed signals:

> Should this Congress tell the children of America that it is a matter of indifference whether they establish families with a partner of the opposite sex or cohabit with someone of the same sex? Should this Congress tell the children of America that we as a society believe there is no moral difference between homosexual relationships and heterosexual relationships? Should this Congress tell the children of America that in the eyes of the law the parties to a homosexual union are entitled to all the rights and privileges that have always been reserved for a man and woman united in marriage? (H7491)

Opponents argued that the measure was a pernicious form of gay-bashing and that Congress should not write its own definition of marriage. "Scapegoating gay men and lesbians for the failure of marriages in this society is very good politics but very terrible social analysis," contended Representative Frank (H7484). Representative Neil Abercrombie (D-Haw.) stated: "I have heard a continuous drumbeat from some Members here about this union of a man and a women. . . . If that is the case, I presume, then, Members are going to forbid divorce and most certainly impose penalties with adultery. But I do not see it in here [legislation]" (H7485). "This bill denies a group of Americans a basic right because they lead a different lifestyle," added Representative Marty Meehan (D-Mass.). "We must be careful when we make legislative determinations on who is different. If gay people are considered 'different' today, who is to say your lifestyle or my lifestyle will not be considered different tomorrow" (H7486)?

The House passed the bill, 342 to 67. Only one Republican voted against the bill: Steve Gunderson (R-Wis.), then the only GOP lawmaker who had publicly acknowledged his homosexuality. Initially willing to affirm marriage as a heterosexual union, Gunderson broke party ranks because he saw the bill as an exercise in political intolerance. This came after Republicans refused to add language calling for a study to examine questions concerning whether same-sex couples should be able to qualify for certain legal rights such as hospital visitation and health insurance (*CQ Almanac* 1996). More quietly, the Senate passed the bill by a vote of 85 to 14, Democrats casting all the votes against the measure.

EXTENDING CIVIL RIGHTS PROTECTION TO HOMOSEXUALS IN THE WORKPLACE

During the debate on the defense of marriage, a second measure—the Employment Non-Discrimination Act (ENDA)—was working its way through the Senate. Antidiscrimination legislation for homosexuals first appeared in the 94th Congress (1975–1977), when it was introduced by Representative Bella S. Abzug (D-N.Y.). ENDA was aimed at banning most bias against homosexuals on the job. Proponents saw the bill in the context of other civil rights legislation—proposed to prohibit job bias against homosexuals by extending federal employment discrimination protections under the 1964 Civil Rights Act to sexual orientation.

Lawmakers did not openly discuss homosexuality in the workplace until the 103d Congress (1993–1995), when the Senate Labor and Human Resources Committee, chaired by Senator Kennedy, gave the issue some attention. Speaking on the measure before the Committee, Kennedy compared removing sexual orientation as a basis for job discrimination to the way that race, gender, religion, national origin, age, and disabilities had been dealt with by previous legislation. "In the past 40 years, the nation has made significant progress in removing the burden of bigotry from our land. We now seek to take the next step on this journey of justice by banning discrimination based on sexual orientation" (Senate 1994, 1). In the 104th Congress, however, following a declaration by three Oklahoma members—Republicans James Inhofe and Ernest Istook and Democrat Bill Brewster—that they would refuse to hire openly gay staffers, legislation was proposed to further expand prohibitions against workplace discrimination.

Senators opposed to the measure framed their arguments either on moral grounds—the definition of sexual orientation—or as a debate on legal issues. Several senators said that the bill would provide homosexuals with special treatment and cause a proliferation of litigation. "We are not speaking of extending rights that every citizen of the United States is guaranteed," argued Senator Dan Coats (R-Ind.). "Rather we are considering special rights for persons based on their lifestyle choice, as evidenced by their behavior" (*Cong. Rec.* 1996, S10131). Senate Majority Leader Trent Lott (R-Miss.) echoed this sentiment: "This is part of a larger campaign to validate or to approve conduct that remains illegal in many States" (S10136).

Senator Nancy Kassebaum (R-Kan.) believed compensatory and punitive damages would only further encourage division and protracted lawsuits when the intent was to encourage employers and employees to get along. "I agree that discrimination does exist," she said. "However, our courts are already clogged with cases which many times only lead to more divisiveness and disruption in the workplace. Relying on our legal system to resolve our differences can be not only counter-productive but fraught with unintended consequences as well" (S9989).

Other opponents objected to the parallels drawn between the ENDA and Title VII of the Civil Rights Act. They argued that the legislation was not on equal footing with Title VII because the issue was a personal choice and behavior. Because an overt choice in lifestyle would be made, there was no need to provide protection from employment discrimination. "Many, many people across America, because of their backgrounds—and maybe that background is a Jewish background or Christian background or Muslim background—have religious beliefs that homosexuality or bisexuality or promiscuity is immoral," Senate Majority Whip Don Nickles (R-Okla.) declared. "To elevate that type of conduct into a protected status or class under the Civil Rights Act I think would be offensive" (S9997).

The Senate took up the measure following the vote on DOMA. Senator Kennedy won agreement for the back-to-back vote in exchange for not offering the job discrimination bill as an amendment. ENDA was struck down 50–49. Several Republicans crossed party lines to support the measure, including moderates such as William S. Cohen (R-Me.), James M.

Jeffords (R–Vt.), Alan Simpson (R–Wyo.), Mark O. Hatfield (R–Ore.), John H. Chafee (R–R.I.), and Olympia Snowe (R–Me.), as well as Senators Alfonse D'Amato (R–N.Y.) and Arlen Specter (R–Penn.)—who were responding to concentrated gay constituencies in New York and Philadelphia. Senator David Pryor (D–Ark.), a likely supporter of the measure, was absent; and Vice President Al Gore was prepared to break a 50–50 vote. The tactic of arranging back-to-back votes, however, had an effect: thirty-five senators who voted to bar gay marriages then got to vote to bar antigay discrimination (*CQ Almanac* 1996, 5–28).

Debate on the two gay rights initiatives was "historic" (*Cong. Rec.* 1996, S10002). For the first time lawmakers had openly discussed sexual orientation and proposed legislation designed to enhance the rights of homosexuals. What was once unthinkable had now briefly taken center stage in Congress, in committee deliberations and on the floor (Biskupic 1996). But the bottom line was that lawmakers were not ready to render a positive judgement on this previously shunned topic.

DID NEW LEADERSHIP FORCE NEW STRATEGIES?

Passage of the Defense of Marriage Act and defeat of the Employment Non-Discrimination Act constituted a major rejection of gay rights. The debate over gay issues on Capitol Hill has frequently divided Republicans and Democrats, with Republicans more apt to view homosexuality as a threat to traditional values and Democrats more likely to define the subject as a civil rights issue (Bull and Gallagher 1996; Haider-Markel 1997). And while gays have received greater support from Democrats, Haider-Markel (1997, 30) suggests that increasing the number of Democrats in Congress would not immediately translate into more progay support. Progay constituencies are already represented overwhelmingly by liberal Democrats; any additions to the party's ranks would necessarily take place in states or districts that are less supportive of gay interests.

The new Republican majority in the House, needless to say, restructured power relationships. Many grassroots groups and their constituents were subject to these partisan shifts (Gimpel 1998, 114). Groups closely aligned with the Democrats were at least temporarily marginalized, while groups allied with the new majority Republicans enjoyed unprecedented access (Campbell and Davidson 1998).

The new institutional arrangements on Capitol Hill forced gay rights organizations to bargain more centrally with the party leadership and to build new relationships. Traditional allies such as Senator Kennedy and Representative Waxman were deposed as heads of relevant committees or subcommittees. These leaders were effective voices in deliberation, in inserting provisions benefitting gay rights, or in mustering winning voting blocs outside the committee system. Cooperative liberal legislative service organizations (LSOs), like the Democratic Study Group and the Congressional Black Caucus (which had vowed not to discriminate based on the sexual orientation or congressional employees), were defunded as well (Price 1995).

The number of lawmakers who indicated in writing to gay rights organizations that they would not consider sexual orientation in hiring, promoting or terminating employees did drop slightly in the 105th Congress (1997–1998). Sixty-six senators and 223 representatives made such a pledge. These numbers mark a slight decrease from the previous Congress (1995–1996), when 71 senators and 225 representatives supported the pledge (Eilperin 1995a; Dewar 1994). This seems to verify the contention that the influence of gay interest groups has increased over time in the House, but decreased in the Senate (Haider-Markel 1997). Several knowledgeable gay aides also cite fewer staffers who belong to the Lesbian and Gay Congressional Staff Association (Eilperin 1995a; Burr and Rosenfeld 1995). The group's request for registration was approved by former Speaker Thomas S. Foley (D-Wash.) and formalized by the House Administration Committee, which allowed them to occupy House office space. Formal membership numbered more than a hundred before the 1994 election but dropped to sixty shortly thereafter (Simpson 1994; Eilperin 1995b).

Others, however, perceive steady improvements, despite continuing harsh rhetoric toward homosexuals by conservative members (Eilperin 1995b). "It used to be that you'd see people at gay bars over the weekend, and then, during the week, they'd ignore you if you ran into them," said one congressional gay aide. "But it's much different now. I've seen huge advances, and I haven't seen any reversal of that since the Republicans took over" (Senior 1995).

Part of this sympathetic change may be attributed to a return of normality in Congress. Two years after the Republican revolution, the 105th Congress witnessed subtle accommodations to moderate viewpoints. Whereas the Republicans of the 104th Congress arrived with a sense of conservative zeal, the 105th Congress found the Republicans in a somewhat mellower frame of mind. Although most remained convinced of the rightness of "traditional values," the majority of the Class of 1994 did temper their conservatism (Rae 1998).

In an unprecedented move, Senator Robert Torricelli (D-N.J.) included a written provision in his office personnel manual that extended the Family and Medical Leave Act to gays and lesbians for the benefit of their domestic partners. "This is making the laws of Congress consistent with a new and rising national standard of equality," Torricelli explained. "Rather than being the last institution to rise to this new standard, Congress should be a part of the change" (Senior 1997).

Similarly, the Committee on House Oversight, chaired by Representative Bill Thomas (R-Calif.), quietly accorded spousal identification passes to the domestic partners of gay members, and the House Ethics Committee granted gift ban waivers to the domestic partners of gay staffers. Neither action implied that Congress formally recognized gay partnerships as marriages, but domestic partners were spared the inconveniences faced in making their way around the Capitol (Bradley 1996). In the case of staffers, they are permitted to receive gifts in amounts appropriate for close personal relationships.

ENDA also picked up renewed interest in the 105th Congress, surprisingly from moderate to liberal Republicans (Sobel 1997) such as the Tuesday Group (formerly known as the Tuesday Lunch Bunch), with forty-five to fifty moderate to liberal members mainly from northeastern, marginal districts, and the newer Main Street Coalition, with thirty or more members. The Tuesday Group had become a vehicle for support of gay rights issues because of the strong influence of Representative Gunderson (who retired in 1994). Another hopeful sign was the elevation of Senator James M. Jeffords (R-Vt.), a cosponsor of the bill in 104th Congress, to the chairmanship of the Senate Labor and Human Resources Committee.

To become active in the legislative process, political groups must build a foundation from which a successful effort at mobilization can be launched (Walker 1991). Organizations must be formed, and advocates must be trained, to adapt to what T. V. Smith (1941) called the "legislative way of life"; resources must be amassed to capture the attention of lawmakers. Elected officials may advance legislation intended to benefit disadvantaged groups without prompting from outside forces. But as Walker (1991, 196) writes, "legislators know that once conflict begins over their proposals, there will be few organizations in place that can mobilize expressions of support, supply information and ideas, or raise financial resources needed to combat the program's critics."

In the years before Stonewall, organizations of gays were nearly invisible on Capitol Hill. Early efforts to organize homosexuals in promoting gay rights proved unsuccessful because of fear of the consequences (D'Emilio

1983, 62). The absence of cohesiveness within the community, combined with substantial structural and moral impediments, inhibited a sense of identity, cohesion, and group consciousness among homosexuals (Hertzog 1996; Wald, Button, and Rienzo 1996; Sherrill 1993). Group activism encompassed a collection of diverse political, social, and service organizations across Capitol Hill. Moderate groups such as the Log Cabin Republicans engaged in quiet politics rooted in personal relationships with limited roles of government over campaigns for equality, while organizations like the National Gay and Lesbian Task Force, the Gay and Lesbian Victory Fund, the Human Rights Campaign, and the Lambda Legal Defense Fund pushed broader rights-based agendas (Kirp 1996).

The identification and threat of AIDS galvanized diverse political initiatives in the gay community, prompting mobilization, fund-raising, and effective political lobbying for legislative remedies (Morgan 1987) as well as efforts to educate lawmakers. Skeptical of Congress's commitment to their well-being, many gay activists began to shift their emphasis from backstairs lobbying for civil rights to more publicly visible and vigorous AIDS activism (Blackwell 1992; Bawer 1994). This entry of AIDS activists into the health care scene added a new dimension to what was previously a genteel dialogue between patient advocates and clinicians, researchers, and policymakers (Blackwell 1992, 128). Increased group activism and the expansion of homosexual issues to include AIDS provided gay rights leaders an entrée to many members of Congress, helping to establish themselves as players with a social stake in the issue (Matlock 1990).

Gay activists have recently explored new ways of making themselves heard on Capitol Hill. A critical part of this political clout is campaign support. Enlarged memberships and budgets have enabled gay political organizations, through their political action committees and independent expenditures, to channel sizeable contributions to congressional campaigns throughout the nation and to even influence legislative voting behavior. Controlling for party affiliation, ideology, religious affiliation, constituency opinion, and past progay support, Haider-Markel's (1997) model of congressional decision-making suggests that, under sub-optimal conditions, gay interest groups can exert some influence over congressional voting behavior through campaign contributions and the mobilization of grassroots supporters. However, although gay and lesbian groups can sway voting behavior at the individual level, this does not necessarily aggregate into legislative victories.

Still, this replaces a situation in which politicians of all stripes, Demo-

Table 14.1 Total Contributions to Congressional Candidates and other PACs from the Human Rights Campaign, 104th–105th Congresses

	Democrat		Republican		
	Primary	General	Primary	General	PACs/Parties
1995–1996	334,974.20	265,180.77	11,000	25,500	110,400
1997–1998	309,872.14	315,881.46	51,500	16,628.36	117,607
Total	644,846.34	581,062.23	62,500	42,128.36	228,007

SOURCE: The Human Rights Campaign (<www.hrc.org/whowthat/whatwedo/pac/pac94.txt.html>, accessed November 11, 1997).

Table 14.2 Total Contributions to Congressional Candidates, 103d–105th Congresses

	1993–1994	1995–1996	1997–1998
Senate			
Democratic candidate	$137,429	$123,500	$23,750
Republican candidate	$18,500	$10,000	0
Other candidate	0	0	0
Total	$155,929	$133,500	$23,700
House			
Democratic candidate	$495,495	$535,848	$114,792
Republican candidate	$18,000	$62,231	$15,000
Other candidate	0	$10,000	0
Total	$513,495	$608,079	$129,792
Total contributions	$669,424	$741,579	$153,492

SOURCE: Data are found in the Federal Election Commission database (<www.fec.gov>).

NOTE: Figures are derived from contributions from four nonpartisan gay rights organizations: Human Rights Campaign Fund PAC, Gay and Lesbian Victory Fund, National Lesbian PAC, and the American AIDS PAC. Figures for the 1997–1998 electoral cycle represent contributions reported to the FEC as of March 1998.

crats and Republicans, often hid or returned financial contributions from homosexuals for fear of being tainted (Schmalz 1992). For example, the Human Rights Campaign donated more than $1 million to mainstream politicians in 1996 (Thomas 1996). Table 14.1 shows the total contributions to candidates and other PACs from the Human Rights Campaign, 104th and 105th Congresses. Table 14.2 details total federal contributions from four nonpartisan gay rights organizations for candidates to the 103d through 105th Congresses. Nearly all the contributions were funneled to like-minded or sympathetic Democratic candidates.

CONCLUSION

The record of Congress on gay rights policymaking is mixed. Some individual members of Congress are sympathetic to gay causes; most, however, are not. The 94th Congress (1975–1977) marked the first time gay rights moved to a visible place on the agenda of the civil rights movement. Since the mid-1980s, congressional action has included AIDS research, civil rights protection, and reforming legislative definitions of "spouse" to accept gay and lesbian identity within state welfare and tax statutes. But as AIDS issues appear less frequently in the 1990s, the level of progay support in Congress weakens (Haider-Markel 1997, 30).

Gay rights issues move through the corridors and committee rooms of Capitol Hill in piecemeal fashion, largely because many lawmakers prefer that they be kept off the floor of the House or Senate. The failure of many gay rights bills reflects this attitude. Most lawmakers, by their own admission, are uncomfortable with the subject as a topic of personal or legislative debate. When measures addressing gay concerns are brought to the forefront of the congressional agenda, members fear political repercussions and purposely pursue the opposite course of legislation, by either obfuscating or by manipulating congressional procedures to thwart proposals. Manipulation was evident when the 104th Congress overwhelmingly approved a federal ban on gay marriages after an emotional debate over the rights of individuals and the nature of love. Even with strong Democratic majorities in the 103d Congress, gay rights advocates were unable to persuade majorities of legislators to repeal the ban on gays in the military, to add sexual orientation as a protected category under the Civil Rights Act, or to vote against repealing antidiscrimination legislation (Wald, Button, and Rienzo 1996).

Continued apprehension about gay rights in the 105th Congress was also evident when the Senate stopped action by placing a hold on the nomination of James C. Hormel to be ambassador to Luxembourg. Conservative Senate Republicans called President Clinton's choice a "payoff" to the homosexual community (Cassata 1998) and contended that, as a homosexual, Hormel would push a gay agenda in a diplomatic post (Cohen 1998). Concurrently, remarks by Senate Majority Leader Trent Lott (R-Miss.), along with some supportive comments from other GOP-related organizations, were interpreted as an effort to activate the party's conservative base. "You should not try to mistreat them [gays] or treat them as outcasts," Lott said while taping an interview for a cable television show. "You should not try to show them a way to deal with that problem, just like alcohol . . . or sex addiction . . . or kleptomaniacs" (*Associated Press* 1998, A6).

Despite the frigid legislative environment, gay organizations are increasingly mobilized. Money is perhaps a potent resource used to influence public policy choices. In 1996, the Human Rights Campaign was active in 170 congressional races (Shin 1997). Raising money for Republicans has earned the Log Cabin Republicans a greater share of trust within the GOP, breaking down the notion among some Republicans that gay organizations support only Democratic lawmakers. Membership in gay organizations is important as well. Group members tend to be voters, and lawmakers pay attention to clusters of voters, especially those who care deeply about an issue, are united, are mindful of change, and are motivated to vote and participate on that basis.

The difficulty Congress has in passing comprehensive gay rights legislation highlights the fact that the climate on Capitol Hill remains generally unreceptive to gay concerns. Still, the congressional process addresses multiple issues and problems concurrently and offers opportunity for delay in implementation, appeals, policy reversals, and compromises to the many interests. Subsequently, the elements of change embodied in public policies, especially those that are controversial, are often marginal rather than sweeping.

Perhaps the tortuous path of civil rights legislation is, in the end, a model. Similar to the Civil Rights Act of 1957, which was not as sweeping in scope as the Civil Rights Act of 1964, issues like ENDA and DOMA represent an important first step toward creating meaningful and much needed gay rights legislation. Although defeated, these legislative efforts opened the door for further debate and additional legislation on the subject in future congresses. The comments of Senator John F. Kerry (D-Mass.) help to illustrate the gradual and invariably contentious evolution of gay and lesbian issues: "When I was first sworn in as a U.S. Senator in 1985, I authorized the gay and lesbian civil rights bill," observed Kerry. "At that time, only five other Senators would join me as cosponsors of that legislation. Last year, I joined sixty-five of our colleagues in signing a pledge that I would not discriminate on the basis of sexual orientation in hiring, promotion and firing" (*Cong. Rec.* 1996, S9997).

NOTES

1. We use the term "gay" to refer to both male and female homosexuals and bisexuals and to describe the issues and policies in terms of "gay rights." The notion of "gay rights" pertains to the relationship of gays, lesbians, and bisexuals to the state, limiting government's power over them as persons, as well as specifying what government should do to aid such individuals and meet their civil needs (Blasius 1994).

2. Authors' interview with Winnie Stachelberg, Political Director for the Human Rights Campaign, 18 November 1997.

3. Excluded were the provisions authorizing $1.2 billion for voluntary blood testing and counseling, with guaranteed confidentiality of test results.

   Donald P. Haider-Markel (1997) suggests that while the institutionalization of a social movement, such as lesbian and gay rights, will likely translate into greater political power, this power will be limited by the ability of formal groups to generate money and mobilize their constituents for legislative campaigns. If groups focus on raising money at the expense of grassroots mobilization, their success is likely to be limited. Conversely, grassroots mobilization without financial contributions is also likely to limit success. To influence policy, therefore, interest groups must coordinate contributions and mobilization.

4. Although the rule permitted a total of twelve amendments to be offered, eight of them by Republicans, Republicans sought to defeat the previous question so they could substitute a rule of their own that permitted thirty other amendments.

REFERENCES

Adam, Barry D. 1993. *The rise of a gay and lesbian movement*, rev. ed. Boston: Twayne Publishers.

Altman, Dennis. 1987. The politics of AIDS. In *AIDS: Public policy dimensions*, edited by John Griggs. New York: United Hospital Fund of New York.

———. 1986. *AIDS in the mind of America*. Garden City, N.Y.: Doubleday.

Associated Press. 1998. Lott: Gays need help "to deal with that problem." *Washington Post*, 6 June, A6.

Bawer, Bruce. 1994. *A place at the table: The gay individual in American society*. New York: Simon and Schuster.

Biskupic, Joan. 1996. Once unthinkable, now under debate; same-sex marriage issue to take center state in Senate. *Washington Post*, 3 September, A1.

Blackwell, Richard E. 1992. AIDS, activism, and the politics of health. *The New England Journal of Medicine* 326 (2): 128–33.

Blasius, Mark. 1994. *Gay and lesbian politics*. Philadelphia: Temple University Press.

Bradley, Jennifer. 1996. House grants gift waivers for "domestic partners." *Roll Call*, 1 July, p. 1.

Bull, Chris, and John Gallagher. 1996. *Perfect enemies: The religious right, the gay movement, and the politics of the 1990s*. New York: Crown Publishers.

Burr, Chandler, and Megan Rosenfeld. 1995. Pink elephants: It isn't easy being a gay Republican. *Washington Post*, 18 October, B1.

Campbell, Colton C. 1996. Creating an angel: Why Congress delegates to *ad hoc* commissions. Ph.D. diss. University of California, Santa Barbara.

Campbell, Colton C., and Roger H. Davidson. 1998. Coalition building in Congress: The consequences of partisan change. In *The Interest Group Connection*, ed. Paul S. Herrnson, Ronald G. Shaiko, and Clyde Wilcox. Chatham, N.J.: Chatham House Publishers, Inc.

Cassata, Donna. 1998. Conservatives, White House step up fight over Hormel. *Congressional Quarterly Weekly Report*, 14 March, 682.

Clines, Francis X. 1992. For gay GOP members, a second closet. *New York Times*, 4 September, A12.

Cohan, A. S. 1992. Obstacles to equality: Government responses to the gay rights movement in the United States. In *Homosexuality and government, politics, and prisons*, edited by Wayne R. Dyes and Stephen Donaldson. New York: Garland.

Cohen, Richard. 1998. Openly gay. *Washington Post*, 3 April, A31.

Congressional Record. 1987. 100th Cong., 1st sess., vol. 133, pt. 26.

———. 1988. 100th Cong., 2d sess., vol. 134, pt. 7.

———. 1990. 101st Cong., 2d sess., vol. 136, pt. 7.

———. 1995. 104th Cong., 1st sess., vol. 141, pt. 2.

———. 1996. 104th Cong., 2d sess., vol. 142, pts. 68, 103, 106, 121, 122, 127.

Congressional Quarterly Almanac. 1987. Vol. 46. Washington, D.C.: Congressional Quarterly Inc.

———. 1988. Vol. 44. Washington, D.C.: Congressional Quarterly Inc.

———. 1990. Vol. 45. Washington, D.C.: Congressional Quarterly Inc.

———. 1996. Vol. 52. Washington, D.C.: Congressional Quarterly Inc.

Crowley, Michael. 1995. Back in the Capitol closet? *National Journal*, 1 April, 818.

Davidson, Roger H. 1999. Leaders and committees in the Republican Congress. In *New majority or old minority? The impact of Republicans on Congress*, edited by Nicol C. Rae and Colton C. Campbell. Lanham, Md.: Rowman and Littlefield, Inc.

Davidson, Roger H., and Walter J. Oleszek. 1998. Congress and its members. 6th ed. Washington, D.C.: CQ Press.

Dejowski, Edmund F. 1989. Federal restrictions on AIDS prevention efforts for gay men. *St. Louis University Public Law Review* 8:275–98.

D'Emilio, John. 1983. Sexual politics, sexual communities: The making of a homosexual minority in the United States, 1940–1970. *UCLA Law Review* 13:643–832.

———. 1989. The homosexual menace: The politics of sexuality in Cold War America. In *Passion and power: Sexuality in history*, edited by Kathy Peiss and Christina Simmons. Philadelphia: Temple University Press.

Dewar, Helen. 1994. Seventy-one senators say they are fair to gay workers. *Washington Post*, 14 June, A10.

Easton, David. 1965. *A systems analysis of political life.* New York: Wiley.

Eilperin, Juliet. 1995a. Clerk's office first draft protects gay staffers from discrimination, but it's not final policy. *The Hill,* 18 September, p. 1.

—————. 1995b. Hill's gay staff club in closet under GOP. *The Hill,* 26 February, p. 1.

Evans, C. Lawrence, and Walter J. Oleszek. 1997. *Congress under fire.* New York: Houghton Mifflin Company.

Freedberg, Louis. 1994. New Congress, old morals. *San Francisco Chronicle,* 27 November, S4.

Gimpel, James G. 1998. "Grassroots organizations and equilibrium cycles in group mobilization and access." In *The interest group connection,* edited by Paul S. Herrnson, Ronald G. Shaiko, and Clyde Wilcox. Chatham, N.J.: Chatham House Publishers, Inc.

Haeberle, Steven H. 1991. The role of religious organizations in the gay and lesbian rights movement. In *The role of religious organizations in social movements,* edited by Barbara M. Yarnold. New York: Praeger.

Haider-Markel, Donald P. 1997. From bullhorns to PACs: Lesbian and gay politics, interest groups, and policy. Ph.D. diss., University of Wisconsin–Milwaukee, Political Science.

Haider-Markel, Donald P., and Kenneth J. Meier. 1996. the politics of gay and lesbian rights: Expanding the scope of the conflict. *Journal of Politics* 58 (2): 352–69.

Herman, Didi. 1994. *Rights of passage: Struggles for lesbian and gay legal equality.* Toronto: University of Toronto Press.

Hertzog, Mark. 1996. *The lavender vote: Lesbians, gay men, and bisexuals in American electoral politics.* New York: New York University Press.

Kirp, David L. 1996. A place at the table: The gay individual in American society. *Tikkun* 11:91–94.

Langbein, Laura I., and Mark A. Lotwis. 1990. The political efficacy of lobbying and money: Gun control in the U.S. House, 1986. *Legislative Studies Quarterly* 15:413–40.

Lewis, Gregory B. 1997. Lifting the ban on gays in the civil service: Federal policy toward gay and lesbian employees since the Cold War. *Public Administration Review* 57 (5): 387–95.

Marwick, Charles. 1988. AIDS commission's next report focuses on four critical issues. *Journal of the American Medical Association,* 259:169–70.

Matlock, Carol. 1990. Gay clout, *National Journal,* 6 January, 16.

Mitniter, Richard. 1994. Gay rights holds GOP in a firm embrace. *Washington Times,* 24 October, A14.

Morgan, Thomas. 1987. Amid AIDS, gay movement grows but shifts. *New York Times,* 10 October, A1.

Newton, David E. 1994. *Gay and lesbian rights: A reference handbook.* Santa Barbara, Calif.: ABC-CLIO, Inc.

Peterson, Mark A. 1995. How health policy information is used in Congress. In *Intensive care: How Congress shapes health policy*, edited by Thomas Mann and Norman Ornstein. Washington, D.C.: American Enterprise Institute and The Brookings Institution.

Polsby, Nelson W. 1969. Policy analysis and Congress. *Public Policy*, 18:61–93.

Pressman, Steven. 1983. The gay community struggles to fashion an effective lobby, *Congressional Quarterly Weekly Report* (3 December): 2543–47.

Price, Deb. 1995. Black caucus: Friend to gay people. *Times-Picayune*. 18 December, B5.

Rae, Nicol C. 1998. *Conservative reformers: The freshmen Republicans and the lessons of the 104th Congress*. Armonk, N.Y.: M. E. Sharpe, Inc.

Rovner, Julie. 1987. Congress is stalemated over AIDS epidemic. *Congressional Quarterly Weekly Report* (5 December): 2986–88.

Schmalz, Jeffrey. 1992. Gay politics goes mainstream. *New York Times*, 11 October, F18.

Schattschneider, E. E. 1975. *Semisoverign people: A realists's view of democracy in America*. Hinsdale, Ill.: Dryden Press.

Senior, Jennifer. 1997. Torricelli extends benefits to gay staffers, partners. *The Hill*, 12 March, p. 4.

———. 1995. For gay GOP staffers, it's a large closet. *The Hill*, 16 August, p. 1.

Sherrill, Kenneth. 1993. On gay people as a politically powerless group. In *Gays and the Military*, edited by Marc Wolinsky and Kenneth Sherrill. Princeton: Princeton University Press.

Shin, Annys. 1997. Gay activists view Hill changes, *National Journal*, 4 January, 30.

Simpson, Glenn R. 1994. Gay aides form club. *Roll Call*. 14 April, p. 1.

Smith, T[homas]. V[ernor]. 1941. *The legislative way of life*. Chicago: University of Chicago Press.

Sobel, Lindsay. 1997. Gay rights battleground shifts, as the GOP leads the charge for gay rights this year. *The Hill*, 7 May, p. 10.

Thomas, Chadwin. 1996. Gays are getting organized, increasing their political clout; Their efforts are no longer on the fringe. *Star Tribune*, 1 November, 18A.

Thompson, Mark, ed. 1994. *The long road to freedom*. New York: St. Martin's Press.

Trejo, Frank. 1994. Gays hoping to join forces with minorities. *Dallas Morning News*, 12 November, 34A.

U.S. House. 1989. Committee on Veterans' Affairs. *National Commission on Acquired Immune Deficiency Syndrome Act*. 100th Cong., 1st sess., H.R. 100-245, pt. 1.

———. 1994. Subcommittee on Select Education and Civil Rights of the Committee on Education and Labor. 1994. *Employment discrimination against gay men and lesbians*. 103d Cong., 2d sess.

U.S. Senate. 1950. Committee on Expenditures in the Executive Departments, Subcommittee on Investigations. *Employment of homosexuals and other sex perverts in government.* 81st Cong., 2d sess. Document No. 241. Washington, D.C.: U.S. Government Printing Office.

――――. 1987. Committee on Labor and Human Resources. *AIDS research.* 100th Cong., 1st sess.

―――― 1989. Committee on Labor and Human Resources. *National Commission on Acquired Immune Deficiency Syndrome Act.* 100th Cong., 2d sess., H.R. 100-400.

――――. 1994. Committee on Labor and Human Resources. *Employment Non-Discrimination Act of 1994.* 103d Cong., 2d sess.

Wald, Kenneth D., James W. Button, and Barbara A. Rienzo. 1996. The politics of gay rights in American communities: Explaining antidiscrimination ordinances and politics. *American Journal of Political Science* 40 (4): 1152–78.

Walker, Jack L. 1991. *Mobilizing interest groups in America: Patrons, professions, and social movements.* Ann Arbor: University of Michigan Press.

Watney, Simon. 1987. *Policing desire.* London: Comedia.

Wright, John R. 1996. *Interest groups and Congress.* Boston: Allyn and Bacon.

Yang, John E. 1996a. Half of Republicans neutral on gay issues, *Houston Chronicle,* 11 February, A7.

――――. 1996b. Advertisement makes appeal to closeted gays in Congress. *Washington Post,* 27 July, A10.

――――. 1997. Gays in the conservative closet; some GOP congressional aides experience dissonance between personal, political, *Washington Post,* 7 November, A23.

15

SEX AND THE SUPREME COURT:
GAYS, LESBIANS, AND JUSTICE

Sarah E. Brewer, David Kaib, and Karen O'Connor

"Cases," says political scientist Richard C. Cortner, "do not arrive at the doorsteps of the Supreme Court like orphans in the night" (1975, iv). Since the 1940s, political scientists have studied the role of organized interests in bringing major cases to the Supreme Court. Beginning with Clement E. Vose's classic works on the National Association for the Advancement of Colored People (NAACP) (1955; 1959) and the National Consumers' League (NCL) (1957; 1972) to more recent accounts of the role of women's groups (O'Connor 1980; Costain 1992), Native Americans (Hermann 1996), and religious organizations (Ivers 1995; Ivers 1992), scholars have paid increasing attention to the subtle political and legal machinations of interest groups who rely on the courts for vindication of what they believe are their constitutional rights. In this chapter, we examine the evolution of constitutional law concerning gay rights. It was not until 1996 that the U.S. Supreme Court interpreted the equal protection clause of the Fourteenth Amendment to apply to classifications based on sexual orientation. In this chapter we attempt to provide a deeper understanding of the Court's decisions and why a majority of the justices remain reluctant or even opposed to providing full constitutional rights to all individuals regardless of their sexual orientation. We also trace the role of organized gay and lesbian groups who, like many other organized interests before them, have resorted to litigation to secure constitutional and statutory rights.

We should note that this chapter deals largely with cases that have resulted in full opinions from the Supreme Court. The Supreme Court has total control over the cases it chooses to hear for oral argument; the Court has accepted very few gay and lesbian rights cases for full review. A note on terminology: we include in our analysis cases that commentators and/or gay and lesbian interest groups have identified as ones with critical ramifications on the legal status of gays and lesbians under U.S. constitutional law. Thus, we analyze some cases when gays and lesbians were not a direct party to the litigation. Moreover, the decisions discussed in detail here are but the tip of the iceberg of the thousands of cases that have been brought in the federal and state courts, particularly since 1980. Since the Supreme Court is the final arbiter of constitutional interpretation, lower federal and state court judges are constantly looking to the High Court for guidance. As we will discuss below, the Supreme Court—at least when dealing with issues of concern to gay and lesbian rights activists—has been notoriously reluctant to enter the legal fray by repeatedly refusing to hear appeals involving important legal issues.

THE ROLE OF ORGANIZED INTERESTS IN THE LEGAL SYSTEM

The NAACP was among the first major organized interest groups to resort to litigation. NAACP leaders quickly recognized that reliance on traditional forms of political pressure would not work for it or its members. Many African Americans, for example, were not even enfranchised so they had no hope of convincing recalcitrant state legislators to remove offensive and discriminatory Jim Crow laws. Likewise, very few African Americans served in any legislatures on the local, state, or national level. In that regard, the reliance by some gay rights groups on litigation to achieve rights, then, is not very surprising. Similarly, gays' and lesbians' political clout has been quite limited historically. Most states, in fact, criminalized oral sex, none recognized gay marriages, and until recently, few states or localities were even willing to accord any form of civil rights protections to any group based on sexual orientation.

Groups who see themselves forced to resort to litigation usually engage in the direct sponsorship of test cases, file amicus curiae briefs in important cases in which they are not a direct party, or more often than not, some combination of both tactics.[1] Interest groups routinely sponsor cases or file amicus briefs either urging the Court to hear a case or asking it to refuse to hear a case, a procedure called a "denial of a writ of certiorari." Even more commonly, groups also file amicus briefs once the Court has decided to hear a case. The participation of numerous groups may highlight lower court and ideological conflicts for the justices by alerting them to the amount of public interest in the issues presented in any particular case. Some areas of the law, however, are inherently controversial given current public opinion. Issues of concern to gay and lesbian rights activists such as discrimination against individuals with HIV/AIDS, the exclusion of gays from the military, or gay and lesbian parents often evoke heated debate, and the Court is well aware of that fact.

Test cases are often well thought out by a group before a lawsuit is even initiated; in other instances, a group will come forward to help someone in trouble because the issue or law at stake or in contention in their case is an area of interest to the group. In the case of *Brown v. Board of Education* (1954), for example, the NAACP Legal Defense Fund actually sought out plaintiffs to be the named parties in an effort to mount a national challenge to racially segregated schools.

Students of the NAACP LDF's litigation strategies initially found that its successes in cases such as those involving racially restrictive housing covenants (*Shelley v. Kraemer* (1948)) and *Brown* were due in large part to thoughtful strategizing by the LDF and its superb lawyers, including Thurgood Marshall, who later was to become the first African American appointed to the U.S. Supreme Court. The successful pursuit of these focused cases, said numerous commentators, was due to the case-by-case "test case" approach adopted by the NAACP LDF, which was facilitated by a network of African American lawyers. Most African-American lawyers were concentrated in but a few cities, were also well connected through the National Bar Association (the American Bar Association barred black members until 1943), and often had a shared law school experience at Howard Law School.

Later, the development of a women's rights litigation strategy to facilitate constitutional change was enhanced by the influx of rights-oriented women into the nation's law schools in the early 1970s. These women, eager to challenge discriminatory laws as well as legal practices, enrolled in "women and the law" courses or participated in specialized "women and the law" clinics. Their collective efforts were fostered by the creation of the National Women's Law Conference as well as by the emergence of women to lead and coordinate litigation efforts, including Ruth Bader Ginsburg. Ginsburg envisioned a test-case strategy to convince the court to find that sex discrimination was unconstitutional under the Fourteenth Amendment. In the first test case she argued, *Reed v. Reed* (1971), the

Supreme Court for the first time found gender discrimination unconstitutional under the Fourteenth Amendment. This success helped her persuade the ACLU to create a Women's Rights Project (WRP). During her tenure at the WRP, Ginsburg was to participate in nearly all of the major cases heard by the Court involving sex discrimination until her appointment to the U.S. Court of Appeals in 1979 (O'Connor 1980). Like Thurgood Marshall before her, Ginsburg ultimately was appointed to the U.S. Supreme Court in 1993.

GAY RIGHTS ACTIVISM BEGINS

As chronicled in other chapters in this volume, the gay rights movement in the United States had its origins in the Mattachine Society, which was formed in the early 1950s in California (Adam 1995, 69; Cain 1993). Throughout the period of the 1950s and well into the 1960s, most organized efforts by gays and lesbians took the form of meeting to discuss their common concerns. There was little attempt made at concerted action in the courts, yet there were a few relatively isolated and individualistic efforts that paved the way for later litigation.

Early Cases

The first major case to reach the Supreme Court during this period was *One, Inc. v. Oleson* (1958). *One, Inc.*, the official magazine of the Mattachine Society, was "the earliest continually published homophile magazine in U.S. history."[2] In reaction to political pressure from the U.S. Senate and the Federal Bureau of Investigation, officials at the U.S. Post Office confiscated the magazine under authority of a federal law that prohibited the use of the U.S. mails to distribute "obscene, lewd, lascivious, or filthy" materials. As legal scholar William N. Eskridge (1997) notes, this action was part of a pattern of government hostility toward homosexuals during the post-war period.

Relying on existing constitutional law, U.S. Court of Appeals upheld the Postal Service's refusal to deliver the magazine. The Mattachine Society then appealed this decision to the U.S. Supreme Court. While *One, Inc.* was on appeal, however, the Supreme Court decided *Roth v. United States* (1957).

In *Roth,* the Court held that for something to be considered obscene, it had to be "utterly without redeeming social importance." On the heels of *Roth,* in deciding *One, Inc.,* the Court rendered but a one-sentence per curiam opinion in which it ruled that the lower court's decision in *One,*

Inc. was inconsistent with *Roth*. Thus, the decision was reversed and the Mattachine Society again was free to mail its official magazine.

One, Inc. did not end the Post Office's campaign against gay and lesbian print media. In *Manual Enterprises v. Day* (1962), at issue was a ruling of the Post Office Department, which was upheld by a district court and a U.S. court of appeals. In 1960, hundreds of magazines were seized by the Alexandria, Virginia postmaster who asked the Post Office for a ruling as to whether the magazines were "nonmailable." The publishers of these magazines argued that even if the magazines aroused the "prurient interest of homosexuals," they were not obscene under *Roth's* definition of obscenity, "the so called 'average person in the community test.'" The Court of Appeals for the District of Columbia Circuit found the magazines to be obscene.

On appeal, Justice John Marshall Harlan, writing for a badly divided Supreme Court, reversed the lower court's ruling. A majority of the Court could not agree on the rationale for the reversal. Harlan, on behalf of himself and Justice Potter Stewart, found that the magazines could "not be deemed so offensive on their face as to affront current community standards of decency." Making up the rest of the majority invalidating the postmaster's refusal to accept the magazines for distribution, Justices William Brennan, William O. Douglas, and Chief Justice Earl Warren concluded that the postmaster had no independent legal authority to close the U.S. mails.[3]

At least two other cases made their way to the Supreme Court during this period, *Smayda v. United States* (1966) and *Boutilier v. Immigration and Naturalization Services* (1967). *Smayda* is illustrative of the kinds of selective harassment that many gays experienced. Joseph Smayda and Wendell Gunther appealed their convictions for oral copulation prohibited under the California criminal code.[4] They claimed that "all the evidence against them was obtained in violation of their Fourth Amendment rights to be free from unreasonable searches and seizures." The Ninth Circuit Court of Appeals agreed. The Supreme Court declined to review the case.

Boutilier is another example of the discrimination faced by homosexuals throughout the 1960s. In 1963, Boutilier, a Canadian living in the United States applied for citizenship. By affidavit, Boutilier admitted to INS officials that he had engaged in homosexual sodomy. In response, the INS issued a deportation order, ruling that Boutilier possessed a "psychopathic personality" excludable under the Immigration and Nationality Act of 1952. Boutilier challenged this action, arguing that the medical term "psychopathic personality" did not extend to homosexuals, and that even if it did, the classification was unconstitutionally vague. The U.S. Supreme Court rejected his arguments, concluding that Congress had clearly intended to exclude homosexuals from naturalized U.S. citizenship and that his exclusion was due to his status as a homosexual, not to any specific sexual activities he engaged in after entering the United States. Despite the fact that at that time the American Psychiatric Association (APA) listed homosexuality as a form of sexual deviance, Justice Douglas dissented, arguing that the majority's ruling that homosexuals were mentally ill was contrary to prevailing medical opinion.

Stonewall and the American Psychiatric Association: A Turning Point

Throughout the 1960s, members of the Mattachine Society lobbied against the medical establishment's classification of homosexuality as a mental illness.[5] The Stonewall riots of 1969 marked a turning point in organized gay activism throughout the United States. New groups created in its aftermath called for an abandonment of apologetic positions on homosexuality and, on a strategic and practical level, became more aggressive in challenging the APA's classification of homosexuality as a mental illness.

The Gay Liberation Front of New York (GLF) was founded in 1969 as a committee of Mattachine New York in direct response to Stonewall. GLF was much more militant than the Mattachine Society in its political philosophy. It struggled to unite numerous radical left movements including the anti–Vietnam War, black civil rights, feminist politics, socialist politics, and the gay and lesbian rights movements to bring about broad social revolution. GLF chapters were founded in Los Angeles, Berkeley, San Francisco, and Minneapolis by the end of 1969. In 1970, GLF groups began disruptive protests at psychiatric, medical, and behavior modification conventions where treatment and correction of homosexuality were being discussed.

The Gay Activists Alliance (GAA) was formed in 1970 by more moderate members of the GLF who believed it was more politically feasible to shift from GLF's focus on broad social revolution to a more specific focus on identifiable gay and lesbian issues. The GAA's strategy was to use all of its resources to fight for gay and lesbian equality. In 1971, GAA members were invited to participate on a panel at the APA national convention called "Lifestyles of Non-Patient Homosexuals." The GAA also held an exhibit at the convention called "Gay, Proud, and Healthy: the Homosexual Community Speaks." This was followed by further participation by GAA members on a panel at the 1972 APA convention, "Psychiatry:

Friend or Foe to Homosexuals? A Dialogue." Despite these inroads, in 1972, GAA dissolved due to internal strife (Adam 1995, 67).

Building on the GAA's strategy, in 1973 the National Gay Task Force (NGTF) was created. (Today it is called the National Gay and Lesbian Task Force (NGLTF).) Its purpose was to work for gay liberation on a national level. The NGTF continued to lobby the APA to change its diagnostic classification of homosexuality as a treatable disease, viewing the APA's categorization of homosexuality as a mental illness as a major stumbling block to its pursuit of a successful litigation strategy. This misunderstanding of homosexuality by psychologists and psychiatrists foreshadowed how many gay and lesbian issues were later to be treated in the courts. In 1973, the APA finally declassified homosexuality as a mental illness and fended off a challenge from its more conservative members in a referendum in 1974, producing a major victory for the NGTF. Most "historians credit the new gay liberation movement for this outcome"; this victory "was equivalent to winning an important test case in the courts" (Cain 1993, 1582–83).

Interest Groups and Gay Rights Litigation

Some groups believed that the courts were their best opportunity for major advances against discrimination. The Lambda Legal Defense and Education Fund, for example, was founded in New York City in 1972 to pursue litigation in cases of discrimination against gays and lesbians in addition to providing educational programs to raise public awareness of gay and lesbian rights. Modeled after the NAACP LDF, Lambda engages in test-case litigation and also files amicus curiae briefs to help provide theoretical and statistical information to improve the courts' understanding of the needs and problems of gays and lesbians. It can probably be correctly called "the NAACP LDF" of the gay and lesbian rights movement, having participated in almost every major case involving gay rights.

Later in the decade of the 1970s, two additional groups largely devoted to litigation were founded. Gay and Lesbian Advocates and Defenders (GLAD) was established in 1978 in Boston. Initially known as Park Square Defenders, Inc., it was created in response to political and legal attacks on the gay and lesbian community. Through its written works (including the *National Attorneys' Directory for Gay and Lesbian Rights*) and public speaking, GLAD seeks to inform the public about discrimination experienced by gays and lesbians in an effort to change public perception and constitutional interpretation.

On the west coast, the Lesbian Rights Project (today called the National Center for Lesbian Rights (NCLR)) was established in San Francisco in 1977 as a public interest law firm specializing in sexual orientation discrimination. It focuses on issues of child custody, housing, employment, the military, and insurance. The project engages in both individual and impact cases and conducts community education projects to inform lesbians and gays of their legal rights. It claims to be the only legal organization in the country that emphasizes litigation and public education in the areas of law of special concern to lesbians.

Two groups were also founded in the 1980s. National Gay Rights Advocates (NGRA) was founded in San Francisco as a nonprofit public interest law firm specializing in litigation to advance the rights of lesbians and gay men. After several years of substantial involvement in important litigation, NGRA was "buried by internal strife" (Slind-Flor 1991) and dissolved in 1991. The Human Rights Campaign (HRC), which was founded primarily to lobby Congress, was also created in 1980. Though it does not focus primarily on litigation strategies, it does, however, lend its prestige and support to other groups through submission or co-sponsorship of amicus curiae briefs.

The American Civil Liberties Union (ACLU), largely through its local and state affiliates on the east and west coasts (especially in California and New York) was instrumental in bringing many early challenges to selective prosecution of gays and lesbians.[6] It was also a key player in challenging obscenity laws that barred the use of the mails to gay and lesbian magazines. In the 1980s, it became increasingly involved in gay and lesbian rights issues on the state and national level. In the mid-1980s, the ACLU formed a Lesbian and Gay Rights Project. Just like the Women's Rights Project and other ACLU projects, this development allowed its attorneys to develop greater expertise in this area of the law as well as to provide assistance to other activist lawyers around the nation.

Interestingly, the new groups that were created to concentrate on litigation were founded in three centers of long-time gay rights activism: San Francisco, New York City, and Boston. Just as the NAACP LDF's pursuit of a legal strategy was facilitated by existing networks of black lawyers in several large cities, so was the gay and lesbian rights movement—at least in terms of access to local networks of attorneys interested (and becoming expert) in areas of the law important to the gay community. Bay Area Lawyers for Individual Freedom (BALIF), for example, was founded in 1980 to take action on questions of law and justice regarding gay and lesbian issues and to promote the appointment of gay and lesbian attorneys to judicial and governmental agencies.

In 1988, the National Gay and Lesbian Law Association was founded; in 1992 it formally affiliated with the American Bar Association. It is the organizer of the Lavender Law Conference, which it initiated in 1992 to provide training and theoretical debates on legal issues pertaining to the gay community, mirroring earlier efforts of Lambda and the ACLU, which held a national meeting in 1983 to strategize about the eradication of sodomy laws. This Lambda / ACLU meeting, in fact, resulted in the creation of the Ad Hoc Task Force to Challenge Sodomy Laws, which, by 1985 became an official Lambda project.

Conferences such as the Lavender Law Conference facilitate communication networks as well as enhance legal expertise. While the first women and the law course was offered in 1970 (Hole and Levine 1973), one author writing in the *Yale Law Journal* notes that in 1983, no classes on "sexual orientation and the law or sexuality and the law" were offered in any national law school (Franke 1997). By 1995, only 25 percent of all law schools offered these kinds of courses (Franke 1997). As more and more law schools began to offer classes dealing with sexual orientation and sexuality legal issues, a growing supply of well-trained lawyers emerged equipped to handle what were to be an exponentially growing number of cases.

GAY RIGHTS LITIGATION AND THE U.S. SUPREME COURT

As gay rights activism spread, interest groups began to challenge a wide array of discriminatory practices in federal courts to complement their other political efforts. For example, student-based interest groups were critical actors in three cases initiated in the 1970s, *Gay Student Organization (GSO) of the University of New Hampshire v. Bonner* (1974), *Gay Alliance of Students v. Matthews* (1976), and *Gay Lib v. University of Missouri* (1978) (later called *Ratchford v. Gay Lib* when it reached the U.S. Supreme Court). In all three cases, federal circuit courts of appeals ruled that state universities could not refuse to allow gay student organizations to meet and use school facilities open to other groups based on these students' constitutional rights to free association and expression protected by the First and Fourteenth Amendments.[7] Only *Ratchford v. Gay Lib* was appealed to the U.S. Supreme Court.

The Supreme Court declined to review the favorable ruling from the Fourth Circuit panel in *Gay Lib*. Justices William Rehnquist and Harry Blackmun, however, forcefully dissented from this denial of certiorari. "The existence of such discretion," wrote Rehnquist of the Court's control over its own agenda, "does not imply that it should be used as a sort of judicial storm cellar to which we may flee to escape from controversial issues." But, the rest of the Court continued to keep its head in the sand when it came to issues of gay or lesbian constitutional rights. While the lower federal courts were willing to protect the rights of gay students to organize, finding those associational rights protected by the First and Fourteenth Amendments, they were much more wary of cases involving the suggestion of sexual activity.

Consensual Sodomy

Throughout the 1970s, myriad gay and lesbian interest groups and public interest law firms initiated test cases throughout the federal courts. An increasingly conservative U.S. Supreme Court, however, remained reluctant to involve itself in issues of homosexuality. In 1973, the Court, in a per curiam opinion, ruled that a Florida sodomy statute was not unconstitutionally vague (*Wainwright v. Stone* 1973). Three years later, in *Doe v. Commonwealth's Attorney*, a Virginia sodomy statute was challenged by a group of gay men who argued that they feared arrest under its provisions. The Supreme Court summarily affirmed a Court of Appeals finding in favor of the law's constitutionality.[8] No gay rights groups were involved, although Lambda filed an amicus brief urging the Supreme Court to review its decision.

Later, in 1981, the U.S. Supreme Court refused to hear a case from the New York State Court of Appeals (New York's highest appellate court), *People v. Onofre* (later called *New York v. Onofre*), in which several homosexual and heterosexual couples had successfully challenged their respective convictions under New York's consensual sodomy law. The New York Court was persuaded by arguments made by the Lambda on behalf of the couples that the New York law was a violation of the right to privacy guaranteed by the U.S. Constitution, regardless of marital status.[9] Thus, while the New York law could no longer be enforced against couples engaging in *consensual* sexual acts, most states continued to prosecute homosexuals with impunity. In fact, twenty-four states and the District of Columbia had sodomy laws; although most banned homosexual *and* heterosexual activity, in general, they largely were enforced selectively against homosexuals (Apasu-Gbotsu et al. 1986, 524–25).

Sodomy laws generally prohibit any form of oral or anal intercourse whether or not it is *consensual*. Like the APA's earlier ruling on homosexuality, the presence of state penal laws criminalizing the private sexual acts engaged in by gays and lesbians continued to be a major legal roadblock to the enjoyment of full rights under the U.S. Constitution. As early as 1965 in *Griswold v. Connecticut,* the U.S. Supreme Court had ruled that a state law that made it a crime for any person who "assists, abets, (or) counsels" a person to use any drug or article to prevent conception violated a married couple's right "of marital privacy which is within the penumbra of specific guarantees of the Bill of Rights." In 1972, the Court expanded this right to privacy in *Eisenstadt v. Baird* to apply to unmarried couples. The Court ruled that the equal protection clause demands similar treatment of similarly situated individuals, i.e. unmarried individuals. Thus, a state law barring unmarried persons access to contraception was unconstitutional. Although the justices seemed very concerned that the reach of the state should not intrude into the privacy of the bedroom, they were unwilling to close the blinds on homosexual behaviors.

Two years after *Onofre,* the New York State Court of Appeals again rendered a decision favorable to gay rights. In *People v. Uplinger* (1983), the Court ruled that "federal constitutional law invalidated a New York statute prohibiting persons from loitering in a public place for the purpose of engaging or soliciting another person to engage in 'deviate sexual behavior.'" The U.S. Supreme Court accepted this case, now called *New York v. Uplinger,* for review and heard oral arguments in 1984. The justices then decided that certiorari had been granted improvidently, concluding that the "case presented an inappropriate vehicle" for resolving the "important constitutional issues" raised by the parties.

Free from Supreme Court review, by 1986 nearly half of states continued to regulate the kinds of sexual activities in which couples could legally engage. And, while many state laws preventing consensual sodomy were written in gender-neutral language without specific reference to sexual orientation, most states used these laws selectively to prosecute rapists or homosexuals.

Gays in the Military

The ACLU and Lambda were particularly active in assisting service men and women who were excluded from the armed services after their sexual orientation became known.[10] During the 1970s and into the 1980s, more and more service members were drummed out of the armed forces because of their sexual orientation. Illustrative of the kinds of cases that made their ways into the federal courts were *Hatheway v. Secretary of the Army* (1981) and *Beller v. Middendorf* (1981). Hatheway was discharged from the Army after being found guilty of engaging in sodomy; Beller was discharged after he admitted to engaging in homosexuals acts. The Supreme Court refused to hear either appeal.

Immigration and Mental Illness Redux

While the Court was turning a deaf ear on cases that often confronted sexual acts head on in one form or another, another line of cases were being filed in the courts—those involving the continued exclusion of homosexuals from the United States on the ground that they suffered from a mental illness and therefore were not "fit" for entry into (or at times, for continuing to reside in) the United States.

In a set of cases that revisited some of the immigration issues addressed in *Boutilier,* the U.S. Supreme Court again refused to hear claims of gay and lesbian petitioners, despite the existence of a split among the federal circuit courts of appeals concerning whether homosexuality could be classified as an excludable mental illness. After the APA declassified homosexuality as a sexual deviance, the U.S. Public Health Service (PHS) informed the INS that it would no longer issue what were called Class "A" certificates, which certified that one was "afflicted with psychopathic personality." The INS used these certificates as its legal basis to exclude homosexuals. Following this action by the PHS, "the INS enforced the exclusion occasionally; more important, some gay immigrants made admissions [of homosexuality] in order to bring test cases" (Eskridge and Hunter 1997, 188).

In *Lesbian / Gay Freedom Day Committee, Inc. v. INS* (1983), the Court of Appeals for the Ninth Circuit ruled that the INS could not enforce the ban on homosexuals without the PHS issuing a Class "A" certificate. About the same time, however, a conflicting ruling was made by the Fifth Circuit, which permitted the exclusion of gays and lesbians without the cooperation of the PHS. Both cases turned on whether the INS was statutorily required to obtain the certificates from the PHS before trying to exclude homosexuals because they were homosexuals. The U.S. Supreme Court refused to take the Fifth Circuit case, *In re Longstaff* (1984). The INS declined to appeal the Ninth Circuit's ruling, fearing an adverse decision from the Supreme Court. In 1984, the PHS, under the conservative Reagan administration, offered to issue the certificates in the Ninth Circuit, which again allowed the INS to exclude gays and lesbians in every circuit in the country. These decisions eventually were overturned by Congress with the passage of the Immigration Act of 1990.

Hundreds of cases were initiated in the federal and state courts concerning the rights of gays and lesbians during this period, but none were deemed worthy of a full hearing by the Supreme Court. Some, like the

Lesbian / Gay Freedom case, were consciously not appealed so as to limit their impact. The Court declined to hear others, such as *In re Longstaff*.

Breaking the Silence

In 1985, just one year after the Court dismissed *Uplinger*, the Court refused to hear *Rowland v. Mad River Local School District* (1985). At issue was the treatment of a high school counselor.[11] Rowland, a bisexual, told some of her colleagues that she had a female lover; her news then was disclosed to school administrators. Rowland was then transferred to a new job and ultimately her contract was terminated. The U.S. Court of Appeals for the Sixth Circuit overturned a lower court verdict against the school district, finding that neither Rowland's equal protection nor free speech rights were violated by her dismissal.[12] The court concluded that her words were not protected by the First Amendment because Rowland's speech "was not made as a citizen on a matter of public concern." According to the appeals court, Rowland needed to provide evidence that heterosexual teachers would have been treated differently if they had disclosed their sexual orientation. Since she had not shown such differential treatment of heterosexual teachers, the Court concluded that there was no equal protection violation.

Rowland then appealed this adverse decision to the Supreme Court shortly before the Court was to accept *Bowers v. Hardwick* for review. Two justices, although not the same dissenters in *Gay Lib*, again urged the Court to take action on this increasingly convoluted area of the law. Justice William Brennan, joined by Justice Thurgood Marshall, dissented from the Court's denial of certiorari. Justice Brennan argued that the Court should take the case because "(T)he determination of the appropriate constitutional analysis to apply in such a case continues to puzzle lower courts and because this Court has never addressed the issues presented. . . . Whether constitutional rights are infringed in sexual preference cases and whether some compelling state interest can be advanced to advance their infringement, are important." Seven other justices were not so moved.

That same term, the Supreme Court actually heard one case involving the constitutionality of a 1978 Oklahoma law that allowed school administrators to fire teachers who "advocate, promote, or encourage homosexual behavior in a manner sufficiently public" to come to the attention of school children or other school employees. The National Gay Task Force (NGTF) challenged the law, arguing that it violated the free speech rights of teachers. The U.S. Court of Appeals for the Tenth Circuit struck down the law as an unconstitutional infringement on free speech rights. The U.S. Supreme Court (with Justice Lewis Powell not participating) divided four to four after hearing oral arguments on the merits of the case. This split in the *Board of Education of Oklahoma City v. National Gay Task Force* (1985) left the lower court's decision in place. This court of appeals decision, then, while binding on the federal courts in the Tenth Circuit, was not binding as precedent outside of the circuit in which the case originally was decided.

HARDWICK AND BEYOND

Since 1986, the U.S. Supreme Court has fully considered and rendered opinions in only six cases involving gay or lesbian rights or decision that potentially affect the gay and lesbian community as revealed in table 15.1. *Bowers v. Hardwick* (1986) was the first major case heard and decided by the Court. *Bowers* arose when a police officer came to the home of Michael Hardwick early in the morning to serve a warrant charging Hardwick with failing to appear in court for drinking in public. A house guest of Hardwick's admitted the officer and allowed him to look for Hardwick. Through a partially open door, the officer saw Hardwick and another man engaging in activities defined as illegal sodomy under Georgia law.[13]

Hardwick was arrested, but the local prosecutor refused to press for an indictment. Hardwick nevertheless challenged the Georgia law in federal court with the help of lawyers from the Georgia ACLU.[14] He was joined in his challenge to the constitutionality of the Georgia Law by a married couple, identified in the court only as John and Mary Doe, because the law prohibited *both* heterosexual and homosexual oral sex. The federal district court judge ruled against the challenge, but he was reversed by the court of appeals. Relying on *Griswold, Eisenstadt, Stanley v. Georgia* (1969),[15] and *Roe v. Wade* (1973), the court of appeals panel concluded that Hardwick's fundamental right to privacy extended to the private sexual acts prohibited by the Georgia law.

The Supreme Court accepted *Bowers* for review in 1985. Throughout his trial and the appeals process, Hardwick was represented by the ACLU; noted Harvard Law professor Lawrence Tribe, an active member of the Ad Hoc Task Force, orally argued his case before the Court. *Bowers* attracted a plethora of amici from a wide array of interest groups on both sides. A total of thirteen amicus briefs were filed—twelve on behalf of interest groups or states. A total of twenty-five interest groups including Lambda, National Gay Rights Advocates, Gay and Lesbian Advocates and Defenders, and

Table 15.1 Major Interest Group Participation in Supreme Court Cases

	Bowers	Webster	Hurley	Romer	Oncale	Bragdon
Amicus						
Americal Civil Liberties Union	S	S	X*	S	X	X
American Psychiatric Association				X		
American Psychological Association	X			X		
American Public Health Association	X					X
Bay Area Lawyers for Individual Freedom	X			X	X	X
Gay & Lesbian Advocates & Defenders	X		S	X	X	S
Human Rights Campaign				X		X
Lambda Legal Defense and Education Fund	X		X	S	X	X
National Center for Lesbian Rights**	X		X	X	X	X
National Gay & Lesbian Task Force***	X			X		X
National Lesbian & Gay Law Association				X		X
National Organization for Women	X			X	X	
U.S. government		S (against)			X	X
Women's Legal Defense Fund	X	X		X	X	

*The ACLU filed in support of neither party in this case.
**Formerly called the Lesbian Rights Project.
***Formerly called National Gay Rights Advocates.
S = sponsored.

the Lesbian Rights Project (now the National Center for Lesbian Rights) urged the Court to find the Georgia statute unconstitutional. The American Psychological Association (joined on its brief by the American Public Health Association (APHA)) also filed an amicus brief to present the Court with the new medical and psychological information that led it to conclude that homosexuality could no longer be considered a sexual deviance.[16]

The Supreme Court narrowly rejected the legal arguments advanced in Hardwick's behalf. Justice Byron White wrote the opinion for the five-person majority. He framed the question presented in *Bowers* as whether a fundamental right to engage in homosexual sodomy existed. He answered that question in the negative, distinguishing *Bowers* from other privacy cases such as *Griswold* and *Roe* by arguing that those cases concerned marriage, procreation, or child rearing. In dissent, Justice Harry Blackmun, the author of the Court's major privacy decision, *Roe,* argued that the majority had posed the wrong question. Writing for himself and Justices Brennan, Marshall, and Stevens, he said the issue in *Bowers* was whether the right of privacy shields private sexual activity taking place in the home from invasion. Blackmun's strongly worded dissent argued that it was, clearly breaking with his support of Justice Rehnquist's dissent from the Court's denial of certiorari in *Gay Lib.*

The Court's decision in *Bowers* was a close one. Many gay and lesbian rights activists had pinned their hopes on Justice Powell, who had not participated in *Board of Education of Oklahoma City v. National Gay Task Force* the term before, to be the tie-breaker in this case. He was, but not on their side. Even more disturbing to the groups involved in *Bowers* were comments later attributed to Powell who reportedly deeply regretted that decision (Greenhouse 1990). In fact, he initially obliged the activists, voting to affirm the lower court's decision on Eighth Amendment cruel and unusual punishment grounds. However, a week after the initial conference, Powell switched his vote to reverse the lower court decision (Greenhouse 1990).

While gay and lesbian groups were disappointed with Justice Powell, they were shocked by the language used in Chief Justice Warren Burger's concurring opinion in which he referred to homosexuality as "an offense of deeper malignity" than rape, a heinous act "the very mention of which is a disgrace to human nature," and "a crime not fit to be named." This language did not bode particularly well for cases now wending their way through the appeals process, unless there were to be personnel changes on the Court. And, with a Republican president in office, the appointment of liberal jurists was highly unlikely.

After *Bowers,* given the composition of the Court and the public's continued hostility toward homosexuality, gay and lesbian rights activists found themselves in a quandary about whether it was advisable to continue to try to bring test cases to the Supreme Court and risk further negative precedent. Moreover, AIDS was taking a growing toll in the gay community and a host of new legal issues were arising concerning insurance, employment discrimination, and health care among others for people with AIDS. Similarly, new reproductive technologies were making it easier for lesbians to have children while many lesbian mothers found themselves locked in battles for custody of their children. Many of these new legal issues facing the gay and lesbian community were issues generally considered to be state issues. Thus, several groups were forced to litigate on the state level, eschewing impact litigation in the federal courts. Those kinds of lawsuits are often costly and aren't the type of impact litigation generally preferred by national interest groups.

Military Discrimination Marches On

There was one area of the law that was national in scope and rife with symbolism as well as discrimination. Until 1993, gay men and lesbians were banned from serving in the military. In general, once it was learned that someone was a homosexual, they often were discharged from the service. A series of challenges were brought to protest releases from the Navy, discharges from the Army Reserves, and the failure of the Army to allow a gay service member to reenlist.[17] The U.S. Supreme Court declined to hear all of these cases.

Historically, the Court has been very reluctant to second-guess the judgment of the military, even when discrimination is alleged. In *Rostker v. Goldberg* (1981), for example, the Court upheld the male-only draft provision of the Military Selective Service Act against the charge that it unconstitutionally discriminated against males. If the Court was unwilling to extend the draft to women, given years of women's relatively successful participation in the military (Francke 1998; Herbert 1998), it was unlikely to protect the rights of gays and lesbians, especially in the absence of any finding that discrimination against them as a group was unconstitutional.

To some extent, the situation was only confused when the Clinton administration finally adopted its "Don't Ask, Don't Tell" policy in 1993. As a presidential candidate, Clinton had run opposed to the ban on gays and lesbians in the military. But shortly after he became president in 1993, the Pentagon and some members of Congress objected so strenuously to his initial recommendation that he unveiled a compromise policy, which permits gays and lesbians to serve in the military so long as they don't publicly state their sexual orientation. In 1993, *United States v. Meinhold* the Supreme Court refused to stay an injunction against this policy.

In an area closely associated to discrimination against gays and lesbians in the military—discrimination in the foreign service or the Central Intelligence Agency (CIA)—the Court did accept one case for review: *Webster v. Doe* (1988), which was sponsored by the ACLU. *Webster* involved a challenge to the dismissal of a covert electronics technician in the CIA's employ after he voluntarily admitted he was a homosexual. Ultimately, the issue presented to the Court was whether the decision to discharge the petitioner was reviewable. A majority of the Supreme Court ruled that the CIA director's decision to terminate Doe in the national interest was reviewable by the lower courts because Doe had alleged constitutional violations of his First and Fifth Amendment rights as well as his right to privacy. The majority, however, *never* addressed any issues pertaining to Doe's sexual orientation The Court's decision in *Webster* dealt solely with the issue of judicial review, with the justices concluding that the director of the CIA's employment decisions could not be above the color of law. Later, in keeping with the Court's general reluctance to deal with issues of sexual orientation, the justices refused to overturn the discharge of a foreign service officer where questions were raised about his conduct and not necessarily his homosexuality, in *KRC v. United States Information Agency* (1994).

Parades and Free Speech

The next case to be accepted for certiorari by the Supreme Court concerning the rights of homosexuals dealt with issues beyond those of specific sexual conduct at issue in *Bowers;* none of the sexual overtones and moralism that seemed to trouble the majority in *Bowers* were present in *Hurley v. Irish American Gay, Lesbian and Bisexual Group of Boston* (GLIB) (1995). Nearly a decade after *Bowers,* an unincorporated group of elected individuals from various veterans' groups who organized Boston's St. Patrick's Day Parade were sued after they refused to allow a homosexual group to march in the annual parade. A group of gay, lesbian, and bisexual potential marchers challenged their exclusion from the parade, arguing that the organizers' actions violated a state law prohibiting discrimination on account of sexual orientation in places of public accommodation. Parade organizers argued that their First Amendment rights would be violated if they were forced to allow a group with whose message they disagreed to march.

Gay and Lesbian Advocates and Defenders sponsored the case before the Supreme Court. They were supported by a number of gay rights groups, as well as several liberal organizations as amici. A number of religious groups including the Christian Legal Society and the National Association of Evangelicals filed amicus briefs in support of the veterans' exclusion of the gay marchers. The ACLU filed in support of neither party. It argued that the Supreme Court should send *Hurley* back to the lower courts for a determination as to whether the veterans' group, which had been authorized by the City of Boston to organize and conduct the parade, was a state actor. If it was, the ACLU argued that it would open up the question of whether GLIB's equal protection as well as free speech and association rights were violated by the state, and not individuals.

The Supreme Court declined to follow the suggestions of the ACLU. Writing for a unanimous Court in *Hurley,* Justice David Souter concluded that the organization of the parade itself was constitutionally protected speech and not a public accommodation. Thus, the state law preventing discrimination in public accommodations could not be applied to force the inclusion of gay, lesbian, or bisexual marchers. Although the Court actually specifically recognized the constitutional authority of the states to enact provisions prohibiting discrimination in public accommodations based on a variety of factors including *sexual orientation,* these kinds of guarantees did not trump the First Amendment rights of parade organizers. So, while the Court recognized the authority of the state to ban discrimination based on status, it ironically upheld the right of some to discriminate for those same status reasons.

A Constitutional Breakthrough: New Gains under the Equal Protection Clause

The next case to come before the Court, *Romer v. Evans* (1996), involved the overt political rights of homosexuals. Unlike *Bowers,* sex acts were not directly in question in *Romer.* Since *Bowers* had been framed in terms of fundamental rights rather than equal protection (Kimball 1996, 221), gay rights advocates hoped that the Court would use the equal protection clause of the Fourteenth Amendment to protect their political rights. Twenty-five years earlier, in *Reed,* the Supreme Court had finally ruled that the equal protection clause could be construed to prohibit some forms of state discrimination against women. Under the guidance of Ruth Bader Ginsburg and the ACLU Women's Rights Project, other cases were quickly brought to the Court in an ultimately unsuccessful attempt to convince the justices to apply the strict scrutiny standard of review to cases involving gender discrimination. While the Court eventually fashioned a new test to determine the constitutionality of state based gender discrimination—the intermediate standard of review—the Supreme Court in 1996 had yet to extend *any* of the protections of the equal protection clause to classifications based on sexual orientation. While homosexuality was no longer officially defined as a mental illness by the APA or the government, the Constitution had yet to be interpreted to prevent discrimination against gays and lesbians as a group, unlike other groups including African Americans and even aliens.

In 1992, the Colorado legislature passed and the voters overwhelmingly approved an amendment to its Constitution that precluded all state action at any level of government to protect the status of persons based on their homosexual orientation, conduct, practices, or relationships. The amendment was passed by popular referendum in response to the actions of several municipalities in the state that had enacted antidiscrimination laws to prevent discrimination based on sexual orientation.

The Colorado amendment was challenged by gays and lesbians as well as by the municipalities whose laws were affected. They argued that the amendment was a violation of the U.S. Constitution's equal protection clause. The Colorado Supreme Court ruled that Amendment 2 was unconstitutional under the U.S. Constitution finding that it violated the "*fundamental rights* of gays and lesbians to participate in the political process" (emphasis added). Like claims based on racial classifications, the U.S. Supreme Court has afforded violations of fundamental rights the highest standard of review, strict scrutiny.

The state of Colorado then appealed this decision to the Supreme Court and the justices granted certiorari in 1995. *Romer* attracted a record number of *amici curiae* from gay and lesbian groups: over eighty interest groups filed briefs in support of Evans. Notable among these were the National Gay and Lesbian Task Force, Gay and Lesbian Advocates and Defenders, the National Center for Lesbian Rights, and the Human Rights Campaign.[18] Seven states and the District of Columbia also filed briefs in support of Evans's claims.

Evans was represented by local counsel, Jean E. Dubofsky, a former Colorado judge. When the case was accepted for review, Matthew Coles, however, the new director of the ACLU's Lesbian and Gay Rights Project, immediately contacted Dubofsky and asked her to turn the case over to the ACLU, a more experienced Supreme Court litigator. As was the case with the NAACP LDF and the Women's Rights Project of the ACLU, civil rights litigators pursuing a test case strategy often find themselves confronted with cases not of their fashioning that have arrived at the doorsteps of the Court without benefit of interest group vetting. Wrote Coles to Dubofsky: "I know how much this case means to you personally and I know how difficult it would be for you to watch someone else argue it at this point, but as you and I have both observed several times this is a difficult case, it could go either way, and the outcome may well depend on oral argument (Biskupic 1996, A19). Dubofsky declined Coles's generous offer and went on to argue the case to "mixed reviews" (Biskupic 1996,

A19). Nevertheless, Dubofsky was soon to become the first lawyer to argue a gay rights case successfully before the Supreme Court.

In *Romer* the Supreme Court held that Colorado's Amendment 2 failed the lowest level of equal protection scrutiny, the rational basis test.

> The Fourteenth Amendment's promise that no person shall be denied the equal protection of the laws must coexist with the practical necessity that most legislation classifies for one purpose or another, with resulting disadvantage to various groups or persons. We have attempted to reconcile the principle with the reality by stating that, if a law neither burdens a fundamental right nor targets a suspect class, we will uphold the legislative classification so long as it bears a rational relation to some legitimate end.

While the majority opinion of Justice Anthony Kennedy did not rest on expansive constitutional grounds, it was certainly a strongly worded opinion. It opened with a quote from Justice Harlan's dissent in *Plessy v. Ferguson* (1896), in which he proclaimed that the Constitution "neither knows nor tolerates classes among its citizens." Kennedy argued that Colorado's Amendment 2 did not, as the state argued, repeal special rights for homosexuals, but rather targeted them to disadvantage them in the political process. Further, he reasoned that these types of laws "raise the inevitable inference that the disadvantage imposed is born of animosity toward the class of persons affected." In an equally strong worded dissent, Justice Antonin Scalia argued that the majority opinion in *Romer* could not be reconciled with the Court's earlier decision in *Bowers.*

Gay rights advocates warmly welcomed the Court's decision, although the Court failed to extend the same degree of constitutional protection to them that already was enjoyed by women or African Americans. Still, one Lambda lawyer called the Court's decision, "a historic shift in the Court's response to antigay discrimination." The Court, said Suzanne B. Goldberg, rejected "gay bashing by referendum," while revealing that "discrimination is discrimination and that antigay sentiment is not a justification for discrimination by government" (Greenhouse 1996, A1).

AFTER *ROMER*: WHAT'S NEXT?

Since *Romer*, the Supreme Court has denied certiorari in more than ten cases involving a wide variety of gay and lesbian rights issues. In late 1995, while *Romer* was pending, it denied certiorari in a case involving a child custody dispute between a lesbian couple in *Knott v. Holtzman* (1995). It also rejected more challenges to the new Clinton policy on gays in the military (*Selland* 1996; *Thomasson* 1996). The Court has also declined to hear a major employment discrimination case involving the dismissal of a lesbian lawyer in *Shahar v. Bowers* (1998).

After declining to hear *Shahar,* the Court decided a case which, although not directly involving the rights of homosexuals or an interpretation of the U.S. Constitution, had the potential to affect gay rights law. *Oncale v. Sundowner Offshore Service* (1998) attracted the attention of a wide array of interested groups largely because of its potential application in future cases. Joseph Oncale, a male employed on an off-shore oil platform, claimed he was sexually harassed by his male coworkers and filed suit under Title VII of the Civil Rights Act of 1964, which prohibits discrimination on the basis of sex. In 1986, the Court had extended the coverage of Title VII to sexual harassment in *Meritor Savings Bank, FSB v. Vinson* (1986).

A lower court held that Oncale could not sue his employer, finding that legally actionable sexual harassment could only take place between members of the opposite sex. Justice Scalia, writing for a unanimous Supreme Court, stated that the lower court had erred. Sexual harassment, concluded the Court, could take place between members of the same sex. Although hailed by gay rights groups, *Oncale* cannot be taken to reflect a change in the Court's attitude about homosexual conduct as reflected in the majority opinion in *Bowers.* However, as Lambda managing attorney Ruth Harlan stated, "Every plaintiff, no matter what their sex or sexual orientation, is now called upon to prove a sexual harassment claim in the same way" (Jackson 1998, 1A). It must be stressed that *Oncale* involved neither a constitutional interpretation nor a gay plaintiff.

HIV/AIDS

Of greater interest to gay rights activists was another case the Court heard during its 1997–1998 term. When the AIDS epidemic hit the United States in the early 1980s (Shilts 1987; Theodolou 1996), gay rights activists were soon called on to help those affected with HIV or AIDS to deal with the wide range of discrimination they quickly began to experience. Both Lambda and the ACLU created specific projects to deal with HIV/AIDS legal problems. The Bay Area Lawyers for Individual Freedom (BALIF) also played an early role in fighting for the rights of those with HIV/ AIDS. BALIF eventually created a separate AIDS Legal Referral Project, which quickly became the model for the creation of other HIV/AIDS legal service providers around the nation.

Although people with AIDS have experienced and challenged discrimination against them since the early 1980s, AIDS cases, most of them with the support of interest groups, are now just finding their way to the apex of the legal system. The Supreme Court has refused to accept several cases involving a wide range of legal issues including employer dismissal of personnel with AIDS (*Reno* 1996; *Wood* 1997) and medical records privacy (*Doe v. SEPTA* 1996). At the close of its 1997–1998 term, however, the Supreme Court decided *Bragdon v. Abbott* (1998), which involved the scope of the Americans with Disabilities Act (ADA). Again, like *Oncale*, the Court was addressing the scope of a federal statute and *not* interpreting the Constitution. And, like *Webster* and *Hurley*, *Bragdon* did not involve issues of homosexuality directly. In fact, the ADA specifically excludes homosexuals, bisexuals, transsexual, and transvestites from coverage.

Sidney Abbott, an HIV-positive woman, sued her dentist, Randon Bragdon, after he refused to provide routine dental care to her in his office. She alleged that Bragdon violated the ADA. The district court granted summary judgment in her favor and the U.S. Court of Appeals for the First Circuit upheld that ruling. When the Supreme Court accepted the case for review, *Bragdon* became the catalyst for gay and lesbian rights groups finally to appraise the Court about their views on discrimination against those with HIV / AIDS as well as the scope of the ADA. In a landmark 5–4 decision, the Court ruled that the ADA protects persons with HIV / AIDS. The Court found that Abbott's HIV status impaired her ability to reproduce and bear children, which constitutes a "major life activity" under the ADA.

THE PROGNOSIS FOR FULL CONSTITUTIONAL RIGHTS

During the 1990s, the gay and lesbian rights community targeted three issues of central legal concern: discrimination against persons with HIV / AIDS, discrimination in the military, and discrimination against lesbian and gay parents and partners.

HIV/AIDS Discrimination

Heartened by the Court's ruling in *Bragdon,* AIDS rights litigation will continue to be a major emphasis of many gay and lesbian rights litigators. AIDS, however, is far more than a legal issue to those in the gay community. AIDS initially derailed many groups' litigation efforts as precious resources and energies were channeled in what were viewed to be more immediate concerns. The gay community and the legal profession have been hard hit by the loss of lead activists and lawyers to the disease (McKee

1993). This resulted in the loss of not only noted leaders in the community but experience and expertise on HIV/AIDS legal issues. The gay male legal community was especially hit hard by AIDS, which has resulted in an increasing number of lesbian lawyers moving into vacated positions. AIDS litigation, however, is unlikely to be the vehicle by which to convince the Court to elevate the minimum rationality standard to Court applied to sexual orientation in *Romer*.

Discrimination in the Military

Discrimination in the military and in other positions of national security has long plagued gays and lesbians. Gay, lesbian, and civil liberties groups initially challenged this kind of discrimination on equal protection grounds; they later were forced to change their strategies when the "Don't Ask, Don't Tell" policy was announced in 1993. Over the years, the Court has rejected scores of cases from gay and lesbians who were dismissed from the military. Often these men and women were assisted by one or more of the numerous groups that have specifically created projects to develop expertise in this complicated area of the law including the ACLU's Lesbian and Gay Rights Project and Lambda. One group, the Servicemembers's Legal Defense Network, concentrates in this area of the law, specifically.

The Court's reluctance to hear three cases, which generally has let stand rulings against gays and lesbians, prompted many activists to change their tactics. Presidential *candidate* Bill Clinton announced that he supported the elimination of the military's ban on gays, and in response many gays and lesbians donated money to his campaign and worked hard for his election, seeing presidential support as more likely to produce change than resort to the courts—at least where military policy was concerned. They were quickly disappointed when as *president* he announced his compromise policy.

The Court clearly has had the opportunity to determine if current military policy (especially the "Don't Ask, Don't Tell" policy) violates the U.S. Constitution either on First or Fourteenth Amendment equal protection grounds. One can argue that a policy that inhibits speech violates the free speech clause of the First Amendment (Strasser 1995; Sullivan 1995). Similarly in the aftermath of *Romer*, gays and lesbians could again argue (this time with some legal authority) that the continued differential treatment of gays in the military violates the equal protection clause. But, historically, the Court has given substantial deference to military claims of necessity, so it is unlikely that the Court will use a military case to announce new or even continued constitutional rights for gays and lesbians (Wachs 1996).[19]

Gay and Lesbian Families

Historically, since the adoption of the U.S. Constitution, issues of family life (including marriage, divorce, and child custody) were presumed to be within the power of the individual states to regulate. Through the 1990s, the federal government and the federal courts have been extremely reluctant to tread into this last bastion of state sovereignty.

State family law, particularly laws or practices that bar prospective gay parents from adopting children, disfavor gay or lesbian parents in child custody matters, or prohibit same-sex marriages and their attendant benefits, have enormous consequences on gays and lesbians. Many gays and lesbian rights groups have tried to change the law in these areas through litigation. Most of their successes, however, have come in the state courts with judges interpreting equal protection–like clauses of *state* constitutions. For example, in Hawaii, the state supreme court ruled in 1993 that there was nothing in the state constitution to prevent gay and lesbian marriage. It sent a challenge to the state's refusal to grant a marriage license to a gay couple back to the lower court with instructions that the state meet the strict scrutiny standard, that is, showing a compelling state interest in denying the license.[20]

Gay and lesbian rights groups have been critical actors on the state and national level in the areas of marriage and family law reform. The National Center for Lesbian Rights (NCLR) and the National Organization for Women's Lesbian Rights Project regularly assist lesbian and gay parents fighting for custody and visitation rights. The ACLU and Lambda have projects that specifically address family and custody issues and are leading advocates for the legalization of same-sex partnership. Issues of children and partnership will continue to top gay and lesbian legal interest groups' agendas well into the future, but for reasons discussed below, these strategies may be better suited to some state courts than pursuit in the U.S. federal courts.

CONCLUSION

What then is the future for gay and lesbian rights? The three areas of major concern to gay and lesbian rights groups—HIV / AIDS, the military, and family law—differ from other legal issues targeted in past efforts, which consisted of more easily defined constitutional challenges to discrimination. Gays first alleged free speech rights in cases involving magazine distribution, then targeted the APA and the federal government's stance on homosexuality as a mental illness. Discrimination in the military (and national security agencies) and in lifestyles (*Bowers*) were next. Neither course produced major advances in the legal status of gays and lesbians under the U.S. Constitution.

The Court's continued refusal to hear cases that involved issues of sexual orientation makes it clear that the Court is reluctant to deal with issues involving intimate sexual conduct. In response, federal litigation sponsored by interest groups has focused on statutory concerns as well as a different mode of constitutional attack. The Court, for example, was willing to extend basic political rights to gays and lesbians in *Romer* finding it unconstitutional for the state to prevent gays from enjoying basic constitutional rights guaranteed by the equal protection clause. The Court was only willing, however, to apply the lowest standard of review in invalidating Colorado's Amendment 2.

Favorable statutory construction is one potentially positive avenue of legal redress for gay rights activists. The Civil Rights Act of 1964, for example, does not include sexual harassment as a specific form of employment discrimination. Yet the Supreme Court found sexual harassment (male to female) actionable in *Meritor Savings Bank* and then extended the ruling to include same-sex harassment in 1998. Similarly, the ADA does not explicitly mention HIV / AIDS as a disability. However, interest groups successfully persuaded the Court in *Bragdon* to interpret the ADA so as to protect those with HIV / AIDS from discrimination. Thus, through statutory construction, the Court may widen opportunities for gays and lesbians in the context of a seemingly neutral law. This strategy may be more productive than constitutional challenges, since courts are more likely to extend specific statutory protections than to construe the Constitution more broadly, especially to a class of people whose activities or states some justices find morally objectionable. Statutory victories are better than no victories at all, but they have less impact initially. But, in the long run, the cumulative impact of these smaller victories on the state and national level, may collectively lessen the public's tolerance of discriminatory laws against gays and lesbians, thereby facilitating more successful constitutional challenges at a later date.

NOTES

1. Amicus briefs are filed by parties and interest groups with an interest in the outcome of the case as a "friend of the court," but actually almost always on one side of the case.

2. All direct quotations used herein are to judicial opinions unless otherwise noted.

3. One year before, in *Kameny v. Brucker* (1961), the Court refused to hear an appeal of Frank Kameny's dismissal from the U.S. Army Map Service after it was reported that he was a homosexual. He then formed the D.C. Mattachine Society, which began to represent individuals discharged from the civil service (Cain 1993, 1547).

4. After receiving numerous complaints about alleged homosexual behavior in public restrooms in Yosemite National Park during the summer of 1963, park rangers and park police cut a hole in the ceiling of a public restroom to conduct night time surveillance.

5. While the Mattachine Society was engaged in traditional forms of lobbying, the Society for Individual Rights was formed in San Francisco in 1964. In 1965, its first foray into litigation occurred after police made arrests at its 1965 New Year's Day Ball. Its lawyers were arrested for obstructing policy entry and its tactics gained considerable publicity for the more radical group (Cain 1993, 1563–64).

6. Prior to the Supreme Court's decision in *Griswold v. Connecticut*, the ACLU held to the view that sodomy statutes were constitutional. All along, however, it acted to protect the due process rights of gays and lesbians.

7. Plaintiffs GSO were themselves part of an interest group and they were assisted by the Lambda Legal Defense Fund in the form of an amicus curiae brief and technical assistance. Similarly, the Gay Alliance of Students was also a group; its members were represented by private counsel and lawyers from the National Gay Task Force.

8. The Supreme Court also denied certiorari to a challenge to a North Carolina sodomy law the same day.

9. Lambda was victorious in *Onofre* and urged the Supreme Court not to accept the case for review. Still, while this case was a victory for gays and lesbians in New York, and of course, in principle, for gays throughout the United States, the Court's refusal to accept the case for review meant that other states still could prosecute homosexual sexual behavior if they wished. The Court could have accepted the case to make the New York ruling apply to all of the states; instead it remained silent.

10. Cases were also brought to the court during this era concerning employment of gays and lesbians in the federal government. In *Singer v. United States Civil Service Commission* (1977), for example, a gay employee was dismissed from the federal service after flaunting his sexual orientation in public.

11. The Court also rejected a case involving the question whether transsexual were a protected class under Title VII of the Civil Rights Act of 1964 during this term in *Ulane v. Eastern Airlines, Inc.*

12. The court specifically rejected this argument that was advanced by National Gay Rights Advocates in its amicus brief.

13. The Georgia law stated: "A person commits the offense of sodomy when he performs or submits to any sexual act involving the sex organs of one person and the mouth or anus of another. . . ."

14. Lambda and its Ad Hoc Task Force provided Hardwick's lawyers with a "legal think tank and central place to discuss constitutionality theory and litigation" (Lambda 1995).

15. In *Stanley*, the Court held that the First Amendment protected the possessions of sexually explicit materials otherwise considered obscene in the home.

16. In 1975, both the American Psychological Association and the APHA passed resolutions supporting the APA's action decategorizing homosexual orientation as a mental illness.

17. These cases include *Woodward v. United States* (1990) (release from the Navy); *Watkins v. U.S. Army* (1990) (Army was prevented from discharging a gay service member because it had knowingly allowed him to reenlist several times despite knowing his sexual preference); *Schowengerdt v. United States* (1992) (discharge from Navy Reserve after a warrantless search revealed bisexuality); and *Pruitt v. Cheney* (1992) (discharge from the army reserve).

18. At the same time gay rights watchers were following *Equality Foundation of Greater Cincinnati v. Cincinnati*, which the Court declined to review just one week after *Romer*. This case involved a challenge to a city Human Rights Ordinance passed in 1992, which prohibited private discrimination in employment, housing, or public accommodation because of sexual orientation. In 1993 Cincinnati voters then overwhelmingly passed a charter amendment barring these kinds of protections based on homosexual, lesbian, or bisexual "orientation, status, conduct, or relationship." A local group then sued and a district court judge ruled that the charter amendment was unconstitutional. He also ordered the city to pay gay rights lawyers nearly $400,000 in attorneys fees and costs. That ruling was overturned by the Sixth Circuit Court of Appeals. The Equality Foundation, represented by the Lambda Legal Defense and Education Fund, appealed to the U.S. Supreme Court in August 1995. The Court decided *Romer* on May 20, 1996. The Supreme Court then vacated the Sixth Circuit Court's ruling sending the Equality Foundation case back to that circuit to reconsider in light of *Romer*.

   Although the Cincinnati amendment was patterned after Colorado's Amendment 2, the Sixth Circuit upheld its earlier ruling deciding that the amendment could withstand constitutional challenge because the state had shown the amendment's rational relationship to legitimate community ends. In late 1997, that court said it was reasonable for a state to try to limit the number of discrimination cases challenging discrimination based on sexual orientation. This ruling was then unsuccessfully appealed by Lambda to the U.S. Supreme Court in 1998.

19. A majority of the court in *Webster*, however, was unwilling to allow the Direc-

tor of the CIA unquestioned or unreviewable authority to fire any individual
when violations of their constitutional rights were alleged.

20. In response, however, the state legislature passed a constitutional amendment
    giving it the authority to restrict marriage to opposite sex couples. That
    amendment is before the voters in November 1998. Federal and state response
    to the specter of gay marriages, however, immediately led over half of the
    states to enact some sort of specific ban on gay marriages.

    Congress succumbed to the fray in 1996 when it enacted the Defense
    of Marriage Act, which should any state allow gay marriage, will permit other
    states not to recognize those unions.

REFERENCES

Adam, Barry D. 1995. *The rise of a gay and lesbian movement.* New York: Twayne
Publishers.

Apasu-Gbotsu, Yao, Robert J. Arnold, Paul DiBella, Kevin Dorse, Elisa L. Fuller,
Steven H. Naturman, Dung Hong Pham, and James B. Putney. 1986. Survey
on the constitutional rights to privacy in the context of homosexual activity.
University of Miami Law Review 40:521–657.

Archer, Belinda. 1998. The G Word; advertisers reluctance to target the gay community. *Campaign.* 30 January, 32.

Beller v. Middendorf, 632 F.2d 788 (9th Cir. 1980), *cert. denied,* 454 U.S. 855
(1981).

Biskupic, Joan. 1996. Legal elite vie for court time in pursuit of supreme challenge.
Washington Post. 2 December, A19.

Board of Education of Oklahoma City v. National Gay Task Force, 470 U.S. 903
(1985).

Boutilier v. Immigration and Naturalization Services, 387 U.S. 118 (1967).

Bowers v. Hardwick, 478 U.S. 186 (1986).

Bragdon v. Abbott, 118 S. Ct. 2196 (1998).

Brown v. Board of Education, 347 U.S. 483 (1954).

Cain, Patricia A. 1993. Litigating for lesbian and gay rights: A legal history. *Virginia Law Review* 79:1551–1641.

Clark, Kenneth B. 1950. Effects of prejudice and discrimination on personality
development. Midcentury White House Conference on Children and Youth.

Cortner, Richard C. 1975. *The Supreme Court and civil liberties policy.* Palo Alto,
Calif.: Mayfield Publishing Co.

Costain, Anne N. 1992 *Inviting women's rebellion: A political process interpretation
of the women's movement.* Baltimore: Johns Hopkins University Press.

Doe v. Commonwealth's Attorney, 403 F. Supp. 1199 (E.D. Va. 1975), *aff'd,* 425
U.S. 901 (1976).

Doe v. SEPTA, 72 F.3d 1133 (3d Cir. 1995), *cert denied,* 117 S. Ct. 51 (1996).

Eisenstadt v. Baird, 405 U.S. 438 (1972).

Equality Foundation of Greater Cincinnati v. Cincinnati, 54 F.3d 261 (6th Cir. 1995), *vacated,* 116 S. Ct. 2519 (1996), 128 F.3d 289 (6th Cir. 1997), *reh'g denied,* 1998 U.S. App. LEXIS 1765 (1998).

Eskridge, William N. 1997. Privacy jurisprudence and the apartheid of the closet, 1946–1961. *Florida State University Law Review* 24:703–838.

Eskridge, William N., and Nan D. Hunter. 1997. *Sexuality, gender, and the law.* Westbury, N.Y.: The Foundation Press, Inc.

Francke, Linda Bird. 1998. *Ground zero: The gender wars in the military.* New York: Simon and Schuster.

Franke, Katherine N. 1997. Homosexuals, torts and other dangerous things. *Yale Law Journal* 106 (June): 2661–83.

Gay Alliance of Students v. Matthews, 544 F.2d 162 (4th Cir. 1976).

Gay Lib v. University of Missouri, 558 F.2d 848 (8th Cir. 1977), *cert. denied sub nom. Ratchford v. Gay Lib,* 434 U.S. 1080 (1978).

Gay Student Organization of the University of New Hampshire v. Bonner, 509 F.2d 652 (1st Cir. 1974).

Greenhouse, Linda. 1990. When second thoughts in case come too late. *New York Times.* 5 November, A14.

———. 1996. The gay rights ruling. *New York Times.* 21 May, A1–6.

Griswold v. Connecticut, 381 U.S. 479 (1965).

Hamill, Katherine M. 1997. *Romer v. Evans:* Dulling the equal protection gloss on *Bowers v. Hardwick. Boston University Law Review* 77:655–85.

Hatheway v. Secretary of the Army, 641 F.2d 1376 (1981).

Herbert, Melissa S. 1998. *Camoflage isn't only for combat: Gender, sexuality and women in the military.* New York: New York University Press.

Hermann, John R. American Indian interests and the Supreme Court agenda setting: 1969–1992 October Terms. *American Politics Quarterly* 25:241–60.

Hole, Judith, and Ellen Levine. 1971. *Rebirth of feminism.* New York: Quadrangle Books.

Hurley v. Irish American Gay, Lesbian and Bisexual Group of Boston, 515 U.S. 557 (1995).

In re Longstaff, 716 F.2d 1439 (5th Cir. 1983), *cert. denied,* 467 U.S. 1219 (1984).

Ivers, Gregg. 1992. Religious organizations as constitutional litigants. *Polity* 25: 243–66.

———. 1995. *To build a wall: American Jews and the separation of church and state.* Charlottesville: University Press of Virginia.

Jackson, David. 1998. Supreme Court ruling allows lawsuits for same-sex harrassment. *Dallas Morning News,* 5 March, A1.

Kameny v. Brucker, 282 F.2d 823 (D.C. Cir. 1960), *cert. denied,* 365 U.S. 843 (1961).

Kimball, Andrea. 1996. *Romer v. Evans* and Colorodo's Amendment 2: The gay movement's symbolic victory in the battle for civil rights. *Toledo Law Review* (fall): 219–45.

Knott v. Holtzman, 193 Wis. 2d 649, *cert. denied*, 516 U.S. 975 (1995).

KRC v. United States Information Agency, 989 F.2d 1211 (D.C. Cir. 1994), *cert. denied*, 510 U.S. 1109 (1994).

Lambda Update: Winter 1995.

Lesbian/Gay Freedom Day Committee, Inc v. INS, 714 F.2d 1470 (9th Cir. 1983).

Manual Enterprises v. Day, 370 U.S. 478 (1962).

McKee, Mike. 1993. A bar under siege: One of the grimmest problems faced by AIDS advocates is that so many veterans of the movement die, taking with them their expertise and leadership skills. *New Jersey Law Journal*, 25 January, p. 15.

Meritor Savings Bank, FSB v. Vinson, 477 U.S. 57 (1986).

O'Connor, Karen. 1980. *Women's organizations use of the courts.* Lexington, Mass.: Lexington Books.

Oncale v. Sundowner Offshore Service, 523 U.S. 75 (1998).

One, Inc. v. Oleson, 355 U.S. 317 (1958).

People v. Onofre, 415 N.E.2d 936 (N.Y.), *cert. denied sub nom. New York v. Onofre*, 451 U.S. 987 (1981).

People v. Uplinger, 447 N.E.2d 62 (N.Y. 1983), *cert. denied sub nom. New York v. Uplinger*, 467 U.S. 246 (1984).

Plessy v. Ferguson, 163 U.S. 537 (1896).

Pruitt v. Cheney, 963 F.2d 1160 (9th Cir. 1991), *cert. denied*, 506 U.S. 1020 (1992).

Reed v. Reed, 404 U.S. 71 (1971).

Reno v. Doe, 518 U.S. 1014 (1996).

Roe v. Wade, 410 U.S. 113 (1973).

Romer v. Evans, 517 U.S. 620 (1996).

Rostker v. Goldberg, 453 U.S. 57 (1981).

Roth v. United States, 354 U.S. 476 (1957).

Rowland v. Mad River Local School District, 730 F.2d 444 (6th Cir.), *cert. denied*, 470 U.S. 1009 (1985).

Schowengerdt v. United States, 944 F.2d 483 (9th Cir. 1991), *cert. denied*, 503 U.S. 951 (1992).

Selland v. Cohen, 100 F.3d 450 (4th Cir. 1996), *cert. denied*, 520 U.S. 1210 (1996).

Shahar v. Bowers, 120 F.3d 221 (11th Cir. 1997), *cert. denied*, 118 S. Ct. 693 (1998).

Shelley v. Kraemer, 334 U.S. 1 (1948).

Shilts, Randy. 1987. *And the band played on.* New York: St. Martin's Press.

Singer v. United States Civil Service Commission, 530 F.2d 247 (9th Cir. 1976), *cert. denied*, 429 U.S. 1034 (1977).

Slind-Flor, Victoria. 1991. NGRA Disbands. *National Law Journal*, 3 June, p. 2.

Smayda v. United States, 352 F.2d 251 (9th Cir. 1965), *cert. denied,* 382 U.S. 981 (1966).

Stanley v. Georgia, 394 U.S. 557 (1969).

Strasser, Mark. 1995. Unconstitutional? Don't ask: If it is, Don't Tell: On deference, rationality, and the Constitution. *Colorodo Law Review* (spring): 375–459.

Sullivan, Andrew. 1995. *Virtually normal: An argument about homosexuality.* New York: Knopf.

Theodoulou, Stella Z. 1996. *AIDS: The political policy of a disease.* Upper Saddle River, N.J.: Prentice-Hall.

Thomasson v. Perry, 80 F.3d 915 (4th Cir. 1996), *cert. denied,* 117 S. Ct. 358 (1996).

Ulane v. Eastern Airlines, Inc., 742 F.2d 1081 (7th Cir. 1984), *cert. denied,* 471 U.S. 1017 (1985).

United States v. Meinhold, 510 U.S. 938 (1993).

Vose, Clement E. 1955. NAACP strategy in the restrictive covenant cases. *Case Western Reserve Law Review* 6:101.

———. 1957. National Consumers' League and the Brandeis Brief. *Midwest Journal of Political Science* 1:178–90.

———. 1959. *Caucasians only: The Supreme Court, the NAACP, and the restrictive covenant cases.* Berkeley, Cal.: University of California Press.

———. 1972. *Constitutional change.* Lexington, Mass.: Lexington Books.

Wachs, Scott W. 1996. Slamming the closet door shut: *Able, Thomasson* and the reality of "Don't Ask, Don't Tell." *New York Law School Review* 41:309–36.

Wainwright v. Stone, 414 U.S. 21 (1973).

Watkins v. U.S. Army, 875 F.2d 699 (9th Cir. 1989), *cert. denied,* 498 U.S. 957 (1990).

Webster v. Doe, 486 U.S. 592 (1988).

Wenner, Lettie McSpadden. 1982. *The environmental decade in court.* Bloomington: Indiana University Press.

Wood v. Garner Food Services, 89 F.3d 1523 (11th Cir. 1996), *cert. denied,* 117 S. Ct. 1822 (1997).

Woodward v. United States., 871 F.2d 1068 (Fed. Cir. 1989), *cert. denied,* 494 U.S. 1003 (1990).

16

GAY RIGHTS IN THE PUBLIC SPHERE: PUBLIC
OPINION ON GAY AND LESBIAN EQUALITY

Clyde Wilcox and Robin Wolpert

Gay and lesbian activists seeking protection from discrimination and access to the same professional and family roles
as heterosexuals have won and lost important victories
in city, state, and national political institutions. Yet ultimately, social movements have their greatest impact when
they change the hearts and minds of the American people.
The labor movement early in the century and the civil
rights and feminist movements in the 1960s and 1970s all
succeeded to some degree in persuading the American
public that the citizens represented by these movements
had not been treated fairly and that new laws were needed
to prevent discrimination. When a social movement wins
its case before the American public, victories in the political arena are likely to follow. Moreover, a favorable climate
of public opinion allows for greater implementation of any
victories that the movement may have won in the courts
and the legislatures.

For this reason, leaders of social movements seek to
define the issues for the public in the most favorable possible terms. Most frequently, this involves framing issues
around the values of equality and fairness. In some cases,
two or more competing social movements seek to frame
the same issues in different ways. The gay and lesbian
rights movement has sought equal treatment in many policy areas (e.g., the right to hold a job, to receive employment benefits such as health insurance for domestic partners, to serve in the military, or to adopt children) without
discrimination based on sexual orientation. The Christian

Right and profamily movements, in contrast, have argued that these policies involve a threat to traditional families and, in some cases, to religious
freedom (Bull and Gallagher 1996). Conservative religious leaders have
also argued that laws that prohibit discrimination against gays and lesbians
would violate their right to fully practice their religion (Morken 1994).
Other elements of the antigay rights coalition have sought to increase levels
of homophobia, suggesting that gays and lesbians seek to recruit children,
spread disease, and undermine the religious character of the United States.
More recently, the movement has sought to convince Americans that homosexuality is simply a sinful choice, and that gays and lesbians can choose
not to be gay. This issue frame would imply that antigay policies constitute
discrimination based on lifestyle choice, not on immutable characteristics,
and therefore can be condoned in the interest of promoting traditional
families. Thus, interest groups in both movements have battled to define
the issues and to mobilize sentiment for or against gay rights groups.

While these competing social movements have struggled to define the
policy issues, increasing number of Americans have discovered that one
or more of their friends or family are gay, and the entertainment media
have gradually exposed Americans to more positive and less stereotypical
images of gays and lesbians. In the 1990s, award-winning movies such as
"Philadelphia" and popular television shows such as "Ellen," "Mad About
You," and "Chicago Hope" portrayed gay and lesbian characters in a generally favorable light. Research suggests that personal contact with gays
and lesbians leads some individuals to abandon stereotypes and to express
more favorable attitudes (Herek 1984; Herek and Glunt 1993; Millham,
San Miguel, and Kellogg 1976; Simon 1995). Although media portrayals
lack the immediacy of personal interaction, they may have a similar impact,
leading to more positive attitudes toward gays and lesbians.

Moreover, President Clinton, by visibly supporting gays in the military,
increased support for that policy (Wilcox and Wolpert 1996). A Senate
debate on a bill prohibiting discrimination on sexual orientation in employment, and Clinton's clear support for that policy in the 1996 presidential
debate, increased public awareness of the issue. The bill failed in the Senate
by one vote, a clear signal that the politics of gay rights have changed
dramatically from an era when the bill would not have made it to the Senate
floor.

There is reason to believe, therefore, that attitudes may be changing in
favor of equal treatment of gays and lesbians in many spheres of life. In
this chapter, we examine attitudes toward policy issues in which gay and

lesbian activists have defined as central to their movement. We begin by exploring the attitudes of Americans toward gays and lesbians themselves. A substantial literature suggests that homophobia, and negative affect toward gays more broadly, is the likely source of an individual's policy positions on AIDS, gay marriage and adoption, and even antidiscrimination laws (e.g., Pryor et al. 1989). We will therefore explore the sources of anti-gay affect, as well as the sources of sympathy for gays and lesbians. Next, we will focus on three issues where gays and lesbians have sought equality: antidiscrimination laws, military service, and adoption. We will first describe these attitudes and then explore their sources: negative affect toward gays and lesbians, basic values, and general ideology, and social sources such as religion, race, gender, education, and age.

THE DATA

The data for this study come from three sources. First, we use General Social Survey data to delineate public reactions to homosexual activity over time. Second, we use National Election Studies (NES) time series data to track overall public evaluations of gay men and lesbians. Such overall evaluations are measured by a "feeling thermometer," which asks respondents to rate homosexuals on a scale ranging from 0 to 100 degrees, where 0 is very cold and 100 is very warm. Although the wording has changed slightly, most commonly the feeling thermometer asked respondents to rate "gay men and lesbians—that is, homosexuals."

Third, we use data from the 1992 National Election Study (NES) and the 1993 NES Pilot Survey. These two studies, which constitute the bulk of our analysis, form a short-term panel that began shortly before the 1992 election, had a second wave immediately after the election, and a final wave in the fall of 1993. The 1992 post-election wave and the 1993 survey both included a feeling thermometer. These surveys also asked respondents whether they strongly favored, weakly favored, weakly opposed, or strongly opposed laws to protect homosexuals against job discrimination. Similar responses were requested with respect to allowing homosexuals to serve in the armed forces and legally permitting homosexual couples to adopt children.

The 1993 survey contained additional questions on reactions toward lesbians and gay men. Respondents were asked:

- whether they believed that homosexuals could change their sexual orientation
- whether homosexuals would try to seduce heterosexuals

- whether homosexuality was natural
- whether homosexuality was against God's will
- whether they were afraid of catching AIDS or some other disease from homosexuals
- whether they were disgusted by homosexuality.

The 1992 survey included measures of ideological self-placement as well as items from which we have constructed scales to measure moral traditionalism and equality values.[1] The survey also included a number of demographic variables that are likely to help us understand attitudes, including religious denomination, doctrine, and attendance, as well as sex, race, age, education, and rural birth.

Although the 1992–1993 NES surveys constitute one of the richest sources of data regarding public attitudes on gays and lesbians and gay rights policy issues, the Pilot Study was conducted on only a relatively small number of respondents. This limits our ability to fully investigate the ways that some variables interact and the full range of religious phenomena that influence attitudes. For this reason, we will identify in the tables below relationships which do not meet the traditional standards of statistical significance for heuristic purposes.

ATTITUDES TOWARD GAYS AND LESBIANS

Public opinion polls over the past twenty years yield two important conclusions about citizens' attitudes toward gays and lesbians. First, a substantial minority of Americans hold very negative views of gays and lesbians. Second, these attitudes have recently begun to change, and this change has been surprisingly rapid.

Trends in Attitudes

Both of these conclusions are evident in the data from the General Social Survey (GSS), which, since 1973, has asked respondents whether "sexual relations between two adults of the same sex" is always wrong, almost always wrong, sometimes wrong, or never wrong. Similar questions ask about premarital and extramarital sex, which most respondents would interpret to refer to heterosexual activity. Figure 16.1 shows the percentage of those who think that homosexual sexual activity is always wrong from 1973 through 1996. Disapproval of homosexual sexual activity reaches its peak in 1988 at nearly 75 percent, then in 1992 begins a sharp plummet, with only 60 percent believing such activity is always wrong by 1996. For comparison we include in the figure similar data regarding extramarital

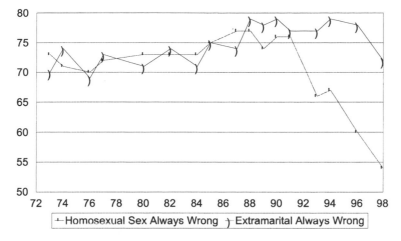

Figure 16.1 Attitudes toward Morality of Sexual Activity
SOURCE: GSS 1972–98; data includes odd-numbered years.

sex. Disapproval of extramarital sex increases slightly after 1992, suggesting that the decreased disapproval of homosexual sex after 1992 is not due to a generalized liberalization of sexual attitudes.

These same trends are also evident in the NES time series, where respondents were asked to rate gay men and lesbians on the feeling thermometer. In 1984 and again in 1988, both the mean and the median public rating for gays and lesbians were 30 degrees, scores which were markedly cooler than for any other group in the surveys. In 1992, the score increased sharply, with a mean of 38 degrees and a median of 50. In 1996 the mean increased to 40 degrees with a median of 50. In these latter surveys, gays and lesbians were still rated more negatively than any of the other approximately 28 groups in the survey. The increase between 1988 and 1992, however, is statistically and substantively significant.

Even more striking is the large percentage of Americans who rated gays and lesbians at 0, the coldest possible rating. In 1984 that figure was 31 percent—far higher than the 20 percent who rated Black Militants (the second lowest group) at 0. In 1988, 35 percent rated gays and lesbians at 0, but in 1992 the figure declined and by 1996 it had dropped to 20 percent. Taken together, these data show considerable negative affect toward gays and lesbians in the United States, although such sentiments have declined rapidly since 1992.

Other surveys show a similar trend of rapidly changing attitudes beginning in 1992 (Yang 1997). Although we are not certain what may have triggered this change, we suspect that part of the explanation lies in the shifting depiction of gays and lesbians in the popular media, particularly television. "Roseanne" and "Melrose Place" had gay and lesbian characters in 1992, and in 1993 Tom Hanks had presented a positive portrayal of a gay man with AIDS in the movie "Philadelphia." By 1996 there were gay and lesbian characters in many television shows (<www.glaad.org>) presenting positive images to the viewing public and perhaps influencing attitudes.

A second explanation for changing attitudes may be that personal contact with openly gay individuals has increased in recent years. There is some evidence that more gay and lesbian Americans are coming out to their friends and family. *Time* magazine reported in 1998 that 41 percent of Americans reported that they had a family member or close friend who is gay or lesbian, a remarkable 9 percent increase over a similar survey just 4 years before (Lacayo 1998). Further surveys are needed to confirm this trend, but if this result holds, it suggests that substantial numbers of Americans are newly aware that someone they care deeply about is gay or lesbian. This is likely to increase support for gay and lesbian equality because contacts with openly gay individuals reduces negative stereotypes and ignorance (Herek 1984, 8).

Regardless of the source of changing attitudes regarding gays and lesbians, such changes have been greater among women than men. In 1988, the correlation between gender and evaluations of gays and lesbians in the NES feeling thermometer was .04; in 1996 it was .16. Why women should be changing their attitudes so much more than men is not entirely clear, but part of the explanation lies in generational replacement. Among men, there is little relationship between age and attitudes. Indeed, the youngest cohort is the most hostile to gays and lesbians. Among women, however, there is a linear relationship between age and attitudes. Those who achieved adulthood before 1960 rated gays and lesbians at 35 degrees on average, while those who came of age after Reagan left office rated them at 53 degrees. Thus as older cohorts are replaced by younger ones, women become more liberal but men do not.[2]

Attitudes toward Gays and Lesbians in the 1990s

In 1993, the NES Pilot study asked a series of questions that helped disaggregate some of the affective and cognitive dimensions of citizen evaluations of gays and lesbians. The responses are shown in table 16.1. Respondents were asked their emotional reaction to "people practicing homosexuality." About 45 percent reported no emotional reaction while more than 35 percent were strongly disgusted. Although this deep divide in emo-

Table 16.1 Affective and Cognitive Sources of Evaluations of Gays and Lesbians (in Percent)

Emotional reaction to gays and lesbians:		Fear disease when working with gays:	
Strong disgust	36	Strongly worry	8
Mild disgust	6	Worry	6
Discomfort	13	Confident no danger	32
No emotional reaction	46	Strongly confident	55
Homosexuality is:		Homosexuality is natural to gays and	
Strongly against God's will	46	lesbians:	
Against God's will	4	Strongly think it is natural	39
Nothing to do with God	34	Think it is natural	6
Acceptable to God	5	Think it is unnatural	15
Strongly acceptable	11	Strongly unnatural	40
Do gays and lesbians try to seduce		Can homosexuals change?	
heterosexuals?		Strongly think they choose	36
Strongly agree	13	They choose to be gay	12
Agree	5	They cannot change	14
Disagree	19	Strongly think cannot change	38
Strongly Disagree	63		

tional reactions is not surprising, it suggests a core of visceral opposition to gay rights that is likely to be slow to change. Other surveys show this as well—one survey by Newsweek in 1998 found that 51 percent of respondents were "very" bothered by gays kissing in public, and another 29 percent were very bothered by same-sex couples holding hands (Peyser 1998). On the other affective questions in the NES data, an overwhelming majority indicated that they did not fear disease when working with gays and lesbians.

Data from the 1993 NES Pilot Study indicate that the public is deeply divided on whether homosexuality is against God's will, with nearly half strongly agreeing that it is opposed to God's will and half either stating that homosexuality has nothing to do with God or that it is acceptable to God. Americans were similarly divided on whether homosexuality is natural, with only a narrow majority in this survey indicating that it is natural.

The data indicate that a narrow majority believe that gays and lesbians cannot change their sexual orientation and an overwhelming majority do not believe that gays and lesbians try to seduce heterosexuals. Two beliefs that will prove important to understanding policy attitudes in our discussion below center on why and how sexual orientation develops (Whitley 1990; Aguero, Bloc, and Byrne 1984). These beliefs are critical to certain fears expressed by conservative Christian activists—that homosexuality is a choice and that adolescents and young adults are seduced by gays and lesbians. Moreover, the belief that sexual orientation is fixed at some point suggests that discrimination against gays and lesbians is like discrimination based on any innate characteristic, while those who believe that sexual orientation can change may argue that no real discrimination exists since individuals could simply change their orientation at any time.

Overall, these data depict a public that is divided in its understanding of homosexuality. Roughly half believe that homosexuality is natural and that gays and lesbians cannot change their orientation. The other half believe that homosexuality is unnatural and that sexual orientation is malleable. These beliefs are associated with emotional reactions, with nearly half showing some level of disgust while somewhat more than half are at most uncomfortable about homosexuality.

In order to determine how these cognitive and affective elements influence overall evaluations of gays and lesbians, as measured by the feeling thermometer scores, we estimated a regression equation predicting feeling thermometer scores with each of the cognitive and affective evaluations as independent variables. The results are shown in table 16.2. All of the beliefs are significant predictors of overall evaluations, but raw emotional re-

Table 16.2 Sources of Evaluations of Gays and Lesbians

	b	t	b	t	b	t
Emotional reaction	5.28	8.59**			5.17	6.93**
Cannot change	2.08	3.29**			2.41	3.23**
Do not seduce	1.94	2.63**			.74	.89
Don't fear AIDS	2.30	2.89**			2.09	2.28*
Homosexuality natural	2.10	3.05**			1.67	2.06*
Not against God's will	1.62	2.19*			1.48	1.59
Evangelical doctrine			−9.87	−3.14**	−.57	−.85
Evangelical denomination			−5.73	−1.97*	−4.90	−1.83@
Catholic			3.80	1.40	−.54	−.21
Attendance			−2.73	−3.79**	−.04	−.94
Age cohorts:						
Pre-sixties			−2.21	−.76	−4.24	−1.55
Sixties			1.57	.50	.96	.31
Reagan			−1.79	−.59	−1.40	−.48
Media			−2.77	−.71	3.90	1.10
Education			1.86	3.89**	1.23	2.63*
White			−8.23	−2.64**	−3.64	−1.19
Rural birth			−1.71	−2.908*	−.67	−1.22
Sex			8.97	4.28**	2.14	1.05
Constant			13.35	11.53**	−.22	−2.45*
N		533		580		447
Adjusted R²		.47		.20		.47

*p < .05   **p < .01   @p < .10

sponses provide most of the explanatory power. An additional equation (not shown) shows that the affective measure alone accounts for 35 percent of the overall variation in the feeling thermometer, while the entire set of variables captures 45 percent. Separate analysis of the predictors for men and women (not shown) reveal that women's evaluations of gays and lesbians are not swayed by the belief that gays and lesbians try to seduce heterosexuals or that homosexuality is against God's will, while these beliefs have a strong influence on the attitudes of men.

The second equation in table 16.2 explores the social sources of evaluations of gays and lesbians. We include measures of evangelical religious doctrine, where evangelicals are those who report a born-again religious experience and believe the Bible is inerrant and all others are nonevangelicals. We have also identified those who belong to evangelical denominations, most of which condemn homosexuality, and members of the Catholic church, which has recently called for accepting gay and lesbian members who abstain from sexual activity. We measure religiosity through frequency of church attendance.[3] Rather than including a simple measure of age, we have identified distinctive cohorts who we suspect have been socialized with different images of gays and lesbians. The various cohorts who reached adulthood before 1960 seem unlikely to differ significantly in their attitudes after controls for other demographic variables,[4] but those who came of age during the 1960s grew up during a period of great emphasis on equality and the evils of discrimination. Those who reached adulthood during the 1970s experienced the feminist movement with its explicit emphasis on lesbian rights and a societal focus on self-actualization and sexual expression. We expect those who came of age between 1980 and 1988 to be influenced by the social conservatism of the Reagan presidency, but those who reached age eighteen after that time to be influenced by the increased positive roles for gays and lesbians in the popular media. We call these cohorts the Pre-Sixties, the Sixties, the Feminist, the Reagan, and the Media cohorts, and exclude the Feminist cohort from our analysis as the comparison group. Finally, we include measures of education, race, sex, and rural birth, all of which have been shown to influence attitudes on social issues in general and on gay and lesbian issues in particular (Irwin and Thompson 1978; Henley and Pincus 1978; Nyberg and Alston 1976; Dejowski 1992; Pain and Disney 1995; Pratte 1993).

The results, shown in table 16.2, indicate that religion is a very important source of evaluations of gays and lesbians. Those who hold evangelical doctrine, those who attend evangelical churches, and those who attend any church regularly are all cooler toward gays and lesbians than other

Americans. Age cohorts do not differ in their evaluation of gays and lesbians after controls for education and religiosity, but the bivariate relationship between cohorts and evaluations is strong—the Pre-Sixties cohort rated gays and lesbians on average at 33 degrees while the Media cohort rated them at 42 degrees. Taken together, these data suggest that younger Americans are more positive toward gays and lesbians because they are better educated and slightly less likely to attend church regularly. Whites are significantly cooler than nonwhites. Bivariate analysis shows that blacks are warmer than Hispanics or Asians and whites are the coolest. Those born in rural areas are significantly cooler than those who grow up in cosmopolitan urban environments.

Women are much warmer toward gays and lesbians than men, a finding that is common in the literature (Kite 1984; Pratte 1993; Weinberger and Millham 1979; Herek 1988). Yet it is not just that men and women differ in their evaluations of gays and lesbians, they also differ somewhat in the sources of those evaluations. We estimated separate equations for men and women (not shown). Evangelical doctrine matters a great deal for women but is not significant for men. Race is a strong predictor for men (white men are the coolest group toward gays and lesbians) but is not a significant predictor for women.

The final equation in table 16.2 shows the combined model of demographic, cognitive, and affective variables. Affective reactions dominate. Emotional reactions to gays and lesbians are by far the most powerful predictor of overall evaluations. Beliefs that homosexuality is natural, that gays and lesbians can change their orientation, and fears of catching AIDS from coworkers are all significant predictors of attitudes. Beliefs about gay and lesbian seduction and that homosexuality is against God's will are not significant in the larger model. None of the religious variables are significant, although evangelical denominaion attains significance at .10, perhaps because they indirectly influence other beliefs about gays and lesbians. Among women, evangelical doctrine is a strong predictor (not shown), but once again among men it is not important. Most of the demographic variables are not significant in the combined model, because these variables influence affective components, which are more important. The exception is education: each additional year of education results in slightly more than one degree of extra warmth in the feeling thermometer toward gays and lesbians. The large gender gap evident in the second model disappears in the combined model, because men and women differ greatly in their visceral reactions to homosexuality.

Overall, these data pose both some discouraging and encouraging evidence for gay and lesbian activists. A significant portion of the public holds very negative views toward gays and lesbians, and much of this is anchored in gut-level affective reactions. Yet overall attitudes toward gays and lesbians are becoming more positive in the 1990s. We suspect that these affective responses are changing also, although we can only trace that change in overall evaluations.

An important part of evaluations lie in a constellation of beliefs that homosexuality is unnatural, that gays and lesbians try to seduce heterosexuals, and that they can change their orientation. These beliefs are probably far more malleable than affective response, and recent Christian Right efforts to portray homosexuality as a choice is probably a realization that recent media and scientific efforts have begun to persuade the public that gays and lesbians are born with a relatively unchanging orientation. As we will see below, these beliefs are also important in understanding policy preferences on basic equality issues.

UNDERSTANDING THE SOURCES OF PUBLIC OPINION
ON GAY AND LESBIAN ISSUES

How do average Americans choose sides on issues of special concern to the gay and lesbian communities? We expect that attitudes toward gays and lesbians themselves will play a central role in determining such attitudes. Research has demonstrated that feelings about groups influence both the policy positions that individuals hold and the way they structure those positions. Individuals are less willing to extend civil liberties protections to members of groups they dislike or fear, and are also more likely to oppose policies that they associate with those groups. Thus negative affect toward gays and lesbians is a likely source of opposition to gay rights in all policy areas. Although extreme dislike of gays and lesbians, and even homophobia, is most likely to be found among the less educated and less cognitively sophisticated Americans, the "likability heuristic" is actually more important in influencing the attitudes of those with at least moderate amounts of political sophistication (Sniderman, Brody, and Tetlock 1991).

Yet visceral reactions to gays and lesbians are not the only likely source of policy preferences. We consider various aspects of attitudes toward gays and lesbians in this chapter, both purely affective reactions and cognitive beliefs. We expect that several beliefs have consequences for policy positions, including whether homosexuality is determined by birth or chosen, whether gays and lesbians try to seduce heterosexuals, whether homosexuality is "natural," whether they spread disease at work, and whether homosexuality is against God's will.

We do not expect attitudes toward gay and lesbian issues to be fully explained by attitudes toward gays and lesbians themselves. Many citizens oppose discrimination against members of groups they dislike or even despise, because they value tolerance of divergent viewpoints and diverse groups. Basic values are also likely to be an important influence on policy preferences. Most importantly, support for general social equality should lead to greater support for antidiscrimination laws, for allowing gays and lesbians to serve in the military, and for other basic civil liberties protections for gays and lesbians. Orthodox religious values and support for traditional morality, in contrast, are likely to lead to greater opposition to such policies. General ideology is also likely to influence attitudes, and it is possible that partisanship will also play a role, especially after the "family values" GOP convention of 1992.

Finally, attitudes toward different policies may also be influenced by other policy concerns. Thus attitudes on gays in the military may also be influenced by attitudes toward various elements of military life, attitudes on antidiscrimination laws may be influenced by attitudes on the role of government in regulating business, and attitudes on AIDS policies may be influenced by a variety of attitudes on public health policy (Jelen and Wilcox 1992).

ATTITUDES ON GAY AND LESBIAN ISSUES

The NES Pilot study included measures of attitudes on three issues of equal treatment for gays and lesbians. First, respondents were asked whether they approved or disapproved of "laws to protect homosexuals from job discrimination." By 1993, many cities had adopted such laws, and in some cases there were heated battles within states as social conservatives sought to pass laws preempting such local laws (Adam 1995). In general, antidiscrimination laws have been discussed in terms of discrimination and fairness. Social conservatives sought to argue that such laws interfered with private business relationships and even that they constituted a violation of religious liberty by forcing Christians to associate with those who they regarded as sinners (Bull and Gallagher 1996). Some small business groups have worried about the health care costs of hiring individuals with AIDS.

Second, respondents were asked whether "homosexuals should be allowed to serve in the Armed Forces." Once again, liberal groups and gay and lesbian activists sought to frame this issue in terms of fairness and equal treatment. Opponents of President Clinton's proposal to lift the ban on military service by gays and lesbians argued that the presence of homosexuals would produce tensions that would undermine discipline, good order and morale, and mutual trust and confidence among service members (Wilcox and Wolpert 1996). This has also been the government's principle defense in the numerous court cases challenging the ban (Wolinsky and Sherrill 1993). Thus, although gays and lesbians have always served in the military, many with distinction and honor (Shilts 1993), concern for military effectiveness is expected to influence public support for lifting the ban. In addition, the public debate on this issue focused on the close and intimate quarters that soldiers are frequently required to share—e.g. pup tents and group showers. The implied or even explicit argument was that gay soldiers might attempt to seduce heterosexual soldiers, possibly provoking tensions within the military unit. For this reason, we expect that beliefs about the nature of sexual orientation and about whether gays and lesbians attempt to seduce heterosexuals will play a special role in explaining these attitudes.

Finally, respondents were asked whether gay and lesbian couples should be allowed to adopt children. Although only three states explicitly prohibit gay men and lesbians from becoming foster or adoptive parents, the Supreme Court's decision in *Bowers v. Hardwick* (1986) is viewed by judges and adoption agencies as an effective legal barrier to gay-lesbian adoptions in the twenty-five states that currently have sodomy laws. Even in states that do not have sodomy laws, adoption by openly gay couples is rare because courts and adoption agencies have held that gays and lesbians as parents are inimical to the natural family (Ricketts and Achtenberg 1989, 103–4). The rationales for this position are that lesbians and gay men are sexually perverted and will molest children or engage in sexual activity in front of children; that children of homosexual parents will probably become homosexual themselves and will be harmed by witnessing affectionate behavior between two persons of the same sex; and that children of gay parents will be especially likely to be subject to peer harassment (Ricketts and Achtenberg 1989; Crawford and Solliday 1996). Because conservatives have argued that homosexual parents will cause their children to be gay, we expect that attitudes on the nature of sexual orientation will influence support for adoption rights. Similarly, the argument that lesbians and gay men will molest their children suggests that views on adoption may be a function of whether individuals believe that homosexuals are sexually promiscuous and will try to seduce people who are not homosexual.

Table 16.3 Public Attitudes on Gay Rights Issues

	1992 (%)	1993 (%)	1996 (%)
Antidiscrimination laws			
strongly favor	33	39	40
favor	28	24	24
oppose	15	14	13
strongly oppose	25	23	23
Gays in the military			
strongly favor	33	45	44
favor	28	17	25
oppose	8	8	7
strongly oppose	31	30	25
Gays adopt children			
strongly favor	12	15	na
favor	16	14	na
oppose	11	9	na
strongly oppose	62	62	na

Table 16.3 shows the distribution of opinion on gay and lesbian-rights issues in the 1992, 1993, and 1996 NES data. Public attitudes became more supportive of gay rights over this period on two of the issues: antidiscrimination laws and gays and lesbians in the military. Indeed, by the 1996 survey, substantial majorities supported these policies. It is striking that support for gays in the military increased in 1993, a year marked by controversy over the issue which expanded the scope of the conflict. Indeed, Wilcox and Wolpert (1996) reported that Clinton's stance in favor of allowing gays to serve persuaded some Democrats on the issue. Public support is lowest for allowing gays and lesbians to adopt children, with more than three in five strongly opposing the policy. Although the NES survey did not measure opinion on other issues of special interest to gays and lesbians, surveys by *Time* and *Newsweek* in 1998 revealed that between 29 percent and 35 percent of Americans would allow gays and lesbians to marry, and 51 percent would allow them to teach in public schools.

What are the sources of policy attitudes on gay and lesbian issues? We have estimated three separate equations for each item in the 1993 NES survey. In the first equation, we include only a measure of affect toward gays and lesbians (feeling thermometer), measures of basic equality values, traditional morality, and general ideology. The second equation adds basic socio-demographic variables, and the final equation includes one or more attitudes that might directly bear on the policy itself, including specific cognitions about gays and lesbians. The results are shown in tables 16.4, 16.5, and 16.6.

Table 16.4   Sources of Attitudes on Gay Rights Issues

	Equation 1		Equation 2		Equation 3	
	b	t	b	t	b	t
Affect toward gays	−.02	−7.45**	−.02	−5.10**	−.01	−2.96**
Moral traditionalism	−.06	−.79	−.01	−.05	.14	1.07
Equality values	.47	5.92**	.53	4.99**	.41	3.52**
General ideology	.15	2.99**	.10	1.55	.05	.71
Evangelical doctrine			−.55	−2.20*	−.13	.50
Evangelical denomination			.10	.46	−.02	−.08
Catholic			.37	1.79@	.61	2.86*
Attendance			−.09	−1.49	−.10	−.54
Cohorts:						
Pre-sixties			−.14	−.64	.08	.35
Sixties			.05	.84	.05	.20
Reagan			−.47	−1.98*	−.54	−2.13*
Post-Reagan			−.43	−1.15	−.49	−1.57
Sex			−.40	−2.45**	−.38	−2.21*
White			−.31	−1.16	−.38	−1.30
Education			.04	.34	.01	.30
Rural residence			.01	.16	.00	.08
Feeling thermometer federal government					.00	.18
Fear AIDS on job					−.17	−2.22*
Gays and lesbians can change					−.14	−2.38*
Gays and lesbians seduce heterosexuals					−.11	−1.52
Constant	4.63	8.29**	5.73	5.84**	5.35	5.88**
Adjusted R²	.27		.29		.35	
N	553		448		436	

*p < .05   **p < .01   @p < .10

The data show that affect toward gays and lesbians is a powerful predictor of attitudes on gay and lesbian rights. Simply put, negative affect toward gays and lesbians is a major source of opposition to antidiscrimination laws and to allowing gays and lesbians to serve in the military or to adopt children. The effect is strong and if the trends (discussed above) of decreasing negative feelings toward gays and lesbians continue, public opinion on these issues might shift markedly.

Moral traditionalism is an important source of attitudes on adoption, probably because the items used to measure this value focus on traditional families. Moral traditionalism has a weak relationship with opposition to gays in the military and it is not a source of attitudes on antidiscrimination laws, perhaps because equality in the workplace would seem to have little to do with traditional families. We suspect, however, that moral traditionalism is relevant to public support for employment benefits for domestic partners.

Table 16.5 Sources of Attitudes on Gays and Military Service

	Equation 1		Equation 2		Equation 3	
	b	t	b	t	b	t
Affect toward gays	−.03	−10.90**	−.03	−8.63**	−.02	−5.47**
Moral traditionalism	−.22	−2.40**	−.22	−2.19*	−.22	−1.92@
Equality values	.16	1.97*	.14	1.52	.10	1.00
General ideology	.14	2.70**	.09	1.46	.07	1.17
Evangelical doctrine			−.41	−1.72	−.18	−.80
Evangelical denomination			.12	.66	−.15	.76
Catholic			.18	1.33	.25	1.37
Attendance			−.06	−1.30	−.06	−1.13
Cohorts:						
Pre-sixties			−.03	−.16	−.06	−.32
Sixties			.09	.05	.05	.22
Reagan			−.31	−1.55	−.37	−1.76@
Post-Reagan			.02	.66	.02	.09
Sex			−.51	−3.62**	−.49	−3.28**
White			.07	.35	−.30	1.18
Education			.02	.86	.05	1.53
Rural birth			−.01	−.14	−.05	−1.37
Affect for the military					−.01*	−1.96*
Gays try to seduce heterosexuals					−.14	−2.15*
Gays and lesbians can change orientation					−.17	−3.41**
Constant	2.91	5.72**	2.71	3.33**	5.14	5.88**
Adjusted R²	.35		.39		.42	
N	553		453		423	

*p < .05   **p < .01   @p < .10

We expected those who placed a strong value on societal equality to be more likely to support an end to discrimination in employment, the military, and adoption. The data show that equality values are especially important in explaining attitudes on antidiscrimination laws, somewhat important in explaining attitudes on adoption, and not at all useful in understanding attitudes toward military service. It is surprising that public attitudes on gays in the military are not affected by equality values, for liberals and gay rights activists framed the issue around equality. The survey was conducted in 1993, which was after the public debate on Clinton's policy, and it appears that the "right to serve" rationale was not clearly articulated to the public. It is possible that equality values do not influence attitudes here because those who hold these values find it difficult to think of military service as a value—much as feminists somewhat reluctantly rally to allow women into combat, liberals may find it difficult to think of the armed services in equality terms. Previous research showed that equality values were significant in 1992 but not in 1993, perhaps because the

Table 16.6   Sources of Attitudes on Gay Adoptions

	Equation 1		Equation 2		Equation 3	
	b	t	b	t	b	t
Affect toward gays	−.03	−11.61**	−.02	−8.96**	−.02	−6.85**
Moral traditionalism	−.37	−4.67**	−.33	−3.38**	−.33	−3.10**
Equality values	.16	2.18*	.20	2.34*	.22	2.37*
General ideology	.09	2.02**	.07	1.41	.07	1.24
Evangelical doctrine			−.25	−1.30	−.35	−1.66@
Evangelical denomination			.07	.45	−.02	−.12
Catholic			.15	.95	−.25	−1.44
Attendance			−.12	−2.56*	−.14	2.87**
Cohorts:						
Pre-sixties			.18	1.01	−.20	−1.08
Sixties			.03	.22	.02	.07
Reagan			−.13	−.72	−.04	−.20
Post-Reagan			.51	1.96*	.49	1.96*
Sex			−.33	−2.59**	−.35	−2.51*
White			.07	.35	−.23	−.99
Education			.05	1.41	.04	1.37
Rural birth			−.08	−.19	−.14	−1.05
Spending for childcare					−.15	−2.13*
Gays try to seduce heterosexuals					−.15	−2.22*
Gays and lesbians can't change						
orientation					−.06	−1.33
Constant	3.96	7.93**	4.50	6.11**	5.12	6.15**
Adjusted R^2	.39		.41		.44	
N	553		453		423	

*p < .05   **p < .01   @p < .10

debate was dominated by talk of seduction and privacy (Wilcox and Wolpert 1996).

General ideology is a significant predictor in the first equation for each attitude, but after controls for religious and demographic variables it loses its usefulness in predicting attitudes. Additional analysis suggests that it is evangelical religion that explains the relationship between ideology and attitudes: in each case adding the simple control for evangelical religious doctrine reduces the coefficient to nonsignificance.

In the second set of equations we add socio-demographic variables. Religious variables are significant predictors of attitudes on antidiscrimination laws and of adoption, although the magnitude of these effects is surprisingly small. Evangelical doctrine leads to greater opposition to antidiscrimination laws, although this effect disappears after one controls for fear of AIDS at work. Evangelical doctrine barely achieves statistical significance in the final equation for gays in the military, and is never a source of attitudes on adoption. Catholics are significantly more supportive of antidiscrimination laws, and this effect is even more significant once controls are added for other beliefs relevant to this issue. Finally, those who attend church regularly (regardless of denomination) are less likely to support adoption by gays and lesbians, after other factors are held constant. We were surprised by the small impact of religious variables on attitudes toward gays and lesbian issues, and experimented with other models. In the 1996 NES, with its larger sample and somewhat larger set of religious variables, we could identify other religious variables as significant predictors, but the substantive impact was still small. Of course, the data in table 16.2 show that religion plays a substantial *indirect* role in shaping these attitudes by influencing beliefs, emotional reactions, and evaluations toward gays and lesbians themselves.

The influence of generational differences on policy attitudes is also primarily indirect. Those who came of age during the Reagan years are less likely to support antidiscrimination laws, while those who came of age during the period of greater media exposure are more likely to favor allowing gay and lesbian adoption. Race, education, and rural birth play no direct role in explaining policy preferences, but there are large gender gaps on each issue—largest for gays in the military and smallest for adoption.

Finally, we estimated equations for each policy question that included measures of attitudes about other dimensions of the policy, and of cognitions about gays and lesbians. For example, antidiscrimination policy involves a willingness to allow the government to interfere in private business transactions. Because no direct measure of beliefs about the role of government was available, we experimented with several items in the NES to tap this dimension and adopted a feeling thermometer toward the federal government as our measure. This variable was not a significant predictor of antidiscrimination attitudes. In addition, we included a measure of fear of AIDS on the job, which was a significant predictor. Thus the minority who fear AIDS through job contact are less willing to support antidiscrimination laws, even after holding constant their personal views of gays and lesbians. Finally, we included beliefs that gays and lesbians try to seduce heterosexuals, which was not a predictor of antidiscrimination beliefs, and beliefs about whether gays and lesbians could change their sexual orientations, which was a significant predictor. Those individuals who believe that gays and lesbians could simply choose to be heterosexual are less likely to support antidiscrimination laws.

Attitudes about gays in the military may also be influenced by beliefs about the importance of military cohesion to overall effectiveness. Lacking such a measure, we included a feeling thermometer measure toward the military, and the data show that those who rate the military highly are less likely to believe that gays and lesbians should be allowed to serve. In addition, we included measures of beliefs that gays and lesbians try to seduce heterosexuals, and that they can change their orientation. Both were statistically significant predictors. This suggests that the references to showers and pup tents in the public debate may have influenced the attitudes of those who believed that gay and lesbian soldiers might use those occasions to attempt seductions. Those who believed that gays and lesbians might try to seduce soldiers, and that those soldiers might allow themselves to be seduced, were significantly less likely to favor allowing gays and lesbians to serve.

Adoption attitudes are also a function of beliefs about child welfare. To help explain attitudes on adoption, we include an item on spending for child care. It is worth noting that those who favored *more* spending for child care were *less* likely to allow gays and lesbians to adopt children. The negative coefficient here is important, for generally it is liberals who favor increased spending on child care. This suggests that one reason that some Americans are more opposed to adoption than to antidiscrimination laws or military service is a fear for the welfare of children. Some of that fear is that gays and lesbians might try to seduce heterosexual children: the data show that this attitude is an important predictor of support for adoption. In contrast to the other policy issues, in this case belief that individuals can change their orientation is not an important predictor, perhaps because some Americans worry more about abuse than seduction.

Taken together, the data in tables 16.4, 16.5, and 16.6 show that gay-related policies do not evoke identical responses from the public. There are similarities across all three policies. In each case, affect toward gays is an important source of attitudes, and there is a large gender gap. Yet the debates around these policies bring into play different values: moral traditionalism is an important source of attitudes on gay adoption but not of antidiscrimination laws, and equality values matter most in attitudes on antidiscrimination laws. Moreover, policy-specific considerations also come into play, affecting each policy attitude. These considerations include concerns for children, for military effectiveness, and possibly attitudes on the role of government regulating business.

Finally, different cognitions about gays and lesbians influence different policy attitudes. Those who believe that gays and lesbians try to seduce heterosexuals do not favor gay adoptions or allowing gays to serve openly in the military. Those who think that people can change their sexual orientation are also more likely to oppose allowing gays in the military and to oppose antidiscrimination laws. Fear of AIDS, although not widespread, influences attitudes on antidiscrimination laws. Attitudes toward these policies is not driven solely by evaluations of gays and lesbians, rather they are a function of a complex mix of values, beliefs about gays and lesbians, and of policy predispositions.

CONCLUSIONS

Taken together, these data tell us some interesting things about American opinion on issues of equal rights for gays and lesbians. First, basic evaluations of gays and lesbians are a central source of attitudes on these equality policies. The data suggest that these evaluations have been moving in the positive direction since 1992, and if this continues, public support for equality policies is likely to follow. Yet there remains significant negative affect toward gays and lesbians in the general public, with a substantial minority voicing strongly negative reactions, often rooted in basic emotional reactions. Although emotional reactions are changing, there is likely to be a core of opposition to gay rights for the foreseeable future.

Second, for many Americans, support for societal equality and for traditional morality are in conflict. To the extent that these policy issues are framed as essentially matters of fairness, gays and lesbians are more likely to make progress. But traditional moral values play an important role on family-life issues such as adoption and presumably marriage, and progress is likely to be much slower on these issues. These conflicting values suggest that the struggle to frame gay and lesbian policy issues is a vital one. If the public ultimately comes to see the issue of gay marriage as involving equality and fair treatment, then they may come to support that policy. If they see it as an assault on traditional families, they may not.

Third, public understanding of the nature of homosexuality is a major source of policy attitudes. Those who believe that sexual orientation is fixed are more likely to support antidiscrimination laws than those who believe that people choose their orientation, and this is true as well for allowing gays and lesbians to serve in the military. Further analysis (not shown) reveals that these attitudes are especially important for those who rate gays and lesbians slightly negatively, but who hold strong equality values. For these individuals, many of whom value traditional morality, equality values are probably called into play precisely because gays and lesbians do not choose their sexual orientation. Moreover, those who believe that gays and lesbians try to seduce heterosexuals are especially unlikely to support allowing them to serve in the military or adopt children. This suggests that the public debate being waged within the gay rights and scientific community on the nature of sexual orientation, coupled with the recent public effort by Christian Right groups to portray homosexuality as a choice that can be reversed, has important implications. If the public comes to believe that gays and lesbians are born with their sexual orientation or acquire it early in life, and that they do not try to seduce heterosexuals, then objections to at least some equality policies will ease.

NOTES

1. The equality scale was composed of items asking whether society should insure equal opportunity, whether we have gone too far in pushing equal rights in the United States, whether the United States would be better off if we stopped worrying so much about equality, whether it is a problem if some people have more of a chance in life, and whether there would be fewer problems if people were treated equally. Alpha = .71. The moral traditionalism scale was constructed from items asking whether moral should be adjusted to a changing world, whether people should tolerate different moral standards, whether the United States should emphasize traditional family ties, whether new lifestyles contribute to the breakdown of society, and whether sex with someone other than your spouse is always wrong. Alpha = .65.
2. It is possible that attitudes for gays and lesbians are mostly a generational phenomena for women, but that there is a substantial life-cycle component for men. We have not yet fully investigated this question.
3. We experimented with other religious variables as well - dummy variables to identify Jews and seculars, and a measure of religious salience. The small number of cases in the pilot survey makes it difficult for measures that are highly skewed or reasonably correlated with other variables to achieve statistical significance.
4. We tested this assumption and found it to be correct.

REFERENCES

Adam, Barry D. 1995. *The rise of a gay and lesbian movement*. New York: Twayne Publishers.

Aguero, Joseph E., Laura Bloch, and Donna Byrne. 1984. The relationship among sexual beliefs, attitudes, experience, and homophobia. *Journal of Homosexuality* 10:95 107.

Bowers v. Hardwick, 478 U.S. 186 (1986).

Bull, Chris, and John Gallagher. 1996. *Perfect enemies: The religious, the gay movement, and the politics of the 1990's.* New York: Crown Publishers.

Crawford, Isaiah, and Elizabeth Solliday. 1996. The attitudes of undergraduate college students toward gay parenting. *Journal of Homosexuality* 30:63–77.

Dejowski, Edmund F. 1992. Public endorsement of restrictions on three aspects of free expression by homosexuals: Socio-demographic and trends analysis 1973–1988. *Journal of Homosexuality* 23:1–18.

Henley, Nancy M., and Fred Pincus. 1978. Interrelationship of sexist, racist, and antihomosexual attitudes. *Psychological Reports* 42:83–90.

Herek, Gregory M. 1984. Beyond "homophobia": A social psychological perspective on attitudes toward lesbians and gay men. *Journal of Homosexuality* 10:1–21.

———. 1988. Heterosexuals' attitudes toward lesbians and gay men: Correlates and gender differences. *Journal of Sex Research* 25:451–77.

Herek, Gregory M., and Eric K. Glunt. 1993. Interpersonal contact and heterosexuals' attitudes toward gay men: Results from a national survey. *Journal of Sex Research* 30:239–44.

Irwin, Patrick, and Norman L. Thompson. 1978. Acceptance of the rights of homosexuals: A social profile. *Journal of Homosexuality* 3:107–21.

Jelen, Ted G., and Clyde Wilcox. 1992. Values as predictors of AIDS policy attitudes. *Social Science Quarterly* 73:737–49.

Kite, Mary E. 1984. Sex differences in attitudes toward homosexuals: A meta-analytic view. *Journal of Homosexuality* 10:69–81.

Lacayo, Richard. 1998. The new gay struggle. *Time,* 26 October, pp. 33–36.

Lewis, Gregory B., and Marc A. Rogers. 1999. Does the public support equal employment rights for gays? In *Gays and lesbians in the democratic process,* ed. Ellen D. B. Riggle and Barry L. Tadlock. New York: Columbia University Press, 1999.

Millham, Jim, Christopher L. San Miguel, and Richard Kellogg. 1976. A factor-analytic conceptualization of attitudes toward male and female homosexuals. *Journal of Homosexuality* 2:3–10.

Morken, Hubert. 1994. "No Special Rights": The thinking strategy behind Colorado's Amendment #2 strategy. Paper presented to the annual meeting of the American Political Science Association, New York, N.Y.

Nyberg, Kenneth L., and Jon P. Alston. 1976. Analysis of public attitudes toward homosexual behavior. *Journal of Homosexuality* 2:99–107.

Pain, Michelle D., and Monique E. Disney. 1995. Testing the reliability and validity of the index of attitudes toward homosexuals in Australia. *Journal of Homosexuality* 30:99–110.

Peyser, Marc. 1998. Battling backlash. *Newsweek,* 17 August, pp. 50–52.

Pratte, Trish. 1993. A Comparative study of attitudes toward homosexuality: 1986 and 1991. *Journal of Homosexuality* 26:77–83.

Pryor, John B., Glenn D. Reeder, Richard Vinacco, and Teri L. Kott. 1989. The instrumental and symbolic functions of attitudes toward persons with AIDS. *Journal of Applied Social Psychology* 19:377–404.

Ricketts, Wendell, and Roberta Achtenberg. 1989. Adoption and foster parenting for lesbian and gay men: creating new traditions in family. *Marriage and Family Review* 14:83–118.

Riggle, Ellen D., and Alan L. Ellis. 1994. Political tolerance of homosexuals: The role of group attitudes and legal principles. *Journal of Homosexuality* 26:135–46.

Shilts, Randy. 1993. *Conduct unbecoming: Gays and lesbians in the U.S. military, Vietnam to the Persian* Gulf. New York: St. Martin's.

Simon, Angela. 1995. Some correlates of individuals' attitudes toward lesbians. *Journal of Homosexuality* 29:89–103.

Sniderman, Paul M., Richard A. Brody, and Philip E. Tetlock. 1991. *Reasoning and choice: Explorations in political psychology.* New York: Cambridge.

Weinberger, Linda E., and Jim Millham. 1979. Attitudinal homophobia and support of traditional sex roles. *Journal of Homosexuality* 4:237–45.

Whitley Jr., Bernard E. 1990. The relationship of heterosexuals' attributions for the causes of homosexuality to attitudes toward lesbians and gay men. *Journal of Homosexuality* 16:369–77.

Wilcox, Clyde, and Robin M. Wolpert. 1996. President Clinton, public opinion, and gays in the military. In *Gay Rights, Military Wrongs*, ed. Craig A. Rimmerman. New York: Garland Press.

Wolinsky, Marc, and Kenneth Sherrill, eds. 1993. *Gays and the military: Joseph Steffan versus the United States.* Princeton: Princeton University Press.

Yang, Alan S. 1997. Attitude toward homosexuality. *Public Opinion Quarterly* 61:477–507.

APPENDIX

All items are taken from the 1993 NES Pilot study, which constituted a panel with the 1992 survey.

Emotional reactions to gays and lesbians	VAR 937347
Homosexuality is against God's will	VAR 937365
Fear disease when working with gays	VAR 937351
Homosexuality is natural	VAR 937355
Homosexuals can change	VAR 937339
Homosexuals try to seduce heterosexuals	VAR 937343
Overall evaluation	VAR 937145

Evangelical doctrine	Coded as 1 if respondent is born again (VAR 923847) and believes Bible is inerrant (VAR 923824), otherwise coded as 0.

Evangelical denomination	Dummy variable coded as 1 if respondent lists evangelical denomination.
Catholic	Dummy variable coded as 1 if respondent lists Catholic church.
Attendance	Scale created from VAR 923826, VAR 923828, VAR 923829). Coded as 0 if respondent never attends, 1 if attends a few times a year, 2 if attends once or twice a month, 3 if attends almost every week, 4 if attends once a week, 5 if attends more often than weekly.
Age cohorts	Pre-sixties cohort reached age 18 before 1960. Sixties cohort reached age 18 between 1960 and 1969. Seventies cohort reached age 18 between 1970 and 1979. Reagan cohort reached age 18 between 1980 and 1987. Media cohort reached age 18 from 1988 through 1993. Variable created by recoding age (VAR 923903).
Education	VAR 923905
Race	VAR 924202
Rural Birth	VAR 924129
Sex	VAR 924201
Antidiscrimination laws	VAR 925924, VAR 937327, VAR 961194
Gays in military	VAR 925926, VAR 937331, VAR 961196
Gays adopt	VAR 925928, VAR 937335
Moral traditionalism	Scale computed as mean of VAR 926115*, VAR 926116*, VAR 926117, VAR 926118, and VAR 926119.
Equality values	Scale computed as mean of VAR 926024*, VAR 926029*, VAR 926025, VAR 926026, and VAR 926027.
General ideology	VAR 923509
Feeling thermometer:	
Toward federal government	VAR 925325
Toward military	VAR 925328
Toward spending for child care	VAR 923813

*indicates item was reversed.

INDEX

Page numbers in italics refer to tables and figures.

Abbott, Sidney, 399
Abercrombie, Neil, 362–63
Able v. United States, 70
abortion, 103, 124, 128, 152, 153, 298, 301
Abzug, Bella S., 62, 296, 363
accommodationism, 33
ACLU. *See* American Civil Liberties Union
"acting out," 16
ACT UP (AIDS Coalition to Unleash Power), 222–23; antidemocratic stridency of, 239; as antihierarchical, 222; "By any means necessary" slogan of, 220; as direct action group, 39; media attention garnered by, 76n. 2; motto of, 223; pink triangle of, 223; political strategy of, 56, 223
ADA (Americans with Disabilities Act), 39, 238, 399, 402
Ad Hoc Task Force to Challenge Sodomy Laws, 385
adoption: in New Hampshire, 292; public opinion on, 195, 421, 422, *422,* 423, 424, 425, 426, 427; sources of attitudes toward, 423, 424, 425, 426, 427; in state family law, 401; strong opposition to, 422; in Washington State, 180

African American civil rights movement. *See* black civil rights movement
African American gays and lesbians, 79–96; black church as influential with, 91; coming out for, 84; and "don't ask, don't tell" policy, 257; in gay identity's formation, 80–81; on "gay" "lesbian," and "queer," 91–92; Gay Men of African Descent, 89, 92; in gay rights movement, 19–20; in Harlem Renaissance, 80–81; identifying with black community issues, 90–91; leaders selected by whites, 84–85, 94; national organization required for, 65, 87; in national organizations, 85–86; paternalistic treatment of, 83; as patronized, 83, 86, 88; and same-sex marriage, 88–89, 92, 93; in Stonewall Rebellion, 82; a strategy for greater inclusion of, 93–96; on symbols of white gayness, 92; as tokenized, 83, 84, 86, 92, 94. *See also* National Black Lesbian and Gay Leadership Forum

AIDS: and antidiscrimination laws, 237–38, 273, 426, 428; California ballot initiatives on, 164–65; Congress on, 198, 228, 232–35, 349, 351–60; conservative constraints on prevention efforts, 132; contradictory impacts on gay activism, 22; "czars" for, 224, 242n. 14; as "de-gayed," 26, 243n. 27, 353; as democratizing disease, 22, 217–48; as divine retribution to some, 218; education as a gay cover for the Christian Right, 144; gay activism on, 22, 38–40, 219–21; as a gay disease, 113n. 8, 352–53; gay issues forced onto national agenda by, 23, 26, 368; as GRID, 113n. 8, 352; as health versus personal behavior issue, 356–60; homosexuals seen as purveyors of, 125; H.R. 2881, 354–56; H.R. 5142, 358; Human Rights Campaign on, 223; institutions and strategies for addressing, 224–27; Lambda Legal Defense and Education Fund in cases involving, 70, 223–24; lesbians in AIDS activist movement, 100, 102, 111, 220; mandatory HIV testing, 165, 219, 233, 239, 351, 356; as mediagenic, 219; medical use of marijuana initiative, 185; minority activism, 220–21; National Black Lesbian and Gay Leadership Forum projects, 66; national organizations made essential by, 58; Office of Personnel Management guidelines on, 351–52; organizations and, 221–24; as overtaking all other issues in 1980s, 48; as policy priority of gay officials, 109; political mainstreaming as consequence of, 64–65; politics of, 218–19; politics of care, 229–30; politics of discrimination, 237–38; politics of drugs, 235–37; politics of prevention, 227–29; politics of spending, 231–35; as portrayed in film "Philadelphia," 414; prognosis for full constitutional rights, 399–400; public health democratized by, 238–41; in reuniting lesbians and gay men, 100; S. 1220, 357–58; safe sex practices, 102, 103, 198, 219, 227, 228; sex and drugs involved in, 219, 353; and sodomy law

repeal, 313; state legislation dealing with in 1998, 301; statewide groups lobbying on, 293; Supreme Court discrimination cases, 398–99
AIDS Action Council, 221
AIDS Arms Network (Dallas), 230
AIDS Atlanta, 230
AIDS Coalition to Unleash Power. *See* ACT UP
Ajello, Edith, 312
Alabama: gay-related policies and interest group resources in, *298;* state government actions on gay issues, *327, 332, 338, 340*
Alaska: gay-related policies and interest group resources in, *298;* same-sex marriage in, 170, 173, 181; state government actions on gay issues, *327, 338*
American Center for Law and Justice, 155n. 8
American Civil Liberties Union (ACLU): in *Bowers v. Hardwick,* 390; gay and lesbian movement supported by, 34, 281; on gay family issues, 401; in gay-related Supreme Court cases, *391;* in gay rights litigation, 384; on gays in the military, 252, 387, 400; in *Hurley v. Irish American Gay, Lesbian and Bisexual Group of Boston,* 395; Lesbian and Gay Rights Project, 69, 384; and *Romer v. Evans,* 396; on sodomy statutes, 403n. 6; Women's Rights Project, 380, 395
American Family Association, 155n. 6
American Psychiatric Association (APA), 37, 62, 382–83, 388, *391,* 401
American Psychological Association, 391, *391,* 404n. 16
American Public Health Association (APHA), 391, *391,* 404n. 16
American Renewal, 173
"Americans Against Discrimination" project, 60
Americans with Disabilities Act (ADA), 39, 238, 399, 402
amicus curiae briefs, 378, 402n
Ann Arbor (Michigan), 270
Antichrist, 142, 146
antidiscrimination laws: and AIDS, 237–

38, 273, 426, 428; civil rights approach to, 270–71; enforcement of, 285–86; factors in state adoption of, 302; gay organizations and, 23; as goal of gays and lesbians, 45, 269; historical quest for, 271–75; impact of, 23, 284–87; at local and state level, 269–87; opposition to, 271; public opinion on, 194–95, 420–28, *422;* sexual orientation in, 11, 23, 167, 174; sources of attitudes toward, 423, 424, 425–26, 428; state groups in adoption of, 292–93; state policies, 301–5, *324–46;* support increasing for, 422. *See also* employment discrimination; local gay rights laws; state gay rights laws

antigay initiatives: elites' positions influencing outcomes of, 182–83; Human Rights Campaign "Americans Against Discrimination" project in, 60; lesbians and gay men as united in opposition to, 111; as more likely to pass in small localities, 170; from 1978 to 1988, 162–67, *164;* "no special rights" strategy in, 133–34; outcomes depending on type, 21, 133, 166–67; as policy priority of gay officials, 109; political entrepreneurs in, 170–73; resources available for, 17; after *Romer v. Evans,* 179–82; social and political effects of, 182–84; strategic environment for, 167–70; surge after 1992, 179–80, *180;* three categories of, 163–64

antigay rhetoric: AIDS epidemic spawning, 38; compared with other social movements, 25; in instrumental opposition to gay rights, 20, 126; "no special rights" slogan, 133; by Republican Party, 40

antisodomy codes: Ad Hoc Task Force to Challenge Sodomy Laws, 385; in almost half the states, 286; American Civil Liberties Union on, 403n. 6; as defined in terms of male sex, 102, 113n. 11; gay interest group strength correlated with, 300; Georgia definition of sodomy, 404n. 13; as legal restraint on gays and lesbians, 9; lesbians in opposition to, 100, 104; policies and gay interest

group resources by state, *298;* as policy priority of gay officials, 111; repeal as goal of gays and lesbians, 45, 49, 269; repeal as virtually stopped in 1980s, 37; repeal until early 1980s, 37; state policies on, 311–13, *324–46;* Supreme Court cases, 386–87. *See also Bowers v. Hardwick*

antiwar movement, 35

APA (American Psychiatric Association), 37, 62, 382–83, 388, *391,* 401

apocalyptic eschatology, 141–42, 153, 155n. 5

Apuzzo, Virginia, 63

Arizona: antigay initiatives in, 174, 186n. 11; gay elected officials in, *320, 322;* gay-related policies and interest group resources in, *298;* Phoenix, 274; on same-sex marriage, 307; state government actions on gay issues, *324, 325, 327, 332, 338, 340*

Arizona Human Rights Fund, 293

Arkansas: Fayetteville, 181; gay-related policies and interest group resources in, *298;* state government actions on gay issues, *327, 332, 340*

armed forces, gays in the. *See* gays in the military

Armstrong, Bill, 185n. 4, 187n. 16

Arno, Peter S., 222

Aspen (Colorado), 166, 174, 275

assimilationist model: activists rejecting, 57; as insider strategy, 55, 57; as limited, 57; same-sex marriage as priority for, 16

Atlanta: AIDS Atlanta, 230; antidiscrimination law in, 270, 273, 315n. 1

Austin (Texas), 131, 271

AZT, 236

Badgett, M. V. Lee, 14, 105, 113n. 10, 114n. 13

Baehr v. Levin (1993), 113n. 10, 199–200, 307

Baehr v. Miike, 307

Baker v. Nelson (1971), 198

Baldwin, James, 20, 82

Baldwin, Tammy, 27n. 6, 348

BALIF (Bay Area Lawyers for Individual Freedom), 384, 398
banks, 285
Barr, Bob, 201
Barry, Marion, 83
Barton, David, 155n. 8
Basile, Vic, 71
bath houses, 99, 219, 228
Bauer, Gary, 143, 173, 295
Baumann, Robert, 348
Baumgartner, Frank R., 42
Bay Area Lawyers for Individual Freedom (BALIF), 384, 398
Bayer, Ronald, 221
Beller v. Middendorf (1981), 387
Berkeley (California), 270, 382
Big Sister Is Watching You (Marrs), 145
Birch, Elizabeth, 59–60
Biskupski, Jackie, 296
black civil rights movement: AIDS activists influenced by, 220; citizens' initiatives used against, 162; gay rights movement affected by, 81–82; gay rights movement compared with, 5, 25; the law used in, 16; NAACP resorting to litigation, 378, 379, 383; national mood affected by, 34
blackmail, 348
Blackmun, Harry, 385, 392
Black Power, 35
Blasius, Mark, 100, 102
Board of Education of Oklahoma City v. National Gay Task Force (1985), 389–90
Bond, Brian, 73
Boozer, Melvin, 82
Boston, 383, 384, 394–95
Boucher, Rick, 361
Boulder (Colorado), 163, 166, 174, 271, 275
Boutlier v. Immigration and Naturalization Services (1967), 381–82
Bowers v. Hardwick (1986), 390–93; and "family, marriage, or procreation," 101; gay adoption affected by, 421; interest group participation in, 390–91, *391;* and legal restrictions on gays and lesbians, 9, 24, 41, 311; right to sodomy as "facetious" in, 198; White on, 101, 178
Bowler, Shaun, 7, 21

Boxer, Barbara, 225, 231
Boykin, Keith O., 19–20, 65, 66
Bradley, Bill, 17–18
Bradley, Tom, 83
Braff, Jeffrey, 221
Bragdon, Randon, 399
Bragdon v. Abbott (1998), *391,* 399, 402
Branch Davidians, 149
Brennan, William, 381, 389, 392
Brewer, Sarah E., 7, 23–24
Briggs, John, 162, 172–73
Briggs Initiative (Proposition 6), 67, 162–63, 272, 292
Brown, Harold, 62
Brown v. Board of Education (1954), 379
Bryant, Anita, 37, 272
Buchanan, Patrick, 201
Bull, Chris, 4, 68
bundling campaign contributions, 73, 76n. 3, 347
Bureau of Alcohol, Tobacco, and Firearms, 148
Burger, Warren, 392
Burstein, Karen, 295
Burton, Dan, 353, 354, 355
Burton, Phil, 225, 231
Bush, George, 224, 359
business community: antidiscrimination law as not affecting business, 287; and opposition to gay rights, 123, 131, 282; small business owners, 123, 282, 285, 420
Buss, Doris, 145
Butterfield, Herbert, 8
Button, James W., 7, 11, 23
Byrd, Robert C., 357

California: AIDS-testing initiatives, 164–65; antidiscrimination law in, 272, 275; anti-immigration Proposition 187, 173; Berkeley, 270, 382; Briggs Initiative (Proposition 6), 67, 162–63, 272, 292; gay elected officials in, *320, 322, 323;* gay-related policies and interest group resources in, *298;* Jarvis and Proposition 13, 171; medical use of marijuana initiative, 185; No on 6, 292; Palo Alto, 270; same-sex marriage poll, 181; San Jose, 162; Santa Clara County, 181;

state government actions on gay issues, *324, 325, 327, 332, 333, 338, 340, 341. See also* Los Angeles; San Francisco

Cammermeyer, Margarethe, 69

campaign contributions, bundling of, 73, 76n. 3, 347

Campaign for Working Families, 295

Campbell, Alan, 197

Campbell, Colton C., 6, 23

Canady, Charles, 202, 362

Carpenter, Chuck, 295, 303

Carrera, Gabriel José, 295

Carter, Jimmy, 37, 62, 197

Carter, Mandy, 60, 90

Casti, David, 302

casual sex, 228

Cathcart, Kevin, 70

Catholicism. *See* Roman Catholicism

CDC (Centers for Disease Control), 225, 226

Celebrating Our Families campaign (National Gay and Lesbian Task Force), 74

Center for Reclaiming America, 133

Centers for Disease Control (CDC), 225, 226

Central Intelligence Agency (CIA), 393–94, 404n. 19

CFV (Colorado for Family Values), 125, 145, 166, 185n. 4

Chafee, John H., 365

Chamber of Commerce, 123

Chicago, 270, 273, 275

child custody, 392, 397, 401

Children at Risk (Dobson and Bauer), 143

Children of the Rainbow curriculum, 131, 277

Christian Civic League of Maine, 132, 167

Christian Coalition: in Carpenter's Oregon reelection campaign, 295; *Contract with the American Family*, 152–53; gay rights issues used in fundraising by, 6, 128; as general purpose group, 125; instrumental opposition by, 127, 128, 129; LifeLine contributing to, 172; in Maine antigay initiative, 167; in Montana sodomy legislation of 1995, 311; reactive opposition by, 131, 132; and same-sex marriage, 200

Christian Identity, 155n. 8

Christianity: and the Constitution, 147, 151; Mormon Church, 122, 170; orthodoxy and an antigay perspective, 139. *See also* Christian Right; Protestantism; Roman Catholicism

Christian Right: on church and state, 150–53, 154; citizens' initiatives as method of, 184; competing groups in, 6; defined, 140, 154n. 2; direct mail targeting gay rights, 128; electoral focus of, 126; emergence of, 272–73; evangelical Protestant traditions in, 20–21, 122, 124, 140; fomenting fear of homosexuals in strategy of, 40; framing gay rights issues, 409–10; on the gay agenda, 139–60; gay candidates targeted by, 295; on gay movement as a conspiracy, 143–47; general purpose groups, 125, 128–29, 130–31; instrumental opposition by, 20, 126, 127–30, 135; Israel supported by, 143; its religious base distinguished from, 122–23; limited purpose groups, 125, 130; methods of, 126; as most notable opponent of gay rights, 282; motives of, 124–25; political influence of, 6; pragmatic discourse of, 153; premillennialism of, 140–43, 153, 154; proactive opposition by, 20, 127, 132–35; public antigay agenda as instigated and led by, 140; reactive opposition by, 20, 127, 130–32, 135–36; as a "religious right," 136n. 3; resources of, 75, 125, 293; restoration of Christianity sought by, 151–52; and same-sex marriage, 200–201, 307, 308, 311; on sexual orientation as a choice, 124, 133, 284, 410, 429; specialized groups, 125–26, 128, 133, 135; and the state, 148–53; state legislatures influenced by, 140, 291; theocracy as goal of, 154; three kinds of opposition in, 126–35; three kinds of organization in, 125–26; Traditional Values Coalition, 100, 126, 140; at United Nations Women's Conference of 1992, 145; working to elect its candidates, 297. *See also* Christian Coalition; Focus on the Family church and state, 150–53, 154

CIA (Central Intelligence Agency), 393–94, 404n. 19

Cincinnati, 18, 125, 181, 274, 404n. 18

Citizens' Alliance of Washington, 171

citizens' initiatives: antiminority initiatives as coming in cycles, 179; for medical use of marijuana, 185; minorities constrained by, 162; opponents of gay rights using, 21, 184; political entrepreneurs in, 170–74; populist roots of, 184; after *Romer*, 161–90. *See also* antigay initiatives; progay initiatives

Civil Rights Act of 1957, 371

Civil Rights Act of 1964, 26n. 4, 363, 364, 371, 398, 402

civil rights for gays and lesbians. *See* gay rights

civil rights movement, black. *See* black civil rights movement

civil rights strategy, 56, 270–71

Clarenbach, David, 73, 303–4, 315n. 9

Class "A" certificates, 388

Clinton, Bill: AIDS activists on, 242n. 13; as campaigning openly for gay support, 40; Defense of Marriage Act signed by, 134, 200; executive order on federal employment, 26n. 3, 197–98, 214n. 10, 287n. 1; gay rights supported by, 274; gays and lesbians supporting, 200, 224, 400; on gays in the military, 10, 40, 198, 252, 393, 400, 410; Hormel nomination, 370; Human Rights Campaign supporting, 61; mainstream lesbian and gay movement as trusting too much, 75; Rutherford Institute opposing, 172; same-sex marriage blocked by, 57

Clinton, Hillary, 145, 172

Coats, Dan, 364

Coburn, Tom, 361

Cohen, William S., 364

Coles, Matthew, 396

collective identity: society's hostility and construction of, 100–101; struggle for, 8–12; visibility and community building, 48. *See also* gay identity

Colorado: antidiscrimination law in, 272; Aspen, 166, 174, 275; Boulder, 163,

166, 174, 271, 275; Denver, 174, 274, 275; Equal Protection, 292; Ft. Collins, 181; gay-related policies and interest group resources in, *298;* state government actions on gay issues, *325, 327, 333, 338, 341. See also* Colorado Amendment Two

Colorado Amendment Two: Christian Right on the media in, 143–44; and coalescence of opponents of gay rights, 40; Colorado for Family Values in, 125, 166; Equal Protection in opposition to, 292; flaws in, 178; Lambda Legal Defense and Education Fund opposing, 69; lesbians and gay men mobilized by, 100, 113n. 9; "no special rights" strategy in, 133–34, 174; Republican Party supporting, 182; Supreme Court rejection of, 18, 24; text of, 186n. 13. See also *Romer v. Evans*

Colorado for Family Values (CFV), 125, 145, 166, 185n. 4

coming out: for African American gays and lesbians, 84; AIDS fight increasing, 39, 273; and antidiscrimination laws, 274; as core strategic impulse, 48, 49, 50; of Ellen DeGeneres, 49; discrimination complaints forcing, 286; gay activists on necessity of, 35, 43, 47–48; Human Rights Campaign's National Coming Out Project, 61; public opinion affected by, 414; relationship with broader gays and lesbian community created by, 100

Commission on Gay and Lesbian Youth (Massachusetts), 279–80

communal protest theory, 282

community building, 48, 49, 50, 97, 102

community protest model of policy change, 136n. 6

Competitive Enterprise Institute, 239–40

computer-based campaigns, 347

Concerned Texans Inc., 131

Concerned Women for America, 140

Conduct Unbecoming (Shilts), 253

Congress, 347–76; Abzug introducing first gay rights bill, 62, 296, 363; on AIDS, 198, 228, 232–35, 349, 351–60; Defense of Marriage Act passed by, 24, 134,

201–11, 350, 360–63; early gay rights politics in, 348–51; Employment Non-Discrimination Act debated in, 203–11, 363–65; first openly gay members of the House, 348; on gay issues, 23–24; gay issues moving piecemeal through, 370; gay-related votes from 95th to 104th Congresses, 350; gay rights bills 1975–99, 349–50; on gays in the military, 198; H.R. 2881, 354–56; H.R. 5142, 358; Human Rights Campaign political contributions, 369, *369;* National Commission on AIDS, 354–56; as not discriminating in its offices, 238, 366; openly gay representatives, 74, 348; out-of-the-closet members winning reelection, 40; public opinion and congressional voting patterns, 203–11, *206;* Ryan White Comprehensive AIDS Resources Emergency Act, 234–35, 359; S. 1220, 357–58; same-sex marriage blocked by, 57; supporters of gays in, 225; total contributions to candidates, 103rd–105th Congresses, *369;* on workplace discrimination, 238

Congressional Black Caucus, 366

Connecticut: antidiscrimination law in, 272; gay elected officials in, *320;* gay-related policies and interest group resources in, *298; Griswold v. Connecticut,* 101, 386–87, 390, *391;* Mantilla's election victory in, 295; progay public opinion in, 205, 207; state government actions on gay issues, *333, 338, 341*

conservatives: and AIDS, 228; on antidiscrimination laws, 420; Christian Right and socioeconomic thought of, 148; on Food and Drug Administration authority, 239–40; libertarians, 123; and opposition to gay rights, 123, 129, 131, 132. *See also* Christian Right

Constitution: and Christianity, 147, 151; Fifth Amendment, 394; First Amendment, 151, 389, 394, 400, 404n. 15; full faith and credit clause, 134, 201, 186n. 6; prognosis for full constitutional rights, 399–401; and recognition of same-sex marriage, 134, 201; sexual orientation provisions lacking in, 11, 26n. 4. *See also* Fourteenth Amendment to the Constitution

Contract with the American Family (Christian Coalition), 152–53

Cortner, Richard C., 377

Cory, Donald Webster, 32, 42

courts, the. *See* judicial branch

Crain, A. Lauren, 230

Creating Change Conference (National Gay and Lesbian Task Force), 63

credit agencies, 11, 285

Cruikshank, Margaret, 98, 99, 112nn. 1, 3

Cullen, Countee, 81

cultural decline, theory of, 4

cultural strategy, 16, 57–58

"culture war," 201, 269, 298, 301

Dade County (Florida), 37, 163, 272

Dallas (Texas), 230, 312

D'Amato, Alphonse, 365

D'Amico, Francine, 10, 22

Dannemeyer, William: on AIDS, 164, 233, 234, 242n. 22, 355, 356–57; antigay activity as advantageous for, 172–73; on gay movement's organization, 143; on a gay takeover, 144

Daughters of Bilitis (DOB), 33, 98, 282

Davidson, Jon, 70

Davidson, Roger H., 6, 23

DeBold, Kathleen, 71

"decency standards," 152

Defense of Marriage Act (DOMA): and antigay initiatives, 180–81; Clinton signing, 134, 200; Congress passing, 24, 134, 201–11, 350, 360–63; Employment Non-Discrimination Act included in, 22, 203; as expanding scope of the conflict, 193; as first step in creating gay rights legislation, 371; as proactive opposition, 134–35; Republican takeover of Congress and passage of, 24, 350

DeGeneres, Ellen, 49, 410

Deitcher, David, 3

Delaware: gay-related policies and interest group resources in, *298;* state government actions on gay issues, *327, 333, 338, 341*

DeMar, Gary, 155n. 8

D'Emilio, John, 6, 13, 19, 64

Democratic Party: antigay state bills introduced in 1997, 300; on Defense of Marriage Act, 203, *208*, 361, 363; on Employment Non-Discrimination Act, 203, *208;* gay elected officials in, 106; gay influence on officials in, 224; gay rights plank in 1980, 37, 82; gay vote courted by, 274; Howard as Vermont state Chair, 315n. 2; Human Rights Campaign political contributions to, 369, *369;* National Stonewall Democratic Federation, 68; and Oregon gay rights bill of 1997, 303; progay constituencies represented by liberal, 365; progay state bills introduced in 1997, 300; supporters of gays in, 225; total contributions to congressional candidates, 103rd–105th Congresses, *369;* and Washington same-sex marriage bills, 309, 310–11

Democratic Study Group, 366

denial of a writ of certiorari, 378

Denver, 174, 274, 275

Department of Education, 148

Deschamps, David, 13

Des Moines (Iowa), 131

Detroit, 270

Diani, Mario, 5

diffusion-of-innovation process, 274

Dinkins, David, 83

direct action tactics, 39, 43, 63

direct democracy: and gay rights initiatives after *Romer*, 161–90; minorities constrained by, 162, 173; opponents of gay rights using, 161; status quo policy usually supported in, 168. *See also* citizens' initiatives; gay rights referenda

direct mail fundraising, 128, 171

discrimination: and antigay attitudes, 97; based on AIDS, 237–38, 273, 426, 428; in housing, 14, 270, 287n. 1; Human Rights Campaign's "Americans Against Discrimination" project, 60; in immigration, 388; legal reform for ending, 270; protection as lacking, 11; in public accommodations, 269, 270, 285, 296, 395; "rational" discrimination, 11, 175, 196. *See also* antidiscrimination laws; employ-

ment discrimination; gays in the military; hate crime laws

diversity, social, 280, 282

DOB (Daughters of Bilitis), 33, 98, 282

Dobson, James, 143, 155n. 8, 166

Doe v. Commonwealth's Attorney (1976), 386

Doe v. SEPTA (1996), 399

Dole, Bob, 68, 359

DOMA. *See* Defense of Marriage Act

domestic partner benefits: antidiscrimination law and, 23, 275, 287; Austin, Texas, policy opposed, 131; for congressional personnel, 367; gay officials in adoption of, 296; as goal of gays and lesbians, 269; increase in granting of, 199; in Philadelphia, 283; public opinion on, 181; in San Francisco, 199, 275; sources of attitudes toward, 423; sympathetic heterosexual officials in adoption of, 296

Domi, Tanya, 63

Donnelly, Richard, 312

Donovan, Todd, 7, 21

"don't ask, don't tell" policy: application and impact of, 253–57; contradictory perspectives in, 252–53; as counterproductive, 260; discharges under, 253–55, *254;* homosexual conduct as grounds for expulsion under, 10, 252; Lambda Legal Defense and Education Fund challenging, 70; "military closet" created by, 252, 256–57, 261n. 2; and physician-patient privilege, 259–60; and recoupment of benefits, 260; and the Supreme Court, 400; *United States v. Meinhold*, 393; as unworkable, 261; violations of, 256; women disproportionately affected by, 249, 257; "zone of privacy" created by, 249, 252, 253, 261

Dorn, Ed, 256

Dornan, Robert, 354

double-blind trials, 236

Douglas, William O., 381, 382

Dreyfus, Lee, 304

drugs: AZT, 236; double-blind trials, 236; Food and Drug Administration, 235–37, 239–40, 351; investigational new drugs, 236, 240, 243n. 29; politics of, 235–37

Duberman, Martin, 62

Dubofsky, Jean E., 396–97
Dudyck (Illinois state senator), 306

Eagle Forum of Rhode Island, 313
East Lansing (Michigan), 270
Edelson, Jonathan L., 7, 10, 21
education. *See* schools
Eisenstadt v. Baird (1972), 387, 390
elected officials: and AIDS, 224–26. *See also* Congress; gay officials
"Ellen" (television show), 410
Emily's List, 71
employment discrimination, 196–98; antidiscrimination laws reducing, 286; *Equality Foundation of Greater Cincinnati v. Cincinnati,* 404n. 18; gays and lesbians reporting, 270; local and state laws forbidding public, 285; opposition to sexual orientation coverage in law, 123; public opinion on, 420–28; public opinion on gay teachers, 205; workplace equity, 49, 103, 114n. 12, 238, 287. *See also* Employment Non-Discrimination Act; federal employment
Employment Non-Discrimination Act (ENDA): congress debating, 203–11, 363–65; and Defense of Marriage Act, 22, 203; as first step in gay rights legislation, 371; Human Rights Campaign supporting, 61; increasing support in 105th Congress, 367; Log Cabin Republicans supporting, 69; public opinion on, 213n. 6; Republican Party in defeat of, 203, *208,* 350–51, 364–65, 367
ENDA. *See* Employment Non-Discrimination Act
end-times scenario, 141–42, 155n. 5
environmentalism, 25, 143, 144
Epstein, Steven, 76n. 2
Equality Begins at Home Campaign (National Gay and Lesbian Task Force), 64, 74, 291–92
Equality Foundation of Greater Cincinnati v. Cincinnati (1998), 181, 404n. 18
equality values, 424, 428
Equal Protection (Colorado), 292
Equal Protection Clause of the Fourteenth Amendment, 175–76, 261, 377, 395, 396–97, 400

"equal rights, not special rights" slogan, 174, 186n. 12
Erikson, Robert S., 204
eschatology, apocalyptic, 141–42, 153, 155n. 5
Eshoo, Anna, 361
Eskridge, William N., 380
espionage, 251
Eugene (Oregon), 272
evangelical Protestantism: antigay initiatives supported by, 163; and attitudes toward gays and lesbians, 417; and the Christian Right, 20–21, 122, 124, 140; diversity within, 122–23; homosexuality stigmatized by, 122; likening themselves to the Israelites, 146; as opposed to gay rights, 20–21, 122, 425–26; resources of, 15
Evans, Richard, 174
Exodus International, 126
extramarital sex, 412–13

FACES (Free Americans Creating Equal Status of South Dakota, Inc.), 309, 315n. 13
Family and Medical Leave Act, 367
Family Protection Act, 37
family relationships. *See* gay family relationships
Family Research Council, 152
"family values," 420
Farrar, Steve, 143, 146
Fayetteville (Arkansas), 181
FDA (Food and Drug Administration), 235–37, 239–40, 351
federal employment: blanket ban on gays and lesbians dropped, 37, 197; campaigns to bar discrimination in, 21; Clinton's executive order on, 26n. 3, 197–98, 214n. 10, 287n. 1; Congress as not discriminating in its offices, 238, 366; denied to gays and lesbians, 10, 348; Senate investigation of gays in, 33; *Singer v. United States Civil Service Commission,* 403n. 10
Federal Gay/Lesbian Civil Rights Bill, 72
Federation of Statewide Gay, Lesbian, Bisexual, and Transgender Political Organizations, 64, 291

Feiden, Karyn L., 222

feminism: and attitudes toward gays and lesbians, 417; gay movement linked to by Christian Right, 144, 145; lesbian and feminist issues as overlapping, 102–3; lesbian feminism, 35, 43, 99–100, 113n. 6; and lesbian separatism, 99–100. *See also* women's movement

Fernandez, Joseph, 277

Fiber, Pamela, 6, 20

Field Action Network (Human Rights Campaign), 61

Fifth Amendment to the Constitution, 394

50 State Action, 291

First Amendment to the Constitution, 151, 389, 394, 400, 404n. 15

Fleischmann, Arnold, 1

Florida: antigay initiatives in, 174, 186n. 11; Christian Coalition's influence in, 293; Dade County, 37, 163, 272; gay-related policies and interest group resources in, *298;* progay public opinion in, 207; state government actions on gay issues, *325, 328, 333, 341, 338, 342; Wainwright v. Stone,* 386

Focus on the Family: antigay initiatives after *Romer,* 180; as general purpose group, 125, 129; governmental activism advocated by, 152; instrumental opposition by, 127; on the media and gay activists, 143; premillennialism of, 140; same-sex marriage opposed by, 307

Foley, Thomas S., 366

Folger, Janet, 133

Food and Drug Administration (FDA), 235–37, 239–40, 351

Ft. Collins (Colorado), 181

Foster, Vincent, 172

Foundation for American Christian Education, 155n. 8

Fournier, Keith, 152

Fourteenth Amendment to the Constitution: Equal Protection Clause of, 175–76, 261, 377, 395, 396–97, 400; gender discrimination found unconstitutional under, 380, 395

Frank, Barney: advice for gay and lesbian candidates, 106; and bundled campaign contributions, 73; and Clinton's executive order on federal employment, 212n. 2; on congressional response to AIDS, 352; Defense of Marriage Act opposed by, 202, 362; low profile on AIDS policy, 225; and National Stonewall Democratic Federation, 68; as openly gay member of Congress, 348

Free Americans Creating Equal Status of South Dakota, Inc. (FACES), 309, 315n. 13

Free Congress Foundation, 123, 129

"freemen," 150

free speech, 389–90, 394–95, 400, 401

Freiberg, Peter, 60

Gaither, Billy Jack, xv

Gallagher, John, 4, 68

Gamble, Barbara S., 132

Gamson, William, 56

Garber, Eric, 81

Gay Activist Alliance (Washington, D.C.), 36

Gay Activists' Alliance (New York City), 62, 382–83

Gay Alliance of Students v. Matthews (1976), 385, 403n. 7

Gay and Lesbian Activists Alliance (GLAA), 104, 114n. 17

Gay and Lesbian Advocates and Defenders (GLAD), 383, 390, *391,* 394, 396

Gay and Lesbian Alliance Against Defamation (GLAAD), 85

Gay and Lesbian Victory Fund (GLVF), 71–74; bundling contributions by, 73, 76n. 3; criteria for choosing candidates to support, 72; executive directors of, 73; grassroots change embraced by, 75; in 1992 elections, 72–73; in 1994 elections, 73; in 1996 elections, 73; in 1997 elections, 73; racial composition of, 85; rights-based agenda of, 368

Gay and Lesbian Violence Project (National Gay and Lesbian Task Force), 62

gay bashing, 9, 253

gay civil rights. *See* gay rights

gay family relationships: child custody, 392, 397, 401; divergent views of, 46; inheritance, 195; for lesbians, 103, 114n. 13; National Gay and Lesbian Task Force attending to, 63; prognosis for full constitutional rights, 401; recognition as goal of gays and lesbians, 45, 49. *See also* adoption; domestic partner benefits; same-sex marriage

gay identity: African American gays and lesbians in formation of, 80–81; formulation of an open, 12; gay liberationists on, 43; other sources of identity contrasted with, 13; as stigmatized, 13. *See also* collective identity

Gay, Lesbian, and Bisexual Veterans of America, 252

Gay Liberation Front, 35, 56, 382

Gay Lib v. University of Missouri (1978), 385, 392

gay marriage. *See* same-sex marriage

gay men: in AIDS activist movement, 100; commonality and difference in priorities of lesbian and gay male elected officials, 105–11; community's meaning for, 99; differentiating lesbian and gay male policy issues, 103–4; discrimination based on AIDS, 237–38; gay organizations disproportionately influenced by, 20; media focusing on compared with lesbians, 98; on pornography, 103; tension between lesbians and, 101–5. *See also* gays and lesbians

Gay Men of African Descent (GMAD), 89, 92

Gay Men's Health Crisis (GMHC), 221–22; ACT UP contrasted with, 222–23; Dannemeyer distributing publications of, 357; "do it yourself" philosophy of, 239; gay men volunteering in, 230; and Helms, 228, 229; as mainstream organization, 222; prevention and care as emphasis of, 230

gay officials: candidates addressing a broader constituency, 294–95; coming out after election, 14, 27n. 6; commonality and difference in priorities of lesbian and gay male, 105–11; in domestic partnership policy adoption, 296; effects of, 23; Gay and Lesbian Victory Fund supporting, 71–74; increase in 1990s, 274, 294; Log Cabin Republicans supporting lesbian and gay candidates, 68, 69; out-of-the-closet candidates winning, 40; representing their constituents, 295–97; Spear as longest-serving legislator, 297; state officials, 293–95, *320–23*

gay politics: African American gays and lesbians in, 19–20, 79–96; AIDS influencing, 22, 217; the arenas of, 267–432; as case of more general political phenomena, 1; civil rights strategy, 56, 270–71; in the congressional arena, 347–76; context of, 1–28; cultural strategy, 16; cycles of accomplishment and quiescence in, 19, 41–45; as embodied in social movements, 5; interest to political scientists, 6; the issues in, 191–265; legal strategy, 16; at local and state level, 269–89; policy priorities of lesbians and gay men compared, 97–115; in political process, 15–18; political strategy, 57–58; public opinion affecting, 24–25, 409–32; reasons for studying, 3–8; understanding, 8–18. *See also* gay rights

gay relationships: casual sex, 228; promiscuity, 227–28; public opinion on, 195, 198–200, 412–13. *See also* sodomy

gay rights: Abzug introduces first bill in Congress, 62, 296, 363; arenas of struggle for, 267–432; attitudes toward, 420–28, *422;* as the civil rights issue of the 1990s, 121; in the congressional arena, 347–76; and Constitutional rights, 11, 26n. 4; context of, 1–28; factors in the politics of, 280–82; as human rights, 58; at local and state level, 269–89; passion in struggle over, 4–5; prognosis for full constitutional rights, 399–401; public opinion on, 194–95, 409–32; as Satanic for the Christian Right, 141, 146; sources of attitudes on, *423;* Supreme Court cases on, 377–408. *See also* antidiscrimination laws; employment discrimination; gay family relationships; gay rights movement; gays in the military; hate crime laws; opponents of gay rights gay rights movement, 29–118; African American gays and lesbians in, 19–20, 79–96; AIDS and its impact on, 38–40; beyond political mainstreaming, 54–78; black civil rights movement affecting, 81–82; black civil rights movement compared with, 5, 25; black politicians supporting, 83–84; civil rights strategy for, 56, 270–71; competing organizations in, 5; as conspiracy for the Christian Right, 143–47; the current movement, 40–41, 50; cycles of accomplishment and quiescence in, 19, 41–45; diversity in study of, 2; diversity of organizations in, 31; divisions in, 37–38, 98; and the gay community, 31–32; goals of, 45–46; historical overview of, 32–41; homophile movement, 98–99; inclusive rhetoric of, 79; interest group politics in, 98; as lagging compared with other movements, 25–26; legal strategy for, 16; lesbians in, 20; political process used by, 12–18; political strategy for, 57–58; post-World War II origins of, 32–34; public opinion and strategies of, 195–200; re-creation of a unified movement, 100–101; reform-oriented organizations, 36, 74; resources available to, 12–15, 55; shared oppression in construction of, 97–98; from Stonewall to AIDS, 34–38; strategies for, 46–50; tension between lesbians and gay men, 101–5; top-down hierarchical approach of, 54, 57. *See also* national organizations

Gay Rights National Lobby, 59

gay rights referenda: antigay activists using, 184; as defeated more often than victorious, 17, 132; Maine's repeal of gay rights statute, 132. *See also* citizens' initiatives

gays and lesbians: affective and cognitive sources of evaluation of, *415;* antigay initiatives affecting opinions about, 182–83; attitudes toward, 412–20; attitudes toward in the 1990s, 414–19; Clinton supported by, 200, 224, 400; electoral process as not kind to, 17; in family law, 10–11; financial status of,

14; isolation and invisibility in experience of, 13; Jews contrasted with, 14–15; legal restraints on, 9–10; and other minority groups, 7; percentage of adults considering themselves, 13, 241n. 6; position as differing across time and space, 8–9; progress made since the 1960s, 25; public dislike of, 13–14, 194, 241n. 7, 392, 413, 419; racism in, 37, 80; as seducing heterosexuals, 415, 418, 419, 421, 426, 427, 428–29; sources of evaluations of, *416;* as a "special interest," 133, 174; statewide interest groups of, 291–93; trends in attitudes toward, 412–14; in urban gay enclaves, 280–81; youth, 275–80. *See also* African American gays and lesbians; coming out; discrimination; gay family relationships; gay identity; gay men; gay officials; gay relationships; gay rights; lesbians; violence against gays and lesbians

gays in the military, 249–65; Cammermeyer case, 69; Clinton's endorsement of, 10, 40, 198, 252, 393, 400, 410; congressional response to, 198; failure to repeal the ban in 1993, 43, 57; fears that change will undermine the mission, 123; habitability issues, 251–52, 421; history of exclusion policy, 249–53; learning from the debacle over, 75; McCarthyite witch hunts, 33; National Gay and Lesbian Task Force attending to, 63; as policy priority of gay officials, 109; prognosis for full constitutional rights, 400; public opinion on, 410, 420–28, *422;* reactive opposition to, 131; Reserve Officer Training Corps (ROTC), 251, 260; security issues, 250–51; Servicemembers Legal Defense Network, 69, 256, 260, 400; as "social experiment," 258–59; sources of attitudes toward, 423, 424–25, *424,* 425, 426–27; support increasing for, 422; Supreme Court cases, 387, 393–94, 397–98, 400, 404n. 17. *See also* "don't ask, don't tell" policy

Gay Student Organization (GSO) of the University of New Hampshire v. Bonner (1974), 385, 403n. 7

gay studies, as recognizable scholarly movement, 3–4
gay youth, 275–80
gender discrimination, 380, 395
general ideology, 425
General Social Survey, 411
Georgia: antisodomy law of, 404n. 13; gay elected officials in, *322;* gay-related policies and interest group resources in, *298;* progay public opinion in, 207; *Stanley v. Georgia,* 390, 404n. 15; state government actions on gay issues, *328, 333, 338, 341. See also* Atlanta; *Bowers v. Hardwick*
Gerstmann, Evan, 196
Gibson, Paul, 276
Gingrich, Newt, 354
Ginsburg, Ruth Bader, 379–80, 395
Gittings, Barbara, 34
GLAA (Gay and Lesbian Activists Alliance), 104, 114n. 17
GLAAD (Gay and Lesbian Alliance Against Defamation), 85
GLAD (Gay and Lesbian Advocates and Defenders), 383, 390, *391,* 394, 396
GLVF. *See* Gay and Lesbian Victory Fund
GMAD (Gay Men of African Descent), 89, 92
GMHC. *See* Gay Men's Health Crisis
Gold, Ronald, 62
Goldberg, J. J., 13
Goldberg, Suzanne B., 18, 397
Goldwater, Barry, 60
Gore, Al, 365
Graham, Billy, 142
Green, John, 5–6, 20
GRID (gay-related immune deficiency), 113n. 8, 352
Griswold v. Connecticut (1965), 101, 386–87, 390, *391,* 392
Gunderson, Steven, 203, 225, 348, 363, 367
Gunther, Wendell, 381

Haider-Markel, Donald P.: on assimilationist strategy, 55; congressional voting modeled by, 204, 350, 368; on Democrats and progay support, 365; on gay

public officials, 7, 23; on gay rights advocates instituting protections quietly, 197; on gay rights opponents expanding scope of the conflict, 196; on gays and policy-making arenas of government, 17; on grassroots organizing versus fundraising, 372n. 3; on heterosexual officials and domestic partner benefits, 296; on Lambda Legal Defense and Education Fund, 69; on National Gay and Lesbian Task Force, 63; and political entrepreneurs, 304
Hamilton, Amy, 98, 102
Hampton, Mabel, 81
Hanks, Tom, 414
Hansberry, Lorraine, 20, 82
harassment: of children of gay parents, 421; of gay bars, 34; in the military, 249, 256; in schools, 270, 276; sexual harassment, 398, 402
Harbeck, Karen, 9, 277
Hardwick, Michael, 390
Harkin, Tom, 357
Harlan, John Marshall, 381, 396
Harlan, Ruth, 398
Harlem Renaissance, 80–81
Hartman, Keith, 15
Harvey Milk Gay Democratic Club, 220, 225
Hatch, Orrin, 235, 243n. 22, 357
hate crime laws: factors in state adoption of, 305; gay organizations and, 23, 293; as goal of gays and lesbians, 45, 269; and Jews, 14, 306; policies and gay interest group resources by state, *298;* as policy priority of gay officials, 109; sexual orientation excluded from coverage by, 10; and Shepard murder, 301; state bills in 1997, 300; state policies on, 305–7, *324–46*
Hate Crimes Prevention Act, xv
Hate Crimes Statistics Act, 39
Hatfield, Mark O., 365
Hatheway v. Secretary of the Army (1981), 387
Hawaii: antidiscrimination law in, 272, 275; *Baehr v. Levin,* 113n. 10, 199–200, 307; gay-related policies and interest group

Hawaii (*continued*)
resources in, *298;* progay public opinion
in, 205, 207; same-sex marriage in, 21,
70, 71, 75, 88–89, 113n. 10, 134, 169–
70, 181, 199–200, 201–2, 307, 308, 360,
401; state government actions on gay issues, *324, 325, 328, 333, 338, 341, 342*
Hay, Harry, 31, 33, 98
Headley, Jubi, Jr., 66–67, 90
Health and Human Services (HHS), Department of, 232
Health Omnibus Act of 1988, 358
Helfley amendment, 198
Helms, Jesse, 228, 229, 233–34, 242n. 22,
356, 357–58, 359
Herman, Didi, 7, 20–21
Hicks, Randy, 185n. 4
HIV. *See* AIDS
HIV testing, mandatory, 165, 219, 233,
239, 351, 356
Hofstadter, Richard, 142
Holmes, Andy, 261n. 3
homophile movement, 98–99
homophobia: antigay groups attempting to
increase, 410; among blacks, 80; different strategies for dealing with, 15, 38,
45–46; policy positions affected by, 411;
and sophistication, 419; and stigma of
homosexuality, 11
Homosexual in America, The (Cory), 32, 42
homosexuality: activity and orientation distinguished, 27n. 5; American Psychiatric Association on, 37, 62, 382–83; and
the antichrist for Pat Robertson, 146; as
choice or biologically-driven, 24–25;
criminalization of homosexual sex, 11;
as dangerous for the Christian Right,
125; fractiousness in debate about, 41;
and God's will, 415, 418, 420; as morally wrong for the Christian Right, 122;
as natural, 415, 416, 418, 419, 420; on
public agenda in U.S., 4; regarded as a
problem, 9; religious community divided over, 15; in school curricula, 276,
277–79, 283–84; as a sin for conservative religious believers, 139, 282; stigma
attached to, 8, 11–12, 221, 294; as subversive for the Christian Right, 125;
therapies for changing, 133. *See
also* gays and lesbians; sexual orientation
Hormel, James C., 370
Horn, Bill, 131
Horner, Maxine, 306
Housh, Michael, 231
Howard, Steve, 315n. 2
Howard University Law School, 379
HRC. *See* Human Rights Campaign
Hughes, Langston, 81
human rights: gay rights seen as, 58; gays
and lesbians excluded from codes of,
270; local human rights commissions,
285
Human Rights Campaign (HRC), 59–62;
AIDS efforts of, 223; "Americans
Against Discrimination" project, 60;
Birch as executive director, 59–60; central activities of, 60; Clinton supported
by, 61; in congressional races of 1996,
370–71; contributions to congressional
candidates by, 369, *369;* criticism of,
60–61; employment discrimination poll,
238, 213n. 6; Field Action Network, 61;
field directors of, 61; fundraising dinners of, 59; in gay-related Supreme
Court cases, *391;* as increasingly professional, 347; joint events with Gay Men
of African Descent, 89, 92; and lesbian
health issues, 104, 114nn. 14, 16; litigation by, 384; Millennium March initiative, 89–90; National Coming Out Project, 61; and National Gay and Lesbian
Task Force, 64; organizing initiatives
of, 61; racial composition of, 65, 85;
rights-based agenda of, 368; in Robb
campaign, 242n. 12; in *Romer v. Evans,*
396; safe, middle-of-the-road approach
of, 61–62; "Speak Out Action Grams,"
61; training of local activists by, 74
Human Rights Campaign Fund (HRCF),
59
human rights commissions, 285
Humphrey, Gordon, 360
Hunt, Roger, 309

Hunter, James Davison, 140
Hurley v. Irish American Gay, Lesbian and Bisexual Group of Boston (1995), *391*, 394–95, 399

Idaho: antigay initiative of 1994, 60, 133–34, 166, 172, 178, 182, 187n. 16, 292; gay-related policies and interest group resources in, *298;* No on One Coalition, 292; state government actions on gay issues, *324, 328, 342*
Idaho Citizens' Alliance, 171
Idaho for Human Dignity, 292
identity politics, 74, 87
ideology, general, 425
Illinois: Chicago, 270, 273, 275; gay elected officials in, *320;* gay-related policies and interest group resources in, *298;* hate crime laws in, 305–6; McKeon's progay measures, 296–97; progay public opinion in, 207; sodomy law repealed in, 312; state government actions on gay issues, *324, 325, 328, 333, 338, 342*
Illinois Federation for Human Rights, 293
Immigration and Nationality Act, 350, 381
Immigration and Nationalization Service (INS), 388
incrementalist proposals, 21, 163, 167, 169, 181
Indiana: gay-related policies and interest group resources in, *298;* state government actions on gay issues, *333, 338, 342*
INDs (investigational new drugs), 236, 240, 243n. 29
inheritance, 195
initiatives. *See* citizens' initiatives
In re Longstaff (1984), 388, 389
instrumental opposition to gay rights, 20, 126, 127–30, 135
interest groups: as force in lesbian and gay state politics, 297; for gay rights litigation, 383–85; gay rights movement reflecting interest group politics, 98; insider and outsider strategies in, 7; interest group liberalism, 74; legal system used by, 378–80; progay laws corre-

lated with, 300; resources for gay groups by state, 298, *298;* statewide gay and lesbian groups, 291–93; in Supreme Court cases, 377, *391*
Internet, 104–5, 114n. 15
investigational new drugs (INDs), 236, 240, 243n. 29
Iowa: Des Moines, 131; gay-related policies and interest group resources in, *299;* legislation on gay youth, 280; state government actions on gay issues, *325, 328, 333, 334, 338, 342*
Iowa City (Iowa), 278–79
Islam, 139
Israel, 142, 143

Jackson, Jesse, Jr., 361
Jackson, Maynard, 83
Janklow, William, 309
Jarvis, Howard, 171
Jefferson, Thomas, 81, 151
Jeffords, James M., 69, 365, 367
Jews: attitudes toward homosexuality, 203, 204; in end-times scenario, 142, 143; gays and lesbians contrasted with, 14–15; and hate crimes, 14, 306; and opposition to gay rights, 122–23, 129; orthodoxy and an antigay perspective, 139
John Birch Society, 123, 129
Johnson, Nancy, 69
Jones, Bryan D., 42
Jones, Paula, 172, 186n. 9
Jones v. Hallahan (1973), 198
judicial branch: and AIDS activism, 226; gays and lesbians turning to the courts, 18, 70; interest groups using, 378–80, 383–85; minority rights in, 173. *See also* Supreme Court

Kaib, David, 7, 23–24
Kameny, Franklin, 34, 62, 403n. 3
Kameny v. Brucker (1961), 403n. 3
Kansas: gay-related policies and interest group resources in, *299;* state government actions on gay issues, *325, 328, 329, 334, 338, 342;* Wichita, 272
Kansas City (Missouri), 274

Kaposi Sarcoma Education and Research Foundation, 230
Kassebaum, Nancy, 364
Kayal, Philip M., 221
Keen, Lisa, 18
Kelsey, Frances, 235
Kennedy, Anthony, 41, 176–77, 397
Kennedy, D. James, 133
Kennedy, Edward M., 353, 356, 357, 359, 363–64, 365
Kennedy, John F., 34
Kentucky: gay-related policies and interest group resources in, *299; Jones v. Hallahan,* 198; sodomy law repealed in, 312; state government actions on gay issues, *324, 329, 338*
Kerry, John F., 371
Kessler (FDA Commissioner), 237
King, Martin Luther, Jr., 81
Kinsey studies, 32, 42
Knight, Robert, 153
Knott v. Holtzman (1995), 397
Koch, Klaus, 155n. 5
Kolbe, Jim, 348
Koop, C. Everett, 232–33
Kramer, Larry, 222, 228
Kraus, Bill, 231
KRC v. United States Information Agency (1994), 394

LaHaye, Beverly, 27n. 7, 152
LaHaye, Tim, 152
Lambda Legal Defense and Education Fund, 69–71; Ad Hoc Task Force to Challenge Sodomy Laws, 385; in AIDS cases, 70, 223–24; board of directors of, 70; in *Bowers v. Hardwick,* 390; criticism of, 70; in *Equality Foundation of Greater Cincinnati v. Cincinnati,* 404n. 18; on gay family issues, 401; in gay-related Supreme Court cases, *391;* in gays in the military cases, 387; in *Gay Student Organization (GSO) of the University of New Hampshire v. Bonner,* 403n. 7; in Hawaii marriage case, 70, 71, 75, 88–89, 199; litigation as purpose of, 383; Marriage Project of, 71; offices of, 70; in *People v. Onofre,* 386, 403n. 9;

racial composition of, 85; as reform-oriented, 36; rights-based agenda of, 368; strategy of, 70
Larouche, Lyndon, 165, 172, 173
Lavender Law Conference, 385
law: gay activists using, 16; as symbol and instrument of gay oppression, 12. *See also* judicial branch; legislation
law enforcement personnel (police), 45, 97, 123, 270
law schools, 385
Legal Marriage Alliance of Washington, 309
Legal Services Corporation Act, 350
legal strategy, 16
legislation: obtaining gay rights through, 17–18. *See also* antidiscrimination laws; Congress; hate crime laws
legislative scorecards, 128
Lesbian and Gay Coalition for Justice (Tennessee), 293
Lesbian and Gay Congressional Staff Association, 366
Lesbian and Gay Rights Lobby (Texas), 293
Lesbian and Gay Rights Project (ACLU), 69, 384
Lesbian and Gay Task Force (Philadelphia), 283
lesbian baiting, 253
lesbian feminism, 35, 43, 99–100, 113n. 6
Lesbian/Gay Freedom Day Committee, Inc. v. INS (1983), 388, 389
Lesbian Rights Project, 384, 390, *391,* 401
lesbians: in AIDS activist movement, 100, 102, 111, 220; antisodomy codes opposed by, 100, 104; breast cancer as concern for, 103; in child custody battles, 392, 397; commonality and difference in priorities of lesbian and gay male elected officials, 105–11; Daughters of Bilitis, 33, 98, 282; differentiating lesbian and gay male policy issues, 103–4; "don't ask, don't tell" policy affecting disproportionately, 249, 257; earnings of, 105; family issues for, 103, 114n. 13; feminist and lesbian issues as overlapping, 102–3; and "gay," 112n. 1; health issues of, 103–4, 109; and the homo-

phile movement, 98–99; as identifying with biological sex more than sexual orientation, 102; lawyers in AIDS litigation, 400; lesbian feminism, 35, 43, 99–100, 113n. 6; and policy agenda of gay rights groups, 104–5; second-class status in gay organizations, 20, 102; tension between gay men and, 101–5; workplace issues for, 103, 114n. 12. *See also* gays and lesbians; lesbian separatism

lesbian separatism: development of, 20, 99–100; male sexism in emergence of, 37; on pornography, 103

Levi, Jeffrey, 240, 351

Levin, Sander M., 352–53

Lewis, Gregory B., 7, 10, 21

Lewis, John, 361

liberationism: of ACT UP, 56; as cultural strategy, 57–58

libertarians, 123

Liebman, Marvin, 67

LifeLine long-distance company, 172, 186n. 7

likability heuristic, 419

local gay rights laws: AIDS in increase of, 39; Christian Right in repeal of, 140; citizens' initiatives in repeal of, 165, 166, 181; and Colorado Amendment Two, 174; impact of, 284–87; passage by early 1980s, 37, 197, 270–73; state government affecting, 290; upsurge in the 1990s, 273–74. See also *cities by name*

Locke (governor of Washington), 309, 310

Locke, Alain, 81

Log Cabin Federation, 67

Log Cabin Republicans, 67–69; Dole contribution controversy, 68; grassroots education by, 75; greater trust within Republican Party, 371; as increasingly professional, 347; lesbian and gay candidates supported by, 69; moderate strategy of, 368; Political Action Committee of, 68; in Texas, 293; and Weld's election in Massachusetts, 68

Lorde, Audre, 82, 94

Los Angeles: AIDS project in, 230; antidiscrimination law in, 270; domestic part-

ner benefits in, 275; Gay Liberation Front in, 382

Lott, Trent, 364, 370

Louisiana: gay-related policies and interest group resources in, *299;* New Orleans, 230, 274; state government actions on gay issues, *324, 325, 326, 329, 334, 342*

Louisiana Lesbian and Gay Political Action Caucus, 293

Loving v. Virginia (1967), 198–99

Mabon, Lon, 165, 166, 169, 171, 172, 173

Macdonald, Douglas Ian, 351

Madison (Wisconsin), 270, 273

Maine: antidiscrimination law in, 275; antigay initiative of 1995, 134, 166, 167–68, *168,* 178; Christian Civic League of Maine, 132, 167; gay elected officials in, *320, 322, 323;* gay-related policies and interest group resources in, *299;* gay rights statute repealed in 1998, 132, 136, 166, 167–68, *168,* 288n. 4; local progay initiatives of 1998, 184–85, 187n. 17; Ogunquit, 185, 187n. 17; Portland, 166, 167; South Portland, 185, 187n. 17; state government actions on gay issues, *324, 326, 329, 334, 338, 342*

mainline Protestants, 122–23, 129, 136n. 2

Main Street Coalition, 367

majority, tyranny of the, 17

Manago, Cleo, 91

mandatory HIV testing, 165, 219, 233, 239, 351, 356

Mantilla, Evelyn, 295

Manual Enterprises v. Day (1962), 381

March on Washington for Lesbian and Gay Rights (1987), 39, 43, 62

marijuana, medical use of, 185

marriage: Christian Right on decay of, 124; Defense of Marriage Act defining, 212n. 3. *See also* same-sex marriage

Marrs, Texe, 145

Marshall, Peter, 155n. 8

Marshall, Thurgood, 379, 389, 392

Maryland: gay elected officials in, *323;* gay-related policies and interest group resources in, *299;* progay public opinion

Maryland (*continued*)
in, 205; state government actions on gay issues, *324, 326, 329, 334, 339, 342*

Massachusetts: antidiscrimination law in, 272, 273; Boston, 383, 384, 394–95; Commission on Gay and Lesbian Youth, 279–80; employment discrimination protection in, 197; gay elected officials in, *320, 322, 323;* gay-related policies and interest group resources in, *299;* Log Cabin Republicans in gubernatorial race, 68; progay public opinion in, 205, 207; state government actions on gay issues, *324, 326, 329, 334, 342*

Matlovich, Leonard, 251

Mattachine Society: civil rights strategy of, 56, 270; in gay and lesbian movement, 33, 42, 98; Gay Liberation Front as committee of, 382; and lesbians, 113n. 5; medical establishment lobbied by, 382; in *One, Inc. v. Oleson*, 380–81; in Philadelphia, 282

Maxey, Glen, 106, 315n. 3

McCarthy, John D., 12

McCarthyism, 33

McCartney, Bill, 185n. 4

McFeeley, Tim, 59, 65

McGiver, John P., 204

McIlhenny, Chuck, 143

McIlhenny, Donna, 143

McKay, Claude, 81

McKeon, Larry, 296–97

McKinney, Cynthia, 361

McVeigh, Timothy, 253

McVeigh v. Cohen (1998), 253

media, the: ACT UP and Queer Nation garnering attention of, 76n. 2; AIDS as mediagenic, 219; Christian Right on gay movement's control of, 143–44, 155n. 6; gay men rather than lesbians as focus of, 98; gays and lesbians portrayed in, 40, 41, 45; positive images of gays and lesbians in, 410, 414; Public Broadcasting System, 147, 148

medical use of marijuana, 185

Meehan, Marty, 363

Meier, Kenneth J., 17, 196, 197, 304

men: attitudes toward gays and lesbians in, 203, 414, 417, 418, 429n. 2; Selective Service Act applying only to, 393. *See also* gay men

Meritor Savings Bank, FSB v. Vinson (1986), 398, 402

Metts, Harold, 313

Michigan: Ann Arbor, 270; Christian Right in, 293; Detroit, 270; East Lansing, 270; gay-related policies and interest group resources in, *299;* state government actions on gay issues, *329, 334, 339, 342*

militant tactics, 44

military, gays in the. *See* gays in the military

Military Selective Service Act, 393

militia groups, 150

Milk, Harvey, 219–20

Millennium March, 89–90, 94, 291

Minneapolis, 270, 275, 382

Minnesota: antidiscrimination law in, 272, 275; *Baker v. Nelson*, 198; gay elected officials in, *320, 323;* gay-related policies and interest group resources in, *299;* Minneapolis, 270, 275, 382; St. Paul, 272; Spear's progay measures, 297; state government actions on gay issues, *324, 329, 330, 334, 335, 339, 342*

Mississippi: antigay initiative petitions in, 174, 186n. 11; gay-related policies and interest group resources in, *299;* progay public opinion in, 205; state government actions on gay issues, *330, 335, 342, 343*

Missouri: antigay initiatives in, 174, 186n. 11; antisodomy law used in, 312; gay elected officials in, *320; Gay Lib v. University of Missouri*, 385, 392; gay-related policies and interest group resources in, *299;* hate crime law in, 301; Kansas City, 274; Privacy Rights Education Project, 293; state government actions on gay issues, *330, 335, 339, 343*

Mitchell, George, 359

Mixner, David, 60

Montana: deviate sexual conduct law, 311;

gay elected officials in, *321;* gay-related policies and interest group resources in, *299;* PRIDE!, 293; sodomy law overturned, 312; state government actions on gay issues, *326, 335, 343*
Montgomery, G. V. (Sonny), 354, 355
Moral Majority, 100, 304
moral traditionalism, 124, 126, 423, 428
Mormon Church, 122, 170
Moskos, Charles, 253, 258, 259
municipal gay rights laws. *See* local gay rights laws
Murray, Ed, 296, 309
Murray, Patty, 310
Murray, Stephen O., 27n. 5

NAACP (National Association for the Advancement of Colored People), 378, 379, 383
National AIDS Clearinghouse, 221
National AIDS Programs Office (NAPO), 224
National Association for the Advancement of Colored People (NAACP), 378, 379, 383
National Bar Association, 379
National Black Lesbian and Gay Leadership Forum, 65–67; AIDS projects of, 66; annual national conference of, 66; board of directors of, 66; first conference of, 65; and the Millennium March, 90; same-sex marriage survey by, 89; Washington, D.C. headquarters of, 66; working with black churches, 74–75; youth council of, 66
National Campaign to Protect Marriage (NCPM), 307
National Center for Lesbian Rights (NCLR), 69, 384, 390, *391,* 396, 401
National Coming Out Project (Human Rights Campaign), 61
National Commission on AIDS, 351, 354–56
National Education Association, 148
National Election Studies (NES), 411
National Endowment for the Arts, 132, 148

National Federation of Independent Businesses, 123
National Gay and Lesbian Law Association, 385
National Gay and Lesbian Task Force (NGLTF), 62–65; and Birch, 59; *Board of Education of Oklahoma City v. National Gay Task Force,* 389–90; Celebrating Our Families campaign, 74; on classification of homosexuality as a disease, 383; Creating Change Conference, 63; Equality Begins at Home Campaign, 64, 74, 291–92; in *Gay Alliance of Students v. Matthews,* 403n. 7; in gay-related Supreme Court cases, *391;* on gay rights referenda, 17; hierarchical model of decision-making in, 64; and Human Rights Campaign, 64; identity crisis of, 63–64; lesbians' status in, 102; political strategies embraced by, 63; progressive political leanings of, 64; racial composition of, 63, 65, 85; as reform-oriented, 36; rights-based agenda of, 368; in *Romer v. Evans,* 396; and South Dakota legislation, 308–9; state-level organizing by, 64; surveys of gay-related bills, 300–301; Task Force Policy Institute, 64; and Wisconsin gay rights bill of 1982, 304; Youth Leadership Training program, 74
National Gay Rights Advocates (NGRA), 384, 390
National Gay Task Force. *See* National Gay and Lesbian Task Force
National Lesbian and Gay Journalists Association (NLGJA), 65
National Lesbian and Gay Law Association, *391*
National Organization for Women, *391,* 401
national organizations: African American gays and lesbians in, 85–86; grassroots organizing and education by, 74–75; strategies of, 58–74. *See also* Gay and Lesbian Victory Fund; Human Rights Campaign; Lambda Legal Defense and Education Fund; Log Cabin Republi-

national organizations (*continued*)
cans; National Black Lesbian and Gay
Leadership Forum; National Gay and
Lesbian Task Force; *and other organiza-
tions by name*
National Organizations Responding to
AIDS, 221
National Stonewall Democratic Federation,
68
National Women's Law Conference, 379
Navratilova, Martina, 174
NCLR (National Center for Lesbian
Rights), 69, 384, 390, *391*, 396, 401
Nebraska: gay-related policies and interest
group resources in, *299;* state govern-
ment actions on gay issues, *324, 326,
330, 335, 339, 343*
Neet, Loretta, 146
Nelson, Janet Cooper, 312
Nevada: antidiscrimination law in, 301; antigay initiatives in, 174, 186n. 11; gay
elected officials in, *321;* gay-related policies and interest group resources in,
299; sodomy law repealed, 312; state
government actions on gay issues, *326,
335, 343*
New Age spiritualism, 144, 145
New Hampshire: antidiscrimination law in,
275; gay adoption ban repealed, 292;
gay elected officials in, *321, 322;* gay-
related policies and interest group resources in, *299; Gay Student Organization (GSO) of the University of New
Hampshire v. Bonner*, 385, 403n. 7; state
government actions on gay issues, *324,
326, 330, 335, 339, 343*
New Jersey: antidiscrimination law in, 275;
gay-related policies and interest group
resources in, *299;* progay public opinion, 205; state government actions on
gay issues, *330, 335, 339, 343*
New Left, 35
New Mexico: gay elected officials in, *321;*
gay-related policies and interest group
resources in, *299;* state government actions on gay issues, *324, 326, 330, 335,
336, 339, 343*

New Orleans, 230, 274
New York AIDS Coalition, 221
New York City: AIDS striking in, 219,
227, 229; antidiscrimination law in, 270,
273; Children of the Rainbow curriculum, 131, 277; domestic partner benefits
in, 275; Gay Activists' Alliance, 62,
382–83; Gay Liberation Front founded
in, 382; Gay Men's Health Crisis
founded in, 221, 230; Stonewall Riot, 3,
35, 42, 82, 270, 382
New York State: antidiscrimination law in,
272; gay elected officials in, *321, 322,
323;* gay-related bills in 1997, 300; gay-
related policies and interest group resources in, *299;* New York AIDS Coalition, 221; *People v. Onofre*, 386, 403n.
9; *People v. Uplinger*, 387; state government actions on gay issues, *324, 326,
330, 331, 336, 339, 343, 344;* Vacco-
Burstein attorney general race, 295. *See
also* New York City
New York v. Onofre (1981), 386
NGLTF. *See* National Gay and Lesbian
Task Force
NGRA (National Gay Rights Advocates),
384, 390
Nichols, Jack, 34
Nickles, Don, 364
Nielson, Howard C., 355
NO AIDS (New Orleans), 230
nonincrementalist proposals, 21, 163–64,
166–67
No on One Coalition (Idaho), 292
No on 6 (California), 292
North, Oliver, 242n. 12
North Carolina: gay elected officials in,
322; gay-related policies and interest
group resources in, *299;* Raleigh, 278;
state government actions on gay issues,
330, 336, 344; teaching about homosexuality in, 280
North Dakota: Equality Begins at Home
campaign in, 292; gay elected officials
in, *322;* gay-related policies and interest
group resources in, *299;* state government actions on gay issues, *336*

Norton v. Macy (1969), 196
"no special rights" slogan, 133–34, 174, 186n. 12
Nugent, Bruce, 81

obscenity, 33, 34
OCA (Oregon Citizen's Alliance), 6, 165–66, 169, 171–72, 180, 295, 302–3
O'Connor, Karen, 7, 23–24
Office of Personnel Management, 351–52
Ogunquit (Maine), 185, 187n. 17
Ohio: Cincinnati, 18, 125, 181, 274, 404n. 18; gay-related policies and interest group resources in, *299;* state government actions on gay issues, *331, 336, 339, 344*
Oklahoma: *Board of Education of Oklahoma City v. National Gay Task Force,* 389–90; gay-related policies and interest group resources in, *299;* hate crime policy in, 306; sodomy law used in, 311; state government actions on gay issues, *331, 336, 344*
Oklahoma City bombing, 148, 150
Omoto, Allen M., 230
Oncale, Joseph, 398
Oncale v. Sundowner Offshore Service (1998), *391,* 398
ONE (magazine), 33
One, Inc. v. Oleson (1958), 380–81
opinion, public. *See* public opinion
opponents of gay rights, 119–90; on antidiscrimination laws, 271, 284; citizens' initiatives used by, 21, 161–90; as coalescing in 1980s, 37; communal protest theory describing, 282; direct democracy used by, 161; future of, 135–36; on the gay agenda, 45; instrumental opposition, 20, 126, 127–30, 135; multiple and competing organizations in, 6; proactive opposition, 20, 127, 132–35; reactive opposition, 20, 127, 130–32, 135–36; resources of, 15; on sexual orientation in school curricula, 277–78; varieties of opposition, 121–38. *See also* antigay initiatives; Christian Right

oral sex: in *Bowers v. Hardwick* (1986), 390; criminalized, 378, 386; in Georgia definition of sodomy, 404n. 13; in *Smayda v. United States,* 381
ordination of practicing homosexuals, 136n. 2
Oregon: antidiscrimination law in, 272, 302–3; Carpenter reelection campaign of 1998, 295; Family Act of 1997, 166; gay elected officials in, *321, 322, 323;* gay-related policies and interest group resources in, *299;* Measure 8 of 1988, 302; Measure 9 of 1992, 40, 133, 164, 165, 169, *169,* 180, 302; Measure 13 of 1994, 60, 133, 165, 169, *169,* 178, 180, 302; Portland, 165; progay bill of 1991, 302; proposed Defense of Marriage Act, 181; Right to Pride, 292, 293, 315n. 7; Right to Privacy, 302–3, 315n. 7; Rural Organizing Project, 292; seemingly contradictory electoral outcomes in, 168–69, *169;* Shibley's progay bills, 296; state employees ruling overturned in 1988, 165, 167, 169, *169;* state government actions on gay issues, *324, 325, 326, 336, 339, 344*
Oregon Citizen's Alliance (OCA), 6, 165–66, 169, 171–72, 180, 295, 302–3
Oregonians for Fairness, 302
Osborn, June, 351
Osborn, Torie, 63–64
OUT (magazine), 13
Out for Office (Gay and Lesbian Victory Fund), 71

paid staff, 43
Palo Alto (California), 270
parades, 394–95
"parallel track" policy (FDA), 237
Park Square Defenders, Inc., 383
patriarchal family, 124
pedophilia, 125
Pennsylvania: antidiscrimination law in, 272; gay-related policies and interest group resources in, *299;* legislation on gay youth, 280; Pittsburgh, 274; progay public opinion in, 205; state govern-

Pennsylvania (*continued*)
ment actions on gay issues, *331, 336, 339, 344. See also* Philadelphia
People v. Onofre (1981), 386, 403n. 9
People v. Uplinger (1983), 387
Perkins, Will, 146
Peron, Dennis, 185
Pettit, Sarah, 13
Phelan, Shane, 112n. 4
Philadelphia: antidiscrimination law in, 271, 273, 282–84; domestic partner benefits in, 275, 283; Lesbian and Gay Task Force, 283
"Philadelphia" (film), 410, 414
Phoenix (Arizona), 274
pink triangle symbol, 99, 223
Pisaturo, Michael, 294–95
Pittsburgh, 274
Plessy v. Ferguson (1896), 396
police (law enforcement personnel), 45, 97, 123, 270
political opportunity structure, 17, 21, 281–82
political strategy, 57–58
pornography, 103, 152, 153
Portland (Maine), 166, 167
Portland (Oregon), 165
postmillennialism, 141, 153
Powell, Colin, 201
Powell, Lewis, 390, 392
premillennialism, 140–43, 153, 154
Presidential Commission on the Human Immunodeficiency Virus Epidemic, 351
Price, Deb, 68
pride, 36, 43
PRIDE! (Montana), 293
Privacy Rights Education Project (Missouri), 293
private sexual acts, 9, 386–87, 390
proactive opposition to gay rights, 20, 127, 132–35
progay initiatives: as defeated more often than not, 163; as more likely to pass in larger jurisdictions, 170; 1978 to 1988, 163; recent use of, 184–85; relative infrequency of, 173–74
promiscuity, 227–28
Promise Keepers, 185n. 4

Proposition 6 (Briggs Initiative), 67, 162–63, 272, 292
protective codes. *See* antidiscrimination laws
Protestantism: attitudes toward homosexuality, 203, 204; mainline Protestants, 122–23, 129, 136n. 2; ordination of practicing homosexuals, 136n. 2. *See also* evangelical Protestantism
Pruitt v. Cheney (1992), 404n. 17
Pryor, David, 365
public accommodations, 269, 270, 285, 296, 395
Public Broadcasting System, 147, 148
public health: AIDS activism as democratizing, 238–41; bureaucrats and AIDS activism, 226–27
Public Health Emergency Fund, 232
Public Health Service (U.S.), 388
public officials. *See* elected officials
public opinion, 409–32; affective and cognitive sources of evaluation of gays and lesbians, *415;* attitudes toward gay rights, 420–28, *422;* attitudes toward gays and lesbians, 412–20; Christian Right trying to influence, 126; citizens' initiatives for shaping, 184; and congressional voting patterns, 203–11, *206;* dislike of gays and lesbians, 13–14, 194, 241n. 7, 392, 413, 419; gay politics affected by, 24–25; on gay rights issues, 194–95, 409–32; and gay rights movement strategies, 195–200; on gay teachers, 205; sources of evaluations of gays and lesbians, *416;* sources of opinion on gay rights issues, 419–20, *423*

quasi-suspect classifications, 196, 199
Queer movement, 102
Queer Nation, 76n. 2

racism, 37, 80
Radicalesbians, 35
radical proposals, 21, 164, 166, 167, 169
Radicec, Peri Jude, 63
Raleigh (North Carolina), 278
RAND, 261

Rapture, 142, 153
Ratchford v. Gay Lib, 385
"rational" discrimination, 11, 175, 196
"rational nexus" test, 196
Rayside, David, 2, 55–56, 57, 58–59
reactive opposition to gay rights, 20, 127, 130–32, 135–36
Reagan, Ronald: AIDS policy of, 228, 231, 233, 351–52; and antidiscrimination law, 37; attitudes toward gays and lesbians influenced by, 417; in Briggs Initiative's defeat, 163; as having little to do with gays and AIDS, 224, 230; and immigration exclusion, 388
Reagon, Bernice Johnson, 81–82
"recruitment," 278
Red Wing, Donna, 92
Reed, Jack, 361
Reed v. Reed (1971), 379–80, 395
Reeves, Kenneth, 66
referenda. *See* gay rights referenda
reform-oriented organizations, 36, 74
Rehabilitation Act of 1973, 238
Rehnquist, William, 385, 392
relationships. *See* gay family relationships; gay relationships
religion: and attitudes toward gays and lesbians, 417–18; Islam, 139; mobilizing against antidiscrimination laws, 272; New Age spiritualism, 144, 145; in opposition to gay rights, 122–23, 139–40. *See also* Christianity; Jews
Reno (1996), 399
reparative therapies, 133
Report, The, 126, 131
Report of the Secretary's Task Force on Youth Suicide (U.S. Department of Health and Human Services), 276
Republican Party: antigay initiatives supported by, 182, 183, 187n. 16; antigay plank in 1992, 40; antigay state bills introduced in 1997, 300; in Defense of Marriage Act's passage, 24, 203, *208*, 350, 361, 363; on Employment Non-Discrimination Act, 203, *208*, 350–51, 364–65, 367; and "family values," 420; gay elected officials in, 106; gay rights movement slowed by, 37; on Hormel

nomination, 370; Human Rights Campaign political contributions to, *369;* and Illinois hate crime laws, 305–6; Main Street Coalition, 367; national organizations made essential by, 58; and Oregon gay rights bill of 1997, 303; pro-gay state bills introduced in 1997, 300; and same-sex marriage and politics, 200–201; support for gays in, 225, 243n. 22; takeover of Congress and gay rights, 24, 350, 365–69; total contributions to congressional candidates, 103rd–105th Congresses, *369;* Tuesday Group, 367; and Washington same-sex marriage bills, 309, 310; and Wisconsin gay rights bill of 1982, 304. *See also* Log Cabin Republicans
Reserve Officer Training Corps (ROTC), 251, 260
resource mobilization theory, 12, 281
Revelation of John, 141
rhetoric, antigay. *See* antigay rhetoric
Rhode Island: antidiscrimination law in, 275; Eagle Forum of Rhode Island, 313; gay elected officials in, *321, 322;* gay-related policies and interest group resources in, *299;* Pisaturo's election in, 294–95; same-sex marriage legislation in, 308; sodomy law repealed in, 312–13
Rhode Island Alliance for Lesbian and Gay Civil Rights, 312–13
Richards, Ann, 71
Rienzo, Barbara A., 7, 11, 23
Right to Pride (Oregon), 292, 293, 315n. 7
Right to Privacy (Oregon), 302–3, 315n. 7
Rimmerman, Craig A., 7, 19
Rivera, Rhonda B., 98
Robb, Chuck, 242n. 12
Roberts, Barbara, 60
Robertson, Pat, 143, 146, 149
Roe v. Wade (1973), 101, 390, 392
Rogers, Marc A., 195
Rom, Mark Carl, 22
Roman Catholicism: on accepting gays and lesbians who abstain from sex, 417; antidiscrimination laws opposed by, 272, 283; antidiscrimination laws supported

Roman Catholicism (*continued*)
by, 425–26; and congressional voting
patterns, 203, 204; as divided on homosexuality, 122–23; and instrumental opposition to gay rights, 129

Romer v. Evans (1996), 174–79, 395–97;
antigay initiatives after, 179–82; antigay
initiatives constrained by, 134, 161, 179,
184; Christian Right's reaction to, 150;
consensus lacking on, 41; decision as extremely narrow in, 178; direct democracy and gay rights initiatives after,
161–90; interest group participation in,
391; lowest standard of review in, 402;
Scalia's dissent, 27n. 7, 177, 178, 187n.
15; Supreme Court as silent apart from,
18

Rosenthal, Donald B., 98, 113n. 5

Rostker v. Goldberg (1981), 393

ROTC (Reserve Officer Training Corps),
251, 260

Roth, William, 360

Roth v. United States (1957), 380–81

Rowland, Roy, 353

Rowland v. Mad River Local School District
(1985), 389

Rubenfeld, Abby, 101

Rural Organizing Project (Oregon), 292

Rustin, Bayard, 20, 82

Rutherford Institute, 172, 186n. 9

Ryan White Comprehensive AIDS Resources Emergency Act, 234–35, 359

safe sex practices, 102, 103, 198, 219, 227,
228

St. Paul (Minnesota), 272

same-sex marriage: African American gays
and lesbians on, 88–89, 92, 93; Alaskan
ban on, 170, 173, 181; assimilationists
seeking legitimation of, 16; *Baehr v.
Levin,* 113n. 10, 199–200, 307; California poll on, 181; Christian Right opposing, 200–201, 307, 308, 311; effects of
prohibiting, 113n. 10; emergence as
mainstream political issue, 200–201; gay
interest group strength correlated with,
300; gay movement strategy and federal
legislation blocking, 76n. 2; gay organizations and, 23; as goal of gays and lesbians, 269; in Hawaii, 21, 70, 71, 75,
88–89, 113n. 10, 134, 169–70, 181,
199–200, 201–2, 307, 308, 360, 401; legal cases on, 198–99; policies and gay
interest group resources by state, *298;*
as policy priority of gay officials, 111;
public opinion on, 195; in South Dakota, 308–9; state policies on, 307–11,
324–46; statewide groups lobbying on,
293; in Washington State, 308, 309–10.
See also Defense of Marriage Act

San Francisco: AIDS striking in, 219, 227,
229; antidiscrimination law in, 270; Bay
Area Lawyers for Individual Freedom,
384, 398; Daughters of Bilitis formed
in, 33; domestic partner benefits in,
199, 275; gay activism in the 1960s, 34;
gay influence on officials in, 224; Gay
Liberation Front in, 382; Harvey Milk
Gay Democratic Club, 220, 225; Kaposi
Sarcoma Education and Research Foundation, 230; Milk elected to board of supervisors, 219–20; National Center for
Lesbian Rights in, 384; National Gay
Rights Advocates in, 384; Society for Individual Rights in, 403n. 5

San Jose (California), 162

Santa Clara County (California), 181

Sarria, Jose, 34

Satan, 141, 146–47

Scalia, Antonin, 27n. 7, 177, 178, 187n. 15,
398

Schacter, Jane S., 101

Scheuer, James, 353

schools, 275–80; antigay initiatives on, 180;
*Board of Education of Oklahoma City v.
National Gay Task Force,* 389–90; Christian Right on education, 148; as concern
to gay community, 49; harassment of
gay youth in, 270; New York City's
Children of the Rainbow curriculum,
131, 277; as policy priority of gay officials, 109; public opinion on gay teachers, 205; *Rowland v. Mad River Local
School District,* 389; school boards as fo-

cus of reactive oppositions, 131; sexual
orientation in curricula, 276, 277–79,
279, 283–84
Schowengerdt v. United States (1992), 404n. 17
Schroedel, Jean Reith, 6, 20
Seattle, 270, 275
Selective Service Act, 393
"self-appointed leaders," 46
Selland (1996), 398
Sensenbrenner, James F., 360
Servicemembers Legal Defense Network
(SLDN), 69, 256, 260, 400
sex: extramarital sex, 412–13; permissiveness, 124; politicization of, 4. *See
also* gay relationships; sexual orientation
sexual harassment, 398, 402
sexual orientation: in antidiscrimination
law, 11, 23, 167, 174; as a choice, 124,
133, 284, 410, 415–16, 418, 419, 427,
429; civil rights legislation extended to,
17–18; Constitution lacking provisions
for, 11, 26n. 4; effects of adding to civil
rights laws, 101; equal protection clause
applied to, 377; excluded from coverage
by hate crime laws, 10; public accommodations discrimination based on, 395;
quasi-suspect status denied to, 199; in
school curricula, 276, 277–79, *279*,
283–84; state legislatures extending legal protections based on, 39. *See also*
gays and lesbians; homosexuality
sexual permissiveness, 124
Shahar v. Bowers (1998), 398
Shapp, Milton, 272
Shays, Christopher, 69
Shelley v. Kraemer (1948), 379
Shepard, Matthew, xv, 301
Sherrill, Kenneth, 13, 14, 17, 55
Shibley, Gail, 296
Shilts, Randy, 251, 253
Simpson, Alan, 365
Singer, Bennett L., 13
Singer v. O'Hara (1974), 198
*Singer v. United States Civil Service Commis-
sion* (1977), 403n. 10
SIR v. Hamilton (1973), 196
small business owners, 123, 282, 285, 420

Smayda, Joseph, 381
Smayda v. United States (1966), 381
Smith, Barbara, 90
Smith, Bessie, 81
Smith, Nadine, 90
Smith, Rhonda, 67
Smith, T. V., 367
Snowe, Olympia, 365
social diversity, 280, 282
social movements: citizens' initiatives as
not used by, 173; gay politics as embodied in, 5; of the 1960s, 35; opponents of
gay rights as, 6; and public opinion,
409; resource mobilization approach to,
12, 281; social and political factors in
policy change, 280–82; strategy determination in, 46. *See also* black civil rights
movement; gay rights movement;
women's movement
social traditionalism: and opposition to gay
rights, 121–24; traditional values, 124,
126, 423, 428
Society for Individual Rights, 403n. 5
sodomy: military discharge for, 250. *See
also* antisodomy codes; oral sex
Solomon, Gerald B. H., 356
Souter, David, 395
South Carolina: gay-related policies and interest group resources in, *299;* state government actions on gay issues, *331, 337,
344*
South Dakota: FACES, 309, 315n. 13; gay-
related policies and interest group resources in, *299;* same-sex marriage ban
in, 308–9; state government actions on
gay issues, *327, 331*
South Dakota Family Policy Council, 308
South Portland (Maine), 185, 187n. 17
"Speak Out Action Grams" (Human
Rights Campaign), 61
Spear, Allan, 297
Specter, Arlen, 365
Stanley v. Georgia (1969), 390, 404n. 15
state, the: Christian Right and, 148–53;
Christian Right on big government,
148–50; Christian Right on church and
state, 150–53, 154

state gay rights laws: impact of, 284–87; passed in 1970s, 272; passed in 1980s, 39; passed in 1990s, 274–75. See also *states by name*

state legislatures: antigay initiatives influencing, 183–84; Christian Right's influence in, 140, 291; gay-friendly and gay-hostile measures passed by, 41; gay presence in, 23; gay rights bills passed in, 197; legal protection based on sexual orientation passed by, 39; local government affected by, 290; proactive opposition in, 134; same-sex marriage banned by, 200

state politics, 290–346; antidiscrimination law, 301–5; gay political representation, 295–97; gay-related legislation and policy in, 297–313, *298, 324–46;* hate crimes policy, 305–7; important forces in lesbian and gay, 297–300; lesbian and gay interest groups, 291–93; openly gay public officials, 293–95, *320–23;* same-sex marriage, 307–11; sodomy laws, 311–13. *See also* state gay rights laws; state legislatures; *and states by name*

Staver, Mathew D., 150

Stein, Marc, 98, 99

Steinmetz, Susan, 231

Stevens, John Paul, 392

Stewart, Potter, 381

Stonewall Riot, 3, 35, 42, 82, 270, 382

strict scrutiny standard, 175–76, 196, 198, 396

Studds, Gerry E., 225, 348

Sullivan, Louis, 239

Supreme Court, 377–408; AIDS discrimination cases, 398–99; *Bragdon v. Abbott, 391,* 399, 402; consensual sodomy cases, 386–87; *Doe v. Commonwealth's Attorney,* 386; and "don't ask, don't tell" policy, 261n. 3; early gay rights cases, 380–82; *Equality Foundation of Greater Cincinnati v. Cincinnati,* 181, 404n. 18; gays in the military cases, 387, 393–94, 397–98, 400; *Griswold v. Connecticut,* 386–87; *Hurley v. Irish American Gay, Lesbian and Bisexual Group of Boston,*
391, 394–95; immigration cases, 388; interest group participation in cases, *391; Kameny v. Brucker,* 403n. 3; *KRC v. United States Information Agency,* 394; *Loving v. Virginia,* 198–99; *Manual Enterprises v. Day,* 381; *Meritor Savings Bank, FSB v. Vinson,* 398, 402; obscenity rulings by, 33, 34; *Oncale v. Sundowner Offshore Service, 391,* 398; *One, Inc. v. Oleson,* 380–81; *People v. Onofre,* 386, 403n. 9; *People v. Uplinger,* 387; *Ratchford v. Gay Lib,* 385; *Reed v. Reed,* 379–80, 395; *Rostker v. Goldberg,* 393; *Roth v. United States,* 380–81; as silent on gay-related issues, 18, 24, 378, 402; since *Romer v. Evans,* 397–99; *Smayda v. United States,* 381; *Stanley v. Georgia,* 390, 404n. 15; in student-based cases, 385–86; *United States v. Meinhold,* 393; *Wainwright v. Stone,* 386; *Webster v. Doe, 391,* 393–94, 404n. 19. See also *Bowers v. Hardwick; Romer v. Evans*

suspect classifications, 175–76, 196

Tafel, Rich, 67, 68

Take Back Cincinnati, 125

Tarrow, Sidney, 17

Task Force Policy Institute (National Gay and Lesbian Task Force), 64

Tebedo, Kevin, 145, 146

Tennessee: gay-related policies and interest group resources in, *299;* Lesbian and Gay Coalition for Justice, 293; sodomy law overturned, 312; state government actions on gay issues, *331, 345*

test cases, 378, 379

Texas: Austin, 131, 271; Dallas, 230, 312; Emily's List in 1990 governor's race, 71; gay elected officials in, *321, 322, 323;* gay-related policies and interest group resources in, *299;* Lesbian and Gay Rights Lobby, 293; Log Cabin Republicans in, 293; progay public opinion in, 207; state government actions on gay issues, *327, 337, 345*

Third World Gay Revolution, 35

Thomas, Bill, 367

Thomasson (1996), 398
Thompson, Bill, 309, 310
Thompson, Mark, 62
Thurman, Wallace, 81
Title VII of the Civil Rights Act of 1964,
    364, 398
Tocqueville, Alexis de, 17
tokenism, 83, 84, 86, 92, 94
Torricelli, Robert, 366–67
traditional values, 124, 126, 423, 428
Traditional Values Coalition, 100, 126, 140
treatment investigational new drugs, 236,
    240, 243n. 29
triangulation paradigm, 84, 94
Tribe, Lawrence, 390
"Truth in Love Campaign, The," 133
Tuchman, Barbara, 79
Tuesday Group, 367
Tyler, Robin, 89
tyranny of the majority, 17

Uniform Code of Military Justice (UCMJ),
    250, 251, 260, 261
United States v. Meinhold (1993), 393
Universal Fellowship of Metropolitan Com-
    munity Churches (UFMCC), 89–90
urbanism, 280
Utah: Biskupski's election in, 296; gay
    elected officials in, *322;* gay-related poli-
    cies and interest group resources in,
    299; state government actions on gay is-
    sues, *327, 337, 345*

Vacco, Dennis, 295
Vaid, Urvashi: on civil rights strategy, 56;
    discrimination experienced by, 112n. 2;
    on grassroots organizations, 58; on hos-
    tility to gays and lesbians, 271; and Hu-
    man Rights Campaign, 61, 63, 64–65;
    on Lambda Legal Issues Roundtables,
    70; on lesbians' second-class status in
    gay organizations, 102; on virtual equal-
    ity, 57
verbal abuse: gays and lesbians reporting,
    270; in schools, 276
Vermont: antidiscrimination law in, 275;
    gay elected officials in, *320, 323;* gay-
    related policies and interest group re-

sources in, *299;* Howard as state Demo-
    cratic Party Chair, 315n. 2; state govern-
    ment actions on gay issues, *339, 345*
violence against gays and lesbians: antigay
    initiatives affecting, 182; in bars and
    bath houses, 99; Bill Bradley on, 18; Na-
    tional Gay and Lesbian Task Force's
    Gay and Lesbian Violence Project, 62;
    in schools, 276. *See also* hate crime laws
Virginia: *Doe v. Commonwealth's Attorney,*
    386; gay elected officials, *322, 323;* gay-
    related policies and interest group re-
    sources in, *299; Loving v. Virginia,*
    198–99; state government actions on
    gay issues, *324, 325, 327, 331, 337, 339,*
    340, 345
Virginians for Justice, 293
virtual equality, 57
Voeller, Bruce, 62
Vose, Clement E., 377
voter guides, 128, 152
Voting Rights Act of 1965, 26n. 4

Waco (Texas), 149
Wainwright v. Stone (1973), 386
Wald, Kenneth D., 7, 11, 23, 57
Walker, Jack, 367
Wallbuilders, 155n. 8
Wallop, Malcolm, 360
Walton, Kelly, 172
Warren, Earl, 381
Washington, Harold, 83
Washington Blade (newspaper), 300, 301
Washington, D.C., 270
Washington State: antigay initiatives in,
    172, 174, 180, 184–85, 186nn. 11, 12;
    gay elected officials in, *321, 322, 323;*
    gay-related policies and interest group
    resources in, *299;* Legal Marriage Alli-
    ance of Washington, 309; Murray's pro-
    gay measures, 296; same-sex marriage
    legislation, 308, 309–10; Seattle, 270,
    275; *Singer v. O'Hara,* 198; state govern-
    ment actions on gay issues, *324, 325,*
    332, 337, 340, 345
Waters, Ruth, 65
Watkins, James D., 233, 351
Watkins v. U.S. Army (1990), 404n. 17

Watson, Rich, 261n. 3

Waxman, Henry A., 225, 231, 232, 356, 365

Waybourn, William, 71, 72, 105

Webster v. Doe (1988), *391*, 393–94, 399, 404n. 19

Weeks, Jeffrey, 113n. 8

Weicker, Lowell P., Jr., 234, 356, 357

Weiss, Ted, 225, 231

Weld, William, 68, 279

Wenzel, Jim, 7, 21

Westmoreland, Tim, 231

West Virginia: gay-related policies and interest group resources in, *299;* state government actions on gay issues, *332, 337, 340, 346*

White, Byron, 101, 278, 391

White, Ryan, 234–35, 359

white flight, 83

Whitehead, John, 155n. 8

Whittier, Nancy, 42

Wichita (Kansas), 272

Wick, Barry, 308–9

Wilcox, Clyde, 7, 13, 24

Wilson, Phill, 65, 82

Wisconsin: antidiscrimination law in, 272, 273, 303–4, 315n. 9; employment discrimination protection in, 197; gay elected officials in, *321, 323;* gay-related policies and interest group resources in, *299;* Madison, 270, 273; state government actions on gay issues, *332, 337, 340*

Witt, Bill, 295

Wolpert, Robin, 7, 13, 24

women: attitudes toward gays and lesbians in, 203, 414, 417, 418, 429n. 2; gender discrimination, 380, 395; Selective Service Act not applying to, 393. *See also* feminism; lesbians; women's movement

Women's Legal Defense Fund, *391*

women's movement: as breaking with mainstream values, 35; and direct democracy, 173; and gender equality, 25; litigation used by, 379–80; and political opportunity structure, 281; *Reed v. Reed* (1971), 379–80, 395; and women's role in homophile groups, 99. *See also* feminism

Women's Rights Project (ACLU), 380, 395

Wood (1997), 399

Woodall, Jim, 146, 153

Woodward, Jim, 255

Woodward v. United States (1990), 404n. 17

workplace. *See* employment discrimination

Wright, Gerald C., Jr., 204

Wyoming: gay-related policies and interest group resources in, *299;* hate crime bills in, 301; state government actions on gay issues, *325, 327, 332, 337, 340, 346*

York, Frank, 143

Yosemite National Park, 403n. 4

youth, gay, 275–80

youth counterculture, 35

Youth Leadership Training program (National Gay and Lesbian Task Force), 74

youth suicide, 276

Zald, Mayer N., 12

Zaller, John, 183